NOVELL'S ®

CNA Study Guide for NetWare® 4.1

NOVELL'S®

CNA Study Guide for NetWare® 4.1

DAVID JAMES CLARKE, IV

AND

KELLEY J. P. LINBERG

Novell Press, San Jose

Novell's® CNA Study Guide for NetWare® 4.1

Published by
Novell Press
2180 Fortune Drive
San Jose, CA 95131

Library of Congress Catalog Card No.: 96-76259

ISBN: 0-7645-4500-0

Printed in the United States of America

10 9 8 7 6 5 4 3 2 1

1A/QW/QV/ZW/FC

Distributed in the United States by IDG Books Worldwide, Inc.

Distributed by Macmillan Canada for Canada; by Computer and Technical Books for the Caribbean Basin; by Contemporantea de Ediciones for Venezuela; by Distribuidora Cuspide for Argentina; by CITFC for Brazil; by Ediciones ZETA S.C.R. Ltda. for Peru; by Editorial Limusa SA for Mexico; by Transworld Publishers Limited in the United Kingdom and Europe; by Al-Maiman Publishers & Distributors for Saudi Arabia; by Simron Pty. Ltd. for South Africa; by IDG Communications (HK) Ltd. for Hong Kong; by Toppan Company Ltd. for Japan; by Addison Wesley Publishing Company for Korea; by Longman Singapore Publisher Ltd. for Singapore, Malaysia, Thailand, and Indonesia; by Unalis Corporation for Taiwan; by WS Computer Publishing Company, Inc. for the Philippines; by WoodsLane Enterprises Ltd. for New Zealand.

For general information on Novell Press books in the U.S., including information on discounts and premiums, contact IDG Books at 800-434-3422 or 415-655-3000. For information on where to purchase Novell Press books outside the U.S., contact IDG Books Worldwide at 415-655-3021 or fax 415-655-3295. For information on translations, contact Waterside Productions, Inc., 2191 San Elijo Avenue, Cardiff, CA 92007-1839, at 619-632-9190. For sales inquiries and special prices for bulk quantities, call IDG Books Worldwide at 415-655-3000. For information on using Novell Press books in the classroom, or for ordering examination copies, contact the Education Office at 800-434-2086 or fax 817-251-8174.

John Kilcullen, *President & CEO, IDG Books Worldwide, Inc.*
Brenda McLaughlin, *Senior Vice President & Group Publisher, IDG Books Worldwide, Inc.*

The IDG Boooks Worldwide logo is a trademark under exclusive license to IDG Books Worldwide, Inc., from International Data Group, Inc.

Rosalie Kearsley, *Publisher, Novell Press, Inc.*

Novell Press and the Novell Press logo are trademarks of Novell, Inc.

Welcome to Novell Press

Novell Press, the world's leading provider of networking books, is the premier source for the most timely and useful information in the networking industry. Novell Press books cover fundamental networking issues as they emerge — from today's Novell and third-party products to the concepts and strategies that will guide the industry's future. The result is a broad spectrum of titles for the benefit of those involved in networking at any level: end-user, department administrator, developer, systems manager, or network architect.

Novell Press books are written by experts with the full participation of Novell's technical, managerial, and marketing staff. The books are exhaustively reviewed by Novell's own technicians and are published only on the basis of final released software, never on prereleased versions.

Novell Press at IDG is an exciting partnership between two companies at the forefront of the knowledge and communications revolution. The Press is implementing an ambitious publishing program to develop new networking titles centered on the current version of NetWare and on Novell's GroupWise and other popular groupware products.

Novell Press books are translated into 12 languages and are available at bookstores around the world.

Rosalie Kearsley, Publisher, Novell, Inc.
David Kolodney, Associate Publisher, IDG Books Worldwide, Inc.

Novell Press

Publisher
Rosalie Kearsley

Associate Publisher
David Kolodney

Market Development Manager
Colleen Bluhm

Associate Acquisitions Editor
Anne Hamilton

Communications Project Specialist
Marcy Shanti

Managing Editor
Terry Somerson

Development Editor
Kevin Shafer

Copy Editors
Kevin Shafer
Suki Gear

Technical Editor
Gamal Herbon

Production Director
Andrew Walker

Supervisor of Page Layout
Craig A. Harrison

Pre-Press Coordination
Tony Augsburger
Patricia R. Reynolds
Theresa Sanchez-Baker

Media/Archive Coordination
Leslie Popplewell
Michael Wilkey

Project Coordinator
Ben Schroeter

Graphics Coordination
Shelley Lea

Production Staff
Diann Abbott
Stephen Noetzel
Chris Pimentel
Andy Schueller
Elsie Yim

Proofreaders
Mick Arellano
Mary C. Oby

Indexer
Lynn Zee Spence

Illustrator
David Puckett

Cartoonist
Michael Kim

Cover Design
Archer Design

Cover Photographer
Jim Kranz

I dedicate this book to the human race for never ceasing to amaze me...
and since you're a human, I guess that in some strange way, I dedicate this book to you!

About the Authors

David James Clarke, IV is the author of *Novell's CNE Study Guide for NetWare 4.1* and *Novell's CNA Study Guide for NetWare 4.1*. He is also the developer of The Clarke Tests v2.0, an interactive learning system, and the producer of the video series *So You Wanna Be a CNE?!* Clarke is a Certified Novell Instructor (CNI), Engineer (CNE), and Administrator (CNA). He speaks at numerous national conferences and currently serves as the president and CEO of Clarke Industries, Inc. He lives in Avila Beach, California.

Kelley J.P. Lindberg, a CNE, joined Novell in 1986. As senior project manager, she has managed NetWare 3.12, NetWare 4.1, and many additional Novell products. she has also written several other books about NetWare software, including *Novell's Guide to Managing Small NetWare Networks* (which won an Excellence award from the Society of Technical Communication) and *Novell's NetWare 4.1 Administrator's Handbook*.

Introduction

By picking up this book, you've just shown that you are interested in taking a step toward furthering your career. Congratulations!

Becoming a NetWare 4.1 Certified Novell Administrator (CNA) demonstrates that you can hold your own as a NetWare 4.1 network administrator. You can make sure users on the network can get to their files, you can keep the printers functioning, you can prevent unauthorized people from breaking into your network, and you can help users learn how to use the network.

As a CNA, you're in prime position to help your users get the most out of your network, to help management get the most out of your users, and to help yourself get the most out of your career opportunities.

Who Needs CNAs, Anyway?

The whole world does, that's who. NetWare networks are, hands-down, the most popular network in the world. According to various surveys, 63 percent to 70 percent of all networks in the world are running some version of NetWare networking software. All other networking companies combined (including Microsoft, IBM, Banyan, and LANTastic) only account for the other 30-some-odd percent.

By mid-1995, there were an estimated 4 million NetWare servers in the world. If you conservatively estimate an average of 10 users per server, you're looking at 40 million users. And those numbers are growing rapidly every month. Just imagine how many users will be out there by the time you read this paragraph. That's a significant number of people who need help with their networks. Lucky thing for them that you're interested in becoming a CNA.

ZEN

"I don't pretend to understand the universe; it's a great deal bigger than I am."

Thomas Carlyle

How Much Trouble Is It?

Achieving CNA status can be one of the best ways you'll find to enhance your position in the computer industry. To become certified, you must prove that you know the fundamentals of networking and can handle the daily needs of a NetWare 4.1 network. To prove this knowledge, you take a single exam.

Taking a test is one thing, but how do you get ready for the test? You must learn all this stuff first, right?

Of course. But it may not be nearly as difficult to learn the networking ropes as you may think.

ZEN

"Anything I've ever done that ultimately was worthwhile... initially scared me to death."

Betty Bender

Understanding how NetWare networks run consists of learning some fundamental principles and a few key tools, then building on those. Once you know the fundamentals, you can begin to see how other aspects of the network fit in, how and where problems might occur, and how to solve those problems.

To learn about NetWare 4.1 and to prepare for this test, you can take a single course, study books like this one, or go the real-world route and learn NetWare on the job. Even better, you can combine these methods.

Most people will tell you that nothing beats actual experience when learning new things. This is true with NetWare, too. You can learn a lot from books and from classes, but until you get your hands into the network yourself, some concepts will still be a little foggy.

On the other hand, the "sink-or-swim" method of real-world learning can be relatively slow and painful by itself. Using a good study guide (such as this book) or taking a course about NetWare networking can give you a terrific jump-start on the way to knowledge. A few days spent in class or with this book can save you several months of trial-and-error.

So, if you're like most people, the best approach to your CNA status may be to combine as much hands-on experience as possible with as much "book larnin'" as you can stand.

This book was designed to help you with this pursuit.

How Can This Book Help?

The first part of this book will deal with some of the more intangible aspects of network administration. For example, you'll find information about how CNA certification can help your career, as well as examples of the types of tasks real CNAs face each day. This type of information isn't on the official CNA exam, but it's the kind of information you'll need to know in the real world.

The second part, which is the bulk of this book, contains the information, exercises, examples, and hints that will help you learn how to keep a NetWare 4.1 network running smoothly. This information applies directly to the material that will be covered in the CNA exam for NetWare 4.1. Not only will this part of the book help you prepare for the exam, but it can also help you skip several months' worth of accidental discovery about how your network works — a bargain by most standards.

ZEN

"A lot of prizes have been awarded for showing that the universe is not as simple as we might have thought!"

Stephen Hawking

The third part of this book contains the appendices, with information about Novell Education, the NetWare 4.1 course objectives, sources for more information, and so on.

Here's a quick rundown of the chapters you'll be reading.

PART I: A DAY IN THE LIFE OF A CNA

Part I begins (oddly enough) with Chapter 1, which describes the benefits that can come from being a CNA. It explains the reasons why certification can be useful, the benefits your management may receive, and the career opportunities that can come with certification. In addition, it talks about the pitfalls of the paper-CNA syndrome, versus real-world experience. There's even some discussion about ways that might be available to you for helping pay for your CNA education.

Chapter 2 takes you through the typical days and duties of a CNA. It describes many of the routine maintenance tasks you'll probably be doing. It even offers some practical advice for setting up and running a Help Desk for your users. This part was written by Kelley Lindberg.

PART II: THE CNA 4.1 PROGRAM

Part II begins with Chapter 3, where it lays down the foundation for understanding NetWare Directory Services (NDS). NDS is the information framework around which the entire NetWare 4.1 network is built.

In Chapter 4, we'll learn about the NetWare file system, which is like the big, electronic filing cabinet that stores all of the data and applications on the network.

Chapter 5 examines network security. Information is now the new commodity — more valuable than money, in many ways. We must take new measures to protect our information. Fortunately, NetWare 4.1 includes a five-layered security model encompassing login/password authentication, login restrictions, NDS rights, file system access rights, and attributes.

Chapter 6 will take you through the five steps of network configuration on a NetWare 4.1 network. This is CNA "childhood."

Then, in Chapter 7, we'll look at what to do with the network once it's been installed and configured — we'll learn the four steps of network management. this is CNA "adulthood."

Chapter 8 tackles network printing, "the great challenge." NetWare 4.1 printing is simple and works great until . . . you add users. It's their fault. In this chapter, we will explore some proven methods for successful NetWare 4.1 printing, setup, and management.

PART III: APPENDIXES

Appendix A introduces us to Novell Education and its certification programs. This appendix also discusses the logistics of taking the exam and obtaining your certification.

Appendix B lists all of the objectives that the authorized NetWare 4.1 Administrator course strives to teach students. However, this appendix doesn't just list the objectives — it goes on to cross-reference each objective to the location in this book where you can learn the related material.

Appendix C contains the solutions to all the quizzes, puzzles, exercises, and case studies that are used throughout Part II.

Appendix D lists some of the many resources you can turn to for more information or technical support about NetWare 4.1 and other Novell products. It also contains a quick look at just what's on the CD-ROM that is included with this book. Finally, this appendix contains the Novell Education Certification Agreement that you'll need to sign and return to Novell when you've passed the exam.

EXERCISES AND CASE STUDIES

Throughout this book, you will find exercises and case studies that will let you flex your newly developed NetWare muscles. The exercises will test your understanding as well as your memory. Some of the exercises are hands-on. You'll be using NetWare utilities and tools to accomplish specific tasks. Other exercises are more brain-stretching in nature. And just for fun, we've thrown in a few puzzles that will keep you entertained while you practice your new grasp of NetWare fundamentals.

ZEN

"The universe is full of magical things, patiently waiting for our wits to grow sharper."

Eden Philpotts

The case studies you will encounter revolve around the ACME organization, an organization made up of dedicated people whose only mission is to Save the World! ACME is staffed by the greatest heroes from our unspoiled history — everyone from Albert Einstein to Wild Bill Hickock to Thomas Jefferson to Mother Theresa. You have joined this illustrious group, and have been designated head of ACME's MIS department. Your goal is to build a pervasive internetwork for ACME, using NetWare 4.1, so that the rest of the heroes can get busy saving the world. The case studies will help you address each type of task along the way.

ICONS

In addition to the exercises and case studies, there are a myriad of other informational tidbits scattered throughout the book. These quips provide instant information in the form of Zen, Quizzes, Tips, Real World, and The Brain. Check them out:

ZEN

These are words of wisdom from people more enlightened than we are. Plus, they make you look really smart in front of your friends.

QUIZ

These brain puzzlers help bring much-needed perspective into your difficult and absorbing journey. It's a great idea to come up for "mental air" every now and then. And these quizzes will appear at just the right time — before you mentally suffocate.

TIP

These icons highlights time-proven management techniques, and action-oriented ideas. These tips are great ways of expanding your horizons beyond just CNAship — they're your ticket to true nerd-om.

REAL WORLD

Welcome to the real world. We don't want you to be a two-dimensional CNA in a three-dimensional world. These icons represent the other dimension. In an attempt to bring this book to life, we've included various scenarios, case studies, situational walk-throughs, and just general real-life bits of advice.

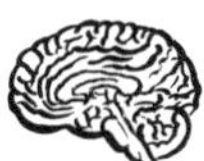

THE BRAIN

Just in case your brain turns to Jell-O, these are great context-sensitive references to supplemental brains-for-hire, like NetWare 4 documentation, Novell Application Notes, Albert Einstein, and so on. Enjoy them, and give your brain a rest.

THE CD-ROM

As if there weren't already enough information in this book to choke a woolly mammoth, we've bound in a CD-ROM for you, too. We want to provide you with the most complete education possible, so this CD-ROM contains an all-star collection of additional learning tools. *The Clarke Tests v2.0* and *Novell Messenger* are waiting for you on the CD-ROM.

ZEN

"As knowledge increases, wonder deepens."

Charles Morgan

And Now a Word...

It would be irresponsible of us to abandon you at the very moment you need the most help — real life! We're here for you — every step of the way.

...FROM DAVID

I spend most of the year traveling around the globe — meeting you! I speak at NetWare Users International conferences, NetWorld+Interop, Networks Expo, and others. But if none of that works for you, I'm always available to chat. Really! I'm sitting by the cyberphone waiting for it to cyberring. You can find me at:

- Internet: dciv@garnet.berkeley.edu

- The Web: Hot Link from novell.com

- CompuServe: 71700,403

- World Wire: DAVID CLARKE, IV

  Sign up at 1-510-254-1193 (on-line)

  Phone: 1-510-254-7283

- The Clarke Tests: 1-800-684-8858

- Cyber State University: 1-510-253-TREK

- NUI Conferences: 1-800-228-4NUI

...FROM KELLEY

I spend all of my days (and too many of my evenings) managing software projects, such as NetWare 3.12 and NetWare 4.1, at Novell. That's why you won't find me at very many conferences or events, but that doesn't mean I don't want to hear from you! You can reach me online at:

- Internet: kelley_lindberg@novell.com

- CompuServe: 74271,3643

TIP

We aren't the only ones willing to help see you through. In fact, Appendix D describes a variety of other resources you can turn to for help, information, advice, or technical support.

Ready, Set...

The main goal of this book is to prepare you for being the best CNA you can be. We'll take you through the mechanics of NetWare, as well as the logistics of CNA-ship. We'll help you pack your CNA toolbox with enough information to ground you solidly in NetWare 4.1 network management.

However, just because the goal is serious, don't think learning about NetWare can't be fun, too! We've worked hard to make this book enjoyable as well as educational.

ZEN

"All the animals except man know that the principle business of life is to enjoy it."

Samuel Butler

So, get prepared for a magic carpet ride through NetWare 4.1 administration. Fasten your seat belts, secure all loose objects, and don't worry about keeping your arms inside the ride at all times – there are no limits to where you can go from here!

Acknowledgments

Wow, this was fun! Even though the pace was fast and furious, we all had a great time exploring the CNA program and inventing ACME - A Cure for Mother Earth. Let's emphasize the word "WE." I know it sounds corny, but we couldn't have written this book without the help and support of numerous friends and family. Let us introduce you to them.

FROM DAVID JAMES CLARKE, IV —

It all starts with my family. I gained a new respect for them while writing this book. Mostly because I continued to test the envelope of sanity. Crazy hours, crazy requests, crazy trips. Mary, my wife, deserves the most credit for supporting my work and bringing a great deal of happiness into my life. She is my anchor. Then there's Leia, my daughter. Somehow she knew just when I needed to be interrupted — daughter's intuition. Most of all, they both have brought much-needed perspective into my otherwise one-dimensional life. For that, I owe them everything.

I also owe a great deal to my parents for their unending support and devotion. They are the architects of my life and I couldn't have accomplished anything without their guidance and love. In addition, my sister, Athena, and her family (Ralph and Taylor) deserve kudos for standing by me through thick and thin. In addition, thanks to my second family for opening their hearts to me. Don and Diane have been wonderfully generous and I appreciate their stability. Also, Keith and Bob have been great brothers to me; and Lisa and Pam have been great sisters to Mary. Finally, Jessica has been a creative and fun influence on Leia.

Now let's meet the true Architects of this book. First, there's Cathy Ettelson. She's the Queenpin. Cathy has been instrumental in all aspects of this book — research, the Mad Scientist's laboratory, exercises, midnight jokes, and the list goes on. I owe a great deal to this brilliant woman and we truly couldn't have done it without her guidance. Next, I want to thank my wonderful co-author Kelley Lindberg. She brought a fresh, new perspective to this Guide and helped round-out the technical education. Thanks for all your hard work, this is a great book because of your involvement. Next, there's Lori Ficklin, who was responsible for bringing my words to life — literally. Also, her husband, Richard, deserves a lot of credit for making sure I didn't ramble on forever. Then there's Mike Kim. He's the collective funnybone of our group. Not only is Mike a gifted cartoonist but he comes from the other side of cyberspace — where most of the world lives. For that, he gives this book unique perspective and readability. I've been blessed to have such wonderful friends who stick with me through good times and bad. This is our eighth book together and I couldn't have done it without them.

Behind every great book is an incredible production team. It all starts with Kevin Shafer - legendary editor. His flawless organization, quick wit, and patience were instrumental in bringing this book to life. And David Puckett deserves equal praise for creating the beautiful illustrations in this book. I've always believed a picture is worth a thousand words. But his pictures are worth a few thousand more. I would also like to thank all the proofreaders, typesetters, artists, and management who made this book possible. And, of course, Anne Hamilton and Jim Sumser for keeping me up to speed on all the exciting adventures at IDG. Finally, thanks to IDG sales, marketing, and bookstores for putting this book in your hands. After all, without them I'd be selling books out of the trunk of my car.

Now let's talk about Novell Press. What an amazing organization. They are truly the future of network publishing. It all starts with Rose Kearsley and David Kolodney. They are Novell Press. Rose has been a wonderful friend and supportive publisher throughout the past four years. I can only hope for greater things in the future. And the dramatic revolution of these Study Guides is due in part to David Kolodney's almost clairvoyant insight — not to mention his uncanny ability to convince people they need to give us stuff. Then there's Marcy Shanti who has been a wonderful friend through thick and thin — always e-mailing, calling, or popping up just at the right time. Marcy has also been my eyes and ears to Novell Education, an invaluable resource. Finally, Colleen Bluhm has had a very positive influence on my work, especially internationally. In addition, she's a rock at Novell Press that I always count on for quick and accurate answers. Together, these great people bring Novell Press books to life. Give them a "thanks" next time you see them.

Life is not one-dimensional. Every now and then, when I leave my cave, I appreciate the support from numerous friends and colleagues. First, I'd like to thank all of my NetWare Users International (NUI) friends for being there with me "on the road." You're all wonderful people and you're doing great things for NetWare users everywhere. Thanks to Daryl Alder for your wisdom; Midge Johnson for you organization; and Shelly, Danielle, Carrie, and Toni for your guidance and collective smile. I'd would be lost without all of you. Next, there's Paul Wildrick, my friend and business partner. Thanks for making my life even more exciting than it already is. Thanks to Ted Lloyd for being, well, Ted Lloyd. Thanks to Lisa and Brian Smith for being friends and keeping the ship afloat. You both have a calming influence. Which is more than I can say for Brent Sharp — although your particular type of chaos I both like and admire.

Finally, thanks to golf courses everywhere for giving me a reason to live; Tears for Fears for inspiration; The Tick for being a superhero role model; and Babs and Buster Bunny for teaching me everything I know about people.

FROM KELLEY LINDBERG —

Once again, I find myself at my favorite point of the writing process — the acknowledgments. When my editor calls and says, "I need your acknowledgments," I know the whole adventure is about to come to a close. Don't get me wrong — it isn't my favorite part just because the work's nearly done (believe me, there's always more work waiting around the corner in the form of a new book or project). The real reason why I enjoy writing the acknowledgments is that I finally get to properly thank all the people who helped make this book happen.

Contrary to popular belief, most authors (even technical authors) aren't lonely, isolated people with an appalling lack of social skills. . . . Okay, you're right, the lack of social skills might be a factor with some, but "lonely and isolated"? Definitely not. You can't possibly write a book like this without working closely with a whole army of people who, for some unknown reason, are perfectly willing to give you the time, encouragement, advice, and knowledge to make the book a success. I'd like to thank all of those wonderful people who gave me those gifts during the writing of this book.

The first person I'd like to thank is my terrific co-author, David James Clarke, IV. He's one of the most ambitious, adventurous writers I've known, and it's been a treat to be associated with him on this project.

Of course, next on the list of my favorite people are the Novell Press crew. David Kolodney has been a steady, positive influence on my writing career since 1992, but I'm sure he tries not to remind himself of that too often. Thanks, David, for keeping the book ideas coming. You always manage to find some way for me to avoid ever having to decide what to do with my weekends. Rose Kearsley, Marcy

Shanti, and Colleen Bluhm, on the Novell side of Novell Press, have been wonderful to me for years — always ready to lend a hand, get permission for something I want to do, or offer encouragement at just the right moment. On the IDG Books side of Novell Press, I send heart-felt gratitude to Anne Hamilton (for her ever-cheerful voice on the other end of the phone line), Jim Sumser (for always staying calm in the face of impending disasters), and Kevin Shafer (for his expert editing, which, of course, kept me from embarrassing myself).

Probably the most important influences on the chapters I wrote have been the outstanding people from Novell Education. I'd especially like to thank Terri Kershaw, the CNA program manager, who was as excited about this project as I was. Terri did everything in her power to make sure I could get as much information to prospective CNAs as possible. My long-time friend and colleague, Grace Whitaker, also came through with valuable information and contacts (and all it cost was a little chocolate!). In addition, my thanks go to Gwen Monette, who helped out in her areas of expertise, too. I offer my thanks and my best wishes for everyone at Novell Education — they've put together a vital program to train the people who will be keeping our planet's networks humming right along into the next century.

Next, I want to thank Novell for letting me spend my free time writing about the best networking technology ever invented, bar none. (Of course, I also thank Novell for keeping me gainfully employed during the day, too!) Novell is an incredible place to work, because the people here are frighteningly smart, and they care passionately about what they do. I couldn't ask for a more rewarding work environment.

Of course, I have to thank the people who mean the most to me in my life — my husband Andy (who keeps the wind in my sails, the sunshine on my back, and the humor in my life), and the rest of my family and friends. Their support and encouragement keep me going every day, even if they don't get to see much of me when I'm in the throes of a book. My brother and great pal, Ray Pollard, who happens to be working his way toward becoming a CNA himself, gave me some great ideas for this book (when he could tear himself away from his new baby daughter, Lauren, that is). Thanks, Ray.

Finally, I want to thank all of the CNAs and CNA candidates who are out there making a difference. I have talked to many of you lately, and you're a dedicated, exciting breed of people. You don't settle for adequate — you know that the future isn't very far off, it's changing daily, and you intend to be a part of it. It's for you that David and I wrote this book. Best of luck in your adventures!

We saved the best for last. Thanks to *YOU* for caring enough about NetWare and your life to buy this book. You deserve a great deal of credit for your enthusiasm and good taste. Thanks again and I'm sure this education will change your life. Good luck, and by the way, thanks for saving the world.

Enjoy the show!

Contents at a Glance

Contents

Part II • The CNA 4.1 Program 99

Chapter 3 • Understanding NDS 101

Chapter 4 • NetWare 4 File System   205

Chapter 6 • NetWare 4 Configuration 401

Chapter 8 • NetWare 4 Printing   **585**

Appendix D • For More Information and Help   759

Life as a CNA

Why Become a CNA?

All over the world, NetWare 4.1 networks are being installed at a breathtaking pace. If you stop and think about how many thousands of users are being added to a NetWare network every month, it's a rather staggering concept.

Over the past ten years, network computing has completely changed how the world communicates. Where were you a decade ago? If a business associate asked for your address back then, chances are good you gave them a street address. If you wanted to send that person a document, you probably stuffed the document in an envelope, typed the address on the envelope, and pasted a stamp in the corner.

Today, when a business associate asks your addresses, you may be inclined to give him or her your e-mail address. It's a safe bet that you haven't touched a typewriter in years (and live in dread of having to find that bottle of white-out), and that you use the Postal Service only on those rare occasions when the recipient needs an honest-to-goodness signature on something.

The rest of the time, when you want to send someone a message or letter, your fingers skip across the keyboard, lightly and quickly typing up an e-mail message. Then, with a click of a button, the message is on its way through cyberspace, arriving within minutes in your colleague's electronic mailbox. No nasty stamp-taste on your tongue, no paper cuts from the envelope, no time wasted while the letter gets carried by trucks or airplanes to its destination.

And let's talk about the information in that letter you just sent via e-mail. A decade ago, you might have spent time at the corporate library (or in the city library downtown) to find the information you needed to write that letter. You would have leafed through stacks of periodicals, research reports, or other types of documents. You would have called experts and played phone-tag while you sat cooling your heels waiting for replies. You would have trekked through buildings, gone up and down elevators, and traipsed down long hallways looking for the person who'd borrowed the manila folder containing the Johannson files. You would have spent time at a terminal, accessing the company's database that was running on an astronomically expensive mainframe.

These days, you can do most or all of that research without leaving your desk. You can access on-line libraries of information, searching for your topic through hundreds of documents in moments. To avoid the phone-tag game (and some long-distance telephone charges), you can send e-mail to colleagues, asking them for the data they have. They, in turn, can send you the Johannson files via e-mail, or you can access them yourself from the document database that your company uses. And better yet for your company's bottom line, you can get all this information from a NetWare network, which is much less expensive than a mainframe.

Today's business world operates at a much higher speed than it did a decade ago. The breakneck rate at which communication travels from colleague to colleague, from customer to company, and from company to company is made possible in large part by the networking infrastructure that is spreading like a huge spiderweb over the planet.

ZEN

"The future is always beginning now."

Mark Strand, *Reasons for Moving*

Do you want to go back to where you were a decade ago? Most people don't. They may gripe about computers, and complain that they're at the mercy of those hunks of plastic and electronics taking up space on their desks. But just watch what happens when those hunks of plastic and electronics suddenly stop working. Mild-mannered accountants suddenly turn into irate bullies. Administrative assistants hide. Deals are put on hold. Transactions get stalled. Whole projects grind to a halt while everyone working on them wanders aimlessly out into the hallways to complain to each other. Frustration becomes tangible.

This is where you, the network administrator, come in.

As a network administrator, you are responsible for taking care of the NetWare 4.1 network on a day-to-day basis. You are the front line of defense for users who have problems. You are the gatekeeper who decides who gets to use the network, and how they get to use it. You are the person who installs new workstations on the network, and who updates old applications.

As a Certified Novell Administrator (CNA), you've not only learned how to do these types of tasks, you've also proven that you can do them to Novell's satisfaction. That can mean a great deal to your manager, and it can mean even more to a prospective employer who doesn't know much at all about you.

Knowledge is the important thing, of course. You can learn all about NetWare 4.1 and be a very competent network administrator, without having to take a test to prove it. This book is designed to help you become a competent network administrator, regardless of whether you choose to take the test. But you may find that there is value in getting officially certified, anyway.

The Importance of Being Certified

As with most fields that offer the opportunity to become certified in a particular skill, the value of that certification varies somewhat with the person who gets it. There are two different ways to look at certification. For the individual who pursues the certification, it can mean

- Tangible proof to show management you know what you're talking about

- Credibility with others in the company or industry

- A fast track to knowledge, as you take classes to prepare for the certification

- Potential college credit

- A valuable asset on your resume

- A competitive edge in the job hunt

- A valid reason to ask for a salary increase or promotion, or to ask for a high salary in a new job

- An admission ticket into user groups or professional organizations

For management, having an employee (or potential employee) with certification means

- Reassurance that the employee really knows the product and has the recommended skills to work with the product

- A way to create a career path for employees

- A clear differentiator between job applicants

> ► A way to save money and time by dividing network support into two
> tiers — CNAs who provide the front-line support for users with their
> day-to-day networking needs, and CNEs (Certified Novell Engineers)
> who work on more technical issues (such as design and implementation
> of networking strategies)

CNA certification is no different in this regard. For the person who becomes a
CNA, the certification can be the ticket to career advancement, credibility, or just a
marginally impressive tidbit to work into conversations at social gatherings.

For management, hiring a CNA (or sending a current employee to class to become
a CNA) means that the manager can be more confident in the employee's ability to
keep the NetWare 4.1 network running smoothly.

The following sections delve a little deeper into ways you can use a CNA
certification to your advantage, as well as how management benefits from having
CNAs in the organization.

TANGIBLE PROOF

Managing a NetWare network can be a challenge. It's even more of a challenge if
you don't have the background knowledge required to keep it running smoothly. If
you've received your CNA certification, you've proven that you were willing and
able to learn about NetWare.

You spent time studying how NetWare 4.1 works. You learned the tools that
make administration easier, the tricks that make each step go a little faster. You
researched how your network works, and found ways to make it work more
efficiently. You've made yourself available to people who have problems, and you've
updated the applications that your people want to use.

Getting your CNA certification proves it. The certificate marks the fact that you've
put in the hours and showed the tenacity required to learn how to run the network.

A piece of paper may not change how you do your job, but every once in a
while, it's nice to be recognized for what you've accomplished. With your CNA
certificate in hand, you can prove to your manager and colleagues that you know
your stuff, and that you have earned the recognition of Novell.

Not to mention that it looks really cool hanging on your wall.

FAST TRACK TO KNOWLEDGE

If you've been assigned to be your network's administrator, but your knowledge of NetWare 4.1 is fairly limited, you will eventually learn what you need to know. Either that, or you'll find another job fairly quickly.

You may learn by trial and error. You might tag along with someone else who understands the system and try to learn at that person's elbow. You can read all the manuals and try to make heads or tails of the correct processes and information that apply to your specific situation. You can experiment with the network (although, hopefully you experiment while everyone else is at home).

Regardless of the methods you use, you will eventually learn enough about the network to keep it going, at least marginally well. However, it's a good bet that it will take you several months (or more) to get to this point if you use these seat-of-the-pants methods.

If, on the other hand, you decide to really focus your attention and learn about NetWare as quickly as you can, choosing the CNA route can be an efficient way to speed up your learning curve.

Take a look at the course objectives (see Appendix B) of the official *NetWare 4.1 Administration* course. The people who designed this Novell course believe that if you understand all the concepts and procedures described by each of the objectives, you will have a solid background of knowledge to help you run a NetWare 4.1 network.

The content of the *NetWare 4.1 Administration* test that qualifies you as a NetWare 4.1 CNA covers this broad range of information. If you can pass the test, you should have a good grasp of all the pertinent areas of network administration on a NetWare 4.1 network.

There will always be more to learn, of course, especially with regard to your individual network's specific characteristics. But these fundamentals will allow you to handle most situations, and will give you enough background to tackle new problems in a logical, educated approach.

How you learn these fundamentals is up to you. Armed with this book and the list of course objectives, the trial-and-error method of learning becomes much more efficient. Instead of a shotgun approach, you can plan the kinds of things you want to learn and tackle them one-by-one.

ZEN

"The only learning that's mattered is what I got on my own, doing what I want to do."

Richard Bach, *Illusions*

Taking the *NetWare 4.1 Administration* course from a Novell Authorized Education Center (NAEC) or from some other source can greatly shorten the time you'll need to learn about the network. A single class can't make you an expert in a week, but it can certainly give you a head-start by giving you a broad overview of the necessary concepts. It can also give you hands-on experience on a lab network, where you don't have to worry about accidentally trashing your manager's account or deleting all the financial reports for 1997.

Whether you take an authorized course, an unauthorized course (there are plenty of people who teach similar courses, some of whom are very good, and some of whom are less so), or adopt some other method of learning, using the CNA objectives as a roadmap can help keep you in the fast lane.

POTENTIAL COLLEGE CREDIT

There are two ways you might be able to get college credit for becoming a CNA. First, you can take the authorized *NetWare 4.1 Administration* course from a college or university that offers the course. Such institutions are called Novell Education Academic Partners (NEAPs). More than 100 such colleges and universities can be found in the United States, as well as some in Canada.

TIP

To receive a list of all the current NEAPs, you can call 800-233-EDUC or 801-222-7800. If you have a fax machine, you can use the Novell Education FaxBack feature. Call one of the same numbers, and follow the instructions to order the FaxBack master catalog of available documents, then order the Novell Education Academic Partner (NEAP) List. Currently, the number of this document is 1235, but document numbers are subject to change.

Second, if you have taken the *NetWare 4.1 Administration* course from an NAEC, you may be able to get college credit for the course transferred from Novell to the college or university of your choice.

College credit is also offered for other authorized Novell courses, as well.

The Novell College Credit Program (NCCP) allows you to get an official transcript from Novell, showing the recommended college credit you may have earned by taking the course and passing the test.

The American Council on Education (ACE) evaluates the Novell courses and recommends the amount of college credit that should be awarded for each course.

Whether or not the college or university you're planning to attend accepts the credit is up to the college or university, however, and not up to Novell.

To apply for college credit, you must first take the full-length *NetWare 4.1 Administration* course from an NAEC. Only authorized courses taught by NAECs are accepted. Next, you must successfully pass the corresponding certification exam at a Sylvan Technology Center or at a Drake Authorized Testing Center (DATC). (Details on how to find NAECs in your area and how to sign up for exams at the Sylvan and Drake testing centers are presented in Appendix A.)

After you've successfully passed the corresponding exam, you can obtain a college credit transcript from the NAEC and have it sent directly to the college or university in which you're interested.

To request a transcript, you must present to the NAEC an original Novell Education course certificate and an original, embossed test score report that shows a passing score. The suggested price for obtaining a transcript is $30 for the first transcript, and $5 for each additional copy made at the same time, although prices are subject to change.

After the college or university receives your transcript, they will evaluate it and decide whether they will award the college credits recommended by the ACE. (Whether the credit is awarded, and how many credits are awarded, is entirely up to the college or university, as with all transferable credits.)

FAST TRACK TO JOBS

Just about anyone you talk to these days will tell you that you must understand computers in order to compete in today's job market, regardless of the field you're in. This is largely true. Computer skills are rapidly becoming a basic requirement in many industries.

However, are general computer skills enough to guarantee you a job? No. Not having those skills may prevent you from landing a particular job, but having them just means you're in the running with everyone else. General computer skills don't differentiate you from the rest of the pack. That's where specialization and planning become important.

REAL WORLD

To make your resume stand out from the rest of the crowd, you must ensure that you have skills necessary in not just today's business world, but tomorrow's as well.

Obtaining your CNA certification can be a step in the right direction. With the range and reach of NetWare networks growing rapidly all over the planet, the number of people needed to manage those networks is increasing at a rapid pace, too. Thousands of people have already recognized this and have begun pursuing their CNA and CNE certifications. The competition has begun.

Gaining a Competitive Edge

Employers have started realizing that a CNA certification can be a differentiating factor in hiring. If a manager is trying to hire someone to administer a NetWare 4.1 network, the applicant with "CNA" on his or her resume will probably move higher up the list of potential interviewees than those without. This is because the employer recognizes that less training may be required for a CNA than for a non-CNA, and training costs money.

REAL WORLD

Take a gander at the help-wanted ads in a city newspaper these days. Every week, more and more positions are being advertised for people to run a company's computer operations. Many of these ads are requesting people who have experience managing Novell NetWare networks, and many even specifically ask for people with CNA or CNE certifications. Your CNA certification will be the first step toward getting an interview at these companies.

The term "CNA" on the resume also helps reassure the hiring manager that the applicant is probably being truthful about his or her knowledge of NetWare 4.1. Some employers have discovered too late that prospective applicants "enhanced" their resumes by claiming to understand NetWare when all they really knew how to do was log in and out of the network.

Being Multitalented Helps, Too

Having CNA status doesn't just help you land a job as a network administrator. Many people running NetWare networks are doing it as a special assignment, in addition to their "real" job. They may actually be accountants, dental hygienists, graphic artists, or account managers who showed an aptitude for computers and got the network administrator assignment as an afterthought.

ZEN

"It takes a fast car to lead a double life."

Lawrence Ferlinghetti

With a CNA certification, you can make that special assignment a forethought rather than an afterthought. If you are applying for a job as an office manager, but you also let the employer know that you are a CNA, the employer may pick you over the competition because you can be of value in more than one area.

In this era of downsizing, more and more people are finding themselves in the sometimes uncomfortable position of having to cover more than one type of job in their company. The people who are surviving the layoffs and restructurings are often those who have more than one valuable skill. If you are capable not only of doing your regular job, but also of taking care of the network, this could possibly help you weather a layoff.

There are no guarantees, of course, but it's always a smart idea to keep yourself diversified and versatile enough that you can move easily from one position to another. Then, even if you do find yourself back out in the job market, you'll still be ahead of much of your competition because you have the marketable quality of being a CNA, in addition to whatever else you have trained for.

Chapter 2 goes into more detail about career opportunities.

GOING AFTER THE BIG BUCKS

Will getting your CNA certification translate immediately into an increase in salary? Possibly, or possibly not. Situations vary widely. It does, however, give you some real negotiating advantages.

If you're applying for a job with a new employer, you may be able to negotiate a higher salary because you are a CNA. The employer will spend less money training you and have more confidence in your abilities right from the start.

Becoming certified as a CNA may help you get a promotion at your current company. It shows a qualitative increase in your skill set, which usually translates into greater productivity for your company. Once again, it may help differentiate you from others in your company who are also vying for that promotion.

Keep in mind, however, that the value of the CNA isn't simply the certificate. It's how you apply the knowledge you received in your pursuit of the certificate. Whether or not you get that job, promotion, or salary increase will be up to you and the effort you show as a direct result of the CNA certification.

JOINING PROFESSIONAL ORGANIZATIONS

As a CNA, you can join the Network Professional Association (NPA) as an associate member. This organization of network computing professionals strives to keep its members current with the latest technology and information about the networking industry. The NPA has more than 100 local chapters that meet regularly to see presentations and hands-on demonstrations of the latest technologies.

NetWare Users International (NUI) is an organization of NetWare user groups. You don't have to be a CNA to join. NUI user groups also meet regularly and try to keep their users current with the latest networking trends.

You may find that because of their experience, members of such organizations can offer advice on issues you've been wrestling with, point out tricks they've found that will save you time and money, and steer you away from decisions that could negatively affect your network (such as buying troublesome hardware, installing incompatible applications, and so on). It may also just be nice to spend time socializing with others who have had the same types of experiences.

Both of these organizations are described more fully in Appendix D.

How Management Benefits from Having CNAs

We've looked at how having CNA certification can benefit an individual. How does that CNA benefit the manager and the company? How do you convince an employer that having a CNA on board will be worth the investment?

One obvious benefit a manager gets from hiring a CNA is the reassurance that the employee has the fundamental background and recommended skills required to maintain a NetWare 4.1 network on a daily basis. Because of the training covered by the CNA program, the new employee will know how to connect workstations to the network, how to control security and access to files on the network, and how to monitor the network's performance. In addition, the CNA will know how to back up the network data and how to take care of the most common networking needs of users.

CNA certification also provides employers with a clear differentiator between job applicants or between current employees who are working their way up the career ladder.

The biggest concerns of employers usually boil down to getting value for their investment. If your company is currently paying outside consultants to handle every support call or issue, you may be able to show how having a qualified CNA on staff could cut those expensive support calls drastically.

Alternatively, if your company doesn't use outside consultants, but does employ an expensive IS staff, you may be able to show them how having an entry-level CNA at the departmental level can benefit them. Such a CNA could provide on-site, personal attention to users' needs, thus improving solution turnaround time (key buzzwords here are "increased productivity in the department"), as well as off-loading many of the time-consuming (but routine) tasks from the more expensive IS employees (key buzzwords here are "efficient resource utilization").

When arguing dollars, do your homework and present an accurate picture. Try to get actual estimates of the costs of support calls, versus how much time you would realistically be able to devote to managing your network.

Also, make sure you're not comparing apples to oranges — as a CNA, you may not be qualified to accomplish everything the consultant does, so you might not be able to completely eliminate those support calls. Be practical and realistic. You don't want your eloquent arguments to backfire on you, setting up in your manager's mind some false expectations that you can't live up to.

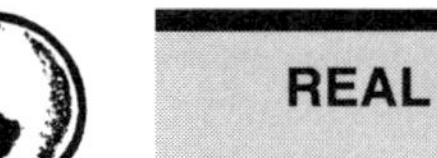

> **REAL WORLD**
>
> A real-world CNA, who is also an accounting manager in Washington, says that when she was convincing her company to pay for her CNA training, "We were paying consultants $95 per hour and travel, so it made sense to have someone [a CNA] in-house. I did not have much of a fight for them to agree to pay for it all."

As an extra benefit, users' confidence in the network may increase if they know they have an on-site CNA available to help them if a problem does arise.

For larger companies, another important benefit of having a CNA aboard is that it allows the company to divide network support tasks into two levels so that support can be managed more efficiently. CNAs can handle the day-to-day administration of the network and act as the front-line support for users' needs. This frees up the more technically advanced support personnel (such as CNEs) to concentrate on more technical, company-wide networking issues (such as design and implementation of networking strategies and research into new technologies).

This division between normal administrative tasks and more advanced issues also allows companies to create a clear career path for their IS departments, from entry-level employee at the CNA level, to advanced employees at the CNE level, to senior-level employees (Master CNEs).

Paper Certification Versus Real-World Experience

Every time someone starts talking about certification, or degrees, or official credentials of any kind, someone else starts arguing about the value of those credentials versus real-world experience. It's an argument that's worth looking into for a minute.

> **REAL WORLD**
>
> Advice from a real-world CNA: "Use hands-on practice whenever possible. Don't try to be a paper CNA."

Official recognition (whether it's in the form of a college degree, a membership in an association, or a certificate) usually is designed to reward and recognize those people who have mastered a new skill or area of knowledge. The requirements to receive that recognition are established by experts in the field, experts who attempt to come up with a set of quantifiable or demonstrable skills or questions that indicate a certain level of proficiency.

Because there is usually no way to absolutely determine a person's full depth of knowledge about anything, the set of requirements the experts establish are more representative than comprehensive.

This unavoidable weakness in the set of requirements can sometimes lead to a certain degree of abuse by some individuals — the kid in school who cheated on exams, the college buddy who could ace any written test but didn't have the common sense promised to a doorknob, or that character at work whose resume looks stellar, but who doesn't seem to have the foggiest grasp of real business sense.

There will always be those types of people in society.

Therefore, when someone argues that a CNA or CNE is a certification that isn't worth the paper it's printed on, it probably means they've encountered one of those individuals somewhere along the line. If this is the case, they have every right to be a little skeptical.

If all someone does is learn how to regurgitate facts, but never bothers to follow up with hands-on experience, then that person really isn't qualified to carry that certification. The CNA program attempts to prevent that situation, as much as possible, but there will always be a few people who manage to get around the system. Most CNAs don't ever fall into that trap, but there will certainly be a few.

So, is it worth it to get a CNA? Or any other degree or credential, for that matter? Yes. Definitely, yes.

But it's a mistake to think that your education begins and ends with certification.

Your CNA certification ensures that you have the foundation you need to do your job. How you build on that foundation is up to you.

REAL WORLD

Advice from a real-world CNA: "Never assume you know all the answers or that any problem will be just like the last. Often, CNEs and CNAs fall into this trap, getting complacent with problems. You need to look at problems with fresh eyes."

BUILDING ON THE CNA FOUNDATION

Once you've received your educational foundation of CNA skills, you will be able to start applying that education immediately on the job. You will quickly discover that what you do on the job will reinforce, enhance, and build upon the education you received. This is where you begin to dispel the argument that paper certification isn't worth as much as real-world experience.

As we've already discussed, pursuing a CNA through formal courses or by studying books such as this one will put you squarely on the fast track toward knowledge. You will eliminate much of the trial-and-error that comes with strictly sink-or-swim hands-on approaches. You can learn several months' worth of accidental discoveries in a few days. Then, once you have those basics down, the on-the-job learning will start at an already advanced point, and you will learn practical tricks and tips for your particular network much more quickly.

So, while the CNA certification is no substitute for hands-on experience, it gives you a definite advantage in achieving that experience rapidly.

Your response to the argument against "paper CNAs" will simply be your own experience. If you are a paper CNA (meaning you've received your CNA certification without much actual hands-on training), your response should be that your certification has prepared you for network administration by giving you the background of knowledge you need, and that you're looking forward to getting that hands-on experience that your challenger is extolling.

If you already have the real-world experience to go with your CNA certification, then your best defense against detractors is simply to show them that you really do know your stuff. That shouldn't be difficult.

GAINING CREDIBILITY

More often than encountering a skeptic, you'll probably encounter people who actually have higher expectations of you because you're a CNA.

There's something about credentials that may change many people's perceptions of you. It may not be a tremendous change, but it's one of those funny quirks of human nature that makes people raise their expectations a little higher when they know someone has a credential.

This can be good or bad, of course. If they raise their expectations of you, and you let them down, it can backfire for you. For example, if the only MBA in the office is the one who makes the most boneheaded decisions, the rest of the people in the office will probably not be impressed with other MBAs they meet in the future. This is the "paper CNA" trap just discussed.

However, what will hopefully happen to you is that they will think to themselves, "Gee, that person is a CNA. I guess all that messing around with computers was beneficial after all. Maybe he/she can help me with my printing problems." Then you take one look at their printing setup, spot the problem (the wrong print driver being used by the application), fix it, and suddenly you've reinforced their new opinion of you.

This may sound silly at first, but think about the last time your company hired an outside consultant. Chances are good that some of the recommendations the consultant made were the same ones that your fellow employees were recommending. But, by virtue of being someone with "credentials," the consultant was listened to, while the regular employees were ignored.

What's going on here? A conspiracy? Not really. It boils down to the fact that some people unknowingly have higher expectations of "officially recognized" people than they do of "home-grown" people.

Becoming a CNA is your opportunity to make this quirk of human nature work for you. If you already have the knowledge, why not make it official and raise their opinion of you a little?

GETTING WHAT YOU NEED OUT OF THE CNA PROGRAM

In the CNA program, you will learn a great deal of information about NetWare. Because the program is trying to cover a representative amount of knowledge that will help the most number of people adequately manage their networks, you will find that not everything in the course objectives may apply to you. However, a significant portion of it will.

REAL WORLD

What you'll have to remember is that you need to strike a balance between what the course objectives teach you, and what you'll need to learn and use on the job. Some of the information you learn in the course (or in this book) may not be of immediate use to you. Of course, you never know what the future will hold for you—the very skills you thought you could ignore in the class may be ones you need urgently in your next job.

In addition, even though you may not immediately apply some of the information you learn, the education may have a more roundabout effect on your job performance. The more exposure you have to the different features and capabilities of NetWare, the more easily you can adapt that knowledge to new problems, even if those specific problems were never covered by the instructor.

In addition to learning some types of information you may not need right away, you might discover that your job involves aspects of NetWare not covered in the CNA program. There are two reasons for this.

First, you may be encountering some of the more advanced, technical issues covered in other courses designed for the Certified Novell Engineer (CNE) program.

Second, your situation may be a less common one, which was simply not covered in either program. Again, this is probably because of the representative nature of the CNA program — the standardized courses attempt to give a broad foundation of knowledge about the most common situations that apply to the highest number of people.

Even if your particular problem isn't covered in the CNA program, the background of knowledge you learned there should help you formulate possible solutions.

Practical Education that Works

In this uncertain economy, where corporations are downsizing and layoffs are occurring with frightening frequency, it's often difficult to predict what skills and training will be in demand over the next few years.

There have been many stories of people who have trained for a skill or gotten a degree that turns out to be obsolete (or at least less in demand) when they are finished with their education. This problem also has affected people who have participated in job retraining after a layoff. Too often, their job retraining has prepared them for jobs that will no longer exist when they graduate.

REAL WORLD

Because lawyers have long enjoyed a reputation for being able to charge astronomical fees, drive fancy cars, wear expensive Italian suits, and spend afternoons at the golf course, prospective law students have been flocking to law schools over the past several years without noticing that the law industry was reaching its saturation point. Now, record numbers of graduating law students are reporting that they are having a difficult time finding jobs.

In addition, there are plenty of training programs out there that are catering to fads — certifying people for unique skills that may only have a shelf life of a year or two. This type of training may land you a job for now, but leave you high-and-dry when you've decided to advance your career to the next step.

There is no surefire way to avoid these fates, but with a little planning, you can better your chances at getting training that will stay in demand for a longer period of time. With the rampant growth of computing and communications, network administration appears to be a career choice that will be growing rapidly for many years to come.

Manufacturing jobs are giving way to computerized processes. The Internet is swelling by thousands of users every month. Businesses are looking for new ways to automate their work and increase the speed of communications. All of these trends appear to be gaining in strength, and show no signs of slowing for the foreseeable future.

Because of this growth, network administration (already a strong career choice) appears to be on the upward side of the growth cycle, poised for much more growth over the coming years. Demand for skilled network administrators is increasing daily, and should continue to rise rapidly as business becomes more and more dependent on communication and computerized processes.

With this kind of predicted growth, choosing to pursue a CNA certification now should be a very good move.

Paying for Your CNA Education

How much does it cost to become a CNA? The answer depends on the route you take to "CNA-dom." If you have been working in a NetWare 4.1 networking environment already, and you feel that this book has rounded out your knowledge sufficiently, then you may be able to simply take the exam and receive your authorization. The cost of the exam is in the neighborhood of $85.

However, if you must get more formal education, you may want to look into taking a course from an instructor — either the Novell-authorized course, or a similar course from an independent trainer. In this case, you'll incur some additional expenses.

The suggested retail price of the Novell-authorized, instructor-led *NetWare 4.1 Administration* course is currently $1,195. The price may vary somewhat. It's really up to the Novell Authorized Education Center (NAEC) that is offering the course.

Courses taught by independent instructors (which are not Novell-authorized) may be a little less expensive.

For many people, paying for the course may not be a problem. If you're fortunate enough to work for a company that understands the value of having a CNA on staff, then you probably will be successful in getting the company to pay for you to attend the necessary courses. Many CNA candidates do work for such an employer. For others, the cost may seem prohibitive at first. Let's look at some of the options you might have for funding your future. Because CNA candidates come from all walks of life, you'll find that the roads they took to get here run all over the map.

FINANCIAL ASSISTANCE

If you don't have the luxury of an employer who's willing to pay for your CNA education, you will probably have to foot the bill yourself.

The good news is, the money you spend on taking the course may be tax-deductible, depending on your particular circumstance. Be sure you do some research or talk to a tax planner about this possibility.

TIP

In the United States, the IRS (Internal Revenue Service) has published a guide to claiming educational deductions on your tax return. To find out more information about this guide, call the IRS at 1-800-TAX-FORM, or write to the IRS Form Distribution Center nearest you. (You can find the address of the nearest office on the income tax package you receive every year.)

Another piece of good news is that you might be able to take advantage of some avenues for financial assistance.

If you're pursuing your CNA certification through a college or university, you may be able to get financial assistance through the school itself. If you aren't going the college route, but still need some financial assistance, you can check into the federal programs that help provide funding for education and job retraining to see if you qualify for those.

In the United States, a variety of federal programs can help provide educational money, such as the Job Training Partnership Act (JTPA) and Trade Adjustment Assistance (TAA). These programs are administered at the state level, and are managed by local employment, job service, and rehabilitation agencies. Because these programs are administered locally, the services they offer may vary from state to state. You can contact any of these agencies in your local area to find out if you qualify for possible financial aid, as well as to find out about any employment opportunities.

TIP

Your local NAEC or NEAP may also be able to point you to some possible sources for financial aid.

If you don't qualify for federal programs, you might try contacting your local banks and credit unions to see if they offer loans (possibly even low-interest student loans) that you can apply toward your educational expenses.

The following sections look at some of the options available in the United States. If you're not in the United States, contact your local government agencies, colleges, and universities for information about similar types of programs in your area.

ZEN

"Education, training and skills [are needed] to seize the opportunities of tomorrow."

President Bill Clinton, 1994 "State of the Union Address"

Financial Aid at School

If you are considering taking the NetWare 4.1 Administrator's course through a college or university that is an NEAP, be sure you check with the school's financial aid office. You may discover that you are qualified to apply for a possible scholarship, low-interest loan, work-study program, or grant to help you pay for your education.

TIP

For more information about possible sources of financial aid at school, you can get a copy of *The Student Guide* by contacting the Federal Student Aid Information Line at 1-800-433-3243.

In addition, some states have private institutions that may help provide financial assistance to students in matriculated schools. These institutions sometimes offer a variety of scholarships, grants, and fellowships based on religious, sports, or heritage affiliations. To find out if such a program exists in your state, talk to your local job service agency, or look for "College Academic Services" in the white pages of your telephone book.

Job Training Partnership Act (JTPA)

Job Training Partnership Act (JTPA) agencies are designed to help people get the education they need to find employment opportunities. These agencies assist the following types of people:

- ▸ Dislocated workers

- ▸ Veterans

- ▸ Youths and adults who are financially disadvantaged

- ▸ Youths and adults whose gross household income is less than government-established poverty levels

If you fall into one of these categories, contact your local job services agency (you can find them listed in the white pages) for information about JTPA programs and eligibility requirements in your area.

JTPA agencies offer financial assistance for education that is designed to land you a full-time career. In addition, they can help you find employment after you've completed your education. Some of the services they provide include:

- ▸ On-the-job training

- ▸ Classroom and customized training

- ▸ Internships

- ▸ Resume-writing assistance

- ▸ Financial assistance for education

- ▸ Help locating educational and professional resources

- ▸ Referrals for employment or educational institutions

Trade Adjustment Assistance (TAA)

If you and your co-workers have been displaced by foreign-import competition, you may qualify for additional unemployment insurance, job retraining, and financial assistance for job search and relocation expenses.

The Trade Adjustment Assistance (TAA) program was designed to help workers in the United States who have lost their jobs as a direct consequence of foreign import competition.

TIP

To be considered for TAA funds, an employer, a group of employees, or an employee representative (such as a labor union) must file a petition with the Department of Labor. If the Department of Labor finds that the claim is valid, the employees (and possibly the employer) can receive TAA services.

The North American Free Trade Agreement (NAFTA) is also connected with TAA. It specifies that employees who lost their jobs because of trade with Mexico or Canada, and who meet eligibility requirements, can receive similar NAFTA benefits.

If you think that you and your co-workers or your employer could be eligible for TAA assistance, contact your local job services agency. Ask for the TAA Coordinator for your state, who will be able to help you find out if you're eligible for TAA services.

Private Industry Councils (PICs)

Private Industry Councils (PICs) are organizations that control how funding is allocated for various government programs. Each PIC is made up of both government representatives and local business representatives. These people act as a governing board that approves contracts for state-allocated money targeted toward lower-income and disadvantaged people.

Because the PIC is run by both government and business representatives, theoretically a balance is maintained for determining the most appropriate and practical funding levels for the programs.

PICs represent many types of government programs. Job services, vocational rehabilitation, and JTPA are a few examples of these programs. For more information about possible opportunities or financial assistance through these or other programs, call your local PIC (listed in the white pages under "Private Industry Council").

Veterans' Administration

If you are a veteran, you should certainly check with your local Veterans' Affairs office for information about any Veterans' programs you may be eligible for. Veterans' programs exist that can provide assistance with education, job training, and vocational rehabilitation. The services you qualify to receive may vary, depending on such factors as your length of service, type of discharge, or a service-related disability.

Advancing Your Career

As a CNA, what are your options for the future?

Immediately, of course, you can apply your knowledge toward managing a NetWare 4.1 network for your company. The longer you experience the hands-on joys of network administration, the more you learn and the more valuable you will become as an employee.

But you may be wondering where you and the networking industry are headed in the future. Let's dust off the crystal ball and take a stab at some possibilities.

ZEN

"Never assume the obvious is true."

William Safire

CURRENT OUTLOOK FOR THE NETWORKING INDUSTRY

Today's international forecast calls for widespread growth of the networking industry, increasing demand for people who understand networking, and widely scattered areas of specialization — an enticing forecast for prospective CNAs.

Want a more specific forecast? Okay. Pick up any recent survey on job trends for the next 10 years or so. Then look through the top jobs. In almost all the recent surveys that have been coming out, jobs relating directly to computing (such as programmers, analysts, and IS personnel) are appearing in the highest-growth categories. Of those jobs that don't specifically deal with computing, most of them require knowledge of computers and software to get the job done.

The world is quickly being engulfed in a tightly woven network of communication. The sheer number of people that will be required to maintain that network is staggering.

Whereas large companies once were the bastion of computer and networking professionals, now everyone from your friendly neighborhood dentist, to your local car dealer, to your small-town church's office worker wants to connect up and dial in to the networked world. All of those businesses need help.

People are already answering the call for qualified networking professionals in large numbers. The CNA program is the fastest growing certification program around. About 10,000 to 12,000 new CNAs are certified every quarter, and the numbers are still growing.

REAL WORLD

Advice from a real-world CNA, on becoming a CNA: "Go for it! We may have to hire a computer person in the future and we would be looking for someone with CNA certification. The world is becoming more and more networked and it needs people *with* that expertise to guide those without."

This isn't just a North American phenomenon, either. Approximately 30 percent of the CNAs being certified as of this book's writing are from outside of the United States and Canada. That number is expected to grow sharply. Because the CNA program was introduced first in the United States, the rest of the world is still considered an emerging market.

The number of CNAs in Asia and Australia is growing incredibly fast. The European market is a little more mature, but numbers there are still growing dramatically. The worldwide growth rate is very impressive.

Does this mean the market will be saturated soon? Probably not. As fast as the CNA numbers are growing, the number of people and devices being hooked up together via computers and communication channels is outpacing them.

ZEN

"Novell networks, applications, and services will serve 1 billion connections by the year 2000."

Bob Frankenberg, CEO of Novell, Inc.

CURRENT OUTLOOK FOR YOUR FUTURE

Even if the market for network administration skills is keeping pace (or outpacing) the number of CNAs available, you can't rest on your laurels if you want to stay marketable over the long haul.

Any certification has a limited shelf life, whether it is a CNA certificate or an engineering degree from the best university. These days, with the lightening speed of growth in the networking and computing industry, it's easy to feel like your entire base of knowledge and skills are obsolete in just a few years. You must take steps to ensure that this doesn't happen to you. Continuing education is vital.

ZEN

*"How we wish we were sunning ourselves
In a world of familiar views."*

Mark Strand, *Reasons for Moving*

The best way to plan out your continuing education needs is to consider your career goals over the long run. Today's goal is to become a network administrator. But then what? Where do you want to go next? Where do you want to be 10 or 20 years from now?

A Career in Network Administration

If network administration is right up your alley, and that's where you want to concentrate on building your career, then you must plan how you will stay current with networking technology over the coming years. For example, as Novell introduces future products, you will probably want to educate yourself in them and recertify on those products.

ZEN

"Even an old cow deserves a new cowbell."

Texas Bix Bender, *Laughing Stock, A Cow's Guide to Life*

Additionally, you will most likely find that a great deal of your time as a CNA isn't just devoted to managing the NetWare side of the network. Chances are very good that you'll exert a considerable amount of energy working with the applications that your users want to use. Staying current on those applications is vital.

Various software manufacturers offer certification programs for their specific applications. For example, Novell has CNA tracks for three applications: GroupWise, InForms, and SoftSolutions. Microsoft and other companies offer similar certification programs for their products.

Upping the Ante

As you begin to delve deeper into the technical workings of your network, you may decide that you want to focus more on design, strategy, and growth aspects of networking technologies. Perhaps you want to expand your depth of knowledge about NetWare networking and advance up the career ladder to IS professional or possibly become a consultant.

If this is the case, you may decide to pursue a CNE, or Master CNE, certification.

ZEN

"Here's the thing with decisions. I can make them. I just don't feel sure about them afterward."

Paul Reiser, *Couplehood*

CNEs are capable of handling jobs where they spend less time managing day-to-day network operations, and more time dealing with the larger, more technical issues of NetWare network management. For example, CNEs are often involved in network design, installation, implementation, and troubleshooting. CNEs specialize in various Novell products (such as NetWare 4 or GroupWare), so that they can concentrate on developing their skills in those critical areas.

To become a CNE, you take additional classes and exams to learn (and demonstrate) advanced techniques and skills for planning and implementing NetWare networks in any size organization.

ZEN

"Never say you don't have enough time. You have exactly the same number of hours per day that were given to Helen Keller, Pasteur, Michelangelo, Mother Theresa, Leonardo da Vinci, Thomas Jefferson, and Albert Einstein."

H. Jackson Brown, Jr., *Life's Little Instruction Book*

The NetWare Administration exam, which you must pass to receive your CNA certification, is one of the required classes for a NetWare 4 CNE certification. Therefore, you've already knocked one requirement off the list to becoming a CNE. Aren't you the clever one?

As a CNE, you may be able to move up in the IS hierarchy, moving into positions requiring greater technical backgrounds, and allowing you to get your hands into some of the more challenging technical aspects of networking. In addition, CNEs are often on the cutting edge of research, exploring new technologies and finding ways to keep their organizations in the fast lane.

A Master CNE has taken his or her education as a networking professional to an even higher level. Master CNEs declare a "graduate major" while they're pursuing their certification. These areas of specialization delve deeper into the integration- and solution-oriented aspects of running a network than the CNE level.

While CNEs provide support at the operating system and application levels, Master CNEs are expected to manage advanced access, management, and workgroup integration for multiple environments. Master CNEs can support complex networks that span several different platforms, and can perform upgrades, migration, and integration for various systems.

Periodically, as Novell introduces new generations of its products, Novell Education requires existing CNEs and Master CNEs to update their certification by learning about and demonstrating their proficiency in these new products. The need for such recertification is obvious. Without recertifying on new products, your skills can become dated, and your certification begins to lose its value.

A Stepping Stone to Other Careers

Of course, nothing says you must spend the rest of your life directly managing networks. Network administration may turn out to be the stepping stone that opens entirely new doors to you.

As we already mentioned, it is becoming increasingly difficult to find a good-paying job in a growing career field that isn't somehow tied into computers. Everywhere you look, knowledge of computers and how they affect your business and your life is becoming more and more important.

Being a network administrator can help you build that foundation of knowledge about business communications, tools, and resources. This background will become invaluable in nearly any aspect of the business world you pursue, whether you start your own business, hop onto a fast-growing startup company, or join a well-established organization.

Another benefit is that if you wisely apply the knowledge and skills you used to get your CNA certification, you will ideally establish a good reputation as a professional who is competent and productive. That reputation may help future employers recognize your ability to take on responsibilities in their organizations, even if the job they are offering is in a completely different area from network administration.

As with any certification, degree, or diploma, it is important to realize that what you make of that piece of paper is up to you. It will never be a free lunch ticket by itself. You must back up its validity by plunging into the real-world aspects of the field. Hard work, talent, skill, and knowledge go hand-in-hand with certification. With that combination, you will definitely have a strong edge over most of the rest of your competition.

ZEN

*"Now I know a refuge never grows
From a chin in a hand in a thoughtful pose,
Got to tend the earth if you want a rose."*

Indigo Girls

A Day in the Life of a CNA

If you're a prospective CNA, you might be wondering what typical CNAs do during the day. How do they spend the bulk of their time? What kinds of situations and tasks do they face on a daily basis? Just what, exactly, are you in for?

If you're already a CNA, you may wonder if you're typical. Do other CNAs do the same types of jobs? Do they have the same problems? Have they set up their work processes the same way you have?

You're probably hoping this chapter will definitively answer these questions, aren't you?

Well, you know that there's no such thing as "typical" in this industry. How you manage a network will depend on many things, such as

- ▶ Your network's size — Are you managing the network for a dentist's office or for a Fortune 500 company?

- ▶ Your experience — Are you new to this whole networking thing, or have you been running networks and troubleshooting PCs for years?

- ▶ Your user's needs — Do they just want to run a few applications and print on a single printer, or do they want to have access to a continuously changing and dizzying array of network resources?

- ▶ Your job description — Are you responsible for installing new workstations and printers, or do you just handle tasks such as helping users figure out their word processing problems?

- ▶ Your personality — Are you an organized, methodical person or a seat-of-your-pants adventurer?

No single approach to network administration will completely please everyone, of course. However, in this chapter, we'll look at some of the processes commonly used by CNAs.

Sometimes just seeing how other people work and solve problems will help you come up with your own plans. Even though those plans may differ, they are most likely rooted in the same principles.

ZEN

"To really succeed in a business or organization, it is sometimes helpful to know what your job is, and whether it involves any duties."

Dave Barry, *Claw Your Way to the Top*

Where Do CNAs Fit in the Organization?

CNAs tend to be the front-line of support for network users. When users have a problem, the first person they call is the CNA. The CNA can handle routine matters, such as creating new user accounts, resetting a user's password, or getting the user's application to print. When the user's problem or situation calls for more technical expertise than the CNA is able to offer, the CNA generally calls on a second line of support for help.

In small companies, the CNA may be the only network administrator on site. If a problem comes up that the CNA can't handle, the CNA may have to call outside support (such as the reseller, a consultant, or the software or hardware manufacturer).

ZEN

"I have personally, with my bare hands, changed my "WIN.INI" and "CONFIG.SYS" settings. This may not mean much to you, but trust me, it is a major data-processing accomplishment. Albert Einstein died without ever doing it. ("Wait a minute!" were his last words. "It erased by equation! It was 'E' equals something!")"

Dave Barry

In a large company, the second line of support may be someone up the hierarchy in the Information Services (IS) department. CNEs often fill these types of roles. The second line of support may handle issues such as new network designs, larger-scale network upgrades, tricky problems that are difficult to track down, and so on.

Another characteristic of CNAs that you might find in larger companies is that the CNAs may be divided up into specialty areas. Certain CNAs might deal with all the spreadsheet issues, for example. Another group of CNAs may cover all the word processing problems. This type of specialization allows users to get answers to their questions more rapidly, because the CNAs are able to focus their attention on those particular areas.

This type of organization also allows the CNAs to add another area of expertise — namely application experience — to their arsenal of networking knowledge. Figure 2.1 illustrates how one company might organize its IS group to handle user problems and manage the company's overall network.

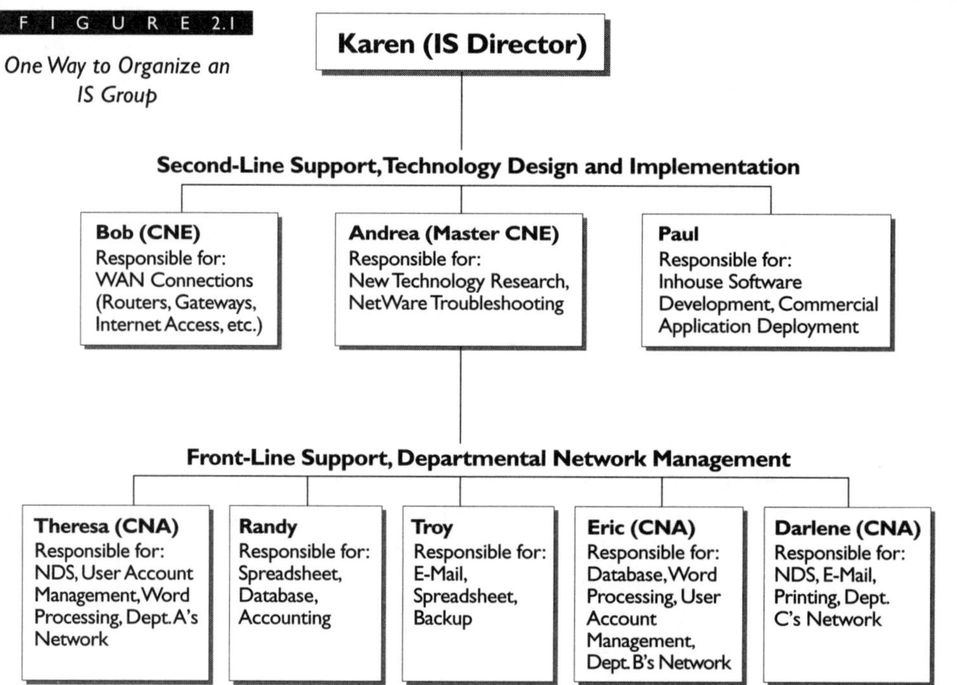

F I G U R E 2.1

One Way to Organize an IS Group

In a smaller company, the lone CNA is generally a jack-of-all-trades, with responsibility for a variety of applications in addition to the regular NetWare features.

Common Day-to-Day Activities

As a network administrator, your primary job responsibility is to keep the network running smoothly so that your users can maintain a high level of productivity. If users aren't productive, management tends to get a little testy, and your job gets a little more high-profile than you might like.

ZEN

"Technology has met its promise of reducing our workload. It does this primarily by preventing us from doing any work at all."

from the "Dilbert" comic strip

In order to keep your users productive

- You make sure the network is set up logically so that users can easily get to the network resources they need when they need them, and so that you can easily manage those resources.

- After the network is set up logically, you monitor it regularly to make sure it continues to be most efficient for your users. An organization's needs can change over time (with reorganizations, new job priorities, the introduction of new technologies or applications, and so on). Your network may need to change with the organization.

- You prioritize and solve network problems quickly. The longer it takes for you to solve network problems, the less productive your users are.

- You minimize the amount of time you spend trying to teach users how to use the network.

- You find ways to streamline your work processes, so that you spend less of your own time trying to deal with network issues. Remember, your own productivity is important, too.

For many CNAs, these types of network-management tasks fall into two basic job responsibilities:

- ▸ Routine maintenance/periodic housekeeping

- ▸ User support

The next sections discuss some of the types of activities that fall into these two categories. Again, you may not be responsible for all of these types of tasks in your current job, but who knows where your career will take you?

Routine Maintenance and Housekeeping

If you own a car, you know that routine maintenance can be the key to extending the life of the car and avoiding costly, unnecessary repairs. You know that, on a regular basis, you must change the oil, check the transmission fluid level, refill the windshield fluid reservoir, rotate the tires, make sure there's enough water in the radiator, change the spark plugs, and so on.

REAL WORLD

It's not absolutely necessary to do routine automobile maintenance on a regular basis, of course. You could just drive the car until pieces start falling off or catching fire. However, that generally isn't the most efficient way to take care of the vehicle. It tends to be a mite expensive, too. Buying a new engine every couple of years is more expensive and more annoying than getting the oil changed every 3,000 miles.

In some ways, the same principle applies to your network. Many types of tasks, if done on a regular basis, will help you stay a few steps ahead of problems.

For example, suppose your server's disk space is gradually getting filled up with users' work. Rest assured, even if you don't do routine maintenance on your network, you'll know when the server runs out of disk space — you'll suddenly have users hysterically calling you, demanding to know why they can't open files or create new ones. You may spend several hours or days finding a new disk and getting the appropriate signatures required to pay for it, and then more time installing it when you finally get your hands on it.

On the other hand, if you make it a habit to periodically spend a few moments monitoring the amount of disk space being used on your server, you can estimate when you'll need to add a new hard disk. If you know ahead of time when to add a new disk, you can have it ordered, installed, and working long before the crisis point. Disaster will have been averted, and your users will quietly continue being productive.

REAL WORLD

Naturally, there will always be the unusual occurrences that create problems, which even the most rigid maintenance regime won't prevent. For example, rotating the tires and keeping them inflated at the correct pressure won't prevent you from driving over a nail. However, with regular maintenance, you may very well reduce the number of additional problems you do have to face — such as discovering that your spare tire is flat.

What types of routine maintenance and periodic housecleaning should you do? The following sections offer some suggestions.

CHECKING UNDER THE HOOD (MAINTAINING THE HARDWARE)

Periodically, you must "check under the hood" to see how the hardware is holding up. You may need to upgrade some pieces of hardware, replace worn items, or add new machinery to accommodate new needs.

A common hardware-related activity is to add new equipment (such as printers or workstations) to your network. As new employees join your organization, you must install new workstations for them to use. If several more employees join, your old printer may not be enough to keep up with printing demands, so you might add a new printer to meet the needs of the new users.

In addition to installing new equipment, you will likely find yourself upgrading existing equipment. Each year, new applications seem to require more memory and disk space, requiring you to add memory and larger hard disks to your current workstations.

Workers who use those workstations have bigger requirements, too — they may want to simply trade in the older computers for faster workstations. They may also start requesting better-quality printers, higher-speed modems, better plotters, and so on. Your old backup system may soon start looking like a dinosaur to you, too, and you'll find yourself hankering after a new one.

ZEN

"The only difference between men and boys is the cost of their toys."

Anonymous

Because of these ever-increasing hardware needs (okay, some are just desires), you'll want to keep up on the latest trends in computer equipment. You must make sure you know about the hardware you already have installed. Take the time to study the hardware settings and to understand what hardware requirements will satisfy the various demands of your users.

Keep records of the equipment currently installed, so that you can predict which machines may need to be upgraded soon. This will help you plan your yearly equipment budget, as well as be proactive in keeping users (and management) happy.

Another area that will bear some attention is the lowly network cabling, and its related hardware. Network cabling and network boards are notorious problem areas. Loose connections and broken wires plague the cables themselves. Network boards seem to spontaneously fizzle. Familiarize yourself with all the types of cabling hardware and network boards on your network, so that you know what types of connectors and terminators, for example, you might need when you're installing a new computer.

Another important recommendation is to keep an adequate supply of spare parts on hand. Keep extra network boards, cables, and connecting hardware handy and clearly labeled.

If you're not sure it's worth the expense to keep spare parts around, calculate the cost of the downtime for a single user, should that user's network board die. If it will take three days to order and receive a new network board, and the user can't work on the workstation for those three days, what will the three days of downtime cost? If three days of lost time costs less than the price of a network board, then you don't need to keep a spare on hand.

In most cases, however, you'll probably find that having an extra board or two available is a negligible expense for a much larger potential gain. Cables and connecting hardware are usually even less expensive, so there's really little reason not to have a ready supply.

REFUELING THE TANK (ADDING TO SERVER CAPACITY)

As your network grows (both in the number of users and in the type of usage it's getting), you'll want to monitor the server's memory and hard disk capacity.

One of the most common causes of server performance problems is a lack of adequate memory in the server. If the network seems to be operating slowly, or if you don't have enough memory to load NLMs, you may need to simply add more RAM to the server.

You should make it a habit to periodically use the Cache Utilization screen of the MONITOR.NLM utility to track the percentage of Long Term Cache Hits. If Long Term Cache Hits shows less than 90 percent consistently, you should add more RAM to the server.

You can also use the MEMORY and MEMORY MAP console utilities to see how much memory the server is using.

TIP

If you can't add more RAM right away, but you still need to make more memory available to NLMs so that they can run, you can use the following temporary solution. Use SERVMAN.NLM to change the Minimum File Cache Buffers and Maximum Directory Cache Buffers parameters. By changing these parameters, you can limit the amount of memory available for file and directory caching, and give that memory to the NLMs. After you change these parameters, reboot the server to make the changes take effect. Remember, only use this as a temporary solution until you can add more RAM to the server.

TIP

If you're using an ISA bus or PCI bus in the server, remember to use the REGISTER MEMORY console utility to register any memory above 16 MB for an ISA bus, or 64 MB for a PCI bus.

Hard disk space on the server is important real estate for your users. If the disk fills up, the users won't be able to open existing files, let alone create new ones. Therefore, it's important to monitor the amount of disk space still available for each volume on your server. By tracking the available disk space, you can predict when you'll have to either clean old files off the server, or add a new hard disk.

TIP

To see how much available disk space a volume has, use the NetWare Administrator utility from a workstation. From the NetWare Administrator's Browser screen, select a volume, then choose Details from the Object menu. When the volume's Details page opens, click on the Statistics page button. The Statistics page will show you how much disk space is still free for the volume to use.

PURSUING HIGH PERFORMANCE (TRACKING HOW THE SERVER RUNS)

Obviously, you want your vehicle to be performing at the highest possible level. Your average mileage per gallon increases, mechanical parts last longer, and your engine sounds really cool at stop lights.

You can keep your server's performance tweaked so that it performs at top levels, too. It might not draw envious looks from passersby, but it will still give you a warm feeling that everything is working well.

When you monitor the server's performance, you look for key indicators that the server is functioning at an optimal level. Some of the things you should monitor include the utilization percentage of the server's processor, the number of cache buffers being regularly used, and the server's memory allocation.

Every network has different needs and usage patterns. By default, server parameters are set so that the server will perform well on most networks, but it's a good idea to monitor the server's performance periodically anyway. By doing so, you can track how your server performs under different conditions, discover potential problems, and make improvements.

TIP

Server parameters (also called SET parameters) are aspects of the server that control things such as how buffers are allocated and used, how memory is used, and so on. You can change these parameters by loading SERVMAN.NLM, or by typing the full SET command at the server's console prompt. Using SERVMAN.NLM is much easier, because you can select the SET parameters you want from menus, and SERVMAN will automatically save the command in the correct server startup file. For more information about SERVMAN, see Chapter 7.

The server will optimize itself over a period of time by leveling adjustments for low usage times with peak usage bursts. Over a day or two, the server will have allocated an optimal number of buffers for each parameter, such as packet receive buffers. If you shut down the server and reboot it, the server will automatically be reset to the default allocation for all parameters.

To speed up the optimization period, record the allocations after one or two days of server usage, then set the given parameters to the recorded values. To set these parameters, use SERVMAN.NLM to select the parameters and change them. Then, when you exit SERVMAN, it will ask you if you want to save the new settings in the STARTUP.NCF and AUTOEXEC.NCF files. Say "Yes," so that these settings will be executed by those files the next time the server is booted.

REAL WORLD

You will probably want to monitor how the server's processor is being utilized by various processes, and how cache buffers and packet receive buffers are being used.

Monitoring Processor Utilization

If one or more server processes monopolize the server's CPU, the server's performance can be degraded, or other processes may have trouble running appropriately.

To see the total percentage utilization of the processor, load MONITOR.NLM and note the percentage in the Utilization field. (This field is in the General Information screen that appears when MONITOR is first loaded.) If the utilization is high, one or more processes may be monopolizing CPU time.

Use MONITOR's Scheduling Information screen to list all server processes and to see which ones have consistently high Load values. Then use the SCHDELAY console utility to prioritize server processes, schedule the processes to use less of the server's CPU, or slow down processes when the server is very busy. Experiment with SCHDELAY times until the CPU load value is acceptable.

Put the SCHDELAY command in the server's AUTOEXEC.NCF file to keep it in effect if you reboot the server.

Monitoring Cache Buffers

If directory searches are slow, you may need to change some SET parameters to increase the allocation and use of directory cache buffers. Use SERVMAN.NLM to change the following SET parameters that relate to directory cache buffers: Directory Cache Allocation Wait Time, Maximum Directory Cache Buffers, and Minimum Directory Cache Buffers parameters.

If disk writes are slow, use MONITOR's General Information screen to see if more than 70 percent of the cache buffers are "dirty" cache buffers. *Dirty cache buffers* are the file blocks in the server's memory containing information that has not yet been written to disk, but needs to be. Then use SERVMAN.NLM to increase the Maximum Concurrent Disk Cache Writes, Maximum Concurrent Directory Cache Writes, Dirty Directory Cache Delay Time, or Dirty Disk Cache Delay Time parameters.

Monitoring Packet Receive Buffers

If the server seems to be slowing down or losing workstation connections, use MONITOR's General Information screen to see how many packet receive buffers are allocated and how many are being used. If the allocated number is higher than 10, but the server doesn't respond immediately when rebooted, or if you are using

EISA or microchannel bus master boards in your server and "No ECB available" error messages appear after the server boots, you may need to increase the minimum number of packet receive buffers. To do this, use SERVMAN.NLM to increase the SET parameter Minimum Packet Receive Buffers so that each board can have at least five buffers.

You can also increase the Maximum Packet Receive Buffers parameter in increments of 10 until you have one buffer per workstation. (Again, if you are using EISA or microchannel bus master boards in your server increase this parameter until each board can have at least five buffers.)

(See Chapter 7 for more information about SERVMAN.NLM.)

ACCOMMODATING PASSENGERS (MANAGING USER ACCOUNTS)

Occasionally, you will have to add, delete, or change user accounts. These are very common, routine types of tasks for CNAs.

When you add a new user to your network, you will need to do more than simply create a user account for that person. Some of the things you may have to set up include:

- ▸ The user's NetWare Directory Services (NDS) account, which is an object for the user, with the object's related properties (information) filled in (such as the user's last name, full name, telephone number, and so on). You'll learn more about NDS in Chapter 3.

- ▸ The user's group memberships

- ▸ A home directory for the user's individual files

- ▸ A login script that maps drives to the directories and applications to which the user will need access

- ▸ NDS trustee rights (to control how the user can see and use other NDS objects in the tree)

- ► File system trustee rights to the files and directories with which the user needs to work (to regulate the user's access and activities in those files and directories)

- ► Account restrictions, if necessary, to control when the user logs in, how often the user must change passwords, and so on

- ► An e-mail account, if necessary

- ► Access to the network printers

- ► A menu program to prevent the user from having to use commands at the DOS prompt

When a user leaves the organization, you'll need to delete the user's account, and clean out any files the user owned. After allowing the user's manager to determine if any of the files should be transferred to another user, you'll want to delete the user's remaining directories, e-mail files, and so on.

In addition to managing user accounts, you will also manage group accounts. A *group* is simply a collection of users. You can create groups of users to allow you to quickly assign identical characteristics (such as trustee rights to a certain directory) to a large number of users at once. Every so often, you will need to update groups to add new users, delete old users, change a group's access rights to an application or directory, and so on.

Some of your most common cries for help probably will be from users who have forgotten their passwords. You can reset their passwords for them by using the NetWare Administrator utility.

All these routine tasks are described in more detail in Chapter 5, "NetWare 4 Security."

TESTING THE ANTI-THEFT SYSTEM (MONITORING SECURITY)

Your network's security can be vital to your organization. Banks must ensure that all their data is completely secure from intruders. Schools must ensure that students can't get in to alter grades or records. Lawyers must protect their client-attorney privileges. Doctors must protect the privacy of their patients.

Even if you don't think you work in a high-risk organization, you should still use some forms of network security. For example, you'll probably want to make sure important files don't get deleted accidentally. And then, of course, users often succumb to that temptation to try to see those payroll files.

The five primary types of security features in NetWare 4.1 are

- ► Login and password authentication, which ensures that only authorized users can log in to the network.

- ► Login restrictions, which control how those authorized users can log in (such as restricting the times of day they can log in, specifying how often they must change their passwords, and so on).

- ► NDS security, which controls whether NDS objects (such as users) can see or manipulate other NDS objects and their properties.

- ► File system access rights, which control whether users can see and work with files and directories.

- ► Directory and file attributes, which protect individual files and directories from various types of user actions.

As part of your normal CNA duties, you will probably be responsible for ensuring that the network security features are all being used wisely. When new users are added to the network, you'll make sure they have the access rights they need (and *only* the rights they need) to the appropriate files and NDS objects.

ZEN

"My current computer, in addition to 'DOS,' has 'Windows,' which is another invention of Bill Gates, designed as a security measure to thwart those users who are somehow able to get past 'DOS.' You have to be a real stud hombre cybermuffin to handle 'Windows.'"

Dave Barry

You'll also want to take a few minutes every once in a while to go through your important files, directories, or NDS objects to verify that everyone who has rights to those items still needs those rights.

For more information about how to set up and manage network security, see Chapter 5, "NetWare 4 Security."

GETTING BACK ON TRACK (BACKING UP FILES)

Suppose you're driving along the freeway, and you miss your exit. In most cases, you have three choices.

First, you can keep going and end up someplace completely different. While this might be an enticing adventure in some cases, if you were headed to Aunt Myrtle and Uncle Fred's golden wedding anniversary, you might not be real popular at the next family gathering.

Second, you could go all the way back home, and start the whole trip over again.

Third, you could return to a point just before you missed the turn-off, and then complete the trip as planned. You'll have backtracked a little, but at least you didn't have to start way back at your front door.

If you chose one of the first two options, you're probably an interesting person to know, but you may not be quite cut out for network management responsibilities.

The third option, of course, is the most efficient. You can get to where you were originally headed, with a minimum of wasted effort.

This is exactly why you make backups of your network files. If your server hard disk crashes and you must replace it, you're going to get a gold star if you can restore the network to where it was yesterday, so that only a few hours of work are lost.

We won't discuss what you get if you don't have backups, and all of the past year's work is lost irretrievably. One of your most important duties as a CNA will be to ensure that network backups are performed regularly (at a minimum, once a week).

ZEN

"When things go wrong, don't go with them."

Texas Bix Bender, *Laughing Stock, A Cow's Guide to Life*

Remember that backups are only useful if they can actually be restored. Therefore, you'll also want to periodically test your restoring processes during nice, calm, nonemergency situations.

For more information about using the backup software in NetWare 4.1, called SBACKUP, see Chapter 7, "NetWare 4 Management."

ADDING NEW ACCESSORIES (INSTALLING APPLICATIONS)

Another aspect of being a CNA is application management. This is the art and science of keeping up with the latest applications that your users need. You'll be installing new applications, upgrading existing ones, and deleting old ones. Then, of course, you must also make sure they all play nicely together once you have them installed.

After a network is up and running smoothly, most of the problems users will report to you will be application-related. Printing problems are common, so you'll want to pay particular attention to how the applications use print drivers, and which print queues the applications are set up to use.

You must also be very familiar with how the applications get installed, both on the server and on individual workstations. Then, you'll need to know how to set up a workstation to access the application.

ZEN

"I have spent countless hours trying to get my computer to perform even the most basic data-processing functions, such as letting me play 'F-117A Stealth Fighter' on it."

Dave Barry

HITTING THE CAR WASH (CLEANING UP THE FILE SYSTEM)

Nothing uses up hard disk space on the server like files do. Okay, maybe that was a little too obvious. But disk space on the server can become in short supply quickly, if your users aren't scrupulous about making sure they only keep important files in their directories.

REAL WORLD

Chances of your users being scrupulous about weeding out obsolete files are about the same odds as having the Boston Red Sox win the SuperBowl. Most users simply don't play that game.

It will probably fall on your shoulders to peruse your file system on a regular basis, looking for obsolete directories or files that could be removed. Now, this doesn't mean that you should go prying through users' files. Not at all. You are the keeper of file security on the network. Don't abuse that security yourself.

All we're recommending is that you look for general areas that could be redundant or obsolete, such as application directories that contain old versions of applications that no one is using anymore. Also, make sure users who no longer work in your organization don't have old directories hanging around.

ZEN

"If you haven't used it in the last three years, throw it out!"

Your mother

If your network has directories divided up by projects, see if there are old project files that you can archive onto another medium (such as backup tapes) and remove the originals from the server's hard disk.

You can also send messages to your users, asking them to take some time to go through their own files and delete the unnecessary ones.

In NetWare 4.1, when files are deleted, they aren't really erased from the disk right away. The file system keeps those files in a salvageable state, so that you can restore them if you need to. NetWare 4.1 will keep these deleted-but-not-gone files around until it begins to run out of disk space. Then it will purge these files from the disk to make more room available for new files. The deleted files are purged in chronological order, so that the ones that were deleted first are purged first.

You may not want all these files to stay on your server in a salvageable state. There may be some files you want to purge immediately whenever they are deleted, or you may want to purge files before the server gets filled to the point where it does it automatically. As part of your routine maintenance tasks, you may want to purge older files to free up disk space.

TIP

To set files or directories so that they are purged immediately when they are deleted, mark those files or directories with the Purge Immediate directory and file attributes. These attributes are explained in Chapter 5, "NetWare 4 Security."

To purge files manually, use the NetWare Administrator utility (also called NWADMIN), the FILER utility (a DOS-based menu utility), or PURGE (a command line utility). These utilities are explained in Chapter 4, "NetWare 4 File System."

LISTENING TO THOSE KNOCKS AND PINGS (MONITORING THE ERROR LOGS)

As the NetWare 4.1 server goes about its merry way each day, it generously keeps log files of any error messages or event notifications that might occur. Because you are probably not sitting at the server console watching the screen 24 hours a day, reading these logs are the easiest way for you to see what you might have missed.

TIP

Not every error message that appears on the screen indicates a real problem with which you must deal. Many messages are simply normal status messages that indicate when a particular event or task occurs. The server might be keeping right on track, running the network just like it's supposed to.

Periodically, such as once a week (or more frequently if you suspect a problem), you should read these error log files to monitor how your network is doing. You can read four different error log files:

▸ SYS$LOG.ERR logs error messages for the server. It is stored in the server's SYS:SYSTEM directory. All the messages or errors that appear on the server's console are stored in this file.

▸ VOL$LOG.ERR logs error messages for a volume. Each volume has its own log file, which is stored at the root of the volume. Any errors or messages that pertain to the volume are stored in this file.

▸ TTS$LOG.ERR logs all data that is backed out by the NetWare Transaction Tracking System (TTS). This file is stored in the SYS: volume. To allow this file to be created, use SERVMAN.NLM to turn the TTS Abort Dump Flag parameter to On. (For more information about using SERVMAN.NLM, see Chapter 7, "NetWare 4 Management.")

▸ CONSOLE.LOG is a file that can capture all console messages during system initialization. To capture messages in this file, type the following in the AUTOEXEC.NCF file:

```
CONLOG.NLM
```

CONSOLE.LOG is stored in the SYS:ETC directory. To stop capturing messages in this file, type **UNLOAD CONLOG** at the server console.

To view any of these error log files, you can either use a text editor from a workstation, or you can use EDIT.NLM from the server. Figure 2.2 shows a portion of an example SYS$LOG.ERR file for a server.

Example SYS$LOG.ERR

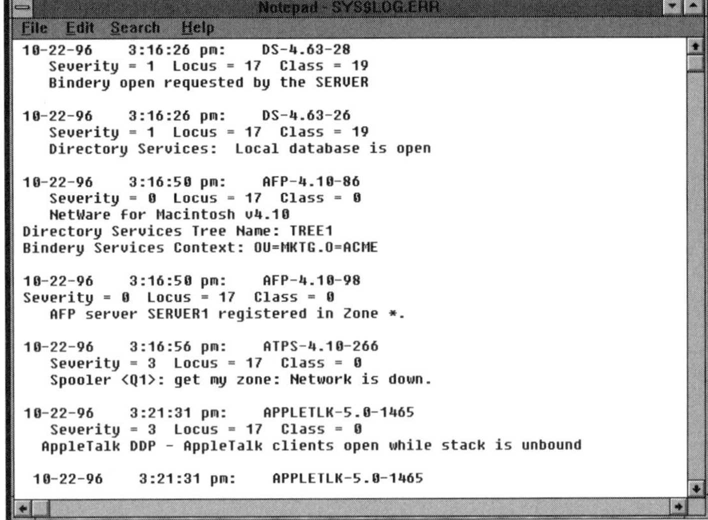

TIP

To use **EDIT.NLM,** type LOAD EDIT at the server console, then specify the path and name of the desired log file. See Chapter 7, "NetWare 4 Management," for more information about using **EDIT.NLM.**

TIP

To limit the size of the **CONSOLE.LOG** file, you can specify its maximum size in the command that loads **CONLOG.NLM.** In addition, you can specify that the previous **CONSOLE.LOG** file be saved under a different name. For example, to specify that the previous file be saved and named **LOG.SAV,** and to limit the new **CONSOLE.LOG** file to be no more than 100K in size, you would type LOAD CONLOG SAVE=LOG.SAV MAXIMUM=100.

To limit the size of the other three error log files (SYS$LOG.ERR, VOL$LOG.ERR, and TTS$LOG.ERR), use SERVMAN.NLM to change the appropriate SET parameters. Server Log File Overflow Size=*number* lets you specify the maximum size (in kilobytes) that the SYS$LOG.ERR file can become. Likewise, Volume Log File Overflow Size=*number* sets the maximum size for VOL$LOG.ERR, and Volume TTS Log File Overflow Size=*number* sets the maximum size for TTS$LOG.ERR.

TIP

To specify what happens to a log file when it reaches the maximum size, use SERVMAN.NLM to change the Server Log File State=*number* parameter, the Volume Log File State=*number* parameter, or the Volume TTS Log File State=*number* parameter. With these parameters, replace *number* with 0 (leaves the log file in its current state), 1 (deletes the log file), or 2 (renames the log file and starts a new one). The default is 1. For more information about using SERVMAN.NLM, see Chapter 7, "NetWare 4 Management."

User Support

As a CNA, ideally you'd like to keep the network running so smoothly that your users never have a single problem or questions. However, being users, they will tend to thwart your best efforts. They insist on forgetting their passwords from time to time. They decide they want to learn a new application. They tinker with their printing setup.

Sometimes, the user's software or hardware gets into the act, as well. A workstation will develop memory problems. A newly installed application will modify a workstation file in a way that conflicts with another application. A cable will get stepped on one too many times and the wires inside it will break.

REAL WORLD

The best-laid network plans of mice and CNAs can't prevent all the problems that users will have. That's why a significant portion of your job as a CNA will most likely be spent supporting your users.

If user support is one of your tasks, you must decide how you can deal with user problems most efficiently. If you don't already belong to a formal "Help Desk" department, setting one up (even if the "Help Desk" is just you) might be beneficial in helping you stay on top of user problems and helping your users get the support they need.

If you are responsible for user training, you will most likely want to standardize how you train them.

Occasionally, Help Desks are also responsible for training, but in most cases, those are separate functions. CNAs may find themselves in either area, however.

HOW DOES A HELP DESK WORK?

If you work in a large organization, you may be part of a formal "Help Desk" department. Help Desks (which may be called by different names) usually have a set of front-line people, such as CNAs, whom users contact when they encounter a problem.

The front-line Help Desk personnel are trained to handle most common problems. They may fix problems over the phone, or they may dispatch someone to go to the user's site to resolve the issue. If the problem is more than the front-line people can handle, the problem may get escalated to a second line of support — people who have even more technical backgrounds in that area (such as CNEs).

Even if you're a one-person Help Desk, you probably have the same basic situation. Users contact you for help, then you try to solve their problem. If it's something you need help with, you call in another expert, which may be someone in another department, an outside consultant, the manufacturer, or so on.

In a nutshell, the steps used to solve a user problem go through the following sequence:

1 • The user reports the problem to the Help Desk.

2 • The Help Desk prioritizes the problem, so that the most critical problems get fixed first.

3 • The problem is assigned to a Help Desk person, if there is more than one person at the Help Desk.

4 • The Help Desk tracks the progress made toward solving the problem, to make sure the user isn't left hanging.

5 • The Help Desk escalates the problem, if necessary.

6 • The Help Desk fixes the problem.

7 • The Help Desk reports the solution to the user.

8 • The Help Desk records the solution, so that if the same problem occurs again later, the solution can be found more quickly.

Granted, if you're a single-handed Help Desk, you may be able to skip a step or two, but the basic sequence is about right.

Let's look at some of the processes Help Desks may use to make each of these steps go smoothly.

Getting Problem Reports from Users

Obviously, you can only fix a problem if someone tells you the problem exists. Right? You'd be surprised how often problems go unreported simply because the user doesn't know there is someone to call.

If you're setting up a Help Desk, or if your Help Desk is fairly new, you may want to look at how well word has spread that the Help Desk is there for users to get assistance. A considerable amount of time can be wasted by users who try to work around a problem on their own, rather than calling in the expert (you).

> **REAL WORLD**
>
> If you think your Help Desk is being under-utilized, look for ways to publicize it. Get an article in the company's newsletter. Get five minutes on the agenda for the next departmental staff meeting and tell everyone about your services. Send an e-mail to everyone you support. Just get the word out. (It doesn't hurt to let the "big guns" see you out and about, too, so that they know they're getting their money's worth out of you.)

If everyone knows about the Help Desk, do they know how to contact you? Most Help Desks have a preferred method for receiving problem reports from users. Some require users to send an e-mail to a particular e-mail account, describing the problem in detail, and including the user's name, location, department, phone number, and so on. Other companies prefer that users phone in their work requests. Still others use a combination, telling users to phone in high-priority problems and use e-mail for lower-priority problems. Especially in smaller departments or companies, users may simply drop by your desk and report the problem to you in person.

Choose the method that works best for you, and make sure your users know how to get their problems reported to you correctly.

Prioritizing Problem Reports

If your Help Desk receives a high number of problem reports, you have probably already devised a way to prioritize those problems. (Again, in smaller organizations, prioritization may be informal, because the requests for help may be less frequent and it's easier to take care of every problem as soon as it is reported.)

Most Help Desks tend to set up priority levels similar to the following:

- *Emergency.* This is a major problem, and needs immediate action from everyone on the Help Desk team who can help.

- *High Priority.* The user who reported the problem needs immediate help. There is no workaround for the problem, and the user cannot work until the problem is solved.

> ▸ *Medium Priority*. The problem is affecting the user's work, but there is a workaround to use until the problem is solved.

> ▸ *Low Priority*. The problem is annoying and should be fixed, but it is not time-critical.

Many Help Desks will ask the users themselves to assign a priority to their problems when they first report them. If you explain the criteria, most users will be able to recognize whether they can get along for a while without the problem being solved. By letting them specify the priority, you may make them realize that other problems may be more important than theirs, and they might be a little more patient with you.

Once you have the priorities lined up, be sure you follow the priority list when fixing the problems. Don't make a high-priority problem wait while you try to solve an annoying medium-priority issue, for example. Give the medium-priority user a good workaround solution, if necessary, then go after the high-priority problem right away.

Assigning Problem Reports to an Available Person

If you have more than one person in your Help Desk area, problem reports usually should be routed to the next available person who has the expertise to handle the issue.

In some cases, Help Desks are set up to route phone calls into the Help Desk to different personnel so that no single person receives all of the incoming problems. In other organizations, a single person may act as a clearinghouse for problems. That person determines the most logical recipient for the problem and forwards the work request to that person. If your Help Desk has specialists in different applications or NetWare features, someone may be responsible for routing work orders to the appropriate specialist.

Your Help Desk should use whatever method seems most efficient for your team.

Tracking the Solution's Progress

Nothing is more frustrating to a user than reporting a problem and then never hearing back from anyone to know if it got fixed, if someone's working on it, or if there's no possible solution.

Many Help Desks use a problem-tracking database to record all incoming problems. The problem is assigned a number when it is first reported. Then, whoever is assigned to the problem reports the status on the problem (such as "In Progress" or "Fixed" or "No solution"). The user can then call the Help Desk, request the status for a particular problem number, and see where it stands. Some systems can fire off an e-mail automatically to the user every time the status in the database is updated.

Not all Help Desks are this fancy, of course. Even if you are running the show by yourself, however, you should still track the problems you receive. One reason to track problems is to keep the users updated, so that they stay happy. Another is simply to remind yourself that a problem is still open.

TIP

Tracking problems allows you to keep a record of the types and frequency of problems being reported. This could help you pinpoint problem areas that may need some extra attention. It may allow you to justify new equipment purchases to management. It can also help you with your next performance evaluation by allowing you to show your manager just how you spent your last year.

It doesn't really matter how you track problems. You can keep these records in a notebook, on cocktail napkins, or in a database. What matters is that you need to be able to tell the user where the problem stands, and you may want to be able to use the records later to compile a picture of your network's problem history.

Escalating the Problem

When the problem is something you can't quite tackle by yourself, you must know who you're allowed to call in for help.

ZEN

"Who ya gonna call?"

from the movie *Ghostbusters*

If your Help Desk has an escalation team or second-line support group, there should be some guidelines for escalating the problem to them. Everyone must understand the types of problems they can escalate, and who, in particular, can be tapped for each type of request.

In addition, your Help Desk may need to establish guidelines for when it's acceptable to call a manufacturer's technical support line. (Since many companies charge fees for technical support, your organization may want to limit such phone calls strictly to higher-priority issues.)

Outside consultants are another resource for escalating problems. Since such consultants tend to be very expensive, this is another area where guidelines should be established. In addition to outlining the types of problems you can take to consultants, these guidelines also should indicate which consultants are approved for you to use.

Resolving the Problem

Resolving the problem, of course, is the most important part of the entire process. This is where you use all your training, your on-the-job experience, your intuition, and your contacts to find a solution for the user's problem.

Sometimes there is no solution. Then you must find a workaround or some other way for the users to get their work done.

ZEN

"There is no such thing as a problem without a gift for you in its hands."

Richard Bach, *Illusions*

Recording and Reporting the Solution

After you've resolved the problem, you must do two things: let the user know what the solution was, and record it so that you don't have to duplicate your efforts the next time it happens.

When telling the user how you solved the problem, decide how much the user must know. If Joe's problem is one that he is likely to encounter again because he was doing something wrong, it will probably be worth your time to carefully explain to Joe how to prevent the problem from happening again. Even if you can't find a solution to the problem, it's still important to let the user know the outcome.

TIP

If the problem wasn't related directly to any action on the user's part, you can probably skip the gory details. It will bore the user and waste time for both of you. Just let the user know that the problem was solved, that it wasn't his or her fault, and that it won't happen again (or who to contact if it does).

Documenting the solution is nearly as important as telling the user about it. In the same database or notebook where you were tracking the problem's progress, be sure to record the final resolution. This will create a history that you can use in case the same type of problem recurs later.

In larger Help Desk organizations, having problems and their solutions stored together in a database can become a kind of "shared brain." Everyone in the Help Desk group has access to the answers that others in the group have already found. Problem-solving can become more efficient throughout the group, and the turnaround time for users' problems decreases. Why go through the whole discovery process again, if someone else has already figured out how to resolve the issue once?

ZEN

"Experience is a wonderful thing; it allows you to recognize a mistake when you make it again."

Anonymous

What if the Help Desk is just you? Even for a team of one, it's still important to record problems and solutions. It will keep you from forgetting how you solved a problem that may have happened a year or two ago. It will give you a history that you can use to plan for future network improvements or hardware purchases, as explained earlier. Finally, it will make it easier for someone else to step into your shoes here when you get promoted or hired away by that great company across the street.

TIP

Some Help Desk systems automatically send an e-mail report to the user when the problem is closed in the database. With a system like this, you kill both of the proverbial birds with one stone — you document the solution and inform the user at the same time. However, the fancy software isn't necessary in a small operation, as long as you simply remember to do the follow-up somehow.

TOOLS FOR HELP DESKS

A variety of tools are available that Help Desk organizations can use to track and solve user problems. Depending on the size of your Help Desk team, you may use some of these tools already. If not, you may want to look at implementing some of them.

ZEN

"The pioneers cleared the forests from Jamestown to the Mississippi with fewer tools than are stored in the typical modern garage."

Dwayne Laws

Help Desk Tracking Software

Many software packages are available that help record and track user-reported problems. The simplest of these software solutions provide basic tracking and reporting functions. Other packages go beyond the basics, providing the ability to research problem histories, integrate with e-mail systems for forwarding assignments or reporting progress, and so on. The software products also vary in degrees of usability.

If you don't already have a tracking application in place, and are contemplating investing in one, decide what you want to accomplish with it. What type of information is important to your company? How many people will it need to support, and how many Help Desk employees will be using it? Do you need the software to be used by one centralized Help Desk, or distributed across multiple Help Desk areas? Do you want to track just the problems themselves, or do you also need to be able to research problem histories to resolve new problems?

ZEN

"The worth of a program cannot be judged by the size of its brochures or by the number of full-page ads that appear in popular computer magazines."

Geoffrey James, _The Zen of Programming_

There's no point in paying extra for features you will never use. On the other hand, there's no point in saving a few bucks on a software package, but then wasting far more than that amount in time spent manually handling problem reports. Be sure you invest in the problem-tracking product that will make your Help Desk the most efficient and productive.

Telephony Systems

Many larger organizations are beginning to use telephony systems as a way to streamline how users report problems. Different types of systems can be used to help automate a Help Desk.

With some of these telephony systems, a user can place a phone call to a single number, and the system will automatically rotate the call to the next available Help Desk person. This feature is sometimes called _automatic call distribution_.

Some systems also provide voice-response features — you know the types. These are the systems that answer with a recording that says something like, "If you need to report a hardware problem, press 1,. . . ." These systems can also include announcements at the beginning of the message, to report on any general news callers may need to know (such as currently downed servers, planned system upgrades, and so on).

ZEN

"More and more, the people in 'Customer Service' won't even talk to you. They prefer to let you interface with the convenient Automated Answering System until you die of old age ('. . . if your FIRST name has more than eight letters, and your LAST name begins with 'H' through 'L' — press 251 NOW. If your first name has LESS than eight letters, and your last name contains at least two E's, press 252 NOW. If your. . .')."

Dave Barry

In addition, telephony systems can be used to track the numbers of calls coming in, how many are on hold, and so on.

Help Desk Handbooks

Any Help Desk, no matter how small, should consider creating and using a Help Desk handbook. Such a handbook could be used to explain everything from Help Desk policies and procedures, to specific remedies for common user-reported problems.

A Help Desk handbook is especially useful for training new Help Desk employees. It also can serve as a record of official policies — for example, noting whose authorization is required for certain procedures.

The following types of topics could be included in a typical Help Desk handbook. You will probably think of additional topics that would be especially useful for your particular organization.

- An overview of how the Help Desk operates.

- The login procedures to get into the Help Desk problem-tracking software.

- An explanation of how to use the Help Desk problem-tracking software.

- A description of any authorization procedures. For example, if your Help Desk charges departments for Help Desk services, the handbook might list approved cost center numbers, people who are authorized to approve such services, and so on.

- Step-by-step procedures for fixing most common user problems, such as how to reset a user's password, how to create a new user account, how to salvage deleted files, how to set up a new workstation's desktop, and so on.

- Procedures for installing new equipment. This may include everything from describing which forms to fill out, to how to check for interrupt and address conflicts in network hardware.

- Instructions for installing or upgrading applications on the network and on workstations.

- A troubleshooting guide, which could include a list of common problem areas, or possibly flowcharts to help isolate the cause of problems.

Figure 2.3 shows a sample table of contents from a Help Desk handbook.

FIGURE 2.3

*Help Desk Handbook,
Table of Contents*

Help Desk Disaster Plans

Having a disaster plan for the Help Desk is critical. A disaster plan outlines exactly what to do in the event of a disaster. For the Help Desk team, the disaster plan should explain which servers and machines to restore immediately, how to set up the Help Desk systems quickly, and so on. Generally, the disaster plan must describe how to get the Help Desk back on-line and functional quickly.

USER TRAINING

Good training is an essential part of ensuring that users stay productive and efficient while working on the network. If you are responsible for ensuring that users know how to access and use the network, you have your work cut out for you.

ZEN

"You teach best what you most need to learn."

Richard Bach, *Illusions*

To plan a training program for users, you must evaluate several factors:

- ▸ How many users must you train?

- ▸ How often must you train new users?

- ▸ What network skills do you have to teach them (such as logging in, selecting print queues, and changing their passwords)?

- ▸ What application skills do you have to teach them? For example, do you need to train them to use the accounting software, a word processing application, or the e-mail system?

- ▸ How much time will you be allowed to prepare the training materials and to present the training itself?

- ▸ Would the users benefit by having a workbook, short manual, or other learning tool that they could refer to later, after the training?

Typical Network Tasks for Users

Some of the most typical tasks you'll need to train the user to do include basic networking activities.

TIP

Ideally, users will not have to know much about the network. In fact, many network administrators set up their networks so that the users have to merely enter a password, then go directly into their applications.

The following list mentions some of the networking tasks you may want to tell users about.

- **Logging in and out of the network.** Tell them how to access and leave the network.

- **Passwords.** Be sure to give them guidelines for passwords. Tell them the minimum number of characters they must use, and explain that they should combine words, characters, and numbers to form words that can't be found in a dictionary.

- **Directory structures.** Tell them how files are organized on the network, and where they should store their own files.

- **Security.** In most cases, users probably do not need to know about the security features of NetWare. However, you will probably want to warn them about storing files on floppy disks, giving their passwords to friends, leaving their workstations without logging out, and so on.

- **Restrictions.** If you've set any time restrictions or disk space restrictions, you may want to tell users about them so they aren't surprised when they encounter such a boundary. It could save you some unnecessary phone calls.

- **On-line documentation.** If you want the users to be able to access the NetWare 4.1 on-line documentation, you'll need to teach them how to set up the viewer on their workstations, and how to use the viewers.

Workstation and Application Skills

The bulk of your training for users may be on their workstation operating system (such as Windows 95 or Macintosh operating system) and the applications that they will be using (such as e-mail, word processing, and spreadsheet applications).

The effectiveness of workstation and application training usually is minimal if the students don't have the opportunity to actually practice the tasks first-hand. Therefore, if at all possible, try to conduct the training in a lab where the students have access to workstations and can try out things such as using the Windows File Manager, sending an e-mail, spell-checking a word-processed document, or creating a spreadsheet.

In addition, you may also want to teach the users how to set up, modify, and upgrade their NetWare workstation software. For example, if you want users to be able to modify their NET.CFG files or login scripts, you'll need to teach them what they can do and how to do it.

Training Tools

As you prepare for the training you'll be doing, consider what types of tools might be most helpful for your users after the training is over. Some ideas you might consider are

- A short reference manual

- A workbook, where students can fill in information or complete exercises during the class

- A one-sheet quick-reference page or card that users can pin up on the wall next to their workstations

- A video, so that new users can watch it without you having to perform a training session every time someone new is hired

If any of these tools will help train the user, as well as minimize the amount of time you must spend training or fielding questions, they may well be worth the time investment. If they aren't going to have lasting value, however, don't waste your own time creating them.

Disaster Planning and Recovery

One area of network administration that is often overlooked until it's too late is disaster planning and recovery. Often, people ignore the "planning" part of the equation, putting it off until they have more time to think about it. (Sound familiar?) Of course, that mystical force that's responsible for enforcing Murphy's Laws views this sort of procrastination as opportunity. If you're one of the unfortunate ones who never got around to planning for a disaster, and then disaster strikes, Murphy's Laws will ensure that you get to enjoy the "recovery" half of the equation in all its full glory.

On the other hand, if you're armed with an up-to-date disaster plan, good backups, and accurate records of your network, the task of reestablishing your network may not seem nearly as daunting.

In the last few years, Mother Nature has been making her presence known in very violent ways. Hurricanes, earthquakes, tornadoes, and floods have rampaged through many parts of the United States as well as the rest of the world, racking up record numbers of casualties and property destruction. The cost of insurance claims from these disasters alone has many insurance companies struggling to stay afloat themselves.

But disasters aren't always caused by nature. Where your network is concerned, disasters can come in many guises.

REAL WORLD

A disaster that affects your network could be anything from a crashed hard disk on your server, to a security breach, to a fire that destroys your building. When it comes to computers, a malfunctioning water sprinkler system can cause as much damage as a hurricane.

How long can your company function without a working network? If your server is fried by a power spike, can everyone who uses the network get by without the network for a few days (or weeks) while you order new hardware and install it?

If your building is burned to the ground, and both your network and your backup tapes are reduced to unrecognizable cinders, what happens to the company? Can it just move into the building next door and be open for business again immediately, or will it take months or years to rebuild the data that was stored on the network? In this era, many businesses are only as good as their information.

If your company depends on the network for business-critical functions, having a disaster plan for your network can be far more important than having insurance that covers the building.

SO WHAT CAN A CNA DO ABOUT DISASTERS?

As anyone who's survived a disaster can tell you, the best way to recover from a disaster is to plan for one ahead of time. It doesn't matter what type of disaster it is. If you're prepared, you can weather the storm more easily and get back to normal much faster.

As a CNA, you can help ensure that your network recovers quickly from any disasters by preparing a disaster plan. A disaster plan documents exactly what to do about the network in case a disaster strikes. Among other things, it lists key people to call, describes how to restore backed-up files to the server, and explains the priority of services provided by the network so that you can restore the critical services first.

If you are in charge of your entire network, the disaster plan will be entirely in your hands. If you are working in conjunction with a consultant (such as a CNE) or an IS (Information Services) department, you will coordinate your disaster plan with them.

For example, if you manage a departmental network, but the IS group is in charge of the company-wide network, you will need to work closely with the IS people to make sure they understand what your needs are if a problem occurs. You can provide them with such information as your key personnel, critical applications, and location of your department's printers and servers.

Then, when the disaster strikes, you will, of course, look like a hero because your department's critical functions will be up and running before the other departments have even figured out what hit them.

PLAN AHEAD

If you haven't already created a disaster plan, do it today. It doesn't need to be that difficult, and it could save you a tremendous amount of wasted time, frustrated users, lost revenue, and sleepless nights. And you know that earthquake or electrical fire isn't going to wait for a convenient time in your schedule to occur, so the sooner you plan for it, the better.

REAL WORLD

Think about it. When would you rather cook up a disaster plan — during your lunch hours this week, or while you're sitting in the middle of a water-soaked server room with your boss screaming at you because he can't log in to the network?

Assuming you're suitably convinced about the need for planning now, here are a few pointers about your disaster plan:

- Write it down

- Make sure someone else knows how to execute the plan in case you aren't available

- Get the plan approved by your management

- Store multiple copies in different locations (not all in the same building)

It's important to have a documented plan because having the plan in your head only works if you happen to be around, of course. It would be just your luck to be vacationing in Tahiti when the roof over your company's headquarters in Denver collapses under the weight of a heavy snowfall.

If your disaster plan is up-to-date and easy to understand, you may be able to avoid a fast trip back home, especially if you've had the forethought to appoint someone else to be the second-in-command.

Just think how smug you'll feel as you dig your toes in the sun-warmed sand on the Tahitian beach, swirl the ice in your beverage, and imagine your second-in-command calmly executing your carefully detailed disaster plan. Ah, bliss.

ZEN

"Nibblin' on sponge cake, watching the sun bake all of those tourists covered in oil…Wastin' away again in Margaritaville."

Jimmy Buffett

Before you go drifting off into a tropical daydream, however, there are a couple of other small details to take care of.

First, now that you've written the plan and selected a faithful sidekick, you'll want to get the plan approved by your organization's heads. This lets you make sure that the people and network services you think are the highest priorities are the same ones your management thinks are. (This is often a useful thing to verify, anyway.)

More importantly, if the CEO has approved your plan to restore the production department's network before the administration department's, you won't have to deal with politics and egos while you're trying to restring cables.

ZEN

"Never make a technical decision based upon the politics of the situation."

Geoffrey James, *The Zen of Programming*

Next, make copies of your disaster plan. Store the copies in several locations so that you'll be able to get to at least one of them should disaster strike. Make sure at least one copy is off-site in case your entire building is demolished.

What Should Be in a Disaster Plan?

What you put in your disaster plan will depend on your particular situation. If you are the only person in charge of your network, you'll need to have a thorough plan that will take you from a mass of smoldering electronics to a functioning network with happy users logging in.

If you manage one part of a network, and other people manage the entire network as a whole, you may need to merely provide those people with your department's specific information. Then the IS department can roll your information into an overall plan to restore the whole company step-by-step.

Everyone's disaster plan will be different, but there are a few key points to consider when planning yours:

▶ Plan who to call in case of an emergency. List key network personnel, such as any network administrators for various branches of the NDS tree, personnel who perform the weekly and daily backups, and so on. You may want to include names of security personnel who should be notified in case of a potential security breach. Be sure to list home phone numbers, pager numbers, and cellular phone numbers, if you can.

▶ Plan the order in which you will restore service on your network. Who needs to be back on-line first? Should a critical department be restored before anyone else? Are there key individuals who need to be reconnected first? If you manage one department in a company, where does your department fit in the priority scheme? Do you need to be back on-line before some other department can function?

▶ Once you've identified the key people who need to be reconnected, is there an order to the files or services they'll need? Which servers need to be restored first? What applications must those users have immediately? Which files will they need right away?

▶ Document the location of your network records. Where do you keep your hardware inventory, purchase requisitions, backup logs, and so forth?

▶ Document the location of your network backup tapes or disks. Don't forget to document instructions for restoring files, or indicate the location of the backup system's documentation, in case the backup operator is unavailable. Record your backup rotation schedule so that other people can figure out how to restore files efficiently.

▶ Include a drawing of the network layout, showing the exact location of cables, servers, workstations, and other computers. Highlight the critical components, so that anyone else reading your plan will know at a glance where to find the priority servers or workstations.

KEEP GOOD RECORDS OF YOUR NETWORK

Another line in your defense against disaster is to maintain up-to-date records about your network. When something goes wrong with your network, it will be much easier to spot the problem if you have accurate documentation.

Good network documentation isn't just helpful in an emergency. Paperwork is always a distasteful task, but you'll be thankful you've done it the next time you have to add new hardware to the network, resolve an interrupt conflict, justify your hardware budget to management, get a workstation repaired under warranty, or train a new assistant.

ZEN

"One of the advantages of being disorderly is that one is constantly making exciting discoveries."

A. A. Milne

How you track your network information is up to you. You may want to keep a three-ring binder with printed information about the network, or you may prefer to keep the information on-line in databases or spreadsheets. Use whatever method works for you. The important part of your network documentation is not the format, but the content.

However you document your network, be sure to keep the information in more than one location. If a disaster occurs, you don't want to lose your only copy of the information that can help you restore the network quickly. Try to keep copies of your network information with your disaster plan, so everything can be accessed at the same time.

What types of network information should you record? Again, networks vary, as do network administrator job descriptions, so your documentation needs will vary, too. The worksheets in this chapter can help you get started. You can photocopy and use those worksheets, or design your own worksheets or databases to keep track of the information you need.

The following sections describe some of the types of information you may want to record for your network.

Hardware and Software Inventory

In any business, it's important to keep track of the company's assets. An up-to-date inventory of hardware and software purchases can help you tremendously with insurance reports and replacements, should a loss occur.

In addition, this inventory isn't just helpful in an emergency. You never know when management will ask for current capital asset information for various business reasons, and you'll avoid a fire-drill if you already have that data available.

In addition, accurate records of past purchases can assist you in predicting how your future computer purchases may grow. This will come in handy when your management asks for your budget plans for the coming year.

ZEN

"'It's a poor sort of memory that only works backwards,' the Queen remarked."

Lewis Carroll from *Alice in Wonderland*

Be sure to record each product's version number, serial number, vendor, purchase date, length of warranty, and so on.

Figure 2.4 is an example worksheet you might use to record hardware or software purchases.

Worksheet: Hardware and Software Purchases

Product: ________________________

Serial number: ________________________

Version number: ________________________

Vendor name: ________________________

    Address: ________________________

                ____

    Phone: ________________________

    Fax: ________________________

Manufacturer name: ________________________

    Address: ________________________

                ____

    Phone: ________________________

    Fax: ________________________

Purchase date: ________________________

Purchase order number: ________________________

Purchase price: ________________________

Warranty card sent in?   Yes ____   No ____   Not applicable ____

Length of warranty: ________________________

Current location of product: ________________________

Comments: ________________________
____
____
____

Installation and Configuration Settings

Whenever you install a new piece of equipment on the network, such as a workstation, printer, or server, there's a good chance the device will have configuration settings that could conflict with some other piece of equipment on the network.

If you keep a record of configuration settings for servers, workstations, printers, and other hardware, you can quickly check existing settings to verify that the new device's settings won't cause a problem, such as interrupt conflicts. Having this information at your fingertips can save you hours of locating and resolving conflicts the hard way.

In addition, there are other types of configuration information you should record so that the data is readily available when you need it.

For example, you should record the names of all the network boards installed in a server, along with the board's LAN driver and frame type being used. In addition, you should note the amount of RAM in the server, the type of time server it is, its IPX internal address, and so on. Figure 2.5 shows an example worksheet for recording a server's installation and configuration information.

For a workstation, you would document the network board installed in it, the LAN driver it uses, its location, station address, and other types of useful information. Figure 2.6 shows an example worksheet for a workstation.

Printers have configuration settings you'll want to record, too. Figure 2.7 is an example worksheet for recording printer data.

You may want to create similar worksheets for documenting other devices on your network (such as modems, tape backup drives, and so on).

*Worksheet: Server
Installation and
Configuration*

Server name: ____

Make and model: ____

Current location: ____

Serial number: ____

Memory: ____

Server's internal IPX network number: _________________________

Directory tree name: ____

Type of time sync server: ___________________________________

Server's time zone: ____

Server's name context in the Directory tree: ___________________

Protocols

PX/SPX (required):   TCP/IP: AppleTalk:

Yes _____ No _____   Yes _____ No _____   Yes _____ No _____

Network Board

   Type: _________________________

   LAN driver: _____________________

   Frame type: _____________________

   Node address: ___________________

   Settings: ________________________

   IP address (for TCP/IP only): ________

   Subnet Mask (for TCP/IP only): ______

Hard disk size: Yes ___ No ___

DOS partition size: Yes ___ No ___

Disk mirrored?   Yes ___ No ___

Disk duplexed?   Yes ___ No ___

SFT III installed?   Yes ___ No ___

CD-ROM drive?   Yes ___ No ___

Network Board

   Type: _________________________

   LAN driver: _____________________

   Frame type: _____________________

   Node address: ___________________

   Settings: ________________________

   IP address (for TCP/IP only): ________

   Subnet Mask (for TCP/IP only): ______

Disk Controller Board

   Name: _________________________

   Disk drive name: _________________

   Settings: ________________________

Other boards

   Name: _________________________

   Settings: ________________________

   Name: _________________________

   Settings: ________________________

Comments: ____

                ____

*Worksheet: Workstation
Installation and
Configuration*

Workstation user and/ or location: _______________________________

Make and model: ____

Serial number: ____

Memory: ____

Size of floppy disk drives: A: ________________   B: ________________

Size of hard disk: C: ________________   D: ________________

CD-ROM drive?   Yes: ________________   No: ________________

PC

DOS version: ____
version: ____

Windows version: ____
version: ____

OS/2 version: ____

NT version: ____

Netware client software version: ___________________________________

Network Board

Type: ____

LAN driver: ____

Frame type: ____

Node address: ____

Settings: ____

Network Board

Type: ____

LAN driver: ____

Frame type: ____

Node address: ____

Settings: ____

Other Boards

Name: ____
Settings: ____

Name: ____
Settings: ____

Comments: ____
____

Worksheet: Printer Installation and Configuration

Printer object's full name: ___________________________________

Make and model: ____

Current location: ____

Serial number: ____

Directory tree name: ______________________________________

Printer number: ____

Print queues assigned: _____________________________________

____

____

____

____

Print server assigned: _____________________________________

How is the printer attached: To server ___ To workstation ______ Direct _______

Print queue operators: ____________________________________

Print server operators: ____________________________________

Printer type (parallel, serial, AppleTalk, etc.): __________________

Interrupt mode (polled or specific IRQ): _____________________

Parallel printer configuration

   Port (LPT1, LPT2, or LPT3): _______________________________

   Poll: ____

   Interrupt (LPT1=7, LPT2=8): ______________________________

Serial printer configuration:

   Port (COM1 or COM2): ___________________________________

   Baud rate: ____

   Word size: ____

   Stop bits: ____

   Parity: ____

   XON/XOFF: ____

   Poll: ____

   Interrupt (COM1=4, COM2=3): _____________________________

Comments: ____

____

Maintenance Histories

The battery in Jason's port replicator for his laptop just died. Didn't that die a few months ago, too? Who fixed it then? Is this the same problem or a new one?

If you've been keeping a maintenance or repair history on all of your computer equipment, you can quickly find the answers to these questions. A maintenance history can help you see if there's a pattern of problems emerging with a particular machine, user, or department. It can also show you if repairs done at a certain facility seem to cost more than others, or if problems recur after a particular facility has repaired a machine.

When you log maintenance histories, be sure to indicate what the problem was, along with the solution. Document when the repair was made, who did the work, and how much it cost. If a warranty for the work was issued, note that as well (and its duration).

You may want to file all paperwork associated with repairs along with the worksheet that documents your original purchase of the item.

Figure 2.8 shows an example worksheet for recording maintenance histories.

*Worksheet: Maintenance
History*

Product:____

Serial number: ____

Repair date:____

Purchase order number: _________________________________

Repair vendor name:_____________________________________

       Address:_______________________________________

         MJ____

       Phone:____

       Fax:____

Repair Cost: ____

   Repaired under warranty? Yes _________ No __________

   New warranty granted? Yes _________ No __________

   Warranty expiration date:______________________

Comments:____

____

____

____

Volumes

If you have several servers and volumes on your network, it wouldn't hurt to keep a written record of the volumes installed on each server. You can document each volume's size, the server on which it is located, and even the types of files it contains. For example, you might indicate that the volume contains applications, users' daily work files, Macintosh-based drawings, or a certain department's database files.

You can also record the name spaces being used on a volume, and you can indicate whether each volume uses data migration or file compression.

Figure 2.9 shows an example worksheet for recording volume information.

Worksheet: Volumes

Server name:_______________________

SYS Volume

  Size: _______________________

  Name spaces:_______________________

    File compression on?   Yes __________ No __________

    Data migration on?   Yes __________ No __________

Other Volume (name): _______________________

  Size: _______________________

  Name spaces:_______________________

    File compression on?   Yes __________ No __________

    Data migration on?   Yes __________ No __________

Other Volume (name): _______________________

  Size: _______________________

  Name spaces:_______________________

    File compression on?   Yes __________ No __________

    Data migration on?   Yes __________ No __________

Other Volume (name): _______________________

  Size: _______________________

  Name spaces:_______________________

    File compression on?   Yes __________ No __________

    Data migration on?   Yes __________ No __________

Comments: _______________________

____

____

____

____

Hot Fix Bad Block Tracking

NetWare 4.1 provides a feature called Hot Fix, which monitors the blocks that are being written to on a disk. When NetWare writes data to the server's hard disk, NetWare writes the data, then verifies that the data was written correctly by reading it again (called *read-after-write* verification).

When a bad block is encountered, the data that was being written to that block is redirected to a separate area on the disk, called the *disk redirection area*, and the bad block is listed in a *bad block table*.

TIP

Some manufacturer's hard disks maintain their own version of data redirection and do not need to use NetWare's Hot Fix feature. If your disk does use Hot Fix, the size of the redirection is set up by default when you first create a volume on the disk.

Periodically, you should monitor the NetWare Hot Fix statistics to see if a disk is showing a high number of bad blocks and is filling up the allocated redirection area. To see the number of redirection blocks being used, use MONITOR.NLM's Disk Information screen. Track the number of bad blocks being found over time, so that you can see if the disk suddenly starts to generate bad blocks at an undesirable frequency.

If more than half of the redirection space has been used for redirected data, or if the number of redirected blocks has increased significantly since the last time you checked it, the disk may be going bad. If this is the case, you may want to refer to the manufacturer's documentation to try to diagnose the disk problem.

Figure 2.10 shows an example worksheet you can use to track the number of bad blocks being found on a server.

Figure 2.10 — Worksheet: Hot Fix Bad Block Tracking

Server: ____

Disk: ____

    Total redirection area: ___________________________________

Date:	Redirection blocks used:
Date:___________	Redirection blocks used: ___________
Date:___________	Redirection blocks used: ___________
Date:___________	Redirection blocks used: ___________
Date:___________	Redirection blocks used: ___________
Date:___________	Redirection blocks used: ___________
Date:___________	Redirection blocks used: ___________
Date:___________	Redirection blocks used: ___________
Date:___________	Redirection blocks used: ___________
Date:___________	Redirection blocks used: ___________
Date:___________	Redirection blocks used: ___________
Date:___________	Redirection blocks used: ___________

Comments: ____
____
____
____
____

Time Synchronization

When a NetWare 4.1 network is set up, each server on the network is designated as a particular type of time synchronization server. A server might be a Reference time server, a Single-Reference time server, a Primary time server, or a Secondary time server.

On larger networks, it's a good idea to keep a list of all the types of time servers on the network, so that you can determine what the effect might be on the network if you add another server or remove one from the tree.

Figure 2.11 shows an example worksheet you can use to record the types of time servers on the network.

<table>
<tr><td>

F I G U R E 2.11

Worksheet: Time Synchronization Servers

</td><td>

NDS Directory tree: ___________________________

Single-reference server: ___________________________

Reference server: ___________________________

Primary servers: ___________________________

____

____

____

____

____

____

____

____

____

Comments: ___________________________

____

____

____

____

</td></tr>
</table>

Network Layout

Another important piece of your network documentation is a drawing of the network layout. If you store this with your disaster plan, you (and others) will be able to locate critical components quickly.

On the drawing, show how all the workstations, servers, printers, and other equipment are connected. The drawing doesn't have to be to scale, but it should show each machine in its approximate location. Label each workstation with its make and model, its location, and its user. Show the cables that connect the hardware, and show what types of cable they are.

Workstation Batch Files and Boot Files

If your idea of spending an exciting afternoon consists of re-creating AUTOEXEC.BAT, CONFIG.SYS, and NET.CFG files on workstations, then there's no need to record the existing files.

However, if you think you may have something better to do, you may want to consider printing out these files and keeping them with the worksheets that document the workstation. You may also want to store copies of the files on diskette. If the workstation must be reinstalled, you can re-create the user's environment quickly if you have these files archived.

Server SET Parameters and Boot Files

If you have modified your server's configuration settings by changing its SET parameters, you can save the settings of those parameters to a file for safe-keeping.

TIP

SET parameters allow you to configure a wide variety of your server's performance characteristics, such as the number of cache buffers it allocates, whether the server is on Daylight Saving Time, or how close a volume can be to running out of disk space before it warns you. You can change SET parameters in several ways: by executing a SET command at the server's console, by putting a SET command in the server's AUTOEXEC.NCF or STARTUP.NCF file, or by selecting the parameter and its value in SERVMAN.NLM (which lets you select the parameters you want from menus).

SERVMAN.NLM allows you to save a server's SET parameters to a file. If you've changed the default SET parameters, you will probably want to print out this file and store the printout and a diskette copy with your network records. This will make it much easier to reinstall the server to the configuration you originally had, should the need arise.

It would also be a good idea to print or archive the server's boot files, including the STARTUP.NCF and AUTOEXEC.NCF files, so that you can re-create them if necessary, too.

Backup Information

Backups are only useful if the data on them can be restored. Sure, that's obvious, but there's more to it than just making sure your backup product works. What if you're not around? You can have the greatest backup rotation schedule in the world, but if you're the only one who knows where the backup tapes are, or in which order to restore them, the tapes are next to useless.

It is very important to record your backup rotation schedule, the location of backup tapes or disks, the names of any backup operators, the labeling system you use on your backup tapes or disks, and any other information someone may need if you're not around to restore the system.

Figure 2.12 shows an example worksheet you can use to record information about your backup schedule.

Worksheet: Backup Schedule

Server name (of server backed up): ___________________________

Server location: ___________________________

Backup system used (hardware and software): ___________________________

____

Location of backup media: ___________________________

____

Backup schedule: ___________________________

   Full backup: ___________________________

   Incremental backup: ___________________________

   Differential backup: ___________________________

   Custom backup: ___________________________

If custom backups are done, describe: ___________________________

____

____

Media rotation schedule: ___________________________

____

____

Media labeling instructions: ___________________________

____

____

Primary backup administrator name: ___________________________

Phone numbers: ___________________________

____

Comments: ___________________________

____

____

WHAT ELSE CAN A CNA DO?

In addition to writing a disaster plan, there are other ways you can plan ahead to avert (or at least diminish) disaster. Some of these preparatory measures include:

- Keeping a faithful schedule of backups, so that files can be restored quickly.

- Implementing disk mirroring (or duplexing), so that a simple hard disk failure in the server won't cause users to lose working time and files.

- ► Implementing SFT III (mirrored servers) on your mission-critical servers. If you can't afford to have the server go down at all, SFT III can be your best fail-safe.

- ► Using NetWare's TTS (Transaction Tracking System) if you're using database applications. TTS ensures that any transactions that are only partially completed when the server dies or the power goes out are backed out completely, so that the database isn't corrupted.

- ► Periodically reviewing your network's security, so that you can ensure that there are no potential security leaks. Investigate security measures such as NCP Packet Signature, access rights, and password security to ensure that your network is as secure as you need it to be.

TROUBLESHOOTING TIPS

Unfortunately, despite the best possible planning, something may still go wrong with your network. The majority of network problems are related to hardware issues — interrupt conflicts, faulty components, incompatible hardware, and so on. However, software creates its own set of problems, such as application incompatibility, Windows problems, and installation errors.

There are endless combinations of servers, workstations, cabling, networking hardware, operating systems, and applications. This makes it impossible to predict and document every possible problem. The closest anyone can do is approach the problem with a methodical system for isolating the problem, then fixing it.

The following troubleshooting guidelines can help you isolate the problem and find solutions.

Narrow Down the List of Suspects

First, of course, you must try to narrow your search to suspicious areas.

ZEN

"Round up the usual suspects."

From the movie *Casablanca*

- Were there any error messages? If so, look up their explanations in the System Messages on-line manual.

- How many machines did the problem affect?

- Can you identify a particular cabling segment or branch of the tree that is having the problem?

- Does the problem occur only when a user is accessing a particular application, or perhaps only when the user executes applications in a particular order?

- If the problem occurred when you installed a new workstation or server on the network, check their network addresses and hardware settings for conflicts with other boards or with machines that already exist on the network. Also, double-check the installation documentation to make sure you didn't misspell a command or accidentally skip a step.

- Are the servers and workstations using the same frame type to communicate? For example, if a server's using Ethernet 802.2 and a workstation is using Ethernet 802.3, they won't see each other.

- Are the servers and workstations using compatible NCP Packet Signature levels to communicate?

- If a user is having trouble working with files or applications, check the security features. Does the user have appropriate rights in the necessary directories? Are the files already opened by someone else? Do the files or directories have attributes assigned that are restricting the user from some actions?

- If some of a user's DOS path commands are gone, look in the login scripts for search drive mappings that are mapped without using the INS keyword (which inserts the mapping into the DOS path instead of overwriting existing paths).

- For printing problems, check that the printer, print server, and print queue are all assigned to each other correctly. You can use the NetWare Administrator to check on your printing setup. Select the print server from the Browser, open its Details page, then open its Print Layout page to see whether the print server, printer, and queue are all assigned together correctly. Verify that applications are using the correct print drivers for your printers. (See Chapter 8 for more information on printing.)

- If a volume won't mount, you may need to run VREPAIR to fix it.

Check the Hardware

Hardware problems can be relatively common in networks. Network cables are notorious for developing problems, partially because of the abuse they get being coiled up, walked on, bent around corners, and so on. A network analyzer, such as NetWare LANalyzer, can be a useful tool for diagnosing cable problems.

If you're suspicious that your problems may be hardware-related, try investigating the following common trouble-spots.

- Cables have an annoying tendency to work loose from their connectors, so check all connections between cables and boards first.

- Test suspicious cables by replacing them with cables you know work, and see if the problem persists.

- Make sure cables are terminated correctly, don't exceed length limits, and don't form endless loops in topologies that don't allow that.

- If the problem is with a computer or printer, try disconnecting it from the network and running it in stand-alone mode. If the problem still shows up in stand-alone mode, it's probably not a problem with the network connection. You can then eliminate the network components and concentrate on the configuration of the machine itself.

> ▶ If the problem occurred when you installed a new workstation or server, or added a board to an existing computer, check hardware settings for conflicts with other boards or with machines that already exist on the network.

Refer to the Documentation

Forget the jokes about only reading the manual as a last resort. The NetWare on-line manuals contain explanations of error messages that may occur. In addition, they include troubleshooting tips, configuration instructions, and so on.

In addition, check the manufacturer's documentation for any network hardware or applications you're using. Some applications have special instructions for installing on a network.

REAL WORLD

Contrary to popular hearsay, most of the network administrators I've known really do read the documentation before they try to install something as complex as NetWare 4.1. Why? Because their jobs are on the line. It's not like installing an application, where, if it doesn't work, it's easy to try again. If you mess up the company's network, it can be a really big deal, and can cost the company far more than your salary. And unfortunately, everyone immediately knows you've done something wrong. Keep this in mind the next time you're tempted to skip the documentation. There are plenty of other potential network administrators out there who would *love* to read the documentation first — and they may be your next replacement.

Look for Patches or Workarounds

When Novell engineers find a problem with NetWare, they usually either solve the problem with a patch (a piece of software that attaches to NetWare on your server and repairs it) or a recommended workaround.

Novell distributes these patches and workarounds on NetWire (on CompuServe and the Internet) and in the Novell Support Encyclopedia (NSEPro), so that you can easily update your server with these fixes. See Appendix D for more information about these resources.

Try Each Solution by Itself

After you've isolated the problem to a suspicious area, try implementing the solutions you've found, but implement them one at a time. The tendency is to try several possible fixes simultaneously to save time.

Start with the easiest, cheapest solution, and work up from there.

Trying solutions simultaneously may save time in the short run, but it could cost you extra money for unnecessary repairs or replacements. In addition, you won't know for sure what fixed the problem, so you'll have to start from scratch again should the problem reappear on another machine or at another time.

Call for Technical Support

There are a wide variety of places you can go to get help, advice, tips, and fixes for your NetWare problems or issues. Appendix D lists several of the resources you should know about. These resources range from Internet user groups, to classes, to publications that deal with NetWare support issues.

ZEN

"Help! I need somebody. Help! Not just anybody."

The Beatles

If you're looking for more formal technical support try these ideas:

- You can often find the technical help you need on-line, through the Internet Usenet groups that focus on NetWare, or through the NetWire forums on the Internet and CompuServe. These forums are moderated by knowledgeable sysops (system operators) and populated by knowledgeable users.

- Try calling your reseller or consultant for help.

- Novell's Technical Support is available by calling 1-800-NetWare. However, Novell's Technical Support is not free. You'll be charged a fee for each incident, so have your credit card handy. (An incident may involve more than one phone call, if necessary.)

> ► Before you call, be sure you've tried your other resources first —
> especially the documentation. It's embarrassing and expensive to have
> Technical Support tell you that the answer to your question is on page
> 25 of the Installation manual.

Document the Solution

When you find a solution, write it down and store it with your network
documentation. This may prevent you or someone else from duplicating efforts
and wasting time going through the same troubleshooting process to fix a similar
problem later.

ZEN

*"The empty page before me now, the pen is in my hand. The words don't
come so easy, but I'm trying."*

Kansas

The CNA 4.1 Program

"We've come halfway across the galaxy to see NetWare 4!"

CHAPTER 3

Understanding NDS

So, you think you know NetWare. Well, I have a surprise for you! Not even Bo knows NetWare. Novell's fourth generation of the NetWare operating system is a completely new ball game — and fortunately nobody is on strike.

Welcome to NetWare 4!

NetWare 4 is the big kahuna. It represents Novell's tenth try at the NetWare network operating system. The original architects of NetWare — Drew Major and Superset — returned to the proverbial drawing board and completely redesigned the interface, communications, and functionality of NetWare. The result is a powerful, flexible, and fast wide area network operating system. There's a mouthful.

NetWare 4 epitomizes transparent connectivity. It unobtrusively provides the user with simultaneous access to multiple network resources from one login — whatever that means. Simply stated, users no longer belong to servers — they belong to the *network* as a whole. All resources of the wide area network (WAN) are created as objects in a hierarchical tree, much like files in a directory structure. Users, servers, printers, volumes, and groups are treated equally and given simultaneous access to each other's resources. It's been a long and winding road, but we've finally achieved NetWare Nirvana in true form. This is all made possible through NetWare 4's newest wonder — NetWare Directory Services (NDS).

NDS is an object-oriented database that organizes network resources into a *hierarchical* tree — now there's a fancy word. The global NDS tree is fully replicated and distributed throughout the network, providing efficient connectivity and network fault tolerance — which is easier said than done. NDS also features a single login and hidden security system that makes access to any server, volume, or network resource completely transparent to the user. NDS takes care of the complexities of network topology, communications, protocol translation, and authentication in the background, far away from the user.

Think of NDS as a friendly cloud of joy overlooking your network! NDS is simplicity through sophistication.

TIP

NDS enables you to manage network resources (such as servers, users, and printers) and services, but it does not control the file system (directories and files). NetWare 4 provides a variety of non-NDS utilities for managing the file system.

In addition to NetWare Directory Services, NetWare 4 offers myriad additional features and benefits. We will explore these in just a moment.

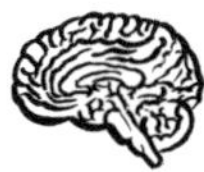

THE BRAIN

For an introduction to NetWare Directory Services, see Chapter 1 ("Understanding NetWare Directory Services") of the *Novell NetWare 4 Introduction to NetWare Directory Services* manual.

NetWare 4 is not an upgrade of NetWare 3.1x — it is a *migration*. NetWare 4 is a completely different way of approaching networking. It splits the role of networking into two halves — logical and physical. The logical half defines organizations and workgroups. The physical half defines users and servers. The beauty of this approach is that NetWare 4 can be as simple or complex as you want it to be. In addition, it includes a feature called *bindery emulation* that enables a NetWare 4 server to look like a NetWare 3.12 server. This is a whole new twist on backward compatibility. All in all, NetWare 4 is a great solution for small-, medium-, and large-size local area networks (LANs), metropolitan area networks (MANs), and wide area networks (WANs). Also, you better get used to it, because NetWare 4 is the foundation of Novell's new Enterprise approach to networking. Before you know it, NetWare 3 will be long gone and you'll be reading *Novell's CNA Study Guide for NetWare 5*.

TIP

NetWare 3.12 is actually more similar to NetWare 4 than you might think. NetWare 3.12 was originated because users of NetWare 3.11 were complaining that NetWare 4.0 had all the cool features. To satisfy these users, Novell released a special version of NetWare 3.11 that included some of the new advanced NetWare 4.0 features (such as VLMs, SMS, a new menu system, on-line documentation, and better Windows support). In reality, NetWare 3.12 is a subset of NetWare 4 without NDS.

If all of this seems a little overwhelming, have no fear, Uncle David is here. NetWare 4 actually isn't as alien as you might think. As a matter of fact, Novell hasn't made any dramatic changes to the fundamental architecture of the core operating system (OS). The Novell designers simply built on top of what exists in

NetWare 3.12. As you can see in Figure 3.1, NetWare 3.12 consists of the core OS and some supplemental services. All of the services shown in this figure are mostly unchanged in NetWare 4.1. These services include:

FIGURE 3.1

The Foundation of NetWare 3.12

> ▶ Core OS — Of course, the core operating system has been "tweaked" a little in NetWare 4.1, but the fundamental 32-bit architecture remains unchanged from NetWare 3.12. NetWare 4 still relies on the console prompt and uses NetWare Loadable Modules (NLMs) to provide additional functionality.

TIP

One of the most exciting enhancements in the NetWare 4.1 core OS is the elimination of overhead instruction sets. The NetWare 4.1 core uses a reduced number of instructions to accomplish the same things it did in NetWare 3.12. This elimination of overhead enables the operating system to run a little bit faster even with the CPU overhead caused by NDS. In addition to cooptimization, the NetWare 4.1 core OS includes UniCode support (with a conversion table for direct multiple languages), CONFIG.NLM, support for the Pentium 4 MB page (ON by default), as well as the ability to automatically detect PCI and PCMCIA bus systems.

> ▶ Internationalization — Both NetWare 3.12 and 4 are designed to support numerous international languages and utilities. By default, NetWare 4 supports English, French, German, Italian, and Spanish.

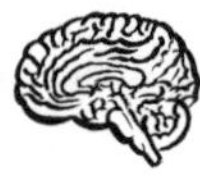

THE BRAIN

For further information on using NetWare 4 in languages other than English, refer to the "International Use of NetWare 4.1" section of the *Novell NetWare 4 Concepts* manual.

- DynaText — The DynaText viewer included with NetWare 4 offers all the functionality of the Novell ElectroText viewer provided in NetWare 3.12, plus a quicker response time, enhanced graphical user interface (GUI), Macintosh and UnixWare support, and compatibility for public or private notes in on-line manuals.

- Client Services (VLMs) — Both NetWare 3.12 and 4 offer better workstation connectivity through the NetWare DOS Requester. The Requester uses Virtual Loadable Modules (VLMs) to provide enhanced workstation support for NDS, NCP packet signing, and advanced user authentication. The latest version also supports connection timeout optimization, auto-reconnect, and much better extended memory management.

- Message Handling Services (MHS) — Novell now includes a sophisticated e-mail engine with NetWare 3.12 and 4. In NetWare 3.12 this engine is implemented as Basic MHS; in NetWare 4, it is termed MHS Services for NetWare 4. Both versions provide a background engine for storing and forwarding NetWare messages. In addition, they provide a starter e-mail application called FirstMail, which includes both DOS and Windows versions. The NetWare 4 version of MHS also provides full integration with NDS and NetWare 4 administration utilities. Furthermore, it takes advantage of specific mail-oriented NDS objects and includes SFT III compatibility.

- Storage Management Services (SMS) — Like MHS, both NetWare 3.12 and 4 include a background engine for backing up and restoring server data. SMS enables data to be stored and retrieved by using a variety of front-end applications. Also, these applications can call on numerous independent storage devices attached directly to the NetWare server. In addition, SMS can back up all file systems — including DOS, OS/2, Macintosh, MS Windows, and UNIX. Another exciting feature of SMS is workstation backup. This might seem a little backward for those of you who are used to backing up servers from the workstation — now we're backing up workstations from the server. NetWare 4's SMS adds support for NDS backup and the System Independent Data Format (SIDF).

▶ Menu System — Since NetWare 3.11, Novell has dedicated itself to providing a better integrated menu system. NetWare 3.12 and 4 use the new Saber-like menu system for building a consistent user interface. It includes better memory management, a higher level of workstation security, and user input options.

ZEN

"The guy who invented headcheese must have been really hungry."

Jerry Seinfeld

As I mentioned earlier, NetWare 4 builds on the foundation of NetWare 3. Now let's take a look at the evolution of NetWare from a server-centric OS to a network-centric OS. As you can see in Figure 3.2, there are five main features that make NetWare 4 the operating system of the next generation. These features build on top of the NetWare 3 foundation and reach to the sky. The most pervasive of these features is NDS:

F I G U R E 3.2

The Evolution of NetWare 4

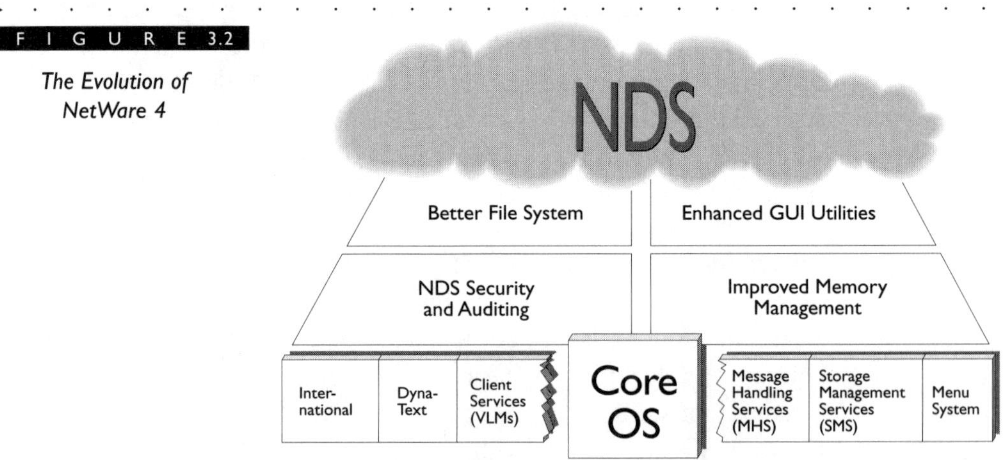

▶ NetWare Directory Services (NDS) — NDS is also known as the "Cloud." It oversees all facets of network operation — from logging in to multiprotocol routing. In short, NetWare 4 is NetWare 3.12 with NDS. It's that simple — or not. Life in the NDS universe is a little more complicated than you might think. The price for user transparency is your blood, sweat, and tears. NDS generates a great deal more administrative overhead than you might be used to. But all of your hard work is worth it. NDS will ultimately increase user productivity and add more value to the network. Some customers are projecting a 300 percent return on their NetWare 4 investment. We'll take a much closer look at NDS in just a moment and spend the rest of this chapter learning its hidden secrets. Welcome to the X-Files.

▸ Better File System — NetWare 4 optimizes the server disk with three new features: file compression, data migration, and block suballocation. File compression automatically reduces the size of infrequently used files by up to 63 percent. Data migration offloads these files to near-line storage devices. Finally, block suballocation decreases storage inefficiencies by allowing multiple files to share a single disk block.

▸ Enhanced GUI Utilities — NetWare 4 has vastly improved the interface for both user and administrator utilities. At the forefront of the new utility revolution is NetWare Administrator (NWADMIN) — a fully integrated Windows-based graphical administrator tool. The NetWare Administrator centralizes all NetWare 4 tasks in one graphical NDS structure. NetWare 4 also offers a text-based menu version of NetWare Administrator, enhanced console commands, server NLMs, and new user command line utilities (CLUs). All in all, NetWare 4 not only works better, it also looks better.

ZEN

"Image is everything."

Andre Agassi

► NDS Security and Auditing — NetWare 4 security is controlled by a five-layer security model. This model looks very similar to the NetWare 3.12 four-layer model, except that it includes an additional layer of login security — NDS security. This layer defines security above the server by controlling movement throughout the NDS tree. NDS access rights apply to both object and property levels. In addition to NDS security, NetWare 4 includes a comprehensive and powerful auditing feature. Independent auditors can track network transactions according to a variety of strategies, including logins/logouts, trustee modifications, file access and modification, NDS activity, queue management, and object management. The beauty of NetWare 4 auditing is that independent auditors can track network resources without having any other rights to the WAN. You will learn more about NetWare 4 NDS security later in Chapter 5, "NetWare 4 Security."

► Improved Memory Management — NetWare 4 manages file server RAM in a completely different way than NetWare 3.12 did. Earlier versions of NetWare allocated memory to multiple pools that served specific purposes. These pools were so inefficient that server applications could run out of RAM even if there was plenty of memory available in the main pool. NetWare 4 has consolidated all server RAM into one central pool, and memory is reallocated as needed. In addition, NetWare 4 includes memory protection that allows NLMs to run in a protected area of RAM. This ensures the safety of the core OS while you are testing third-party NLMs. Shields up!

As you can see from this discussion, NetWare 4 represents the peak of OS evolution. It builds on the foundation of NetWare 3.12 to create a more powerful platform for the next generation of networking. For an even more detailed comparison of the NetWare 3 and NetWare 4 features, refer to Table 3.1.

T A B L E   3.1

NetWare 4 and NetWare 3 Features Comparison

FEATURE	NETWARE 4	NETWARE 3
ARCHITECTURE		
Maximum number of user connections per server	1,000	250
Nondedicated server	Yes (NetWare 4 for OS/2)	No
Single login to network	Yes	No
Additive licensing	Yes	No
Memory protection	Yes	No
Global directory services	Yes	No
FILE SYSTEM AND STORAGE		
File compression	Yes	No
Data migration	Yes	No
Block suballocation	Yes	No
NETWORK SECURITY		
RSA public/private key encryption	Yes	No
Restrict login to specific Macintosh addresses	Yes	No
Security auditing	Yes	No
NETWORK MANAGEMENT		
GUI utility with view of entire network	Yes	No
Remote console session security	Yes	No
Remote console modem callback	Yes	No
Maximum shared printers	256 per print server	16 per print server
RAM used with remote printer	4.6 to 5.4 KB	4 to 20 KB
Integrated messaging	Yes	No
Network Link Services Protocol (NLSP)	Yes	Yes (add-on required)

(continued)

T A B L E 3.1

NetWare 4 and NetWare 3 Features
Comparison
(continued)

FEATURE	NETWARE 4	NETWARE 3
CLIENT SUPPORT AND INTEROPERABILITY		
LPT ports on client	LPT-1 to LPT-9	LPT-1 to LPT-3
NetWare for Macintosh user licenses included	Limited to total number of new user licenses	5
GUI user tools	Yes	Yes
NetWare DOS Requester support	Yes	Yes

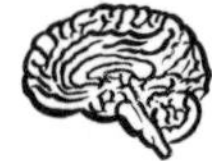

THE BRAIN

For a quick overview of new features in NetWare 4, refer to the *Novell NetWare 4 New Features* manual.

So, you bought NetWare 4 and now what do you do with it? How do you design your NDS tree? Where do you put your user accounts? What steps should you take to optimize performance, transparency, and system fault tolerance? Who shot Mr. Burns? What did you get yourself into? Don't panic — these are good questions.

This book is dedicated to *YOU*. I hope to get you through NetWare 4 with the least amount of pain. Who knows — you might even enjoy yourself along the way. We're going to start this first technical chapter with a detailed exploration of NetWare Directory Services (NDS). Then, we'll journey through all the exciting technologies that make life as a NetWare 4 CNA so wonderful.

Here's what's in store:

- ▶ NetWare Directory Services

- ▶ NetWare 4 File System

- ▶ NetWare 4 Security

- ▶ NetWare 4 Configuration

- NetWare 4 Management

- NetWare 4 Printing

In this chapter, we'll expand on the heart of NetWare 4 — NDS. But this is only the beginning. Once you've been introduced to the technology, you must learn what to do with it. Imagine what could happen if this power falls into the wrong hands. Imagine what Napoleon could have done with a turbocharged water cannon! No, we must harness the power of NetWare 4 by learning how to manage it. That's the true focus of *Novell's CNA Study Guide for NetWare 4.1*. Aah, but let's not get ahead of ourselves. It all begins with NetWare Directory Services.

QUIZ

I'm in a giving mood; it must be your birthday. I have three gifts for you — small, medium, and large. Each gift is wrapped with a different color paper that is red, green, or silver. In addition, I've placed a different color bow on each package, either red, green, or gold. In order to earn your gifts, describe the wrapping and bow combination for each present. Here are some clues:

- **The small gift has a green bow.**

- **The large gift is the only one that matches.**

Remember, puzzles help stretch your imagination. But whatever you do, don't pull a frontal lobe!

(Q3-1)
(See Appendix C for all quiz answers.)

Getting to Know NDS

Every cloud has a silver lining. Even Daisy-Head Mayzie had 15 minutes of fame. But she let it go to her head — literally. One sunny afternoon, sweet little Mayzie sprouted a Daisy out of her head! How odd.

After she got over the initial shock, Mayzie got a "big head." She left her family and friends to become a star in Hollywood. But all the money and fame didn't change the fact that she had a plant growing out of her cranium. And what's money worth anyway without somebody to share it with? So, Daisy-Head Mayzie realized her mistake and left the afternoon talk shows to return home. Yes, HOME. Not a SYS:USERS directory, not a base in baseball. No, this home is where everybody loves her for who she is, not what she has growing out of her head. Everybody lived happily ever after.

This could happen to you. You could become "NDS-Head Fred!" As a matter of fact, you can probably feel a slight twinge even as you read this. You knew that your new life as a NetWare 4 CNA would be exciting, but nobody prepared you for this. The more you learn about NDS, the faster your tree will sprout. Until one day you'll be as rich and famous as Daisy-Head Mayzie. But don't make the same mistakes that she did. Don't abandon the people who got you here — your family, your friends, Novell, and Ortho Weed Killer. Keep your head out of the clouds and your two feet planted firmly *in* the ground.

ZEN

"Congratulations! Today is your day. You're off to great places! You're off and away!"

Dr. Seuss

I'm here to help you deal with this whole cranial gardening thing. NDS is a virtual tree structure that helps you organize network resources. It's also referred to as the "Cloud" because it floats above physical resources — servers, printers, and users. In order to be an effective NetWare 4.1 CNA, you'll need an NDS tree growing out of your head. That's the goal of this chapter. We hope to generate enough neurokinetic energy to stimulate cranial growth. In other words, we're going to make you think until it hurts. So, without any further ado, let's start at the beginning — with the NDS database.

NDS is your friend. It may seem a little intimidating at first, but when you get to know NDS, it's actually pretty fun. Really. NDS is a big Sta-Puff marshmallow man that keeps track of your network's resources. In more technical terms, it's a distributed object-oriented hierarchical database of physical network objects. Huh? Just think of it as a huge WAN phone book. NDS classifies all network resources into 24 different objects. These objects can be organized by function, location, size, type, or color — it doesn't matter. The point is, NDS organizes network resources independently from their physical locations. When a user logs into the network, he/she can access any object in the tree regardless of its location. This type of openness, however, does not come without a price. One obvious problem is security — which is why NDS is controlled by a complex, impenetrable set of armor known as *NDS access rights*.

So, what does NDS look like? From the outside, it looks like a big cloud hovering over your network. On the inside, however, it's a hierarchical tree similar to the DOS file system. As you can see in Figure 3.3, NDS organizes resources into logical groups called *containers*. This is like Tupperware gone mad. In Figure 3.3, servers are organized according to function, then users are placed in the same container to simplify connectivity. In addition, productivity increases because users are near the resources they use. NDS also creates a global method of interconnectivity for all servers, users, groups, and other resources throughout the WAN. The bottom line is this — users don't access physical resources anymore. Instead, they access logical objects in the NDS tree. This means they don't need to know which NetWare server provides a particular resource. All they need to know is where the server exists in the logical NDS world.

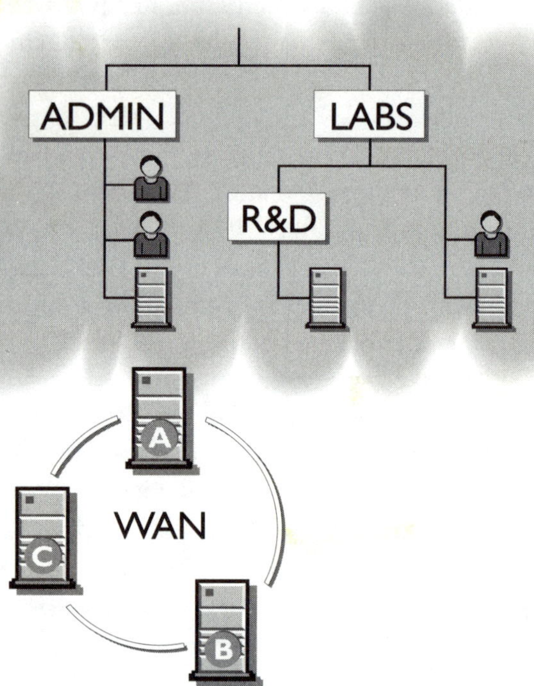

So, is NDS worth it? Well, you have to make that decision for yourself. But here are some of its benefits:

- ▸ Global database providing central access to and management of network information, resources, and services.

- ▸ Standard method of managing, viewing, and accessing network information, resources, and services.

- ▸ Logical organization of network resources that is independent of the physical characteristics or layout of the network.

- ▸ Dynamic mapping between an object and the physical resource to which it refers.

So, what do you think? Is NDS for you? Before you answer, let's take a moment to get to know NDS. Who knows — you might even like it.

THE "CLOUD"

NDS has many different names — the Directory, the tree, the "Cloud," the Sta-Puff marshmallow man. In reality, it's all of these things. But the most appropriate description is the "Cloud." NDS oversees physical network resources and provides users with a logical world to live in. This differs dramatically from what you're used to — NetWare 3.12. As you can see in Figure 3.4, the NetWare 3.12 bindery is server-centric. This means that every physical resource exists within and/or around the server. If Leia wants to access files or printers on multiple servers, she must have a login account and security access on every one. This system makes access and management both repetitive and time consuming. Also note that nothing exists above the server. The server itself represents the highest level of the network organization structure. Users, volumes, files, and printers all exist within each server.

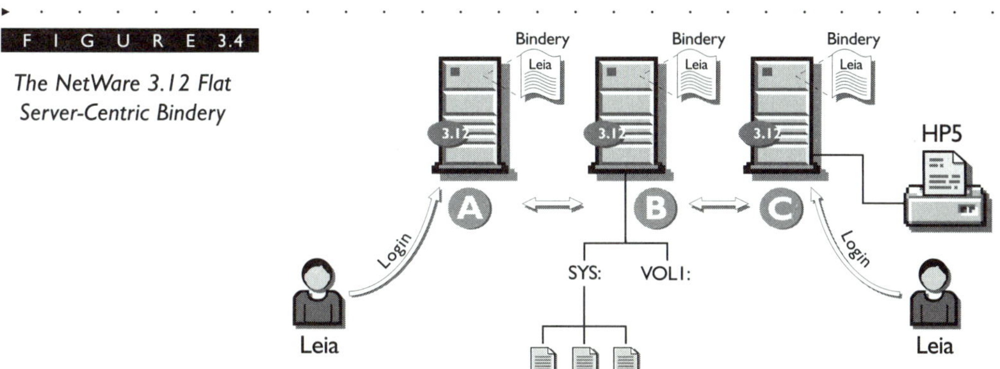

F I G U R E 3.4

The NetWare 3.12 Flat Server-Centric Bindery

NDS, on the other hand, creates a whole new world *above* the server. As you can see in Figure 3.5, each network resource exists only once as a logical object in the "Cloud." NDS is *network-centric* in the sense that everything happens in the NDS hierarchy. Suddenly the server has gone from being at the top of the network organizational chart to being a physical object at the bottom. The beauty of this system is that Leia only logs in once and has instant access to all network resources. She doesn't log into each server — she logs in to the NDS tree, and it tracks where her files and printers are. All logins, attaches, and access rights are handled in the background by NDS. This is the epitome of user transparency. The beauty is that users don't need to see inside the "Cloud"; all they need to know is that their stuff is there.

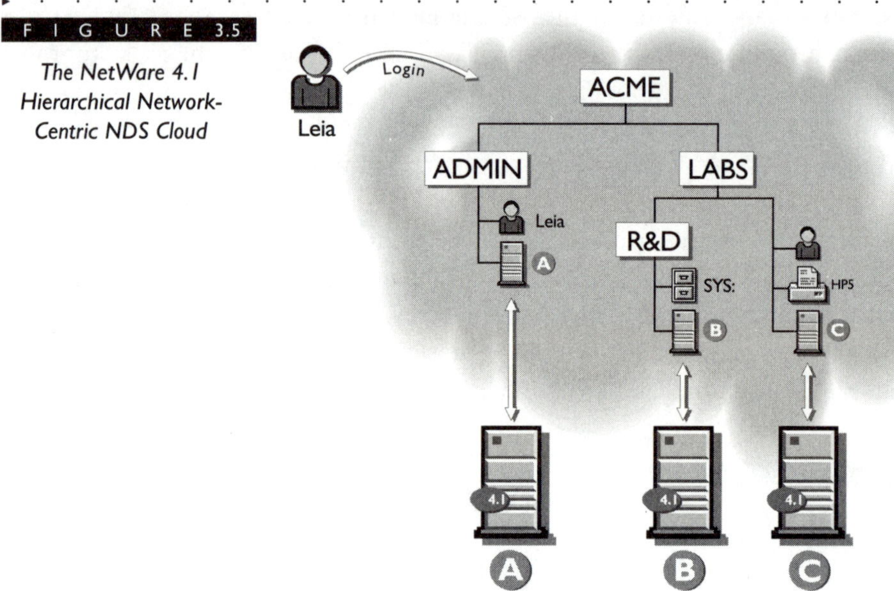

F I G U R E 3.5

The NetWare 4.1 Hierarchical Network-Centric NDS Cloud

The main lesson to learn from the accompanying graphics is the direction of the arrows. In Figure 3.4, the arrows of communication are horizontal. This means that all communication exists within and between NetWare 3.12 servers. If Leia wants access to another resource, she must follow the horizontal communications path to another server by either re-logging in or attaching. In contrast, Figure 3.5 shows the communication arrows running vertically. This means that communication occurs from within and between the NDS Cloud and its physical resources. The NDS Cloud handles the problem of locating resources and transparently grabs whatever Leia wants. This vertical communication structure makes finding and using network resources much easier for the user. In addition, and this is the part you'll like, it provides a single point of central network management for CNAs.

Let's take a closer look at the difference between NDS and the NetWare 3 bindery.

QUIZ

Let me tell you a little story. Maybe you've heard it before. It's about this little girl named Alice, who traveled through the "looking glass." Are you with me, here? When Alice entered the Forest of Forgetfulness, she didn't forget *everything* — only certain things. She often forgot her name, and the one thing she was most likely to forget was the day of the week.

Now, the Lion and the Unicorn were frequent visitors to the forest — strange creatures. The Lion lies on Mondays, Tuesdays, and Wednesdays and tells the truth on the other days of the week. The Unicorn, on the other hand, lies on Thursdays, Fridays, and Saturdays, but tells the truth on the other days of the week. One day Alice met the Lion and the Unicorn resting under a tree. They made the following statements:

Lion: Yesterday was one of my lying days.
Unicorn: Yesterday was one of my lying days.

From these two statements, Alice (who was a very bright girl) was able to deduce the day of the week. Can you?

(Q3-2)

NDS VERSUS THE BINDERY

The bindery is a flat-file database that tracks network resources on each server. It's stored as the files NET$OBJ.SYS, NET$PROP.SYS, and NET$VAL.SYS in the SYS:SYSTEM directory. The bindery uses these three files to track network objects, properties, and values. When users need to access a server's resources, they must log in and register with its respective bindery. If the server doesn't recognize them, it disallows access. Then the administrator must create a special entry with different access security for this user. This is painstaking and dumb.

NDS, on the other hand, stores information about network resources in a global database, called the Directory. This database is distributed on all servers in the WAN so that users can instantly get access to what they need. Suddenly, you've been escalated from a lowly bindery user to the top of the NDS food chain. As an object, you exist at the same level as the NetWare 4 server. How does it feel?

Following is a brief comparison of NDS and the NetWare bindery. In each case, focus on NDS's network-centric approach.

▶ Database — The bindery is a flat-file database consisting of three files in the SYS:SYSTEM directory. Each server retains its own database. NDS, on the other hand, is an object-oriented hierarchical database, called the Directory. The Directory encompasses all objects in the WAN and is distributed across servers. It also consists of database files on the SYS: volume. These files are, however, protected in a system-owned special directory.

REAL WORLD

The Sta-Puff marshmallow man has to come down to Earth sometimes. With all this flowery talk of clouds and trees, this simple fact remains — NDS is a database with parts of it stored on the SYS: volume of every NetWare 4 server. More specifically, the database is made up of four protected files in SYS:_NETWARE directory:

▶ BLOCK.NDS

▶ ENTRY.NDS

▶ PARTITIO.NDS

▶ VALUE.NDS

These files are very hard to find. Take my word for it, however, they are there. If you need to see them yourself, use the Directory Scan option of RCONSOLE. See Chapter 7, "NetWare 4 Management," for more details.

▶ Server — In NetWare 3, the server is king of the hill. It houses the bindery and controls all network resources. In NetWare 4, however, the server's importance diminishes quite a bit. It's simply another logical object in the global NDS tree. Network resources are accessed through the "Cloud" — independently from the physical server. But don't get caught up in the logical insignificance of the NetWare 4 server. In the physical realm, it's still king of the hill. After all, NetWare 4 has to be installed somewhere, files have to be stored somewhere, and users have to log into something.

▶ Users — In NetWare 3, users are defined as objects in the server-based bindery. You must maintain a user entry for every server to which a user needs access. In NDS, however, users are logical objects in the NDS "Cloud." Each user is defined only once. The system takes care of tracking the resources to which they need access. This is made possible using a concept called *context*, which we'll explain a little bit later.

▶ Login — Bindery logins are server-centric. This means that users must log in or attach to every server they use a resource from — files, printing, or applications. NDS logins are network-centric. This means that users issue one login statement for access to the entire "Cloud." Once they're in, the world is at their fingertips.

TIP

In order for NDS to identify you, you must provide your "full NDS name" at context. This includes your login name and user "context." There's that word again. A user's full name is a combination of who they are and where they live. My login name, for example, would be DAVID in CALIFORNIA in the USA. We'll talk about this later in the "NDS Naming" section in this chapter.

▶ Network Resources — In a bindery network, resources are owned by the server. Volumes and printers, for example, are tracked according to the server to which they're attached. User access to these resources requires login or attachment to the host server. NDS, on the other hand, distributes network resources independently from the server to which they're attached. It might seem strange, but volumes can be organized across the tree from their host servers. It's possible for users to have access to the NetWare 4 file system without logical access to its host server. Very cool. But don't get too carried away. Physical volumes still reside inside NetWare 4 servers. We haven't figured out how to separate the two yet — that's NetWare 5!

As you can see, NDS is a huge improvement over the NetWare 3 bindery. NDS is actually not even an improvement — it's a complete revolution. Nothing is as it appears. So, if NDS isn't what you think it is, what is it? Let's take a closer look.

ZEN

"The truth is out there."

The X-Files

COMPOSITION OF THE TREE

Plant a tree in a "Cloud" — it's good for the environment.

As in nature, the NDS tree starts with the [Root] and builds from there. Next, it sprouts container objects, which are branches reaching toward the sky. Finally, leaf objects flutter in the wind and provide network functionality to users, servers, and the file system. As you can see in Figure 3.6, the tree analogy is alive and well.

FIGURE 3.6

The Figurative NDS Tree

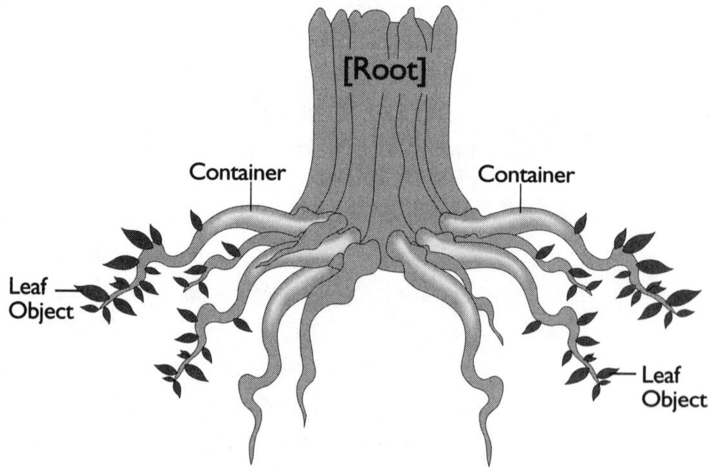

The real NDS tree is made up of special logical objects. NDS objects define logical or physical entities that provide organizational or technical function to the network. As you can see in Figure 3.7, they come in three different flavors:

- [Root]

- Container objects

- Leaf objects

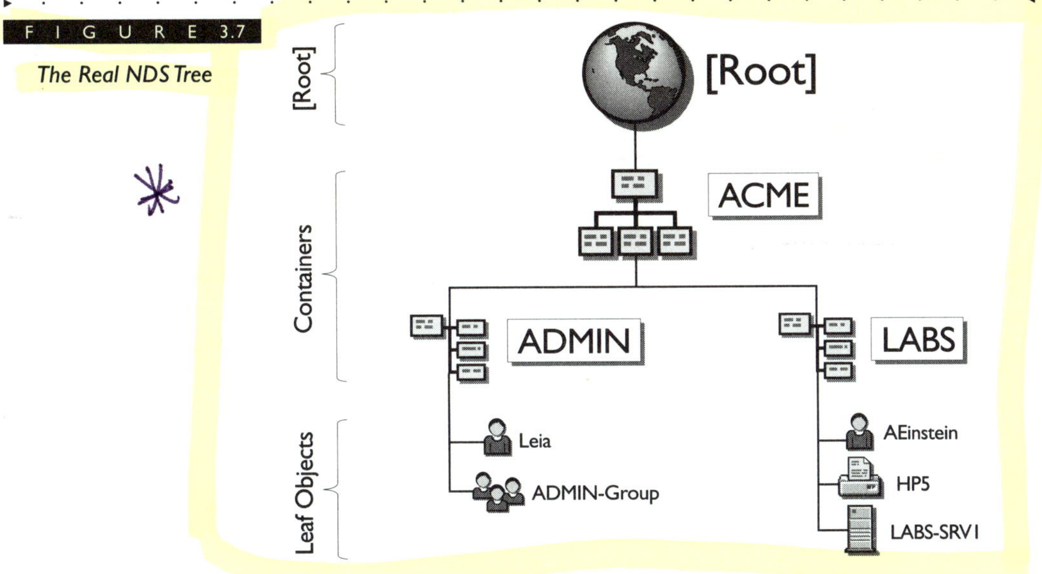

FIGURE 3.7

The Real NDS Tree

The [Root] is the very top of the NDS tree. Because it represents the opening porthole to our NDS world, its icon is appropriately a picture of the earth. Container objects define the organizational boundaries of the NDS tree and house other container objects and/or leaf objects. In Figure 3.7, we use container objects to define the ACME organization and its two divisions — ADMIN and LABS. Finally, leaf objects are the physical network resources that provide technical services and WAN functionality. Leaf objects define the lowest level of the NDS structure. In Figure 3.7, leaf objects represent users, a printer, a server, and a group. NDS supports 21 different leaf object types. We'll discuss these types in detail in the next section.

The tree can be organized any way you want, as long as it makes sense. AEinstein, for example, is placed near the resources he uses — the HP5 printer and LABS-SRV1 file server. In the ACME Case Study at the end of this chapter, we'll learn more about the ACME organization and rules for building their tree. For now, just focus on the conceptual framework of NDS and its tree structure.

On a more fundamental level, the NDS tree is stored in a fully replicated, globally distributed, object-oriented database, called the Directory. The Directory consists of multiple hidden system files in the SYS:_NETWARE directory on each server. These files are replicated and distributed throughout the WAN in order to provide fault tolerance and increased connectivity. Although all NetWare 4 servers use NDS, they don't have to contain their own directory database. If a server contains a portion of the database, that portion is called a partition. If a server doesn't have a copy of the database, then it must access it from some other server — which is less efficient. The bottom line is that a NetWare 4 server can contain the entire directory database, pieces of it (partitions), or none at all.

In addition, NDS requires a temporal assurance system, called time synchronization. This means that everybody has to agree on what time it is. Time is critical to NDS because NetWare uses time stamps for synchronization, auditing, and NDS security. Time synchronization is implemented by using a variety of different time server types, as you'll see later in this chapter.

Typically, a single network has only one directory. Although it's possible for a WAN to have multiple NDS trees, users can only be logged into one at a time. Also, resources cannot be shared between multiple trees. For this reason, Novell is pushing toward a single tree for the whole world. We'll see, but it sure explains the world icon for the [Root].

ZEN

"So be sure when you step, step with care and great tact. And remember that life's a great balancing act. Just never forget to be dexterous and deft. And never mix up your right foot with your left."

Dr. Seuss

Now that you understand the fundamental architecture of NDS, let's take a closer look at its different container and leaf objects. Remember, plant a tree in a "Cloud" — it's good for the environment.

NDS Objects

When you sprout a cranial conifer and become NDS-Head Fred, leaf objects and the [Root] will become important to you. I'd like to take this opportunity to help you out a little and explain them more. After all, even Daisy-Head Mayzie studied botany.

As we just learned, the NDS tree consists of three different classes of objects — [Root], container, and leaf objects. What we didn't learn is that these objects have specific properties and values. Remember, NDS is, after all, a database. An object is similar to a record or row of information in a database table. The property is a field in each database record. For example, the properties of a sales database may be Name, Phone Number, and Last Item Purchased. Finally, values are data strings stored in each object property. These values define the information around which the database is built. Let's take a closer look.

UNDERSTANDING NDS OBJECTS

So, how do we store things in NDS? The NDS database can contain all kinds of information stored as objects. An NDS object is defined by its properties. For example a USER is an object in NDS that can store information like LOGIN NAME, TITLE, LOCATION, and PASSWORD. Take a look at Table 3.2. It shows several different object types, their properties, and property values.

TABLE 3.2	OBJECT	PROPERTY	VALUE
NDS Objects, Properties, and Values	User	Login Name	AEinstein
		Title	Super smart scientist
		Location	NORAD
		Password	Relativity
	Printer	Common Name	HP5
		Default Queue	HP5-PQI
		Print Server	LABS-PSI
	NCP Server	Full Name	LABS-SRVI
		Version	NetWare 4.10
		Operator	Admin
		Status	Running just fine

The blueprint of all the object types, which are called *classes*, and their properties is called the *Schema*. One of the extraordinarily powerful features of NDS is that we can add things to the Schema. We might decide that it is important to store our Social Security Numbers as a property of the USER class. We can even add this property dynamically without interfering with users that are currently logged into NDS.

Many programs that run in a NetWare 4.1 environment add new object classes and properties to the Schema and, as a result, we will need to manage them. These databases are said to have an "Extended Schema." In this chapter, we will explore the objects that are created in the "Base Schema" of NetWare 4.1, plus some special objects created by the NetWare Application Manager.

Let's start our exploration of NDS objects with an introduction to the three different categories NetWare 4.1 offers:

▸ [Root]

▸ Container Objects

▸ Leaf Objects

[ROOT]

Whether you have used NDS before, or are just encountering it for the first time, you are probably familiar with how it is organized. We all know how the DOS file system works and NDS works in pretty much the same way. How, you ask? Well, let's take a look at the way a DOS file structure is organized.

DOS has a root for each file system such as C:\ or A:\. C:\ represents the top of the directory structure for drive C. Underneath C:\ are directories and subdirectories (such as "DOS" or "GAMES"). Files can be contained in directories or subdirectories and represent the end of the line. Files are the things that we use in the DOS file system.

Now, let's compare the way DOS file systems work with NDS. Every NDS tree has a single root, called [Root], that is just like C:\ in DOS. Underneath the NDS [Root] are containers, just like directories and subdirectories. Instead of having just one type of container like DOS, NDS has three — Country, Organization, and Organizational Unit. Leaf objects in NDS are just like files in the DOS world. They represent the end of the line. In general terms, Leaf Objects are the network resources we use on a daily basis. Check out Table 3.3 for a quick comparison between NDS and the old familiar file system.

T A B L E 3.3	OBJECT TYPE	DOS FILE SYSTEM	NDS
NDS looks like the old familiar file system	Root	C:\ - Top of the DOS file system	[Root] - Top of the NDS tree.
	Container	DOS - Directory	ACME - Organization
	Leaf	WP.EXE - File	Fred - User

In fact, we generally organize information in the NDS tree the same way we organize things in DOS. After all, NDS is a directory structure just like the DOS file system. In the DOS world we create directories to contain each of our applications in order to keep them separate and organized. In reality, there is nothing stopping us from putting all our applications in one big bucket, except programs that use the same filename. So, we keep each application executable separate and put it in a container with all the files it will need to run correctly. In NDS we do something similar. Instead of putting an executable and all its resource files together we put a USER and all the resources they typically need in the same container. We will talk more about organizing NDS and naming of NDS objects later in this chapter.

Now, let's explore each of the NDS object classes in more detail, starting with the [Root]. You never know which objects you're going to have sprouting from your cerebellum.

[Root] is a special object that is created for us by the NDS install program and there is only one for any given NDS database. It is used to represent the top of the NDS tree structure. In fact, it is an object of Schema class *TOP*. It only has one property that we can modify — *Access Control List* (ACL). We cannot create other [Root] objects and all NDS containers and leafs must exist under [Root].

By default, the Admin user is created at the same time, and the Admin user is granted supervisory privilege over the [Root] object. Check out Chapter 5 for more security information.

Each NDS object has a specific icon that depicts its purpose graphically. The [Root] object's icon is particularly interesting. Because the [Root] object represents the opening porthole to the NDS world, its icon is appropriately a picture of the earth. As you can see in Figure 3.8, the [Root] defines the top of our tree and houses the ACME container object.

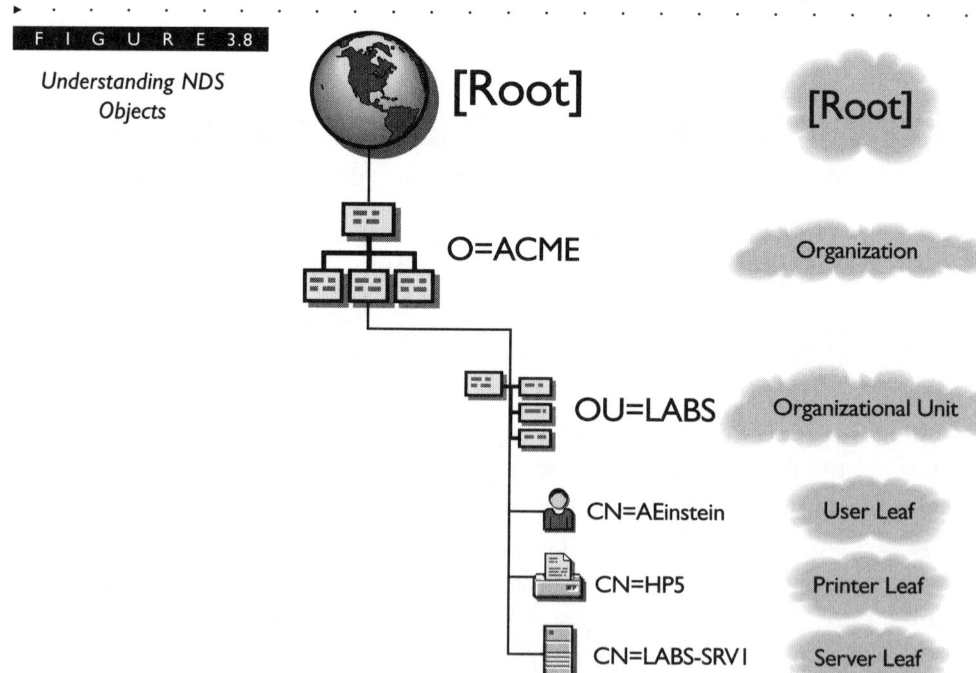

FIGURE 3.8

Understanding NDS Objects

The [Root] can hold only these specific container objects:

▶ Country — An optional container object that designates the country where your network resides.

▶ Organization — A one-dimensional container that typically represents your company.

▶ Alias — A logical NDS pointer to any other object existing elsewhere in the tree. In this case, the Alias can only point to Country and Organization objects.

All in all, the [Root] is a cool object, but you can't do much with it. Most of your CNA tasks will involve container and leaf objects.

REAL WORLD

You might notice the square brackets ([ ]) surrounding the [Root] object. These brackets designate the object as a special NDS entity. NetWare 4 supports two other such entities — [Public] and [Supervisor]. [Public] is a special trustee that applies security to all other objects in the tree. Users can inherit the rights of [Public] without having to log in. They simply need to attach. As we'll see in Chapter 5, this creates a serious NDS security loophole.

[Supervisor] is a special superuser for bindery emulation. Users from the NetWare 3 world can log into NDS using [Supervisor] and inherit all its special rights. [Supervisor] has other important properties that allow you to manage NetWare 3 and 4 coexistence.

CONTAINER OBJECTS

Although [Root] is a container object there is only one allowed per NDS tree. As a result, NDS give us three types of containers to help us build a directory tree.

▶ Country — Designates the country where certain parts of the organization reside.

> ▸ Organization — Represents a company, university, or department. NDS only supports one layer of Organization objects, hence, the term "one-dimensional."

> ▸ Organizational Unit — Represents a division, business unit, or project team within the Organization. Organizational Units hold other Organizational Units or leaf objects. They are multidimensional.

Refer to Figure 3.8 for an illustration of the relationship between the [Root] and container objects. The ACME Organization houses other Organizational Units (including LABS), which in turn house leaf objects (like AEinstein). Let's take a closer look at these three different container objects.

The Country object can only exist under the [Root] of the tree and there can be more than one. It has only three properties that we can modify — *Name*, *Description*, and *Rights to Files and Directories* (the ACL). It is largely used as an organizational object for very large WANs. On the downside, the Country object limits the use of typeless naming. This is very inconvenient. We will talk more about typeful versus typeless naming in the next section.

The country object is required by the X.500 specification. So, if you're going to plug into the "global village" anytime in the future, you'll need to insert a Country object. Here's why: the X.500 specification was designed to create a global directory for the entire planet. In one of the scenarios, the tree would begin with [Root], which would contain country objects. The problem with this idea is that we need to build NDS trees around our companies, not around our countries. In fact, many companies span more that one country. In most cases, the Country object is not used, and replaced with the Organization container.

The Organization object (O) can also only exist under [Root]. It is what most companies use as the top level of their NDS tree. You can create as many as you like and, in fact, the AT&T NetWare Connect Service (ANCS) is an NDS tree with many Organizations. When two separate NDS trees are combined into one, the "merge" happens at the Organization level in NDS. Once the merge of two NDS trees is complete, there will be a single [Root] with multiple Organization containers.

The Organization object has quite a few more properties than the Country object and, as a result, is a lot more useful. Keep in mind, however, it typically only represents the name of your company. One of the most important Organization properties is the Access Control List (ACL). The ACL allows us to use the Organization to grant rights that will be inherited by everyone in the Organization. We might want to grant everyone in the ACME company the privilege of using GroupWise. By granting ACME (organization object) rights to use GroupWise, we have also granted everyone in the ACME company access to GroupWise in one fell swoop. Pretty powerful stuff!

Because Organization and Organizational Unit objects perform similar tasks, they use pretty much the same properties. See Figure 3.9 for a detailed look at ACME's properties (using NWADMIN). The main difference between an Organization and Organizational Unit is that Organizations can only exist at one level. Any further subordinate structure must be created by Organizational Units. That's why the Organization icon is primarily horizontal in design.

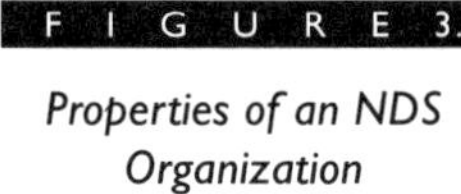

F I G U R E 3.9

Properties of an NDS Organization

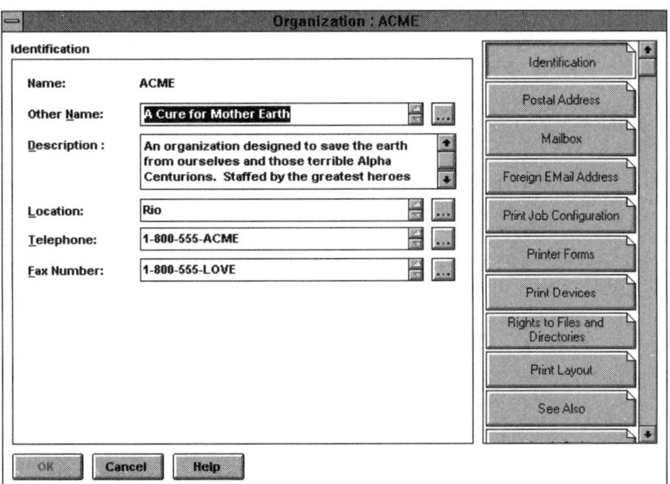

Before we move on to the Organizational Unit container, here's a few things to remember about the Organization object:

- ▸ Organization exists only under the [Root].

- ▸ There can be as many as you want.

- ▸ When two trees are merged together, the merge happens at the organization level.

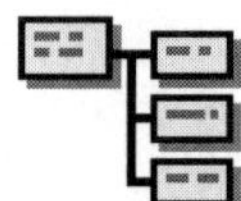 We now come to the most commonly used grouping object in NDS — the Organizational Unit (OU). As you discovered earlier, the OU is a lot like a directory. It can be contained by an Organization or another OU. Both the Organization and OU can contain leaf objects like users, printers, directory maps, and so on. Since the O and OU can contain similar objects they have similar properties, so let's explore.

The most important property of the OU, like the O, is the ACL. The ACL allows us (as administrators) to grant the OU container privileges to use a resource, and everyone in the container inherits the new privileges. We will talk more about how to effectively use the ACL in Chapter 5.

For now, let's take a closer look at some of the most important O / OU properties (see Figure 3.9):

- ▸ Login Script — User objects that reside in the O or OU run the Login Script as part of the login process. This login script is called the container login script and replaces the system login script in NetWare 2 and 3. For more information, see Chapter 6.

- ▸ Print Job Configurations — These define a printer or queue, form, and device information that is inherited by all the users in the O or OU. This is different from NetWare 2 and 3 in that we do not have to assign a configuration to each individual user. We can now assign configurations for whole Os or OUs. For more information, see Chapter 8.

- ▸ Printer Forms — These define a form type to be used by printers in the O or OU. Forms have names and a unique number that identifies them, as well as a length parameter and a width parameter. When a job prints with a form that is different from the form mounted in the printer, NetWare will stop the print job and ask the operator to mount the correct form in that printer. For more information, see Chapter 8.

- ▸ Print Devices — These define special commands that are to be sent to the printer before or after print jobs are completed. Print devices are used less in NetWare 4 than in NetWare 3 because most applications now control the printer directly and send special commands as part of the text or graphics to be printed.

▶ Print Layout — This shows the print servers, in addition to all associated printers and queues, for the print servers that are contained in the O or OU at which you are looking. For more information, see Chapter 8.

▶ Rights to files and directories — This stores privileges to the file system that users in the O or OU can use. This is a separate property because NDS and the NetWare file system are still separate, even though they work together. For more information, see Chapter 5.

▶ Intruder Detection — This defines the rules that govern how the intruder detection lockouts get tripped. In NetWare 2 and 3, we had to assign the rules to each user. Now we can assign them to the container and all the users in that container follow the rules. For more information, see Chapter 5.

There are other properties associated with both the O and OU, but the ones we have talked about here are the most often used. That does it for Container objects. Now let's take a look at the real stars of our NDS show — the leafs.

LEAF OBJECTS

As we learned earlier, the NDS leaf object is a great deal like a file in the NetWare file system. Leafs are the actual resources we need on a daily basis — like printers, users, file servers, volumes, directory maps, and so on. In this section we will talk about all 21 leaf objects that are included in the Base NDS Schema, plus Application objects used by the NetWare Application Manager. The Application objects are added to NDS when you install the NetWare Application Manager and won't be there if you haven't installed it yet. Also, remember, some of your applications may create their own objects and will not be listed here. Not to worry though. Onward to the leaves. . . .

There are 21 leaf objects available right out of the NetWare 4.1 box, plus 5 application objects created by the Application Manager. I have further organized these resources into six simple categories (see Table 3.4). These categories help you understand the relationships between related NDS resources. Let's start with User Leaf Objects.

T A B L E 3.4	OBJECT	CATEGORY
NDS Leaf Object Categories	User Leaf Objects	User Group Profile Organizational Role
	Server Leaf Objects	Communications Server NetWare Server Volume Directory Map
	Printer Leaf Objects	Printer Print Server Print Queue
	Messaging Leaf Objects	Distribution List External Entity Message Routing Group
	Informational Leaf Objects	AFP Server Computer
	Miscellaneous Leaf Objects	Alias Application (DOS) Application (Windows 3.x) Application (Windows 95) Application (Windows 95) Application (Windows NT) Bindery Bindery Queue Unknown

QUIZ

Look, there's that mischievious Alice again. She's trying to figure out when to believe the Lion. He says he'll help her escape from this crazy world. On what days of the week is it possible for the Lion to make the following two statements:

1. I lied yesterday.
2. I will lie again tomorrow.

Please help Alice find her way home.

(Q3-3)

User Leaf Objects

Users are the center of your universe. After all, they are the ones that "use" the network. NDS supports four different leaf objects that help users do what they do. Let's check them out.

User

Since the user object is the most important leaf object in NDS, we're going to take a really detailed look at all of its properties. The most important thing that the user object does is give the users their names and rights, based on the object's location in the NDS tree. Like all objects in NDS, it has its own ACL and with it we can grant specific privileges to each user. Users also inherit privileges from the containers they live in and their parents all the way to the [Root]. When you look at a user object in the NetWare Administrator graphical utility (see Figure 3.10), you'll find that all the properties are grouped into detailed pages of related properties. Here's a quick look:

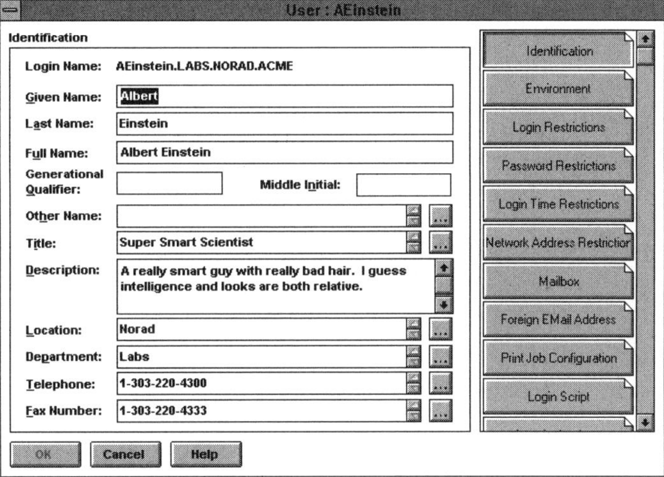

FIGURE 3.10

Properties of an NDS User Object

▶ Identification — The only mandatory property is Login Name and it is determined for you when you create the user. It is the full NDS name. For example, AEinstein.LABS.ACME. The remainder of the properties on this page are merely informational and here is a list of them: Given

Name, Last Name, Full Name, Generational Qualifier, Middle Initial, Other Name, Title, Description, Location, Department, Telephone Number, Fax Number.

▸ Environment — There are two important properties on this page: Language and Home directory. Language specifies what language you will see in the NetWare utilities. Home directory specifies where the users home directory will be located. This is used in login scripts by mapping to "%Home_Directory." This differs from NetWare 3 in that we no longer must use %LOGIN_NAME and can be more flexible. Network Address and Default server are populated when you login and are usually considered informational properties.

▸ Login Restrictions — Account Enabled, Account Has Expiration Date, and Limit Concurrent connections allow us to control whether a user can log in to NetWare NDS. This works exactly the same way as in NetWare 3.1x (see Chapter 5).

▸ Password Restrictions — Allow User to Change Password, Require Password, Force Periodic Password Changes, Require Unique Passwords, and Limit Grace Logins all are rules that force users to practice safe passwording (see Chapter 5).

▸ Login Time Restrictions — This is a graph of the times that this user may log into the network. Many administrators use this to kick users off the network when backup is running late at night (see Chapter 5).

▸ Network Address Restrictions — With NetWare we can restrict the user to specific stations on the WAN. To do this, we must know what the addresses are of the stations allowed. Since NetWare supports multiple protocols (such as IPX, TCP/IP, and AppleTalk), we must tell NetWare what protocols will be used by specific users. That's what this NWADMIN page is for.

▸ Mailbox — If MHS Services for NetWare 4.1 (the Messaging service included in the NetWare box) is installed on your server, you can

automatically add users with this NWADMIN page button. If Novell
GroupWise is installed, there is also a message on this page to use the
GroupWise detail page for administration. It saves tons of time, take my
word for it.

▸ Foreign E-mail Address — If your e-mail system is hooked up to the
Internet or another mail world, your mail name outside NetWare may be
different from your NetWare mail name. Foreign addresses are where we
store your e-mail name on other mail systems. This is mostly
informational and rarely used.

▸ Print Job Configuration — We can create custom configurations for
NetWare 4.1 printing. This page performs the same functions as the
O / OU page, but only for a specific user.

▸ Login Script — Login scripts are used to automate important drive
mapping and printing parameters. As the name implies, these scripts are
run at the time the user logs into NDS. There are four login scripts that
run in NetWare 4.1 and they run in the following order: Container,
Profile, User, and, finally, Default. User login scripts are difficult to
administer and are rarely used. We'll talk more about login scripts in
Chapter 6.

▸ Intruder Lockout — Sometimes hackers try to break into your network
by getting someone's username and trying to guess the password.
Intruder lockout prevents a great deal of wrong guesses by shutting
down the account temporarily if the user gets the password wrong too
many times (see Chapter 5).

▸ Rights to Files and Directories — The NetWare file system is still
separate from NDS and we must assign rights to it separately. For the
user, these rights are usually just rights to home directories and special
applications (see Chapter 5).

▸ Group Membership — Groups grant additional rights to their members.
They may be rights to places in NDS, or to places in the file system. This
property shows the groups of which the user is a member.

▸ Security Equal To — Shows what NDS objects to which the user has the same privileges. The rule in NDS is that all users are security equivalent to anything in their NDS Name. For example, Aeinstein.LABS.ACME is equivalent to himself ("Aeinstein"), the "LABS" OU, and the "ACME" O. We can expand this rule by granting trustee rights elsewhere in NDS and this is where we see the additional priveleges.

▸ Account Balance — If accounting has been enabled, this shows the account balance of the user.

▸ See Also — This is an informational page that allows us to reference another person in the company. If the user is away, this is the next person in line. The user's boss is a good example.

Group

Groups grant their members additional privileges. An example might be a group called "Payroll" that has all the privileges to access the payroll applications and databases. When a user is added to the group the rights are added to the users own rights, and when the user is removed, the rights are taken away.

Profile

Profiles are additional login scripts that run between the container login script and the user login script. These allow us to be a little more modular in writing login scripts. If the user is a member of the profile, the profile login script runs and does the additional configuration programmed into it. Simply speaking, it's a "group" login script.

Organizational Role

The organizational role is a little bit like a group. It grants new rights and privileges to the occupants of the role. Many organizations use the Organizational Role to implement Help Desk administrators. Think of it as a *JOB*, not a user.

Server Leaf Objects

The NetWare 4.1 server is still king of the physical hill. Even though it loses a great deal of its significance in the logical realm, NetWare still resides on it, users still log into it, and printers still attach to it. NDS supports four different leaf objects that apply to the logical server. Let's take a closer look.

Communications Server

Communications servers are those servers running NetWare Connect or NetWare SAA. This is also largely an informational object. In order to administer services such as SAA on the communications server, the user needs to have privilege to at least see and modify the communications server object.

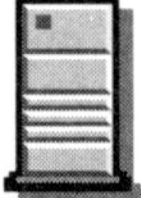

NetWare Server

This is also mostly an informational object but there are some special behaviors. Any user that has Supervisor rights over the NetWare Server object also has Supervisor privileges over the file system on that server. There's also a special login behavior that relates to the server object. When users log into NDS they usually need to type in their full names. For example, Albert types "AEinstein.LABS.ACME". However, if Albert is attached to a server that is located in the LABS.ACME container, then he can log in as "AEinstein". Much easier. As you can see, the NetWare Server object does have some significance in NDS. Check out Figure 3.11 for more details about the "WHITE-SRV1" server object. The page buttons provide some interesting informational categories including Identification, Error Log, Blocks Read, Blocks Written, Connect Time, and other dynamic statistics.

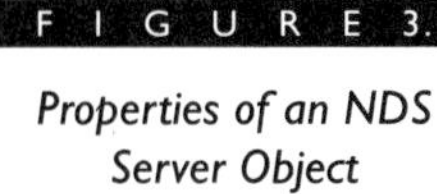

*Properties of an NDS
Server Object*

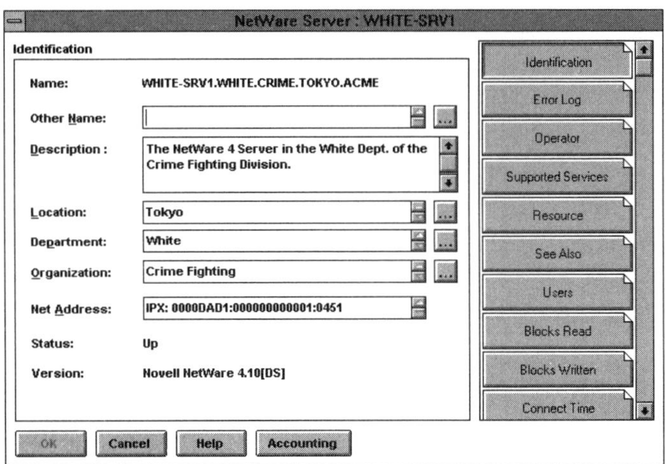

Volume

Volumes are important in NDS because they are no longer logically related to a server. We can map to a volume using its NDS name — "SYS.LABS.ACME," for example. Then, if the server on which the volume is located changes, we don't have to change our login scripts. Any user who has Supervisor NDS rights over the volume object also has Supervisor rights over the file system on that volume. The volume object is also where we view statistics about the space being used, where we set user space limitations for storage space, and control default rights to files created on the volume. All in all a very important object!

Directory Map

The Directory Map object is an abstraction object. What it allows us to do is create an object with an application name such as WordPerfect in NDS and point it to the actual physical location of WordPerfect. Here's an example. In our login scripts, we will map to "WordPerfect.LABS.ACME". If for any reason, and this never happens, the location of WordPerfect changes we do not have to rewrite our login scripts. Although the physical location of WordPerfect changed, the location of the directory map object in NDS is the same and as a result the name is the same. We'll talk more about how to use the Directory Map object later in this chapter and in Chapter 4.

ZEN

"We see them come. We see them go.
Some are fast, and some are slow.
Some are high, and some are low.
Not one of them is like another.
Don't ask us why; go ask your mother."

Dr. Seuss

Printer Leaf Objects

Like previous versions, NetWare 4.1 printing relies on three main elements — print queue, print server, and printer. Each of these printing elements is represented in the NDS tree as a leaf object. Users print to print queues where jobs are stored until the printer is ready. Once a job gets to the top of the queue, the print server redirects it to the appropriate printer. Sounds pretty simple to me — you be the judge. Here's a quick look at these three critical printer NDS objects:

Printer

The printer object defines a physical printer and important properties about it. Printers can be parallel, serial, or remote. The printer object also defines what print queues will be serviced by the printer. When there are problems with the printer, such as paper out, the printer object also contains the rules as to who will be notified. Check out Figure 3.12 for more information about the NDS Printer object.

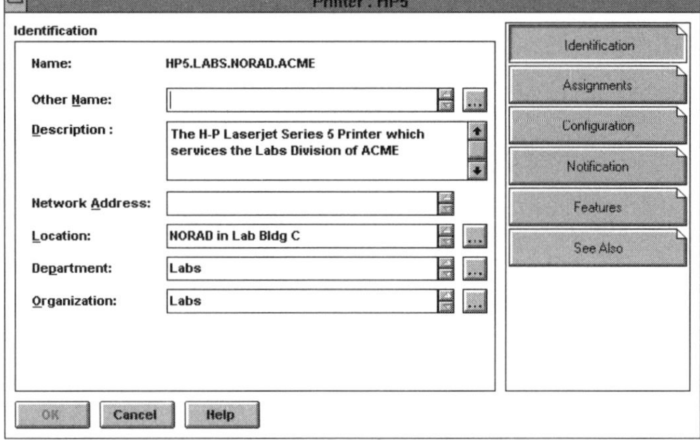

FIGURE 3.12

Properties of an NDS Printer Object

Print Server

The print server object is where we define the rules for the print server NLM. In NetWare, the print server's role is to make sure print jobs get from print queues to appropriate printers. Also, they make sure jobs are ultimately printed correctly (Print Job Configurations and Forms). The logical NDS print server must log in to the WAN to access the print queue's file system. To this end, you must be sure to give it a valid password. The print server object also contains a list of all the printers for which it is responsible.

Print Queue

The print queue is the object that the end user will select to get a job printed on the network. It tells the network where jobs will be spooled (stored) while they are being printed and who can use the queue. Print queue objects are primarily used by the "CAPTURE" command. Here's the good news: NetWare 4.1 gives you the flexibility to assign print queues to any volume — not just SYS:. See Chapter 8 for more information.

ZEN

"My shoe is off, my foot is cold.
I have a bird, I like to hold.
My hat is old, my teeth are gold.
And now my story is all told."

Dr. Seuss

Messaging Leaf Objects

NetWare 4.1 includes an impressive messaging engine called MHS Services for NetWare 4.1. It utilizes the Message Handling Service (MHS) standard. When you install and configure MHS, a variety of messaging objects are created. These objects allow you to control communications between users throughout the WAN. For a complete discussion of MHS Services, see Chapter 6 ("Netware 4 Configuration"). For now, here's what they look like

Distribution List

The Distribution List is a list of NDS users that will receive any MHS mail messages sent to the list. It also determines the owner responsible for administering the list. Lists can contain users, groups, and other Distribution Lists, but does not grant any additional privileges to the members of the list. This differs from the group object.

External Entity

Sometimes we would like to include people in our mailing lists who are not on our e-mail system. In this case they wouldn't be in NDS, since NDS is the mail address book. We can add users outside the NDS world using the External Entity (EE) object. EE contains the NDS name to which we will send messages and the foreign e-mail address where the user really resides. Since the External Entity is an NDS object, using MHS mail we can send messages to it and include it in our Distribution Lists.

Messaging Server

Represents a messaging server residing on any NetWare 4.1 server. This object is created automatically during MHS Services installation. The messaging server sends, receives, and manages user e-mail.

Message Routing Group

The Message Routing Group defines a domain in which all the member messaging servers can send messages to each other. This is a control object for the MHS services mail system included with NetWare 4.1.

Informational Leaf Objects

Most of the leaf objects so far have performed an obvious network function. Two other objects, however, exist for one purpose only — to store information. The AFP Server and Computer objects allow you to categorize information about noncritical physical resources (such as AppleTalk servers and workstations). Let's take a closer look.

AFP Server

This is primarily an informational object, but any NDS user who has Supervisor right over the AFP Server object also has Supervisor rights to its Macintosh file system. As an informational object, the AFP server stores interesting AFP information, including the resources it provides, who to contact in the event of a problem, and who uses the server.

Computer

The computer is also an informational object and merely provides a place to store information about physical workstations in the logical NDS structure. One application that will eventually take advantage of the computer object is software distribution. Software is distributed to workstations, not users. By creating computer objects, we can then select them as targets for software distribution using NDS-enabled software distribution products. In the future, CNAs will be able to install software from the comfort of their own desks.

QUIZ

Once again, we return to the Land of Forgetfulness and find Alice in cranial combat with the Lion. She still hasn't figured him out. Here's the question on the table: When can the Lion say, "I lied yesterday and I will lie again tomorrow"? *Warning!* **The answer is** *not* **the same as that of the preceding problem!**

Hmmm.

(Q3-4)

Miscellaneous Leaf Ojbects

No list would be complete without the final category — miscellaneous. There are four NDS leaf objects that don't fall into any other category. They're dominated by the Alias object, which points to any of the 23 previous resources. In addition, there are Bindery objects, Bindery Queues, and, of course, the Unknown leaf object — whose icon, interestingly enough, is a user with a paper bag over its head.

Finally, I've included some Application-based leaf objects because they perform an important role in the NetWare Application Manager. Let's check them out, starting with the Alias:

Alias

The Alias is a very powerful object that allows us to create a copy of any object in NDS and put it in a different location. Any rights and privileges associated with the original are also valid for the copy. However, in order to determine those rights and priveleges, you must go to the original object. It is really useful when, for example, a container full of users wants to use a printer that must reside in a different container. We can use an alias to make a copy of the printer and place it in the users' container. Additionally, we can place copies of users throughout the try for easier administration and logging in. In Figure 3.13, we place a copy of AEinstein in the ADMIN container. Now he gets all the privileges of both LABS (his home container) and ADMIN. Keep in mind, that when you administer an alias it actually affects the original object.

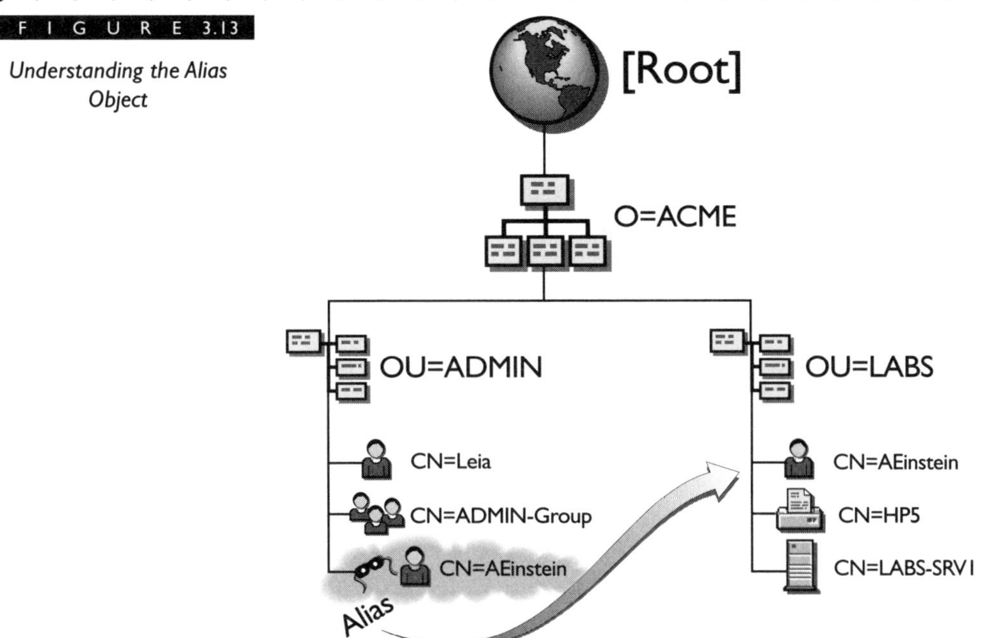

F I G U R E 3.13

Understanding the Alias Object

Application (DOS and/or Windows)

Application objects are created by the NetWare Application Manager and are containers for all the dependencies that must be met to run a given application. These include drive mappings, printer captures, scripts, and the location of the application. Using the information contained in the application object, the Application Manager will make sure the computer is configured just right to run the application. This is a very powerful object and we will be talking more about it later in this chapter.

Bindery

Bindery objects cannot be created directly by the NetWare Administrator tool, but are the result of creating an object using old bindery based utilities that do not have a corresponding NDS object type. These rare leaf objects can also be created by third-party utilities that extend the Bindery and need to be present for these applications to run. They only have meaning in the bindery context of a NetWare 4.1 server and are not manageable from NDS.

Bindery Queue

Bindery Queue objects are created during upgrade of a NetWare 3.1x server to NetWare 4.1 if "PUPGRAD.NLM" is not run. This normally only happens when using the "Across-the-Wire" migration method. When doing a same server upgrade, the PUPGRADE.NLM is run automatically and bindery queues are automatically upgraded to NDS queues. Bindery queues are not manageable from NDS and should be upgraded.

Unknown

Unknown objects exist in two ways. The first is the most common. The NetWare Administrator as an application has no way to know about new object types that are created in NDS. To handle and administer the new objects, the NetWare Administrator tool must load a snap-in module that knows what to do with the new objects. If the snap-in module is not loaded, NWADMIN will display all new objects as unknown simply because it simply doesn't know what to do with them. Objects of Unknown class are different. Objects of class *Unknown* will always show up in the NetWare Administrator as unknown and are created by the server to restore an object whose class is no longer known by the Schema. This could be due to corruption or because we deleted an entire Schema class.

That's all of them. We've discussed every NDS object supported by NetWare 4.1. You'll want to get to know them well because all future discussions center around how to organize, design, and manage these cute little network entities. Once you understand the relationships between NDS objects, you can start building your tree. As you've seen in this discussion, every leaf and container object is represented by an icon graphic that depicts its purpose. For example, printers are printers, servers are computers, and users are people. These icons are used throughout this book and in graphical NDS utilities. NWADMIN, for example, uses icons to provide a snapshot of the entire NDS tree in a hierarchical structure. This feature makes it easier for administrators and users to locate and use NetWare 4 resources.

ZEN

"Look what we found in the park in the dark. We will take him home, we will call him Clarke. He will live at our house, he will grow and grow. Will our mother like this? We don't know."

Dr. Seuss

NDS Management

So, how's your cranium feel? Are you getting a twinge from all this neural stimulation? Well you haven't seen anything yet. So far, we've explored the fundamentals of NDS and all it's wonderful objects. Now, we need to learn what this means for you as a NetWare 4.1 CNA.

In this section, we will explore the entire world of NDS Management. We will learn about planning, naming, the CX Command, and special NDS administration rules. Then, at the end of the chapter, we'll dive deeply into a case study of our own — ACME (A Cure for Mother Earth). Who knows, you might even save the world along the way. So, without any further adieu, let's get on with the show.

PLANNING A DIRECTORY TREE

One of the most important uses of NDS is security. By using the NDS security features you can allow or deny users access to any resource in NDS. In fact, if you deny a user access to, say, a printer, they don't even know what they're missing. Users only can see the things you have allowed them to see. This is because the NetWare security system consumes the directory. As administrators, we control what each user sees in NDS.

The user has a different view of the NDS tree. It is still a database, but to them it is also a list of network resources they are allowed to use. NDS is where users go to find and use things on the network. NDS is where users go to locate a printer on the network, capture to it, and print a pretty picture.

So, what's the point here? NDS is different things depending on who is looking at it. For us as administrators, NDS is a catalog of all the things on the network and how they should interact with users. To users, NDS is a catalog from which they can "order" services and resources to help them do their jobs. As we move through this chapter we will talk about both viewpoints. Let's start with design.

When designing an NDS tree we need to keep three goals in mind:

1. Keep things that users are going to use intuitive and easy to find.

2. Make things as easy as possible for us to administer.

3. Provide fault tolerance for the tree.

Now, all that sounds like NDS is difficult to deal with and plan. Not the case. NDS, just like your company, is a living, breathing entity. When we start creating NDS trees, we are creating models of the way our companies work. Our companies change all the time, and so must NDS. NDS is easy to change. In fact, it is expected and encouraged. But, before you get too carried away, you must be intimately familiar with the NDS structure.

NDS STRUCTURE

We can conceptually think of NDS as a six-dimensional database. It's not really as bad as it sounds. We can break it up into three 2-dimensional planes.

- ▶ Logical — This is where users, fax servers, file servers, volumes, and so on are located. It is the plane where we handle security and access control and it is also the plane that users view while looking for and using network resources. We will be spending a lot of time talking about this plane and the way that it works.

- ▶ Physical — NDS is a database, and just like any other database it is a set of files. It is stored on the SYS: volumes of the NetWare 4.1 servers in the tree. Since the information in the NDS database is very important to the operation of the network, it is partitioned and replicated. Partitioning allows us to break up the NDS database into smaller databases that can then be copied (replicated) around to other servers for fault tolerance and performance. Partitioning and replication are usually set up once and rarely changed. NDS will take care of itself. We will not be spending time on this aspect of NDS, but you can get more information from Novell White Papers, the NetWare Support Encyclopedia, and, of course, *Novell's CNE Study Guide for NetWare 4.1.*

▸ Schema — The Schema is the blueprint of what can be stored in NDS. We will not be talking about the Schema either, but remember from earlier in this chapter that the Schema can be changed. New object types can be created in NDS and the Application object is a good example.

The logical plane and the physical plane are related and affect planning of NDS. Since NDS can get pretty big for large companies, we really want to take advantage of the partitioning and replication features of NDS. These allow us to distribute the NDS database to other servers in our network and protect the tree from server crashes.

As a general rule, we want to create NDS trees that follow the logical model of the way our company works. Often this will look similar to the organizational charts. I said "similar" because it's pretty rare that the organizational chart is up to date. Larger multi-site companies will use partitioning across WAN links to keep local copies of the NDS database close to the people that use them. This means introducing physical location information into NDS much like this:

```
LABS.NORAD.ACME
```

```
CRIME.TOKYO.ACME
```

In a tree that has these two containers, we will put a copy of the NORAD part of the tree in NORAD, Colorado and the Tokyo part of the tree in Japan. This make things convenient for the users in the local offices but it does mean creating a container that has a location as its name.

We may also need to study the way workgroups share information and resources to get an idea of what our tree should look like. We will also need to think about who is going to run the NDS tree. If more than one administrator will have responsibility for maintaining NDS, then we may create Admin "domains" where each Admin has rights to administer only a part of NDS.

Earlier in the chapter, we talked about organizing NDS objects in containers much like files are stored in file system directories. In the file system, we create application containers (subdirectories) for the program executable and all the files that the program needs to run. In NDS, we place users and all the resources they need in the same container. Often, however, a user will need to access a resource outside his or her container. That's where NDS access management comes in. Let's take a closer look.

ZEN

"Waiting for the fish to bite or waiting for wind to fly a kite. Or waiting around for Friday night or waiting perhaps for their Uncle Jake or a pot to boil or a better break or a string of pearls or a pair of pants or a wig with curls or another chance. Everyone is just waiting."

Dr. Seuss

GENERAL NAMING RULES

Chances are you will be administering an NDS tree that has already been designed and built. In this case, your job is to make sure that users can get to the resources they need. This will mean creating objects and teaching users how to access them. Efficient resource access centers on good naming fundamentals. Let's start there.

All objects in NDS are accessed via their names. There are two types of NDS names:

▶ Distinguished Names (known as Fully Distinguished Names — FDN)

▶ Relative Distinguished Names (RDN)

Table 3.5 summarizes the differences between FDNs and RDNs.

TABLE 3.5

Getting to Know Distinguished Naming

	DISTINGUISHED NAMES	RELATIVE DISTINGUISHED NAMES
What it is	Complete unique name	Incomplete name based on current context
How it works	Lists complete path from object to [Root]	Lists relative path from object to current context
Abbreviation	FDN	RDN
Leading period	Leading periods required	No leading periods allowed
Trailing periods	No trailing periods allowed	Trailing periods optional

Believe it or not you are already an expert in NDS naming. Earlier, we explored the similarities between NDS and the DOS file system. Naming works almost exactly the same way — check it out.

For the moment let's assume that DOS has no search paths and that we have a laptop computer with the following directory structure.

```
C:\
        →11DOS
        →APPS
                →WP51
                →QPRO
```

This is a really simple computer and it doesn't have a menu program. When the laptop fires up it greets you the the with standard "C:\>" prompt. If you want to run WordPerfect, what do you have to do? Can you type WP at the C:\> prompt? Nope, the computer will respond with "program not found." Remember, we are assuming no search paths. This is because WP.EXE is not in the current directory. The real problem is that DOS names, just like our real names, are multi-part.

Mary Todd Lincoln, wife of Abraham Lincoln, is an example of a multi-part name. In the western world if we see someone else with the last name "Lincoln" we assume that the person is a possible relation. If we come across someone with "Todd" and "Lincoln" in their name we assume closer relation. Perhaps a brother or sister. In order to distinguish Mary from everyone else, we use her full name. However, when we are in a personal situation like dinner with Mary, we need only to use her first name.

ZEN

"Who am I? My name is Ned. I do not like my little bed. This is no good. This is not right. My feet stick out of bed all night."

Dr. Seuss

In NDS, Fred.ADMIN.ACME is just like our "Mary Todd Lincoln" example — "Fred" is his first name, "ADMIN" is his middle name, and "ACME" is his family name. Check out Figure 3.14. Barney.LABS.ACME is related to him because he is also part of the ACME organization. Wilma.ADMIN.ACME is an even closer relation to Fred because she is not only a member of the ACME organization, she is also a member of the ADMIN organizational unit (she's his wife). Since Fred and Wilma live in the same container (and house), they can address each other by their first name. This is called a common name. We'll talk more about common names later.

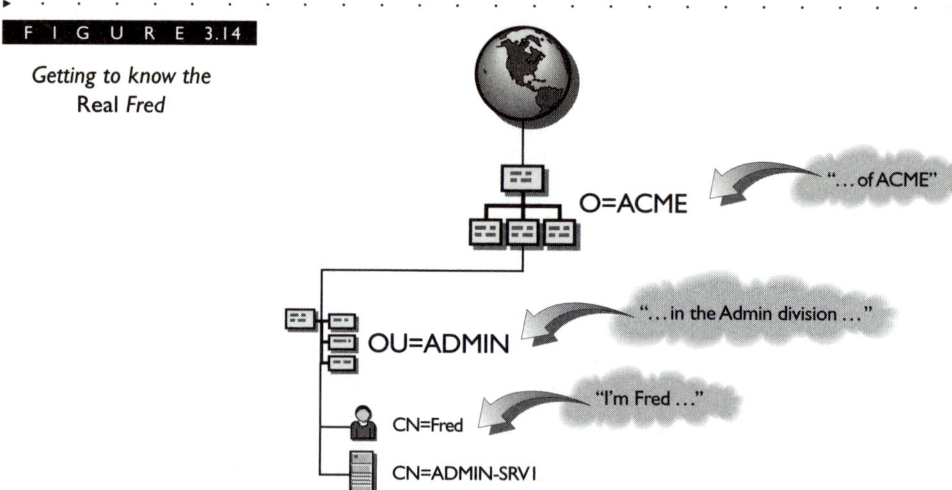

FIGURE 3.14

Getting to know the Real Fred

In the previous DOS example, with no search paths, the reason we could not run WordPerfect at the C:\> prompt is because we were not on a first name basis with WP.EXE. Our current directory in DOS tells us that we can use the first name of the programs in the current container. Since WP.EXE is not stored in C:\>, DOS could not run the program.

There are two ways that we can run WordPerfect in this example. First, we can type WordPerfect's full name or enough of it to distinguish where it is from our current directory. Secondly, we could use the CD command to change to the C:\APPS\WP directory and put ourselves on a first name basis with WP.EXE.

Let's take a closer look at full and/or partial DOS names. At the C:\> prompt we could type the following commands:

```
C:\> c:\apps\wp\wp.exe — a fully distinguished name (FDN)

C:\> apps\wp\wp.exe — a relative distinguished name (RDN)
```

Nothing new here. After all, you've been working with DOS file systems for years. This is exactly how names work in NDS. Of course, the syntax is a little different. But, we'll talk about that a little later.

Now let's take a look at using the CD command to get on a first name basis with WP.EXE. At the C:\> prompt we can type the following commands:

```
C:\> CD C:\APPS\WP — an FDN

C:\> CD APPS\WP — an RDN
```

Both commands result in the DOS computer displaying the following prompt: "C:\APPS\WP>". At this point, we are on a first name basis with all the programs in C:\APPS\WP. Now all we have to do is type "WP.EXE" at the command line and the program will run. Effectively, we have changed our current DOS directory and we're now standing in Fred and Wilma's house. In NDS, we call this "Current Context". That's the container we are currently on a first name basis with. Things are so similar to DOS that we even use a similar command to walk the NDS tree. In DOS we use the CD command, in NDS we use the CX command.

ZEN

"Oh, the thinks you can think up if only you try!"

Dr. Seuss

So, what have we learned up to this point (see Figure 3.15). Let's see now….

► NDS Names are just like DOS filenames in the way that we use them.

► NDS Current Context is just like the DOS current directory.

In NDS, we use the <u>CX</u> command (instead of CD) to move around the directory tree.

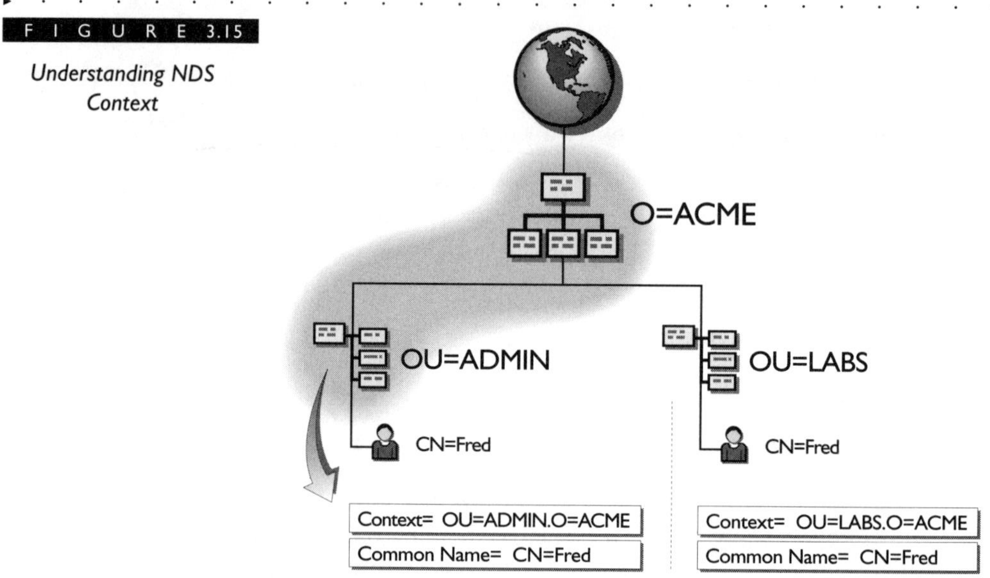

F I G U R E 3.15

Understanding NDS Context

NDS isn't quite so intimidating after all! It works a bit like the DOS file system we all know and love. After all, the DOS file system IS a directory — just like NDS. Now, let's take a closer look at when to use names and how they operate in the NDS world.

QUIZ

Numbers can be challenging, fascinating, confusing, and frustrating, but once you have developed an interest in them, a whole new world is opened up as you discover their many characteristics and patterns. Numbers can be divided into many different categories, including amicable, abundant, deficient, perfect, and delectable numbers.

Amicable numbers **are pairs that are mutually equal to the sum of all their aliquot parts: for example, 220 and 284. The aliquot parts of 220 are 1, 2, 4, 5, 10, 11, 20, 22, 44, 55, and 110, the sum of which is 284,** while the aliquot parts of 284 are 1, 2, 4, 71, and 142, the sum of which is 220. There are seven known pairs of amicable numbers, the largest of which are 9,437,056 and 7,363,584.

Abundant, deficient, and perfect numbers can be linked together because all numbers fit into these categories. An *abundant number* is one such that the sum of all its divisors (except itself) is greater than the number itself: for example, 12, because its divisors (1, 2, 3, 4, and 6) total 16. The opposite of this is a *deficient number,* where the divisors total less than the number itself: for example, 10, whose divisors (1, 2, and 5) total 8. If a number is not abundant or deficient, then it must be a *perfect number,* which means that it equals the sum of its aliquot parts: for example, 6, where its divisors (1, 2, 3) also total 6. Perfect numbers were first named in Ancient Greece by the Pythagoreans around 500 BC, and to date only 30 have been discovered. The first four perfect numbers were discovered before AD 100, and they include 6 and 496. However, the next (33,550,336) was not found until the fifteenth century. With the help of computer technology, the process of discovering new perfect numbers has been speeded up and the latest to be found has no fewer than 240 digits. One fact that has emerged is that all the perfect numbers now known are even numbers. However, no one from the time of Euclid to the present day has been able to prove that it is mathematically impossible for a perfect odd number to exist.

So, having dealt with amicable, abundant, deficient, and perfect numbers, what, may you ask, is a *delectable number?* The answer is that a nine-digit number is delectable if (a) it contains the digits 1 to 9 exactly once each (no zero) and (b) the numbers created by taking the first n digits (n runs from 1 to 9) are each divisible by n, so that the first digit is divisible by 1 (it always will be), the first two digits form a number divisible by 2, the first three digits form a number divisible by 3, and so on. Only one delectable number is known. Can you find out what it is?

Matching:

A) Abundant   1) 10
B) Perfect   2) 220
C) Deficient   3) 381654729
D) Amicable   4) 12
E) Delectable   5) 8128
6) 284
7) 386451729
8) 28

(Q3-5)

LOGGING IN

Whenever you want to use a resource in NDS, you need to identify it using a valid name. This also applies when you want to login. For example, when Fred wants to log into NDS he needs to tell NDS exactly "who" he is and "where" he lives:

```
login .Fred.ADMIN.ACME
```

In this example Fred uses his Full Distinguished Name. You can never go wrong using your FDN; NDS will always know who you are. Figure 3.14 above shows Fred's full name and how to construct it. Fred is lazy, though, and like all users he is getting bored with typing his FDN everytime he logs in. Good news! There are several shortcuts that you can use to help Fred reduce his typing. You can set a default context on Fred's workstation or you can take advantage of the server's context. We'll talk more about this later. Finally, you can change Fred's current context to his home container before he logs in. This is accomplished using the "CX" command. Let's take a closer look.

THE CX COMMAND

As we learned earlier, the CX command works a whole lot like the DOS "CD" command — it changes the current NDS context. CX is a DOS utility, but it does a few things in NDS that CD doesn't do for DOS. It can be used to list containers in the NDS tree. Let's look at CX in detail.

The CX command is located in the SYS:PUBLIC directory and has the following switches:

- ▶ **/T — Tree.** View all the container objects below the current context. Works like DIR /S in DOS.

- ▶ **/CONT — Container.** Show only containers in the current context. Works like the DOS DIR*. command.

- ▶ **/A — All.** Show all objects at or below the current context. Works like the DOS DIR*.* command. Note: This switch is used to modify the /T or /CONT switches. It does not work by itself

- ▶ **/R — Root.** Do whatever CX command we are trying relative to the [Root].

- ▶ **/VER — Version.** Display version information for the CX command.

- ▶ **/C — Continuous.** Scroll the output of the CX command continuously if more than one page of information is going to be generated.

- ▶ **/? — Help.** Displays the CX help screen. This switch can be used with all NetWare 4.1 DOS utilities to display help screens.

Furthermore, here are some common CX commands and what they display:

- ▶ **CX /T** — Displays the directory tree below the current context.

- ▶ **CX /T/R** — Displays the entire directory tree below the [Root].

- ▶ **CX /R/A/T** — Displays all the objects in the entire NDS tree below the [Root]. See Figure 3.16 for a picture of "CX /R/A/T" command.

FIGURE 3.16

Using CX /R/A/T in the ACME Tree

```
*** Directory Services Mapping ***

[Root]
  └ACME
      ├NORAD
      │   ├LABS
      │   │   ├LABS-SRV1
      │   │   ├R&D
      │   │   │   ├R&D-DL
      │   │   │   ├LDaVinci
      │   │   │   ├POLL
      │   │   │   ├NUC
      │   │   │   ├VR
      │   │   │   └R&D-PS1
      │   │   ├WHI
      │   │   │   ├CBabbage
      │   │   │   ├CANONBJ-PQ1
      │   │   │   ├CANONBJ-P1
      │   │   │   └WHI-PS1
      │   │   ├AEinstein
      │   │   ├LABS-SRV1_SYS
      │   │   └LABS-SRV1_MSG
      │   ├NOR-Admin
      │   ├CHARITY
>>> Enter = More    C = Continuous    Esc = Cancel
```

ZEN

"My alphabet starts with this letter called YUZZ. It's the letter I use to spell YUZZ-A-MA-TUZZ. You'll be sort of surprised what there is to be found once you go beyond 'Z' and start poking around!"

Dr. Seuss

The CX command can be a little crazy for users at the command line. Fortunately for MS Windows users, life is a little bit easier. When an MS Windows user wants to select an object to use with the NWTOOLS application, an NDS tree browser pops up. It displays stuff that looks exactly like the output of "CX /T/A" in DOS. Well, almost exactly. The tree browser uses icons for leaf objects, and filters the leafs according to function. For example, if you're trying to capture to a printer or queue, only printers and queues are displayed. Most users, if they are using MS Windows, will prefer the NWTOOLS utility to the DOS commands of CX and CAPTURE. But before they can do anything, they need to understand the difference between Full Distinguished and Relative Distinguished names.

FULL DISTINGUISHED AND RELATIVE DISTINGUISHED NAMES

Earlier, we learned about FDNs and RDNs. Now, let's take a closer look at how they behave in the virtual NDS universe. To begin, FDNs are quite simply the full name of any given object in NDS. In our DOS file system example, this is the complete file name. For example, C:\APPS\WP51\WP.EXE. In NDS this is the same as ".AEinstein.R&D.LABS.ACME" in Figure 3.17.

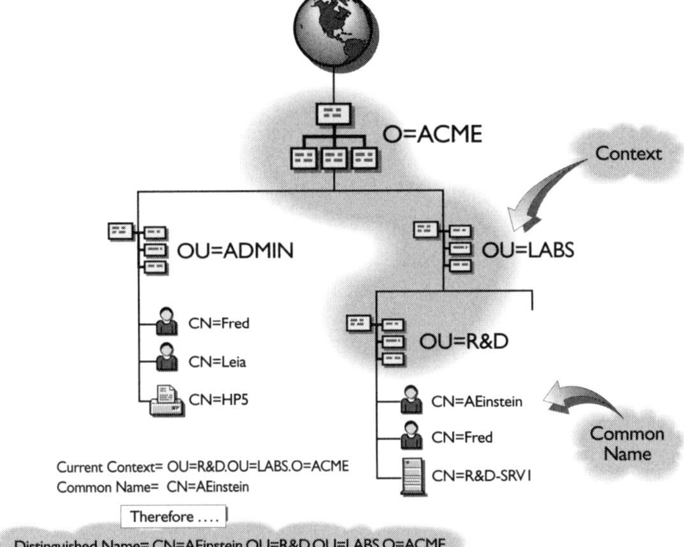

F I G U R E 3.17

Building AEinstein's Distinguished Name

RDNs are the name of any NDS object relative to your Current Context. In our DOS example it works like this. If our current DOS directory is C:\APPS then the relative name of the WP.EXE program is WP51\WP.EXE. In our NDS example, if our current context is LABS.ACME then the RDN for AEinstein is "AEinstein.R&D". It's just simple math — the RDN added to the current context always equals the FDN. So, for this example see Figure 3.18:

```
AEinstein.R&D + LABS.ACME = AEinstien.R&D.LABS.ACME
```

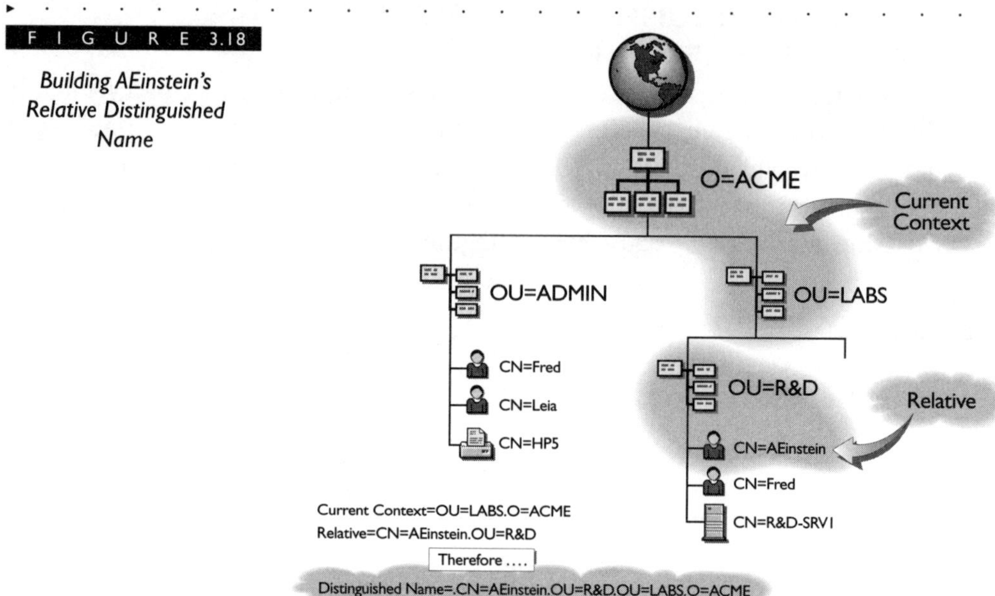

FIGURE 3.18

Building AEinstein's Relative Distinguished Name

So why do we care about FDNs and RDNs? Good question. You can always use the complete FDN and find any object in the NDS tree. But this soon becomes cumbersome. And sometimes you want to find the nearest version of the object, not the absolute version of it. So, for these reasons, RDNs become important. Now let's take a closer look at NetWare 4.1's use of periods. Yes, even the dots have significance in NDS.

ZEN

"The Scientific Theory I like best is that the rings of Saturn are composed entirely of lost airline luggage."

Mark Russell

LEADING AND TRAILING PERIODS IN NDS NAMES

Up to this point all the fully distinguished names in our examples have included a preceding dot (.). It's not a typing error! In fact, when we construct NDS names we can use trailing dots as well. Why? Well, let's check it out.

A preceding dot in NDS means that the name will be an FDN. Remember, FDN identifies a specific object in NDS and will not be "mistaken" for a different object by NetWare. How could this even get "confused?" Actually this can happen quite easily since we will often deliberately create objects of the same name in different contexts. By using the preceding dot we are telling NDS that we don't give a hoot about what our current context is and the name we are asking for is complete. That way NDS doesn't try to add anything to the name (like the current context). On the other hand, if there's no leading period, NDS assumes it's an RDN and appends the Current Context to the end of the name. See Figure 3.18 above.

Trailing dots are a lot more fun. The best way to understand trailing dots in NDS is to once again use our DOS example. In DOS, we can use dots with the CD command to move back one or more directories. Here is an example that you probably use yourself. If our current directory is C:\APPS\WP51 and I want to move up only one directory level, then I use the following CD command:

```
CD ..
```

In DOS, ".." means parent, so "CD .." translates to "go to my parent directory". In NDS, a single dot means parent. A double dot means grandparent (go up two levels). Three dots means go up three levels.

Let's take Leia, for example. She lives in the ADMIN container. If we were in LABS, she couldn't use a relative distinguished name to identify herself — or could she? A single trailing period would move her current context up to O=ACME. Then she could use an RDN to move down the ADMIN side of the tree (see Figure 3.19). Her current context would be OU=LABS.O=ACME, and her relative distinguished name would be:

```
Leia.ADMIN.
```

The resulting distinguished name would be Leia's relative name plus her new current context (remember, the trailing period moved the current context from LABS.ACME up to O=ACME). That is, her distinguished name would be:

```
.Leia.ADMIN.ACME
```

Piece of cake. It gets even weirder if Leia's current context is:

```
OU=R&D.OU=LABS.O=ACME
```

In this case, her relative distinguished name would be:

```
Leia.ADMIN..
```

Are we having fun yet? Just like anything in life, it's very important where you place your dots. Here's a quick summary:

▸ All objects in the NDS name are separated by dots.

▸ Distinguished names are preceded by a dot. This identifies them as complete.

▸ Relative distinguished names are not preceded by a dot. This identifies them as incomplete.

Trailing dots can only be used in relative distinguished names, and they modify the current context. Each dot moves the context up one container.

F I G U R E 3.19

Using Trailing Periods

 **ZEN**

"Did I ever tell you how lucky you are?
Thank goodness for all the things you are not!
Thank goodness you're not something someone forgot
and left all alone in some punkerish place.
Like a rusty tin coat hanger hanging in space."

Dr. Seuss

TYPEFUL AND TYPELESS NAMING

Great news, we're almost done with naming. In closing, I'd like to explore Typeful and Typeless naming.

If you remember back to our discussion of NDS objects, we learned that they are classed by their types. We had containers (O and OU) and leaf objects (CN). In *Typeful* naming, we tell NDS how to read the name by specifying the type of each part of the name. For example, Fred's Typeful name is ".CN=Fred.OU=ADMIN.O=ACME". We have told NDS that "Fred" is a Common Name, "ADMIN" is an Organizational Unit, and "ACME" is an Organization. NDS knows the rules about CNs, OUs, and Os so there is no mistaking this name. We mean Fred, specifically.

The annoying thing about Typeful naming is all the typing. There are a great deal of extra characters to create on the command line. Nah, Typeless naming is much more fun. *Typeless* naming allows us to specify the full NDS name without telling NDS about the type of each object. NDS utilities make some assumptions about the parts of the name and try to figure out the types on their own. The operative word here is "try." There are some situations where typeless naming will not identify the same object. Fred's typeless name is the same name we have been using in all our examples: ".Fred.ADMIN.ACME". This is eight characters shorter than the typeful name. A savings of 30 percent in typing! Definitely the way to go.

However, it's important to note that Typeless naming is not perfect. We trade some ambiguity for less typing. Take a look at Figure 3.20. Here we have a container, ACME, that has two objects in it of the same name. They are, however, of different type. One is a user and the other is an Organizational Unit. This is perfectly legal in NDS, but suddenly Typeless naming falls apart. Fortunately, NetWare 4.1 has some guidelines for "guessing" what the object types should be:

1. The leftmost object is a common name (leaf object).

2. The rightmost object is an Organization (container object).

3. All middle objects are Organizational Units (container objects).

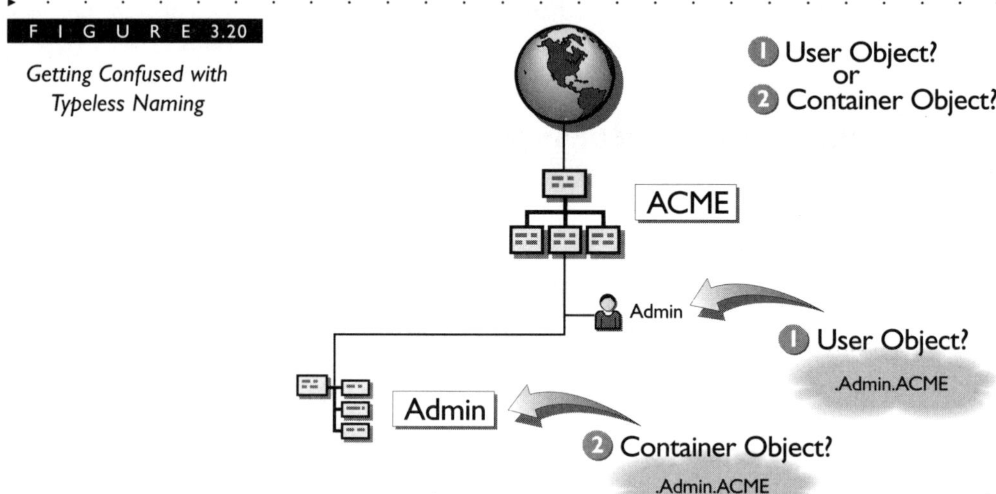

Getting Confused with
Typeless Naming

Although this works for most cases, it's only a general guideline. Many times, typeless names are more complex. Take our example in Figure 3.20, for instance. We know now that the rightmost object is an Organization, but what about "Admin?" Is it a common name or an Organizational Unit? We still don't know. Fortunately, NetWare 4 includes numerous exceptions to deal with complex typeless scenarios. Here's how it works:

Exception Rule 1: Container objects — NetWare 4 utilities are intelligent enough to resolve their own typeless names depending on what they are trying to accomplish. CX, for example, is used primarily for changing context. If you apply the CX command to a typeless name, it assumes the leftmost object is an Organization or Organizational Unit. This is because you can't change context to a leaf object. Other utilities that allow you to change context include NETADMIN and NWAdmin. In summary, here's how our example from Figure 3.20 would look with the CX utility:

```
CX .ADMIN.ACME-.OU=ADMIN.O=ACME
```

Exception Rule 2: Leaf objects — Similarly, resource-based utilities recognize the leftmost object of a typeless name as a leaf object. Many of these utilities are expecting to see a common name. The most prevalent are LOGIN, MAP, and CAPTURE. Here's how it works for our example in Figure 3.20:

```
LOGIN .Admin.ACME-.CN=Admin.O=ACME
```

Exception Rule 3: Mixed naming schemes — It is possible to generate an NDS name that mixes both typeless and typeful naming. In this case, the typeful abbreviation is used as a reference point for resolving the typeless portion of the name. NDS simply focuses on the typeful portion and moves to the left. All subsequent typeless objects are assigned one less abbreviation. Here's an example from Figure 3.20:

```
.ADMIN.O=ACME-.OU=ADMIN.O=ACME
```

Of course, this mixed NDS name would be resolved differently if CX or LOGIN were involved. Some exception rules take precedence over others.

Exception Rule 4: Using current context — If all else fails, NDS uses the current context as an example of NDS naming. If your typeless name has the same number of objects as the current context, it assigns attribute abbreviations accordingly. For example, if your current context was .OU=LABS.O=ACME, the typeless name in Figure 3.20 would become .OU=ADMIN.O=ACME.

In another example, let's assume the Country object is involved. If your current context was OU=LABS.O=ACME.C=US, then .ADMIN.ACME.US would become .OU=ADMIN.O=ACME.C=US.

If, however, the typeless name has a different number of objects as the current context, the default NDS naming rules apply. That is, rightmost Organization, leftmost common name, and all intervening Organizational Units.

Exception Rule 5: Country object — The Country object messes up NDS defaults in almost all cases. Naming is no exception. The Country object is a special circumstance and is assumed not to exist. If you introduce the Country object in either the current context or a typeful portion of the name, you'll run into trouble. In this case, NDS tries to resolve the name using any of the exception rules above. If they don't apply, it isolates the Country object and applies the defaults to the rest of the typeless name. Pretty weird, huh?

There you have it. This completes our discussion of typeless names and NDS naming in general. As you can see, this is a very important topic because it impacts all aspects of NDS design, installation, and management. No matter what you do, you're going to have to use the correct name to login or access NDS resources. As we've learned, an object's name is a combination of "who they are" (common name) and "where they live" (context).

Congratulations! You are now a professor of NDS nomenclature.

ZEN

"Oh! The places you'll go! You'll be on your way up! You'll be seeing great sights! You'll join the high fliers who soar to high heights!"

Dr. Seuss

That's everything you need to know about the "Cloud." Well, not really, but it's a very good start. Remember, every cloud has a silver lining and this chapter has been yours. Can you feel the twinge in the crown of your cranium? Has your NDS tree begun to sprout? Pretty soon, you'll be NDS-Head Fred!

The goal of this chapter was to make you think until it hurt — to generate enough neurokinetic energy to stimulate cranial growth. Have we succeeded? You be the judge. It all started with an NDS getting-familiar period. Once you were comfortable with the concept of a tree in a cloud, we learned about the 24 different objects that live there — including the [Root] and leaves. We learned that NDS objects come in two different flavors: Tupperware containers and physical leaf resources. We learned about Countries, Users, Distribution Lists, and the Alias object (if that's what it's really called).

With objects comes management. We delved into the world of NDS management with a brief look at tree planning and resource access. Then we explored naming in much more depth. We learned that names uniquely identify "who we are" and "where we live." It works much the same way in NDS. We learned about the common name (who) and context (where). And we learned how these two are combined to create the distinguished name.

So, here we are — NDS-Head Fred! So far, we've explored the basics of NetWare 4 and the intricacies of NetWare Directory Services. That completes our discussion of CNA basics. Now you're ready to start the real journey:

> ▸ NetWare 4 File System

> ▸ NetWare 4 Security

> ▸ NetWare 4 Configuration

> ▸ NetWare 4 Management

> ▸ NetWare 4 Printing

Don't be scared — I'll be with you every step of the way. And we'll return to these topics many times again. This is only the beginning and I can't wait for you to become a full-fledged superhero....

Speaking of Superheroes, let me introduce you to an organization full of them. As a matter of fact, this company's single purpose is to Save The World!! Check it out.

QUIZ

If my three were a four,
And my one were a three,
What I am would be nine less
Than half what I'd be.
I'm only three digits,
Just three in a row,
So, what in the world must I be?
Do you know?

Hint: Synergy.

(Q3-6)

Getting to Know ACME

The world is in a lot of trouble. If we keep abusing the Planet Earth at our current pace, there'll be nothing left in a few decades.

As a matter of fact, the Alpha Centurions have discovered this and decided to do something about it. As it turns out, they are great fans of the Planet Earth and would hate to see us destroy it. They have given us a deadline before which we must clean up our act — or else.

To save the world, we have created an organization called ACME (A Cure for Mother Earth). ACME is staffed by the greatest heroes of all time. They are the founding mothers and fathers of Earth's Golden Age.

We've traveled back in time to recruit the ACME management. Now it's your turn. You will serve as ACME's MIS department. You will build a pervasive internetwork for ACME using NetWare 4. The clock is ticking and connectivity is the key.

 **ZEN**

"Don't Panic!"

The Hitchhiker's Guide to the Galaxy

In the social hierarchy of needs, the world is pretty screwed up. The Pyramid of Needs states that basic fundamental needs, like food and shelter, preclude us from enjoying higher needs, like art, education, and corn dogs. This pyramid exists at many different levels throughout the world. Almost two-thirds of our population doesn't have sufficient resources to satisfy the lowest basic needs — medicine, food, shelter, and peace — while a smaller percentage takes higher needs — like digital watches — for granted. Something needs to change.

As a matter of fact, the Alpha Centurions have discovered this and have decided to do something about it. The good news is they are a benevolent and intelligent race. They understand the Pyramid of Needs and recognize that everyone should be able to enjoy digital watches. They have discovered that the top 1 percent of the Earth's population is destroying the world at an alarming pace, while the other 99 percent are just trying to survive. In an effort to save the world, they have issued an ultimatum:

Clean up your act or find another planet to exploit!

They have given us until January 1, 2000, to clean up our act — or else! It's safe to say that the fate of the human race is in your hands. To help measure our progress, the Alpha Centurions have developed a World Health Index (WHI). The WHI is a balanced calculation of seven positive and seven negative factors that determine how good or bad we're treating the Earth. They've decided that 100 is a good number to shoot for. It represents a good balance between basic and higher needs. Once the world achieves a WHI of 100, almost everyone will be able to afford a digital watch. Here's a quick list of the 14 positive and negative WHI factors:

WHI Positive	**WHI Negative**
Charity	Crime
Love	Pollution
Birth	Starvation
Education	Disease
Health	War
Laughing	Poverty
Sports	Corruption

Bottom line: The Alpha Centurions have given us a little more than three years to increase our WHI from its current level (− 2) to 100. We have until January 1, 2000. If we don't clean up our act by then, they will mercifully eradicate all humans and let the animals and plants live peacefully on the Planet Earth.

ZEN

"This magnificent butterfly finds a little heap of dirt and sits still on it. But man will never on his heap of mud keep still."

Joseph Conrad

ACME has been staffed by the greatest heroes from our unspoiled history. These are the founding mothers and fathers of Earth's Golden Age — before instant popcorn, talking cars, and daytime television. It's clear that somewhere along the human timeline, progress went amuck. We need help from heroes before that time. In order to vortex back in history and grab the ACME management, we've used the prototype Oscillating Temporal Overthruster (OTO). We've hand-chosen only the brightest and most resourceful characters, then meticulously trained each one of them for special tasks. They're a little disoriented, but more than happy to help.

These historical heroes have been placed in an innovative organizational structure. As you can see in Figure 3.27, ACME is organized around five main divisions. They are

- ► Human Rights (Gandhi) — Taking care of the world's basic needs, including medicine, food, shelter, and peace. These tasks are handled jointly by Albert Schweitzer, Mother Teresa, Florence Nightingale, and Buddha. This division's work has the most positive impact on the WHI.

- ► Labs (Albert Einstein) — Putting technology to good use. This division is the technical marvel of ACME. In addition to research and development (R&D) efforts, the Labs division is responsible for the WHI tracking center in NORAD. This division is staffed by the wizardry of Leonardo da Vinci, Sir Isaac Newton, Charles Darwin, Marie Curie, Charles Babbage, and Ada, "The Countess of Lovelace."

▸ Operations (King Arthur) — Saving the world can be a logistical nightmare. Fortunately, we have King Arthur and the Knights of the Round Table to help us out. In this division, ACME routes money from caring contributors (Charity) to those who need it most (Financial) — there's a little Robin Hood in there somewhere. Also, with the help of Merlin, we distribute all the Human Rights and Labs material to the four corners of the globe.

▸ Crime Fighting (Sherlock Holmes and Dr. Watson) — Making the world a safer place. This division tackles the almost insurmountable task of eradicating world crime. It's a good thing we have the help of Sherlock Holmes and some of our greatest crime-fighting superheroes, including Robin Hood, Maid Marion, Wyatt Earp, and Wild Bill Hickok. These heroes deal with the single most negative factor in WHI calculations — crime. This is very important work.

▸ Admin (George Washington) — Keeping the rest of ACME running smoothly. It's just like a well-oiled machine with the help of America's Founding Fathers — George Washington, Thomas Jefferson, Abraham Lincoln, FDR, and James Madison. Their main job is public relations under the command of one of our greatest orators, Franklin Delano Roosevelt (FDR). In addition to getting the word out, Admin tracks ACME activity (auditing) and keeps the facilities operating at their best.

ACME Organizational
Chart

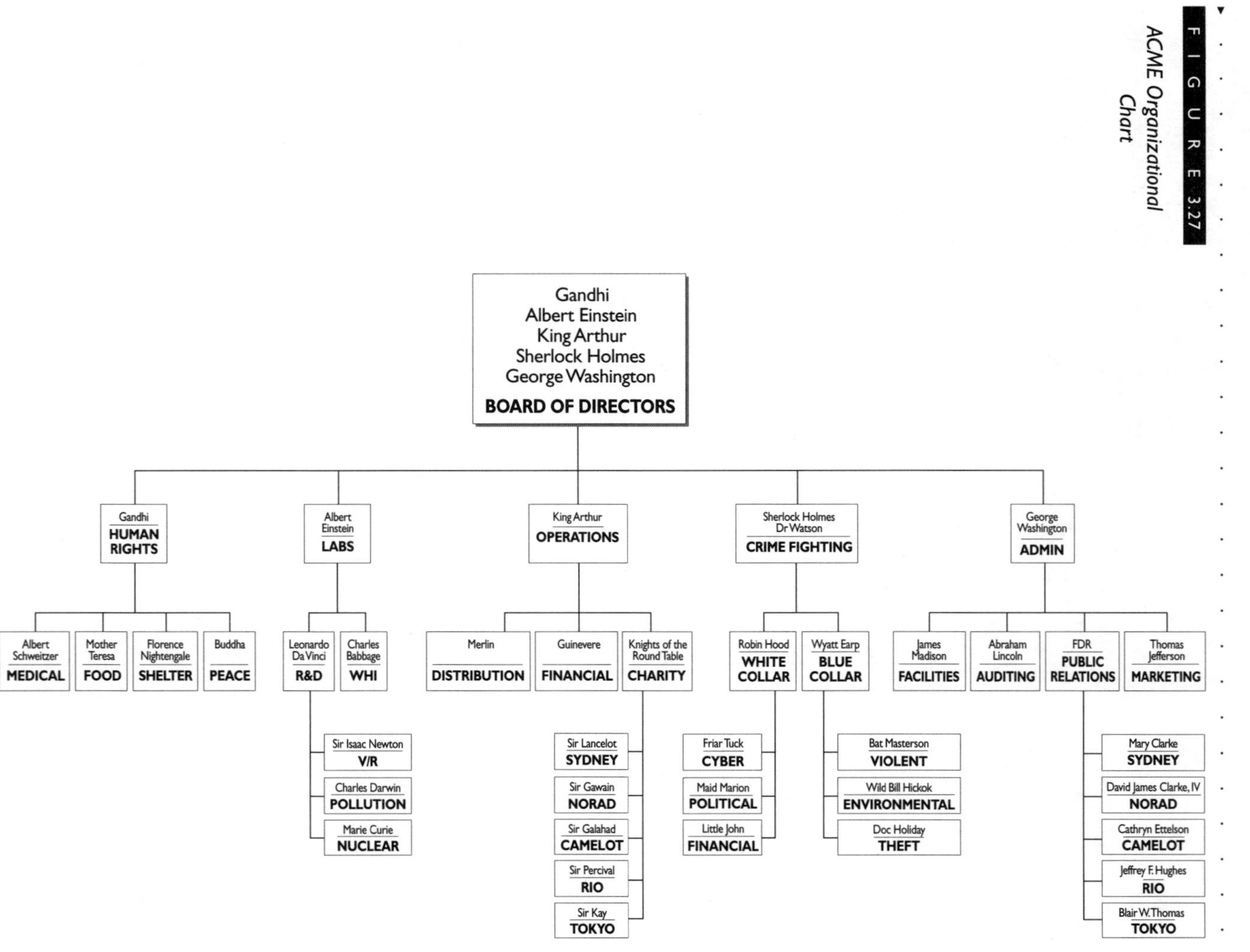

Now it's your turn. You are the final piece in our globe-trotting puzzle. You are ACME's MIS department. We have recruited you as the architect of our communications strategy. As a NetWare 4 CNA, you come highly recommended. Your mission — should you choose to accept it — is to build the ACME WAN. You will need courage, design experience, NDS know-how, and this book. If you succeed, you will save the world and become a CNA! All in a day's work.

ACME has a daunting task ahead of it, so we don't have any time to mess around. I'd like to begin by thanking you for choosing to accept this mission. You'll find a few design inputs included with this book. They are for your eyes only. Once you have read the inputs, eat them! There's other good news — you don't have to save the world alone. The project team is here to help you. Remember, we're counting on you. Be careful not to let these facts fall into the wrong hands. Believe it or not, there are forces at work that don't share our love for the human race.

ACME CHRONICLES

A day in the life. . .

What you're about to read is for your eyes only. This is extremely confidential information. The ACME *Chronicles* (an hourly interactive newsletter) is a detailed look at the life and times of ACME. This is an exceptional organization created for a singular purpose — to save the world. As you can see in Figure 3.27, ACME is organized around five main divisions:

- ▶ Human Rights

- ▶ Labs

- ▶ Operations

- ▶ Crime Fighting

- ▶ Admin

Let's go inside and see what makes them tick.

Human Rights — Gandhi in Sydney

This is the "heart" of ACME's purpose. Human Rights has the most profoundly positive effect on the WHI. Efforts here can save lives and increase our chances of surviving into the next century. The goal of Human Rights is to raise people from the bottom of the Pyramid of Needs. By satisfying their basic needs (medicine, food, shelter, and peace), we hope to give humans the strength to fight for higher needs (equality, justice, education, and digital watches). This makes the world a better place and dramatically improves the WHI.

All Human Rights materials developed here are distributed every day through 10 different distribution centers around the world. This is ACME's manufacturing facility for food, shelter, and medical aid. In addition, the peacekeepers use any means necessary to thwart global wars. Let's take a closer look at the four different departments of Human Rights.

- ▶ Medical (Albert Schweitzer) — This department is collecting basic medical materials and training doctors and nurses for field work. Also, ACME is eagerly developing vaccines and working overtime to cure serious diseases. Finally, their medical staff is taking steps to clean up the sanitation of "dirty" countries. This is all accomplished with the help of Albert Schweitzer and his dedicated staff.

- ▶ Food (Mother Teresa) — With the help of her country-trained culinary heroes, Mother Teresa will determine how much Opossum Stew the whole world can eat. In addition, they are developing a series of genetically engineered organisms that will transform inedible materials into food stock. Finally, ACME's Food department has teamed up with R&D to create virtual reality (V/R) programming that teaches people how to grow food of their own. After all, if you give a person a fish, they eat for a day; but if you teach them to fish, they eat for a lifetime (and get a guest spot on ESPN's *Outdoor World*).

- ▶ Shelter (Florence Nightingale) — With all the new healthier and happier people in the world, our attention shifts to shelter. Fortunately, Florence Nightingale and her crack construction team have developed a cheap, recyclable, geodesic dome called a Permaculture. It has central heating, air conditioning, water, plumbing, and computer-controlled maid service. The most amazing thing about the dome is that it can be constructed from any native materials — that's cacti and sand in the desert, lily pads in the marsh, and snow in the Arctic. If all else fails, they're edible.

- ▶ Peace (Buddha) — One of the most overlooked basic needs is peace. All the other stuff doesn't mean a hill of beans if you're living in a war zone. Buddha's job is to somehow settle the 101 wars currently plaguing our Earth. He relies on a combination of wisdom, diplomacy, military presence, and fortune cookies.

This completes our discussion of Human Rights. See Figure 3.28 for an illustration of the Human Rights portion of the NDS tree in Sydney. Now let's take a look at the ACME Labs division.

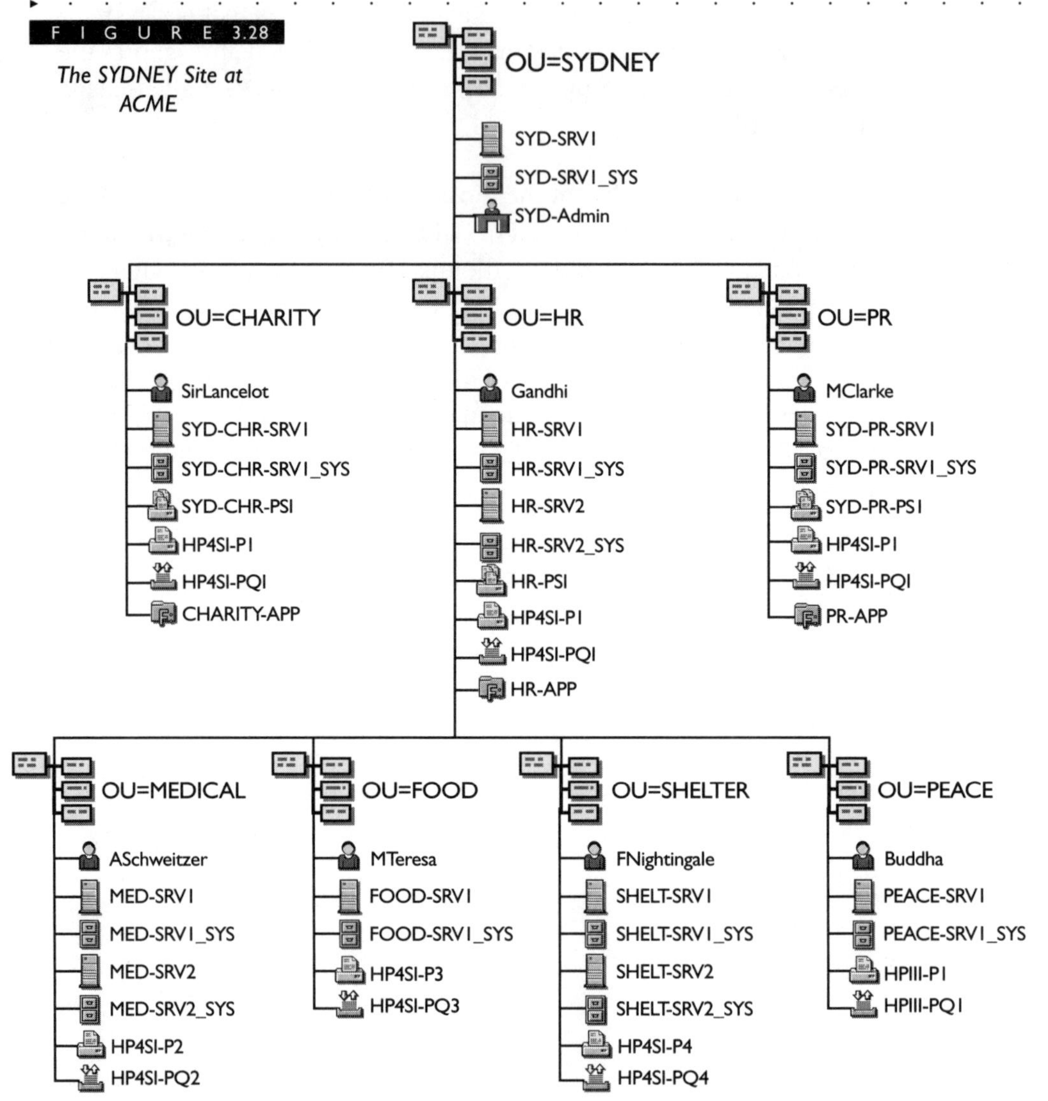

FIGURE 3.28

The SYDNEY Site at
ACME

OU=SYDNEY
SYD-SRV1
SYD-SRV1_SYS
SYD-Admin

OU=CHARITY
SirLancelot
SYD-CHR-SRV1
SYD-CHR-SRV1_SYS
SYD-CHR-PS1
HP4SI-P1
HP4SI-PQ1
CHARITY-APP

OU=HR
Gandhi
HR-SRV1
HR-SRV1_SYS
HR-SRV2
HR-SRV2_SYS
HR-PS1
HP4SI-P1
HP4SI-PQ1
HR-APP

OU=PR
MClarke
SYD-PR-SRV1
SYD-PR-SRV1_SYS
SYD-PR-PS1
HP4SI-P1
HP4SI-PQ1
PR-APP

OU=MEDICAL
ASchweitzer
MED-SRV1
MED-SRV1_SYS
MED-SRV2
MED-SRV2_SYS
HP4SI-P2
HP4SI-PQ2

OU=FOOD
MTeresa
FOOD-SRV1
FOOD-SRV1_SYS
HP4SI-P3
HP4SI-PQ3

OU=SHELTER
FNightingale
SHELT-SRV1
SHELT-SRV1_SYS
SHELT-SRV2
SHELT-SRV2_SYS
HP4SI-P4
HP4SI-PQ4

OU=PEACE
Buddha
PEACE-SRV1
PEACE-SRV1_SYS
HPIII-P1
HPIII-PQ1

Labs — Albert Einstein in **NORAD**

Albert Einstein is one of the greatest minds in our history, but how far can he push technology? The U.S. Military has loaned us the NORAD facility in Colorado as a base for technical wizardry. In addition to Research & Development (R&D), this is the central point of a vast WHI data-collection network.

ACME's R&D efforts are controlled by Leonardo da Vinci and his dream team of scientists. They use technology and a little bit of magic to save the Earth. Current projects include alternative power sources, V/R programming, anti-pollutants, NDS, and a cure for bad hair days. Let's take a closer look:

- V/R (Sir Isaac Newton) — V/R programming is being developed to convince the world that a cure is necessary. The V/R devices will be sold as video games and will help ACME tap the minds of the world. This borders on mind control but in a good way (if that's possible). There's nothing that brain power and a little bit of magic can't cure.

- Pollution (Charles Darwin) — This department is developing anti-pollutants and methods of transforming garbage into fuel. Also, this group is working to eradicate the world's largest scourge — ElectroPollution. Currently, Leonardo da Vinci and Charles Darwin are working on airplanes powered by pencil erasure grit.

- Nuclear (Marie Curie) — Cybernetic soldiers (Nuclear Disarmament Squads or NDS) are being designed to infiltrate and neutralize nuclear weapons facilities. Finally, somebody's splitting atoms for good.

In addition to R&D, NORAD is the central point of a vast WHI data-collection network. This network is the pulse of ACME. Collection of world data and calculation of the WHI occur here every day. Currently, the WHI sits at -2. And as we all know, it must climb to over 100 by January 1, 2000. Charles Babbage and Ada diligently guard the computers and make daily adjustments to WHI calculations. Ada's sacrifice is particularly notable because she used to be the "Countess of Lovelace." But fortunately for us, she had a soft spot in her heart for mathematics and Mr. Babbage.

Distributed world data-collection centers are scattered to all four corners of the Earth. There are 10 ACME WHI hubs — one in every divisional headquarters — and five more scattered to strategic points around the Earth. From each of these sites, world data is sent to NORAD and calculated on a daily basis. The results are distributed to every major newspaper so the world can chart ACME's progress. In addition to the 10 WHI hubs, there are hundreds of collection clusters distributed around each hub. Each cluster sends data directly to the closest hub (via dial-up lines), and eventually, back to the central site at NORAD.

ZEN

Techno-hip — comfortable with the use of the modern jargon of computers and other recent technological developments. Just think — all you have to do is memorize all the CNA nomenclature in this book and you will be a "techno-hipster." An unexpected side effect of becoming a CNA.

That completes our journey through ACME technology. See Figure 3.29 for an illustration of the Labs portion of the NDS tree in NORAD. Now let's take a look at the Operations division.

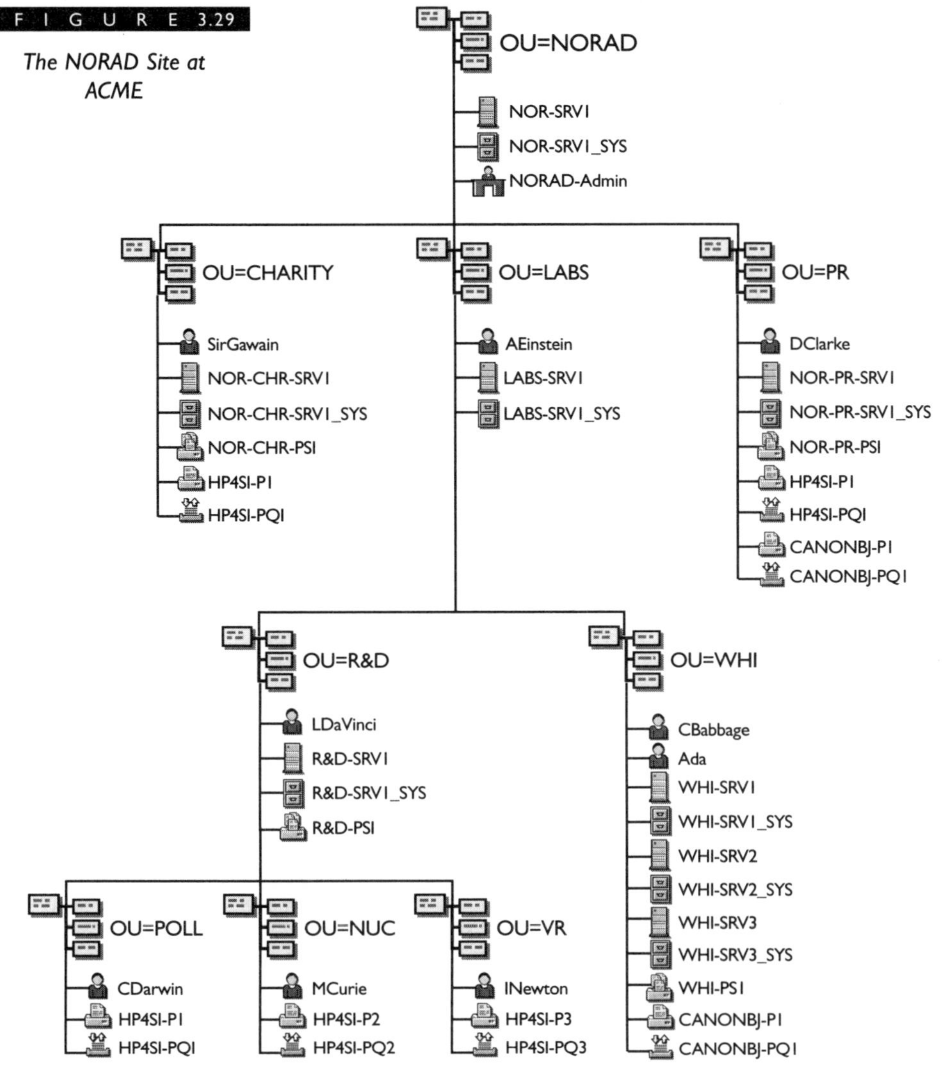

*The NORAD Site at
ACME*

Operations — King Arthur in Camelot

King Arthur and his court will keep ACME financed through charity drives and financial spending. After all, "money makes the world go 'round." Never before has it been more true. In addition, the Operations division handles the arduous task of distributing ACME aid to all the people who need it. Here's how it works:

▶ Distribution (Merlin) — We're going to need all the magic we can get. This department handles the distribution of human rights materials, medical supplies, doctors, nurses, food, hardware, building supplies, and prefabricated geodesic domes. No guns! It also handles implementation of WHI devices from R&D, such as anti-pollutants, Nuclear Disarmament Squads (NDS), anti-hacking viruses, and V/R programming. The latter is handled through satellite TV transmissions and video games. ACME distribution takes place through the same 10 hubs as WHI.

▶ Financial (Guinevere) — This is the money-out department. Guinevere handles the distribution of charity contributions, including the purchase of human rights material, bailing-out of bankrupt nations, and the funding of internal ACME activities. For a more detailed discussion of Financial operations, refer to the "ACME Workflow" section later in this chapter.

▶ Charity (Knights of the Round Table) — This is the money-in department. The Knights collect charity from world organizations and distribute it to the Financial department for disbursement. Each of the five major Knights oversees one of five charity centers — in each of the divisional headquarters. Sir Lancelot is in Sydney, Sir Gawain is in NORAD, Sir Galahad handles Camelot, Sir Percival oversees Rio, and Sir Kay is in Tokyo. I haven't seen such dedication since the medieval ages.

Well, that's how ACME's Operations work. See Figure 3.30 for an illustration of the Operations portion of the NDS tree in Camelot. Now let's take a look at Crime Fighting.

The CAMELOT Site at ACME

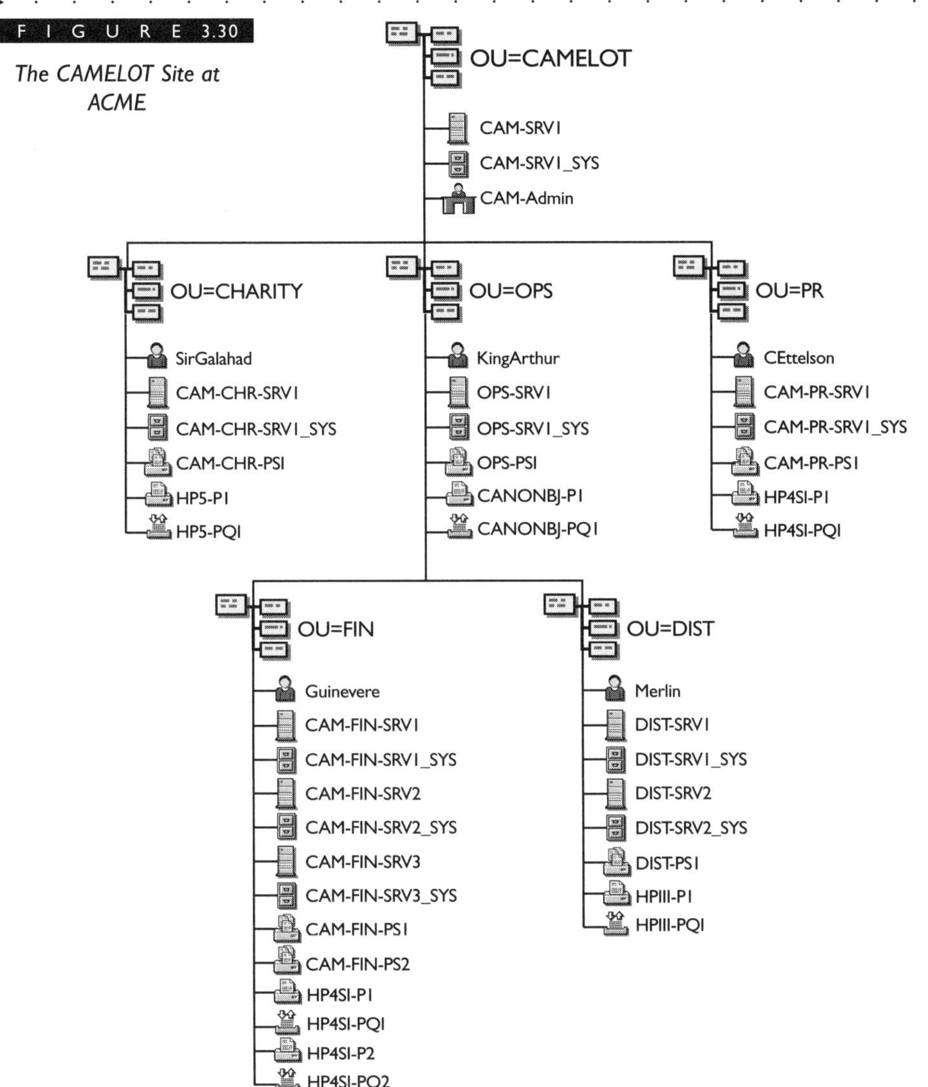

Crime Fighting — Sherlock Holmes in Tokyo

Crime has one of the most negative effects on the WHI. Fortunately, we have history's greatest crime-fighting mind to help us out — Sherlock Holmes. With the help of Dr. Watson, he has identified two major categories of world crime:

- White Collar

- Blue Collar

White-collar crimes include cyberhacking and political espionage. Robin Hood and his Band of Superheroes direct white-collar crime-fighting efforts from Tokyo. Here are some of the different types of crimes they're concerned with:

- Cyber (Friar Tuck) — With the help of the *Cyberphilia* underground, Friar Tuck attempts to thwart cyber crime. Most cyber crimes occur on The Net, so ACME must constantly monitor global communications. Tuck also has the help of an off-shoot group of guardian angels known as the Cyber Angels.

- Political (Maid Marion) — She can charm her way through any politically tense situation. Political crimes are especially rampant in emerging nations, so Maid Marion enlists the help of the United Nations.

- Financial (Little John) — With some creative financing and the help of ex-IRS agents, Little John thwarts financial crimes throughout the world. These crimes especially hurt the middle class, so he has recruited some key Yuppies as undercover agents.

Blue-collar crimes are a little more obvious — such as violence and theft. This is familiar ground for Wyatt Earp and his band of western heroes. They're not glamorous, but they're effective. Here's a look at ACME Crime Fighting from the blue-collar point of view:

- ▸ Violent (Bat Masterson) — This cowboy is in his own element. He thwarts violent crime by getting inside the criminal's mind — literally.

- ▸ Environmental (Wild Bill Hickok) — A great fan of the environment, Mr. Hickok uses his country charm to thwart environmental crimes such as excessive deforestation, toxic waste, whaling, oil spills, ElectroPollution, and forced extinction.

- ▸ Theft (Doc Holliday) — With his legendary sleight of hand, Doc Holliday stays one step ahead of the world's thieves.

So, that's what's happening on the crime fighting front. See Figure 3.31 for an illustration of the Crime Fighting portion of the NDS tree in Tokyo. Now let's take a close look at the final ACME division — Admin.

The TOKYO Site at ACME

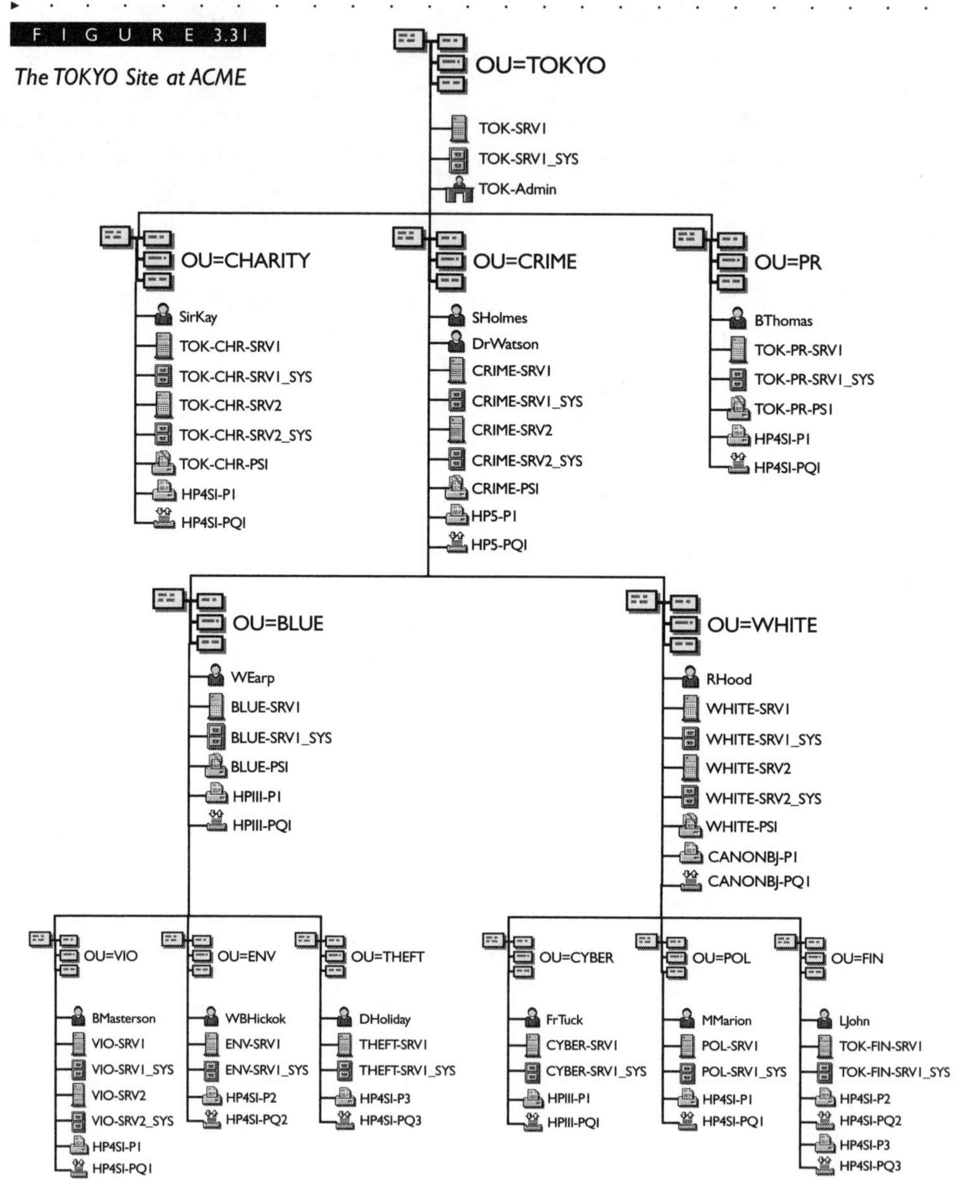

Admin — George Washington in Rio

Ever since the beginning of time, humans have quested for wisdom and knowledge. Now we'll need to put all of our enlightenment to good use — or else. A few centuries ago, the United States' Founding Fathers joined a growing group of men and women called Illuminoids. These people were dissatisfied with everyday life on Planet Earth and began to reach above, within, and everywhere else for a better way. The Illuminoids formed a variety of organizations dedicated to creating a New World Order including the Masons, Trilateral Commission, Council on Foreign Relations (CFR), and the Bilderberg Group.

Regardless of their ultimate motivation, the Illuminoids' hearts were in the right place — "let's make the world a better place." The founder of the Trilateral Commission has always claimed they are just *a group of concerned citizens interested in fostering greater understanding and cooperation among international allies.* Whether or not it's true, it sounds like a great fit for ACME. Once again, we've used the OTO to grab some of the earliest Illuminoids and solicit their help for ACME administration.

George Washington keeps the ACME ship afloat. Along with FDR, he keeps things running smoothly and makes sure the world hears about our plight. In addition, James Madison keeps the facilities running, while Abraham Lincoln makes sure ACME is held accountable for all its work. For years, the Trilateral Commission has been rumored to covertly run the world. Now they get a chance to overtly save it!

Now let's take a look at the four departments that make up ACME's administration:

- ▸ Public Relations (Franklin Delano Roosevelt) — This department solicits help from the rest of the world by enlisting the help of heroes from our own age — the 1990s. We're not going to be able to save the world alone. The PR department is responsible for communicating our plight to the four corners of the Earth. Department members inform everyday citizens about the Alpha Centurion ultimatum, daily WHI quotes, and requests for charity. There is a local PR office in each major location. See the organizational chart in Figure 3.27 for more details.

- ► Marketing (Thomas Jefferson) — Educating the rest of the world and soliciting help is another Marketing department responsibility. In addition to advertising, this department develops materials for distributed PR offices. Its goal is to rally all nations around ACME and our cause in order to save the Earth. They also bake really good apple pies and chocolate chip cookies.

- ► Auditing (Abraham Lincoln) — He makes sure that everyone stays in line. Financial trails for all charity moneys and complete records of all changes to the WHI are tracked by the Auditing department. Although it's part of the internal ACME organization, Auditing is an independent tracking company that generates bonded reports.

- ► Facilities (James Madison) — This department keeps everyone working, happy, and fed. The Facilities department also organizes field trips and ACME parties. Imagine the doozy they're going to have when we finally succeed!

Well, there you have it. That's everything you need to know about ACME. See Figure 3.32 for an illustration of the Administration portion of the NDS tree in Rio. I hope these *Chronicles* have helped you and your project team better understand what ACME is up against. This is no normal organization. If ACME goes out of business, the world is either lost or saved — it's up to you.

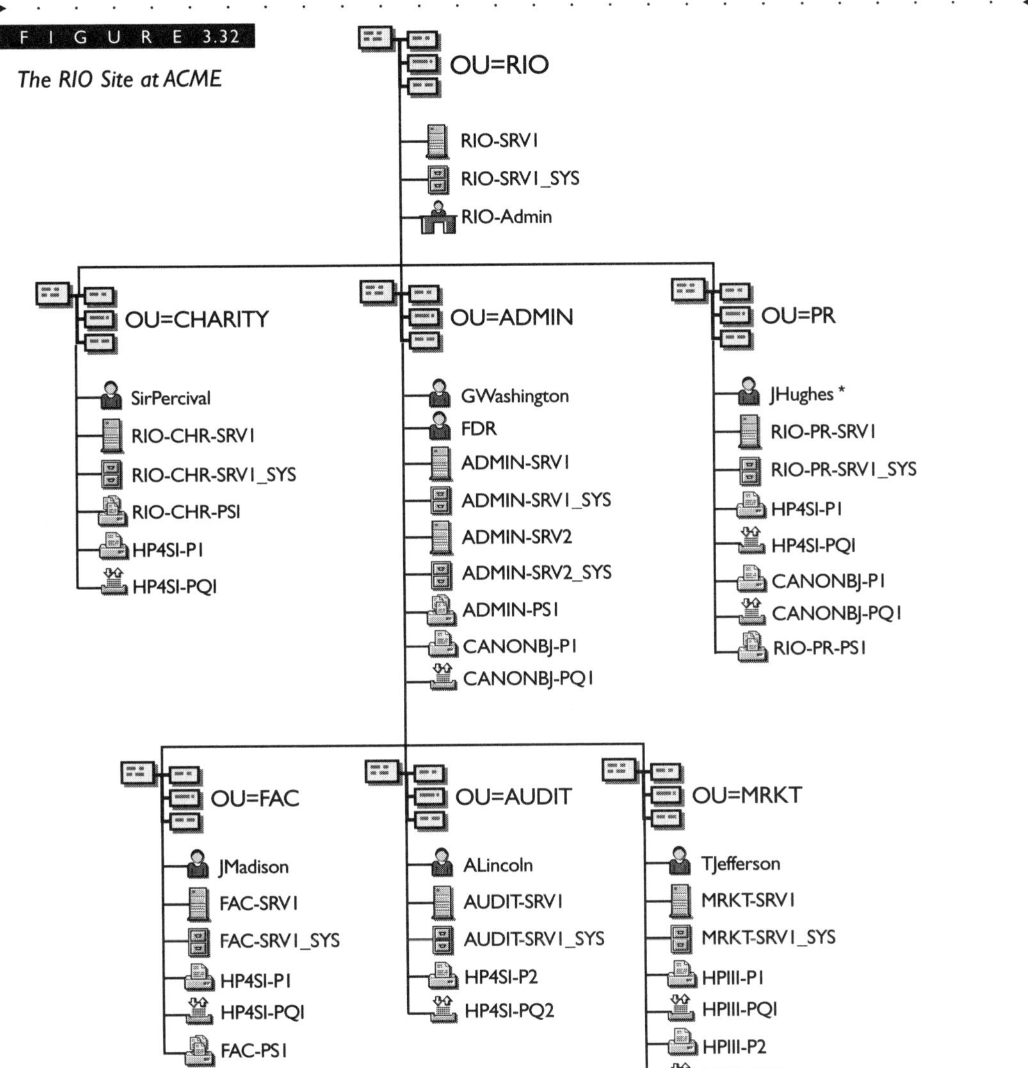

The RIO Site at ACME

ZEN

Chaos theory — the systematic approach to describing very complex events in mathematics and science by rounding off numerical data to reveal very general patterns. This theory can be used to describe the irregular patterns of a dripping water faucet, fluctuations in insect populations, stock-market price changes, or the daily grind of a CNA. In all cases, chaos theory relies on the strange attractor, which is a complex and unpredictable pattern of movement — much like a user's interface with NetWare workstations or your understanding of ACME.

ACME WORKFLOW

Although it may look complicated, the daily grind at ACME is really pretty simple. It's a combination of workflow and dataflow. *Workflow* describes the daily operations of ACME staff and their task-oriented responsibilities. *Dataflow* describes the daily or weekly movement of data from one location to another. Although the two are not always the same, they should be compatible. This is the goal of ACME synergy.

In this section, we're going to take a detailed look at how work and data flow through the ACME organization. This data has a dramatic impact on NDS design. Afterall, work and data flow over the WAN infrastructure. Refer to Figure 3.33 as you follow along. Here's how it works.

ACME Workflow Diagram

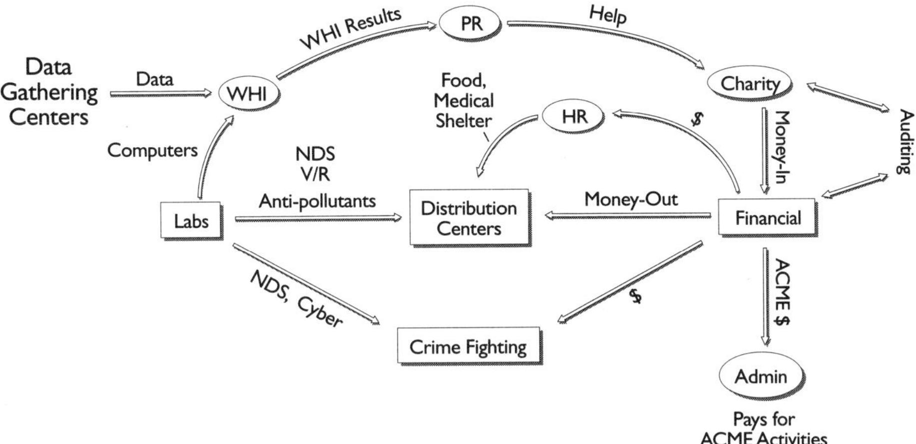

Financial Money-Out

Of course, money makes the world go 'round! The Financial department has two main responsibilities:

- ▸ Money-in

- ▸ Money-out

Money-in focuses on funding ACME activities and distributing charities to needy people. In funding ACME activities, Guinevere pays for Human Rights materials, Admin work, and Crime Fighting tools. Next, she disburses charity money through distribution centers. Money-in comes from the various Charity activities. All financial activity is audited by the internal Auditing organization.

Technically, this is accomplished from a central database at the Financial headquarters in Camelot. No money changes hands. Quarterly budgets are developed in Camelot and distributed to local banks for Human Rights, Crime Fighting, Distribution, and Admin. Each of these distributed sites sends weekly updates to the central database with the help of local servers.

Distribution Centers

The Distribution department is the hub of ACME achievements. Distribution centers disburse three kinds of aid:

- Human Rights materials (such as food, medicine, and shelter)

- Money from the Financial department

- Exciting inventions from Labs

Each of the 10 distribution centers maintains its own distributed database. They move material to local warehouses for delivery to needy people. Weekly summary updates are sent to the central inventory management database in Camelot. The central database oversees the big picture of aid distribution.

If a center runs out of a particular resource, one of two things happens:

1 • Camelot updates the center's budget, and they purchase the resource locally.

2 • Camelot orders the movement of resources from another distribution center. This option makes sense for finite materials such as special inventions from Labs or medical supplies.

Labs and Their Inventions

This is where the brainiacs hang out. Scientists in the Labs division develop world-saving toys for:

- Crime Fighting — NDS and cyberviruses

- Distribution — V/R programming and anti-pollutants

The Labs division supports WHI and all its technical needs. New product updates are sent to Distribution and Crime Fighting for internal consumption. This is secure information.

WHI Calculations

Labs is also where the WHI (World Health Index) is calculated. Charles Babbage and Ada collect data from data-gathering centers (DGCs) throughout the world. These DGCs are housed in divisional headquarters and distribution centers throughout the ACME WAN. They are

NORAD	Seattle
Rio	Cairo
Camelot	New York
Sydney	Moscow
Tokyo	St. Andrews

Ironically, the distribution centers send aid *out* and the DGCs pull data *in* — from the same 10 locations. Daily WHI summary calculations are sent to NORAD each day so the final WHI calculation can be made. Results are then distributed to PR daily for inclusion in global periodicals — including the ACME *Chronicles*.

Public Relations

This is the voice of ACME. In addition to distributing daily WHI reports, Public Relations (PR) educates the world and helps solicit money for Charity. PR pulls the daily WHI results from NORAD twice a day. They're also the on-line editors of the ACME *Chronicles*, which gives them some great financial leads for Charity.

Charity — Money-In Charity is ACME's open door. It is the funnel for ACME contributions. There is a charity center in each of the five divisional headquarters. This is how the top one percent helps the rest of us. Their motto is:

Spread the Wealth, or the Alpha Centurions will eat you!

All money collected by Charity is sent to the Financial department for disbursement. Two of the most important uses for this money are Crime Fighting and Admin. Note that the money doesn't actually change hands. It is deposited in local divisional banks, and daily updates are sent to the central financial database in Camelot.

Crime Fighting

Remember, crime has one of the greatest negative effects on the WHI. The Crime Fighting department relies on the following sources:

- Labs' inventions (NDS and cyberviruses)

- Money from the Financial department

- The guile of Robin Hood, Wyatt Earp, and their respective heroes

ACME Administration

The ACME staff has to eat. Admin relies on money from Financial to keep things running smoothly. You can't fight bureaucracy. In addition, the Auditing department needs audit-level access to the central financial database in Camelot. They are responsible for tracking money-in from Charity and money-out from Financial.

That's all there is to it. No sweat. As you can see, ACME runs like a well-oiled machine. Someone sure put a lot of effort into designing its organizational structure — and it shows! We're in good hands with ACME.

Good luck; and by the way, thanks for saving the world!

ZEN

"Today is gone. Today was fun. Tomorrow is another one. Every day from here to there funny things are everywhere."

Dr. Seuss

EXERCISE 3-1: NDS – PLANT A TREE IN A "CLOUD"

Circle the 20 NDS terms hidden in this word search puzzle using the hints provided.

```
G  L  E  A  D  I  N  G  P  E  R  I  O  D  N  X  G  X  T  Q  W
Y  C  O  U  N  T  R  Y  R  F  T  I  O  V  S  I  H  R  R  I  Q
M  U  X  C  P  S  K  V  O  O  U  N  K  N  O  W  N  E  L  M  F
G  R  S  W  A  K  S  K  F  B  U  D  A  L  I  A  S  K  A  X  J
E  R  N  H  T  L  W  Y  I  N  J  P  V  M  M  M  U  U  A  I  I  N
R  E  G  A  J  R  I  B  L  U  Z  E  C  E  P  C  W  B  E  Q  H
Y  N  L  S  N  H  P  T  E  H  D  W  C  E  Y  X  V  Q  X  Q  O
L  T  X  P  B  F  H  R  Y  H  H  O  R  T  A  W  V  E  S  C  T
I  C  B  B  F  H  I  R  X  D  N  V  G  H  R  Q  K  E  B  Q  E
B  O  R  G  A  N  I  Z  A  T  I  O  N  A  L  R  O  L  E  T  K
V  N  Y  T  L  Y  B  X  E  S  E  R  H  F  K  F  W  G  U  Y  K
J  T  D  Y  V  R  N  X  O  T  V  G  E  E  B  T  L  Y  E  P  X
K  E  T  P  S  J  T  R  W  I  L  A  N  C  S  E  J  V  B  E  U
R  X  F  E  H  E  S  F  G  V  H  N  A  M  T  F  B  D  Y  L  L
M  T  W  F  A  S  Q  L  H  A  Q  I  D  K  R  O  D  Q  I  E  R
T  I  N  U  L  A  N  O  I  T  A  Z  I  N  A  G  R  O  W  S  Z
M  Y  D  L  H  S  W  N  C  X  D  A  U  Q  I  S  N  Y  V  S  S
O  D  B  N  L  R  C  G  T  J  O  T  O  O  Y  D  A  E  M  N  M
R  J  P  A  A  T  J  X  N  G  F  I  T  B  V  H  J  Y  F  A  B
Q  O  H  M  H  D  I  R  E  C  T  O  R  Y  S  C  A  N  P  M  P
W  U  N  E  Z  T  R  A  I  L  I  N  G  P  E  R  I  O  D  E  V
```

Hints:

1. Object that represents a logical NDS pointer to another object in the tree.
2. Container object that uses predetermined two-character names.
3. The context that would be displayed if you issued the CX command with no options.
4. Command line utility used to view or change your current context.
5. Object that represents a logical pointer to a physical directory in the NetWare 4 file system.
6. RCONSOLE menu option that can be used to display the four main files that comprise the NetWare 4 NDS database.
7. An object that represents a set of users and is used for assigning rights.
8. Identifies a name as a distinguished name.
9. Similar to a Country object, except that it can exist in a Country, Organization, or Organizational Unit container.
10. Command that can be used in NET.CFG to set the current context.
11. Item that represents a resource in the NDS database.
12. Container object that is often used to represent a company, university, or association.
13. Object that represents a position or role with an organization.
14. Container object that is considered a "natural group."
15. Object that represents a login script that is used by a group of users who reside in the same or different containers.
16. Special superuser used for bindery emulation.
17. Allows you to change the current context while using relative distinguished naming.
18. Name that contains object attributes abbreviations.
19. Name that does not contain object attributes abbreviations.
20. NDS object that has been invalidated or cannot be identified as belonging to any of the other object classes.

See Appendix C for answers.

EXERCISE 3-2: NETWARE 4 BASICS

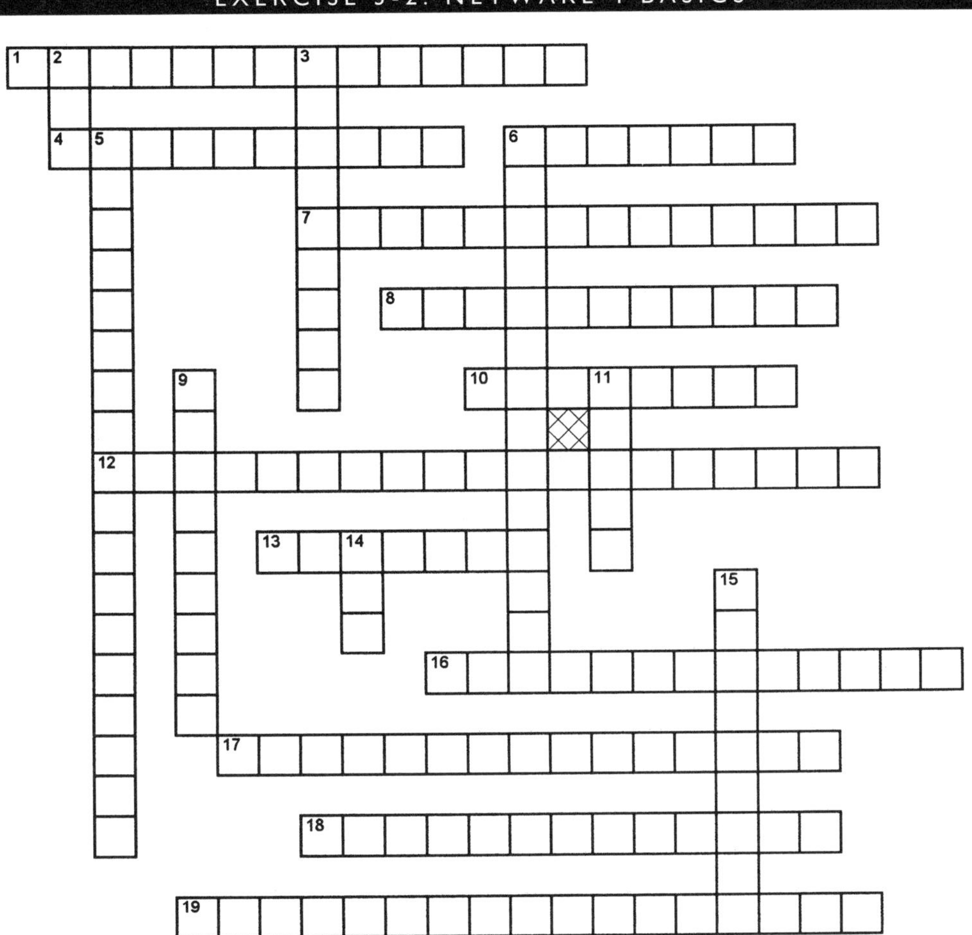

Across

1. Where am I?
2. Who you are, not where you live
5. The "old way" of storing users
7. Login interrogation in NetWare 4
8. The "time keepers" of NetWare 4
10. "Red books" in electronic form

12. Creating a "superbindery"
13. Where you live
16. Off-loading out-of-date files to near-line
17. Saving space
18. No more wasted space
19. Your name and address combined

Down

2. Also GMT
3. Tupperware
5. Multiple layers of Tupperware
6. Two-dimensional slice of 3-D NDS
9. When
11. NetWare 4 incognito
14. The cloud
15. A piece of the "Cloud"

See Appendix C for answers.

EXERCISE 3-3: "TREE WALKING" FOR TODDLERS

To complete this exercise, you will need Admin-level access to a NetWare 4 NDS tree. You will explore the NDS tree structure using three different utilities: NetWare Administrator (NWADMIN), NETADMIN, and CX. Before beginning this exercise, you'll need to make sure that your network administrator has set up the NetWare Administrator icon in MS Windows on your workstation.

NETWARE ADMINISTRATOR

The NetWare Administrator (NWADMIN) utility is undoubtedly the most versatile utility available in NetWare 4. It can be used to perform a variety of functions, including the type of network administrator tasks that are available in FILER, NETADMIN, PARTMGR, and PCONSOLE.

During NetWare 4 installation, the files for the MS Windows version of this utility are stored in the SYS:PUBLIC directory. The files for the OS/2 version are stored in the SYS:PUBLIC\OS2 directory. Before you run the NetWare Administrator in MS Windows or OS/2 on a workstation for the first time, you'll need to create an NWADMIN icon. From then on, you can select the icon to activate the utility. As stated earlier, this exercise assumes that your network administrator has already set up the NetWare Administrator icon for you in MS Windows.

In this exercise, we are going to use NWADMIN to explore the NDS tree.

1. Exploring the browser window. Execute the NetWare Administrator (NWADMIN) utility in MS Windows by double-clicking on its icon. At least one NDS container object should be displayed. If not, select the Browse option from the Tools menu to open a browser window.

   a. What container and its objects are displayed when you activate the NetWare Administrator utility? How can you determine what your current context is? How was your current context determined? Is it the same current context that would be displayed using the CX command at the DOS prompt?

b. How many containers are displayed? What type of containers are represented? How many leaf objects, if any, are displayed? What type of leaf objects are represented?

2. Changing context

a. Keying in a new context. Keying in the name of a new context is one of the two methods available for changing your current context. Change your context to the [Root] by selecting Set Context. . . from the View menu. Type **[Root]** and press Enter. The [Root] icon should then be displayed at the top of the screen.

b. Walking the tree. Next, let's try the "walking the tree" method to change your current context. Select Set Context. . . from the View menu.

(1) Click on the Browser button to the right of the New Context field to display the Select Object window.

(2) To navigate the tree, double-click on a container in the Directory Context list box on the right side of the screen to move down one level in the tree or double-click on the double-dot (..) to move up one level in the tree. The objects that are located in each container that you select will be displayed in the Objects list box on the left side of the screen. Practice walking up and down the tree. When you are finished, walk all the way up the tree, so that the [Root] icon is displayed at the top of the Object list box on the left side of the screen.

(3) The Name Filter field in the middle of the main NWADMIN browser screen allows you to restrict the objects that are listed in the Object list box on the left side of the screen by using wildcard characters or object names. The Directory Context filter field allows you to restrict the containers that are displayed on the right side of the screen by using wildcard characters or container names. Practice using these filters to limit what is displayed on the screen. When you are finished, delete any filters in either field.

(4) When the container you want to select as the current context is displayed in the Objects list box (which in this case is the [Root] object), click on it, then click on the OK button at the bottom of the window. The container that you have selected will appear in the New Context field in the Set Current Context window. Click on the OK button at the bottom of the Set Current Context window to return to the main NWADMIN browser screen.

3. Opening a container object and viewing its contents. There are two methods available for opening a container and viewing its contents:

   a. Double-clicking on the container's object name or icon.

   b. Clicking on the container object to select it, then selecting the Expand option from the View menu.

   Practice using both of these methods to view the contents of various containers. Determine the type of containers that are in each container, as well as the type of leaf objects.

4. Viewing the object dialog (object details) of a container object. The object dialog lets you display and edit information relating to an object's properties. When you open an object dialog, you'll notice that there is a column of page buttons along the right side of the screen. You can click on each button, one at a time, to view the category of information indicated on the button. There two methods available for viewing the information relating to a container object:

   a. Clicking on the container object with the left mouse button to select it, then selecting the Details option from the Object menu.

   b. Clicking on the container object with the right mouse button to select it, then selecting Details from the pull-down menu that appears on the screen.

Practice using both of these methods to look at the information available for various types of container objects, including the [Root], a Country object (if one exists), an Organization object, and Organizational Unit objects.

5. Viewing the object dialog (object details) of a leaf object. There are three methods for viewing the information relating to a leaf object:

   a. Double-clicking on the leaf object.

   b. Clicking on the leaf object with the left mouse button to select it, then selecting the Details option from the Object menu.

   c. Clicking on the leaf object with the right mouse button to select it, then selecting Details from the menu that appears on the screen.

   Practice using all three of these methods to look at the information available for various types of leaf objects, including Users, Groups, Print Servers, Printers, Print Queues, and so on.

   When you are ready to exit the NetWare Administrator utility, select the Exit option from the File menu.

NETADMIN

The NETADMIN utility is a menu utility that can be used to manage NDS objects and their properties. It is much more limited in scope than the NetWare Administrator Utility.

1. Changing context. In order to change your current context for purposes of the NETADMIN utility, choose the Change context option from the NetAdmin Options menu. There are two methods of changing your context for the purposes of this utility. (When you exit the utility, you will return to the current context that was set before you ran the utility.) One is keying in the name of a new context in the field provided; the other is pressing the Insert key and walking the tree.

a. Press Insert. The contents of the current directory will be displayed, as well as a dot (.) representing the current directory and a double-dot (..) representing the parent directory. You will *not* need to select the dot (.) for purposes of this exercise.

b. Practice walking up and down the tree by double-clicking on the double-dot (..) to move up one level in the tree and double-clicking on a container to move down one level in the tree. You'll notice that the current context is displayed at the top of the screen. Go ahead and walk all the way up the tree by double-clicking on the double-dot (..) until the [Root] is listed as your current context, then walk down the tree by double-clicking on a container object, then double-clicking on a container object below that container object, and so on. When the current context you want is selected, press F10 to return to the NetAdmin Options menu.

2. Managing objects. In order to view and manage objects and their properties, select the Manage objects option from the NetAdmin Options menu. You'll notice that you can walk the tree from this screen as well.

a. In order to display information about an object, select the object using the up-arrow and down-arrow keys, then press F10 to select it. You'll notice that the name and type of the object that you selected will be listed at the top of the menu that appears. Select the View or edit properties of this object menu option and press Enter. A list of categories will be displayed. Select the category desired and press Enter. Review the information displayed for this category, then press Esc to return to the previous menu. Use this method to display the various properties of this object, then press Esc to return to the Object, Class menu.

b. Practice using this technique to display the properties of various types of container and leaf objects. When you're ready to exit the NETADMIN utility, press Esc twice when the Object, Class menu is displayed, then select Yes and press Enter when asked if you want to exit.

CX

The NetWare 4 CX command line utility can be used to display or modify your context, or to view containers and leaf objects in your Directory tree. Open a DOS window in MS Windows (or exit MS Windows) and perform the following steps at the DOS prompt:

1. Change to the F: drive.

   F:

2. Display your current context.

   CX

3. Display online help for the CX command.

   CX /?

4. Display containers in the current context.

   CX /CONT

5. Display containers and objects in the current context.

   CX /A /CONT

6. Display containers at or below the current context.

   CX /T

7. Display containers and objects at or below the current context.

   CX /A /T

8. Display all of the containers and objects in the Directory tree, starting at the [Root], without changing your current context.

   CX /R /A /T

9. Create and display a file that contains a visual representation of the NDS tree structure.

   CX /R /A /T > TREE.NDS

   TYPE TREE.NDS

10. Change your current context to the [Root].

    CX /R

11. Display containers in the [Root].

    CX /CONT

12. Move down one level in the NDS tree.

    CX *context*

    (where *context* is the name of a container that was listed in Step 11)

13. Move up one level in the NDS tree (which in this case happens to be the [Root]).

    CX .

14. Display all containers below the current context ([Root] in this case).

    CX /T

15. Move to a container several levels below the current context ([Root] in this case).

    CX *context*

    (where *context* is a context such as .WHITE.CRIME.TOKYO.ACME)

16. Move up four levels in the NDS tree.

    CX ....

    (where you indicate one dot for each level you want to move up in the NDS tree)

See Appendix C for answers.

EXERCISE 3-4: UNDERSTANDING NDS NAMING

Answer the following questions using the directory structure listed in Figure 3.34 below.

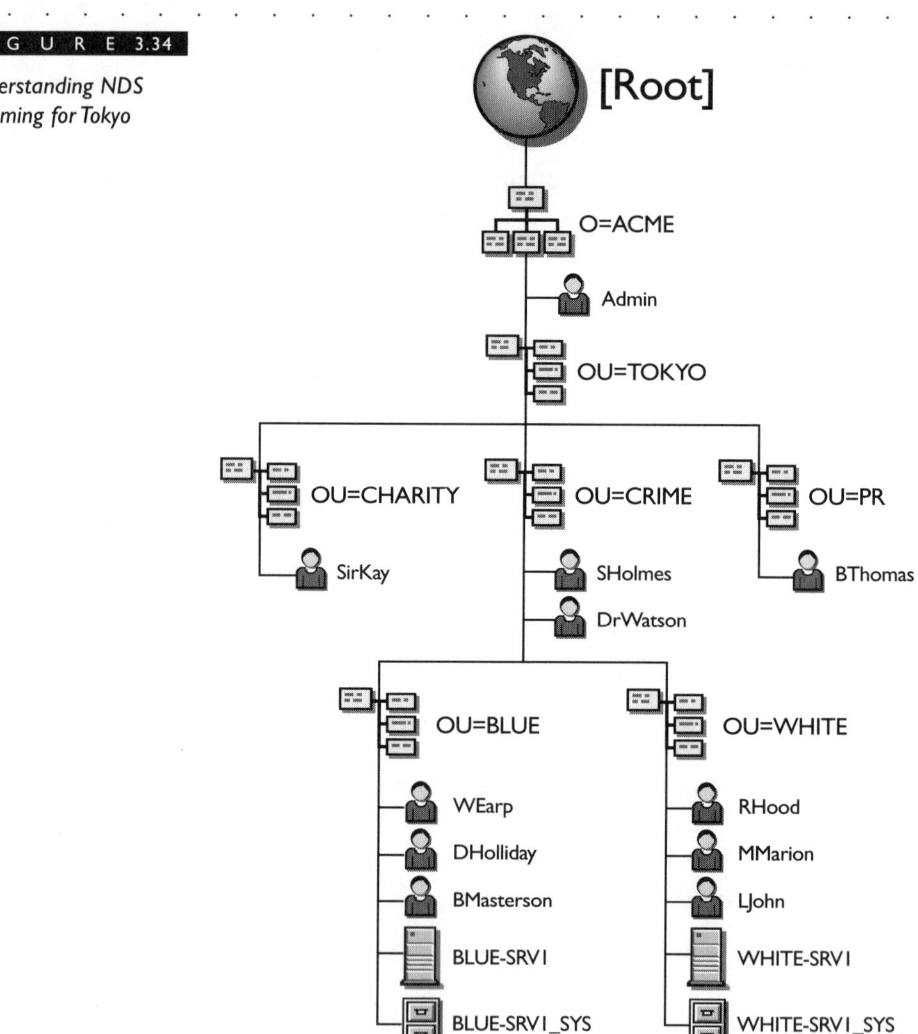

1. Indicate a typeless distinguished name for BMasterson.

2. Provide a typeful distinguished name for RHood.

3. List a typeless relative distinguished name for the CRIME Organizational Unit, assuming that your current context is the [Root].

4. Show a typeful relative distinguished name for the BLUE-SRV1 server object from the default current context.

5. If your current context is .CRIME.TOKYO.ACME, what is the shortest name that accurately references the SHolmes User object?

6. Assume your current context is .TOKYO.ACME. Indicate a typeless relative distinguished name for the LJohn User object.

7. If your current context is .PR.TOKYO.ACME, what would be a typeful relative distinguished name for SirKay?

8. Assume your current context is .WHITE.CRIME.TOKYO.ACME. Provide a typeless relative distinguished name for Admin.

9. If your current context is .BLUE.CRIME.TOKYO.ACME, what would be a typeful relative distinguished name for Sir Kay?

10. Assume your current context is .WHITE.CRIME.TOKYO.ACME. What is the longest possible typeful relative distinguished name for the SYS: volume on the BLUE-SRV1 server?

11. If DHolliday attaches to the BLUE-SRV1 server by default, what's his current context after login? Give two LOGIN commands for DHolliday.

12. How would MMarion visit SirKay?

13. How can you make sure that SirKay's workstation drops him into his home context when he attaches to the "Cloud"?

14. Provide 10 LOGIN commands for SHolmes from
    BLUE.CRIME.TOKYO.ACME:

15. What is the easiest way to move above ACME from the .PR.TOKYO.ACME
    context?

See Appendix C for answers.

NetWare 4 File System

Just when you think you have NetWare 4 and NDS figured out, a little voice inside your head whispers, "There is another. . . ."

Another what? Listen more closely, ". . . directory structure."

Another directory structure? How could that be? You may think that there's only one NetWare directory structure and it's the foundation of NDS. Well, that's where you're wrong. If you look closely at Figure 4.1, you'll see *two* directory trees — one above the server and one below it.

The Two NetWare 4
Directory Trees

The directory tree above the NetWare 4 server is NDS. It organizes network resources into a logical WAN hierarchy. The directory tree below the server is the file system. It organizes network data files into a functional application hierarchy. Pretty simple, huh? The important thing is to separate the two in your mind. NDS handles resource data and the file system handles application data. Think of it as the "File Cabinet of Life."

ZEN

"To me, if life boils down to one significant thing — it's movement. To live is to keep moving. Unfortunately, this means that for the rest of our lives we're going to be looking for boxes!"

Jerry Seinfeld

In the past, cave-LANs relied on "sneakernet" for file sharing. First, they copied files to a diskette, then ran them down the hall to a coworker's machine. Finally, the coworker transferred the files from diskette to his or her own directory structure. Voilá!

With the advent of NetWare (and coaxial cabling), society experienced the dawning of a new age — the file server. The file server became the central repository for shared data and applications. Life was good.

Then, NetWare 4 came along. Once again, society experienced the dawning of a new age — NDS. The file server suddenly became a small fish in a very large, global pond. Volumes took on a life of their own. People started treating them as independent objects; free from the servers that house them. Is this progress? I'm not so sure. It underemphasizes the importance of the file server. Let's be honest. It's still the most important resource in the WAN. And what do file servers do? They serve files. How? Through the NetWare 4 file system.

Let's check it out.

Understanding the NetWare 4 File System

Every NetWare 4 file server contains a hierarchical directory structure for storing shared data files and applications. It is called the *file system*. The file system organizes internal disks into one or more volumes. Volumes are then divided into directories that contain subdirectories or files. On the surface it looks a lot like DOS. But don't be fooled; it's a whole new world. Check out Figure 4.2!

The NetWare 4 File
System

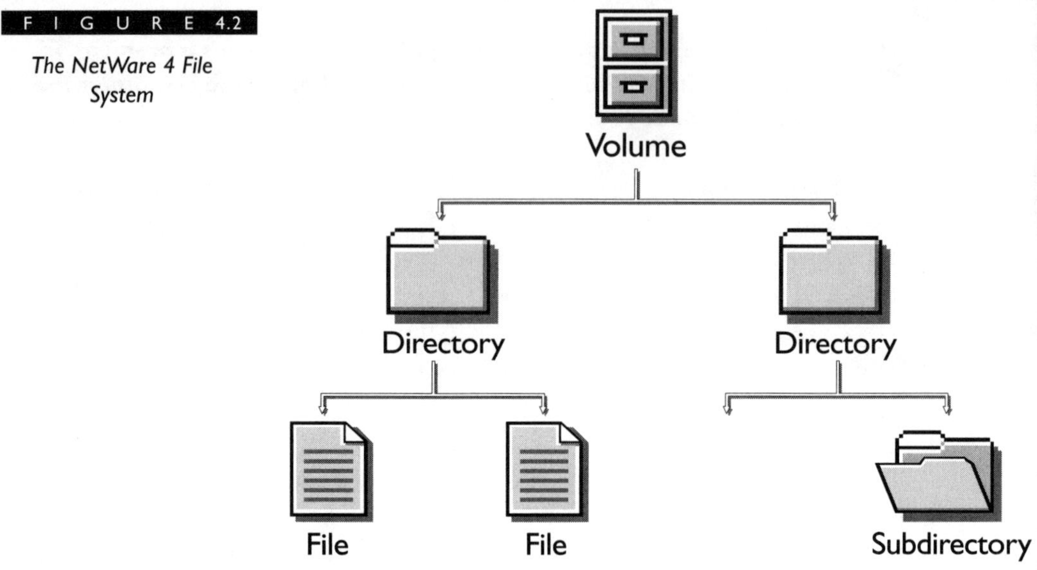

TIP

In earlier versions of NetWare, the "file system" was referred to as the "directory structure." In NetWare 4, it is referred to as the "file system" to distinguish it from the NDS directory structure.

Earlier we called the NetWare 4 file system the "File Cabinet of Life." It fits. See Figure 4.3. In such an analogy, the file server is the filing cabinet, and the volumes are the drawers. Similarly, the directories are hanging folders, the subdirectories are file folders, and the files become individual sheets of paper. Pretty nifty, huh?

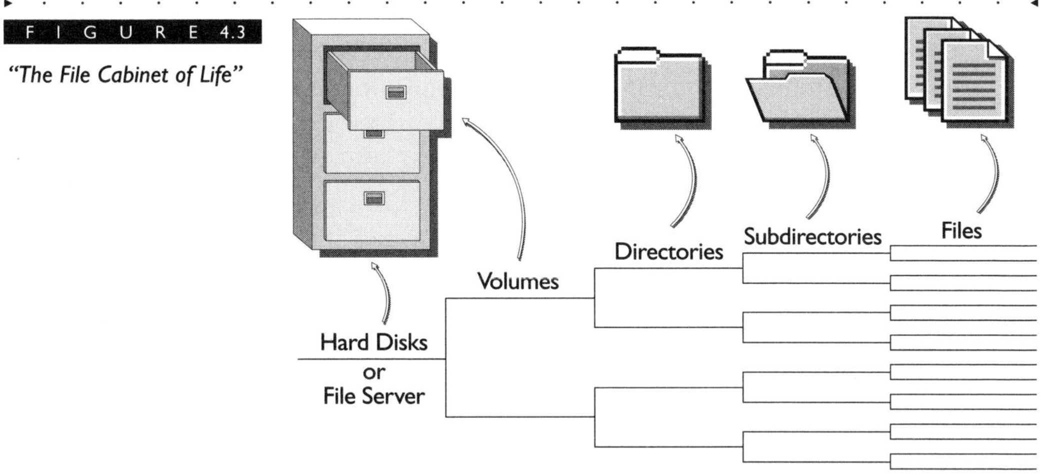

"The File Cabinet of Life"

With this analogy in mind, let's explore the key components of NetWare 4's exciting new file system: volumes and directories. In the first section, we will discover the volume, and learn about its dual personality as a logical NDS object and physical disk resource. Then, we'll focus our journey even further into the Netware 4 directory structure — starting with system-created directories, which are defined automatically within the SYS: volume during NetWare 4 server installation. Next, we'll expand our horizons beyond default directories and into the realm of DOS, application, configuration, home, and shared directories. Finally, you'll get a taste of two different directory designs — shallow and deep.

And that's only the first section. Later in the chapter, we'll explore file system management and the land of drive mapping. Wow! So much to learn and so little time. So, without any further interruptions, let's get on with the show.

UNDERSTANDING NETWARE 4 VOLUMES

Volumes are cool — mostly because they're so unique. They can span multiple disks, or they can be subdivisions of a single disk. They are physical storage units within the file server, but also independent logical objects that stand alone. They are neither here nor there — they are everywhere!

The volume represents the highest level in the NetWare 4 file system. It is the root of the server directory structure. Volumes can also be leaf objects in the NDS directory tree. Because of this unique position, they act as a bridge between NDS and the file system. The first volume on each NetWare 4 server is named SYS:. It is created automatically during NetWare 4 installation. In addition, an NDS leaf object is created in the server's home container. For our example, this is called WHITE-SRV1_SYS — a logical representation of the physical SYS: volume on WHITE-SRV1.

None of this is set in stone, of course. You can change the context of a Volume object using NetWare Administrator (NWADMIN) or NETADMIN. You can also rename volumes. To rename a physical volume, you'll need to change its server definition with INSTALL.NLM. To rename a logical volume, you can use either NWADMIN or NETADMIN. Finally, you can create a special pointer to a different physical volume using the Alias object type.

ZEN

Infobit — An individual item of information, such as a recipe or a description of a place, that meets the requirements for inclusion in a databank. Also used to describe properties of NDS objects.

So, what are they? NetWare 4 *volumes* are fixed units of hard disk storage. They can be formed from any hard disk that contains a NetWare partition. Think of it as NetWare formatting. You can place 64 volumes on a NetWare 4 server, and each one can span up to 32 hard disks. Do the math. That means a NetWare 4 server can support 2,048 disks — wow!

How does it work? Volumes are divided into physical volume segments. Different segments can be stored on one or more hard disks. Each volume can support 32 segments, and/or each hard disk can support 8 volume segments from one or more volumes. Because of this, a volume can

- ▸ Contain a portion of a hard disk

- ▸ Occupy an entire hard disk

- ▸ Span multiple hard disks

The simplest configuration is, of course, one hard disk per volume. The advantage of spreading a volume across multiple hard disks is performance. It allows the server to read from or write to different parts of the same volume simultaneously — thus speeding up disk input/output. The disadvantage of such a technique, however, is fault tolerance. If you span volumes across multiple disks, it increases the chances that something will go wrong. If any disk fails, the entire volume fails, and you lose all your data. Consider protecting your volumes with mirroring, duplexing, or RAID (Redundant Array of Inexpensive Disks).

TIP

RAID provides numerous performance and SFT (System Fault Tolerance) advantages. From a performance standpoint, it uses *data striping*, which means that files are stored across multiple disks. Read and write performance is enhanced dramatically because blocks can be accessed simultaneously. In addition, RAID employs a parity algorithm that protects volumes even when a disk crashes. Cool.

NetWare 4 volumes are further organized into *directories* and *files*. Directories are logical volume subdivisions that provide an administrative hierarchy for network applications and data files. They allow you to further organize your data into content-specific file folders. Directories can contain other directories (called *subdirectories*) or files.

Files are individual items of data. They represent the bottom level of the file-server food chain. Files can contain valuable user data or network applications. It doesn't matter. What does matter is their location. Files should be stored in logical subdirectories according to their purpose and security level. That's the ultimate goal of the NetWare 4 file system — to organize the user's data so that it's secure and easy to find.

To accomplish this goal, you must follow specific file syntax and naming rules. As with NDS object naming, filenames define the data's name and location:

```
Server\Volume:Directory\(Subdirectory)\Filename
```

Standard directory names and filenames support eight characters plus an optional three-character extension. Special non-DOS filenames can extend as far as 32 characters (Macintosh) or even 255 characters (OS/2 and Windows 95). These special files require an additional volume feature called *name space* (see Chapter 7). Also, make sure to support the path conventions of standard or special filenames.

NetWare allows 255 characters in a directory path (counting the drive letter and delimiters), whereas DOS only allows a maximum of 127 characters. Refer to Table 4.1 for more NetWare 4 file system naming rules.

T A B L E 4.1	PATH COMPONENT	RULES
NetWare 4 File System Naming Rules	File Server	Name is limited to 2 to 47 characters.
		First character in name cannot be a period.
		Name cannot contain spaces or special characters such as * + , \ / | : ; = < > [ ].
	Volume	Name length is limited to 2 to 15 characters.
		Physical name must end with a colon (:), which is added automatically.
		First volume on server must be SYS:.
		Two physical volumes on the same server cannot have the same name.
		Name cannot contain spaces or special characters such as * + , \ / | : ; = < > [ ].
	Directory	Name length is limited to a maximum of 11 characters (a directory name consisting of 1 to 8 characters plus an optional directory name extension of up to 3 characters).
		A period (.) is used to separate the directory name from the (optional) extension.
		Directories should be limited to functional groups.
		Name cannot contain spaces or special characters such as * + , \ / | : ; = < > [ ].
	Subdirectory	Name length is limited to a maximum of 11 characters (a directory name consisting of 1 to 8 characters plus an optional directory name extension of up to 3 characters).
		A period (.) is used to separate the directory name from the (optional) extension.
		Subdirectories share common functionality.

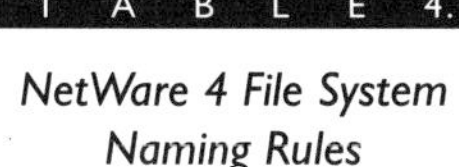 T A B L E 4.1	PATH COMPONENT	RULES
NetWare 4 File System Naming Rules	Subdirectory	The size of subdirectories is limited by disk size.
		Name cannot contain spaces or special characters such as * + , \ / | : ; = < > [ ].
	Files	Name length is limited to a maximum of 11 characters (a filename consisting of 1 to 8 characters plus an optional filename extension of up to 3 characters).
		A period (.) is used to separate the directory name from the (optional) extension.
		Name cannot contain spaces or special characters such as * + , \ / | : ; = < > [ ].

Before you get too carried away with NetWare 4 configuration and management, you should design the basic structure of the file system. This is just as important as designing the NDS tree. In both cases, you need to consider a number of important WAN factors, including security, administration, and accessibility. Except, this time we're working below the server, not above it.

ZEN

Nonchaotic attractor — A pattern of movement in a system with motion that settles down to an easily describable and predictable pattern, such as a pendulum or NetWare 4 volume. This can also be thought of as a normal attractor in that it is the opposite of a "strange" attractor.

Because volumes are at the top of the file system tree, they should be planned first. Here are a few things to think about:

▸ The simplest strategy is one-to-one. That is, one volume for each internal disk. In this scenario, stick with the default SYS: volume and let it occupy your entire internal disk. Then rely on directories and subdirectories for file organization and security.

▶ If the one-to-one strategy isn't for you, be sure to reserve the SYS: volume for files needed by the NetWare 4 operating system. Additional volumes can be created for applications, data files, and print queues.

▶ Create a separate volume for each client operating system that allows long filenames. For instance, if you have both Macintosh users and DOS or OS/2 users, you might want to create a separate volume for the Macintosh files. This is particularly important because it enhances administration, backup procedures, and disk space usage. Also, name space adds performance overhead to *all* files on the host volume, so, minimize the files on that volume.

▶ If fault tolerance is more important than performance, create one volume per disk. If performance is more important than fault tolerance, span one NetWare volume over multiple hard disks (with one segment of the volume on each hard disk). If fault tolerance and performance are equally important, you can still spread volumes across multiple hard disks, but you should make sure that they are duplexed or RAIDed.

Once the volumes are in place, it's time to shift your focus to directories. This is when it gets interesting. Fortunately, NetWare 4 gives you a big head start with system-created directories and files. Let's check them out.

SYSTEM-CREATED DIRECTORIES

With the NetWare 4 server installation, you get a default user (Admin) and two directory trees:

▶ The default NDS tree (server context)

▶ The default file system on SYS:

In our discussion of the NetWare 4 file system, we will explore the default tree and go a few steps beyond:

- ► System-created directories

- ► DOS directories

- ► Application directories

- ► Configuration directories

- ► Home directories

- ► Shared data directories

System-created directories contain NetWare 4 operating system files, NLMs, and utilities. They are divided into two main categories: Admin directories and User directories. This is a security issue. The Admin directories (SYSTEM, for example) are reserved for administrators only — they require Supervisor access rights. User directories, on the other hand, contain public utilities and are open to all users throughout the WAN (PUBLIC, for example). Next, with the system-created directories as a platform, you will spring forward into the world of file-system creativity.

DOS directories are optional. They are required only if you want users to access DOS from the server instead of from their local drives. Application directories contain third-party application programs such as word processing, spreadsheet, or database programs. Configuration directories hold user- or group-specific configuration files. These files help you manage network applications. Home directories hold special user files and create a cozy, productive network environment. Finally, shared data directories contain global files for all users throughout the WAN.

Let's start our discussion with a detailed look at the nine system-created directories. Refer to Figure 4.4. Here they are:

LOGIN	ETC
SYSTEM	QUEUES
PUBLIC	DELETED.SAV
MAIL	DOC
NLS	

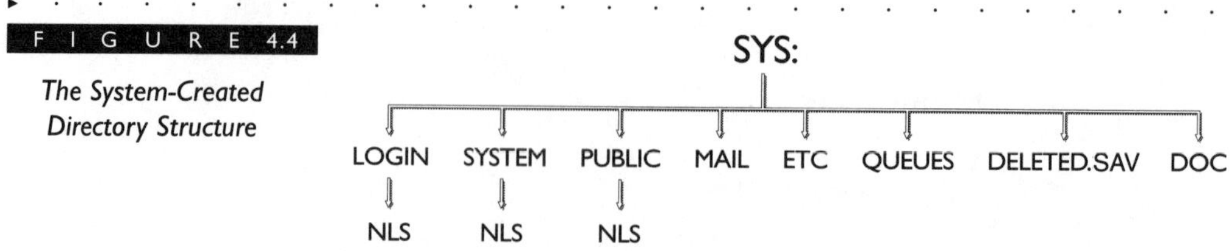

F I G U R E 4.4

The System-Created Directory Structure

LOGIN

LOGIN is your doormat to the WAN. From there you can knock on NetWare's door and provide the secret password for entrance. This is all accomplished with the help of LOGIN.EXE. In addition to logging in, there are other administrative tasks you (and users) can perform from the LOGIN directory — such as changing context (CX), viewing the NDS tree structure (NLIST), and mapping drives (MAP).

LOGIN is the only directory available to users prior to login. Be careful which programs you place there, because they are available to users without any security. Finally, there's an additional subdirectory under LOGIN, called OS2, which contains login programs for OS/2 clients.

Once you log in and pass through the magic NDS gates, the rest of the world opens up to you — namely, the other eight system-created directories.

SYSTEM

SYSTEM is Admin's workroom. This directory contains special administrative tools and utilities, including OS files, NLMs, and dangerous NDS programs. For this reason, SYSTEM should be kept out of the reach of users and small children. Fortunately, it contains a "child-proof cap" in the form of Supervisor access rights. Only Admin can gain access by default.

PUBLIC

PUBLIC, on the other hand, is the user's playground. This directory contains general user commands and utilities, such as NWADMIN, NETADMIN, NWUSER, and MAP. By default, all users in the server's home container have access to PUBLIC — but only after they've logged in. In addition, a subdirectory under PUBLIC, called OS2, contains NetWare programs and utilities for OS/2 users.

MAIL

MAIL is left over from the old days when NetWare shipped with an e-mail application. Well, guess what — it does again (see Chapter 6), but it doesn't use the MAIL directory. Go figure. Instead, the MAIL directory is a repository for old user-specific system configuration files, like bindery login scripts (LOGIN.) and print job configurations (PRINTCON.DAT). Of course, with Netware 4, these files are now properties of each user object. Ah, NDS.

Oh yeah. MAIL is sometimes used by third-party e-mail applications, but not very often.

NLS

NLS is NetWare 4's translator. It stands for NetWare Language Support (or something like that). Each of the main system-created directories has its own NLS subdirectory. These NLS directories contain message and help files for multilingual NetWare 4 utilities. If multiple languages have been installed, each language has its own subdirectory under NLS.

Here's a quick review of how multiple languages work. Each utility and message file has a general language pointer. The workstation determines which language the user wants to use and tells the pointer where to go for the language-specific modules (that is, which NLS directory). NLS then displays the utility or message in the appropriate language. It is very cool.

ETC

ETC is aptly named. It contains a bunch of other stuff, like sample TCP/IP configuration files and, you know, other stuff.

QUEUES

QUEUES is one of the great advancements in NetWare 4. Earlier versions stored print queues on the SYS: volume only. This caused serious problems if the print job was large and SYS: ran out of space — namely, the server crashed. Now, CNAs can offload print queue storage to any volume they want. When you do, NetWare 4 automatically creates a QUEUES directory off the root of the host volume.

DELETED.SAV

DELETED.SAV is file heaven. This is where files go when they die. You see, files can be brought back to life in NetWare 4 — it's called *salvaging*. But the files must be salvaged from their parent directory. If, in some horrible plane crash, their parent directory was also deleted, the children files can be salvaged from DELETED.SAV. This directory is only created when it's needed.

DOC

Welcome to NetWare 4's electronic documentation — DynaText. The interesting thing about DynaText is that it becomes available *after* you need it. For example, the NetWare 4 installation instructions are available once you install DynaText — *after* the server's been installed! Life has a funny way of surprising you. Remember, Murphy's law number 142: "I'm an optimist."

Anyway, NetWare 4 DynaText is installed in the DOC directory using INSTALL.NLM at the tail-end of server installation.

ZEN

"Pioneers took years to cross the country. Now people will move thousands of miles just for the summer. I don't think any pioneers did that, 'Yeah, it took us a decade to get there, and we stayed for the summer. It was nice, they had a pool, the kids loved it. And then, we left about ten years ago and we just got back. We had a great summer, it took us twenty years, and now our lives are over!'"

Jerry Seinfeld

This completes our brief pilgrimage through the NetWare 4 system-created directory structure. Be sure that you do not accidentally delete, move, or rename any of these system-created directories — especially LOGIN, SYSTEM, PUBLIC, MAIL, and NLS. These directories are critical to the server and bad things will happen if they're removed.

Okay. We're cruising now. Next, let's expand our horizons beyond the default directory structure and explore the land of additional directories. You'll be amazed at what you can find there.

EXPANDING BEYOND THE DEFAULT DIRECTORY STRUCTURE

NetWare 4 provides you with a big head start by building the default directory tree (see Figure 4.4). The next step is to add some productive DOS, user, application, and data directories. Think of it as a transition from Figure 4.4 to Figure 4.5. It boils down to five suggested directory components:

- ▸ DOS directories

- ▸ Application directories

- ▸ Configuration directories

- ▸ Home directories

- ▸ Shared data directories

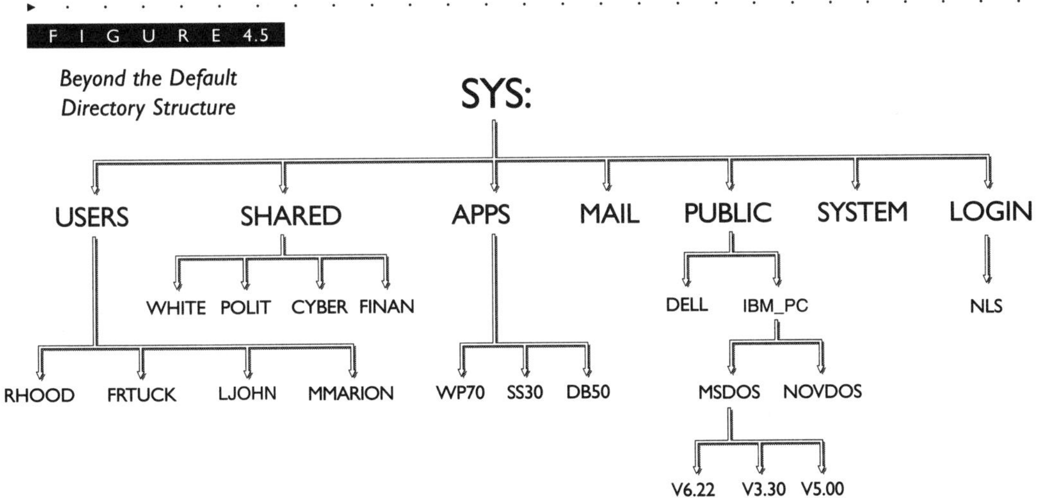

F I G U R E   4.5

Beyond the Default Directory Structure

Let's take a closer look.

DOS Directories

DOS directories are vital because they provide support for various workstation operating systems (namely DOS and OS/2). They are, however, optional. You can choose to have users execute DOS commands and utilities from their local workstation drives, or from a shared DOS directory on the server — it's up to you.

If you choose to have users run DOS from the server, you'll need to make a separate subdirectory for each version of DOS. It is preferable, of course, to have all users run the same version of DOS, but dream on — it'll never happen. Here's the trick: You'll need to somehow interrogate each workstation and point the user to the correct version of DOS. Fortunately, NetWare 4 supports login script identifier variables for this very purpose. We'll explore them in more depth later in Chapter 6, "NetWare 4 Configuration."

For now, you'll need to create a DOS directory structure that supports all the different types of machines and DOS versions on your WAN. As you can see in Figure 4.5, the DOS structure starts under SYS:PUBLIC because users already have access there. Next, you'll need to create a subdirectory structure for each of the following three components:

- MACHINE — IBM_PC, DELL, or other

- OS — MSDOS, NOVDOS, OS2, and so on

- OS VERSION — V7.01, V6.22, or whatever version you're using

So, why should you bother? Many users simply access DOS utilities from their local drives. Well, if you're using a diskless workstation, you'll need to get DOS somewhere else — such as the server. Also, some users get better performance from the server because of file caching and a slow local disk channel. Finally, a centralized DOS structure allows you to update DOS once (on the server), instead of hundreds of times on each distributed workstation. The bottom line is that it's your choice, DOS central or DOS local — whatever you do, just DOS it!

Application Directories

A subdirectory structure should be created under SYS:APPS for each network application. For security's sake, restrict this structure to application files only — no data. Users can store their data in home directories, group areas, or SYS:SHARED — a global data directory (see the "Shared Data Directories" section).

Configuration File Directories

What about application configuration files, such as templates, interface files, and style sheets? It depends on the type of configuration file it is. For instance, application-specific configuration files, like style sheets, should be placed in a CONFIG directory under the application. User-specific configurations, on the other hand, such as interface files, should be placed in user home directories. Let's take a closer look.

Home Directories

Each user needs a place he/she can call home. A special subdirectory under SYS:USERS gives each of them a private, secure retreat for his or her own stuff. User directories serve two functions: security and organization. From a security viewpoint, they provide a secure place for private user files — a place away from coworkers' prying eyes. (Of course, you can look at their files because you are a NetWare 4 CNA.) From an organizational viewpoint, user directories become the parent of a complex user-specific directory structure — a place for personal games and applications.

Each user's home directory should exactly match their login name — or at least be very close. This simplifies administration and makes them easy to find. Also, be sure to give users sufficient access rights to move around in there (see Chapter 5).

Shared Data Directories

The proper organization of network data strongly impacts user productivity. Let's be honest — the sole purpose of the NetWare 4 file system is to organize data efficiently. This is accomplished in three ways:

▶ Personal data — should be stored in user home directories

▶ Group-specific data — should be stored in special group data directories under SYS:SHARED

▶ Globally-shared data — should be stored in the SYS:SHARED directory off of the root of SYS:

There you go. That's the NetWare 4 file system. So, the only question that remains is, "What should it look like?" You have two choices: shallow or deep. Check it out.

QUIZ

I'm on this numbers kick. Numbers have an unavoidable fascination. Try this one on for size:

What is the five-digit number, no zeros, in which the first number is one-fourth of the second, the second is twice the third, the third is two-thirds of the fourth, and the fifth is half of the fourth, with the sum of all the digits being 23?

(Q4-1)
(See Appendix C for quiz answers.)

DESIGNING YOUR DIRECTORY STRUCTURE

Now that you know what the file system is made of, you need to decide what it's going to look like. You can either create a flat tree with many directories stored off the root of the volume, or you can have a deep directory structure with many levels of subdirectories (see Figure 4.6). Novell recommends that, for ease of administration, you design a directory structure that is no more than five levels deep.

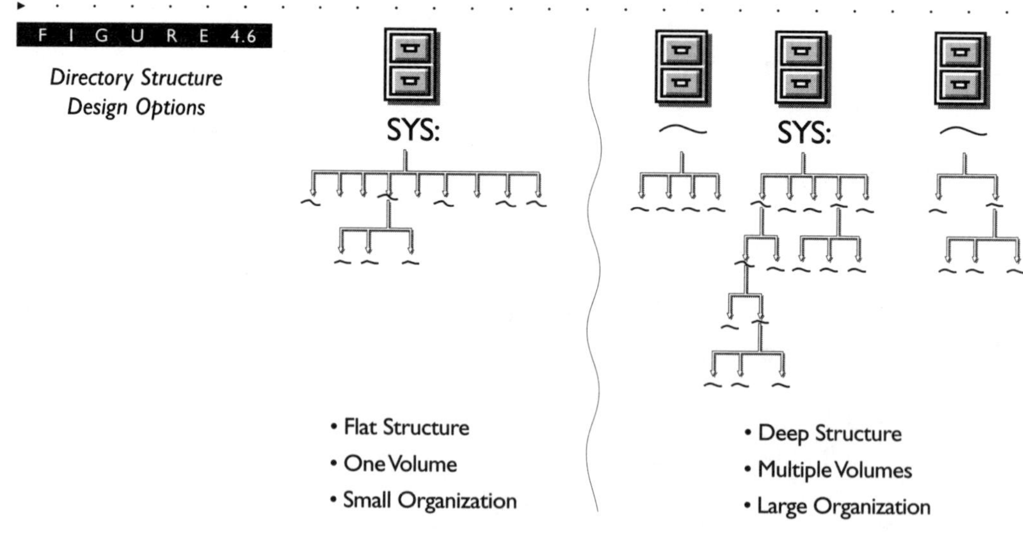

FIGURE 4.6

Directory Structure Design Options

A flat directory structure, such as the one in Figure 4.7, could be used for a very small company with few users. In this example, all home directories are stored in the root of the volume — not recommended, but easy to use. On the up side, this design limits file storage to a single volume, and the path names are very short. Also, the application programs are separated from data files.

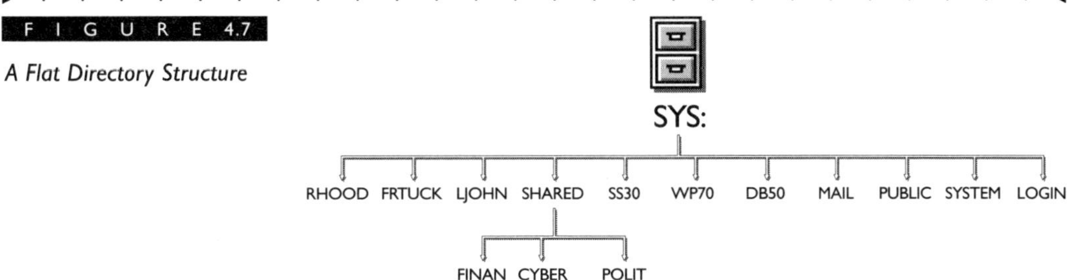

FIGURE 4.7

A Flat Directory Structure

On the down side, the SYS: volume shares its space with everyone else. Sometimes it just needs to be alone. Also, home directories are located in the root of the volume, and there is no shared data area.

A deeper directory structure is shown in Figure 4.8. In this design, system-created directories and applications share SYS:, while all other components have their own volumes. On the up side, the SYS: volume is more stable, because files are not added or deleted very often. Also, applications are more secure because they hang out with SYS:. Finally, you can consider using a different file system administrator for each volume.

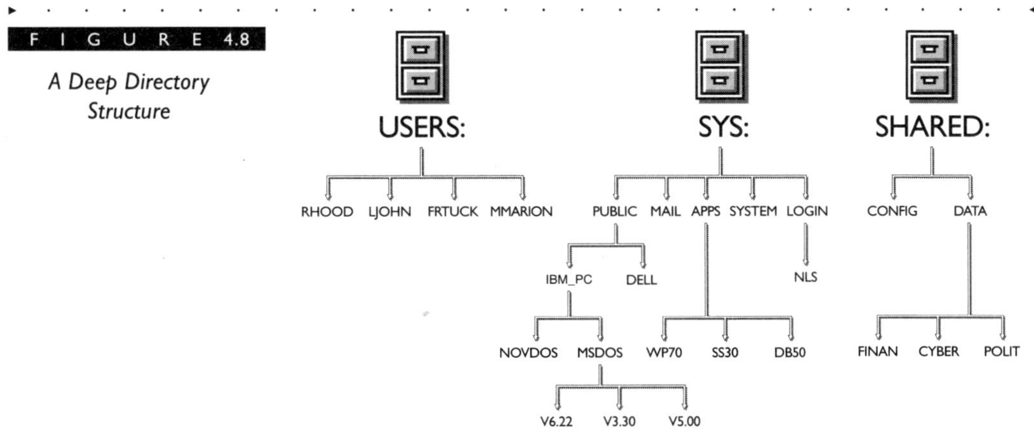

FIGURE 4.8

A Deep Directory Structure

On the down side, this design places users on different volumes, which makes security much more difficult to administer. Also, you may run out of room on a given volume, even though you have sufficient disk space on the server.

So, there you are. The "other" NetWare 4 directory structure. It's not so bad. It's a lot easier than those crazy leaf objects and distinguished names. As you can see, the NetWare 4 file system provides a simple, straightforward structure for sharing valuable WAN files. But what about management? How do you keep it running on a daily basis? I'm so glad you asked. That's the next topic.

Managing the NetWare 4 File System

Once you've designed your file system, you'll need to develop a plan to maintain it — every day! You'll need to ask yourself the following questions:

- How much disk space is left on each volume?

- How much disk space is still available to users with volume space restrictions?

- How much room is being taken up by files that have been deleted but not yet purged?

- Which files have not been accessed in a long time?

- Are there any directories or files with no owner?

For the most part, the NetWare 4 file system looks like DOS. For this reason, you can perform many DOS file management tasks in NetWare 4 as well. In addition, DOS tools such as DIR, COPY, and the MS Windows File Manager work just fine in the NetWare environment.

This is not nearly enough, however. Networking, in general, puts a great strain on file management. Fortunately, NetWare 4 includes a number of file management utilities that are specifically designed to work in a network environment, such as:

- FILER — A text-based utility that is used to manage directories and files, display volume information, and salvage and purge deleted files.

- FLAG — Allows you to view or modify directory and file attributes. It can also be used to modify the owner of a directory or file and to view or modify the search mode of executable files.

- NCOPY — Allows you to copy network files from one location to another.

- NDIR — Lets you view the files once they've been copied. In addition, this utility allows you to view a plethora of information about volumes and directories — but you can't modify anything with it.

- NLIST — A new NetWare 4 NDS utility that displays information about NDS objects and/or properties. It can be used to display information about volumes, as long as they're represented as Volume objects in NDS.

- NWADMIN (runs under MS Windows) and NETADMIN (runs under DOS) — NDS-based tools that can be used to perform a variety of file management tasks such as creating, deleting, renaming, copying, or moving directories and/or files. You can also use them to assign trustee rights, determine effective rights, and modify inherited rights filters. In addition, they display Volume object information and, finally, allow you to purge and salvage deleted files. Wow!

It's a good thing you have so many friends to help you out. In this section, we will explore these and other NetWare 4 file management tools. But we're going to approach them in a slightly unique way. Instead of talking about each utility alone, we are going to explore how they combine to help you manage three key file-system components:

- Volumes

- Directories

- Files

In each area, we will explore all the file management tools that apply to that component. Also, we'll provide some examples of how they can be used to simplify your life. This makes sense, because we're managing volumes, directories, and files — not utilities. So, without further ado, let's start with NetWare 4 volumes.

ZEN

"My parents live in Florida now. They moved there last year. They didn't want to move to Florida, but they're in their seventies now and that's the law!"

Jerry Seinfeld

MANAGING NETWARE 4 VOLUMES

Volumes are at the top of the file-system food chain. They also represent a bridge between physical files on server disks and logical leaf objects in the NDS tree. For your managing pleasure, NetWare 4 includes five key tools for managing volumes:

- ▸ FILER

- ▸ NWADMIN

- ▸ NETADMIN

- ▸ NLIST

- ▸ NDIR

Let's check them out.

FILER

The FILER DOS-based menu utility can be used to display a variety of volume information, including:

- ▸ Volume statistics relating to space usage, directory entries, and compression

- ▸ Volume features such as volume type, block size, name space, and installed features (such as compression, migration, suballocation, or auditing)

- ▸ Date and time information, including creation date/time, owner, last modified date/time, last archived date/time, and archiver

To view information relating to the current volume, choose the "View volume information" option from the Available options menu, as shown in Figure 4.9. A Volume menu will appear that gives you the option of viewing volume statistics, features, or dates and times.

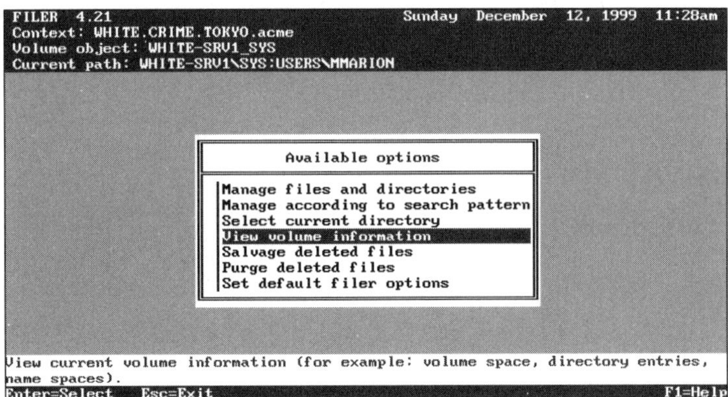

F I G U R E   4.9

Available Options Menu in FILER

If you select the "Volume statistics" option, a screen will appear that is similar to the one in Figure 4.10. This screen lists statistics relating to volume space usage, maximum and available directory entries, and file-compression space usage.

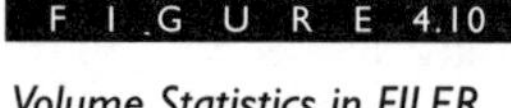

F I G U R E 4.10

Volume Statistics in FILER

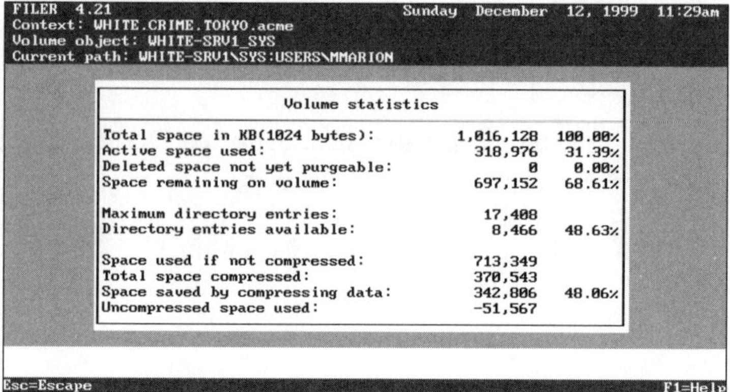

```
FILER  4.21                                 Sunday  December  12, 1999  11:29am
Context: WHITE.CRIME.TOKYO.acme
Volume object: WHITE-SRV1_SYS
Current path: WHITE-SRV1\SYS:USERS\MMARION

                        Volume statistics

        Total space in KB(1024 bytes):          1,016,128   100.00%
        Active space used:                         318,976    31.39%
        Deleted space not yet purgeable:                 0     0.00%
        Space remaining on volume:                 697,152    68.61%

        Maximum directory entries:                  17,408
        Directory entries available:                 8,466    48.63%

        Space used if not compressed:              713,349
        Total space compressed:                    370,543
        Space saved by compressing data:           342,806    48.06%
        Uncompressed space used:                   -51,567

Esc=Escape                                                            F1=Help
```

If you select the "Volume features" option, a screen will appear that is similar to the one in Figure 4.11. This screen includes information about the volume type (that is, non-removable), the block size, the name space(s) installed, and installed features (such as compression, migration, suballocation, or auditing).

F I G U R E 4.11

Volume Features in FILER

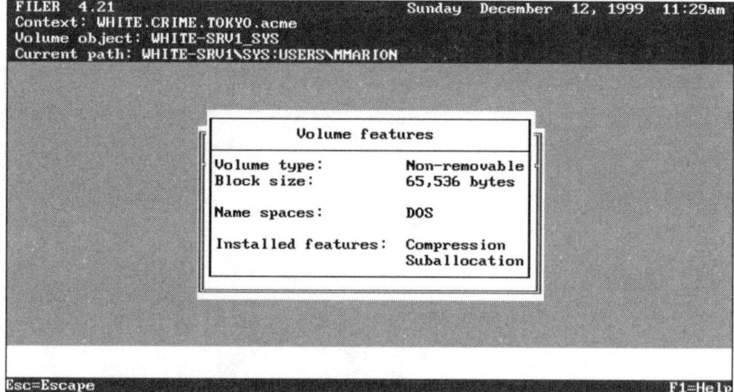

```
FILER  4.21                                 Sunday  December  12, 1999  11:29am
Context: WHITE.CRIME.TOKYO.acme
Volume object: WHITE-SRV1_SYS
Current path: WHITE-SRV1\SYS:USERS\MMARION

                        Volume features

            Volume type:            Non-removable
            Block size:             65,536 bytes

            Name spaces:            DOS

            Installed features:     Compression
                                    Suballocation

Esc=Escape                                                            F1=Help
```

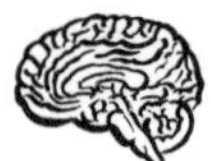

THE BRAIN

Some of the most exciting NetWare 4 volume features are file compression, data migration, and block suballocation. Learn them, use them, live them. Refer to NetWare 4 documentation for more details.

Finally, if you choose the "Dates and times" option, a Volume dates and times window will be displayed. This window displays information such as the volume creation date/time, owner, the last modified date/time, the last archived date/time, and the archiver.

FILER is the most useful non-NDS file management tool. It focuses on volumes, directories, and files as physical storage units within the NetWare 4 server — no NDS nonsense to confuse you. This is appealing to many CNAs. If you want fancy NDS footwork, refer to NWADMIN.

Hey, good idea!

NWADMIN

The NetWare Administrator (NWADMIN) tool treats volumes as NDS objects. It displays roughly the same information as FILER, but from a slightly different point of view:

- ▸ Identification

- ▸ Dates and Times

- ▸ User Space Limits

- ▸ Trustee Security

- ▸ Attributes

To display volume information using NWADMIN, walk the tree until you find your desired volume — in our case it's .CN=WHITE-SRV1_SYS.OU=WHITE. OU=CRIME.OU=TOKYO.O=ACME. When you select a volume, the Identification page button activates by default. Because of this, a screen similar to the one in Figure 4.12 magically appears. It's marginally interesting, containing information on volume name, host server, NetWare version, host volume, and location.

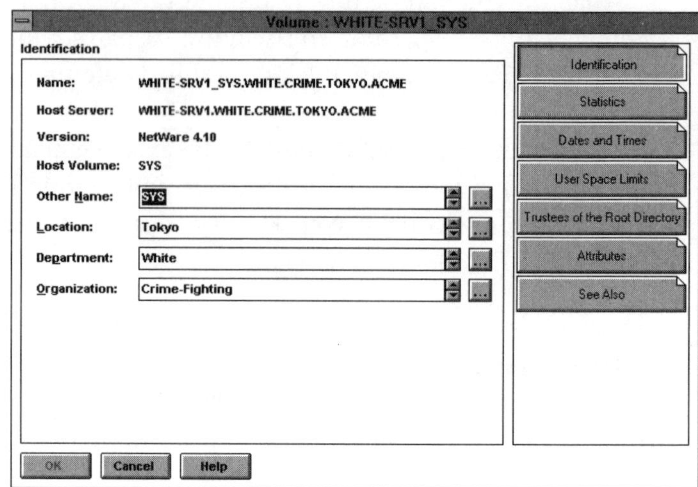

F I G U R E 4.12

Identification Page for Volumes in NWADMIN

The Statistics page is the really interesting NWADMIN volume page (see Figure 4.13). It displays statistical information relating to the volume type (non-removable), deleted files, compressed files, block size, name spaces, and installed features (such as suballocation, data compression, and data migration). Colorful pie charts are also displayed, showing the percentage of disk space and directory entries used. Very cool.

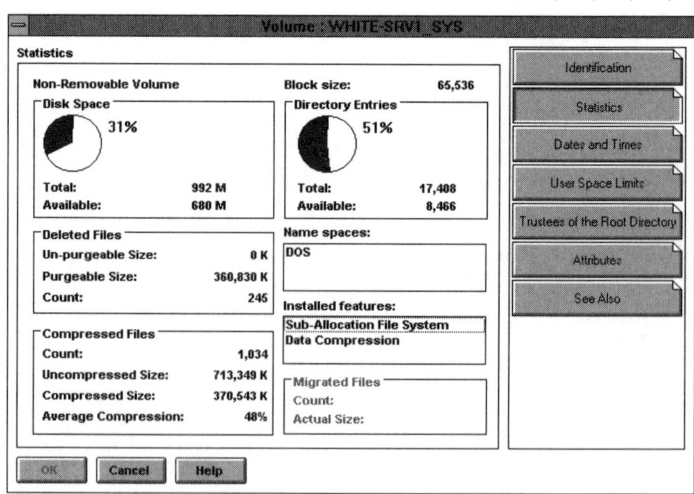

F I G U R E 4.13

Statistics Page for Volumes in NWADMIN

In addition to Identification and Statistics, NWADMIN provides numerous other volume-related page buttons:

▸ Dates and Times — Displays values for the volume creation date and time, owner, last modified date, last archived date, and user last archived by. The latter option offers valuable information for managing data backup (see Chapter 7).

▸ User Space Limits — Displays information regarding user space limits imposed on particular users (if any). This is an effective way of controlling "disk hogs."

▸ Trustees of the Root Directory — Displays security information concerning the trustees of the root directory, their effective rights, and the directory's inherited rights filter. You should be careful about who gets access rights to the root directory of *any* volume — especially SYS:.

▸ Attributes — Displays directory attributes for the root directory of the given volume. This is another security option (see Chapter 5).

▸ See Also — Displays who and what is related to the volume object. This is basically a manual information record for tracking special volume details.

NETADMIN

NETADMIN is the DOS-based version of NWADMIN for those of you who break out into hives every time you touch a mouse. It provides the same type of information as NWADMIN, but in a slightly (or greatly) less user-friendly way. That means it's very hard to use.

To view volume information with NETADMIN, you have to find the volume first. This involves a labyrinth of tree-walking through three menu choices: Manage Objects, Object class, and View or edit properties of this object. Once you arrive at your destination, it looks something like Figure 4.14.

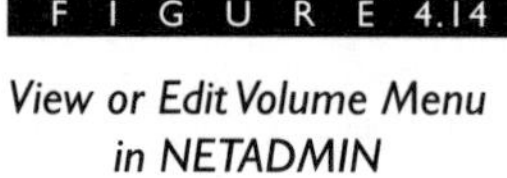

FIGURE 4.14

View or Edit Volume Menu in NETADMIN

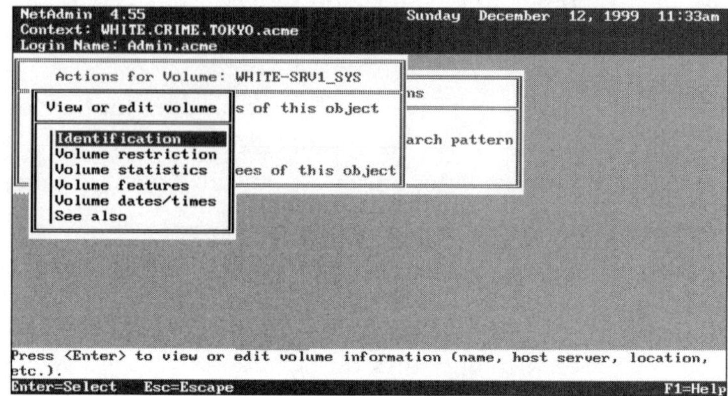

If you select the Identification option from this menu, a screen appears showing the same type of NDS information as the NWADMIN Identification page, including volume name, host server, NetWare version, host volume, and location. Once again, the really interesting data is in the Volume statistics screen (see Figure 4.15). This screen lists numerous statistics related to volume space, maximum and available directory entries, and file-compression space. As a matter of fact, it looks a little familiar — like the Statistics screen in FILER. It's exactly the same data, just using a different DOS-based menu tool. Hmmm.

FIGURE 4.15

Volume Statistics in NETADMIN

```
NetAdmin  4.55                               Sunday  December  12, 1999  11:33am
Context: WHITE.CRIME.TOKYO.acme
Login Name: Admin.acme

                            Volume statistics

Total volume space in KB (1024 bytes):              1,016,128  100.00%
Active space used:                                    318,976   31.39%
Deleted space not yet purgeable:                            0    0.00%
Space remaining on volume:                            697,152   68.61%

Maximum directory entries:                             17,408
Available directory entries:                            8,466   48.63%

Space used if not compressed:                         713,349
Total space compressed:                               370,543
Space saved by compressing data:                      342,806   48.06%
Uncompressed space used:                              309,265


This is information pertaining to the physical volume.  These fields can't be
changed.  Press <Esc> when done.
Esc=Escape                                                              F1=Help
```

In addition to Identification and Statistics, NETADMIN provides a combination of options from both NWADMIN and FILER, including:

- Volume restrictions

- Volume features

- Volume dates/times

- See also

NLIST

As we learned earlier, NLIST is a special NetWare 4 NDS command line utility. It displays all related property information for any NDS object — including volumes. For our purposes, NLIST gives us access to:

- Object class

- Current context

- Volume name

- Host server name

- Physical volume name

- The number of Volume objects in the NDS tree

- Property values for Volume objects

NLIST can only be used to display information about NDS objects — it cannot be used to modify NDS information. Some of the most common commands used to display NDS volume information are included in Table 4.2. Check it out.

T A B L E 4.2	COMMAND	RESULT
Partial List of NLIST Options	NLIST VOLUME	Lists information for all volumes in the current context
	NLIST VOLUME /D	Lists detailed information about a specific volume in the current context
	NLIST VOLUME /N	Lists the names of the volumes in your current context

Output from the NLIST VOLUME /D command is shown in Figure 4.16. Notice the detailed volume-based information you can view from the command line.

F I G U R E 4.16

Results of the NLIST VOLUME /D Command

```
Object Class: Volume
Current context: WHITE.CRIME.TOKYO.acme
Volume: WHITE-SRV1_SYS
        Name: WHITE-SRV1_SYS
        Name: SYS
        Object Trustees (ACL):
                Subject: [Root]
                Property: Host Resource Name
                Property Rights: [ R    ]
        Object Trustees (ACL):
                Subject: [Root]
                Property: Host Server
                Property Rights: [ R    ]
        Host Resource Name: SYS
        Host Server: WHITE-SRV1
        Object Class: Volume
        Object Class: Resource
        Object Class: Top
        Revision: 1
--------------------------------------------------------------

One Volume object was found in this context.

One Volume object was found.
>>> Enter = More   C = Continuous   Esc = Cancel
```

Now let's explore the final volume management tool — NDIR. Just imagine "the forest moon of NDIR."

NDIR

NDIR, as its name implies, is mostly a directory and file utility. It does, however, offer a few statistics for NetWare 4 volumes, namely:

- ▸ Volume space statistics

- ▸ Directory entry statistics

- ▸ Compression space statistics

Figure 4.17 shows an example of the type of information that can be displayed by typing **NDIR /VOL**.

You'll notice that it lists a variety of volume information, including space used, space remaining, deleted space not yet purged, space available for use by you, maximum and available directory entries, as well as compression statistics, such as space used by compressed files, space saved by compressed files, and uncompressed space used. It's amazing that all this information can be viewed from such a small utility!


```
F:\USERS\MMARION>NDIR /VOL

Statistics for fixed volume WHITE-SRV1/SYS:
Space statistics are in KB (1024 bytes).

Total volume space:                        1,016,128   100.00%
Space used by 4,888 entries:                 318,976    31.39%
Deleted space not yet purgeable:                   0     0.00%
                                           ----------   -------
Space remaining on volume:                   697,152    68.61%
Space available to Admin.ACME:               697,152    68.61%

Maximum directory entries:                    17,408
Available directory entries:                   8,466    48.63%

Space used if files were not compressed:     713,349
Space used by compressed files:              370,543
                                           ----------
Space saved by compressing files:            342,806    48.06%

Uncompressed space used:                     -51,567

F:\USERS\MMARION>
```

There you go. That's everything you wanted to know about volume management but were afraid to ask! Now that you've gotten cozy with some of NetWare 4's finest file system tools, let's see what they can do with directories and files. Who knows, you might even meet some new tools along the way.

ZEN

"If professional wrestling didn't exist, could you come up with this idea? Could you envision the popularity of huge men in tiny bathing suits pretending to fight?"

Jerry Seinfeld

MANAGING NETWARE 4 DIRECTORIES

Volumes are important, but directories win the prize. These are the true organizational containers of the NetWare 4 file system. As we learned earlier, a logical directory design can save hours of security and file management. In this section, we will explore many of the same utilities, but from a totally different point of view:

- ▸ FILER

- ▸ NWADMIN

- ▸ NDIR

- ▸ NCOPY

- ▸ RENDIR

So, let's get started.

FILER

FILER is NetWare 4's most comprehensive directory and file management tool. Earlier we learned about its volume savvy, but you ain't seen nothing yet. In its natural element, FILER can

- ▸ Create, delete, and rename directories

- ▸ Copy and move entire subdirectory structures

- ▸ View or change directory information such as owner, directory creation date/time, directory attributes, trustees, inherited rights filter, and space limitations

► View your effective rights for directories

► Set up search and view filters (include and exclude options)

The first step is to select the default directory. If you look at the top of the screen, you'll notice that it lists the current path. To choose a different directory, choose the "Select current directory" option from the Available options menu, as shown in Figure 4.18. You can either modify the path manually or walk the tree by pressing Insert. If you walk the tree, don't forget to press Esc when you're finished selecting directories. When the correct directory is selected, press Enter to return to the Available options menu.

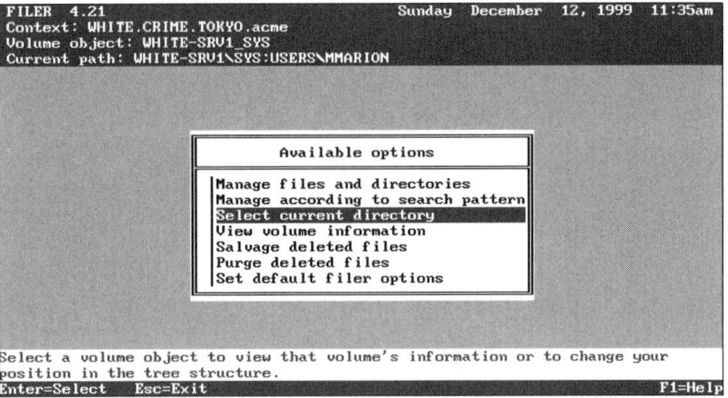

F I G U R E   4.18

Available Options Menu in FILER

The next step is to determine if you want to use any search or view filters to limit the directories that are displayed. If so, select the "Manage according to search pattern" option from the Available options menu. As you can see in Figure 4.19, a screen appears with the directory include and exclude patterns. You can also specify Hidden and/or System directories. After you've made your selections, press F10 to return to the Available options menu.

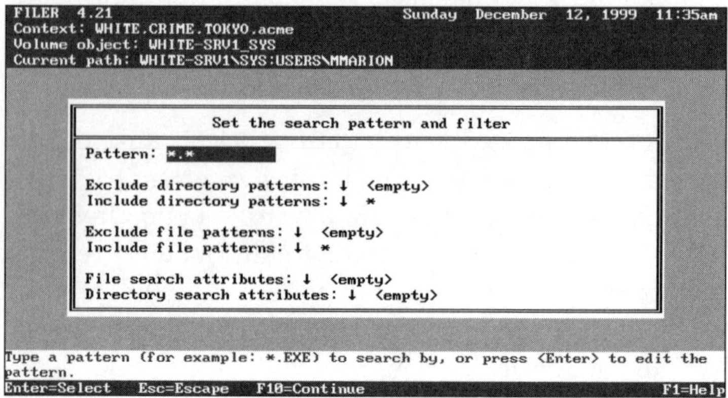

F I G U R E 4.19

Set the Search Pattern and Filter Menu in FILER

Now you're ready to go exploring — inside the selected directory. Select the "Manage files and directories" choice from the Available options menu. You'll notice that the subdirectories and files in the current directory appear as well as a double-dot (..), representing the parent directory, and a dot (.), representing the current directory.

You can do a number of different things with this screen. For instance,

- ► If you want to make another directory the current directory, you can walk the tree again.

- ► If you want to create a new subdirectory, press Insert and type in the name.

- ► If you want to delete a subdirectory, press Del. If you want to delete multiple directories at once, mark them all using F5 before pressing Del.

- ► If you want to rename a subdirectory, highlight it and press F3, then enter the new name.

To display information about this directory, highlight the period (.) and press F10. The Subdirectory options menu will be displayed. Press Enter to select the View/Set directory information option. A directory information screen will pop up, similar to the one in Figure 4.20. This screen lists information about the directory, such as the owner, the creation date/time, the directory attributes, the inherited rights filter, the trustees of the directory, the directory space limitations, and your effective rights for this directory.

If you have the appropriate rights, you can change any parameter listed, except for effective rights, which are a calculation completed by NetWare 4 (as you'll see in painstaking detail in Chapter 5). Go ahead and press Esc twice to return to the Directory contents screen.

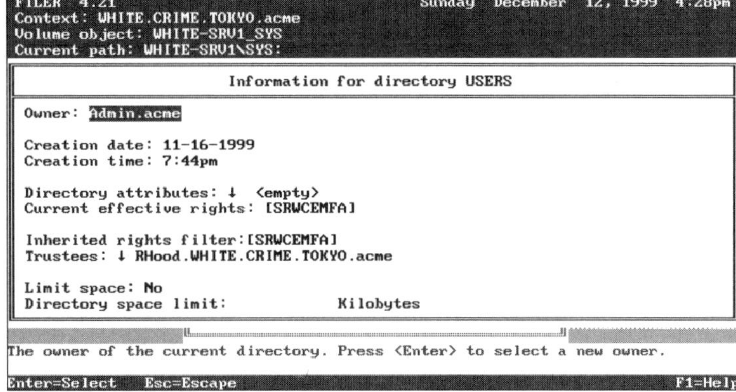

F I G U R E 4.20

Directory Information in FILER

If you highlight a subdirectory and press F10, a Subdirectory options screen will be displayed, as shown in Figure 4.21. Two of the most interesting options allow you to move or copy an entire branch of the tree at one time. Cool.

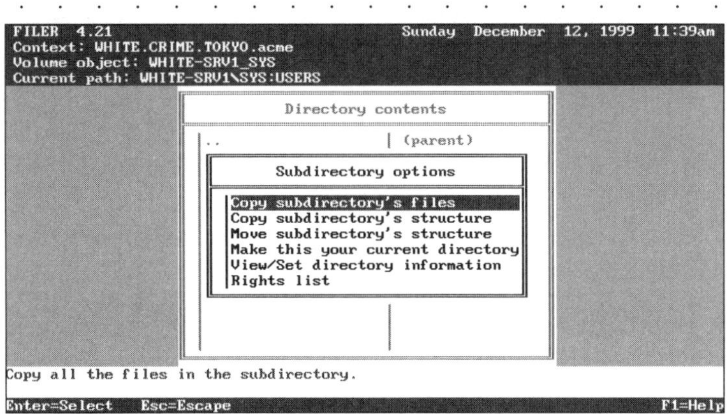

F I G U R E 4.21

Subdirectory Options in FILER

That does it for FILER. Now let's see what NWADMIN can do for NetWare 4 directories.

QUIZ

Here's another numbers game:

Find the product of $(x-a)(x-b)(x-c)\ldots(x-z)$, where x is any number between 22 and 42.

(Q4-2)

NWADMIN

NWADMIN (the NetWare Administrator utility) is primarily an NDS-management tool; however, it offers a few directory-related functions, such as:

- Create, delete, and rename directories

- Copy and move entire subdirectory structures

- View or change directory information, such as owner, attributes, trustees, inherited rights filter, or space limitations

- Set up search and view filters (include and exclude options)

First of all, walk the tree until the directory with which you want to work is in view. Click on the directory, then click on the Object menu. If you look at the options in the Object menu, you'll notice that you can perform the following file management tasks: create a directory; delete a directory; rename, copy, and/or move a directory. You can also select the Details option to view information about your directory.

If you select Details, the Identification page button is activated by default. As you can see in Figure 4.22, this page includes two important pieces of information: the directory name and the name spaces available on the volume.

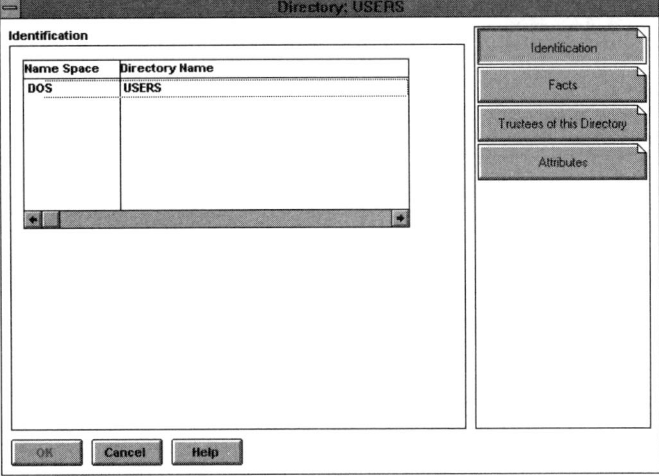

F I G U R E 4.22

Identification Page for Directories in NWADMIN

If you select the Facts page button, as shown in Figure 4.23, another screen appears with more detailed directory information, including the owner, the directory creation date/time, the last modified date/time, the last archived date/time, and the archiver. It also lists the volume space available on this directory and the space limitations (if any).

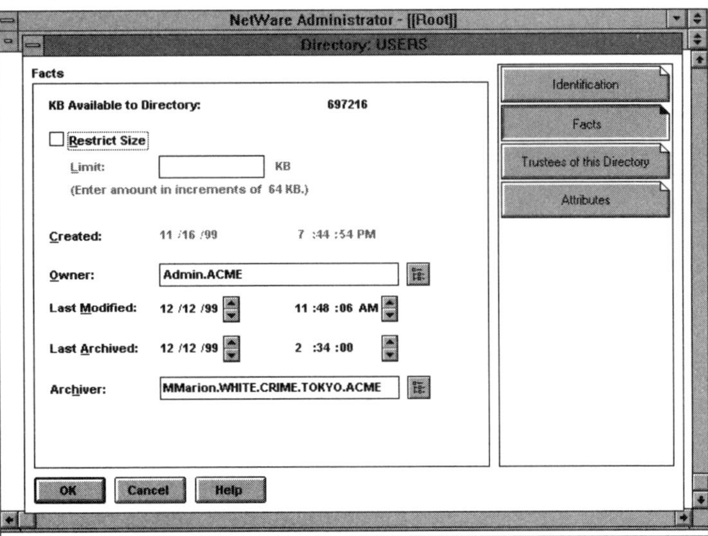

F I G U R E 4.23

Facts Page in NWADMIN

Figure 4.24 illustrates the first of two directory-specific security options in NWADMIN — the Trustees of this Directory page. This page allows you to list trustees and their effective rights as well as the inherited rights filter for this directory.

F I G U R E 4.24

Trustees of this Directory Page in NWADMIN

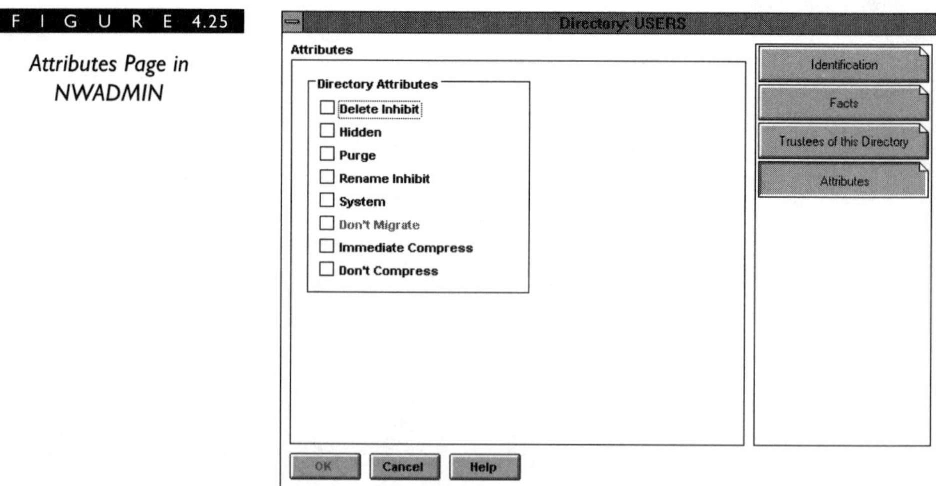

The second NWADMIN file system security option deals with Attributes (see Figure 4.25). Don't worry, you'll get plenty of chances to work with security in Chapter 5.

F I G U R E 4.25

Attributes Page in NWADMIN

That's enough of NWADMIN for now. As you can see, it augments the FILER functions in a prettier Windows-based user interface. Now, for something completely different. Let's go back to the command line — starting with the forest moon of NDIR.

NDIR

NDIR gives us limited functionality at the volume level — because it's not a volume utility — it's a directory/file utility. NDIR opens a new world of directory information to you, including:

- ▸ Owner, creation date, attributes, and archive information

- ▸ Subdirectories/files

- ▸ Inherited rights filter

- ▸ Effective rights

In addition, directory information can be sorted according to almost any criteria (owner, creation date, attributes, and so on). If you don't specify any formatting options, NDIR lists the following information about each directory: the directory name, inherited rights filter, your effective rights, the creation date/time, and the owner.

By default, NDIR lists all subdirectories and files in the specified directory (unless otherwise noted). You can display directory information selectively by using wildcards, and/or display options. For example, use /C to scroll continuously or /SUB to include subdirectories and their files. You can also list directories that contain (or do not contain) a specific directory attribute.

The beauty of NDIR is its logic searching capabilities. NDIR also supports date options such as AFT (after), BEF (before), and EQ (equals); size options such as LE (less than), EQ (equal to), and GR (greater than); and sorting options such as /REV SORT (reverse order), /SORT CR (creation date), /SORT OW (owner), and /UN (unsorted).

Some of the more common NDIR directory commands are listed in Table 4.3.

COMMAND	RESULT
NDIR	Displays subdirectories and files in the current directory
NDIR /DO	Displays directories only
NDIR /DO /SUB	Displays directories and subdirectories only
NDIR /SPA	Displays space limitations for this directory
NDIR /DO /C	Displays directories only — scrolls continuously when displaying information
NDIR /DO CR AFT 10/01/99	Displays directories only — those created after 10/01/99
NDIR /DO /SORT REV CR	Displays directories only — sorts by directory creation date, with newest listed first

Figure 4.26 shows an example of output from the NDIR /DO command. Use it or lose it.

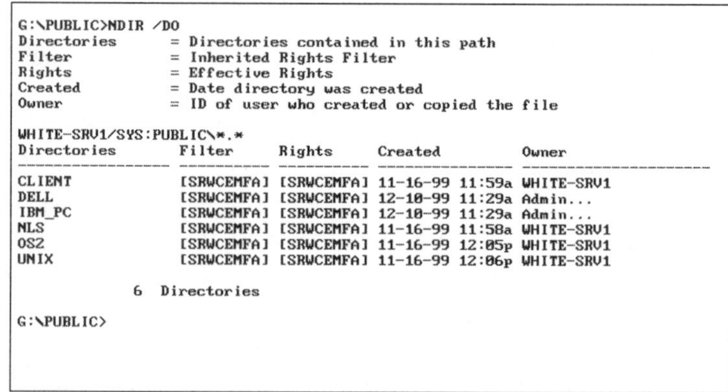

NCOPY

NCOPY is the NetWare version of COPY. Can you guess what it does? Very good — it copies stuff. NCOPY is similar in function to the DOS XCOPY command and allows the use of the same wildcards. Benefits of using NCOPY include:

▸ Directory/file attributes and name space information are automatically preserved.

▸ Read-after-write verification feature is ON by default. (You must use the /V switch to use verification if you're copying files on local drives.)

▸ NetWare volume names can be specified in a path.

TIP

Because NCOPY is a NetWare utility, it accesses the NetWare file allocation table (FAT) and directory entry table (DET) more efficiently than the DOS COPY or XCOPY commands. It is faster than COPY and XCOPY if the files are being copied from one directory to another on the server, because it works within server RAM rather than copying the directories and/or files to and from workstation RAM. It is also a safer method because it uses the NetWare 4 read-after-write verification fault tolerance feature by default.

Some of the more common NCOPY commands are listed in Table 4.4.

T A B L E 4.4	COMMAND	RESULT
Common NCOPY Commands	NCOPY G:REPORTS C:REPORTS	Copies the REPORTS directory from the G: drive on the server to the default directory on your workstation's C: drive
	NCOPY F:DATA C:DATA /S	Copies the DATA directory from the F: drive to the C: drive, including subdirectories
	NCOPY G:1995 ..\ ARCHIVE /S /E	Copies the 1995 directory on the G: drive (as well as its subdirectories and their files, including empty subdirectories) to an ARCHIVE directory under the current directory's parent directory
	NCOPY .TEMP /V	Copies the current directory to the TEMP directory and verifies that the procedure was accurate (only needed if copying files on a local drive)

RENDIR

RENDIR allows you to rename directories — what a surprise. Wildcards can be used, as well as a period (.) to represent the current directory or a colon followed by a forward slash (:/) to represent the default drive and volume. Check out Table 4.5 for some examples of the more common RENDIR commands in Netware 4.

T A B L E 4.5	COMMAND	RESULT
Common RENDIR Commands	RENDIR REPORT REPORTS	Renames the directory called REPORT under the current directory to REPORTS
	RENDIR U:USER USERS	Renames the directory on Drive U: called USER to USERS
	RENDIR S: SAMPLES	Renames the directory to which drive S: is mapped as SAMPLES
	RENDIR . DATA	Renames the current directory to DATA
	RENDIR :/ QTR1 95QTR1	Renames the directory called QTR1 on the current drive and volume to 95QTR1
	RENDIR /?	Displays on-line help for the RENDIR command

TIP

If you rename a directory, don't forget to modify any configuration files that reference it — like login scripts.

That completes our discussion of directory management. Wasn't that fun? There's only one more file system component left — and we've saved the best for last. Hold onto your hats; we're entering the file management zone.

ZEN

Sick-building syndrome — A condition found in humans, caused by a substance that pollutes the environment becoming trapped in a building, especially as a result of poor design or hazardous materials being used in construction. How are you feeling? Need some fresh air?

MANAGING NETWARE 4 FILES

Earlier, I said that directories win the prize — I lied. Files are really the most important components. After all, what's the ultimate goal of the NetWare 4 file system? File sharing. What do users ask for when they log in to the "Cloud"? Files. Why are we here?

Anyway, file management looks a little like directory management, and it uses the same tools. But that's where the similarities end. Directories are for organization; files are for productivity. And what's more important? Here's a list of the tools we'll explore in this section:

▸ FILER

▸ NWADMIN

▸ NDIR

▸ NCOPY

Don't just sit there; get moving. There are only a few utilities left. Ready, set, go.

FILER

Let's visit our old friend FILER just one last time. Now we're focusing on real file management, including:

▸ Creating, deleting, renaming, copying, and moving files

▸ Managing files attributes

▸ Setting up search and view filters (include and exclude options)

▸ Salvaging and purging deleted files

As before, the first FILER step is to select the default directory. Refer to the directory management section for more details. Once you're there, you can alter the include and exclude filters for specific files or even check out Hidden and/or System documents. After you've made your selections, you can press F10 to return to the Available options menu.

In addition to the search/view filters, FILER presents Copy and Delete options when working with files. First, select the "Set default filer options" choice from the Available options menu. A Filer settings screen will appear, as shown in Figure 4.27. You can set a number of defaults for copying and deleting files, including confirmations and messaging help. When all of the file management settings are correct, press Esc to return to the Available options menu.

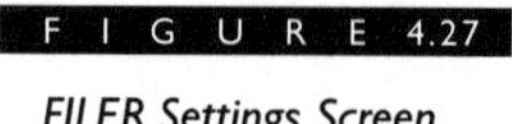

FIGURE 4.27

FILER Settings Screen

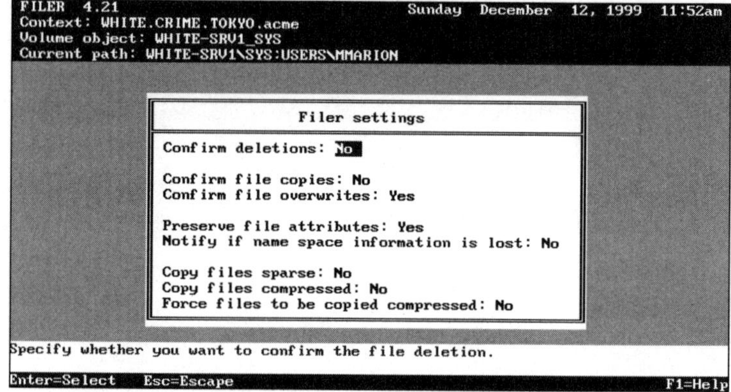

Now you're ready to display your files. Select the "Manage files and directories" option from the Available options menu. You'll notice a plethora of subdirectories and files in the current directory, as well as a double-dot (..) representing the parent directory and a dot (.) representing the current directory. Now, you're ready to get busy:

- ► Walk the tree to select another directory as the current directory.

- ► Delete a file by highlighting it and pressing Del. If you want to delete multiple files at once, mark them all with the F5 key before pressing Del.

- ► Rename a file by highlighting it and pressing F3.

Next, select a particular file to work with by highlighting it and pressing F10. The File options menu appears. This menu gives you the option of copying, viewing, or moving the file; displaying trustees of the file; or viewing/modifying file information. If you select the View/Set file information option from the File options menu, a file information screen pops up that is similar to the one in Figure 4.28. This screen lists information about the file such as the owner; access, archive, creation, and modification dates; file attributes; the inherited rights filter; the trustees of the file; the owning name space; the file size and EA size; as well as your effective rights.

If you have appropriate rights, you can change most of the parameters listed, except for effective rights, owning name space, file size, and EA size. Press Esc three times to return to the Available options menu.

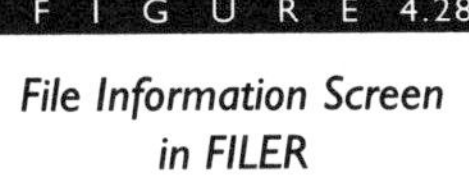

F I G U R E 4.28

File Information Screen in FILER

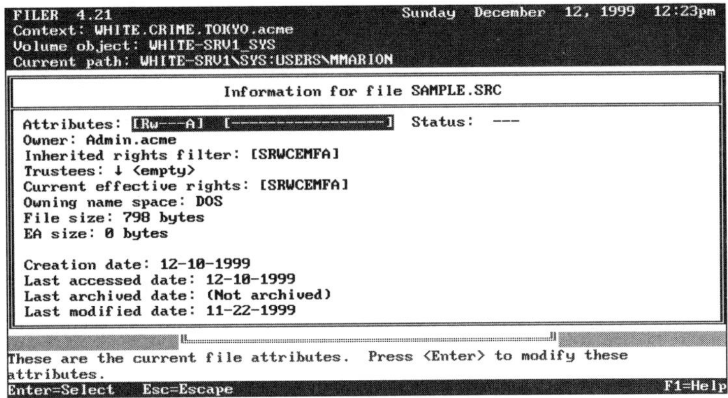

There are two more choices in the Available options menu that relate to files, namely "Salvage deleted files" and "Purge deleted files." Salvage allows you to recover deleted files that have not yet been purged. Purge is the process of permanently removing deleted files from the system.

If you choose "Salvage deleted files," you will be given three options:

- ▶ Salvage files from an existing directory

- ▶ Salvage files from DELETED.SAV (because the parent directory has been deleted)

- ▶ Set salvage options (that is, indicate whether to sort the list by filename, file size, deletion date, or deletor)

If you choose "Purge deleted files" from the Available options menu, you can specify the filename pattern to be used when selecting purged files. It will also allow you to choose whether to purge files in the current subdirectory only, or to purge the files in the entire subdirectory tree structure. Be very careful when purging files: You can never recover these files.

That completes our discussion of FILER. It's been a wondrous journey, and I hope you have learned to appreciate how helpful it can be for volume, directory, and file management. Now, let's visit NWADMIN one last time.

QUIZ

I like these number brainiacs so much, I thought I'd try another one:

What is the five-digit number in which the first digit is two-thirds of the second, the third is one-third of the second, the fourth is four times the last, and the last is one-third of the first? The digits total 28.

(Q4-3)

NWADMIN

NWADMIN is another important file management tool. It allows us to perform any of the following functions from a friendly Windows-based interface:

- ► Create, delete, and rename files

- ► Copy and move files

- ► View or change file information such as owner, attributes, trustees, and inherited rights filter

- ► Set up search and view filters (include and exclude options)

- ► Salvage and purge deleted files

First of all, walk the tree until the desired file is in view. Click on the file, then click on the Object menu. If you look at the options in the Object menu, you'll notice file management options that allow you to delete the file, rename it, copy it, and move it. The same options can be accessed from the Details menu as well.

If you select the Facts page button, a screen appears with the file's owner, size, file creation date/time, last modified date/time, last archived date/time, and archiver. If you have the appropriate rights, you can modify all of these parameters except for the size and creation date.

If you select the Trustees of this File page button, you will be allowed to view, add, or modify trustees and display their effective rights, as well as view or change the inherited rights filter for the file. Similarly, if you select the Attributes page button, you can view the attributes that have been set for this file, and you can change them if you have the appropriate access rights (see Chapter 5).

In addition to the usual file management stuff, NWADMIN allows you to salvage or purge deleted files. Interestingly, both of these functions are handled by the same menu option: Choose Salvage from the Tools menu (see Figure 4.29).

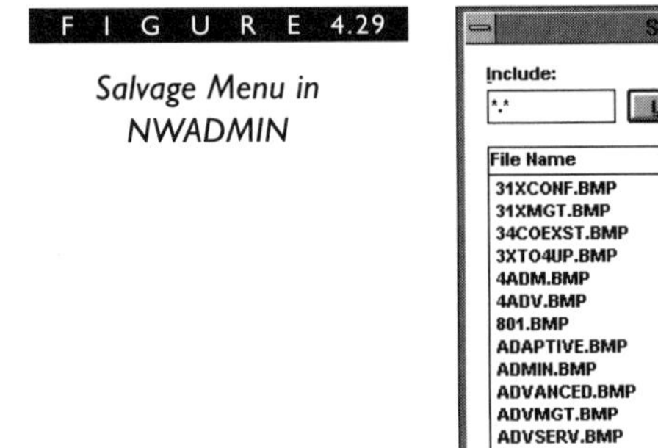

F I G U R E   4.29

Salvage Menu in NWADMIN

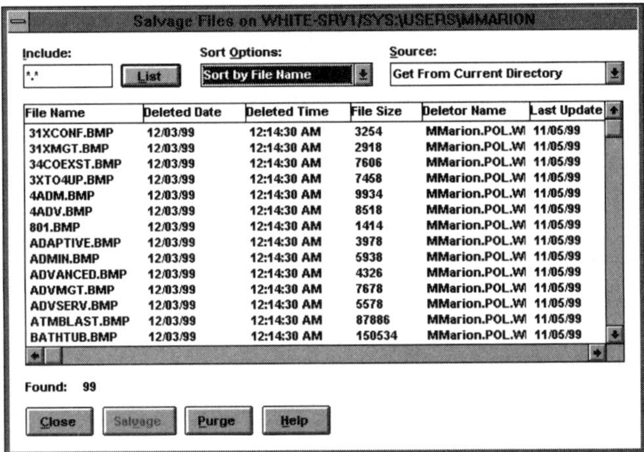

You can set three sets of options from the Salvage menu:

- ▸ Include pattern using wildcards or filenames

- ▸ Sort options (deletion date, deletor, filename, file size, or file type)

- ▸ Source (current directory or deleted directories)

When all of the options are set correctly, click on the List button to list the files indicated. As with other MS Windows utilities, to select the desired files, you can

- Select a single file by clicking on it

- Select sequentially listed files by clicking on the first file, holding down the Shift key, then clicking on the last file in the range

- Select nonsequentially listed files by holding down the Ctrl key while selecting files

When you have selected all of the desired files, you can click on either the Salvage or Purge button at the bottom of the screen to salvage or purge the selected file(s). Finally, when you're finished, click on the OK button to return to the NWADMIN browse screen.

From there you can bid the utility one last fond farewell. It's time to leave this Windows scene and check out the NetWare 4 command line. NDIR awaits!

NDIR

As we discussed earlier, NDIR is a very versatile command line utility that allows you to selectively list a large variety of directory and file information, sorted by a number of different parameters. From a file management standpoint, NDIR displays:

- Filename

- Owner

- Creation date and time

- Last modified date and time

- Size

- File attributes

- Access rights

- ▸ Macintosh files

- ▸ Version information for application files

- ▸ Extended details

If you don't specify any formatting options, NDIR lists the following information about each file: the filename, size, last update (modified) date, and owner. You can customize the output by specifying one of the following formatting options: /COMP (compression statistics), /DA (Dates), /D (detail), /L (long names), /M (Macintosh), and /R (rights).

By default, NDIR lists all subdirectories and files in the current directory, unless otherwise noted. You can selectively list the information by specifying a particular file, using wildcards, or by indicating a display option such as /C (scroll continuously), /FI (list every occurrence within your current directory and path), /FO (list files only), /SUB (include subdirectories and their files). You can also list files that contain (or do not contain) a specific file attribute.

NDIR also lets you restrict files by specifying date options such as AFT (after), BEF (before), and EQ (equals); size options such as LE (less than), EQ (equal to), and GR (greater than); and NOT (all except).

NDIR lists files in alphabetical order by default. You can change the order files are sorted in by specifying one of the following options: /REV SORT (reverse order), /SORT AC (access date), /SORT AR (archive date), /SORT CR (creation date), /SORT UP (update date), /SORT OW (owner), /SORT SI (size), or /SORT UN (unsorted).

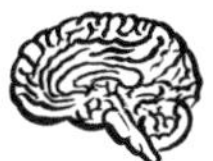

THE BRAIN

For further information on the options available with the NDIR command, refer to the NDIR section of the *Novell NetWare 4 Utilities* manual.

Get to really know the NDIR command by checking out Table 4.6.

T A B L E 4.6

Common NDIR Commands

COMMAND	RESULT
NDIR /FO	Displays files only — those in the current directory
NDIR /FO /C	Displays files only — scrolls continuously
NDIR /FO /SUB	Displays files only — those in the current directory and its subdirectories
NDIR /FO /REV SORT SI	Displays files only — sorts by size, starting with the largest file
NDIR /FO /SORT UP	Displays files only — sorts by last modified date
NDIR /FO /SORT OW	Displays files only — sorts by owner
NDIR /FO OW EQ DAVID	Displays files only — where the owner is David
NDIR R *.* /FO	Displays files only — those that begin with the letter "R"
NDIR *.BAT /FO	Displays files only — those in the current directory with an extension of .BAT
NDIR /FO /AC BEF 06-01-99	Displays files only — those not accessed since 06/01/99
NDIR \WHOAMI.EXE /SUB /FO	Displays files only — lists all occurrences of the WHOAMI.EXE file, starting the search at the root of the volume
NDIR Z:*.EXE /VER	Displays the version number for those files on the Z: drive with an .EXE extension
NDIR *.* /R /FO	Displays files only — lists your effective rights for each file
NDIR Z:NWADMIN.EXE /D	Displays detailed file information for the Z:NWADMIN file
NDIR SYS:SHARED*.* /RO	Displays those files in the SYS:SHARED directory that have the Read Only attribute set
NDIR *.* /FO /NOT RO	Displays files only — those that do not have the Read Only attribute set
NDIR F:*.* /FO /REV SORT AC	Displays files only — sorts by access date, listing the file with the most recent access date first
NDIR /FO DA	Displays files only — lists access, archive, creation, and update dates

Output from the NDIR /FO command is shown in Figure 4.30. And that does it for NDIR. Now, let's explore the final NetWare file management tool — NCOPY.


```
F:\ETC>NDIR /FO
Files                = Files contained in this path
Size                 = Number of bytes in the file
Last Update          = Date file was last updated
Owner                = ID of user who created or copied the file

WHITE-SRV1/SYS:ETC\*.*
Files                         Size Last Update       Owner
--------------------  --------------- -----------------  ------------------------
ATTYPES.CFG                    237  9-23-93   6:56p  WHITE-SRV1
BUILTINS.CFG                 9,951  8-26-94  10:19a  WHITE-SRV1
GATEWAYS                       500  9-24-93   1:06p  WHITE-SRV1
HOSTS                          441  9-11-92   2:31p  WHITE-SRV1
NETWORKS                       288  9-11-92   2:31p  WHITE-SRV1
PROTOCOL                       370  9-11-92   2:31p  WHITE-SRV1
SERVICES                     1,570  9-11-92   2:31p  WHITE-SRV1
TRAPTARG.CFG                 1,697  3-17-93   8:50a  WHITE-SRV1


        15,054  bytes (when the files are not compressed)
         8,192  bytes (disk space used by compressed and non-compressed files)
             8  Files

F:\ETC>
```

NCOPY

NCOPY can be used to copy files as well as directories. What a surprise. As we discussed earlier, NCOPY is similar in function to the DOS XCOPY command, except that directory attributes and name space information are automatically preserved. Refer to Table 4.7 for an exploration of NCOPY from a file management point of view.

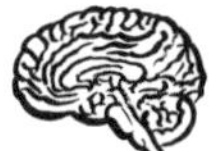

THE BRAIN

For further information on the options available with the NCOPY command, refer to the NCOPY section of the *Novell NetWare 4 Utilities* manual.

COMMAND	RESULT
NCOPY JULY.RPT F:	Copies a file in the default directory called JULY.RPT to the F: drive.
NCOPY F:PHONE. NUM C:	Copies the PHONE.NUM file from the F: drive to the C: drive.

(continued)

<table>
<tr><td colspan="2">T A B L E 4.7
Common NCOPY
Commands
(continued)</td><td>COMMAND</td><td>RESULT</td></tr>
</table>

COMMAND	RESULT
NCOPY F:*.RPT A: /A	Copies files with a *.RPT extension that have the archive bit set (and thus, need to be backed up) from F: to A:.
NCOPY DOC1. WP TEMP1.* /C	Copies the DOC1.WP file and renames the new version TEMP1.WP, without preserving extended attributes and name space information.
NCOPY F:R*. G: /F	Copies files beginning with the letter "R" from the F: drive to the G: drive, forcing the copying of sparse files.
NCOPY *.DOC A: /I	Copies files with a .DOC extension from the current directory to the A: drive and notifies you when extended attributes or name space information cannot be copied because the target volume doesn't support these features.
NCOPY F: *.DOC A: /M	Copies files with the *.DOC extension that have the archive bit set (and thus need to be backed up) from F: to A:, then turns off the archive bit of the source files. (This allows NCOPY to be used for backup purposes.)
NCOPY C:FRED.LST C:TOM.LST /V	Copies FRED.LST to TOM.LST on the C: drive using the verify option.
NCOPY /?	Displays on-line help for the NCOPY utility.

Well, there you have it — the wonderful world of NetWare 4 file system management. Aren't you a lucky camper? Now you are an expert in gardening NDS and non-NDS trees. In this section, we focused on the three main components of the NetWare 4 file system — volumes, directories, and files. We discovered a variety of tools and learned how they help us manage each of these components. The important thing is to focus on the file system, not the tool — a unique, but effective approach.

I guess we're done then, huh? Wrong! We haven't journeyed into the mysterious land of drive mapping yet. I'm sure you'd rather not go there, but buck up soldier, you're a CNA — you can handle it. But can your users?

ZEN

"Fear of success is one of the newest fears that I've heard about lately. I think it's definitely a sign that we're running out of fears. A person suffering from fear of success is scraping the bottom of the fear barrel."

Jerry Seinfeld

Drive Mapping

Drive mapping is one of the great mysteries of life. Forget about the pyramids, alien cornfields, or quarks — drive mapping has them all beat.

It doesn't have to be this way. As a matter of fact, drive mapping is really pretty simple. The problem is that it requires you to unlearn the fundamentals of DOS. Let me explain. In the DOS world, drive letters point to *physical* devices. In Figure 4.31, the A: and B: letters point to floppy drives, C: and D: point to hard drives, and the E: drive is a CD-ROM. Pretty simple, huh? Well, it works fine on workstations, because they typically use multiple storage devices.

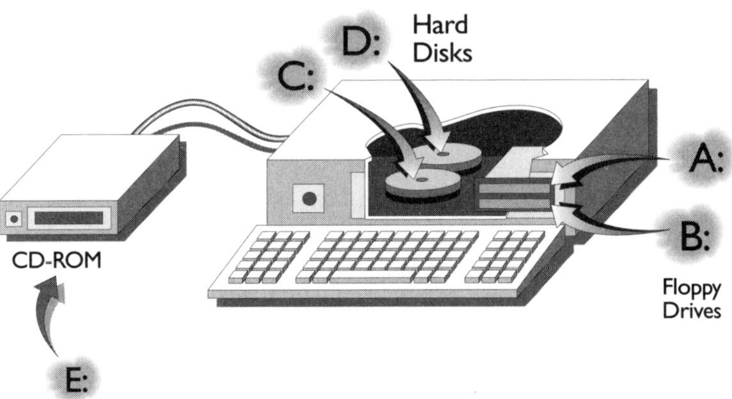

FIGURE 4.31

Drive Mapping to Physical Local Devices

So, how does this theory apply to NetWare drives? If we extrapolate from the local theory, we would use 21 different drive letters (F–Z) to point to 21 physical devices — not very likely. So, Novell returned to the proverbial drawing board and came up with a slightly different approach — just different enough to confuse you, me, CNAs, and especially users. Here's how it works:

NetWare 4 drive letters point to logical directories instead of physical drives.

This is also pretty simple; a little too simple (see Figure 4.32). As a matter of fact, users treat the NetWare drives just like local drives — which is a big mistake. The first time they use the CD command, all heck breaks loose. Let me tell you a little story — ironically, about Little John.

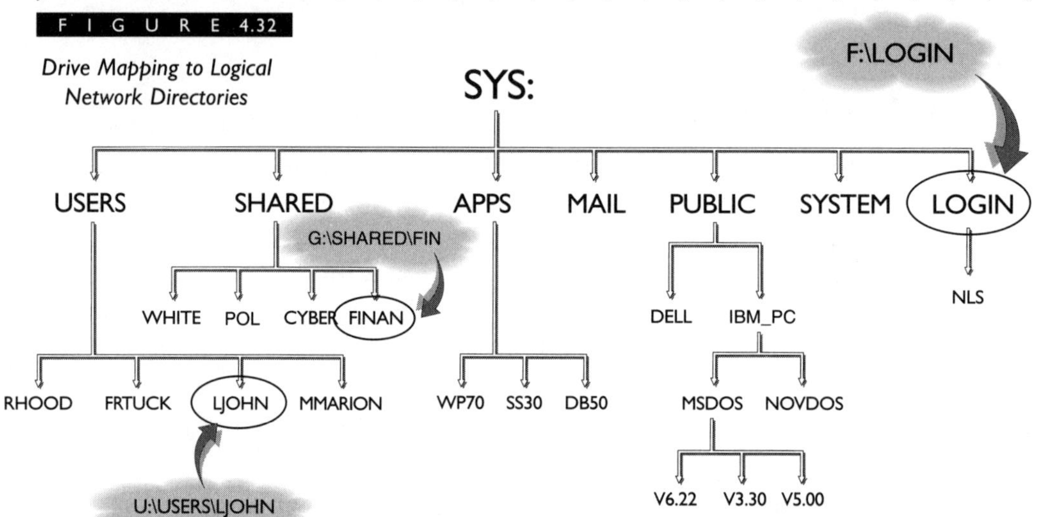

*Drive Mapping to Logical
Network Directories*

One seemingly innocent summer day in August, Little John was working on his financial files in the SYS:SHARED\FIN directory. For his convenience, you have mapped this directory to drive letter G: (see Figure 4.32). He suddenly realizes that his report templates are at home, that is, SYS:USERS\LJOHN (drive map U:). Any other time he would simply type U: and press Enter to get home, but not today. Today he confuses his network and local drives. Today is a bad day for Little John.

Instead of using the existing U: drive mapping, Little John types **CD\USERS\LJOHN** from the G: drive. This would work fine in the DOS world, but it's unforgivable in the NetWare world. What has he done? Correct. Little John has inadvertently re-mapped his G: drive to SYS:USERS\LJOHN. Remember, NetWare drive letters are logical pointers to NetWare directories, not physical devices. As you can see in Figure 4.33, Little John now has two letters mapped to his home directory. Of course, he doesn't realize this. Let's return to the story.

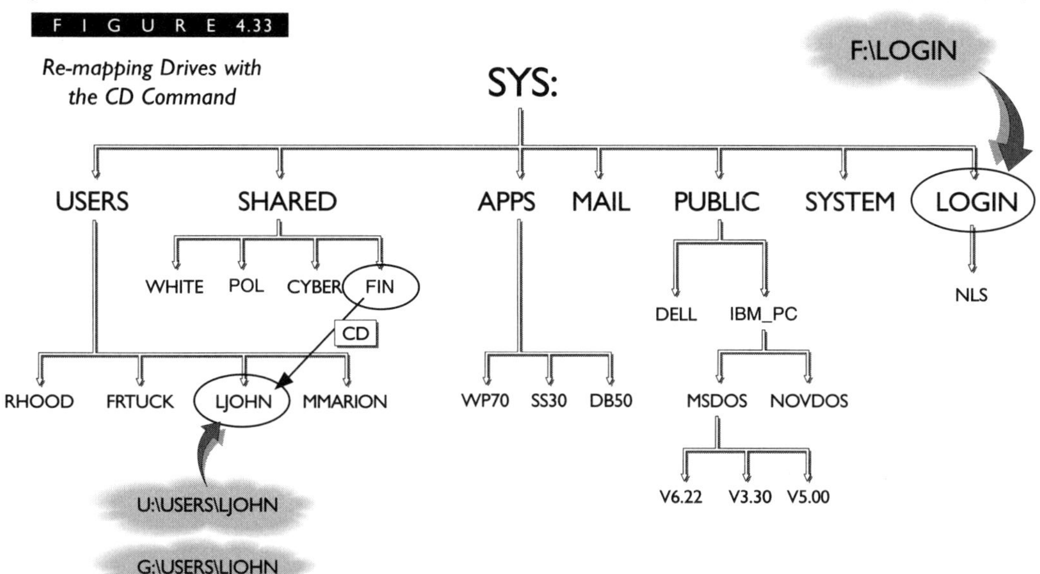

Re-mapping Drives with the CD Command

Oblivious to the changes in his world, Little John searches the G:\USERS\LJOHN directory for his report templates. He can't find them. "Ah," he thinks. "They're in my home directory. That's drive U:." He quickly switches over to U:\USERS\LJOHN, unaware that this is the same directory. Remember, he thinks the G: and U: drives are different hard disks. He searches in vain and doesn't find the report templates on the U: drive either — he wouldn't. This is where it gets interesting.

Disgruntled, Little John decides to return to his financial directory and continue work without the missing templates. Naturally, he types **G:** and presses Enter to return to the G:\SHARED\FIN directory — it doesn't work. "That's odd," he thinks. "It's always worked before." Much to his dismay, all of the financial files have been removed from the G: drive and replaced by a duplicate copy of his home files. At least that's how it appears to Little John. Remember, he thinks the G: and U: drives are different hard disks. In actuality, Little John has re-mapped the G: drive to G:\USERS\LJOHN with the CD command. Oops.

In a panic, Little John deletes the duplicate copy of his home files — hoping it will clear enough space for his financial files to return. Of course, he has inadvertently deleted *all* his home files, because they are *not* duplicates. It's simply a duplicate drive mapping. He comes rumbling down the hall to your office, screaming at the top of his lungs, "Somebody has deleted my financial files!" Incidentally, Little John is not a little man. After picking yourself off the floor, you proceed to explain to him that the NetWare CD command doesn't change directories as it does in DOS. Instead, it *cancels data*. Of course this is a lie, but it stops him from using the CD command in the future. Fortunately, you're a CNA and you can save the day! Use SALVAGE to undelete his files, and MAP to return G: back to \SHARED\FIN where it belongs. Just another day in the life of a NetWare 4 CNA.

ZEN

"I once had a leather jacket that got ruined in the rain. Now why does moisture ruin leather? Aren't cows outside a lot of the time?"

Jerry Seinfeld

This story has been brought to you by NetWare 4 and your local neighborhood DMV (Drive Mapping Vehicle). It's a great example of what can happen when users get local and network drive mappings confused. For this reason, you have a choice to make: Do you perpetuate the myth or tell your users the truth? If you perpetuate the myth that NetWare drives point to physical disks, you'll need to use the MAP ROOT command to make them appear as such. This will also nullify the effects of CD. If you decide to tell your users the truth, consider that knowledge is power. Also consider that they may not want to know the truth. Either way, NetWare 4 provides you with three different approaches to drive mapping:

- ▸ Network Drive Mapping

- ▸ Search Drive Mapping

- ▸ Directory Map Objects

Network drives use a single letter to point to logical directory paths. The previous example used network drives. *Search* drives, on the other hand, provide additional functionality by building a search list for network applications. Finally, *Directory Map objects* are centralized NDS resources that point to logical directory paths. They help ease the transition from one application version to another. Let's take a closer look.

NETWORK DRIVE MAPPINGS

Network drive mappings have a singular purpose — convenience. They provide simple directory navigation for accessing data files. As we learned earlier, NetWare 4 supports 21 network drives by default: F–Z. In Figure 4.32, the F: drive points to SYS:LOGIN and the U: drive points to SYS:USERS\LJOHN. These mappings make it easy for users to find their stuff — as long as they don't use the dreaded CD command. Little John simply types **U:** followed by Enter to get home to U:\USERS\LJOHN. Without drive mappings, movement throughout the directory tree would be cumbersome and time consuming. It would involve long path names and confusing directory searches. Yuck!

TIP

The availability of network drives is dictated by the NetWare DOS Requester configuration at the workstation. By default, the VLMs specify F: as the first network drive. You can change this by removing the FIRST NETWORK DRIVE = F statement from NET.CFG. As a matter of fact, you can use 26 network drive letters by overwriting all existing local drives. Cool!

Network drive mappings are user-specific, temporary environment variables. Each user has a different set of drive mappings within his or her workstation RAM. These mappings are created each time the user logs in. When the user logs out or turns off the machine, these mappings are lost. For this reason, you'll want to automate the creation of drive mappings in System and Profile login scripts (see Chapter 6).

Network drive mappings are created using the MAP command. We'll explore this command in depth later in this chapter. For now, consider creating any or all of the following drive mappings for your users:

- ▶ U: — each user's home directory (for example, SYS:USERS\LJOHN)

- ▶ F: — SYS:LOGIN

- ▶ G: — group-specific data directories (for example, SYS:SHARED\FIN)

- ▶ H: — global shared directory (for example, SYS:SHARED)

Now, let's expand our understanding of NetWare 4 drive mapping with search drives. They help us build an internal search list for network applications.

SEARCH DRIVE MAPPINGS

Search drive mappings extend one step beyond network mappings by helping users search for network applications. When a user executes an application, NetWare searches two places for the program file:

1 • The current directory.

2 • The internal NetWare search list. Search drive mappings build the internal search list. They are the NetWare equivalent of local PATH statements.

The beauty of the NetWare search list is that it allows you to prioritize application directories. NetWare searches for programs in the order in which they are listed. The list can be a combination of local and network directories. For example, the following search list would find Windows on the local drive first; otherwise, it would use the network version in SYS:APPS\WINDOWS:

```
S1:=SYS:PUBLIC

S2:=SYS:PUBLIC\IBM_PC\MSDOS\V6.22

S3:=C:\WINDOWS

S4:=SYS:APPS\WINDOWS

S5:=SYS:APPS\SS30
```

Because search drive mappings are primarily used to build search lists, you should be more concerned with the order of the list than with the letter assigned to each directory. As you can see from this list, NetWare assigns search drive mappings in search order — and each is preceded by the letter S. As a matter of convenience, NetWare automatically assigns a drive letter to each search directory — in reverse order (to avoid using network drive letters). For example, the first search drive (S1:) inherits the letter Z:, the second mapping (S2:) gets the letter Y:, and so on (see Figure 4.34). This allows you to navigate through search directories if necessary, although I don't recommend it. You are limited to a total of 16 search drives that inherit network drive letters. That is, you can have more than 16 search drives, but the extra ones will have to point to already-existing drive letters — such as C:.

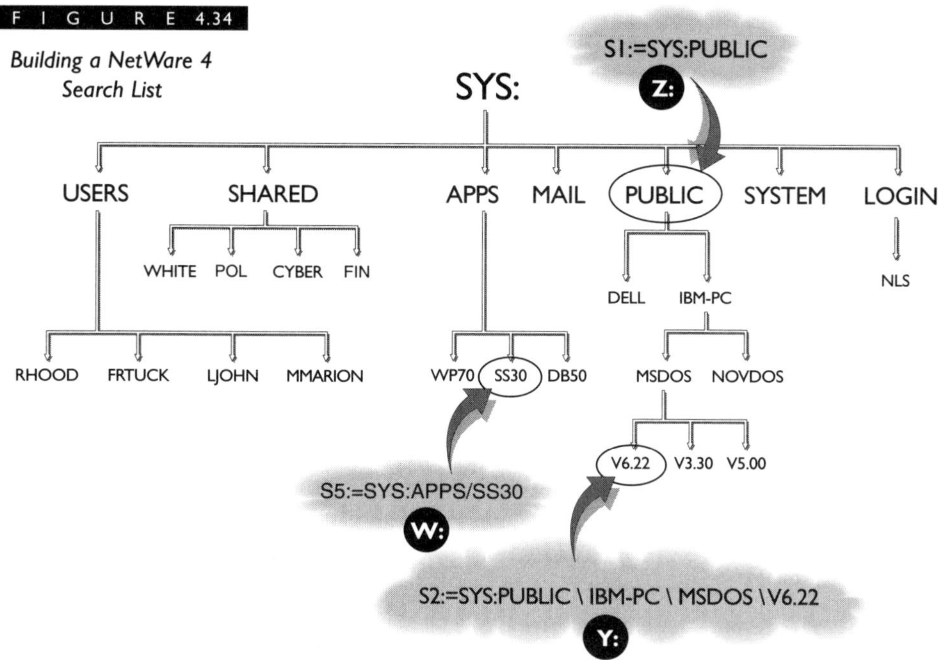

F I G U R E 4.34

Building a NetWare 4 Search List

TIP

If a search drive encounters an existing network letter, the drive skips the letter and inherits the next one. For this reason, you should always assign network drive mappings first.

Because the NetWare search list and DOS PATH statements accomplish the same thing, there's a little conflict of interest. As a matter of fact, the NetWare search list systematically eliminates directories in the DOS path. To avoid this problem, consider incorporating your DOS path into the NetWare search list. This is accomplished using the MAP INSERT command (see the "Drive Mapping" section).

That completes our discussion of network and search drive mappings. Refer to Table 4.8 for a summary of how they work.

T A B L E 4.8	FUNCTION	NETWORK	SEARCH DRIVE MAPPING
Comparing Network and Search Drive Mappings	Purpose	Movement	Searching
	Assignment Method	As the letter	In search order
	Letter Assignment	By you	By NetWare
	First Letter	F:	Z:
	Directory Types	Data	Applications

Now, let's take a moment to explore Directory Map objects before we dive into the MAP command.

DIRECTORY MAP OBJECTS

In Chapter 3, we learned about a special NDS leaf object that helped us deal with drive mapping in the NetWare 4 file system — the Directory Map object. This special-purpose object allows us to map to a central logical resource instead of to the physical directory itself, mainly because physical directories change and logical objects don't have to.

This level of independence is very useful. Let's say, for example, that you have a central application server in the TOKYO container that everybody points to. On the server is an older copy of WordPerfect (WP5). You have two options for adding this application to your internal search lists:

1 • Search Drive Mapping — Use a traditional search drive mapping in each container's login script (five of them). This mapping points to the physical directory itself — TOKYO-SRV1\SYS:APPS\WP5.

2 • Directory Map Object — Create a central Directory Map object in TOKYO called WPAPP. Then, each of the five search drive MAP commands can point to the logical object instead of the physical APPS\WP directory. Finally, here the WPAPP object points to the physical directory as TOKYO-SRV1\SYS:APPS\WP5.

Both of these scenarios accomplish the same thing: They create a search drive mapping to WordPerfect 5 for all users in the Tokyo location. But, once you upgrade WordPerfect, you'll find the second option is much more attractive. In the first scenario, you'll need to change five different search drive statements in five distributed login scripts on five different servers. This is a lot of work!

In the second scenario, however, you'll only need to change the one Directory Map object reference, and all the other MAP statements automatically point to the right place. Amazing! In the next section, we'll explore the MAP command and learn how it can be used to reference Directory Map objects.

ZEN

"The movie ad I don't get is this one:'If you see only one movie this year....'Why go at all? You're not going to enjoy it — there's too much pressure. You're sitting there, 'Alright, this is it for 51 more weekends, this better be good!'"

Jerry Seinfeld

USING THE MAP COMMAND

So, now that you know everything there is to know about network, search, and NDS drive mappings, the next logical question is, "How?" It's simple — the MAP command. The NetWare 4 MAP command allows you to

- ▸ View drive mappings

- ▸ Create or modify network or search drive mappings

- ▸ Point to Directory Map objects

- ▸ Map drives to a fake root — to fool users or install special applications

- ▸ Change mappings from one type to another

- ▸ Integrate the network and local search lists

- ▸ Do all sorts of other stuff

As I'm sure you've probably guessed, the MAP command is the heart and soul of NetWare 4 drive mapping. Now, let's take a closer look at some fun and exciting MAP commands — starting with plain, old MAP. Also, there's a MAP summary table at the end of this section for your review. Ready, set, MAP!

MAP

You can use the MAP command without any options to display a list of your current drive mappings. As you can see in Figure 4.35, the local drives (A: through E:) are listed first, followed by the network drives, and finally, the search drives. Also, note the cool dashes in the middle. They separate the network drives from the search drives.

<table>
<tr><td>F I G U R E 4.35

The Plain Old MAP
Command</td><td>

```
U:\USERS\MMARION>MAP

Drives A,B,C,D,E map to a local disk.
Drive F: = WHITE-SRV1_SYS.WHITE.CRIME.TOKYO: \LOGIN
Drive G: = WHITE-SRV1_SYS.WHITE.CRIME.TOKYO: \SHARED\FIN
Drive U: = WHITE-SRV1_SYS.WHITE.CRIME.TOKYO: \USERS\MMARION
       ------     Search Drives     ------
S1:  = Z:. [WHITE-SRV1_SYS.WHITE.CRIME.TOKYO: \PUBLIC]
S2:  = Y:. [WHITE-SRV1_SYS.WHITE.CRIME.TOKYO: \PUBLIC\IBM_PC\MSDOS\V6.22]
S3:  = C:\WINDOWS
S4:  = X:. [WHITE-SRV1_SYS.WHITE.CRIME.TOKYO: \APPS\WINDOWS]
S5:  = W:. [WHITE-SRV1_SYS.WHITE.CRIME.TOKYO: \APPS\SS30]

U:\USERS\MMARION>
```

</td></tr>
</table>

TIP

NetWare 4 does not track information on local drive assignments. Even though a map list will show that drives A: through E: are assigned to local drives, that doesn't necessarily mean they point to real devices. If you really want to mess with your users, map network drives to local devices. Or, even better, map local drives to network directories.

MAP G:=WHITE-SRV1\SYS:SHARED\FIN

You can use the MAP command followed by a drive letter (A: through Z:) to create network drive mappings. In this case, the G: drive is assigned to the SYS:SHARED\FIN directory on the WHITE-SRV1 file server.

 **TIP**

We also could have used the relative distinguished name or distinguished name for the volume instead of using the physical volume name. For instance, we could have typed

```
MAP G:=WHITE-SRV1_SYS:SHARED\FIN
```

or

```
MAP G:=.WHITE-SRV1_SYS.WHITE.CRIME.TOKYO.ACME:SHARED\FIN
```

If the G: drive already exists, it will replace the existing assignment without displaying a warning. However, if you attempt to re-map a local drive (that is, Drive A: through Drive E:), you will receive a warning that the drive is currently assigned to a local device. NetWare 4 is polite and will ask you if you want to assign it to a network drive anyway.

MAP NP E:=SYS:MAIL

Using the NP parameter allows you to overwrite local or search drives without being prompted. It must be listed first or second. In this example, the E: drive would be re-mapped without the usual warning:

```
Warning: You are attempting to re-map a local drive.
```

MAP S3:=SYS:APPS\WP70

You can use the MAP SEARCH command followed by a search drive number (S1: through S16:) to map a directory to a specific search drive. The number in the search drive defines the pointer's place in the search list (that is, its priority).

 **TIP**

Search drive mappings share the same environment space as the DOS path. As a result, if you assign a NetWare search drive number using the MAP SEARCH command, it will overwrite the corresponding pointer in the DOS path. (For instance, if you use the MAP S1: command, it will overwrite the first pointer in the DOS path.) The only way to retain existing pointers in the DOS path is to use the MAP INS or MAP S16: commands (listed later in this section), which insert new search drives into the DOS path, rather than replacing existing ones.

In this example, the SYS:APPS\WP70 directory will be assigned as search drive S3:, which is the third item in the search list. It will also map the directory to the next available drive letter, starting with Z: and moving backward. Review the section "Search Drive Mappings."

TIP

There is a way to specify which network drive letter is assigned when creating a search drive. In the previous example, if you want to assign network drive letter W: to the S3: search drive, you can use the following command:

```
MAP S3:=W:=APPS\WP70
```

REAL WORLD

A very interesting thing happens if you re-map an existing search drive number. NetWare assigns the new directory, as specified, without warning you that an existing search drive with the same number already exists. It does not, however, overwrite the network drive letter that was originally associated with the search drive number. Instead, it assigns a new network drive letter to the new directory and converts the old network drive letter into a full-fledged network drive mapping — thus stripping away its searching ability. Conversely, if you attempt to re-map the network drive associated with a search drive, you will receive a warning that the drive is already in use as a search drive and will be asked if you want to overwrite it. If you say Yes, both the network drive and its associated search drive will be mapped to the new directory. Weird, huh?

MAP INS S1:=SYS:PUBLIC

The MAP INSERT command can be used to insert a new search drive into the search list, at the number specified, without overwriting an existing drive mapping. All existing search drives below the new pointer are then bumped up one level in the list and renumbered accordingly.

In this example, we are inserting a new drive as S1:. Therefore, NetWare bumps up and renumbers all other search drives in the list. Then, it inserts the new drive at the top of the list as search drive S1:.

The interesting thing about this scenario is that it has no effect on existing network drives. All previous drives retain their original drive letters, even though they change positions in the search list.

Earlier, we learned that both the MAP INSERT and MAP S16: commands could be used to preserve the DOS path. This way, when you log off the network, your NetWare search drives will be deleted, but your local PATH statements will remain intact. Remember, DOS PATH drives don't count toward your limit of 16 network search drives.

TIP

So, what happens when you mix the **MAP INSERT** and **MAP S16:** statements? You create a strange "genetic" breed. The resulting command, **MAP INSERT S16:** places your search drives in the NetWare search list but *after* the **DOS PATH** directories. Weird.

QUIZ

One final numbers game: This is one of my personal favorites (see if you can figure out why). Change the position of only *one* number to make this a palindromic sequence:
1, 4, 2, 9, 6, 1, 5, 10, 4

Hint: When in Rome...

(Q4-4)

MAP DEL G:

The MAP DEL command deletes an existing drive mapping. This command can be used with both network and search drive pointers. The MAP REM command performs the same function. Network drive mappings and search drive mappings are deleted automatically if you log off the network or turn off your workstation.

MAP ROOT H:=SYS:ACCT\REPORTS

You can use the MAP ROOT command to create a false root. This command solves user problems like the one we had with Little John. The user sees this drive as if it were the root directory; therefore, he can't wander off too far with the dreaded CD command.

MAP ROOT can also be used for application programs that need to be installed in the root directory. For security reasons and administrative purposes, you should never install applications in the actual root, so here's a great compromise. The INSTALL program thinks it's installing WordPerfect, for example, in the root directory, when it's actually a false root pointing to SYS:APPS.

To determine if a drive mapping is actually a false root, use the MAP command alone. As you can see in Figure 4.36, the H: drive is shown differently than are the other network drives. Instead of showing a blank space between the volume name and the directory name, it shows a blank space followed by a backslash following the directory name. This clues you in that we're dealing with a different breed — a false root.


```
U:\USERS\MMARION>MAP

Drives A,B,C,D,E map to a local disk.
Drive F: = WHITE-SRV1_SYS.WHITE.CRIME.TOKYO: \LOGIN
Drive G: = WHITE-SRV1_SYS.WHITE.CRIME.TOKYO: \SHARED\FIN
Drive H: = WHITE-SRV1_SYS.WHITE.CRIME.TOKYO:ACCT\REPORTS \
Drive U: = WHITE-SRV1_SYS.WHITE.CRIME.TOKYO: \USERS\MMARION
          --------    Search Drives    --------
S1: = Z:.  [WHITE-SRV1_SYS.WHITE.CRIME.TOKYO: \PUBLIC]
S2: = Y:.  [WHITE-SRV1_SYS.WHITE.CRIME.TOKYO: \PUBLIC\IBM_PC\MSDOS\V6.22]
S3: = C:\WINDOWS
S4: = X:.  [WHITE-SRV1_SYS.WHITE.CRIME.TOKYO: \APPS\WINDOWS]
S5: = W:.  [WHITE-SRV1_SYS.WHITE.CRIME.TOKYO: \APPS\SS30]

U:\USERS\MMARION>
```

MAP N SYS:DATA

You can use the MAP NEXT (N) command to assign the next available drive letter as a network drive mapping. It doesn't work, however, with search drive pointers.

 **TIP**

Although the MAP NEXT command doesn't work with search drives, there is another technique that you can use to achieve the same effect, namely the MAP S16: command. The MAP S16: command assigns the next available search drive number to the specified directory. Because search drives update the DOS Path, NetWare 4 does not allow you to assign search drive numbers that would cause holes to exist in the DOS path. For instance, if only search drives S1: through S4: exist, NetWare would not let you create search drive S7:. Instead, it would just assign the next search drive number in the list (S5:, in this example).

MAP C I:

The MAP CHANGE (C) command can be used to change a regular NetWare drive to a search drive, or vice versa. In this example, Drive I: will still point to the same directory to which it was originally assigned, but it would also be added to the end of the NetWare search list. Conversely, if you use the MAP CHANGE command with a search drive, the search drive number is deleted from the search list, but the network drive letter originally associated with it is retained as a network drive mapping.

MAP S5:=.WPAPP.TOKYO.ACME

You can also map a drive to a Directory Map object (WPAPP) instead of to the directory itself. This is especially useful if the directory name changes from time to time — such as every time you upgrade WordPerfect or Microsoft Word — but you don't want to change every MAP statement in every login script.

In this case, you only need to change the reference in the central Directory Map object. All other drive mapping commands will reflect that change instantly. It's fun at parties.

MAP /?

The MAP /? command displays on-line help for all variations of the MAP command.

MAP /VER

The MAP /VER command lists the version of the MAP utility that you are using, as well as the files the utility needs to execute. If you use the /VER option, all other parameters will be ignored.

Table 4.9 provides a quick summary of all the really amazing MAP commands you've learned today.

T A B L E 4.9

Getting to Know the MAP Commands

COMMAND	RESULT
MAP	Displays a list of current drive mappings.
MAP G:=WHITE-SRV1\SYS:	Maps the G: drive as a network drive that points to SHARED\FIN the SHARED\FIN directory on the SYS volume of the WHITE-SRV1 server (using the physical volume name).
MAP G:=.WHITE-SRV1_SYS. WHITE. CRIME.TOKYO. ACME:SHARED\FIN	Maps the G: drive as a network drive that points to the SHARED\FIN directory on the SYS volume of the WHITE-SRV1 server (using the Volume object name).
MAP NP E:=SYS:HR\EVAL	Maps the E: drive to the HR\EVAL directory, suppressing the warning that you are about to re-map a local drive.
MAP S3:=SYS:APPS\WP70	Maps the S3: search drive to the SYS:APSS\WP70 directory and assigns the next available drive letter in reverse alphabetical order as a network drive.
MAP S3:=W:=SYS:APPS\WP70	Maps the S3: search drive to the SYS:APPS\WP70 directory and assigns W: as the associated network drive.
MAP INS S1:=SYS:PUBLIC	Inserts a new S1: search drive at the beginning of the search list, renumbering all existing search drives accordingly. Also assigns the next available drive letter in reverse alphabetical order as a network drive.
MAP DEL G:	Deletes the G: network drive (see the MAP REM command).
MAP REM G:	Deletes the G: network drive (see the MAP DEL command).
MAP ROOT H:= SYS:ACCT\REPORTS	Maps the H: drive as a false root pointing to the ACCT\REPORTS directory.
MAP N SYS:DATA	Maps the next available network drive letter to the SYS:DATA directory.

T A B L E   4.9

Getting to Know the MAP Commands

COMMAND	RESULT
MAP C I:	Changes the I: network drive to the next available search drive number.
MAP C S4:	Changes the S4: search drive to a network drive.
MAP S5:=WPAPP	Maps the S5: search drive to a Directory Map object called WPAPP.
MAP /?	Displays on-line help information for the MAP command.
MAP /VER	Displays version information about the MAP utility, including the files it needs to execute.

In the beginning. . . there was the NDS directory tree. We discovered the [Root], leaf objects, proper naming, and Read/Write replicas. We learned how to build it, name it, manage it, and groom it. Just when we thought we understood the true meaning of NetWare 4 life, another tree appeared — the non-NDS directory tree.

This strange new tree is very different. Instead of a [Root], it has a root; instead of leaves, it has files; and instead of replicas, it has duplexing. But once you get past its rough exterior, you'll see that the non-NDS tree shares the same look and feel as the NDS one. And they approach life together with a similar purpose — to logically organize user resources, except this time the resources are files, not printers.

In this chapter we learned everything there is to know about our non-NDS friend. We learned how to name it, partition it, design it, install it, manage it, and groom it. All in a day's work.

ZEN

Megatrend — A far-reaching or widespread change in society such as the advent of computers and the information revolution, aerobics and physical fitness, microwave ovens and convenience food, or, most importantly, CNAs becoming florists.

So, what does the future hold? Well, now that we've learned everything about NDS and non-NDS trees, we can expand our minds to the rest of the NetWare 4 CNA program. We will combine our "treeologist" skills and forge ahead into the great CNA abyss:

> ▸ Security

> ▸ Configuration

> ▸ Management

> ▸ Printing

During your journey through the remainder of this book, look back to the fun times you had in gardening class. Count on your NDS and non-NDS gardening skills — because you will need them. Oh yes, you will.

Good luck, and by the way. . . thanks for saving the world.

EXERCISE 4-1: NETWARE 4 FILE CABINET

Circle the 20 NetWare 4 File System terms hidden in this word search puzzle using the hints provided.

```
S   Y   S   T   E   M   C   T   E   R   R   B
Y   E   U   U   J   N   E   Q   E   K   B   U
S   N   E   A   K   E   R   N   E   T   S   R
I   W   L   L   S   J   Q   X   Y   F   Q   Z
X   A   U   C   P   P   T   V   Q   L   V   G
T   D   E   L   E   T   E   D   S   A   V   C
E   M   Z   O   V   X   V   M   W   G   P   Q
E   I   F   N   C   O   P   Y   P   L   U   N
N   N   N   I   G   O   L   P   R   I   B   G
R   I   D   N   L   S   D   U   A   A   L   Q
V   Q   U   E   U   E   S   I   M   M   I   K
T   A   N   B   H   K   R   W   M   E   C   D
```

Hints:

1. Directory that contains deleted files from directories that no longer exist.
2. Directory that contains NetWare on-line documentation files.
3. Directory that contains sample programs for use in configuring the network for TCP/IP.
4. NetWare 4 file management menu utility that can be used to salvage and purge files.
5. Command line utility that can be used for assigning directory or file attributes.
6. The only directory available to users prior to login.
7. This directory may or may not contain User ID subdirectories.
8. Command line utility used for assigning network or search drive mappings.

9. Command line utility that be used for copying files from one location to another.
10. Command line utility that can be used to selectively list volume, directory, and file information.
11. Directory that contains subdirectories for different languages.
12. MS Windows-based file management utility.
13. Directory that contains NetWare utilities available to network users.
14. Directory that contains print queue subdirectories.
15. Another name for Redundant Array of Inexpensive Disks.
16. Maximum number of network search drives available.
17. Process used for filesharing before the advent of LANs.
18. First volume on every NetWare 4 server.
19. A directory that contains operating system files, NLMs, and administrator utilities.
20. The highest level in the NetWare 4 file system.

See Appendix C for answers.

CASE STUDY: CREATING A DIRECTORY STRUCTURE FOR ACME

You're ready to create the basic file system directory structure for the WHITE-SRV1 server. Using the scenario listed here, design the directory structure on paper first, then use the DOS MD command or the NetWare 4 FILER utility to create the directory structure on the system.

As you know, initially, the Crime Fighting division, the White-Collar Crime department, and the three White-Collar Crime units (Cyber Crime, Financial Crime, and Political Crime) will all be sharing the same server (WHITE-SRV1.WHITE.CRIME.TOKYO.ACME). Although there will be some sharing of programs and data, each group will essentially function as an independent workgroup with a separate network administrator.

Because the WHITE-SRV1 server has already been installed, the system-created LOGIN, SYSTEM, PUBLIC, MAIL, and ETC directories already exist.

The USERS directory should be created in the root of the volume. It will serve as the parent directory of the home directories for each user. (The home directories will be created when you actually create the users at a later time.) Each of the workgroups will have access to the SHARED directory, which will be located in the root of the volume. This directory will be used for the sharing of files between workgroups. In addition, each workgroup will have exclusive access to its own group directory under the SHARED directory (called WHITE, CYBER, FIN, and POL, respectively).

The users in the various workgroups will be running different versions of DOS. Although each user will normally run DOS off his/her local workstation, there will also be a copy of each DOS version stored on the server in case anything happens to the copy on a particular workstation. Because the DOS versions differ in manufacturer, type, and version, you will want to use the standard DOS directory structure recommended by Novell (that is, a three-level directory structure under the SYS:PUBLIC directory: the machine type on the first level, the DOS type on the second level, and the DOS version on the third). So far, you know that there will be

▶ Two types of machines (DELL and IBM_PC)

▶ Two types of DOS (MSDOS and NOVDOS)

▶ Three versions of MSDOS (v3.30, v5.00, and v6.22).

The first three applications that will be installed on the server include:

- ▸ A word processing application (in the WP70 directory)

- ▸ A spreadsheet application (in the SS30 directory)

- ▸ A database application (in the DB50 directory)

Each of these subdirectories will be stored under the APPS directory, which will be located in the root of the volume.

EXERCISE 4-2: UNDERSTANDING DRIVE MAPPING

Follow these steps to create sample drive mappings for the directory structure that was created in the case study, "Creating a Directory Structure for ACME."

1. Display on-line help information for the MAP command.
2. Display your current drive mappings.
3. Map drive F: to the USERS directory. (Normally, it would point to each user's individual home directory, but they have not been created yet.)
4. Map drive G: to the POL subdirectory under the SHARED directory, using the physical name of the volume.
5. Map the J: drive to the same directory as the F: drive.
6. Map drive S: to the SHARED directory, using the Volume object name.
7. Map the S1: search drive to the SYS:PUBLIC directory without overwriting the existing pointers in the DOS path.
8. Map the S2: search drive to the V6.22 directory without overwriting the existing pointers in the DOS path.
9. Map the S3: search drive to the SS30 subdirectory.
10. Map the S4: search drive as a false root to the DB50 subdirectory.
11. Display your current drive mappings again. How does the system indicate a false root?
12. Map the S5: search drive to the WP70 subdirectory, specifying that W: be assigned as the associated network drive. Did it work?
13. To view the effect of the CD command on search drive mappings, switch to the Z: drive. Type **CD ..** and press Enter to switch to the root directory. Type the MAP command to list your current drive mappings. What happened? What should be done to fix the problem? Fix the problem.
14. Delete the J: drive.
15. Delete the S3: search drive using a different command than you did in Step 14. What happened to your other search drive mappings? What happened to the network drive associated with those search drives?
16. Change the S4: drive from a search drive to a network drive. What happened to the search drive itself? What happened to the network drive associated with it?

See Appendix C for answers.

NetWare 4 Security

"You won't find a more secure system anywhere."

Security is an interesting thing. Everyone wants it but how much are you willing to pay? On the one extreme, you could live in a titanium vault — secure but very uncomfortable. On the other extreme, you could live in a 1960s Woodstock fantasy — fun but way too risky. No, I believe you live somewhere in between. Whether you know it or not, your security requirements fall in a spectrum between a titanium vault and the 1960s. The key to security is gauging the range of your boundaries.

Goal: Let the good guys in and keep the bad guys out!

Security in the Information Age poses an even more interesting challenge. Computers and communications have made it possible to collect volumes of data about you and me — from our last purchase at the five-and-dime to our detailed medical records. Privacy has become a commodity to be exchanged on the open market. Information is no longer the fodder of afternoon talk shows. It has become *the* unit of exchange for the 21st Century, more valuable than money.

A recent study has shown that 92 percent of the Fortune 500 companies think security is important enough to do something about. Even the government is getting involved with the "clipper chip" and other anti-theft policies. I bet you thought you left cops and robbers behind in childhood. Well, this is a variation on the game and the stakes are very high. As a CNA, it is your responsibility to design, install, and manage the NetWare 4 network. But, most importantly, you must protect it. You need a brain filled with sophisticated security strategies and a utility belt full of advanced protection tools. Think of this chapter as your impenetrable network armor.

NetWare security, in general, is pretty good. But for many of today's WANs, it's not good enough. As a matter of fact, most of NetWare's security features need to be "turned on." It's not secure right out of the box. A truly *secure* network protects more than just user data — it protects everything! So, what is "everything"? The definition of "everything" has changed in NetWare 4. Now the world exists in a nebulous cloud full of Tupperware containers and User objects. As the NetWare universe becomes more open and interconnected, security becomes more and more important.

So, what is "security"? Simply stated, security is freedom from risk. Therefore, network security can be considered as any effort you take to protect your network from risk. Of course, it's difficult to protect your network from things you cannot see or understand. So, the first thing you need to do in developing a security model is to learn about risks.

So, what is "risk"? Risk is a combination of value and threat. The value you determine is the cost of your network resources should you lose them. Value extends well beyond monetary value — it encompasses data integrity, confidentiality, and the value of data to competitors. The threats are more difficult to define. Threats come from a variety of different sources, including people, technology, and the environment. The very nature of computer networks puts them at continual risk. In summary, sharing data makes it harder to protect data. Of course, you don't have a choice. The first step toward true network security is *risk analysis*.

The goal of risk analysis is to define your network security principles and identify the threats against them. A "threat" is a person, place, or thing that poses some danger to a network asset. Threats can be physical (file servers and workstations), topology (wire tapping), network-related (back/trapdoors, impersonation and piggybacking), data (logic bombs and Trojan horses), and people (intentional sabotage or unintentional bumbling).

The goal of your threat-based security model is to determine how likely your network is to experience any of these threats. What are the chances, for example, that your system has a back/trapdoor in place? Is wiretapping a possibility? How about impersonation or, even worse, logic bombs? The best approach is to make a realistic judgment of each threat's probability on your WAN. This becomes the foundation of your network's risk index. You can then use this index to develop a successful system of security countermeasures.

Countermeasures are actions that create a protective barrier against network threats. In many cases, countermeasures can reduce the probability of serious threats. In addition, vulnerability decreases as countermeasures increase. There is, however, never a vulnerability level of zero because countermeasures themselves have vulnerabilities built in. The bad news is countermeasures cost money. As a matter of fact, the more serious the threat, the higher the cost of the countermeasure. And it's difficult to quantify the decrease in threat probability because of countermeasures. Therefore, cost justification becomes a challenge. But all in all, countermeasures are necessary to keep your network running and, therefore, money needs to be spent on them. After all, money makes the world go 'round.

As a CNA, it's your job to identify the network's threats and implement appropriate countermeasures to eliminate them. This isn't easy. You have many factors working against you — including money, office politics, and user productivity. But there are some quick and easy countermeasures that can dramatically improve your network security:

- Restrict physical access to file servers.

- One of your network's most insecure entry points is through virtual links.

- Consider using dial-back systems with multilayered password protection. Remember, anyone with a modem and phone line can gain access to your network.

- Background authentication and NCP packet signing protect data packets as they travel over topology lines. In addition, data is encrypted for further protection.

- Many advanced routers allow you to filter SAPs, RIPs, and specific frame types. Consider filtering non-essential packets to increase performance and keep out the bad guys.

- Don't use the Supervisor or Admin accounts — use an equivalent instead. Also, don't delete the original Admin account once you have made yourself equivalent. There are some existentialist ramifications in there somewhere.

- Always create a backdoor. Consider using Alt+255 as a null character. It's hard to track. The beauty of null characters is they appear as spaces. Intruders will see a username or password with a space and never assume it's a null character. Also, many times you can't tell how many null characters are involved — especially when they're sequentially added to the end of a username.

- NetWare 4 includes an extensive auditing system that allows you to audit login events as well as file/directory events. Use it!

▶ Consider restricting the following file server access rights: Supervisory, Access Control, and Modify [SAM].

▶ Track rights carefully and make sure you know what you're doing before you get started. Calculating effective rights can be very tricky, especially if you use an inherited rights filter (IRF). Many times users end up with rights they shouldn't have.

▶ Classify people into security levels and identify the highest security risks. Then implement countermeasures against these people, including training sessions, tracking, or extensive auditing.

▶ Be careful when assigning distributed administrative responsibility. Remember, power corrupts and absolute power corrupts absolutely.

Well, there you go. Risk analysis and countermeasures. These are key factors in protecting your NetWare 4 WAN. Sometimes NetWare security isn't good enough. You need to develop appropriate countermeasures for *all* network threats, not just a few. After all, the '60s was a great decade, but welcome to the '90s. This is the Information Age and your data is a valuable commodity.

Fortunately, NetWare 4 has a dramatically improved security model for creating and maintaining your impenetrable network armor. This model allows us to perform risk analysis at five different levels. It also includes numerous countermeasures for dealing with "bad guys." Whatever you do, don't let this information fall into the wrong hands. Let's take a closer look.

ZEN

As you progress through this chapter, you'll find that "true security" is a mystery. What is it? How do you get it? Many times, it's not what it seems. You'll find it in the least likely places. As an example, let's rewind a few years to one of the greatest mysteries of our time — "Who shot Mr. Burns?" It all started with a simple question, from a key witness: "Who shot who in the what, now?"

Old Man

NetWare 4 Security Model

NetWare 4 improves on earlier NetWare security models by adding supplemental front-end barriers for filtering unauthorized users. Once again, the same security goal applies:

Let the good guys in and keep the bad guys out!

As you can see in Figure 5.1, the NetWare 4 security model consists of five different barriers. They are

- ▸ Layer One: Login/Password Authentication

- ▸ Layer Two: Login Restrictions

- ▸ Layer Three: NDS Security

- ▸ Layer Four: File System Access Rights

- ▸ Layer Five: Directory/File Attributes

The NetWare 4 Security
Model

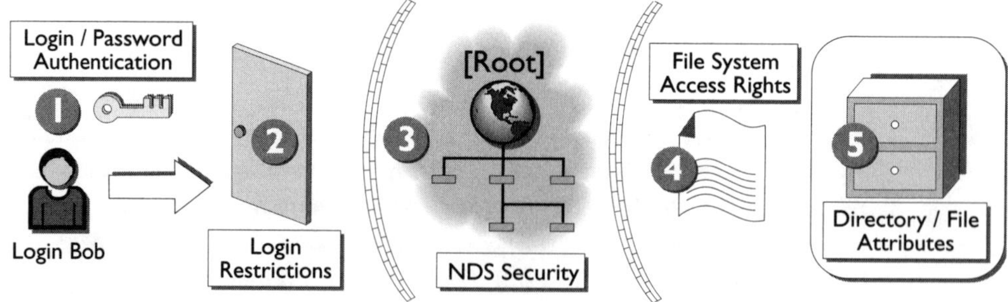

As you can see, each layer creates an increasingly strong barrier against user access. Each time you pass through a door, you are greeted with an even stronger barrier. This works much the same way as the opening to the TV show *Get Smart*.

Maxwell would have to travel through numerous barriers until he finally reached the telephone booth. After entering the correct code, he was allowed access to Control headquarters. Users pass through similar barriers on their way to the ultimate prize — data.

Let's take a quick look.

LAYER ONE: LOGIN/PASSWORD AUTHENTICATION

As you can see from Figure 5.1, it all starts with login/password authentication. Remember, users don't log in to NetWare servers anymore — they log in to the "Cloud." First, the user requests access by typing **LOGIN** followed by a valid username. Once this occurs, authentication begins. There are two phases:

▶ Initialization — The server and workstation authenticate the session with an encrypted key. You are required to enter a valid password to decrypt the key.

▶ Background — NetWare continues to attach the key to all messages to ensure data integrity. This process is known as *background authentication*. In addition, you can enhance background security with a related feature called *NCP packet signing*. We'll explore both features later in this chapter. In addition to authentication, NetWare 4 accepts passwords up to 127 characters. This is a substantial improvement over earlier versions. The limit is decreased significantly, though, for Macintosh clients. Once you have been authenticated, NetWare matches you against a list of global and personal login restrictions. These restrictions allow for conditional access according to a variety of criteria. That's Layer One.

LAYER TWO: LOGIN RESTRICTIONS

Once you provide a valid login name and password, you are authenticated. Congratulations! NetWare responds with conditional access and NDS rights take over. At this point, I stress the word *conditional* access. Permanent access is made possible by a variety of login restrictions. These login restrictions include:

- ▶ Account Restrictions — Includes anything from "Account locked" to "Force periodic password changes."

- ▶ Password Restrictions — Includes "Minimum password length" and "Force unique passwords."

- ▶ Station Restrictions — Limits users to specific workstation node IDs.

- ▶ Time Restrictions — Determines when users can and cannot use the system.

- ▶ Intruder Detection/Lockout — A global feature that detects incorrect password attempts and locks bad guys out.

Each of these restrictions are configured by *you* using a variety of NetWare 4 tools, including NWADMIN and NETADMIN. We'll learn all the details of how and why later in this chapter.

LAYER THREE: NDS SECURITY

Once you enter the "Cloud," your ability to access leaf and container objects is determined by a sophisticated NDS security structure. At the heart of NDS security is the Access Control List (ACL). The ACL is the property of every NDS object. It defines who can access the object (trustees) and what each trustee can do (rights). The ACL is divided into two types of rights:

- ▶ Object Rights — Defines an object's trustees and controls what the trustees can do with the object.

- ▶ Property Rights — Limits the trustees' access to only specific properties of the object.

Here's a great example (see Figure 5.2). Let's say the Group object Admin-GROUP has rights to the User object Leia. Admin-Group has the Browse object right, which means that any member of the group can see Leia and view information about her. But Leia is shy. She wants to limit what the group can see (reasonable enough). She only wants them to see her Last Name, Postal Address, and Telephone Number. So

Leia limits the group's rights by assigning the Read property right to only these three properties: Last Name, Postal Address, and Telephone Number. No sweat.

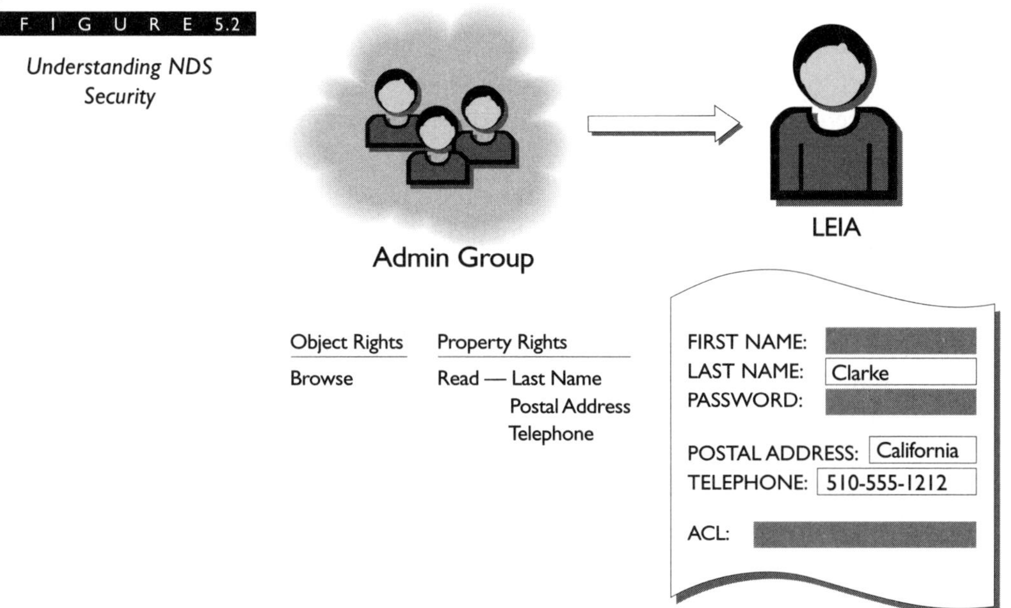

F I G U R E 5.2

Understanding NDS Security

Object and property rights are designed to provide efficient access to NDS objects without making it an administrative nightmare. You be the judge. Users can acquire object rights in a variety of ways, including trustee assignment, inheritance, and security equivalence. Property rights, on the other hand, are a bit trickier. Global property rights can be inherited, but rights to specific properties must be granted through a trustee assignment.

Trustee assignments occur when an object is given explicit access to another object or its properties. These trustee assignments are administered by adding the user to a host object's ACL property. This is accomplished using NWADMIN or NETADMIN menu utilities.

Inheritance is a little simpler. If rights are granted at the container level, they are inherited for all container and leaf objects below. This means that rights assigned to the [Root] object, for example, are inherited by every object in the NDS tree. Be very careful. Fortunately, NetWare 4 includes an inherited rights filter (IRF), which blocks inherited rights.

Finally, there's *security equivalence*. This means objects can absorb rights by being associated with other objects. Sometimes the associations are obvious, but most of the time, they're not. In reality, users can inherit rights ancestrally from containers, groups, organizational roles, and [Public].

Regardless of how you acquire object and property rights, the concept of *effective rights* still applies. This means the actual rights you can exercise with a given object are the combination of explicit trustee assignments, inheritance, and the IRF. The mathematical product of this mess is known as *effective NDS rights* — "modern math." That effectively ends our discussion of NDS security and moves us on to Layer Four of the NetWare 4 security model — file system access rights.

LAYER FOUR: FILE SYSTEM ACCESS RIGHTS

Well, here we are. Congratulations! You've finally made it to NetWare Nirvana. You've passed through three very difficult barriers of network armor and the search is over — your files await you. Ah, but not so fast! Before you can access any files on the NetWare 4 server, you must have the appropriate file system access rights. Once again, another barrier pops up to bite you. Following is a list of the eight rights that control access to NetWare 4 files (they almost spell a word):

▶ W — Write: Grants the right to open and change the contents of files.

▶ (O) — Doesn't exist but is needed to spell a word.

▶ R — Read: Grants the right to open files in the directory and read their contents (or run applications).

▶ M — Modify: Grants the right to change the attributes or name of a file or directory.

▶ F — File Scan: Grants the right to see files and directories.

▶ A — Access Control: Grants the right to change trustee assignments in the IRF.

▶ C — Create: Grants the right to create new files and subdirectories.

▶ E — Erase: Grants the right to delete a directory, its files, and subdirectories.

▶ S — Supervisor: Grants all rights to a directory and the files and subdirectories below. This right cannot be blocked by the IRF.

Holy anatomical nematodes, Batman! That spells "WoRMFACES." It's not a pretty sight but certainly a name you will not forget. NetWare 4 file system access rights are administered in much the same way as NDS object rights. They are granted with the help of trustee assignments, inheritance, and ancestral inheritance. In addition, file system rights are subject to most of the same rules as NDS effective rights. All in all, NDS and file server security parallel one another — one operating in the clouds (NDS) and one with its feet firmly planted on the ground (file system).

Well, that completes the majority of the NetWare 4 security model. There's only one layer left, and it is seldom used — directory/file attributes. Let's take a closer look.

LAYER FIVE: DIRECTORY/FILE ATTRIBUTES

Directory and file attributes provide the final and most sophisticated layer of the NetWare 4 security model. These attributes are rarely used, but provide a powerful tool for specific security solutions. If all else fails, you can always turn to attribute security to save the day.

NetWare 4 supports three different types of attributes:

▶ Security Attributes — The main attribute category. Some attributes apply to both directories and files.

▶ Feature Attributes — Applies to three key features: backup, purging, and the Transactional Tracking System (TTS).

▶ Disk Management Attributes — For file compression, data migration, and block suballocation.

QUIZ

There's a hidden message in everything. The following coiled sentence contains a profound truth. Start at the correct letter, move to any touching letter, and you will find a mystery unfold.

```
V   E   O   E   T

E   U   Y   L   P

R   Y   S   L   A

H   T   R   O   M

I   N   A   A   D

G   E   X   R   T

E   C   O   E   I

P   O   T   F   D

T   H   W   O   L
```

(Q5-1)
(See Appendix C for all quiz answers.)

Well, there you have it. That's a brief snapshot of NetWare 4's five-layered security model. Now we'll take a much closer look at each of these layers and learn how they can be used to create your impenetrable network armor. Now it's time to attack the first layer of NetWare 4 security — login/password authentication.

REAL WORLD

In October 1967, a task force was assembled by the Department of Defense (DOD) to address computer security safeguards that would protect classified information and computer networks. The task force was formed primarily because networks were just beginning to make an impact on all the world's computers. Of course, they had no idea what they were in for during the next 30 years. The DOD now explores security alternatives through the National Computer Security Center (NCSC). In December 1985, the DOD published a document affectionately known as "the Orange Book." Yes, I've seen it — it is orange. The document was entitled *The Department of Defense Trusted Computer System Evaluation Criteria* (TCSEC). The Orange Book was designed to provide security guidelines for both developers and administrators. The major goal of the document is "to encourage the computer industry to develop trusted computer systems and products making them widely available in the commercial marketplace." The book basically consists of a spectrum of evaluation criteria for differing levels of security. It lists basic requirements for very low and very high levels of security.

In order to be truly secure, your system must satisfy six fundamental requirements:

1 • It must have a clear and well-defined security policy enforced.

2 • All system elements must be associated with access control labels.

3 • All individuals accessing the system must be identified.

4 • Audit information must be selectively kept and protected so that all security actions can be traced.

5 • The computer system must contain hardware/software mechanisms that can be independently evaluated.

6 • The countermeasures that enforce these basic requirements must be continuously protected against tampering and/or unauthorized changes.

So, there you have it. Is your system truly secure? Well, in addition to these six requirements, the Orange Book includes evaluation criteria for four different divisions of security — A through D. Just like in school, A is good and D is bad. Working your way from the bottom, Division D is simply the bottom of the totem pole. This classification is reserved for those systems that have been evaluated, but have failed to meet the requirements for a higher evaluation class.

(continued)

(continued)

Division C, on the other hand, provides security on a "need to know" basis. Division C security includes auditing and accountability. The Orange Book further classifies Division C into two classes — C-1 and C-2. Most of today's network operating systems, including NetWare 4 and NT, vow to meet C-2 requirements at the very minimum (the Government requires it). Class C-2 is entitled "Controlled Access Protection." Systems in this class enforce a more finely grained discretionary control than C-1 systems. C-2 users are individually accountable for their actions through login procedures, auditing of security-related events, and resource isolation. The idea here is to permit or refuse access to any single file.

The bottom line is NetWare 4.1 satisfies C-2 security. Some of the new features that were implemented to meet this classification include login authentication, distributed NDS administration, and auditing. While you may yearn for level B or A security, you don't want to pay the price. C-2 should be fine.

Layer One: Login/Password Authentication

When you log in to a NetWare 4 server, the world changes. Suddenly you have access to a plethora of resources that weren't available before — printers, files, users, and e-mail. Whatever you do, don't take the login process for granted. It's a complex series of sophisticated communication steps between your client and the server.

As you'll see in the next two chapters, logging in involves ODI drivers, VLMs, context, and STARTNET.BAT. But the real goal of logging in is security. After all, this is the only way to differentiate between real users and "bad guys." Now let's take a closer look at how hard it is to get into a NetWare 4 server.

GETTING IN

The first two layers of the NetWare security model are concerned with gaining access to the network, that is, "getting in." Once you're in, the bottom three layers take over. They control what you can do once you get there — access to NDS resources and the file system. As you can see in Figure 5.3, there's a lot going on during the login process. Also notice that there are three ways to be denied, and only two ways to be granted access to, a NetWare 4 "Cloud." This is because of authentication. Let's take a closer look at the flowchart in Figure 5.3.

FIGURE 5.3

Login Process Flowchart

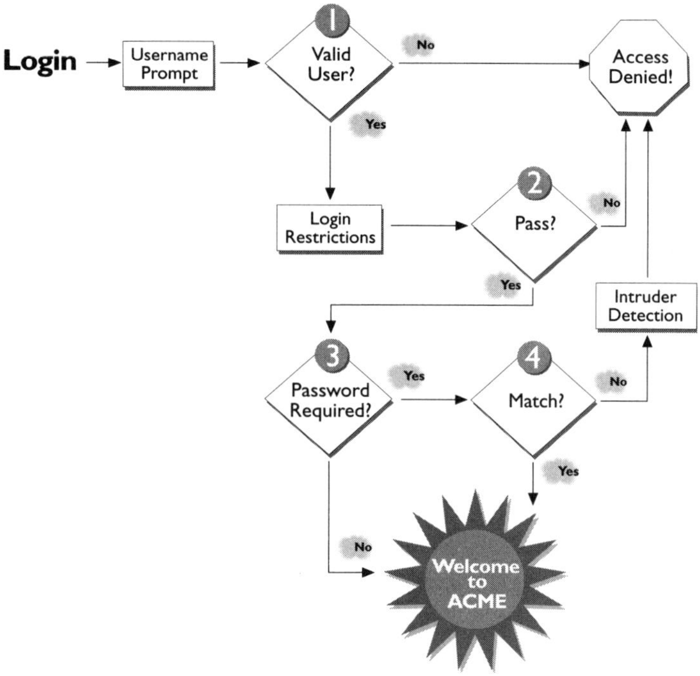

It all starts with the LOGIN command. NetWare responds with a username prompt. You'll need to provide your login name with complete NDS context. This is so that NetWare 4 can match you against specific user properties in the NDS database. Once you enter a username, NetWare goes to the nearest Read/Write replica of your parent partition to verify that you exist. If you don't exist in the context specified, you'll be denied access and the following two error messages will be displayed:

```
LOGIN - 4.12 - 895: The user does not exist in the specified
context.

LOGIN - 4.12 - 130: Access has been denied and you have been
logged out.
```

If you do provide a valid username and context, the system continues to decision two — login restrictions. Using the information provided by the Read/Write replica, NetWare 4 checks all your major login restrictions including time restrictions, station restrictions, and account lockout. If you try to log in from an unauthorized workstation or during the wrong time of day, access will be denied and the following error message appears:

```
LOGIN - 4.12 - 860: You have tried to login during an unauthorized
time period.
```

If you pass login restrictions, NetWare moves on to the final two decisions — passwords. First, it uses your NDS information to determine whether a password is required. If the password is not required, you are authenticated automatically and access is granted. Bad idea. If a password is required, you are prompted for it. Good idea. That brings us to the final login decision: Does the password you provided match the one in the NDS database? If not, access is denied, Intruder Detection is incremented, and the following brief error message appears:

```
LOGIN - 4.12 - 100: Access has been denied.
```

If you provide the correct password, NetWare 4 uses it to decrypt the private authentication key. This completes the initialization phase of login authentication and access is granted. We'll discuss the two phases of authentication in just a moment.

In summary, the NetWare 4 login process consists of four decisions:

1 • Are you using a valid username?

2 • Do you pass login restrictions?

3 • Is a password required?

4 • Does your password match?

If all these conditions are met, access is granted. As you can see in Figure 5.3, there are three ways to be denied access — invalid username, you don't pass login restrictions, or you provide the incorrect password. Now you should have a new appreciation for all the work that's involved when you type that one magic word: **LOGIN**.

ZEN

"Nancy Drew says that all you need to solve a mystery is an inquisitive temperament and two good friends."

Lisa Simpson

INITIAL AUTHENTICATION

From a security standpoint, the entire login process points to one goal — authentication. This is the only way you can gain access to a NetWare 4 network. Authentication involves the username, the password, the client, NDS, and the NetWare 4 server. There sure are a lot of cooks in the kitchen. Once you've been initially authenticated, NetWare 4 activates a secondary authentication scheme — background authentication. Background authentication keeps the user validated throughout the current session. An additional feature, called *NCP packet signing*, validates *every* user packet as they're sent from the workstation to the server. This also applies to the active session only.

In both cases, NetWare 4 authentication guarantees the following:

- Only the purported sender built the message.

- The message came from the workstation where the authentication data was created.

- The message pertains to the current session.

- The message contains no information counterfeited from another session.

- The message has not been tampered with or corrupted.

- You are who you say you are.

- You're doing what you say you're doing.

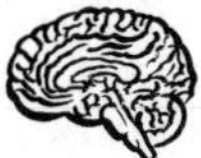

THE BRAIN

A more detailed explanation of the authentication process can be found in my Novell's CNE Study Guide for NetWare 4.1 book, published by Novell Press/IDG Books.

Layer Two: Login Restrictions

Login restrictions further scrutinize WAN access by matching the login name with a variety of NDS qualifications:

- Is this user authorized to log in during this time period?

- Is this user authorized to log in from this particular workstation?

- Is this user authorized to log in on this date?

- Will this user ever get the password right?

- Will this user ever change the password?

- Who shot Mr. Burns?

- What is the meaning of life?

The first layer of NetWare security (login authentication) restricts INVALID users. Login restrictions, on the other hand, restrict VALID users. At this point, NetWare assumes a valid username has been provided and authentication can probably be guaranteed.

As you can see in Figure 5.4, NDS supports a variety of login restriction properties. A quick scan of the right side of Figure 5.4 shows four obvious user restrictions — login, password, login time, and network address. In addition, NetWare 4 supports a password tracking feature called Intruder Detection/Lockout. This security feature tracks unauthorized login attempts and automatically locks accounts when the attempts exceed a given bad login threshold count. The user account can only be unlocked by an administrator.

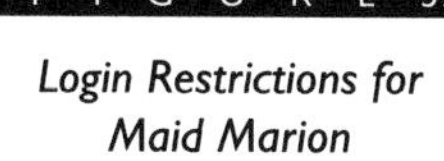

F I G U R E 5.4

Login Restrictions for Maid Marion

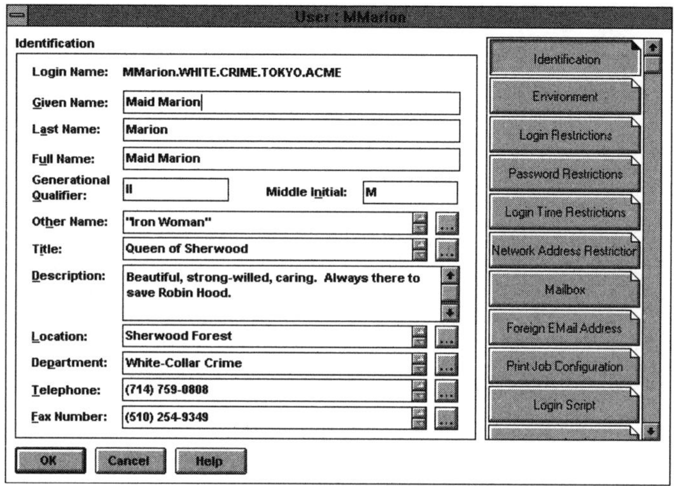

In summary, NetWare 4 login restrictions fall into five different categories:

- ▸ Account Restrictions

- ▸ Password Restrictions

- ▸ Time Restrictions

- ▸ Station Restrictions

- ▸ Intruder Detection/Lockout

Account restrictions apply only to specific users. Maid Marion, for example, can have her account expired, concurrent connections limited, or access disabled altogether. Password restrictions impact login authentication. In this screen, we can define a variety of Maid Marion's password settings, including allowing her to change her password, requiring a minimum password length, forcing periodic password changes, requiring unique passwords, and limiting grace logins. Remember, the password is used by the client to decrypt the authentication private key.

The next option is time restrictions. These limitations simply apply to when users can be connected to NDS. Time restrictions are not login restrictions per se, they are *connection restrictions*. This means users cannot log in or be connected to the tree during inactive time periods.

Similarly, station restrictions do not allow users to log in or attach from unauthorized stations. NWADMIN calls this *network address restrictions* because it allows you to limit user access to a specific protocol, LAN address, or node ID.

Finally, Intruder Detection/Lockout is a global feature that is activated at the container level. All objects within the container are tracked according to a variety of parameters, including Incorrect Login Attempts, Intruder Attempt Reset Interval, and Account Lockout. If, for example, Maid Marion logs in with her correct context and an incorrect password seven times within an hour, intruder lockout activates. Once her account has been locked, she has two options — wait the Intruder Lockout Reset Interval or have an administrator unlock her account. This feature allows you to sleep better at night knowing that NetWare 4 is doing all it can to keep intruders out of your WAN.

All of these restrictions (except Intruder Detection/Lockout) are activated at the user level. This means you have to set them for each individual user — too much work. Fortunately, NetWare 4 includes a USER_TEMPLATE object for global configurations. If, for example, you'd like to set a minimum password length for all users in the WHITE container, you could create a USER_TEMPLATE object with the correct settings. Then all users created from this point forward would inherit the properties of the USER_TEMPLATE. This applies to all properties, not just login restrictions. Figure 5.5 shows a sample USER_TEMPLATE configuration screen for the WHITE container. Notice all the page buttons listed on the right-hand side. I'm a big believer in the theory "Less work and more play makes life worth living." And the USER_TEMPLATE object is right up my alley. Use it or lose it.

USER_TEMPLATE Saves the Day!

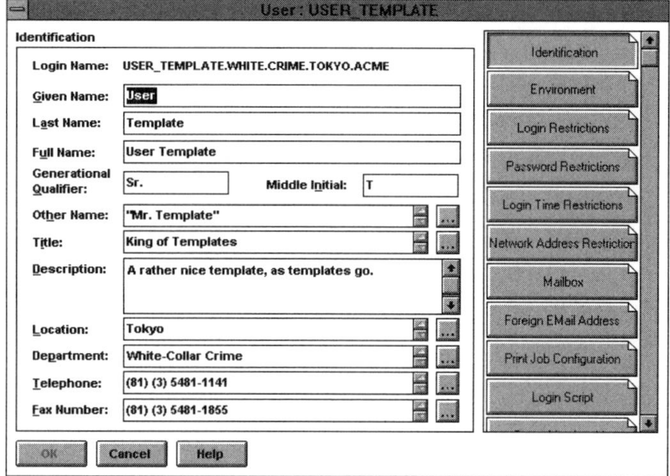

ZEN

"And when he tried to steal our sunlight, he crossed over that line between everyday villainy and cartoonish super-villainy."

Mr. Wayland Smithers

Now let's take a much closer look at each of the five NetWare 4 login restrictions, starting with account restrictions.

ACCOUNT RESTRICTIONS

NetWare 4 account restrictions provide a method for controlling and restricting user access to the NDS tree. Account restrictions can be found in the Login Restrictions screen of NWADMIN (see Figure 5.6). As you can see, there are four main options:

- ▸ Account Disabled

- ▸ Account Has Expiration Date

- ▸ Limit Concurrent Connections

- ▸ Last Login

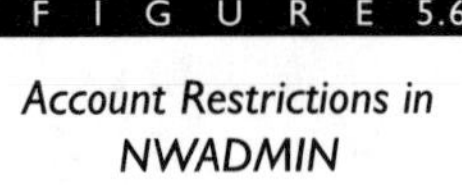

FIGURE 5.6

Account Restrictions in NWADMIN

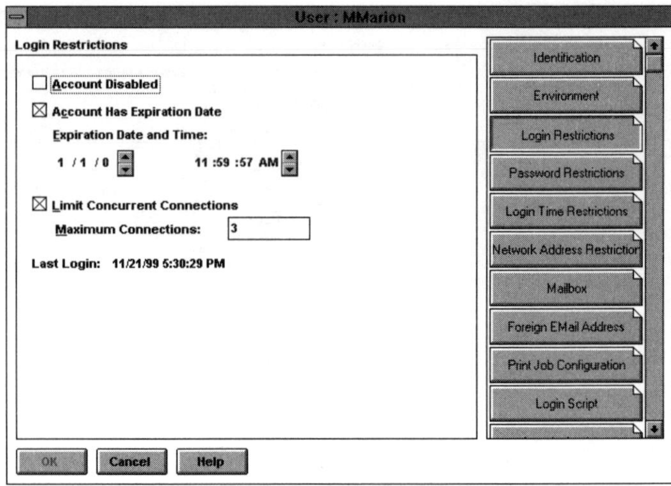

Account Disabled

This option is pretty self explanatory. The account is either disabled or not. This option is not related to Intruder Detection/Lockout. It is possible for an account to be locked but not disabled. In both cases, the effect is the same — the user can't log in. In order to disable a NetWare 4 account, you have two choices — manually check this box or use an expiration date.

Account Has Expiration Date

This option is a useful tool for temporary employees or students in an academic environment. It allows you to lock an account after a specific date. The default is inactive. If you check the Account Disabled box, NOW appears as the default date and time. This means as soon as you exit NWADMIN, Maid Marion's account will be disabled. Be sure to increase the value before you leave. In Figure 5.6, Maid Marion's expiration parameters have been set to just before noon on January 1, 2000. At this point, she will either be gone or celebrating the success of ACME.

Limit Concurrent Connections

Let's face it, users are nomadic. They like to migrate throughout the WAN and log in from multiple workstations. You can limit a user's concurrent connections by changing the inactive parameters in Figure 5.6 to something greater than zero.

As you can see, an ideal setting is three concurrent connections. This means that Maid Marion can only log in from three workstations simultaneously. That's plenty. This account restriction works in conjunction with station restrictions. You can enhance a user's concurrent connection limitation by combining it with a specific physical workstation address. In this case, Maid Marion can only log in from three specific machines simultaneously.

Last Login

The Last Login parameter allows users to track activity on their login account. You should train users to periodically check this parameter for intruder logins. If, for example, Maid Marion was gone for a week, but saw that the last login was three days ago, she would have reason to believe an intruder had used her account.

That does it for login restrictions. Now let's take a closer look at password restrictions.

PASSWORD RESTRICTIONS

The next set of login restrictions properties deal with passwords. As you can see in Figure 5.7, there are five main options:

- ▶ Allow User to Change Password

- ▶ Require a Password

- ▶ Force Periodic Password Changes

- ▶ Require Unique Passwords

- ▶ Limit Grace Logins

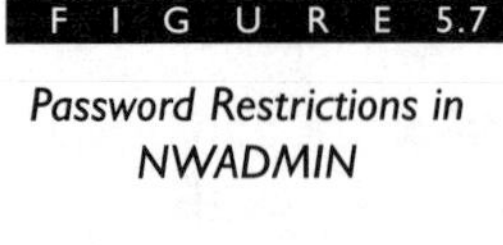

F I G U R E   5.7

Password Restrictions in NWADMIN

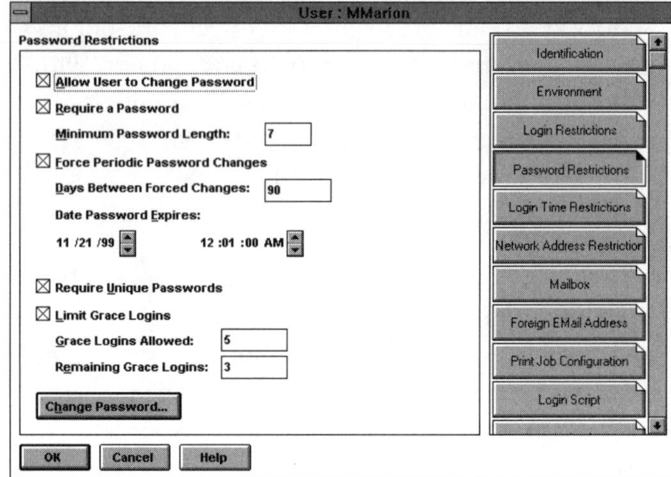

Password restrictions directly impact login authentication. As we learned in Figure 5.3, NetWare 4 access can be granted in one of two ways — by providing the correct password (if one is needed) or automatically (if no password is required). Requiring a password is absolutely mandatory. Otherwise, authentication is crippled. Once you require a password, the question remains, "Who manages it?" If you place the burden of password management on the user, the other four password restriction parameters become important. Let's take a closer look.

Allow User to Change Password

If you allow users to change their passwords, you're opening a can of worms. On the one hand, it shifts the burden of password management from you to them — this is a good thing. On the other hand, it allows them to mess around with an important authentication parameter — this is a bad thing. Most annoying user complaints deal with password management and printing. Well, one out of two ain't bad. If you don't allow users to change their passwords, all the work falls on you. It's your call — a balance between security and practicality.

Require a Password

By default, NetWare 4 does not require a password — this is bad. This should be the very first parameter that you change when creating user accounts. If you activate Require a Password and Force Periodic Password Changes, the system will ask for a password the very first time users log in. Once you activate the Required Password parameter, it's a good idea to set a minimum password length of more than five characters. There are many password hacking routines that can guess a five-character password in less than 20 minutes. On the other hand, you want a password length that doesn't intimidate fragile users. Consider most users can't easily remember strings in excess of 7 to 10 characters. The last thing you want to do is force large passwords so that users have to write them down on a piece of paper and tape them to the front of their monitors. NetWare 4 supports passwords up to 127 characters in length. It also supports any alphanumeric and ASCII characters. Consider creating passwords that join two unrelated words with a punctuation mark such as

- ► DOOR!GROUND

- ► SHOE;QUARK

- ► LATCH PURPLE

Note the last example did not use a space — it used a null character (Alt+255). Funny, it looks like a space — that's the whole point. Intruders will assume it's a space. Also, it's even trickier when used in succession at the end of a password or username. I bet you can't tell there are seven successive null characters at the end of the second example. Once you've required a password, all the other restrictions light up.

Force Periodic Password Changes

Once a password has been required and a minimum password length of seven characters has been set, you should explore using the Force Periodic Password Changes restriction. This parameter forces users to change their passwords at periodic intervals. If you activate the option, NetWare asks you to input the number of days between forced changes. The default is 40 days. This is a little short and can become a nuisance very quickly. Remember, users love to complain about password problems. A periodic password interval of 90 days seems to be optimal.

Password expiration seems to be a touchy topic for users and administrators alike. We want the interval to be short for better security, and they want the interval to be long for less interference. Either way, someone has to track it. You can train your users to check NWADMIN periodically and view the Date Password Expires property within Password Restrictions. This will tell them exactly on what date and at what time their password will expire. Once the password interval has expired, the user is required to change his/her password. This is where grace logins come in. We'll talk about them in just a second.

REAL WORLD

Many times password expiration and grace logins cause unneeded friction between CNAs and users, especially when users abuse the privilege and CNAs ultimately have to change the passwords anyway. Consider making password expiration a big "event." Use the PASSWORD_EXPIRES login script identifier variable to count down the number of days until password expiration (see Chapter 6). Then when the day arrives, throw a party, bring in balloons and cake, and have everyone change their passwords at once. Turning this event into a party makes password transition every 90 days fun and unobtrusive. It's also a great excuse to have four parties a year.

Require Unique Passwords

The Require Unique Passwords restriction works in conjunction with forcing periodic password changes. When the periodic password interval expires and the user must change his or her password, unique passwords forces him/her to enter a new *different* value. If you're going to endure the effort of forcing periodic password changes, do yourself a favor and make them unique. It doesn't make sense to have users change their passwords every 90 days if they're going to use the same ones. NetWare 4 only tracks the last 20 passwords. Don't let your users learn this. They will create numerical intervals such as FIFI1, FIFI2, FIFI3, and so on. Also, I've seen users change their passwords 20 times in succession so they can reuse the original one. Perpetuate the myth that NetWare keeps track of all passwords forever.

Limit Grace Logins

When the periodic password interval has expired, NetWare responds with the following statement during login:

```
Your password has expired. Would you like to change it now?
```

This provides the users with an opportunity to change their passwords right away. If they do not, the system will lock their accounts. The problem with this message is the words, "Would you like." It should say something like, "You better change your password now or your computer will explode." Unfortunately, this message is not configurable. So, many users see it as a choice and decide to move on using their existing password. This is where *grace logins* come in. Grace logins allow the users to log in without changing their passwords. This is a temporary situation because even grace logins expire. As you can see in Figure 5.7, we're giving Maid Marion five grace logins. This means she can log in five times without changing her password. But then her account will be locked. Once again, encourage your users not to rely on grace logins. There's a convenient Change Password button on the Password Restrictions screen for user access. Otherwise, they can use the SETPASS command at the NetWare prompt.

QUIZ

Even numbers have a certain mystery. Try to find the five-digit number, no zeros, in which the first digit is the sum of the last two digits, the second digit is twice the first digit and three times the fourth digit, and the total of all five digits is 16.

Hmmm.

(Q5-2)

That completes our discussion of password restrictions. Aren't they fun? As you can see, there's much more to NetWare 4 passwords than meets the eye. Remember, this is the foundation of our login authentication strategy. Don't underestimate the importance of passwords. Use them or suffer the consequences.

TIME RESTRICTIONS

The next two login restrictions deal with *when* and *where* you get to log in. Time restrictions determine *when*. How many of you have suffered from the curious custodial syndrome (CCS)? Let's see a show of hands. Ah, just as I thought — just about all of you. CCS is a problem that afflicts most of today's modern businesses.

It's caused by the simple fact that the network stays up 24 hours a day and you don't. Since nighttime janitors have access to your equipment, they can easily hack into your networks. One simple solution is time restrictions. Deactivate the network after 9:00 at night and before 6:00 in the morning. This way, no matter how curious the custodial staff is, they can't access the network after hours.

Each square in Figure 5.8 represents a 30-minute interval. The shaded area represents inactive time periods. The white area shows that users can log in any time between 6:00 a.m. and 9:00 p.m. Time restrictions go beyond login restrictions and become connection restrictions. Not only can they not log in, but they can't be connected. If Maid Marion is using the network at 8:55 p.m., she will receive a message:

```
Time expires in five minutes. Please log out.
```

F I G U R E 5.8

Time Restrictions in NWADMIN

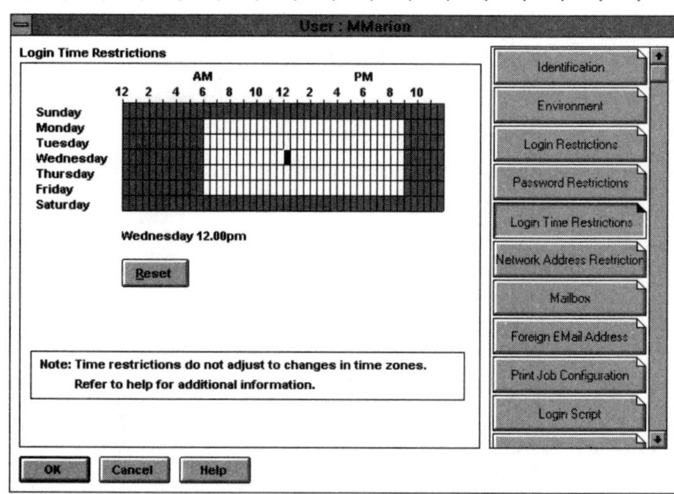

She will get this message at five- and one-minute intervals. When a time restriction is encountered and the user connection is cleared, the system does not perform a proper logout. The system simply *clears* the connections without saving the file. This is a very serious problem. Clearing Maid Marion's connection could result in bindery corruption, hardware failure, or even worse, data loss. When you see a five-minute or one-minute message, be sure to pay attention and log out.

Here are some common time restriction strategies:

▸ Restrict After Hours — ACME doesn't expect employees to work between the hours of 9:00 p.m. and 6:00 a.m. They want to avoid burnout. Setting a time restriction during this period protects them from curious custodians.

▸ Restrict Weekends — Also to avoid burnout, ACME restricts anybody from accessing the network during the weekend. Remember, all work and no play. . . .

▸ Activate Backup Periods — One down side of time restrictions is that it doesn't allow a window for backup. If you're backing up the system late at night, you'll have to activate a backup time window. Test your backup to determine how long it takes and give the system a large enough window — let's say from 11:00 p.m. till 1:00 a.m.

▸ Restrict Specific Users — Remember, time restrictions are a user configuration. You can restrict everybody in a container using the USER_TEMPLATE object or specific users individually. If temporary users, for example, only work on Tuesdays and Thursdays, consider deactivating their accounts on other days.

Don't go crazy with time restrictions. Intelligent time restrictions increase network security, but careless time restrictions can significantly hinder user productivity. You want to give users time to work but not leave the network susceptible to CCS.

STATION RESTRICTIONS

Station Restrictions are the other half of the when/where dynamic duo. They deal with *where*. Now that we've solved our CCS problem, another one will arise — Nomadic User Syndrome (NUS). NUS hinders network security for a variety of reasons. First, nomadic users take up multiple network connections and block access to other users. Secondly, NUS implies that users are logging in from workstations other than their own. And, finally, NUS impairs your ability to limit intruders from accessing physical workstations.

Station restrictions solve NUS. They allow you to virtually chain users to specific machines. Instead of restricting them with passwords, disk restrictions, or time slots, you're physically restricting the workstation from which they can log in. As you can see in Figure 5.9, NetWare 4 station restrictions go a few steps farther:

- ▶ Protocol Restrictions

- ▶ Network Address Restrictions

- ▶ Node Restrictions

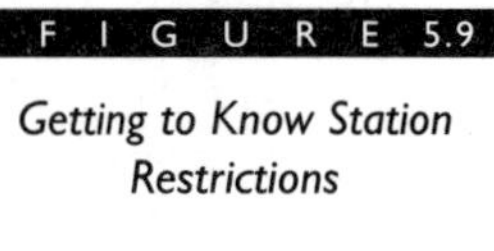

Getting to Know Station Restrictions

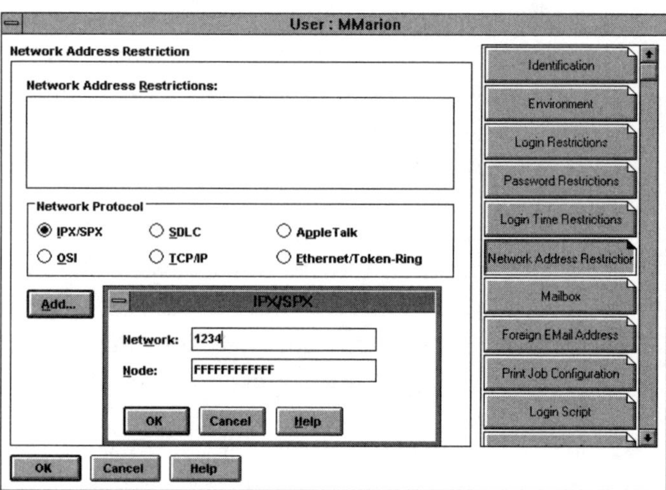

First you pick a protocol. NetWare 4 defaults to the IPX/SPX protocol. Other options include OSI, SDLC, TCP/IP, AppleTalk, and Ethernet/Token Ring. Each protocol treats network address restrictions differently. The IPX/SPX address format consists of an 8-digit external network address and 12-digit hexadecimal node ID. The network address identifies an external LAN segment, while the node ID identifies a specific workstation. Maid Marion, for example, is restricted to any workstation (FFFFFFFFFFFF) on the 1234 LAN. We could further refine her restriction by listing one or more physical node IDs on the 1234 LAN.

The TCP/IP address format expresses logical and physical IDs in the dotted-dash decimal notation. In this case, you can also restrict to all workstations on a logical network or a specific physical machine. Finally, the Ethernet/Token Ring address format uses a SAP (Service Access Point) address, block ID, and PU ID (physical unit). Once again, these values specify all stations on a LAN segment or a specific workstation.

Unfortunately, NWADMIN doesn't dynamically interrogate the LAN to determine addresses for you. You must use other NetWare or third-party utilities to gain network and node ID information. As a word of warning, don't go hog-wild with station restrictions. Use it only if you suffer from NUS. Like other login restrictions, if it's abused or mishandled, station restrictions can significantly impede user productivity. What happens, for example, when Maid Marion travels to another location? Or, what if we restrict her to one workstation and the machine goes down? These are all important considerations. Although station restrictions are a useful security tool, they can also be detrimental to user relationships.

That completes our discussion of what, when, and where. Now only one question remains: "Who?"

ZEN

"If you've ever handled a penny, the government's got your DNA. Why do you think they keep them in circulation?"

Scientist Smith

INTRUDER DETECTION/LOCKOUT

Welcome to Whoville. This is not so much a restriction as it is a security tracking feature. Intruder Detection/Lockout tracks invalid login attempts by monitoring users who try to log in without correct passwords. As you recall from Figure 5.3, this feature increments every time a valid user provides an incorrect password. It also leads directly to Access Denied! Once Intruder Detection has reached a threshold number of attempts, the account is locked completely.

There's one very important thing you need to know about this final login restriction — it's a container-based configuration. All the previous restrictions have been user-based. As you can see in Figure 5.10, intruder detection is activated at the Organization or Organizational Unit level. Once an account has been locked, it must be reactivated at the user level. There are two main configuration elements:

▶ Intruder Detection Limits

▶ Lock Account after Detection

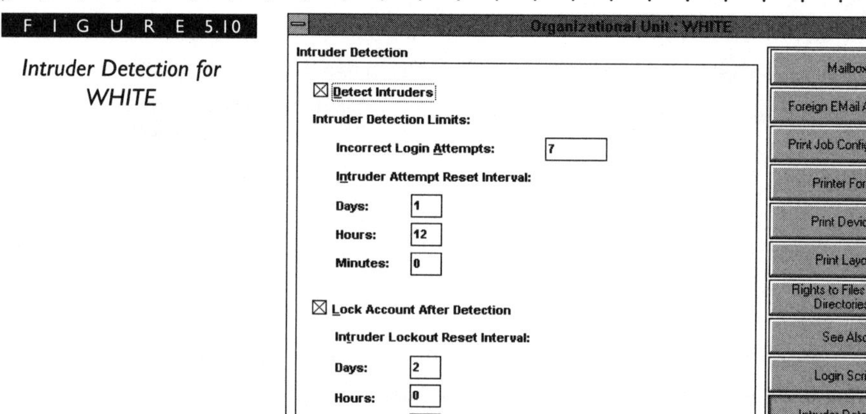

F I G U R E 5.10

Intruder Detection for WHITE

Once Intruder Detection/Lockout has been activated at the container level, all users in that container are tracked. Let's take a closer look.

Intruder Detection Limits

Intruder Detection is turned off by default. In order to activate it, you simply check the Detect Intruders box. Once you activate Intruder Detection, it begins tracking incorrect login attempts. This parameter is set to seven by default. As soon as the incrementing number exceeds the threshold, account lockout occurs. Finally, the Intruder Attempt Reset Interval is a window of opportunity, so to speak. The system uses it to increment the incorrect login attempts. It is set to 30 minutes by default.

Here's how it works. Assume the Incorrect Login Attempts parameter is set to 7 and Intruder Attempt Reset Interval is set to 1 day, 12 hours (see Figure 5.10). The system will track all incorrect login activity and lock the user account if the number of incorrect login attempts exceeds 7 in the 36-hour window. Pretty simple, huh? Now let's take a look at what happens once Intruder Detection is activated.

Lock Account After Detection

This is the second half of Intruder Detection/Lockout. After all, the feature wouldn't be much good if you didn't punish the intruder for entering the wrong password. When you activate the Lock Account After Detection parameter, NetWare asks for an Intruder Lockout Reset Interval. By default, this value is set to 15 minutes. Doesn't make much sense, does it? This invites the hacker to come back 15 minutes later and try all over again. Typically, a value equal to or exceeding the Intruder Attempt Reset Interval is adequate. As you can see in Figure 5.10, we're locking the account for two days, therefore giving you enough time to track down the intruder.

So, what happens to the user when the account is locked? As you can see in Figure 5.11, NetWare tracks account lockout at the user level. The Intruder Lockout screen provides three important pieces of information:

- ▶ Incorrect Login Count — A dynamic parameter that tells the user how many incorrect login counts have been detected during this reset interval. If the account is locked, the incorrect login count should equal the lockout threshold.

- ▶ Account Reset Time — Informs the user how much time is remaining before the account is unlocked automatically.

- ▶ Last Intruder Address — Shows the network and node address of the workstation that attempted the last incorrect login. This parameter provides you with valuable information regardless of whether the account is locked. This is pretty undeniable evidence that someone tried to hack this account from a specific workstation. You don't have to worry about disputed evidence or planted gloves.

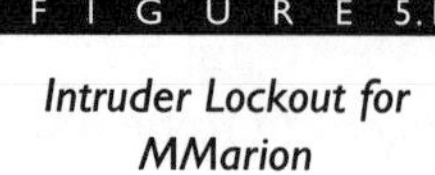

FIGURE 5.11

Intruder Lockout for MMarion

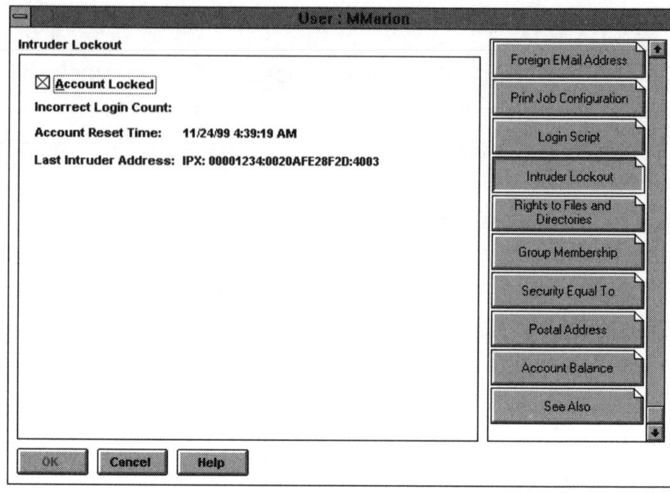

So, who's going to unlock Maid Marion's account? You! Only Admin or distributed administrators can unlock accounts that have been locked by the Intruder Detection feature. But what about Admin? After all, Admin is the most commonly hacked account — with good reason. If you don't have an Admin-equivalent user to unlock the Admin account, consider using **"ENABLE LOGIN"** at the file server console. It's always nice to have a back door.

There you have it. That completes our discussion of Intruder Detection/Lockout and login restrictions in general.

Congratulations, you are in! You've successfully navigated the first two layers of the NetWare 4 security model — login/password authentication and login restrictions.

In login/password authentication, we discussed the first two phases of WAN access — initial authentication and background authentication. Initial authentication is a sophisticated four-step process that develops a user-specific, session-specific signature and proof. This signature is then used by background authentication to validate incoming workstation packets. Once you've been authenticated, NetWare grants you conditional access to the WAN. Permanent access relies on login restrictions.

Login restrictions are the second layer of the NetWare 4 security model. They define what, when, where, and who gets access to the system. "What" is account and password restrictions, "when" is time restrictions, "where" is station restrictions, and "who" is Intruder Detection/Lockout.

NetWare has never been more secure. And we haven't even accessed any resources yet. The first two layers get us in, but what we do inside the "Cloud" relies on NDS and file system security. How secure do you feel now?

Layer Three: NDS Security

Welcome to the "Cloud"!

The NDS park is a great place to hang out. It has trees, swings for the kiddies, a bike trail, and external entities. Feel free to look around. Browse all day if you'd like. But don't touch anything. You haven't been secured yet.

Access to the tree is one thing; being able to do anything there is another. Until you've been granted sufficient NDS access rights, all the pretty objects are useless to you. No trees, no swings, no bike paths. Once you enter the NDS park, your ability to access leaf and container objects is determined by a sophisticated NDS security structure. At the heart of NDS security is the Access Control List (ACL). The ACL is a property of every NDS object. It defines who can access the object (trustees) and what each trustee can do with it (access rights).

This strategy poses two important questions:

- ▶ What rights do I need to do stuff?

- ▶ How do I get these rights?

These are good questions. Fortunately, I have some simple answers. First, NDS supports two types of access rights — object and property. *Object rights* define an object's trustees and control what they can do with the object. *Property rights*, on the other hand, further refine NDS security by limiting access to only specific properties of the object. Fortunately, these rights are fairly self explanatory. Browse, for instance, allows you to see an object. Hmmmm, no "brain drain" there.

So, that leaves us with an answer to the second question: "How do I get these rights?" It's a simple three-step process:

> ▶ Step One: Assigning Trustee Rights — Someone gives you specific rights to specific objects through trustee assignments, inheritance, and/or security equivalence.

> ▶ Step Two: Filtering IRF Rights — Someone else can filter certain rights if they want to.

> ▶ Step Three: Calculating Effective Rights — The result is effective rights, which define what you can actually do to the object.

As easy as A-B-C. And you thought NDS security was going to be hard — nope. It can get weird, though. As I'm sure you can imagine, the potential combination of object/property rights can be staggering — almost infinite. So, you're going to want to try to keep it under control. In this section, we'll talk about default NDS rights and how you can use the simple three-step method for limiting potential loopholes. Finally, we'll talk about NDS administration and explore Admin, distributed administrators, and "special" cases. So, without any further ado, let's get on with the show — starting with NDS access rights.

QUIZ

While establishing the credibility of Mr. Smithers' testimony, we learned a few interesting things about him. He prefers pneumonia to a cold. He likes sequoias, but not pine trees. He is facetious, but not amusing. So, the question remains, is he abstemious or sober?

(Q5-3)

UNDERSTANDING NDS ACCESS RIGHTS

Access to NDS objects is controlled by 10 different NDS access rights — sounds reasonable. These 10 rights are organized into 2 functional groups:

▸ Object rights

▸ Property rights

Let's use the famous "box analogy" to understand the difference between these two different sets of NDS access rights. Think of an NDS object as a box. Like any other three-dimensional rectangloid, the box has external characteristics. You can look at the box and describe its color, size, and shape. By describing the outside of the box, you have a good idea of the type of box it is. But you don't know anything else about it, especially what's inside the box. With object rights, you can look at the box, destroy the box, relabel the box, or create a new one. But you can't get specific information about what's inside the box — that requires property rights.

The contents of the box are similar to what's inside an NDS object — properties. In most cases, the contents of different boxes will vary. One box may contain caviar while the other contains video games. In order to see what's inside the box, you need permission to open it and look inside. With the proper rights, you can compare properties in this box with properties in other boxes, you can read the packing list, or you can change the contents of the box altogether. It all depends on which property rights you have.

If you're feeling a little boxed in, that's okay. We'll try and take it slow. But before we can move on to the three-step NDS security model, we need to explore each of these 10 rights in depth, plus you'll need to have a firm understanding of default NDS rights before you start changing things around. The default rights in NetWare 4 are very sophisticated. In many cases, they're good enough. Let's start with a closer look at object and property rights.

Object Rights

Object rights control what a trustee can do with any object. As you can see in Figure 5.12, the five object rights spell a word — BCDRS. So, what do NDS object rights have to do with dinosaurs? Absolutely nothing, but it's an easy way to remember the five rights. Just visualize *Jurassic Park* and all the sick dinosaurs. What would they do without dinosaur doctors?

F I G U R E 5.12

A Jurassic Set of Object Rights

Following is a description of the five object rights and their functions:

- Browse — Grants the right to see objects in the directory tree. With this right, you can see the outside of the box.

- Create — Grants the right to create a new object within this container. Obviously, the Create right is only available on container objects. With this right, you can create a new box.

- Delete — Grants the right to delete the object from NDS. With this right, you can throw away the box.

- Rename — Grants the right to change the name of the object, in effect changing the naming property. This is the only object right that has any impact on properties except Supervisor. With this right, you can relabel the box.

- Supervisor — Grants all access privileges. Anyone with Supervisor rights to an object has access to all its properties. The Supervisor right *can* be blocked with the Inherited Rights Filter (IRF). In effect, anyone with Supervisor rights owns the box.

Except for a few minor exceptions, object rights have no impact on properties. Remember, we're dealing with the outside of the box at this point. If you want to have control over the contents of the box, you'll need to be granted property rights.

Property Rights

Property rights control access to the information stored within an NDS object. They allow users to see, search for, and change the contents of the box. At the very minimal level, you must be a trustee of an object in order to be granted rights to its properties. As you can see in Figure 5.13, the property rights almost spell a word — SCRAW(L). In order to cure the dinosaur, you'll have to write a pretty big prescription. This involves that unique medical skill known as SCRAWling — wait until you see my signature.

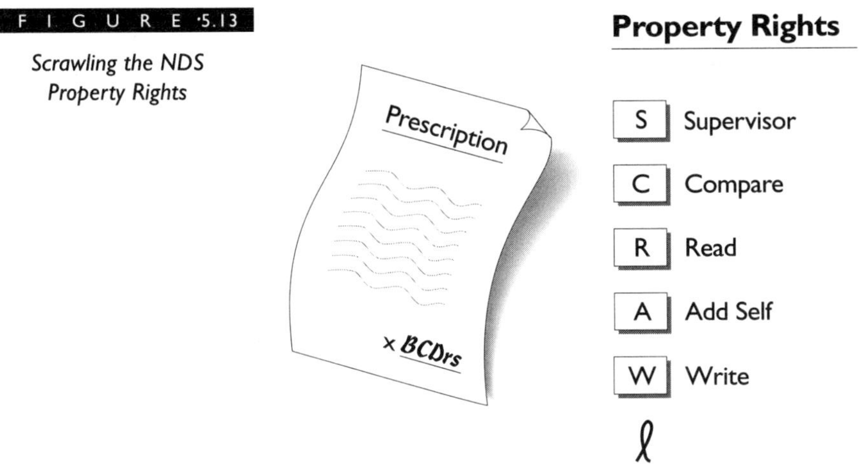

Scrawling the NDS Property Rights

Here's a description of the five NetWare 4 property rights:

- Supervisor — Grants all rights to the property. The Supervisor right *can* be blocked by an object's inherited rights filter (IRF).

- Compare — Allows you to compare any given value to the value within the property. This is analogous to saying, "I'm not going to tell you what my phone number is, but I'll let you guess at it." With the Compare right, an operation can return True or False, but will not give the value of the property. Compare is automatically granted when users have the Read property right.

- Read — Grants the right to read values of the property. This is better than Compare because it actually allows you to view the value.

▸ Add Self — Allows you to add or remove yourself as a value of a property. This right is only meaningful for properties that contain object names as values such as group membership lists and mailing lists. This right is automatically granted with the Write right.

▸ Write — Grants the right to add, change, or remove any values of the property. This is better than Add Self because it allows you to change any value, not just yourself.

▸ (l) — This is not a property right but is needed to spell a word.

Property rights can be assigned in one of two ways — All Properties and/or Selected Properties. As you can see in Figure 5.14, NWADMIN provides two choices. The All Properties option assigns the rights you choose to *all* properties for the object. A list of these properties is displayed in the Selected Properties window. The Read All Properties right selection, for example, would allow you to view the value of all the properties for a given object.

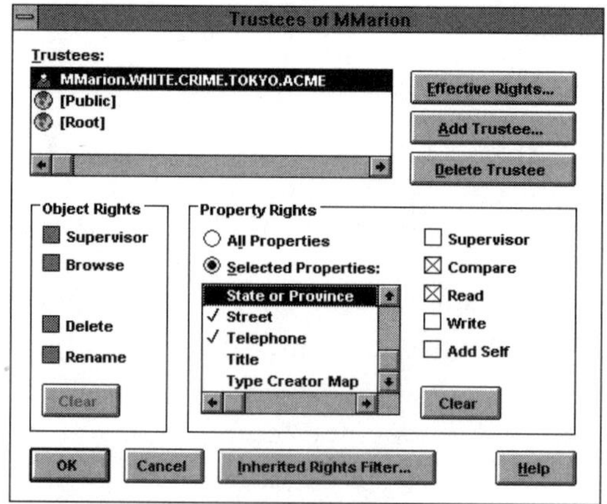

F I G U R E 5.14

Assigning Selected Property Rights in NWADMIN

The Selected Properties option, on the other hand, allows you to fine-tune NDS security for specific properties. Simply choose the right you want to assign and highlight one or more properties from the Selected Properties window. It's important to note that the list will change for each object type. Users, for example, have 55 properties, whereas groups have only 23. Finally, granting rights to selected properties overwrites anything granted through the All Properties option. This is very powerful because it allows you to get very specific with certain properties even though a general assignment already exists.

TIP

Later, in Step One of the NDS security model, we're going to learn about a concept called *inheritance*. Inheritance is based on the concept that object and property rights flow down the NDS tree from container to container to leaf objects. It's a fairly simple concept, but there's one exception you need to be aware of. Object rights and All Properties rights are inherited, but Selected Properties rights are not. This means rights you assign to selected properties work with the specific object only — they do not flow down the tree. Keep this in the back of your mind when we get to inheritance later.

Now that you understand the 10 different NDS access rights, it's time to start our three-step model. Before we do, however, let's take a detailed look at default NDS security. This discussion will help you determine when, where, and if you need to assign additional object and property rights.

Default NDS Rights

You have to start somewhere, and default NDS rights are a great place. As I said earlier, default NetWare 4 security is extremely sophisticated. In many cases, it's enough. Every time a Server and/or User object is created, NetWare 4 assigns a variety of object and property rights to them. Before you move on to the three-step model, you'll want to learn what these defaults are in case you can use them. There's no sense in re-inventing the wheel. Use NetWare 4's default NDS rights as a foundation and build from there.

NetWare 4 assigns default NDS rights during three major events:

- ▸ Initial NDS installation

- ▸ File server installation

- ▸ User creation

Let's take a closer look.

Initial NDS Installation

When NDS is installed on the very first server, two key objects are created — [Root] and Admin. [Root] represents the very top of the NDS tree (the Earth) and Admin has Supervisor control over the entire network. Incidentally, Admin is placed in the Organization level of the first server's context. The following default rights are granted when NDS is first installed:

- Admin — Granted Supervisor [S] object rights to [Root]. This allows the first User object to administer the entire NDS tree. Distributed administrators can be created using supplemental rights. We'll take a look at this later in the chapter.

- [Public] — A special system-owned trustee object also created at initial installation. Every object in the NDS tree inherits the rights of [Public]. This is analogous to the EVERYONE group in NetWare 3. By default, [Public] is granted Browse [B] object rights to [Root]. This allows every object in the NDS tree to see every other object.

REAL WORLD

A special trustee called [Public] is created during initial NDS installation and granted Browse [B] object rights to the [Root]. This trustee establishes a global assignment for all objects. Think of it as a minimum trustee assignment. There's one problem, though — users do not have to be logged in to inherit the rights of [Public]. They simply need to be *attached*.

Therefore, any hacker with a notebook and VLMs can attach to your network and download the entire NDS tree. Consider removing [Public] as a trustee of the [Root] object and assign each Organization or Organizational Unit container Browse [B] rights to itself. This will allow users to see their portion of the NDS tree and not the entire tree. But, more importantly, users must be logged in (not just attached) to inherit these rights.

File Server Installation

When a new file server is installed in NDS, default rights are given to the creator of the server object, the server itself, and [Public]. Remember, in order to create a server object, you must have Supervisor object rights to that portion of the tree. By default, INSTALL.NLM asks for the Admin password. If Admin doesn't exist or has been locked out of this portion of the tree, a container administrator's username and password is sufficient. In either case, this person is known as the *Creator*. Let's take a look at the default rights assigned during server installation.

▸ Creator — Either Admin or a container administrator. By default, this user is granted Supervisor [S] object rights to the server. This allows Admin or the container administrator to manage the server object.

▸ Server — The server itself is granted Supervisor [S] object rights to itself. This allows the server to modify the parameters of its own object. Of course, in order for this to occur, the server would have to sprout arms.

▸ [Public] — Granted the Read [R] property right to a specific server property — Messaging Server. This allows any network client to identify the messaging server assigned to this file server. As you'll see in Chapter 6, this is required for MHS Services for NetWare 4.

TIP

Layers Three and Four of the NetWare 4 security model are completely independent. This means rights assigned at the NDS level do *not* apply to the file system. These rights only apply to network resources like printers, users, and servers. There is, of course, one exception. If you grant anybody Supervisor [S] object rights to a Server object, they also inherit Supervisor file system rights to the Root of all volumes on that server. Therefore, by default, the creator of a server gets all rights to its NDS properties and file system. If you're lucky, this could be you.

User Creation

When you create a new User object in NDS, certain necessary rights are granted automatically. These rights are granted to provide the user with some degree of access to WAN resources. Remember, default NDS rights provide a very good beginning. In many cases, these rights are enough for users to be productive. In general, the User object receives enough rights to modify its own login script and print job configurations. If you don't like this idea, consider revoking these rights. Let's take a closer look:

- User — Each user is granted three sets of property rights by default. First, he/she is granted the Read [R] right to All Properties. This allows users to view information about themselves. Next, he/she is granted the Read and Write [RW] property rights to two selected properties — Login Script and Print Job Configuration. This allows users to execute and change their own User script and/or print job configurations. As you will learn in Chapter 6, this is a moot point since User login scripts are avoided at all costs. Finally, an obvious object right assignment is missing — Browse [B] rights to yourself. While this is not explicitly granted at user creation, the right is inherited from initial NDS installation. Remember, [Public] is granted Browse [B] rights to the [Root], and, therefore, all users can see all objects including themselves.

- [Root] — Granted the Read [R] property right to two specific user properties — Network Address and Group Membership. This allows anyone in the tree to identify the user's network address, location, and any groups he/she belongs to.

- [Public] — Granted the Read [R] property right to a selected user property — Default Server. This allows anyone to determine the default server for this user. The difference between the [Public] and [Root] assignment is that [Public] rights are granted upon attaching, where [Root] rights imply a valid login authentication.

That completes our discussion of the default NDS rights. Refer to Table 5.1 for a summary. Hopefully, you've gained an appreciation for the sophistication of NetWare 4 default security. As you can see, users and servers are well taken care of. The only additional security you'll need to add are for special container administrators, traveling users, or groups. We'll discuss these special NDS circumstances later in the chapter.

But for now, let's put our understanding of object, property, and default rights to the test. Let's learn the simple three-step model for assigning NDS security:

- ► Step One: Assigning trustee rights

- ► Step Two: Filtering IRF Rights

- ► Step Three: Calculating effective rights

T A B L E   5.1

Default NDS Security Summary

NDS EVENT	TRUSTEE	DEFAULT RIGHTS
Initial NDS installation	Admin	[S] — Supervisor object rights to [Root]
	[Public]	[B] — Browse object rights to [Root]
File server installation	Creator	[S] — Supervisor object rights to server
	Server	[S] — Supervisor object rights to self
	[Public]	[R] — Read right to selected server property (Messaging Server)
User creation	User	[R] — Read right to All Properties
		[RW] — Read and Write rights to selected user property (Login Script)
		[RW] — Read and Write rights to selected user property (Print Job Configuration)
	[Root]	[R] — Read right to two selected user properties (Network Address and Group Membership)
	[Public]	[R] — Read right to a selected user property (Default Server)

ZEN

*"When I took your father's name, I took everything that came with it —
including his DNA!"*

Marge Simpson

STEP ONE: ASSIGNING TRUSTEE RIGHTS

I keep talking about how simple the NDS security model is — as easy as 1-2-3.
Well, now I get a chance to prove it. A lot has been written about NDS security and
most of it is intimidating. Granted, there are a lot of complexities involved, but if
you approach it with an open mind, everything falls into place. So far we've talked
about object and property rights. Understanding these rights is a prerequisite to
building an NDS security model. But it's certainly not enough. Now you have to
learn how to implement these rights in the ACME NDS tree.

Step One deals with assigning these rights. In many cases, this is enough. You
only need Steps Two and Three under special circumstances. NDS rights can be
assigned in one of three ways:

- ► Trustee assignments

- ► Inheritance

- ► Security equivalence

Trustee assignments involve work — this is bad, of course, since our goal is to
minimize the amount of work we do. But you have to start somewhere. Trustee
assignments are granted using NWADMIN, NETADMIN, and/or RIGHTS.
Inheritance, on the other hand, doesn't involve work — this is good. Inheritance
happens automatically when you assign trustee rights at the container level. Just
like water flowing down a mountain, trustee rights flow down the NDS tree —
from top to bottom. The beauty of this feature is that you can assign sweeping
rights for large groups of users with a single trustee assignment.

Finally, security equivalence gives us the added flexibility we need in today's
modern world. There are a variety of security equivalence strategies including
ancestral inheritance (AI), Organizational Roles, Groups, and Directory Map objects.

You'll learn that security equivalence is a way of augmenting the other two trustee assignment strategies. Let's take a closer look at Step One, starting with trustee assignments.

Trustee Assignments

You have to start somewhere and Step One starts with work. A trustee is any NDS object with rights to any other object. Trustees are tracked through the ACL (Access Control List) property. Every object has an ACL property, and the ACL lists the trustees of that object and the rights they have. NetWare 4 supports a variety of trustees, including:

▶ User — A leaf object in the NDS tree. It represents a person with access to network resources. Individual users can be assigned specific NDS rights through the User trustee type.

▶ Group — A leaf object with a membership list. The membership list includes users from anywhere in the NDS tree. When NDS rights need to be assigned to unrelated users (in different containers), the group object is a great option. Rights granted to a group object are passed to all members of the group.

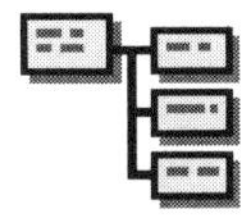

▶ Container — All container objects are considered "natural groups" and can be used to assign NDS rights to multiple trustees. If you make any container object a trustee of any other object, all users and subcontainers inherit those same rights.

▶ Organizational Role — A leaf object much like groups, except users are identified as occupants. This object is used to specify a particular role in the organization and not a group of unrelated users. Container administrators, for example, inherit the rights from the Organizational Role they occupy.

▶ [Public] — A special system-owned trustee. Rights granted to [Public] are passed to every object connected to the network. This means users do not have to be logged in order to inherit [Public] rights. Be very careful when using the [Public] trustee.

Once you identify *who* is going to get the rights, you have to determine *what* rights you're going to give them and *where* the rights will be assigned. *What* consists of any of the 10 object and property rights — simple. *Where* can be any object in the NDS tree — also simple. Take Figure 5.15, for example. As you can see, Sherlock Holmes is granted all object rights to the .OU=TOKYO.O=ACME container. In the figure, we have satisfied all three of the trustee assignment elements — who, what, and where.

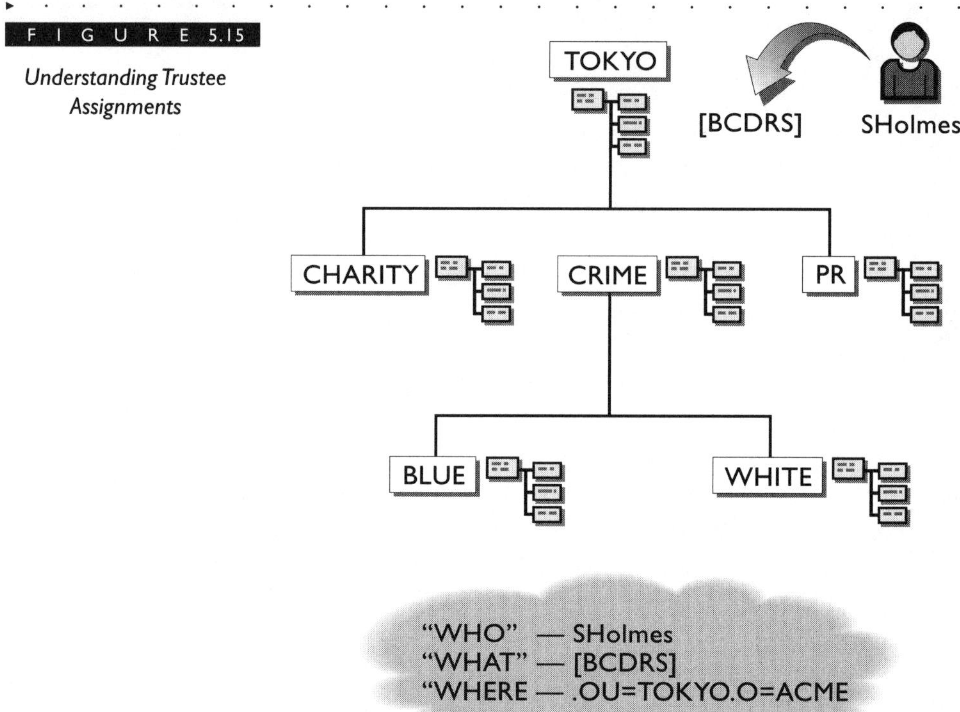

F I G U R E 5.15

Understanding Trustee Assignments

So, how is this accomplished in NWADMIN? It depends on your point of view. You have two choices:

▶ Rights to Other Objects — This is from Sherlock Holmes's point of view.

▶ Trustees of this Object — This is from OU=TOKYO's point of view.

It really doesn't matter which option you choose. You can either assign rights from the user's point of view or the object's point of view. In the first example, we assign security from Sherlock Holmes' point of view. In NWADMIN, highlight SHolmes and click on the right mouse button. An abbreviated dialogue box appears. As you can see in Figure 5.16, there are two security options. In this case, we're interested in Rights to Other Objects.

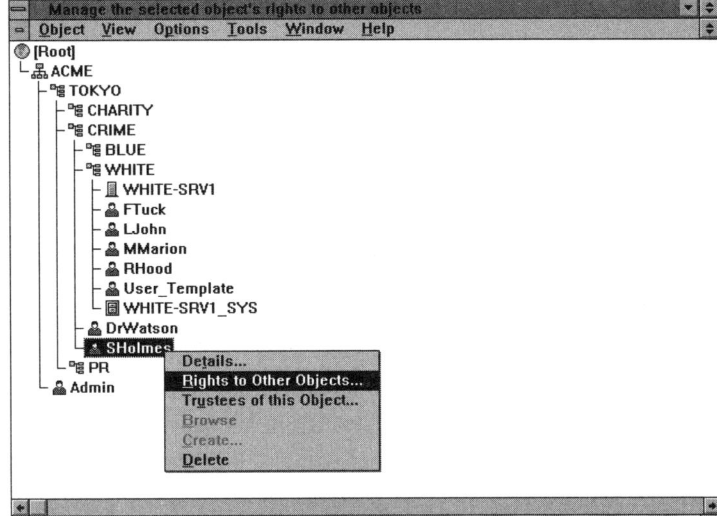

FIGURE 5.16

NWADMIN Security Window for SHolmes

The SHolmes menu appears. Figure 5.17 shows the security window from Sherlock Holmes' point of view. As you can see, he has been granted all object rights to the TOKYO Organizational Unit. Specifically, the Supervisor object right implies the Supervisor property rights to All Properties. This was accomplished using the "Add assignment" button.

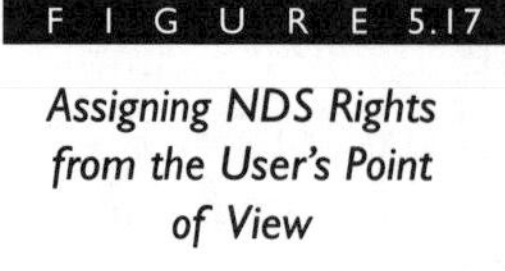

Assigning NDS Rights from the User's Point of View

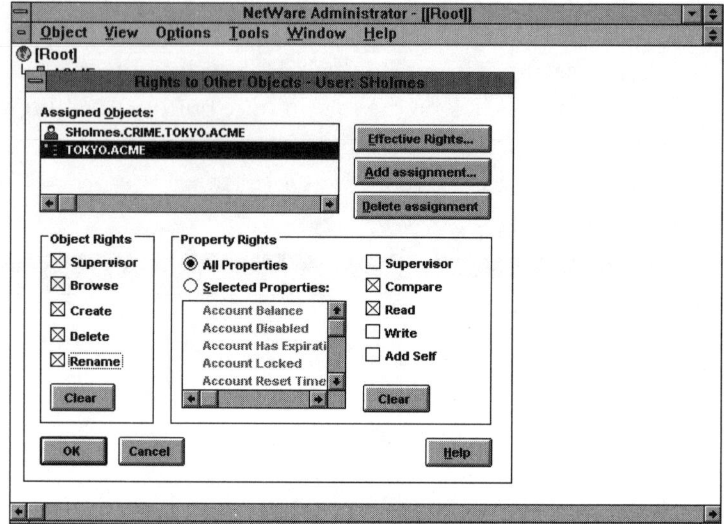

The second option allows you to assign NDS rights from TOKYO's point of view. In this case, you would select OU=TOKYO.O=ACME from the Browse window and click on the right mouse button. The same window will appear (as shown in Figure 5.16). This time, though, choose Trustees of this Object. Figure 5.18 shows the NDS security window from TOKYO's point of view. Notice the default trustees. In addition, SHolmes has been added with all object and property rights. This was accomplished using the "Add Trustee" button.

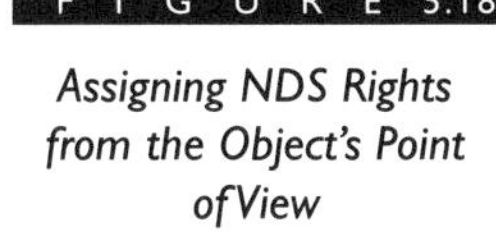

*Assigning NDS Rights
from the Object's Point
of View*

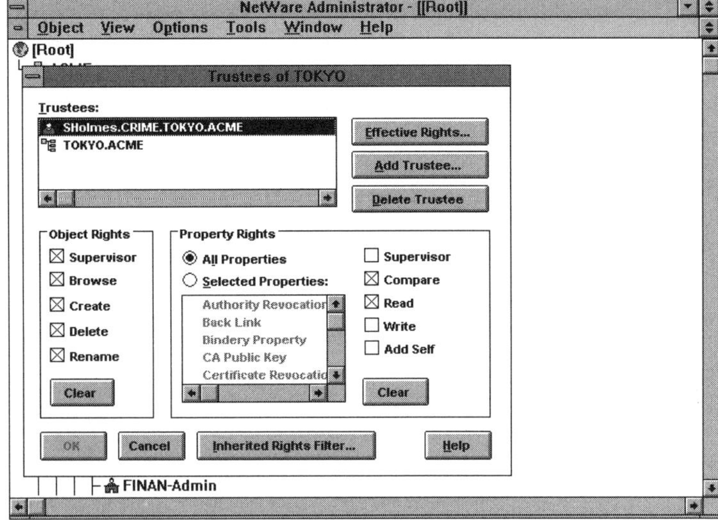

There you have it. As you can see, it doesn't matter how we assign trustee rights. Both methods accomplish the same thing — Sherlock Holmes (who) is granted [BCDRS] object rights (what) to .OU=TOKYO.O=ACME (where). I told you trustee assignments would be simple. Now that we've explored the "work" part, let's take a closer look at inheritance — the "no work" part.

Inheritance

NDS rights can also be assigned through inheritance. This is an automatic side effect of trustee assignments. As you can see in Figure 5.19, Sherlock Holmes got a lot more than he bargained for. When you assigned him the [BCDRS] object rights to .OU=TOKYO.O=ACME, he actually inherited these rights for all containers and objects underneath TOKYO as well. Now he has all object rights to all containers and all objects in that portion of the tree — this might not be a good thing.

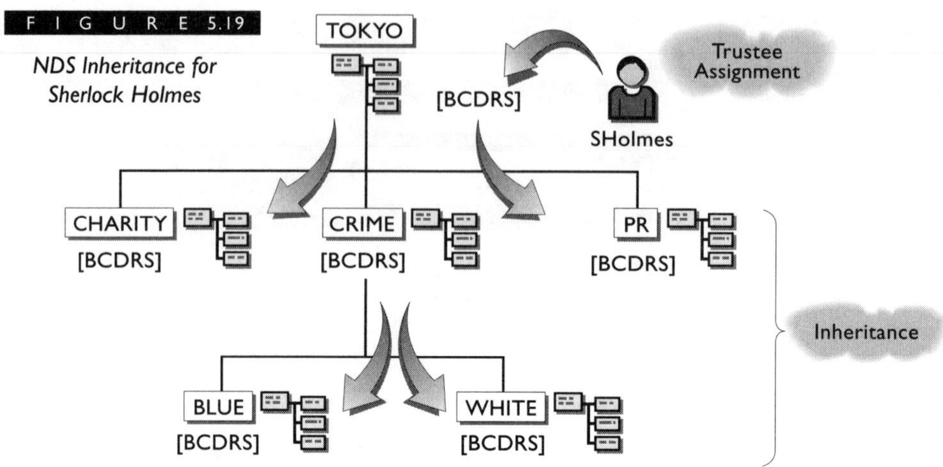

F I G U R E 5.19

NDS Inheritance for Sherlock Holmes

As you recall from our ACME overview in Chapter 3, Sherlock Holmes heads up the Crime Fighting division. He probably shouldn't have Supervisor object rights to Charity and PR. Fortunately, we can rectify the situation. NetWare 4 provides two methods for overriding inheritance:

▸ New trustee assignment — Trustee assignments override inherited rights. If we assigned SHolmes Browse [B] rights to Charity and PR, he would lose his inheritance in these containers. The new trustee assignment would become his effective rights and inheritance within these containers would reflect the changes.

▸ Inherited Rights Filter (IRF) — The IRF is much more serious. It overrides inherited rights for all objects in the tree. A [B] filter on Charity and PR wouldn't allow anybody to inherit [CDRS] including SHolmes. So who manages these containers? What about SirKay and BThomas? Stay tuned for the answer.

Inheritance is a great thing. It allows you to assign sweeping NDS object rights with minimal effort. Remember, as a CNA, "work" is a bad word. As far as property rights go, only one type is inherited. Remember, there are two ways of assigning property rights — All Properties or Selected Properties. The rights assigned using the All Properties option are inherited. Rights assigned to Selected Properties are not. Combine this with what we learned about trustee assignments and we could have an effective strategy for property customization.

Here's an example. Let's assume Maid Marion is shy as well (just like Leia). She's a user in the .OU=WHITE.OU=CRIME.OU=TOKYO.O=ACME container. She doesn't want Sherlock Holmes to see any of her properties except Telephone and Postal Address. This can be a problem since he inherits all rights from his [BCDRS] assignment to the TOKYO container. Fortunately, as a CNA, you have a solution. You simply assign SHolmes the Read [R] property right to Maid Marion's Selected Properties — Telephone and Postal Address. This trustee assignment overrides his inheritance through All Properties. Voilà, Maid Marion is safe. (See Figure 5.20.)

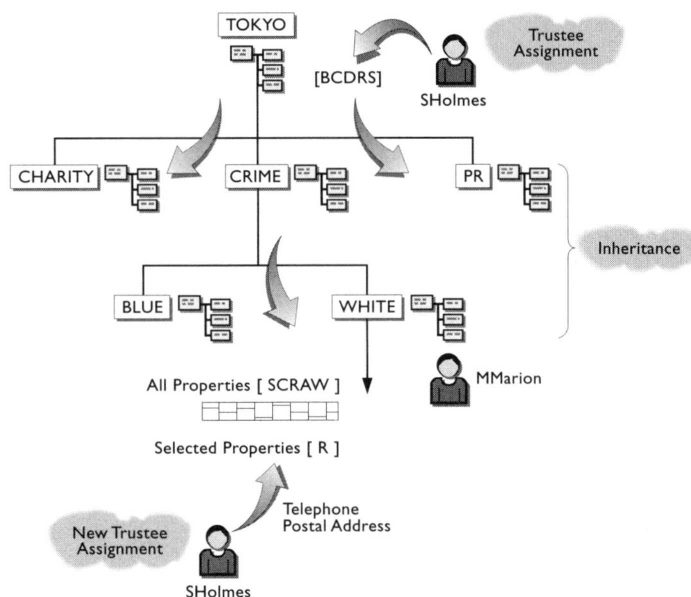

F I G U R E 5.20

Protecting Maid Marion with a New Trustee Assignment

Trustee assignments and inheritance are the two main strategies of Step One. But special situations may arise when you need something more. This is where security equivalence comes in. Let's take a closer look.

Security Equivalence

If trustee assignments or inheritance aren't quite getting the job done, security equivalence may be the answer. Security equivalence simply states "one object is equivalent to another with respect to NDS rights." Users, for example, are security equivalent to their parent container. Security equivalence is different from inheritance in that it operates at the trustee assignment level. Please do not confuse the two. Security equivalence applies when an object is made equivalent to another object's explicit trustee assignments. Therefore, security equivalence overrides the IRF.

NetWare 4 provides four strategies for security equivalences:

▸ Ancestral inheritance (AI)

▸ Organizational Role

▸ Groups

▸ Directory Map objects

Ancestral Inheritance (AI)

Ancestral inheritance (AI) is a very cool term. But, before you get too caught up in it, you should know a little secret — it doesn't really mean anything. AI simply implies that an object is security equivalent to its ancestor (parent container). This means any rights you assign to an NDS container are absorbed by all the objects in the container. This is not inheritance; this is security equivalence. Therefore, AI can get very strange. Earlier we learned that containers can be trustees and they're thought of as "natural groups." This is true. But, remember, any rights that you assign to a container are implicitly assigned to all objects within the container. For example, suppose we assigned OU=CRIME [BCDRS] rights to TOKYO instead of SHolmes (see Figure 5.19). Now, both users in OU=CRIME — Sherlock Holmes and Dr. Watson — gain the same trustee assignments and inheritance shown in Figure 5.19. Pretty simple.

Well, that's not all. Not only do the objects in OU=CRIME absorb its trustee assignments, but all objects underneath CRIME as well! This means Maid Marion, Robin Hood, and all their friends would get the same trustee assignments as Sherlock Holmes and Dr. Watson. Wow. This concept is also called implied security equivalence. However tempting it is, avoid AI unless you know what you're doing.

> **REAL WORLD**
>
> AI allows you to make broad trustee assignments at high levels in the tree. For example, you could place a mail server at O=ACME and grant the container rights to it. Because of AI, all objects in the ACME organization will have immediate access to the mail server. This also applies to file system rights. You could place all the CRIME files on a single server in the OU=CRIME container. Then assign appropriate file system rights to OU=CRIME. Because of AI, all users in the CRIME division would have immediate access to the central server.

Organizational Role

Organizational Roles are another type of security equivalence. These special NDS objects are designed as task identifiers. Jobs that require multiple temporary users are excellent candidates for Organizational Roles. Postmaster, for example, is a job that can be assigned to multiple users on a rotating basis. When a user is performing the Postmaster duties, he/she will need special NDS and file system rights. Let's say the White Collar Crime Division has a Postmaster OR that changes occupants every three months. This person needs special NDS security to e-mail objects and the file system. Instead of continually moving trustee assignments around, you can define security once for the Organizational Role. Then switch occupants. Let's say it's Little John's turn, for example. When you remove Maid Marion from the Postmaster OR and replace her with LJohn, he immediately absorbs the NDS security of that object. Suddenly, Little John has all the security he needs to perform Postmaster duties. An elegant solution. Later we'll explore the Organizational Role as one solution for creating distributed administrators. For now, let's move on to the next security equivalence option — Groups.

Groups

As we learned earlier, groups were another trustee type for assigning NDS rights. This allows us to distribute similar rights to unrelated users. That is, users not within the same area of the NDS tree. First, create a group, then assign it rights, and finally add members. This is similar to the Organizational Role object in that it works on the security equivalence concept. Members of any group absorb (not inherit) rights assigned to the host Group object. Groups also differ from AI containers in that they don't involve "implied inheritance." Rights assigned to groups only apply to specific members of the group. And, as we all know, users can be easily removed from groups.

Directory Map Objects

In very special circumstances, security equivalence can be used to facilitate Directory Map objects. As we learned in Chapter 4, these objects allow us to map directory paths to a centralized object instead of to a physical location. To accomplish this, you must first create a Directory Map object that points to a physical location in the file system. Then create a logical drive pointer to the Directory Map object using the MAP command. There's one problem with this scenario: The drive mapping doesn't work until the user is assigned explicit or inherited file system rights to the physical directory. This involves a lot of planning, a lot of work, and some careful tracking. An easier solution would involve assigning the file system rights to the Directory Map object itself, then making each user a security equivalent of the NDS object. This makes security assignments much clearer.

In summary, when you create a Directory Map object, be sure to assign adequate file system rights to its physical directory. Then when you use the MAP command to create logical pointers, be sure to assign the host user security equivalence to the Directory Map object. Believe me, this will make drive mapping and security much easier to manage. Really!

There you have it — Step One. Don't get discouraged — this is the tricky part. Once you assign NDS rights, the rest takes care of itself. In Step One, we learned there are three different ways of assigning rights to NDS trustees — trustee assignments, inheritance, and security equivalence. We also learned there are a variety of different trustee types and to be aware of ancestral inheritance (implied security equivalence). The good news is, most of your work stops here. Only in special cases do you need to go on to Steps Two and Three. Of course, you remember Murphy's Law Number 342 — special cases will appear just when you least expect them. So, in honor of Murphy and to decrease your stress level, let's take a quick look at Steps Two and Three.

ZEN

"DNA.... Positive ID....Those won't hold up in any court. Run Dad!"

Bart Simpson

STEP TWO: FILTERING IRF RIGHTS

Earlier we learned there are two ways of blocking unwanted inherited rights:

- New trustee assignments

- Inherited rights filter (IRF)

We propose a problem with Sherlock Holmes' inheritance. Since he's been assigned [BCDRS] object rights to .OU=TOKYO.O=ACME, he becomes distributed administrator of that entire section of the tree — this is bad. Sherlock Holmes is responsible for the Crime Fighting division. He has no authority over Charity or PR. However, his inheritance model shows [BCDRS] object rights to both OU=CHARITY and OU=PR (see Figure 5.19). We're going to have to do something about this right away.

Welcome to planet IRF. NetWare 4 includes an inherited rights filter that blocks inherited rights at any point in the tree. Right off the bat, you'll to need to understand two very important points about how the IRF works:

- It's an inclusive filter, which means the rights that are in the filter are the ones that are allowed to pass through.

- The IRF applies to everyone in the NDS tree. Once you've assigned an IRF to a container, everyone is blocked, including Admin.

TIP

The Supervisor object right can be blocked by an NDS IRF. It cannot be blocked, however, by an IRF in the file system. If you attempt to block the Supervisor [S] right with an IRF, NWADMIN will first require you to make an explicit Supervisor [S] trustee assignment to someone else (assuming, of course, that one does not already exist). This is so that access to that portion of the tree is not permanently removed. Imagine how much fun it would be if the Supervisor object right was filtered for everybody. Does the term _reinstall_ mean anything to you?

The IRF can be used to block inheritance of either object rights or property rights assigned through the All Properties option. Remember, Selected Properties aren't inherited. Figure 5.21 shows how the IRF can be used to solve our Sherlock Holmes problem. We create an inclusive IRF of [B] to block everything but the Browse right. His inheritance in OU=CRIME, however, remains unaffected.

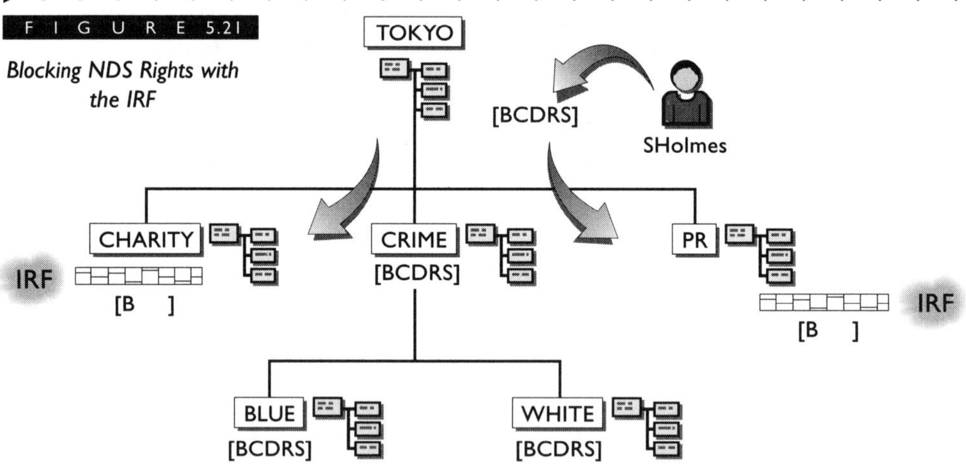

FIGURE 5.21

Blocking NDS Rights with the IRF

So, how do we assign an IRF? Once again, NWADMIN is our friend. Earlier we learned that trustee assignments can be assigned in one of two ways — "Rights to other objects" and "Trustees of this object." IRFs are accomplished using one of these two choices. Can you figure out which one? Correct — it's "Trustees of this object." Remember, IRFs are host-object specific. They work from the host's point of view and apply to every object in the NDS tree. Figure 5.22 shows how to get to the IRF input screen for OU=PR. Once you get there, downward arrows will appear next to each rights box. These differentiate IRF rights from trustee assignments. Anywhere you see a downward arrow, you can assume it's an IRF filter.

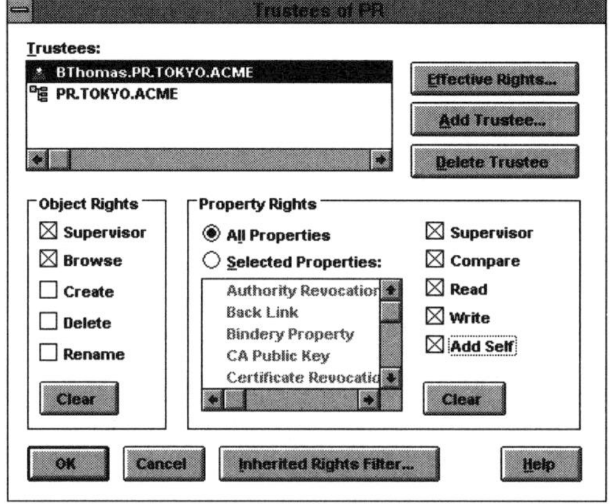

FIGURE 5.22

Filtering NDS Rights in NWADMIN

REAL WORLD

Even though the IRF input window in NWADMIN gives you the option of choosing Selected Properties, it's not a feasible configuration. Why? Because Selected Properties are *not* inherited. Therefore, the IRF is useless. Please don't let the utility confuse you. That's my job.

If the IRF applies to all objects in the tree, who is going to administer the OU=CHARITY and OU=PR containers? As you can see in Figure 5.21, nobody can have the [CDRS] object rights. Fortunately, trustee assignments override the IRF. Remember, the "I" in IRF stands for "inherited." It only works on inherited rights. Figure 5.23 introduces two new players — SirKay (the administrator of OU=CHARITY) and BThomas (the administrator of OU=PR). We will simply assign BThomas the [BCDRS] object rights to OU=PR. Now he is the container administrator for this section of the tree and everyone else, including Sherlock Holmes and Admin, has been locked out. The same holds true for SirKay and OU=CHARITY.

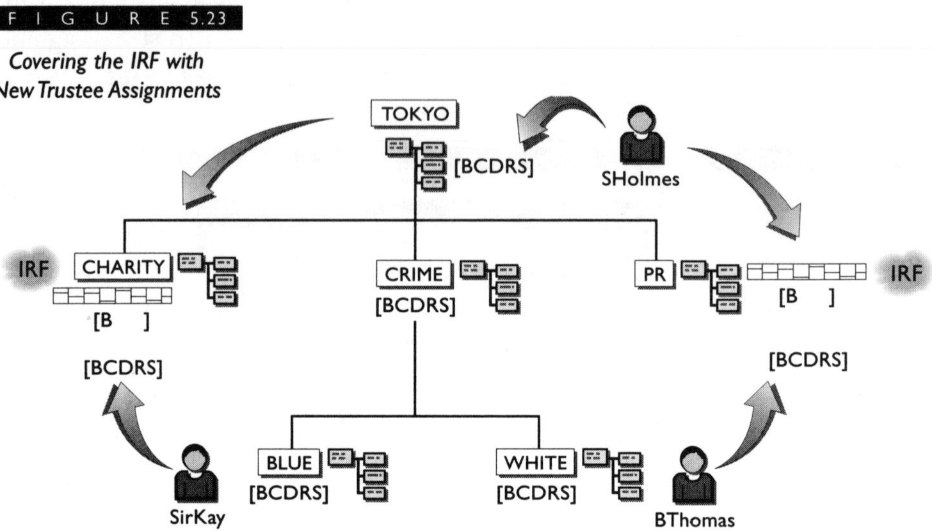

F I G U R E 5.23

Covering the IRF with New Trustee Assignments

So, let me ask you — which activity occurs first? The IRF or the new trustee assignment? Correct, the new trustee assignment. Remember, NWADMIN will *not* allow us to set an IRF for OU=PR until someone else has explicitly been granted Supervisor privileges. So, first we assign BThomas [BCDRS] privileges, then we set the IRF to [B].

Good work.

So, what's the bottom line? What can Sherlock Holmes *really* do in the TOKYO portion of the tree? "It's elementary, my dear Watson, elementary." More accurately, it's Step Three: calculating effective rights.

STEP THREE: CALCULATING EFFECTIVE RIGHTS

Effective rights are the bottom line. This is the culmination of our three-step process. In Step One, we assign the rights. In Step Two, we filter the rights. In Step Three, we calculate exactly what the rights are.

Calculating effective rights is about as simple as modern math. Any object's effective rights are the combination of NDS privileges received through any of the following:

- Trustee assignments made to the user

- Inheritance minus rights blocked by the IRF

- Rights granted to the special [Public] trustee

- Security equivalences to parent containers, groups, or Organizational Roles

I don't know if you've ever done modern math, but it's ugly. It would be easy if any of the assignments shown above canceled out the others. But, unfortunately, life isn't easy. These assignments work in combination with each other. Consider it modern math in the 7th Dimension.

Let's start with a simple example. Refer to Figure 5.24. In this first example, Sherlock Holmes is assigned [BCDRS] object rights to OU=CRIME. On the right side of the figure, we've created an effective rights calculation worksheet. This is an *effective* (pun intended) tool for helping you get through modern math. You can create one at home with paper, a pencil, and a ruler.

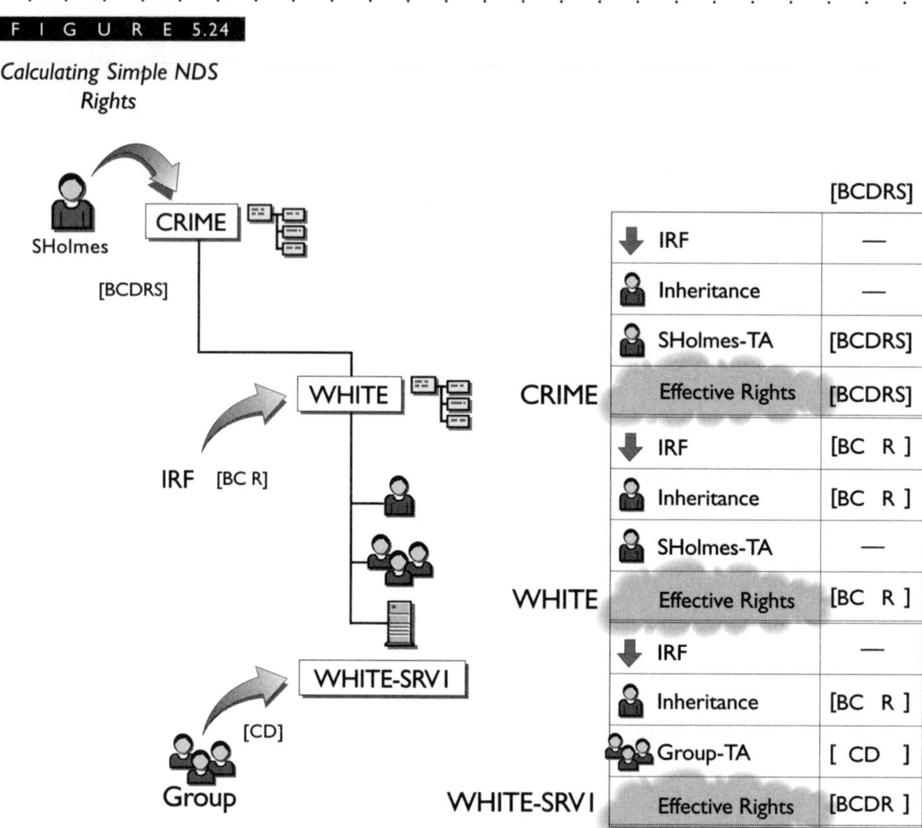

It starts with SHolmes' trustee assignment to OU=CRIME. Since there's no inheritance or IRF involved, his effective rights in this container are the same. Those effective rights become inherited rights in all subcontainers — one of which is OU=WHITE. To further complicate things, there's an IRF of [BCR] on the WHITE container. Since the IRF blocks [DS], Sherlock Holmes' inherited rights become [BCR]. With no other trustee assignments, his effective rights in OU=WHITE are the same — [BCR].

Finally, we arrive at the WHITE-SRV1 server object. It has no IRF so SHolmes' inherited rights are equal to the effective rights of the WHITE container — [BCR]. In addition, one of Sherlock Holmes' groups is assigned the [CD] object rights to the WHITE-SRV1 server. These rights combine with his inherited rights to create ultimate effective rights of [BCDR] for the server object. You see, that wasn't so hard. In this simple example, we had a limited number of different elements — one user trustee assignment, one group trustee assignment, and one IRF. Of course, the world is not always this simple. Now let's take a look at a more complex example.

Just when you think you understand it, they throw something like this at you. In this example (see Figure 5.25), there's one user assignment, one group trustee, an Organizational Role equivalent, AI, and three IRFs. Hold on to your hat!

Calculating Complex NDS Rights

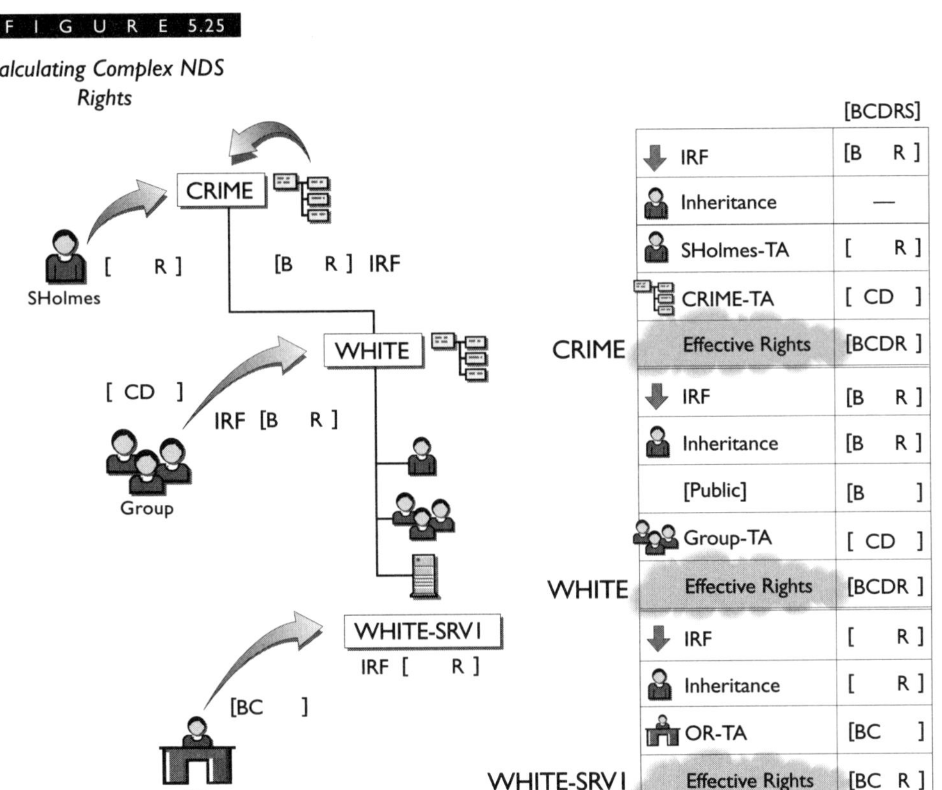

		[BCDRS]
	IRF	[B R]
	Inheritance	—
	SHolmes-TA	[R]
	CRIME-TA	[CD]
CRIME	Effective Rights	[BCDR]
	IRF	[B R]
	Inheritance	[B R]
	[Public]	[B]
	Group-TA	[CD]
WHITE	Effective Rights	[BCDR]
	IRF	[R]
	Inheritance	[R]
	OR-TA	[BC]
WHITE-SRV1	Effective Rights	[BC R]

Once again, we're going to use the effective rights calculation worksheet in Figure 5.25. As before, it begins with Sherlock Holmes at the OU=CRIME container — trustee assignment of [R]. In addition, the container is granted [CD] rights to itself. Since Sherlock Holmes lives in this context, he gains an ancestral inheritance of

[CD]. This, combined with his user assignment, gives the effective rights [CDR]. In this case, the IRF is useless — simple window dressing. Remember, trustee assignments override the IRF.

Sherlock Holmes's effective rights in OU=CRIME become his inherited rights in OU=WHITE. The IRF, however, blocks [CDS] so his inheritance becomes [R]. This combines with a group trustee assignment of [CD] to give the effective rights [CDR]. But, wait a minute, we're not done. Remember, [Public] is granted [B] rights to the [Root]. Assuming no other IRFs, these rights are inherited throughout the tree. Since the OU=WHITE IRF allows [B], SHolmes gets it as well. Therefore, his real effective rights in OU=WHITE become [BCDR].

The above effective rights pass through the [R] filter at WHITE-SRV1. These inherited rights combined with his OR equivalence give effective rights of [BCR] at the WHITE-SRV1 server object. Piece of cake.

As you can see, effective rights get very hairy very quickly — just like modern math in the 7th Dimension. This is probably because there're so many forces at work. Remember, effective rights are the combination of trustee assignments, inheritance, [Public], and security equivalence. The default NDS rights are looking better and better all the time.

There you have it. The simple three-step NDS security model:

▶ Step One: Assigning NDS Rights — through trustee assignments, inheritance, and/or security equivalence.

▶ Step Two: Filtering IRF Rights — The inclusive filter allows you to block inherited rights. Remember to avoid isolating sections of the tree by using new trustee assignments with IRFs.

▶ Step Three: Calculating Effective Rights — just like modern math in the 7th Dimension.

Now I bet you're glad you made it through the simple steps of NDS security. Fortunately, there's a sophisticated foundation of NDS default rights to start from. And Steps Two and Three are optional. Your security system doesn't need to be this complex, but in case it is, you have *Novell's CNA Study Guide for NetWare 4.1* to fall back on.

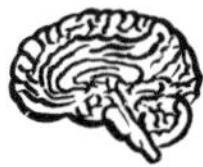

THE BRAIN

For more expert tips on NDS rights, see "Designing NetWare 4.x Security" in the November 1993 Novell Application Notes.

Before we move on to the Fourth Layer of the NetWare security model (file system access rights), let's spend a few moments exploring NDS administration. These are some supplemental strategies to help you deal with the daily grind of NDS security management.

QUIZ

OK, Bart. To prove your innocence, tell me: What is the English word most often pronounced wrong?

(Q5-4)

NDS ADMINISTRATION

NDS security is a daunting task. Don't feel like you have to accomplish it all alone. The advantages of NDS are that it enables you to section off certain areas of the network and delegate network administration tasks. You can, for example, delegate portions of the tree to distributed container administrators. On the other hand, what if it's a very highly secured government installation? You may only be involved in setting up the network. The daily administration tasks may be accomplished by a high-security workgroup.

NDS allows you to approach administration in one of two ways:

- ▸ Central administration

- ▸ Distributed administration

Central administration means you have only one user (Admin) with Supervisor rights to the entire tree. This is the NetWare 4 default. Distributed administration, on the other hand, allows you to designate users with Supervisor rights to branches of the directory tree. This container administrator can either work in conjunction with Admin or replace him/her for that portion of the tree. Let's take a closer look.

Admin

The user Admin is created during installation and initially has all rights to manage NDS. As you saw in our earlier discussion, Admin is granted the [S] object right to the [Root] by default. He/she consequently inherits all rights to the rest of the tree unless an IRF is applied. These rights also extend into NetWare 4 file systems unless blocked by an IRF in the NDS tree.

Centralized administration is appropriate for small organizations or large implementations with a central MIS department. Some tasks that could easily be centrally administered include:

- Naming the Directory tree

- Installing the first server

- Creating the top layers of the NDS tree

- Partition management and synchronization

- Assigning container administrators

It may be difficult for one person to administer the entire tree. A central Admin may not be able to meet the daily requests of user creation, file system rights, login scripts, and so on. Therefore, you may consider assigning container administrators for busy portions of the tree.

TIP

The Admin user has few special properties beyond [S] rights to the [Root]. This user can be deleted, replaced, or generally abused. This is unlike the special Supervisor account from previous versions of NetWare. The moral of the story is, "Don't get delusions of grandeur if you log in as Admin."

Distributed Administrators

Distributed administration means that designated users are given enough NDS rights to manage distributed branches of the NDS tree. This special type of user is often referred to as a container administrator. Distributed administration tends to allow you to respond to users' needs more quickly, especially in a large implementation. The following tasks can be distributed:

▸ Creating user accounts

▸ Creating and configuring print services

▸ Backing up and restoring data

▸ Assigning file system trustees

▸ Installing additional servers

▸ Creating workgroup managers

Of course, the optimum administrative strategy combines a central Admin with a few distributed administrators. As we saw in our earlier discussion, there are two ways of creating distributed administrators — IRF/new trustee assignments and Organizational Role. If only one person will administer a container, consider using the first option. Otherwise, Organizational Roles can act as a host to rotating administrators. Remember our Postmaster example.

REAL WORLD

There is a third way of creating distributed administrations — security equivalence. You can create a single container administrator and then make other users security equivalent to that object. This is not recommended, however. If you happen to delete the host administrator, all security equivalent users lose their rights. If the host was an exclusive container administrator, you've just lost all administrative control over a section of the tree. Does the term *reinstall* mean anything to you?

As we saw in an earlier example, it's possible to create an exclusive container administrator. Refer back to Figure 5.23. When the IRF was used to block all rights in the PR container, all administrators, including Admin, were locked out. Then BThomas was granted [BCDRS] object rights — thus making him an exclusive container administrator. Remember, NWADMIN requires you to make the trustee assignments first, then assign the IRF.

There are two other distributed administrators in addition to Admin and the container administrator:

- ▸ Print server operator — Responsible for managing print services. This role is often incorporated into the role of the container administrator.

- ▸ Print queue operator — Can assist the print server operator or container administrator in managing print jobs.

Table 5.2 summarizes the actions and requirements of central and distributed administrators. For now, suffice it to say — you don't have to do it alone. No matter who you are, there will always be some special circumstances to deal with. Let's take a look at some clever solutions for Profile login scripts, Directory Map objects, mailing list administrators, and traveling users.

T A B L E 5.2

Summary of Distributed Administrators

ROLE	ACCOUNT INFORMATION	FUNCTIONS
Admin	Default Admin User Object [S] object rights to [Root] (by default).	Name the Directory tree; install the first server; create the top levels of the NDS tree; handle partition management and synchronization; assign distributed administrators; issue initial auditor password; and upgrade servers, clients, and applications.

T A B L E   5.2

Summary of Distributed Administrators

ROLE	ACCOUNT INFORMATION	FUNCTIONS
Distributed Administrator	Exclusive container administrator or Organizational Role. Requires [BCDRS] object rights to appropriate container.	Install supplemental servers; perform data backup and restoration; create and configure print services; write and maintain login scripts; monitor file server performance; track errors; monitor disk space usage, assign file system security; and upgrade respective servers, clients, and applications.
Print Server Operator	Print Server Operator object or Organizational Role. Must be added to Print Server Operator property of the respective Print Server object.	Load and shut down the print server, manage and maintain print server configurations.
Print Queue Operator	Print Queue Operator object or Organizational Role. Must be added to the Print Queue Operator property of the respective print queue.	Delete print jobs, change the order of print jobs, change queue status.

"Special" NDS Security

If you only learn one thing in this crazy chapter, I hope it's this:
Expect the unexpected.

ZEN

"Doh!"

Homer Simpson

There are many special circumstances that require a unique approach toward NDS security. Certain objects in the tree, for example, require additional NDS rights beyond the defaults. This usually occurs when a user is defined in a different container than the resource he/she is trying to access. Also, there are special considerations for traveling users and mailing list administrators. Here are some proven solutions for dealing with special security circumstances:

▶ Profile Login Scripts — As you'll learn in Chapter 6, NetWare 4 provides a facility for group login scripts — the Profile object. In order for a user to access a Profile script, he/she requires special rights. If the User and Profile objects are in the same container, no additional rights are required because he/she gets them by default. If, however, the User is in a different container, the Read [R] right to the Profile Login Script property is required.

▶ Directory Map — In Chapter 4, we discovered the Directory Map object as a way of reducing redundant network administration. It allows you to map logical pointers to NDS objects instead of physical volume locations. In order to access Directory Map objects, users need two sets of rights. First, NDS rights (Read [R] to the "Path" selected properties of the Directory Map object) and, second, file system rights to the volume in question. If the user resides in the same container as the Directory Map object, no additional NDS rights are required. Otherwise, you'll need to make the above NDS assignment.

▶ Mailing list administrator — Postal workers are special people, too. Mailing list administrators need special NDS rights to manage certain user properties. Specifically grant him/her Read and Write [RW] properties rights to the following Selected Properties of each user in the mailing list — Telephone, Street, City, State or Province, Postal (Zip) Code and other postal office box properties. Whatever you do, don't use the All Properties option. This would give the mailing list administrator unintended power. Remember, if you grant anyone the Write [W] property right to a user's ACL property, he/she can change the user's security. This is a bad thing.

▶ Traveling user between two offices — Traveling users can create havoc in NDS administration. These users typically bounce from location to location, demanding access to distributed and centralized resources. Several of the NDS security issues you should consider when working with traveling users include access to applications, file storage in a central volume, access to distributed files, access to local and distributed printers and e-mail, login authentication, and the type of computer they're using (notebook or desktop). The user who divides his/her time between two offices needs similar resources in two different locations. The easiest way to approach this problem is create two User objects, one in each location. Give appropriate rights to any resources needed in the local location. Then give him/her the Read [R] property rights to the Profile Login Script and Directory Map objects (as shown above).

▶ Traveling users between various locations — Users who travel to various locations on a regular basis require a slightly different type of NDS security. In this case, you may want to create an Alias object in each location. You can also use Groups or Organizational Roles. Then assign the appropriate rights to the Alias for access to directories and network resources. Finally, don't forget the Profile Login Scripts and Directory Map objects. This strategy can also be used for traveling users who find themselves stuck in a remote location for a temporary period of time.

Wow. That's NDS security! In this section, we've explored the simple three-step model for configuring NDS access rights. We've learned about trustee assignments, inheritance, and security equivalence. The IRF came along to help us lock inherited rights and quickly became the foundation of modern math in the 7th Dimension — calculating effective rights. That's all there is to it. Finally, we learned you don't have to do it alone. You can share all this fun with distributed administrators.

At the beginning of the chapter, we learned that security is "freedom from risk." At this point in the discussion, you're probably thinking NDS security is freedom from sanity. Don't worry — it's not as crazy as you think. We've provided a detailed exploratorium at the end of the chapter for your enjoyment. And in the next section

— file system access rights — you'll get a chance to review the three-step approach. Here's the good news. File system security is very similar to NDS security. Let's check it out.

QUIZ

So, you wanna be the next Sherlock Holmes? Let's see if you've got what it takes. Each of the following six words is the odd one out for a different reason.

ABORT

ACT

AGT

ALP

OPT

APT

Can you find all six answers? If so, you are well on your way to answering the question, "Who shot Mr. Burns?"

(Q5-5)

Layer Four: File System Access Rights

NetWare 4 security exists on two functional planes:

- Above the server

- Within the server

In order to understand the two functional planes of NetWare 4 security, use the server as a midpoint (see Figure 5.26). NDS security occurs above the server — the "Cloud." In this plane, the server is at the bottom of the tree. It is treated as any other leaf object, just like Users, Printers, and Groups. NDS security applied above the server ends when it gets to a leaf object. There's no transition into the file system.

*The Two Functional Planes
of NetWare 4 Security*

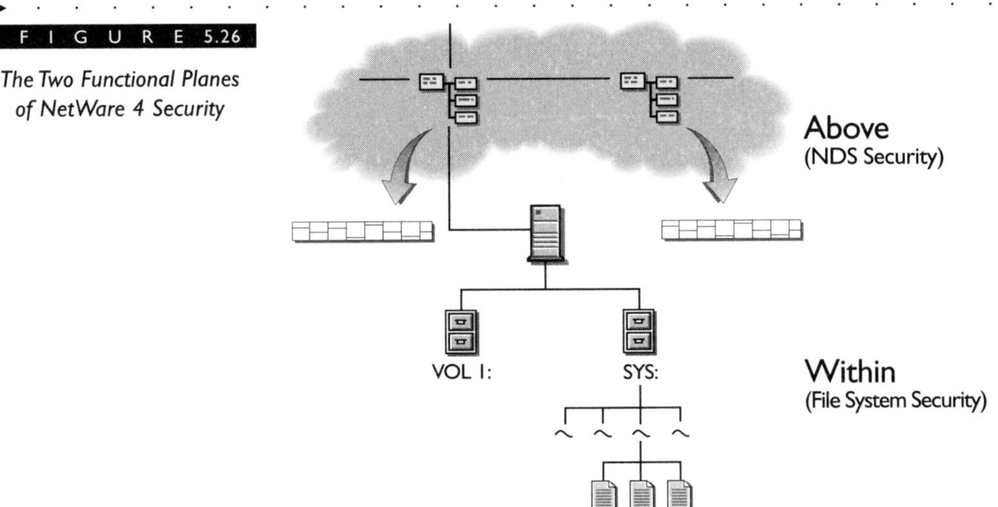

File system security, on the other hand, occurs within the server. In this case, the server is the top of the tree. The server contains the volumes that contain the directories that house the files. Again, file system security ends once it gets to the server. There's no transition into the NDS security structure. Understanding the server's point of view will help you understand NDS and file system security.

The good news is that NDS and file system security have a lot in common. You don't have to learn a whole new model. The same simple three-step approach applies. There're trustee assignments, inheritance, and security equivalence. The file system uses an IRF and calculating effective rights is still ugly. There are, however, a few minor differences between NDS and file system security:

> ▸ NDS has 10 access rights broken into two groups — object and property. The file system uses eight access rights.

▶ Rights do not flow from NDS into the file system except in one special instance — Supervisor [S] object rights to the Server object. This grants the trustee Supervisor file rights to the [Root] of all the server's volumes.

▶ The Supervisor NDS right can be blocked by the IRF. The Supervisor file system right, on the other hand, *cannot* be blocked by the IRF.

That does it. As you can see, the file system and NDS have much more in common than you think. Let's start our discussion of security *within* the server by describing the eight file system access rights.

UNDERSTANDING FILE SYSTEM ACCESS RIGHTS

Welcome inside the server. It's kind of dark and cold in here, but very secure. Before you can access any files, though, you must have appropriate file system access rights. As you can see in Figure 5.27, they also spell a word — WoRMFACES (the "O" is implied). Holy anatomical nematodes, Batman! It's not a pretty sight but certainly a name you will not forget. Let's check them out.

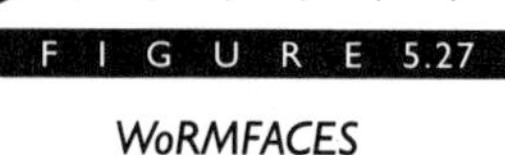

F I G U R E 5.27

WoRMFACES

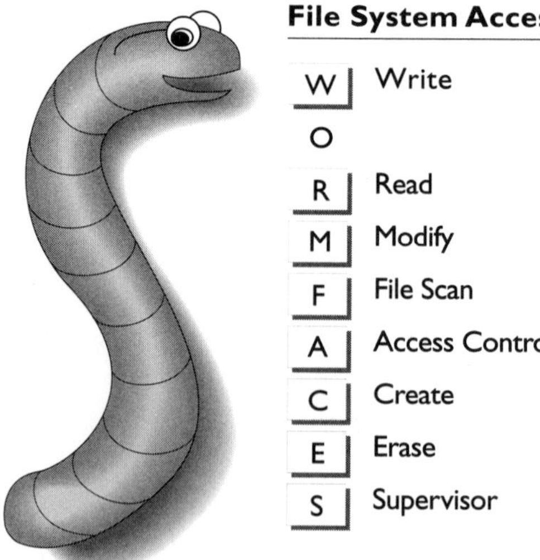

- W — Write: Grants the right to open and change the contents of files and directories.

- (O) — Doesn't exist but is needed to spell a word.

- R — Read: Grants the right to open files in the directory and read their contents or run applications.

- M — Modify: Grants the right to change the attributes or name of a file or directory. As we'll learn in just a second, the Modify right has a dual personality.

- F — File Scan: Grants the right to see files and directories.

- A — Access Control: Grants the right to change trustee assignments and the IRF.

- C — Create: Grants the right to create new files and subdirectories.

- E — Erase: Grants the right to delete a directory, its files, and subdirectories.

- S — Supervisor: Grants all rights to a directory and its files and subdirectories. This right *cannot* be blocked by the IRF (unlike NDS security).

In this list, there are three rights you may want to steer clear of — [SAM] (and they also spell a word). The Supervisor right grants all privileges to files and directories and it cannot be filtered. Users with the Supervisor right can make trustee assignments and grant all rights to other users as well. Access Control also allows users to make trustee assignments, but they can only grant the rights they possess. In addition, these users can modify the IRF. Finally, the Modify right has a split personality — Dr. Jekyll and Mr. Hyde. As Dr. Jekyll, Modify allows users to rename files and directories. Many applications require this. As Mr. Hyde, Modify allows users to change file and directory attributes. As we'll see a little later, attributes constitute the fifth layer of the NetWare 4 security model. I don't think you want users messing around with it.

> **REAL WORLD**
>
> The Supervisor access right is just as dangerous in the file system as it is in NDS. The tricky part is it can leak its way into the file system without you knowing it. Any user with the Write [W] property right to a server's ACL will implicitly receive Supervisor file rights to the [Root] of all volumes on the server. And to make things worse, the user will not appear on any file or directory trustee list. There's a variety of ways to get the Write [W] property right to a server's ACL, including Supervisor object rights, Supervisor All Properties rights, and security equivalence. You may consider blocking these rights with a server IRF.

Recognizing the eight file system access rights is only the beginning. In order to effectively configure and manage file system security, you must understand what they do. Individually, the rights are useless. But in combination, they become valuable security tools. Table 5.3 summarizes the file system rights requirements for common network tasks. Believe me, this will be an invaluable aid when it comes time to configure application and data security. Use it or lose it.

T A B L E 5.3	FILE SYSTEM TASK	RIGHTS REQUIREMENTS
Rights Requirements for Common File System Tasks	Open and read a file	Read
	See a filename	File Scan
	Search a directory for files	File Scan
	Open and write to an existing file	Write, Create, Erase, and Modify
	Execute an .EXE file	Read and File Scan
	Create and write to a file	Create
	Copy files *from* a directory	Read and File Scan
	Copy files *to* a directory	Write, Create, and File Scan
	Make a new directory	Create
	Delete a file	Erase

	FILE SYSTEM TASK	RIGHTS REQUIREMENTS
T A B L E 5.3 *Rights Requirements for Common File System Tasks*	Salvage deleted files	Read and File Scan for the file, and Create for the directory
	Change directory or file attributes	Modify (Mr. Hyde)
	Rename a file or directory	Modify (Dr. Jekyll)
	Change the IRF	Access Control
	Change trustee assignments	Access Control
	Modify a directory's disk space restrictions	Access Control

So, where do you begin? As with NDS, file system security starts with the defaults. NetWare 4 provides a sophisticated set of default file system access rights. These rights should become the foundation of your application and data security strategies. They aren't, however, as comprehensive as NDS defaults. You'll need to assign security whenever you create new application and data directories. Let's take a quick look at the NetWare 4 defaults:

- ▶ User — A unique User directory is created under SYS:USERS during User object conception. By default, the user gets all file system rights except Supervisor to the directory — [RWCEMF]. This directory will exactly match the User object name unless otherwise specified. Its location is also configurable.

- ▶ [Supervisor] — The Bindery Services Supervisor object is granted Supervisor [S] file rights to the [Root] of all volumes. This user performs special bindery functions using the Admin password.

- ▶ Creator — Whoever creates the file server object (usually Admin) automatically gets Supervisor [S] file system rights to all volumes. This can be blocked by filtering the Supervisor [S] object right with a server IRF.

- ▶ Container — The server's parent container is granted Read and File Scan [RF] access rights to SYS:PUBLIC. This way, all users and objects in the server's home container can access NetWare 4 PUBLIC utilities.

That completes our discussion of file system access rights. As you can see, there's a lot more than meets the eye. Be sure to use Table 5.3 when assigning rights to new application and data directories. Also, test these rights before you let the users loose. Many times, applications have strange unobvious requirements. Now that you know what to do, let's learn how to do it. Remember, the NetWare 4 file system behaves exactly the same as NDS:

- ▸ Step One: Assigning Trustee Rights

- ▸ Step Two: Filtering IRF Rights

- ▸ Step Three: Calculating Effective Rights

Ready. Set. Go!

ZEN

"I am Melvin Van Horn, and this is my associate Hershel Krustovsky. Officers, you have arrested an innocent man!"

Krusty's Sidekick

FILE SYSTEM THREE-STEP SHUFFLE

This gives us an opportunity to review the three-step NDS security model. Fortunately, file system security imitates it to the letter. Remember, NetWare 4 security starts with two simple questions:

- ▸ What rights do I need to do stuff?

- ▸ How do I get these rights?

Well, so far we've learned about the eight file system access rights and what rights are needed for common network tasks. Now we get to answer the question, "How do I get these rights?" As with NDS, file system security is as easy as 1-2-3:

- ▸ Step One: Assigning Trustee Rights — You assign the access rights through trustee assignments, inheritance, and/or security equivalence.

- ▸ Step Two: Filtering IRF Rights — In special circumstances, you can filter inherited rights at the directory level.

- ▸ Step Three: Calculating Effective Rights — The result is effective rights (that is, what users can actually do to directories and files).

Once again, it's as easy as A-B-C. Except in this case, we're assigning access rights to files and directories, not NDS objects. Let's take a closer look at this simple three-step model from the file system's point of view.

Step One: Assigning Trustee Rights

You have to start somewhere, and Step One starts with work. A trustee is any NDS object with rights to directories or files. Trustees are tracked through the DET (directory table). The file system supports the same trustee types as NDS — users, groups, containers, Organizational Roles, and [Public]. Once you identify who is going to get the rights, you have to determine what rights you're going to give them and where the rights will be assigned. This is shown in Figure 5.28. MMarion is granted all rights except [SAM] to the SYS:SHARED directory. These rights are then inherited for all subdirectories underneath. As you can see, the *who* is MMarion, the *what* is [RWCEF], and the *where* is SYS:SHARED. This is an explicit trustee assignment.

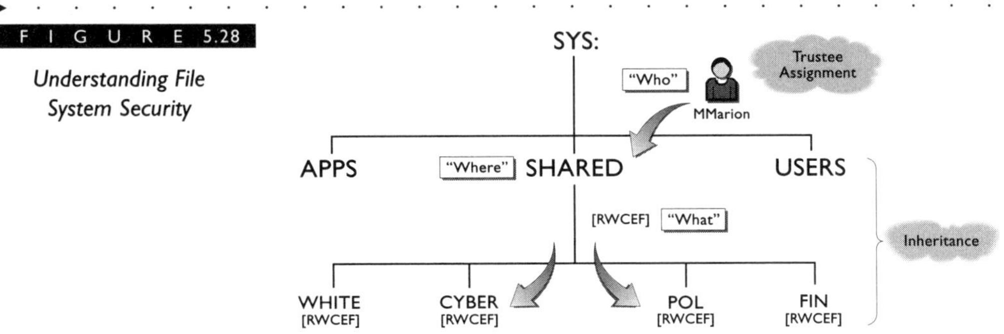

FIGURE 5.28

Understanding File System Security

So, how is this accomplished in NWADMIN? Once again, it depends on your point of view, and you have two choices:

- Rights to Files and Directories — This is from Maid Marion's point of view.

- Trustees of this Directory — This is from SYS:SHARED's point of view.

It really doesn't matter which option you choose. You can either assign rights from the user's point of view or the directory's point of view. In the first example, we assign security from Maid Marion's point of view. In NWADMIN, double-click on Maid Marion and her User Information window appears. Choose Rights to Files and Directories from the right-hand list and voilà — Figure 5.29 appears.

Figure 5.29 shows the security window from Maid Marion's point of view. As you can see, she has been granted [RWCEF] access rights to SYS:SHARED. In addition, she's also a trustee of SYS:\USERS\POL\MMARION — by default. You can create trustee assignments by using the Add... button.

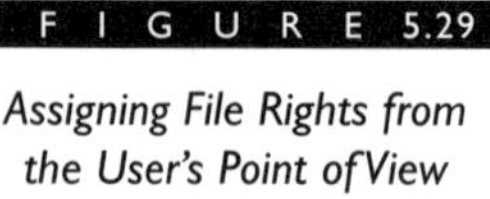

FIGURE 5.29

Assigning File Rights from the User's Point of View

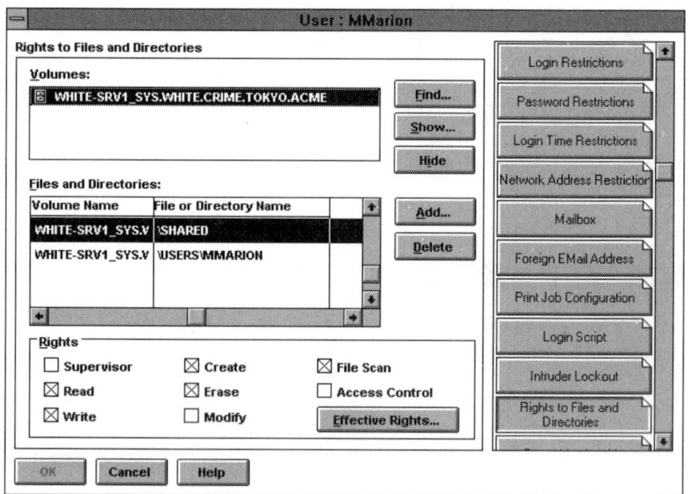

REAL WORLD

The Security Information window shown in Figure 5.29 only displays trustee assignments for a single volume at a time. By its very nature, NDS allows you to view information about multiple volumes throughout the WAN. In order to bring up the trustee assignments for a different volume, use the Show... button. You can also explore for other volumes by using the Find... button. In Figure 5.29, we're only looking at Maid Marion's trustee assignments for WHITE-SRV1_SYS.

The second option allows you to assign access rights from SYS:SHARED's point of view. In this case, you would double-click on WHITE-SRV1_SYS from the Browse window of NWADMIN. All of its directories should appear. Then, highlight SHARED and click the right mouse button. A pull-down menu will appear — choose Details. Once the SYS:SHARED Details window appears, choose Trustees of this Directory from the right-hand list (see Figure 5.30). In this screen, NWADMIN gives you the choice of adding trustees or setting the IRF (Inherited Rights Filter). Notice that MMarion has been added with the [RWCEF] access rights. You can create other trustee assignments for SYS:SHARED using the Add Trustee... button. Also notice the IRF allows all rights to flow through — this is the default.

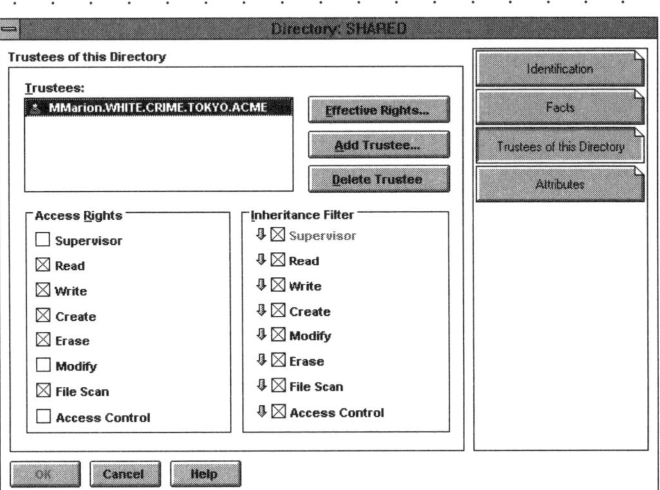

F I G U R E 5.30

Assigning File Rights from the Directory's Point of View

There you have it. As you can see, it doesn't matter how we assign access rights. Both methods accomplish the same thing — Maid Marion (who) is granted [RWCEF] trustee rights (what) to SYS:SHARED (where).

Now that we've explored the "work part," let's take a closer look at inheritance — "no work."

As we learned earlier, access rights are also assigned through inheritance. This is an automatic side effect of trustee assignments. As you can see in Figure 5.28, Maid Marion inherits [RWCEF] access rights in all subdirectories of SYS:SHARED. Inheritance is a great thing. It allows you to assign sweeping file system access rights with minimal effort. Remember, as a CNA, work is bad.

But many times, inheritance gets out of hand. Fortunately, NetWare 4 allows you to override inheritance using a new trustee assignment or an IRF. We'll explore these topics in just a moment.

If trustee assignments or inheritance aren't quite getting the job done, security equivalence may be the answer. Security equivalence simply states "one object is equivalent to another with respect to file system access rights." As we learned earlier, users, for example, are security equivalent to their parent container. We also learned that security equivalence operates at the trustee assignment level — this is *not* inheritance. Therefore, security equivalence overrides the IRF.

NetWare 4 provides four strategies for security equivalence:

▶ Ancestral Inheritance (AI) — Any object is security equivalent to its ancestors (parent containers). This means any rights you assign to an NDS container are absorbed by all the objects in the container. This is not inheritance — this is security equivalence.

▶ Organizational Role — Our special NDS objects designed as task identifiers. Jobs that require multiple temporary users are excellent candidates for Organizational Roles. Simply assign file system access rights to the Role and they are absorbed by all occupants of the Role. Once again, this is not inheritance.

- ▶ Groups — Allows you to distribute similar rights to unrelated users. That is, users that do not exist within the same area of the NDS tree. Members of any group absorb (not inherit) rights assigned to the host Group object.

- ▶ Directory Map — In very special circumstances, security equivalence can be used to facilitate Directory Map objects. When you create a Directory Map object, be sure to assign adequate file system rights to its physical location. Then when you use the MAP command to create logical pointers, be sure to assign the host user's security equivalence to the Directory Map object.

That completes Step One of the file system security model. Remember, this is the hard part. Step Two and Step Three are optional. Step Two allows us to filter inherited rights, and Step Three combines all rights assignments into a single mathematical formula — math in the 7th Dimension. Let's keep rolling!

Step Two: Filtering IRF Rights

Earlier we learned there are two ways of blocking unwanted inherited rights: new trustee assignments and the inherited rights filter (IRF). The IRF blocks inherited rights at any point in the tree. There are, however, two very important points you must understand about how the IRF works:

- ▶ It's an inclusive filter, which means the rights that are in the filter are the ones that are allowed to pass through.

- ▶ The IRF applies to everyone in the NDS tree. Once you've assigned an IRF to a directory, everyone is blocked *except* Admin.

This is the only place where file system and NDS security differs. The NDS IRF blocks the Supervisor right. The file system IRF, on the other hand, *cannot* block the Supervisor right. As you can see in Figure 5.30, the IRF is assigned using the Trustees of this Directory option. Also notice that the Supervisor right has been grayed out. This means it cannot be removed. Also notice the downward arrows that appear next to each option box. These differentiate IRF rights from trustee assignments. Anywhere you see a downward arrow, you can assume it's an IRF filter.

When you assign an IRF, all sorts of crazy things happen. My word of advice is, "Avoid them at all cost." But if you can't, you'll need to deal with Step Three — calculating effective rights.

Step Three: Calculating Effective Rights

As we learned earlier, effective rights are the bottom line. This is the culmination of our three-step process. In Step One, we assign the rights. In Step Two, we filter the rights. In Step Three, we calculate exactly what the rights are. We also learned that calculating effective rights is as simple as modern math — in the 7th Dimension! Any object's effective rights are the combination of file system privileges received through any of the following:

- ▶ Trustee assignments made to the user

- ▶ Inheritance minus rights blocked by the IRF

- ▶ Rights granted to the special [Public] trustee

- ▶ Security equivalences to parent containers, groups, or Organizational Roles

As we learned earlier, calculating effective rights for NDS can be mind-boggling and fun. The file system is no different. Let's use Maid Marion as an example. Suppose we're concerned about users making changes to our political database. To protect it, we assign an [RF] filter to SYS:SHARED\POL. This will block MMarion's inherited rights of [RWCEF]. Therefore, her effective rights must be Read and File Scan [RF]. But as you can see in Figure 5.31, her effective rights in SYS:SHARED\POL are, in fact, [RWF]. How did this happen? She must be getting the [W] right from somewhere else. Ah, I remember. She's a member of the POL-Group and they've been granted Write privileges to SYS:SHARED\POL. Therefore, her effective rights become inherited rights minus the IRF *plus* group trustee assignments.

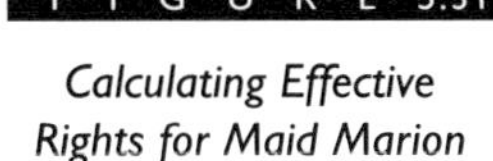

FIGURE 5.31

Calculating Effective Rights for Maid Marion

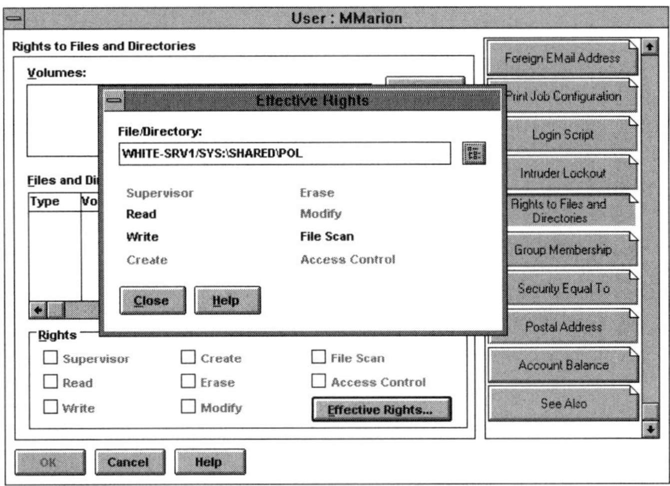

NWADMIN provides an excellent tool for viewing effective rights — check out Figure 5.31. All you have to do is identify the user (MMarion) and the directory (SYS:SHARED\POL) — NWADMIN does all the rest.

There you have it. The simple three-step file system security model:

▶ Step One: Assigning NDS Rights — Through trustee assignments, inheritance, and/or security equivalence.

▶ Step Two: Filtering IRF Rights — The inclusive filter allows you to block inherited rights.

▶ Step Three: Calculating Effective Rights — Just like modern math in the 7th Dimension.

That was a fun review. It's fortunate for us that NetWare 4 uses the same model for both NDS and file system security. Even though these two layers apply to dramatically different network elements, they approach security in a similar way. Hopefully, now you have a firm handle on access rights, default assignments, trustees, inheritance, the IRF, and effective rights. They all work together as a synergistic solution for risk management. Of course, there's always that isolated exception when four layers of security aren't quite enough. You never know when a hacker will show up with armor-piercing bullets. Fortunately, NetWare 4 has one more layer for just these emergencies — file/directory attributes. Let's check it out.

ZEN

"Shot... by you? I'm afraid not my primitive friend. Your kind has neither the cranial capacity nor the opposable digits to operate a firearm."

Mr. Montgomery Burns

Layer Five: File/Directory Attributes

Welcome to the final layer. I bet you never thought you'd get here. Directory and file attributes provide the final and most sophisticated layer of the NetWare 4 security model. These attributes are rarely used, but provide a powerful tool for specific security solutions. If all fails, you can always turn to attribute security to save the day.

Attributes are special assignments or properties that are assigned to individual directories or files. Attribute security overrides all previous trustee assignments and effective rights. Attributes can be used to prevent deleting a file, copying a file, viewing a file, and so on. Attributes also control whether you can share files, mark files for backup purposes, or protect them from data corruption using the Transactional Tracking System (TTS).

Attributes allow you to manage what users can do with files once they have access to them. Attributes are global security elements that affect all users, regardless of their rights. And they override all previous levels of security. Let's say, for example, Maid Marion has all rights except [SAM] to the SYS:APPS\WP directory — [RWCEF]. You can still restrict her from deleting a specific file by assigning it the Read-Only attribute. Therefore, the true effective rights for Maid Marion in this directory are the combination of her effective file system rights *and* file attributes.

NetWare 4 supports two types of attributes: directory and file. Directory attributes apply to directories only, whereas file attributes can be assigned to files. In both these cases, attributes fall into one of three categories:

- Security attributes

- Feature attributes

- Disk management attributes

Security attributes affect users' security access — what they can do with files. Feature attributes, on the other hand, affect how the system interacts with files. That is, whether the files can be archived, purged, or transactional tracked. Finally, disk management attributes apply to file compression, data migration, and block suballocation.

Let's take a closer look at NetWare 4 attribute security, starting with security attributes.

SECURITY ATTRIBUTES

Security attributes protect information at the file and directory level by controlling two kinds of file access — file sharing and file alteration. File access security controls not so much *who* can access the files but *what kind of access* they have. Once users have been given the proper trustee assignments to a given directory, they're in the door. Security attributes tell users what they can do with the files once they're there. Here's a list of NetWare 4's security attributes and a brief description. An asterisk (*) indicates an attribute that affects both directories and files.

- Copy Inhibit (Ci) — Only valid on Macintosh workstations. Prevents users from copying the file. Even if users have been granted the Read and File Scan [RF] rights, they still can't copy this specific file. Macintosh users can, however, remove the Ci attribute if they have been granted the Modify [M] access right.

- Delete Inhibit (Di)* — Prevents users from erasing the directory or file.

- ▸ Execute Only (X) — This is an extremely sensitive attribute and provides a very high level of NetWare security. Only the Supervisor, Admin, or anyone with the Supervisor [S] right can set this file attribute and it *cannot* be cleared. The only way to remove X is to delete the file. The Execute Only attribute can only be assigned to .EXE and .COM files. These files cannot be copied or backed up — just executed or deleted. You should note that many applications don't work on files with the Execute Only attribute assigned.

- ▸ Hidden (H)* — Valid on both DOS and OS/2 machines. Hidden is reserved for special files or directories that should not be seen, used, deleted, or copied over. However, the NDIR command shows the directory if the user has File Scan [F] access rights.

- ▸ Normal (N)* — No directory or file attributes have been set. This is the default. Normal files are typically flagged non-sharable, Read/Write automatically.

- ▸ Read-Only (Ro) — No one can write to the file. When Read Only is set or cleared, NetWare 4 also sets or clears the Delete Inhibit and Rename Inhibit attributes. Consequently, a user can't write to, erase, or rename a file when Read Only is set. A user with the Modify access right can remove the Di and Ri attributes without removing Ro. In this case, the file can be deleted or renamed, but not written to.

- ▸ Read/Write (Rw) — Allows users to change the contents of the file. This attribute is assigned automatically through Normal (N).

- ▸ Rename Inhibit (Ri)* — Prevents a user from renaming the file or directory.

- ▸ Sharable (Sh) — Allows the file to be accessed by more than one user at a time. This attribute is usually used in combination with Ro for application files. The default Normal setting is non-sharable.

▶ System (Sy)* — Applies to DOS and OS/2 workstations. The NetWare 4
OS assigns this attribute to system-owned files and directories. System
files are hidden and cannot be deleted, renamed, or copied. However,
the NetWare NDIR command shows the file if the user has File Scan
access rights.

That does it for security attributes. Now let's take a closer look at feature attributes.

FEATURE ATTRIBUTES

Feature attributes provide access to special NetWare functions or features. These
features include backup, purging, and transactional tracking. As a matter of fact,
there are only three feature attributes in NetWare 4, and one of them (P) applies to
both directories and files. Here's how they work:

▶ Archive Needed (A) — A status flag set by NetWare. Indicates that the
file has been changed since the last time it was backed up. NetWare sets
this attribute when a file is modified and clears it during SBACKUP full
and incremental sessions. We'll learn more about this in Chapter 7.

▶ Purge (P)* — Tells NetWare to purge the file when it is deleted. The file
then cannot be salvaged with FILER. Purge at the directory level clears
all files and directories from the salvage table once they're deleted. This
attribute is best used on sensitive data.

▶ Transactional (T) — Indicates that the file is protected by NetWare 4's
internal Transactional Tracking System (TTS). TTS prevents data
corruption by ensuring that either all changes are made or no changes
are made when a file is being modified. The Transactional attribute
should be assigned to TTS-tracked database and accounting files.

That does it for NetWare 4 feature attributes. Now let's take a quick look at disk
management.

DISK MANAGEMENT ATTRIBUTES

The remaining seven file and directory attributes apply to NetWare 4 disk management — file compression, data migration, and block suballocation. File compression allows more data to be stored on a volume by compressing files that are not being used. Once you enable this disk management feature, volume capacity increases up to 63 percent. Data migration is the transfer of inactive data from a NetWare volume to an external optical disk storage device — called a *jukebox*. The process is transparent to the user because files appear to be stored on the volume. Data migration is made possible because of NetWare 4's internal High Capacity Storage System (HCSS). Finally, block suballocation increases disk storage efficiency by segmenting disk allocation blocks. Suballocation is also automatic, and you can turn it off using one of the following seven attributes. Here's a quick look at NetWare 4's disk management attributes. An asterisk (*) indicates that an attribute affects both directories and files.

▸ Can't Compress (Cc) — A status flag set by NetWare. Indicates that the file can't be compressed because of insignificant space savings. To avoid the overhead of uncompressing files that do not compress well, the system calculates the compressed size of a file before actually compressing it. If no disk space will be saved by compression, or if the size difference does not meet the value specified by the "Minimum Percentage Compression Gain" parameter, the file is not compressed. This attribute is shown on attribute lists, but cannot be set by users or CNAs.

▸ Compressed (Co) — A status flag set by NetWare. Indicates that the file has been compressed by the system. Once again, this attribute is shown on attribute lists, but cannot be set by the user or CNAs.

▸ Don't Compress (Dc)* — Marks a file or directory so that it is never compressed. This is your way of managing file compression. This attribute is used in combination with Ic (immediate compression). We'll check this out in just a moment.

- Don't Migrate (Dm)* — Marks a file or directory so that it is never migrated to a secondary storage device. This is the only way you can directly manage data migration. Otherwise, all files are automatically migrated once they exceed the timeout threshold.

- Don't Suballocate (Ds) — Prevents an individual file from being suballocated even if suballocation is enabled on the volume. This is typically used for files that are huge or appended to frequently — such as databases. This attribute is your only tool for managing suballocation once it's been activated.

- Immediate Compress (Ic)* — Marks a file or directory for immediate compression. NetWare 4 will compress the file as soon as it can without waiting for a specific event to initiate compression — such as a time delay. As a CNA, you can use Ic to turn on compression and Dc to turn it off. Both attributes operate at the file and directory level.

- Migrated (M) — A status flag set by NetWare. Indicates that the file has been migrated. This attribute is shown on an attribute list, but can't be set by the user or CNA.

TIP

Any of these attributes can be modified using the FLAG command line utility or NETADMIN menu utility and/or NWADMIN graphical utility. In addition, they can be viewed using the NDIR command line utility, FILER menu utility and/or NWADMIN graphical utility.

These file and directory attributes can be used in combination to create effective security tools to control who has access to do what with specialized NetWare files. The default attribute combination for all files is Normal — nonsharable Read/Write.

There are special instances, however, when you can justify customizing these attributes, such as

- Stand-alone applications that are not to be shared should be flagged nonsharable Read-Only.

▸ Data files that are shared but not written to simultaneously should be flagged nonsharable Read/Write.

▸ Data files that are part of larger multiuser applications can be flagged Sharable Read/Write only if the application supports internal record locking and it is activated.

▸ Application files that are accessed by simultaneous users should be flagged Sharable Read-Only.

▸ Large important database files should always be flagged with the Transactional (T) attribute.

▸ Sensitive archive files should be flagged with the attribute Hidden. These include records that are only accessed once a month.

▸ All System files owned by NetWare should be flagged System. This is an attribute assigned by NetWare, not you.

▸ Sensitive application files that cost lots of money should be flagged Execute Only by the network administrator.

Congratulations! You've completed the NetWare 4's five-layered security model. Wow, what a wild ride. It all started with risk analysis and countermeasures. We learned the absolute goal of NetWare 4 security:

Let the good guys in and keep the bad guys out.

We also learned that NetWare 4's five-layered security model is an increasingly more secure series of barriers against network threats — users. In Layer One, they log in to the "Cloud" with initial and background authentication. Then login restrictions take over. This barrier controls the user's conditional access through five different types of restrictions — account, password, station, time, and Intruder Detection/Lockout. Once the user passes through the first two barriers, their ability to access leaf and container objects is determined by a sophisticated NDS security structure. At the heart of NDS security is a simple three-step process — trustee assignments, IRF, and effective rights.

But what about security *within* the server? NDS security isn't enough. Now we must protect the file system. File system security operates in much the same way as NDS object rights. They're granted with the help of trustee assignments, inheritance, and security equivalence. We learned how the eight different access rights can be used to protect NetWare 4 files and directories. But sometimes this isn't enough. That's where attributes come in. The final barrier allows you to override previous security with three different attribute types — security, feature, and disk management.

Well, there you have it. The NetWare 4 five-layered security model. As a NetWare 4 CNA, it is your responsibility to manage the NetWare 4 network. But more importantly, you must protect it. Hopefully now you've gained a new appreciation for the value of an impenetrable network armor.

So, where do you go from here? The world is your oyster. It's amazing what a little security can do for your fragile psyche. Once all your risks are in check, there's no limit to what you can do. So far you can manage NDS, build a tree, map drives, and secure the WAN. I'd say you're becoming a full-fledged "NetWare 4 gardener"! But what about the big picture? Now I think you're ready to journey through the life-span of a LAN — starting with childhood (NetWare 4 configuration) and continuing through adulthood (NetWare 4 management). It all starts with a single seed.

EXERCISE 5-1: HOW SECURE DO YOU FEEL?

Circle the 20 NetWare 4 Security terms hidden in this word search puzzle using the hints provided.

```
S  E  C  U  R  I  T  Y  Z  P  K  C  G  M  G  L  S  M  Y
T  J  Z  U  N  I  Q  U  E  P  A  S  S  W  O  R  D  S  Y
A  C  M  C  K  R  S  S  Z  P  Z  T  V  G  O  K  B  O  W
T  P  R  O  O  F  S  K  P  P  W  T  T  O  M  D  R  H  P
I  R  U  G  R  A  C  E  L  O  G  I  N  S  N  M  X  L  Q
O  I  O  B  J  E  C  T  R  I  G  H  T  S  J  U  T  H  S
N  V  D  Z  L  I  T  L  T  U  T  I  Y  A  B  T  Z  W  R
R  A  J  S  G  I  N  H  E  R  I  T  A  N  C  E  C  T  V
E  T  E  F  F  E  C  T  I  V  E  R  I  G  H  T  S  J  Q
S  E  C  U  R  I  T  Y  E  Q  U  I  V  A  L  E  N  C  E
T  K  R  P  R  Y  B  V  D  N  F  D  G  M  L  F  D  W  R
R  E  S  B  Q  P  G  W  P  X  G  F  W  T  W  B  H  P  J
I  Y  Y  O  B  G  V  X  L  G  O  T  B  B  M  C  A  V  M
C  L  H  F  W  T  Y  N  B  B  T  G  Y  P  T  Q  Y  E  K
T  I  M  E  R  E  S  T  R  I  C  T  I  O  N  S  U  F  P
I  N  T  R  U  D  E  R  D  E  T  E  C  T  I  O  N  X  U
O  R  U  S  T  H  G  I  R  Y  T  R  E  P  O  R  P  Q  F
N  C  P  P  A  C  K  E  T  S  I  G  N  A  T  U  R  E  F
S  N  W  P  B  Z  S  T  H  G  I  R  E  E  T  S  U  R  T
```

Hints:

1. Property of an object that lists trustees of the object.
2. The rights that an object can actually exercise for an object, directory, or file.
3. The number of times a user can log in with an expired password.
4. Flowing down of money or trustee rights.

5. Feature that tracks invalid login attempts.

6. Controls the rights that can be inherited from a parent container or directory.

7. Security feature that protects servers and workstations by preventing packet forgery.

8. Privileges that are assigned to an object and that control its access to other objects, directories, or files.

9. An encryption scheme element that is user-specific and that can only be decrypted with a valid password.

10. A temporary encryption that is constructed from the signature, a message, the user's private key, and a randomly generated number.

11. Privileges required to view or modify the property of an object.

12. Special trustee that is similar to the EVERYONE Group found in earlier versions of NetWare.

13. Is a combination of value and threat.

14. Risk prevention strategies.

15. Method of granting a User object the same rights as another object.

16. Login restriction that limits a user to specific workstation node IDs.

17. Login restriction that limits the hours during which a user can log in.

18. Privileges granted to an object that determine its access to another object, directory, or file.

19. System Fault Tolerance feature that protects database applications from corruption by backing out incomplete transactions.

20. Login restriction that requires a User to supply a new password that is different from previous passwords.

See Appendix C for answers.

EXERCISE 5-2: NETWARE 4 MANAGEMENT

Across

1. Automatically granted with Read property right
4. Keeping the bad guys out
6. Central application control
9. Required for changing file system IRF
10. Automatically granted with Write property right
11. Graphical administrator tool

12. Object being security equivalent to parent
13. Object for global configuration
15. DOS text administrator tool
17. What is the 'O' for?
20. Can be blocked by an NDS IRF
21. Third layer of NetWare 4 Security
22. Property rights that can be inherited

Down

1. Preventative actions against threats
2. Required for changing file attributes
3. Required for seeing objects in the NDS tree
4. File system rights to consider restricting
5. Assigned to individual files or directories
7. Required for looking at file contents
8. Required for deleting a directory or file
14. Danger
16. Tracking important network events
17. Required for changing file contents
18. Initially is granted access to entire tree
19. For granting rights to unrelated users

See Appendix C for answers.

CASE STUDY: ACME SECURITY

In this exercise, we are going to explore the exciting world of NetWare 4 NDS and file system security. In order to complete this exercise, you will need to install a server called WHITE-SRV1 in the WHITE.CRIME.TOKYO.ACME container.

Initially, the Crime division, the White-Collar Crime department, and the three White-Collar Crime units (Cyber Crime, Financial Crime, and Political Crime) will be sharing the same server (.WHITE-SRV1.CRIME.TOKYO.ACME) — but not the same data. The Users in the Crime division office will be located in a container called CRIME.TOKYO.ACME. The White-Collar Crime department and its three Crime units will be located in a subcontainer called WHITE.CRIME.TOKYO.ACME.

You will need to create Group objects for each of these workgroups (namely, CRIME-Group, WHITE-Group, CYBER-Group, FIN-Group, and POL-Group).

Temporarily, the managers of each workgroup will act as network administrators for their respective workgroups. Because these administrator assignments are temporary, you will need to create an Organizational Role for each (called CRIME-Admin, WHITE-Admin, CYBER-Admin, FIN-Admin, and POL-Admin, respectively).

Each workgroup will be given rights to the SYS:SHARED directory as well as to its own subdirectory under the SYS:SHARED directory (namely, SYS:SHARED\CRIME, SYS:SHARED\WHITE, SYS:SHARED\CYBER, SYS:SHARED\FIN, and SYS:SHARED\POL). The SHARED directory will contain those files that are shared by the entire division, whereas the individual subdirectories will contain those files that are shared by each workgroup. An inherited rights filter will be placed on each of the subdirectories under SHARED, so that users from one department cannot see the files from another.

Everyone in these five workgroups will have access to the word processing program (stored in SYS:APPS\WP70). In addition, the Financial Crime unit will have access to the spreadsheet program (stored in SYS:APPS\SS30) and the Cyber Crime unit will have access to the database program (stored in SYS:APPS\DB50). Each workgroup is currently generating a list of other applications that they'd like on the server.

User Templates will be used for consistency in creating User objects and will contain the following account restrictions:

▸ Each User will be limited to logging in on one workstation at a time (that is, one concurrent login).

▸ Each User will be required to have a *unique* password consisting of seven characters or more, and will be required to change their password every 45 days. Each User will be allowed six grace logins.

▸ Because employees in this division work long hours and travel a lot, there will be no time restrictions on anyone's account except between 3:00 a.m. to 4:00 a.m. daily (when system backups and network maintenance are done).

▸ Intruder detection will be set to lock for 24 hours after 7 incorrect attempts in 24 hours. Intruder detection statistics will be kept for 10 days.

Now that you know the plan, let's go ahead and implement it!

1. Execute the NetWare Administrator Utility. Log into the network as .ADMIN.ACME and double-click on the NetWare Administrator icon in MS Windows.

2. Change the current context to [Root]. You'll want to get a visual perspective of where these containers are located in the NDS tree. If the [Root] is not displayed on the screen, set the context by clicking on Set Context in the View menu, typing in **[Root]** as the new context, and clicking on OK. To display the portion of the tree with which we will be working, double-click on the ACME container, then double-click on the TOKYO container, then double-click on the WHITE container.

3. Create the basic file system directory structure. Double-click on the WHITE-SRV1_SYS Volume object in order to display the directories under it.

    a. Press the Insert button to display the Create Directory window. To create the USERS directory, type **USERS** in the Directory Name field, then click on the Create Another Directory box, then click on the Create button.

b. To create the SHARED directory, type **SHARED** in the Directory name field, then click on the Create Another Directory box to de-select it, then click on the Create button.

c. To create the CRIME subdirectory under the SHARED directory, click on the SHARED folder icon. Type **CRIME** in the Directory Name field, then click on the Create Another Directory box, then click on the Create button. Follow the same procedure to create the WHITE, CYBER, FIN, and POL directories under the SHARED directory.

d. Finally, use the same procedure to create a SYS:APPS directory, then create the following directories under it: DB50, SS30, and WP70.

4. Set Intruder Detection/Lockout defaults for the CRIME and WHITE containers. Click on the CRIME container with the right mouse button and select the Details option from the menu displayed. Click on the Intruder Detection page button. (You'll have to use the scroll bar on the right side of the screen to bring it into view.) Click on the Detect Intruders box, then type the following Intruder Detection limits:

Intruder Attempt Reset Interval: **10 days, 0 hours, 0 minutes**

Next, click on the Lock Account After Detection box and type in the following information:

Intruder Lockout Reset Interval: **1 days, 0 hours, 0 minutes**

Use the same procedure to set the Intruder Detection/Lockout parameters for the WHITE container.

5. Create a User Template for the TOKYO container. As you know, changes to a User Template object affect only those Users created after the changes are made. Since no Users have been created yet, this will not be a problem. In actuality, a User Template is just a User object with the name USER_TEMPLATE. Make sure that the TOKYO container is highlighted, and press Insert. The New Object window will be displayed. Use the scroll bar along the right side of the window to bring the User icon into view, then double-click it to select it. Type **USER_TEMPLATE** in the login Name *and* Last Name fields, then click on the Define Additional Properties box. Finally, click on the Create button at the bottom of the window to create the User Template. The object dialog will be displayed. You will notice a set of page buttons along the right side of the screen. Select the page buttons listed below and make the changes indicated.

    a. Identification page button. You'll notice the Identification page button is selected by default. Type the following information on this screen:

       Location: **Tokyo, Japan**

       Telephone: **813-5481-1141**

       Fax Number: **813-5481-855**

    b. Environment page button. Click on the Environment page button. Walk the tree to select the following Home Directory information:

       Volume: WHITE-SRV1_SYS.WHITE.CRIME.TOKYO.ACME

       Path: USERS

    c. Login Restrictions page button. Click on the Login Restrictions page button.

       Click on the Limit Concurrent Connections box. A value of 1 will be displayed in the Maximum Connections field.

d. Password Restrictions. Click on the Password Restrictions page button, then perform the following tasks:

Click on the Allow User to Change Password box.

Click on the Require a Password box.

Indicate a Minimum Password length of 7.

Click on the Force Periodic Password changes box.

e. Indicate a value of 45 for Days Between Forced Changes.

Click on the Require Unique Passwords box.

Click on the Limit Grace Logins.

Accept the default of six Grace Logins Allowed.

Click on the Change Password button. Change the password to one that you will remember, so that no one can actually log in to the network using this account.

f. Login Time Restrictions page button. Next, go ahead and restrict login privileges between 3:00 a.m. and 4:00 a.m. every day. Click on the Login Time Restrictions page button. A grid will be displayed on the screen showing days of the week along the left edge and time of day across the top. Each box in the grid represents a half-hour period during the week. You'll notice that when you place the mouse cursor in a box, the day and time the box represents is displayed. White boxes represent times during which the User is allowed to log in; gray boxes indicate times that the User is prevented from logging in. Click on the 3:00 and 3:30 boxes for each day of the week. (Alternately, you can click on the box corresponding to 3:00 a.m. Sunday, and while holding down the mouse button, drag the mouse cursor to the rectangle representing 3:30 a.m. Saturday before releasing the mouse button.)

g. Postal Address page button. Click on the Postal address button and fill in the following information:

Street: **Toei Mishuku Building; 1-13-1, Mishuku**

City: **Setagaya-ku, Tokyo 154**

State or Province: **Japan**

When you have finished updating the User Template, click on the OK button at the bottom of the screen to accept the changes that you have made.

6. Copy the TOKYO User Template to the CRIME and WHITE containers. Click on the CRIME container. Select the User Template menu option from the Object menu. Click on the Yes button when asked whether you want to copy the properties of the User Template from the TOKYO.ACME container. The Identification screen for the new User Template will be displayed. Click on the Cancel button since you don't need to make any changes at this time. Follow the same procedure for copying the User Template to the WHITE container.

7. Create Group objects. Before you can create Users, you will need to create the Group objects that they will be members of. Click on the CRIME container and press Insert. The New Object window will appear. Double-click on the Group icon to select it. Type **CRIME** in the Group Name field, click on the Define Additional Properties box, and click on the Create button. The Group Object Identification screen will be displayed. Fill in the following information:

Location: **Tokyo, Japan**

Department: **Crime-Fighting**

Organization: **ACME**

Click on the OK button when you are finished. Follow the same procedure for creating the WHITE, CYBER, FIN, and POL groups in the WHITE container.

8. Create User objects. Next, you need to create the SHolmes and DrWatson User objects in the CRIME container and the RHood, LJohn, MMarion, and FrTuck User objects in the WHITE container.

   a. Click on the CRIME container and press Insert. Double-click on the User object icon. Type **SHolmes** for the login name and **Holmes** for the Last Name. The Use User Template and Create Home Directory boxes should already be checked. Click on the Define Additional Properties box. The Identification screen for the SHolmes User object will be displayed.

   b. Click on the Group Membership button, then on the Add... button. Double-click on the CRIME Group in the Objects box on the left side of the screen. Click on OK to accept the changes to the properties of this User object.

   c. Follow the procedure listed above for adding the DrWatson User Object to the CRIMES container and the RHood, LJohn, MMarion, and FrTuck User objects to the WHITE container, indicating the WHITE, FIN, POL, and CYBER groups, respectively.

9. Create Organizational Role objects. Your next task will be to create an Organizational Role object for each workgroup manager. Create an Organizational Role object for SHolmes by clicking on the CRIMES container, then pressing Insert. Double-click on the Organizational Role icon, then type **CRIME-Admin** as the Organizational Role Name. Click on the Define Additional Properties box, then click on the Create button. The Identification screen for the Organizational Role object will be displayed. Click the browser button to the right of the Occupant field, then click on the Add... button. Double-click on the SHolmes icon in the Objects list box on the left side of the screen, then click on the OK button in the Occupant Window. Click on the OK button at the bottom of the screen to accept the changes you've made to this Organizational Role object. Using this same technique, create Organizational Roles for the following Users in the WHITE container: RHood (WHITE-Admin), FrTuck (CYBER-Admin), LJohn (FIN-Admin), and MMarion (POL-Admin).

10. Now that you've created the Organizational Roles for container administration, let's give them the rights they need. In this section, we will create an exclusive container administrator for CRIME (SHolmes) and WHITE (RHood). As you remember, an exclusive administrator has all NDS rights to a container and blocks most rights (especially S) from everyone else.

    a. To start, assign SHolmes as the administrator for .CRIME.TOKYO.ACME. Click on this container, and press the right mouse button. Choose Trustees of this Object from the dialog box. Click on the Add Trustee... button and walk the tree to select SHolmes.

    b. Next, we'll need to assign SHolmes' object rights. Click on Supervisor, Create, Delete, and Rename, because the Browse box is already selected. With all rights in place, he's well on his way.

    c. Finally, click on the OK button on the bottom of the screen. Good work.

11. You have successfully made SHolmes an administrator of the
     .CRIME.TOKYO.ACME container. He currently shares this role with
     Admin. Now comes the "exclusive" part. We need to create an IRF of [B]
     for the CRIME container. This will block Admin, but not SHolmes.

     a. The CRIME container should still be highlighted in the NWADMIN
         Browser. Press the right mouse button, and choose Trustees of this
         Object again. Click on the Inherited Rights Filter... button.
         Currently, the defaults are selected — that is, all five object rights
         [BCDRS].

     b. To make SHolmes an exclusive administrator, click on all rights
         except Browse. This will leave an IRF of [B]. Then click on OK
         twice to return to the browser window.

     c. Very good work. Now, repeat these steps (10 and 11) to make
         RHood the exclusive container administrator of
         .WHITE.CRIME.TOKYO.ACME.

12. Assign file system rights to the file system. You are now ready to start
     assigning rights to the file system.

     a. Assign rights to the SHARED directory. Because all five workgroups
         will have the same level of access to the SHARED directory, you can
         grant these rights at the container level rather than at the Group
         level. Click on the SHARED folder, then select the Details option
         from the Object menu. Click on the Trustees of this Directory page
         button, then click on the Add Trustee button. Walk the tree until
         the CRIME container is displayed in the Objects list box on the left
         side of the screen, then double-click on it. You'll notice that the
         container is automatically granted the Read and File Scan rights.
         Click on the Write, Create, and Erase rights, then click on the OK
         button to accept this trustee assignment. (You don't need to make
         the same trustee assignment to the WHITE container, because the
         rights will be inherited by the members of the WHITE container
         from above.)

b. Assign rights to the CRIME directory under the SHARED directory. Double-click on the WHITE-SRV1_SYS volume. (Use the scroll bar on the right side of the screen, if necessary, to see the subdirectories under the SHARED directory.) Double-click on the SHARED directory, then click on the CRIME directory under it. Select Details from the Object menu, then click on the Trustees of this Directory page button. Next, click on the Add Trustee button, then select the CRIME-Group and click on OK. Finally, click on CRIME-Group.WHITE.CRIME.TOKYO.ACME in the Trustees box.

c. As you can see, Read and File Scan rights are assigned by default when you create a trustee. Click on the Write, Create, and Erase rights, then click on OK. Next, you'll want to change the Inherited Rights Filter for this directory so that rights are not inherited from above. Click on each of the rights, except for the Supervisor right, in order to de-select them. The net effect will be to assign an IRF of [S].

13. Assign trustee rights for the APPS subdirectories. Now that you know how to grant trustee rights for directories to containers and Group objects, use the same techniques to make the trustee assignments. If you'd really like a challenge, see if you can make these assignments from the trustee's perspective (that is, container or Group) rather than the directory's perspective. (Hint: You can use the Rights to Other Objects option in the Object menu.)

a. Grant the CRIME container [RF] rights to the SYS:APPS\WP70 directory (since all five workgroups will have access to the word processing application).

b. Grant the FIN Group [RF] rights to the SYS:APP\SS30 directory.

c. Grant the CYBER Group [RF] rights to the SYS:APPS\DB50 subdirectory.

14. Assign trustee rights to Organizational Role objects. Grant the trustee rights listed below to the Organizational Roles indicated:

    a. All five Organizational Roles should be granted all rights to the SHARED directory.

    b. Each Organizational Role should be granted all rights to their corresponding workgroup's subdirectory under the SHARED directory.

    c. Each Organizational Role should be granted all rights to the home directories of each User in their workgroup.

15. Verify effective rights. You can verify an object's effective rights to a directory from the object's perspective or the directory's perspective.

    a. To verify an object's effective rights from the directory's perspective, you can click on the object with the right mouse button, then select the Details option from the menu that is displayed. Next, click on the Trustees of this Directory page button, then click on the Effective rights... button. An Effective rights window will be displayed. Click on the Browser button to the right of the Trustee field. Walk the tree until the desired object is displayed in the Object list box on the left side of the screen. Double-click on the object to select it. The Effective rights screen will again be displayed. This time, the effective rights for this object will be displayed in black. (The rights they do not have will be displayed in gray.)

    b. Practice verifying the effective rights of different objects for various directories that we worked with in this exercise from the directory's point of view.

    c. Practice verifying the effective rights of different objects for various directories that we have worked with in this exercise from the object's point of view. (**Hint:** Use the Rights to Other Objects menu option.)

EXERCISE 5-3: CALCULATING NDS EFFECTIVE RIGHTS

Okay, now that you're a pro with NetWare 4 security, let's experiment with "modern math." Earlier in the chapter, we explored NetWare's version of calculus — calculating effective rights. We learned that both NDS and the file system have their own versions of effective rights — and they work exactly the same:

Effective Rights = trustee assignments + inheritance - IRF (inherited rights filter)

In this exercise, we'll begin Calculus 101 with NDS access rights. Then, in Exercise 5-4, you'll get an opportunity to explore file system access rights. Also, we've included some beautiful graphic worksheets to help you follow along. You can create your own at home with a pencil, some paper, and a ruler.

So without any further ado, let's get on with CASE #1.

CASE #1

In this case, we are helping Sherlock Holmes gain administrative rights to the Crime Fighting division. Refer to Figure 5.32. It all starts at .CRIME.TOKYO.ACME. He is granted [CD] NDS privileges. Also, he ancestrally inherits Browse rights from the special [Public] trustee. There is no IRF or inheritance in CRIME.

In the next container, WHITE, SHolmes gets [S] from his "CRIME-Group" group. Also, there's an IRF of [D]. Finally, these privileges flow down to the WHITE-SRV1 server object and become inherited rights. But the server's IRF is set to [BR], so some of them are blocked. Also, SHolmes has an explicit trustee assignment of [D] to the WHITE-SRV1 server. Finally, Sherlock's home container, WHITE, is granted [C] privileges to the server object.

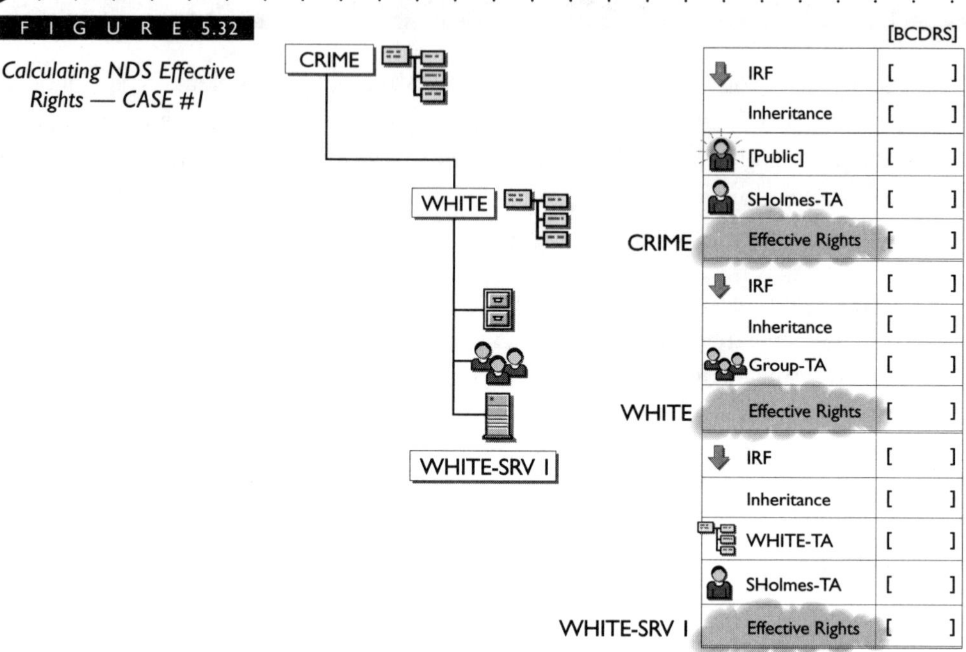

F I G U R E 5.32

Calculating NDS Effective Rights — CASE #1

CASE #2

After careful consideration, you decide that the above rights are inappropriate. So, let's try it one more time. But, in this case, we're going to use the WHITE-Admin Organizational Role instead of the "WHITE-Group" group. This gives us more administrative flexibility and narrows the scope of rights assignments. For this case, refer to Figure 5.33.

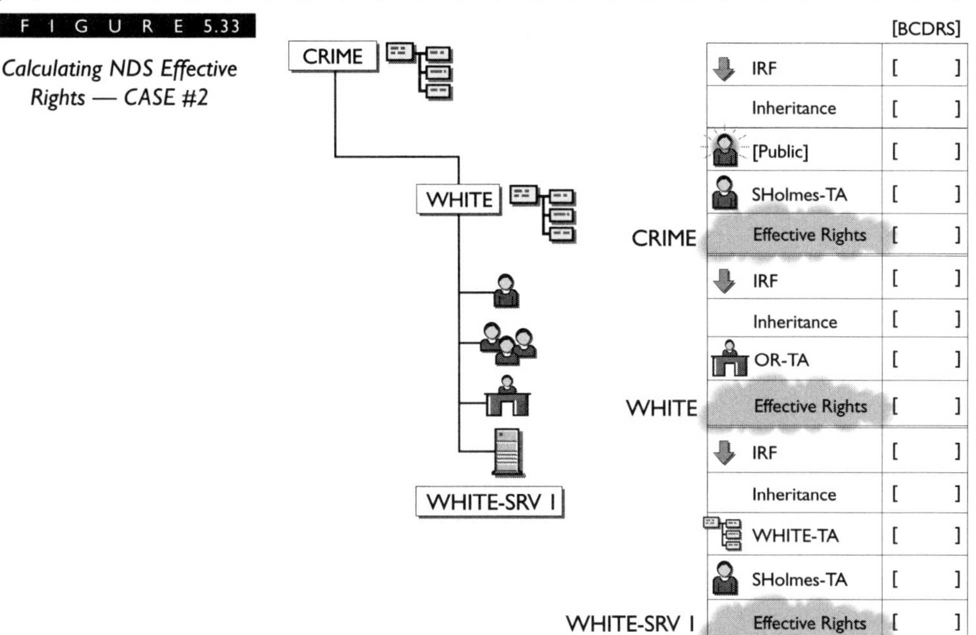

F I G U R E 5.33

Calculating NDS Effective Rights — CASE #2

As before, it starts in the .CRIME.TOKYO.ACME container. Sherlock Holmes is granted the [BR] rights to the container. Also, he ancestrally inherits [B] from [Public]. Finally, there is no inheritance in CRIME, but the IRF has been set to [CD] anyway.

In the next container, WHITE, SHolmes gets [BCD] through his CRIME-Admin Organizational Role. Also, there's an IRF of [CDRS]. Finally, the container's effective rights flow down to the WHITE-SRV1 server object and become inherited rights. But the server's IRF is set to [BR], so some of them are blocked. In addition, SHolmes has an explicit trustee assignment of [CD] to the WHITE-SRV1 server. Finally, Sherlock's home container, WHITE, is granted [B] privileges to the server object. Now, let's see what he ends up with.

CASE #3

In this final case, let's bounce over to the .BLUE.CRIME.TOKYO.ACME container and help out Wyatt Earp — their administrator. Refer to Figure 5.34. As with most NDS trees, it actually starts much higher up — above TOKYO. Wyatt Earp inherits [BCDR] to .TOKYO.ACME. The IRF is identical, so all rights are allowed to flow through. In addition, he's granted Rename privileges as a user and Browse privileges through his home container — BLUE.

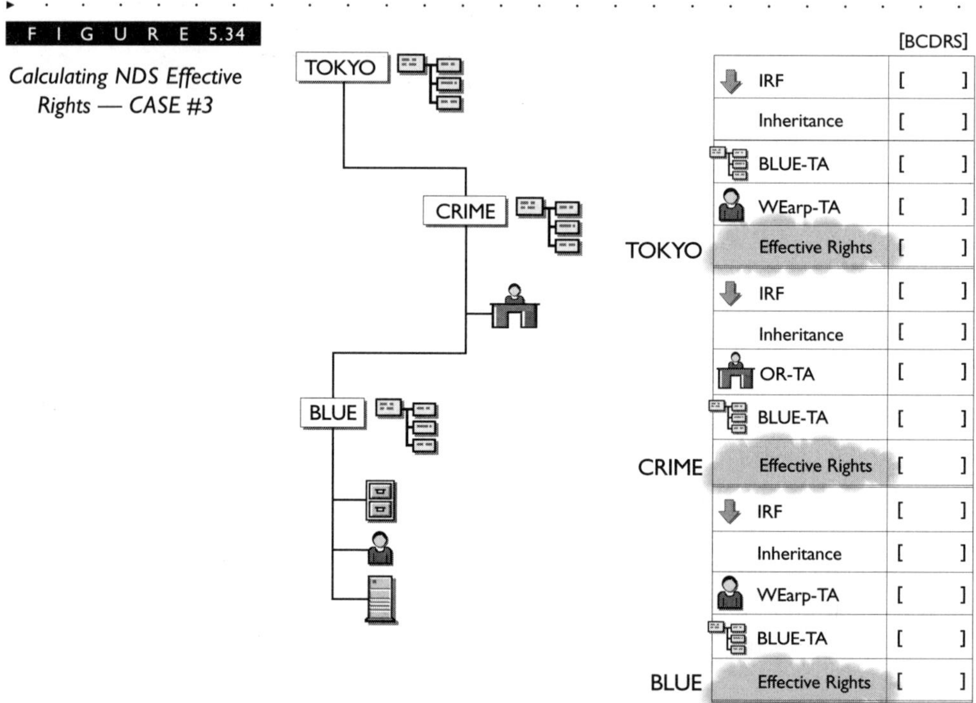

F I G U R E 5.34

Calculating NDS Effective Rights — CASE #3

In the next container, CRIME, WEarp gets all object rights through his BLUE-Admin Organization Role. This overshadows the Browse privileges he ancestrally inherits from BLUE. Also, don't forget the CRIME IRF of [BCD]. Finally, all rights flow down to the BLUE container and become inherited. But the Organizational Unit's IRF is set to [DR], so most of them are blocked. In addition, WEarp has an explicit trustee assignment of [C] to BLUE. This assignment is enhanced by the Browse privilege he inherits from BLUE. Good luck.

Well, there you have it. Great work. Now that you're a security guru, let's dive into file system access rights. Rustle on over to Exercise 5-4.

Good luck, and by the way, thanks for saving the world!

See Appendix C for the answers.

EXERCISE 5-4: CALCULATING FILE SYSTEM EFFECTIVE RIGHTS

Here you are. In case you're lost, here is modern math, part 2. In this exercise, we're going to explore the wonderful world of file system effective rights. Now that you've helped "administrate" Sherlock Holmes and Wyatt Earp, it's time to "liberate" the rest of the crime-fighting team, namely Robin Hood, Maid Marion, Dr. Watson, Little John, and Friar Tuck. Ah, a CNA's job is never done.

CASE #1

FrTuck has been made a trustee of the SYS:SHARED directory and granted Read, Write, Create, and File Scan rights. The IRF for the SYS:SHARED directory contains all rights; the IRF for the SYS:SHARED\CYBER directory contains Supervisor, Read, and File Scan; and the IRF for the CYBER.DOC file contains Read, Write, Create, and File Scan. Calculate FrTuck's effective rights in the SYS:SHARED directory, the SYS:SHARED\CYBER directory, and the CYBER.DOC file, using the worksheet in Figure 5.35.

FIGURE 5.35

Calculating File System Effective Rights — CASE #1

SYS:SHARED	S	R	C	W	E	M	F	A
Inherited Rights Filter								
Inherited Rights-User								
Inherited Rights-Group								
Trustee Assignment-User								
Trustee Assignment-Group								
Effective Rights								

SYS:SHARED\FIN	S	R	C	W	E	M	F	A
Inherited Rights Filter								
Inherited Rights-User								
Inherited Rights-Group								
Trustee Assignment-User								
Trustee Assignment-Group								
Effective Rights								

99QTR4.RPT	S	R	C	W	E	M	F	A
Inherited Rights Filter								
Inherited Rights-User								
Inherited Rights-Group								
Trustee Assignment-User								
Trustee Assignment-Group								
Effective Rights								

CASE #2

LJohn was made a trustee of the SYS:SHARED\FIN directory and granted all rights except Supervisor and Access Control. The FIN group, of which he is a member, was granted the Read, Write, Create, and File Scan rights to the SYS:SHARED directory. In addition, the FIN group was granted Read rights for the 99QTR4.RPT file. The IRF for the SYS:SHARED directory contains all rights; the IRF for the SYS:SHARED\FIN directory contains the Supervisor right; and the IRF for the 99QTR4.RPT file contains Supervisor, Read, Write, and File Scan rights. Calculate LJohn's effective rights in the SYS:SHARED directory, SYS:SHARED\FIN directory, and 99QTR4.RPT file, using the worksheet in Figure 5.36.

FIGURE 5.36

Calculating File System Effective Rights — CASE #2

SYS:SHARED	S	R	C	W	E	M	F	A
Inherited Rights Filter								
Inherited Rights-User								
Inherited Rights-Group								
Trustee Assignment-User								
Trustee Assignment-Group								
Effective Rights								

SYS:SHARED\CYBER	S	R	C	W	E	M	F	A
Inherited Rights Filter								
Inherited Rights-User								
Inherited Rights-Group								
Trustee Assignment-User								
Trustee Assignment-Group								
Effective Rights								

CYBER.DOC	S	R	C	W	E	M	F	A
Inherited Rights Filter								
Inherited Rights-User								
Inherited Rights-Group								
Trustee Assignment-User								
Trustee Assignment-Group								
Effective Rights								

CASE #3

DrWatson was granted the Read, Write, Create, and File Scan rights to the SYS:SHARED directory. The CRIME Group, of which he is a member, was granted Read, Write, Create, Erase, Modify, and File Scan rights to the SYS:CRIME directory. The CRIME Group was also granted Read and File Scan rights to the CRIME.DB file. The IRF for the SYS:SHARED directory is all rights; the IRF for the SYS:SHARED\CRIME directory is Supervisor and Access Control; and the IRF for the CRIME.DB file is Supervisor, Read, Write, Create, and File Scan. Calculate DrWatson's effective rights in the SYS:SHARED directory, the SYS:SHARED\CRIME directory, and the CRIME.DB file, using the worksheet in Figure 5.37.

SYS:SHARED	S	R	C	W	E	M	F	A
Inherited Rights Filter								
Inherited Rights-User								
Inherited Rights-Group								
Trustee Assignment-User								
Trustee Assignment-Group								
Effective Rights								

SYS:SHARED\CRIME	S	R	C	W	E	M	F	A
Inherited Rights Filter								
Inherited Rights-User								
Inherited Rights-Group								
Trustee Assignment-User								
Trustee Assignment-Group								
Effective Rights								

CRIME.DB	S	R	C	W	E	M	F	A
Inherited Rights Filter								
Inherited Rights-User								
Inherited Rights-Group								
Trustee Assignment-User								
Trustee Assignment-Group								
Effective Rights								

CASE #4

MMarion was granted the Modify and Access Control rights to the SYS:SHARED\POL directory. In addition, the POL Group was granted the Read, Write, Create, Erase, and File Scan rights to both the SYS:SHARED and SYS:SHARED\POL directories. The IRF for the SYS:SHARED directory contains all rights; the IRF for the SYS:SHARED\POL directory contains the Supervisor right; and the IRF for the CRIME.RPT file contains all rights. Calculate MMarion's effective rights to the SYS:SHARED directory, the SYS:SHARED\POL directory, and the CRIMEP.RPT file, using the worksheet in Figure 5.38.

Calculating File System Effective Rights — CASE #4

SYS:SHARED	S	R	C	W	E	M	F	A
Inherited Rights Filter								
Inherited Rights-User								
Inherited Rights-Group								
Trustee Assignment-User								
Trustee Assignment-Group								
Effective Rights								

SYS:SHARED\POL	S	R	C	W	E	M	F	A
Inherited Rights Filter								
Inherited Rights-User								
Inherited Rights-Group								
Trustee Assignment-User								
Trustee Assignment-Group								
Effective Rights								

CRIME.RPT	S	R	C	W	E	M	F	A
Inherited Rights Filter								
Inherited Rights-User								
Inherited Rights-Group								
Trustee Assignment-User								
Trustee Assignment-Group								
Effective Rights								

CASE #5

SHolmes was granted all rights to the SYS:SHARED directory. The CRIME Group, of which he is a member, was granted Read, Write, Create, and File Scan rights to the SYS:SHARED\CRIME directory. The CRIME Group was also granted Read and File Scan rights to the CRIME.DB file. The IRF for the SYS:SHARED directory contains all rights; the IRF for the SYS:SHARED\CRIME directory contains the Supervisor right; and the IRF for the CRIME.DB file contains Supervisor, Read, and File Scan rights. Calculate SHolmes' effective rights to the SYS:SHARED directory, the SYS:SHARED\CRIME directory, and the CRIME.DB file, using the worksheet in Figure 5.39.

FIGURE 5.39

Calculating File System Effective Rights — CASE #5

SYS:SHARED	S	R	C	W	E	M	F	A
Inherited Rights Filter								
Inherited Rights-User								
Inherited Rights-Group								
Trustee Assignment-User								
Trustee Assignment-Group								
Effective Rights								

SYS:SHARED\CRIME	S	R	C	W	E	M	F	A
Inherited Rights Filter								
Inherited Rights-User								
Inherited Rights-Group								
Trustee Assignment-User								
Trustee Assignment-Group								
Effective Rights								

CRIME.DB	S	R	C	W	E	M	F	A
Inherited Rights Filter								
Inherited Rights-User								
Inherited Rights-Group								
Trustee Assignment-User								
Trustee Assignment-Group								
Effective Rights								

CASE #6

RHood was made a trustee of the SUMMARY.RPT file and granted the Read, Write, Create, Erase, and Modify rights. He was also made a trustee of the SYS:SHARED\WHITE directory and granted all rights. [PUBLIC] has been granted the Read and File Scan rights to the SYS:SHARED directory. The IRF for the SYS:SHARED directory contains the Supervisor, Read, File Scan, and Access Control rights; the IRF for the SYS:SHARED\WHITE directory contains the Supervisor, Read, and File Scan rights; and the IRF for the SUMMARY.RPT file contains the Supervisor right. Calculate RHood's effective rights for the SYS:SHARED directory, the SYS:SHARED\WHITE directory, and SUMMARY.RPT file, using the worksheet in Figure 5.40.

<table>
<tr><td>F I G U R E 5.40

Calculating File System
Effective Rights —
CASE #6</td></tr>
</table>

SYS:SHARED	S	R	C	W	E	M	F	A
Inherited Rights Filter								
Inherited Rights-User								
Inherited Rights-Group or [Public]								
Trustee Assignment-User								
Trustee Assignment-Group or [Public]								
Effective Rights								

SYS:SHARED\WHITE	S	R	C	W	E	M	F	A
Inherited Rights Filter								
Inherited Rights-User								
Inherited Rights-Group or [Public]								
Trustee Assignment-User								
Trustee Assignment-Group or [Public]								
Effective Rights								

SUMMARY.RPT	S	R	C	W	E	M	F	A
Inherited Rights Filter								
Inherited Rights-User								
Inherited Rights-Group or [Public]								
Trustee Assignment-User								
Trustee Assignment-Group or [Public]								
Effective Rights								

The answers to all of these cases are in Appendix C.

NetWare 4 Configuration

The birth of a LAN.

There are many different definitions of "life." The one that you choose depends entirely on your point of view. Regardless of your choice, the fundamental question remains — is your LAN alive? Judging from the following guidelines, I think so:

▸ Carbon-based organic life form — Silicon is close enough.

▸ Consumes food — Your LAN processes valuable information.

▸ Propagates — Most NetWare 4 WANs include multiple servers.

▸ Self-awareness — Many times your network has a mind of its own.

There you go — your LAN must be alive. And, as a living, breathing life form, it must pass through the three phases of "life span" — birth, childhood, and adulthood. This evolution (that we all experience) can be both painful and rewarding. But there's nothing more exciting than watching it happen and being involved from Day One.

During birth, the NetWare 4 server is installed. In the grand scheme of things, this event is theoretically quick and painless (although I don't know about the latter part). Decisions you make during installation may have an irrevocable impact on the server, LAN, and WAN. Birth is especially important in NetWare 4 because of the importance of the NDS infrastructure.

Once the server has been installed, you are left with a simple directory structure, some workstations, and a few users — a LAN version of a cute little baby girl. Over time, this adorable little monster will learn to walk, talk, and start getting along with others. She will go to school and learn some valuable skills — ranging from how to climb the social ladder to how to deal with integral calculus. Finally, at some point, she will make an abrupt transition to adulthood — buy her first car, get her first job, and move into her first apartment.

In NetWare 4, childhood is dominated by *NetWare 4 Configuration*. During configuration, your server undergoes five important steps:

- ▸ Step 1: Workstation connectivity — Leia takes her first steps. In NetWare 4, workstation configuration files provide an initial attachment to the server and NDS. This is accomplished using CONFIG.SYS, AUTOEXEC.BAT, STARTNET.BAT, and NET.CFG.

- ▸ Step 2: Login scripts — Leia finally begins to talk (and doesn't stop for 85 years). In NetWare 4, login scripts enable you to customize user connections and establish important login settings.

- ▸ Step 3: Menu system — She learns how to share and begins getting along with others. In NetWare 4, the menu system provides a vital interface between users and the network. Just as Leia learns to get along with others, your users learn to get along with NetWare 4.

- ▸ Step 4: Network applications — Leia goes to school and learns important (and not so important) skills. In NetWare 4, applications are productivity tools that give the network value. These tools are undeniably bound to the aforementioned menu system — just like Leia is likely to make most of her friends in school.

- ▸ Step5: E-mail — Leia makes a quick transition into adulthood by getting her first car, first job, and first apartment — all in the same week. In NetWare 4, e-mail provides a vital link between applications, interface, and management. Think of it as "the force that binds the network together."

ZEN

"Life is like a 10-speed bike. Most of us have gears we never use."

George Schultz

The third and final phase of "life span" is adulthood. At this point, your LAN is secure in its new purpose and the goal shifts from conception to "keeping it going." These are the golden years. During adulthood, your LAN will get married, have children of its own, plan for the future, and finally retire. Where do I sign up? This phase is controlled by *NetWare 4 Management*. It goes something like this:

▸ Server management — Your LAN gets married and becomes part of a team. Remember LAN synergy — the whole is greater than the sum of its users. In NetWare 4, marriage takes the form of startup management, NDS configuration, internationalization, internetworking, and server protection. In addition, you'll learn to use console commands and NLMs as parent tools.

▸ Workstation management — The family grows larger with the addition of three little "rug rats" — aka, children. Life suddenly takes on a whole new meaning. Your thoughts switch from "me" to "them" — cute little people who rely on you. In NetWare 4, these cute little people are represented by users and workstations. Workstation management relies on ODI files, the NetWare DOS Requester, non-DOS support, virus prevention (colds), and diskless workstations. You'll never truly understand the frustration and joy of running a network until you have children of your own.

▸ Storage Management Services (SMS) — With the family firmly in place and your children advancing through childhood, focus shifts to the future. You need to develop disaster recovery plans and begin saving for retirement. This is life's little backup (insurance) policy. In NetWare 4, backup management ensures job security. Remember Murphy's Law Number 107 — the network WILL crash!

▸ Remote Management Facility (RMF) — Your children leave home and are off to a LAN of their own. Now it's time for you to take it easy. Through remote management, you can retire to Happy Acres and enjoy the good life. There's no reason to be involved in the daily grind anymore. In NetWare 4, RMF enables you to manage the central server from the comfort of your own office. And if you really want luxury, you can attach to the server from the comfort of your own sofa.

Wow, I bet you didn't think becoming a CNA would be such a life-changing experience! So far, the LAN has been relatively quiet — this will change. Remember, babies are cute until they learn to walk and talk and eat furniture. The daily bustle of humming workstations and crazed users will quickly take its toll on an unorganized NetWare LAN. That's why it's important to carefully configure it now — while things are still under control. It's imperative for you to establish workstation connections, write login scripts, and develop menu systems before the network goes into hyperactivity — configuring an active network is like tuning a moving car.

Consider this scenario: Guinevere walks into her office every morning, eager to begin a new day. She hangs up her coat, turns on the radio, and shifts her focus to the center of worklife — the computer. She gracefully reaches for the on/off switch and gives it a gentle nudge. Voilà! The day begins! During the booting process, Guinevere takes an opportunity to slip out for a quick cappuccino. When she returns, the machine displays a friendly network menu and her e-mail for the morning.

Magic! Although Guinevere doesn't pay much attention to what occurs while she's sipping her cappuccino, the LAN has undergone an entire childhood in only an instant. As a CNA, it's your responsibility to configure the system so that Guinevere doesn't have to worry about connectivity software, login scripts, VLMs, NMENU.BAT, or MHS. As a parent, it is your responsibility to make childhood as painless as possible.

Let's start our journey through the life span of a LAN with the first step — workstation connectivity.

Step 1: Establishing Workstation Connectivity

Leia begins to walk.

The first step is always the most exciting. I hope you have your camcorder. While Leia's taking her first step, the network begins life anew as well. During this step, the client computer boots and activates a variety of configuration files. These configuration files establish the client environment and attach Guinevere to the network. All of this magic occurs with the help of just four simple files:

- CONFIG.SYS — The first configuration file loaded during the boot process. Because DOS and the NetWare DOS Requester share drive table information, CONFIG.SYS must include the LASTDRIVE command.

- AUTOEXEC.BAT — This autoexecuting batch file is modified to activate STARTNET.BAT from the default C:\NWCLIENT subdirectory.

- STARTNET.BAT — Automates the workstation connection. By default, it resides in the C:\NWCLIENT subdirectory and initializes the workstation-specific ODI and VLM drivers.

- NET.CFG — The final workstation configuration file is used to customize ODI and VLM settings.

ZEN

"In walking, just walk. In sitting, just sit. Above all, don't wobble."

Yun-Men

Once the first step of configuration has been taken, Leia is well on her way toward childhood and Guinevere is well on her way toward LAN productivity. Let's take a closer look at these respective first steps, starting with CONFIG.SYS.

CONFIG.SYS

CONFIG.SYS is the first configuration file loaded when Guinevere turns on her computer. It is used by DOS for registering devices, managing memory, and establishing local drives. In addition, the NetWare DOS Requester uses CONFIG.SYS to identify a range of letters available for network drives. Here's how it works.

Because the NetWare DOS Requester and DOS share drive table information, we need a convention to determine where the local drives end and the network drives begin. Fortunately, the NetWare 4 VLMs do this for us. They read the workstation hardware configuration and determine where the local drives end. From that point forward, they make all remaining drive letters available to the network. The key is determining exactly which drive letters are available. This is accomplished using the LASTDRIVE command.

If you place the following statement in each workstation CONFIG.SYS file, all drive letters from A through Z will be available for local and network drives:

```
LASTDRIVE=Z
```

Remember, you don't have to determine where the network drives begin because VLMs do it for you. For example, most standard workstations have a single floppy drive (A:), an internal hard disk (C:), and a CD-ROM (D:). This means that the first available network drive is E:. Similarly, if you have only a local floppy drive (A: — a more simple configuration), your first network drive will be B:. Undoubtedly, this sounds strange because you're used to pointing to F: as the first network drive. Fortunately, NetWare 4 includes a statement in NET.CFG (by default) that ignores drives A: through E: and treats F: as the first network drive regardless of what your workstation thinks.

Once CONFIG.SYS is loaded and the LASTDRIVE statement has been activated, control shifts over to AUTOEXEC.BAT.

 **TIP**

The LASTDRIVE statement works a little bit differently when used with NETx. In the NETx universe, the LASTDRIVE statement identifies local drives only — which means that the LASTDRIVE=Z command has an entirely different effect. In such a case, users are left with no network drives at all.

This is not entirely true because NetWare 4 reserves certain ASCII characters for emergencies. If you use the LASTDRIVE=Z statement with NETx, the first available network is [: (a smiley-face). It really works. Try it — it's fun at parties.

AUTOEXEC.BAT

AUTOEXEC.BAT is a DOS configuration file used for activating a variety of workstation parameters, including PATH statements, the PROMPT command, SET parameters, and internal TSRs (terminate-and-stay-resident programs). By default, the NetWare 4 client installation creates a file called STARTNET.BAT and places it in the C:\NWCLIENT subdirectory. It then adds the following line to the top of AUTOEXEC.BAT:

```
@CALL C:\NWCLIENT\STARTNET.BAT
```

This is a great way to automatically load workstation connectivity files while separating them from normal DOS operations. There is, however, one problem with this strategy. By placing this line at the top of AUTOEXEC.BAT, none of the other DOS statements load until STARTNET.BAT is finished — which is never. Remember, the goal of workstation connectivity is to load the drivers, automatically execute login scripts, and leave Guinevere in a menu system. This means NetWare will never execute the remaining statements in AUTOEXEC.BAT. A better solution is to move the @CALL C:\NWCLIENT\STARTNET statement to the end of AUTOEXEC.BAT.

Speaking of STARTNET.BAT, let's take a closer look.

STARTNET.BAT

NetWare 4 workstation connectivity consists of two main components:

- ▸ Communications — ODI drivers

- ▸ NetWare DOS Requester — VLM files

STARTNET.BAT automates the loading of these files — isn't that special. By default, it consists of the following commands:

```
C:
cd \NWCLIENT
LSL.COM — the first ODI file
NE2000 — or other MLID driver
IPXODI.COM — or other communications protocol file
VLM.EXE — loads the NetWare DOS Requester
F: — switches to the first network drive
LOGIN Guinevere — or other username
```

By default, this file is stored in the C:\NWCLIENT subdirectory. This is also where the NetWare 4 client installation process stores ODI drivers and VLMs. The beauty of this scenario is that it enables you to separate workstation connectivity files from other DOS programs. Also, it gives you a central point of workstation management. Once STARTNET.BAT has loaded and the workstation connectivity files are initialized, control shifts from the workstation to server login scripts.

QUIZ

Here's an easy one to warm up your gray matter. Twenty-four red socks and 24 blue socks are lying in a drawer in a dark room. What is the minimum number of socks I must take out of the drawer that will guarantee that I have at least two socks of the same color?

(Q6-1)

(See Appendix C for quiz answers.)

But not so fast. Before we move on to Step 2, you need to learn a little bit more about how these workstation connectivity files are configured. That is, you need to learn more about NET.CFG.

REAL WORLD

As a CNA, you'll decide how transparent the login process should be. Do you want Guinevere to input her login name and password, or have the system do it for her? While the latter is not the most secure alternative, it certainly removes the burden from Guinevere. The following line inputs Guinevere's username and password automatically:

```
LOGIN GUINEVERE < C:\NWCLIENT\PASSWORD.TXT
```

This statement logs Guinevere into the network and redirects her password from a text file on the C: drive. In order for this to work, make sure to place only her password (followed by a carriage return) in the text file. Although this isn't great security, you can deter would-be hackers by placing the text file in a hidden directory or on a secure boot disk. Remember, there's always a compromise between user transparent and security.

NET.CFG

The final workstation connectivity file is NET.CFG. This file is not executed, it's simply used as a support file for customizing ODI and VLM settings for STARTNET.BAT. By default, NET.CFG must be stored in the same subdirectory as the other workstation connectivity programs. You only need to create a NET.CFG file if you plan to deviate from the established ODI/VLM defaults. You can create NET.CFG with any DOS text editor, and it must follow these general conventions:

- ► Left-justify section headings

- ► Place options under each section heading and indent them with a tab or at least one space

- ► Use upper- or lowercase for section headings and options

- ► Precede comments with a semicolon (;) or pound sign (#) for documentation purposes

► End each line with a hard return

► Write all numbers in decimal notation, except where noted

NET.CFG is your friend. Use it to customize ODI and VLM parameters as well as to automate the login process. In this section, we will explore NET.CFG as a CNA workstation management tool. You'll have a lot of parameters to think about, but keep in mind that many times the defaults are just fine. All in all, NET.CFG configurations fall into three categories:

► LINK DRIVER section

► NETWARE DOS REQUESTER section

► Other NET.CFG parameters

LINK DRIVER

LINK DRIVER is the section heading for ODI support. You use this section to name the MLID driver and specify hardware and software settings for items such as interrupt, memory address, and frame type. Recall that ODI is a modular communications strategy that relies on NET.CFG for specific hardware settings. The IPX.COM file used in earlier versions of NetWare had these settings hardcoded into it during WSGEN configuration. This is not the case with ODI. LINK DRIVER enables you to specify nondefault MLID settings and incorporate a variety of different frame types at the NetWare workstation. Following is a sample format for Guinevere LINK DRIVER heading:

```
LINK DRIVER 3C5X9
        INT 3
        PORT 300
        MEM D0000
        FRAME Ethernet_802.2
```

Refer to Table 6.1 for a complete listing of the NetWare 4 LINK DRIVER parameters.

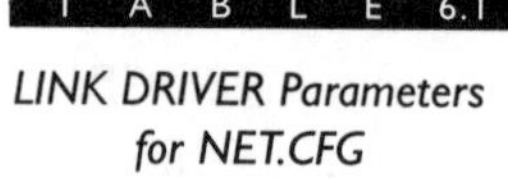

T A B L E   6.1

LINK DRIVER Parameters for NET.CFG

PARAMETER	RANGE	DESCRIPTION
INT	2 to 15	Interrupt value for the NIC (in decimal notation).
PORT	240 to 4AFF	I/O port address for the NIC (in hexadecimal format).
MEM	8000 to EFFF	Memory address for the NIC (in hexadecimal format).
DMA	1 to 7	Direct memory access (DMA) channel number for the NIC.
NODE ADDRESS	000000000000 to FFFFFFFFFFFE	Physical address for the NIC. This parameter enables you to override the physical address that is burned into each NIC at the factory. This is especially important for ARCNet.
SLOT	1 to 8	A MicroChannel and EISA parameter that identifies the NIC slot.
FRAME	Ethernet_802.2, Novell_RX-Net	Determines the frame type for workstation communications. By default, NetWare 4.1/3.12 use Ethernet_802.2, whereas NetWare 3.11/2.2 use Ethernet_802.3.

NetWare DOS Requester

The majority of NET.CFG customization occurs under the NETWARE DOS REQUESTER section heading. Here you get an opportunity to specify configurations for VLM operations. Some of the activities you can control include preferred trees, preferred servers, name context, first network drive, and packet signing. In addition, you can use NET.CFG to specify which VLMs are loaded and their order of execution. Here's a sample NETWARE DOS REQUESTER section for Guinevere's NET.CFG file:

```
NETWARE DOS REQUESTER

    Preferred Tree=ACME

    Name Context="OU=FIN.OU=OPS.OU=CAMELOT.O=ACME"

    First Network Drive=F

    PB Buffers=10

    Signature Level=3
```

QUIZ

What is Bullwinkle Moose's middle initial? You have a 1 in 26 chance of guessing it correctly!

(Q6-2)

Refer to Table 6.2 for a list of some of the most important NETWARE DOS REQUESTER parameters. Remember, this is the best way to customize the workstation attachment.

T A B L E 6.2

NETWARE DOS REQUESTER Parameters for NET.CFG

PARAMETER	RANGE	DESCRIPTION
PREFERRED TREE	Any tree name	Forces the workstation to attach to a specified tree. By default, it will find the tree defined by the nearest available server.
PREFERRED SERVER	Any server	Forces the workstation name to attach to a specified server. By default, NET.CFG will find the nearest available server.
NAME CONTEXT	Any NDS container	Places the workstation in a specified container once a connection is established. By default, the system will use the [Root] as the workstation context.
FIRST NETWORK DRIVE	A to Z	F by default. Establishes the first available network drive provided that the command LASTDRIVE=Z appears in the workstation CONFIG.SYS file. This is used for convenience and convention.
PB BUFFERS	0 to 10	3 by default. This sets the number of buffers used by packet bursting. Larger values increase performance but occupy additional workstation RAM.
SIGNATURE LEVEL	0 to 3	I by default. Sets the level of packet signing at the workstation. Higher values increase security but decrease performance.
USE DEFAULTS	ON or OFF	ON by default. If set to OFF, you must specify which VLMs are loaded using the VLM=name parameter.
VLM	Complete VLM filename	Enables you to load specific VLMs in a specific order. Be forewarned: Most VLMs are load-order dependent.

T A B L E   6.2

PARAMETER	RANGE	DESCRIPTION
CONNECTIONS	2 to 50	8 by default. This represents the maximum number of connections available to the workstation. You may need to increase this value if your NetWare 4 WAN has many active servers.
LOAD LOW CONN	ON or OFF	ON by default. When set to OFF, this parameter causes the CONN VLM to load in upper memory. This saves workstation RAM, but degrades performance.
LOAD LOW IPXNCP	ON or OFF	ON by default. When set to OFF, this parameter causes IPXNCP to load in upper memory.
MESSAGE TIMEOUT	0 to 10,000	0 by default. This controls how long the workstation waits before clearing broadcast messages. The default of 0 means users must press Ctrl+Enter to clear a broadcast message. If you want these messages to clear without user intervention increase the value up to 6 hours — where each number equals 1/18th of a second.
NETWORK PRINTERS	0 to 9	3 by default. This sets the number of printer ports the workstation can capture. Setting the value to 0 will cause PRINT.VLM not to load and disable network printing at the workstation.
CACHE BUFFER SIZE	512 to 4096 bytes	512 by default. This parameter sets the size of each cache buffer and can be used to increase performance. The size should be equal to (or at least an increment of) the maximum packet size.
CACHE BUFFERS	0 to 64	5 by default. This parameter sets how many cache buffers are available for sequential network files. Increasing this value speeds the movement of files across the LAN.

TIP

One important aspect of logging in is "context." In order for you to log in, the "Cloud" must be able to differentiate you from everybody else in the NDS tree. This means you have to tell the system where your home container is. In addition, most users access resources in their home container, and, therefore, should be guided there during login. You can specify a user's context during login in one of two ways. You can include the context with the login statement

LOGIN .CN=Guinevere.OU=FIN.OU=OPS.OU=CAMELOT.O=ACME

Alternatively, you can use the NAME CONTEXT parameter to specify the user's context before logging in:

NAME CONTEXT="OU=FIN.OU=OPS.OU=CAMELOT.O=ACME"

Note that the NAME CONTEXT line specifies a full distinguished name without a preceding period. This is one of those exceptions that Murphy keeps talking about.

Other NET.CFG Parameters

In the past, CNAs used SHELL.CFG to define parameters for the old IPX/NETx connectivity files. Fortunately, NetWare 4 supports these parameters by enabling you to include them at the top of NET.CFG. Following is a list of some of the most useful of these parameters, and remember — they must be left-justified.

- ▸ IPX RETRY COUNT — The IPX/SPX protocol uses this parameter to determine how many times to resend packets. This setting should be increased for an active network with heavy traffic and WANs that cover long distances. It works in conjunction with the SPX ABORT TIMEOUT parameter.

- SPX ABORT TIMEOUT — Adjusts the amount of time SPX waits without receiving any response from the other side. If this timeout value is exceeded, SPX aborts the connection. SPX ABORT TIMEOUT should be combined with IPX RETRY COUNT, for instance, if the workstation is using RPRINTER over routers. The default SPX ABORT TIMEOUT should be increased from 540 to about 1080 and the IPX RETRY COUNT should be doubled from 20 to 40.

- LONG MACHINE TYPE — You should use this parameter to specify the value returned by the %MACHINE login script variable. The default is IBM_PC. This parameter can be up to six characters long and should specify the type of machine being used — Altima, Compaq, Dell, NEC, and so on. This is a very important part of configuring the workstation DOS settings (as shown in Chapter 4 and the section, "Step 2: Creating Login Scripts," in this chapter).

- SHOW DOTS — Enables you to emulate the "dot" (.) and "double dot" (..) graphics in directory entries. The default is OFF, but should be set to ON for Windows support.

In addition to the above SHELL.CFG settings, NET.CFG supports one more section heading — LINK SUPPORT. This section is used for configuring receive buffers, the size of memory pools, and the number of boards and stacks for TCP/IP support. The BUFFERS option configures the number and size of receive buffers that LSL maintains. Because the IPX protocol stack does not use LSL communication buffers, this heading is rarely configured. TCP/IP, on the other hand, requires at least two link support buffers.

As a CNA, you can create NET.CFG files in one of two ways:

- Edit NET.CFG *after* client installation

- Edit INSTALL.CFG *before* client installation

After installing the NetWare DOS Requester, you will need to customize each user's NET.CFG file with additional settings. You can use any DOS text editor or the Windows WRITE application. Regardless of how you do it, each user's NET.CFG must be configured individually.

On the other hand, you can edit INSTALL.CFG before client installation and the system will automatically create a special NET.CFG for each user. During the NetWare 4 server installation, INSTALL.CFG is placed in the SYS:PUBLIC\CLIENT\DOSWIN subdirectory. You can use any DOS text editor to change the NetWare DOS Requester settings in INSTALL.CFG. The client installation program will then recognize INSTALL.CFG and create an identical NET.CFG for each user.

ZEN

"If you gaze for long into the abyss, the abyss also gazes into you."

Nietzsche

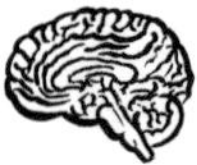

THE BRAIN

For additional information on configuring the NetWare DOS Requester and NET.CFG settings, see these *Novell Applications Notes:* "Using the DOS Requester with NetWare 4.0" (April 1993), "The Functions and Operations of the NetWare DOS Requester v1.1" (June 1994), and "Support Issues for the NetWare Requester (VLM) 1.2" (March 1995).

This completes our discussion of NET.CFG and workstation connectivity files in general. Now that the first step of configuration has been completed, Leia is well on her way to toddlership and Guinevere is well on her way to LAN productivity. At this point, the workstation computer has booted, the connectivity software has been activated, and Guinevere has been logged in. The next step is to customize Guinevere's network connection via login scripts. Let's dive in.

Step 2: Login Scripts

Chatterbox.

The next step in Leia's development is learning to talk. One day, your LAN's mindless babbling will begin to form words. Of course, we all know her first word will be "Daddy." Embrace these early days because soon she'll begin to form sentences and "Daddy" will become "Daddy, where're the car keys?" or "Daddy, I'm getting married" or, even worse, "Daddy, I want to be a CNA." Aah, the innocence of youth!

ZEN

"But the Emperor has nothing on at all!," cried the little child.

Hans Christian Andersen

Login scripts are an expression of your LAN's vocal cords. Once Guinevere has been authenticated with a valid username and password, NetWare 4 greets her with login scripts. In short, login scripts are batch files for the network. They provide a simple configuration tool for user customization — drive mappings, text messages, printer redirection, and so on.

Login scripts are one of your most important configuration responsibilities. From one central location, they enable you to customize *all* users or just specific groups of users. Many of the configurations we've talked about are session-specific and disappear when users log out. Login scripts give you the ability to reestablish these settings every time Guinevere logs in. Don't underestimate the power of NetWare 4 login scripts.

NetWare 4 supports four types of login scripts, which are executed in systematic progression. As you can see in Figure 6.1, there's a flowchart logic to how login scripts are executed. Here's a quick look:

- *Container login scripts* are properties of Organization and Organizational Unit containers. They enable you to customize settings for all users within a container.

- *Profile login scripts* are properties of the Profile object. These scripts customize environmental parameters for groups of users. This way, users who are not directly related in the NDS tree can share a common login script.

- *User login scripts* are properties of each User object. They are executed after the Container and Profile scripts and provide customization all the way to the user level.

- *Default login scripts* are executed for any user who does not have an individual User script. This script contains some basic mappings for the system and a COMSPEC command that points to the appropriate network DOS directory.

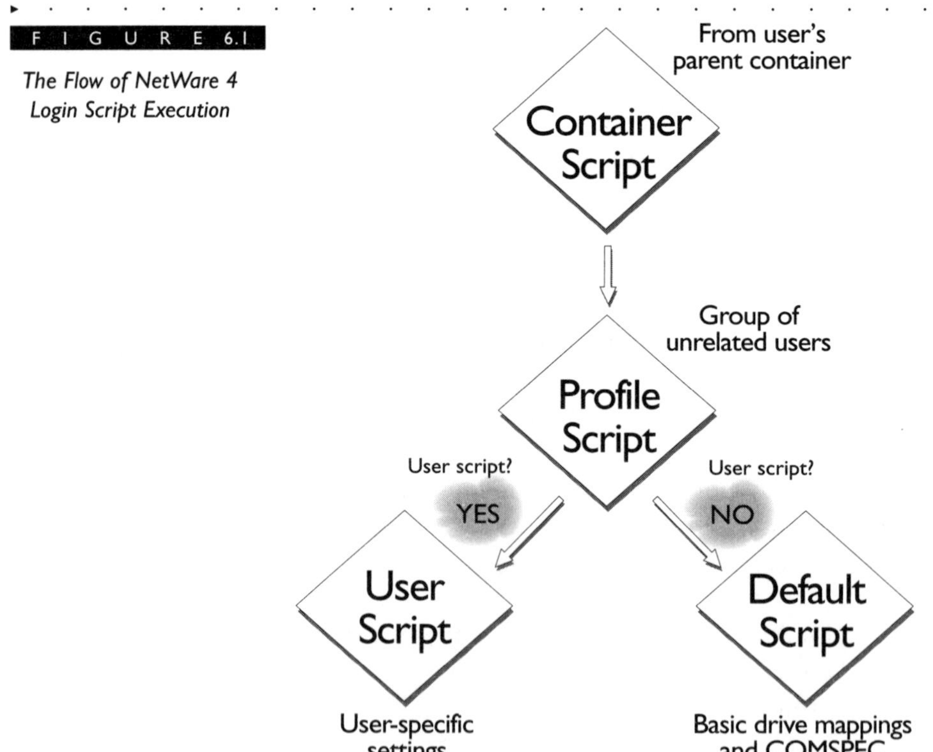

F I G U R E 6.1

*The Flow of NetWare 4
Login Script Execution*

Login scripts consist of commands and identifiers just like any other program or batch file. In addition, login script syntax must follow specific rules and conventions. Let's start our discussion with a more detailed look at the four login script types and then explore the commands that make them productive.

LOGIN SCRIPT TYPES

We just saw that there are four types of NetWare 4 login scripts — Container, Profile, User, and Default. All four work in concert to provide LAN customization for containers, groups, and users. As you'll quickly learn, login scripts are an integral part of your daily CNA grind. Let's start with a description of the four different login script types.

Container Login Script

Container login scripts are properties of Organization and Organizational Unit containers. In previous versions of NetWare, there was one System login script that was executed for all users. In NetWare 4, it is possible for every container to have its own login script. As you can see in Figure 6.1, the container is the first login script executed — Profile and User scripts follow.

There is one important difference between the NetWare 4 Container login script and earlier System login scripts. A Container script only executes for users *within* the container. As you can see in Figure 6.2, the Admin user executes the ACME Container login script. SHolmes, on the other hand, doesn't execute any Container login script because the CRIME Organizational Unit doesn't have a script. Similarly, RHood executes the WHITE Container login script, whereas AEinstein executes none.

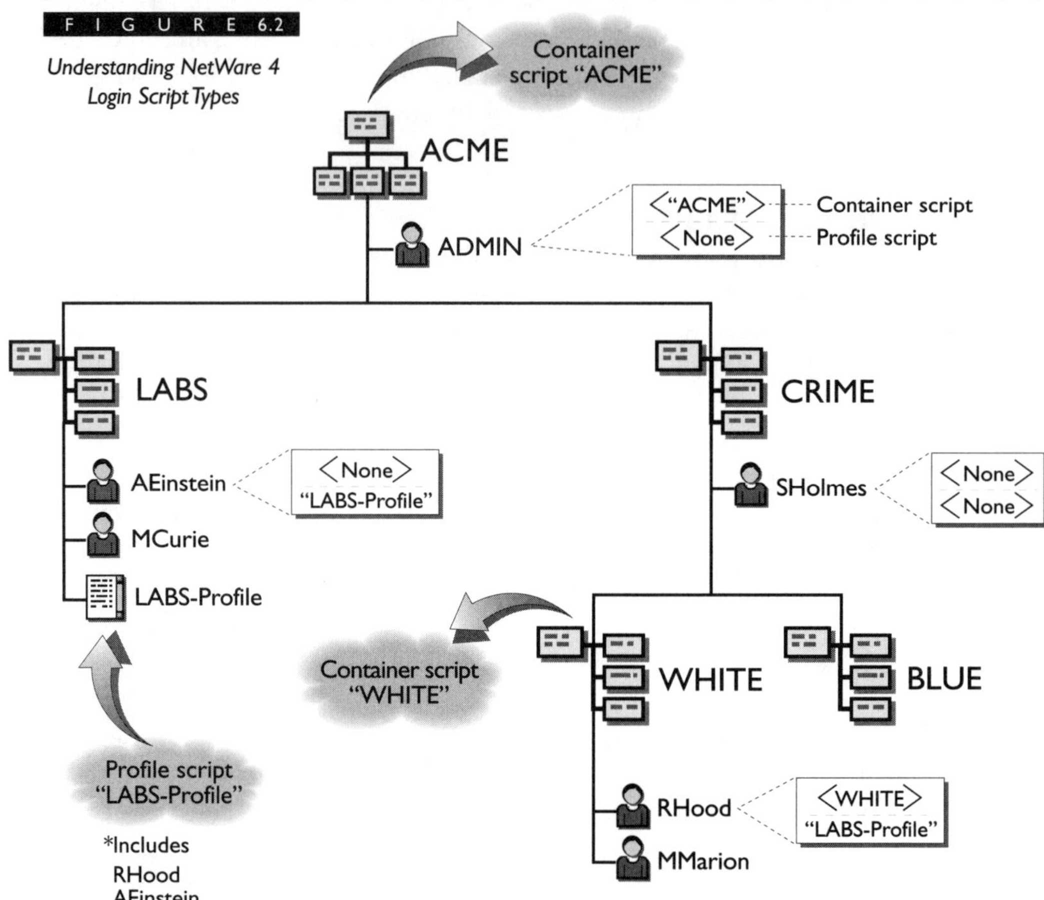

This is an important point because many CNAs assume that Container login scripts can be inherited by lower containers. This is *not* the case. If you wish to have one login script for all users to share, you have three options: (1) You can create a Profile login script and have all users point to it; (2) you can use the cut-and-paste feature within NWADMIN to copy one script to all containers; or (3) you can use an INCLUDE statement in each Container login script, which executes a text file containing these commands. Regardless, the moral of the story is that NetWare 4 no longer provides a single script for all users.

As you plan login scripts for your network, keep in mind that, at some point, you'll need to maintain them. Use Container login scripts to provide access to network resources, Profile scripts for a specific group's needs, and User login scripts only in special circumstances. Following are the types of things you might do within a Container login script:

- ▸ Send messages to users within a container

- ▸ Establish the first search drive mapping to SYS:PUBLIC

- ▸ Establish the second search drive mapping to DOS directories

- ▸ Create other search drive mappings for application directories

- ▸ Establish a network drive mapping U: to each user's home directory

- ▸ Connect users within a container to appropriate network printers

- ▸ Use IF...THEN statements for access to specific resources based on times, group memberships, and other variables

- ▸ Transfer users to an appropriate container-based menu system

Profile Login Script

The Profile login script is a property of the Profile object. This script customizes environmental parameters for groups of users. Each User object can be assigned a single Profile script — that's all. This way, users who are not directly related in the NDS tree can share a common login script. For example, Figure 6.2 shows how AEinstein and RHood can share the LABS-Profile login script even though they live in different parts of the tree. Also, note how the Profile login script executes after the Container script and in Mr. Einstein's case, the Profile login script is the only script that executes.

Figure 6.3 shows an example of how the Profile login script is created in NWADMIN. Once the script has been defined, two things must happen so you can use it. One, each user must have the Browse right to the object and the Read property right to the Profile object's login script property. Two, the complete name of the Profile object must be defined in the user's Profile login script property. See the case study at the end of this chapter.

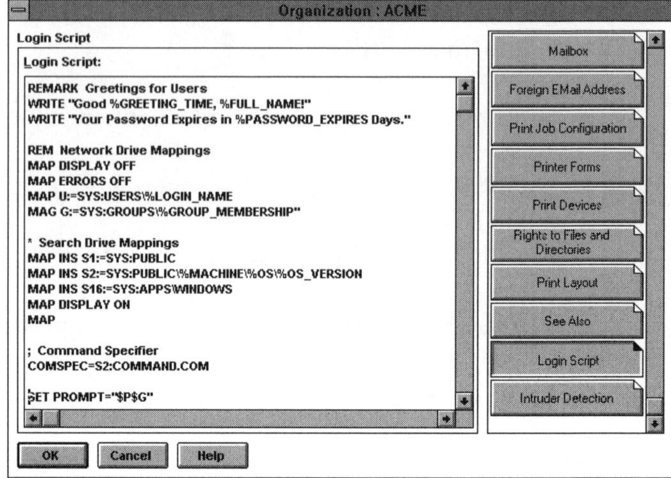

FIGURE 6.3

Creating the LABS Profile Script in NWADMIN

TIP

Remember, users can be assigned to only one Profile object, but other Profile login scripts can be specified at the command line. For example, the following line would allow RHood to execute the "WHITE-Profile" script in addition to his default "LABS-Profile" script:

LOGIN RHOOD /PR.CN=WHITE-Profile.OU=WHITE.OU=CRIME.OU=TOKYO.O=ACME

Wasn't that fun?

Profile login scripts should be used to customize specific group configurations. Some tasks you can accomplish with Profile login scripts include

▶ Send messages to users within a group

▶ Establish network drive mappings to special data directories, report files, or other servers that contain critical group information

- Establish search drive mappings to group application directories

- Connect to group-specific printers such as high-resolution LaserJets, plotters, or faxes

User Login Script

The User login script is a property of each User object. The User script is executed after the Container and Profile scripts, and provides customization all the way down to the user level. Although User scripts are a nice feature, they can quickly become a maintenance nightmare — imagine hundreds and hundreds of User login scripts constantly screaming for attention. Nope, one baby is enough. A better strategy is to use Container and Profile scripts as much as possible and eliminate the User scripts altogether.

The primary purpose of the User login script is user-specific customization. This level of customization can be accomplished in the Container and Profile scripts by using IF...THEN logic commands. But, if you absolutely have to create a user-specific script, it's nice to know that it's there.

User login scripts should be created only in special circumstances. Remember, you have to *maintain* any scripts you create. Some instances when a User script might be justified include

- Establish network drive mappings to specific user directories, provided that these directories do not correspond with the drive mappings made in the Container script

- Connect to commonly used printers, in addition to the ones selected in the Container and Profile scripts

- Send weekly messages to remind the user about time-sensitive tasks

- Activate a special user-specific menu system

Default Login Script

The Default login script is executed for any user who does not have an individual User script. This poses an interesting dilemma. Earlier we said it's a good idea not to have a User script. This means the Default script will automatically execute. Oops. This is a problem because the default script typically corrupts already-established drive mappings and COMSPEC settings. Fortunately, Novell has recognized this problem and provides you with the means to disable the Default login script using the following statement:

```
NO_DEFAULT
```

This command must be placed in a Container or Profile login script.

TIP

The Default login script cannot be edited because it is included in the LOGIN.EXE command code. It can, however, be disabled by including the NO_DEFAULT command in a Container or Profile script.

QUIZ

So, you think you're so smart? Let's see if you can think in three dimensions. A man is 100 yards due south of a bear. He walks 100 yards due east, then faces due north, fires his gun due north, and hits the bear.

What color was the bear?

Don't underestimate this one. The answer is much more involved than you think.

(Q6-3)

This completes our discussion of the different login script types. In leaving this little discussion, consider the factors that determine how you use login scripts and which types you'll need. These factors include the needs of users, their knowledge level, the size of your network, the complexity of the WAN, the type of groups, and access requirements for different containers. Remember, login script design can go a long way toward increasing your CNA quality of life and decreasing your daily workload. This is your first shot at parenthood (system customization); don't underestimate it.

LOGIN SCRIPT COMMANDS

Login scripts consist of commands and identifiers just as any other program or batch file. In addition, login script syntax must follow specific rules and conventions. The syntax for login script programming is quite simple, but you must be sure to organize identifier variables and commands with appropriate grammar — much like learning to talk. For example, consider the following line:

```
MAP U:=SYS:USERS\%LOGIN_NAME
```

This line uses proper login script syntax — it starts with the login script MAP command and uses appropriate identifier variable grammar — %LOGIN_NAME. The cool thing about this line is that it changes for each user. For example, when Dr. Watson logs in, the system creates a U: drive for him, and it points to SYS:USERS\DRWATSON. On the other hand, when SHolmes logs in, his U: drive points to SYS:USERS\SHOLMES. Cool!

Another good example of login script vernacular is the WRITE command. Consider the following statement:

```
WRITE "Good %GREETING_TIME, %FULL_NAME!"
```

Depending on the time of day and user who logs in, this single statement will provide a custom message. For example, Guinevere gets the following message when she turns on her machine in the morning:

```
"Good Morning, Guinevere Wannamaker!"
```

This can go a long way in making users feel warm and fuzzy about the LAN. As a matter of fact, some users get the perception that NetWare actually *cares* about them and is personally wishing them a nice day. Regardless of the LAN's motivation, the point is that users feel good about using the network!

All this configuration magic is made possible because of two login script elements — identifier variables and commands. Let's take a closer look at how they work.

Identifier Variables

Identifier variables enable you to enter a variable (such as LAST_NAME) rather than a specific name (Wannamaker). When the login script executes, it substitutes real values for the identifier variables. This means that you can make your login scripts more efficient and more flexible. In addition, it makes the concept of a single Container script feasible. As we saw in earlier examples, identifier variables are preceded by a percent sign (%) and written in all uppercase. This is the ideal syntax for identifier variables because it allows you to use them anywhere in the script, including inside quotation marks (" "). Table 6.3 lists all the identifier variables available in NetWare 4. Learn them. These cute little guys can go a long way in customizing Container and Profile scripts.

	CATEGORY	IDENTIFIER VARIABLE	DESCRIPTION
T A B L E 6.3			
Login Script Identifier Variables for NetWare 4	Date	DAY	Day number 01 through 31
		DAY_OF_WEEK	Day of week (Monday, Tuesday, and so on)
		MONTH	Month number (01 through 12)
		MONTH_NAME	Month name (January, February, and so on)
		NDAY_OF_WEEK	Weekday number (1 through 7, where 1 equals Sunday)
		SHORT_YEAR	Last two digits of year
		YEAR	All four digits of year
	Time	AM_PM	a.m. or p.m.
		GREETING_TIME	Time of day (morning, afternoon, or evening)
		HOUR	Hour of day on a 12-hour scale
		HOUR24	Hour of day on a 24-hour scale

CATEGORY	IDENTIFIER VARIABLE	DESCRIPTION
	MINUTE	Minutes (00 through 59)
	SECOND	Seconds (00 through 59)
User	CN	User's full common name as it exists in NDS
	ALIAS_CONTEXT	Y if REQUESTER_CONTEXT is an Alias
	FULL_NAME	User's unique full name as it appears in both NDS and the bindery
	LAST_NAME	User's last name in NDS or full name in bindery-based NetWare
	LOGIN_CONTEXT	Context where user exists
	LOGIN_NAME	User's unique login name truncated to eight characters
	MEMBER OF "*GROUP*"	Group object that user is assigned to
	NOT MEMBER OF "*GROUP*"	Group object that the user is *not* assigned to
	PASSWORD_EXPIRES	Number of days before password expires
	REQUESTER_CONTEXT	Context when login started
	USER_ID	Unique hexadecimal ID assigned to each user.
Workstation	MACHINE	Type of computer (either IBM_PC or other name specified in NET.CFG)
	NETWARE_REQUESTER	Version of Requester being used (NetWare Requester for DOS or OS/2)

(continued)

TABLE 6.3

Login Script Identifier Variables for NetWare 4 (continued)

CATEGORY	IDENTIFIER VARIABLE	DESCRIPTION
	OS	Type of operating system on the workstation (MSDOS, OS/2, and so on)
	OS_VERSION	Operating system version loaded on the workstation
	P_STATION	Workstation's 12-digit hexadecimal node ID
	SHELL_TYPE	Version of the work-station's DOS shell for NetWare 2 and 3 users
	S_MACHINE	Short machine name (IBM, and so on)
	STATION	Workstation's connection number
Miscellaneous	FILE_SERVER	NetWare server name that workstation first attaches to
	NETWORK_ADDRESS	IPX external network number for the cabling system (eight-digit hexadecimal number)
	ACCESS_SERVER	Shows whether the access server is functional (true or false)
	ERROR_LEVEL	An error number (0 equals no errors)
	%n	Replaced by parameters entered after the LOGIN command (starting with %0)

In addition to these identifier variables, you can use any NDS property name within a NetWare 4 login script. Just be sure to use the same syntax — that is, uppercase and preceded by a percent sign.

REAL WORLD

Here's a list of things to think about when creating NetWare 4 login scripts. It's always a good idea to have a few guidelines in mind before you begin exploring all the possibilities:

- Minimum — None. All four login script types are optional. Of course, if no User script exists, the default will run. So, at the absolute minimum, you must have one User script with one command — EXIT.

- Case — Not case-sensitive, except for identifier variables in quotations. They must be uppercase and preceded by a percent sign (%).

- Characters per line — 150 maximum, although 78 is recommended for readability.

- Commands per line — One. Also press Enter to mark the end of each line. Lines that automatically wrap are considered one command.

- Blank lines — Have no effect. Use them to visually separate groups of commands.

- Documentation — Use any version of the REMARK command to thoroughly document what's going on.

These identifier variables have to be used with valid login script commands. As you can see in Figure 6.4, NetWare 4 includes a plethora of commands that can be used in various configurations. In this discussion, we'll present the commands as part of a productive NetWare 4 Container login script. In each case, refer to Figure 6.4 for appropriate syntax.

```
A   {   REMARK Greetings for users
        WRITE "Good %GREETING_TIME, %FULL_NAME!"
        WRITE "Your Password Expires in %PASSWORD_EXPIRES DAYS"

B   {   REM Network Drive Mappings
        MAP DISPLAY OFF
        MAP ERRORS OFF
        MAP U:=SYS:USERS\%LOGIN_NAME
        MAP G:=SYS:GROUPS\"%Group Membership"

C   {   *Search Drive Mappings
        MAP INS S1:=SYS: PUBLIC
        MAP INS S2:=SYS: PUBLIC \%MACHINE\%OS\%OS_VERSION
        MAP INS S16:=SYS:APPS\WINDOWS
        MAP DISPLAY ON
        MAP

D   {   ; Command Specifier
        COMSPEC= S2: COMMAND.COM

E   {   SET PROMPT= "$P$G"
        SET TEMP= "U:\USERS\%LOGIN_NAME\TEMP"

F   {   IF DAY_OF_WEEK= "Friday" THEN BEGIN
            MAP R:=.REPORTS.LABS.NORAD.ACME
            DISPLAY R:FRIDAY.TXT
            PAUSE
        END

G   {   IF MEMBER OF "OPS-Group" THEN #CAPTURE P=HP4S1-P1 NT1=10
        IF MEMBER OF "ADMIN-Group" THEN #CAPTURE P=HP5-P1 NFF NT
        IF MEMBER OF "LABS-Group" THEN #CAPTURE P=CANONBJ-P1 NB

H   {   NO_DEFAULT

I   {   PCCOMPATIBLE
        DRIVE U:
        EXIT "Start"
```

A: WRITE and REMARK

Login scripts should always start with documentation. This is accomplished using the REMARK command. Any line beginning with REMARK is ignored. It does, however, provide a useful tool for documenting the many different sections of your Container and Profile scripts. Besides the word REMARK, NetWare 4 supports three other uses — REM, an asterisk (*), and a semicolon (;). As you can see in Figure 6.4, all possibilities have been used. Another use of documentation is edit tracking. When multiple supervisors are maintaining the same Container login script, it's a good idea to document who does what when. Finally, documentation is necessary for CNAs who follow you. After all, you do plan on winning the lottery, don't you?

ZEN

"Miami Beach is where neon goes to die."

Lenny Bruce

One of the most popular login script commands is WRITE. With it, you can display a variety of friendly messages during login script execution. One of the friendliest is shown in Figure 6.4. Other identifier variables you can use with the WRITE command include:

```
Your password expires in %PASSWORD_EXPIRES days.
Today is %MONTH_NAME %DAY.
At the tone, the time is %HOUR:%MINUTE %AM_PM.
You're connected as workstation %STATION.
You're attached to %FILE_SERVER.
```

Don't underestimate the power of communication. Goodwill flourishes with a quick note to your users now and again.

B: Network Drive Mappings

The next section in Figure 6.4 establishes user-specific and group-specific drive mappings. Drive mapping is the single, most important purpose of login scripts. Mappings are essential to NetWare navigation and provide a facility for representing large directory paths as drive letters. The problem with mapping is that it's both session-specific (meaning drive pointers disappear when users log out) and user-specific (meaning they're unique for each user). The temporary nature of drive mappings makes them particularly annoying — because complex MAP commands must be entered each time a user logs in. Fortunately, this process can be automated using NetWare 4 login scripts.

Before you get too excited about network and search drive mappings, it's a good idea to turn off the display of drive mapping and drive mapping errors. MAP DISPLAY OFF stops complex mappings from displaying during execution, and MAP ERRORS OFF avoids confusing users with mappings to directories they don't have rights to. Don't worry, we'll turn them back on later.

The MAP command is most useful when combined with identifier variables. This way, you can accomplish user-specific and group-specific mappings with only one command. Notice the second network drive mapping in Figure 6.4. Here we're using the Group Membership property from NDS. The trick is getting the quotes in the right place.

C: Search Drive Mappings

Once the network drive mappings have been established, it's time to shift your attention to search drive mappings. By default, the first two should always be SYS:PUBLIC and the network DOS directory structure. Notice our creative use of identifier variables in search mapping 2. This single statement intelligently maps every workstation to the appropriate version of DOS. Of course, these statements must be combined with the exact DOS structure outlined in Chapter 4. The three key identifier variables are

- %MACHINE — Identifies the machine such as IBM_PC, Dell, NEC, and so on. These values are established using the LONG MACHINE TYPE parameter in NET.CFG.

- %OS — Identifies the operating system as MSDOS, OS/2, PCDOS, DRDOS, and so on.

- %OS_VERSION — Identifies the specific version of DOS running on the workstation (for example, v5.00, v7.01, v6.22).

Next, you should create a search drive mapping for every application that users are likely to access. In these cases, you can use MAP INS S16 to systematically create mappings in order. In each case, S16 will drop to the next available search number. Finally, turn MAP DISPLAY back on and issue one final MAP command to show the user what he/she has available.

 **TIP**

Remember from Chapter 4 that NetWare search mappings systematically replace the DOS path statement. Also remember that using MAP INSERT eliminates this problem by adding the DOS path to the end of the NetWare search list. In addition, an interesting thing happens when you use "MAP INS S16." The NetWare search drives are added *after* the DOS path. This means users will execute local applications before network ones. Sometimes, this is a good thing!

 **QUIZ**

What is the name for the upper portion of the BRAIN? You know, the part that really hurts right now.

(Q6-4)

D: COMSPEC

The next step is to create a COMSPEC for the new DOS directory mapping. COMSPEC stands for "Command Specifier," and it helps NetWare find COMMAND.COM when it's lost. This happens all the time when TSRs and Windows applications need extra space. If COMMAND.COM cannot be found, your users will get one of these messages:

```
Invalid COMMAND.COM
COMMAND.COM cannot be found
Insert Boot Disk in Drive A
```

Interestingly, this causes the hair to stand up on the back of your neck — especially if it happens all day. This must be a kinetic reaction.

COMSPEC solves the "lost DOS" problem by telling the system where to search for appropriate COMMAND.COM files. Keep in mind that each version of DOS on each of your workstations supports a different type of COMMAND.COM. You must make sure to point to the correct file. This is accomplished by using the S2: drive mapping we created earlier. Remember, it points to the correct DOS directory structure for each workstation.

TIP

Sending COMSPEC to a network directory for COMMAND.COM has its advantages. However, many CNAs still insist on pointing to a local drive such as C:\DOS. It's your choice. Here are some reasons to use the NetWare 4 DOS directory structure:

- ▶ **Speed (with file caching)**

- ▶ **Central management (all workstations point to the file server)**

- ▶ **Diskless workstations (it's required)**

E: SET

The SET command enables you to configure DOS environment variables within the login script. You can use the SET command exactly the same as you would in DOS (except that you'll need to surround the values with quotation marks). Otherwise, most SET variables are configured in the user's AUTOEXEC.BAT file. In Figure 6.4, we've included two important SET variables:

```
SET PROMPT="$P$G"
```

This configures the local and network prompt to display the current directory path. We want users to feel like they're at home.

```
SET TEMP="U:\USERS\%LOGIN_NAME\TEMP"
```

This points the Windows TEMP directory to a NetWare drive under the user's area. Whatever you do, don't use the SET PATH command in a Container login script; it overwrites local and network search drives.

F: IF...THEN... ELSE

The IF...THEN command enables you to use script programming logic. It checks a given condition and executes your command only if the condition is met. In addition, you can add the ELSE statement to selectively execute another command only when the condition is *not* met. For example, you can have the system display a fancy message and fire phasers whenever it is the user's birthday (using MONTH and DAY identifier variables). Otherwise, display a message pointing out that it's not his/her birthday the other 364 days of the year.

The IF...THEN command is the most versatile login script tool. Learn it, use it, be it. IF...THEN effectively enables you to execute any command based on condition, including login name, context, day of the week, or group membership. As you can see in Figure 6.4, we are executing these three commands only on Friday:

- MAP — Maps the R: drive to a Directory Map object.

- DISPLAY — Displays a text file that is stored on the R: drive.

- PAUSE — Temporarily stops execution of the login script to allow the user time to read the display. Just as with the DOS PAUSE command, execution resumes when the user presses any key.

Also notice the use of BEGIN and END. If you plan on including multiple commands within a nested IF...THEN statement, you must use BEGIN to start and END to mark the bottom of the nest. As a sidenote, IF...THEN statements can be nested up to 10 levels.

You can do anything with an IF...THEN statement. Don't be shy. Before you resign yourself to creating Profile and User login scripts, explore the use of IF...THEN statements in Container scripts.

G: # (DOS Executable)

The DOS executable (#) command has been included by Novell to support external programs. Because NetWare 4 has a limited number of login script commands, you might run across a case where you need to run a non-login script program. The most obvious oversight that comes to mind is CAPTURE, which is a NetWare 4 printing command that redirects local ports to shared network printers.

This command should be included in Container and Profile scripts for user and group automation. You can do so with the following command:

```
#CAPTURE P=HP4SI-P1 NT TI=10
```

There is one problem with this scenario. While CAPTURE is running, the entire login script and LOGIN.EXE is swapped to workstation RAM. Once the # command is finished, NetWare reloads the login script from memory. But what if the external program is a TSR or never returns stolen RAM to the workstation? In both of these cases, you run the risk of wasting 70K to 100K of workstation RAM. This is a bad thing. By default, NetWare 4 swaps login scripts and LOGIN.EXE into extended or expanded memory.

Fortunately, CAPTURE is not one of those misbehaving # commands. As you can see in Figure 6.4, we've combined the #CAPTURE program with IF...THEN statements to customize group-specific printing captures within a single Container login script. Once again, the goal is to satisfy all your users' needs from within a single, centrally managed login script.

H: NO_DEFAULT

Here's another command that helps you avoid conflicts between a central Container script and the Default login script. As you remember from our earlier discussion, the Default login script is contained in LOGIN.EXE and cannot be edited. In addition, it conflicts with drive mappings and the COMSPEC command from Container and Profile scripts. Finally, the Default login script executes only if there is no User script, and this conflicts with our goal of having one centrally managed Container login script. Fortunately, by using the NetWare 4 NO_DEFAULT command you can skip the Default login script even without a User script. Simply place it toward the end of your Container or Profile script and everything will be fine. Sometimes life can be so easy.

I: EXIT

Congratulations, you've made it to the end of our mammoth Container login script. Don't forget Guinevere. She's counting on finding a menu system and e-mail somewhere in her future. As a CNA, it is your job to orchestrate a smooth transition from Guinevere's login script to her menu system. Fortunately, you have the EXIT command.

EXIT terminates any login script and executes a specific network program. The program can be an .EXE, .COM, or .BAT file and must reside in the default directory. When combined with the DRIVE command (as shown in Figure 6.4), EXIT can facilitate a smooth transition from login script to menu system. In the case of Figure 6.4, we're exiting to a START batch file residing in either SYS:PUBLIC or the user's home area. Here's what START looks like:

```
ECHO OFF
CLS
CAPTURE P=HP4SI-P1 NFF NT
TSA_SMS /SE=CAM-FIN-SRV1 /P=RUMPELSTILTSKIN /D=C /B=30
NMENU GUINEVER.DAT
```

In this scenario, the DRIVE command dumps Guinevere into her own home directory where the menu system resides. Otherwise, she would be placed in the first available network drive (by default). In addition, the PCCOMPATIBLE line ensures that her clone workstation returns a %MACHINE value of IBM_PC.

It's important to note that the EXIT command skips all other login scripts. For this reason, you'll want to be careful where you place it. Only use EXIT in a Container login script if you're convinced there are no Profile or User scripts, or if you'd rather not execute those scripts because they've been created by nonauthorized managers. All in all, this is a great strategy for skipping unnecessary login scripts and making a smooth transition to Guinevere's menu system.

ZEN

"When love and skill work together, expect a masterpiece."

John Ruskin

Before we move on to Step 3: Menu System, let's take a quick look at some other powerful login script commands.

Other Login Script Commands

In addition to the commands shown in Figure 6.4, NetWare includes a potpourri of other login script commands. For a complete listing, refer to THE BRAIN after this discussion.

- ▸ BREAK — If "BREAK ON" is included in a login script, you can press Ctrl+C or Ctrl+Break to abort the normal execution of a login script. This is not a good thing, especially in the hands of users. The default is BREAK OFF.

- ▸ CLS — Use CLS to clear the user's screen during login script execution.

- ▸ CONTEXT — This command changes the workstation's current NDS context during login script execution. It works similarly to the workstation CX utility.

- ▸ FDISPLAY — Works the same as DISPLAY, except it filters formatting codes before showing the file on the screen. It can be used to display the text of an ASCII file without showing all the ASCII formatting codes.

- ▸ FIRE PHASERS — Beam me up, Scotty. FIRE PHASERS can also be combined with identifier variables to indicate the number of times the phaser sound should blare. For example, FIRE PHASERS %NDAY_OF_WEEK will fire five phasers on Thursday.

- ▸ GOTO — This command enables you to execute a portion of the login script out of regular sequence. GOTO jumps to login script labels — text followed by a colon (TOP:, for example). Do not use GOTO to enter or exit a nested IF..THEN statement. This will cause the keyboard to explode. You can go through a lot of users this way.

▶ INCLUDE — As if one login script isn't enough. The INCLUDE command branches to subscripts from anywhere in the main Container script. These subscripts can be text files with valid login script syntax, or entire login scripts that belong to different objects in the NDS tree. Once the subscript has been completed, control shifts to the next line in the original script. Now we're really getting crazy. Consider using INCLUDE subscripts with IF...THEN statements to ultimately customize Container login scripts. Now there's no excuse for using Profile, User, or Default scripts. As a matter of fact, everyone in the WAN can share the same Container script by distributing INCLUDE statements to all Organizational Units. Think of the synergy.

▶ LASTLOGINTIME — As you've probably guessed, displays the last time the user logged in. This can be combined with WRITE statements to ensure that nobody is logging in as *you* while you're on vacation. When the cat's away, the mice will play.

▶ SWAP — As you recall from our earlier discussion, the # command swaps 100K of stuff into workstation RAM and doesn't always give it back. The SWAP command can be used to force the 100K out of workstation RAM onto the local or network disk. Simply identify a path with the SWAP command and LOGIN.EXE will bother you no more. When the # command is completed, LOGIN.EXE continues on its merry way. If this bothers you, NOSWAP will force LOGIN.EXE into conventional workstation RAM.

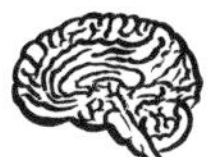

THE BRAIN

For a complete list of NetWare 4 login script commands and identifier variables, refer to page 187 of *Supervising the Network I*. Another good reference is "Using NDS User Object Properties in NetWare 4.1 Login Script" in the May 1995 *Novell Application Notes*.

That completes our discussion of NetWare 4 login scripts. I hope you've gained an appreciation for how these cute little tools help you customize user and group connections. Once the Container and Profile scripts have been executed, NetWare 4 automatically loads Guinevere's menu. As we saw, this is accomplished by using the EXIT login script command.

QUIZ

Now that you're warmed up, let's try something a little more interesting. Besides, Guinevere could solve it — how about you?

Alice, Brett, Catherine, and Deirdre went to school together. They became, but not necessarily respectively, an author, a biologist, a cartoonist, and a doctor. Years before, they belonged to A, B, C, and D sororities, and they came from Australia, Brazil, Canada, and Denmark. The letters of each woman's house, the initial letters of her profession, her home, and her name are all different from each other. The doctor had never been to Brazil, and the biologist had never been to Canada. Back at school, Catherine, the girl from Australia, and the biologist used to spend all their spare time together.

What was the profession, the home, and the house of each of them?

Good luck.

(Q6-5)

She can walk, she can talk; your LAN is an unstoppable bundle of joy. Now that all of the fundamentals have been accomplished, it's time to put her to the test — preschool. It's time for your LAN to learn how to get along with others.

Step 3: Creating the Menu System

Leia goes to preschool.

One of the most rewarding aspects of a child's development is watching how she gets along with others. You can't beat the thrill of discovery and the sight of two toddlers bonding. Of course, this peaceful picture hinges on the ability of children to "share" — a lesson the world hasn't quite caught onto yet. Although with Barney the dinosaur as our ambassador of sharing, I can understand why some people have resorted to violence. Not my baby! Leia's going to learn how to share without resorting to Barney-isms.

Social interaction is a valuable skill on any level. It's how the world works. Learning to get along with others is as practical a skill as tying your shoes or signing your name. As a matter of fact, you'll run into questions on your CNA job application that deal with this very topic.

Social interaction is also important to our NetWare 4 LAN. In order for Guinevere to get anything done, she needs a friendly menu interface for all her network applications and e-mail. A turnkey custom menu environment provides transparent access from "point A" (turning on the computer) to "point Z" (accessing her e-mail with cappuccino in hand). Fortunately, NetWare 4 has a built-in menu system that provides custom NetWare-looking menus. This system uses a simple script format and is versatile enough to support large groups of users with a single menu file.

Menus are a good thing. They provide a comfortable, friendly interface for Guinevere and eliminate the need to learn NetWare command line utilities. They present information in multiple layers instead of all in one place. But let's be honest. You're probably using MS Windows. On the most fundamental level, MS Windows is a simple graphical menu. It controls what kind of information is presented and enables users to launch applications from a single place. If you're using MS Windows, you don't need this menu system. However, it does have merits as a simple network-oriented interface for small NetWare 4 LANs. So, with that in mind, you're prepared to learn about it.

TIP

The NetWare 4 menu system is a partial version of the Saber Menu System. This software acquisition falls into the Novell category of "if you can't build it, buy it." As a partial version, NetWare 4 menus have limitations. For example, you can't specify the location of menus on the screen nor avoid the default color palette — blue and gold. In addition, NetWare's internal menu system is limited to 11 cascading screens — 1 main menu and 10 submenus. Finally, there's limited security and many missing features. So, if you're intrigued by what you learn here, consider contacting Saber and buying the full-blown version.

NetWare 4 menus are built using two simple command types:

- ▸ Organizational commands — providing the menu's look and feel

- ▸ Control commands — doing the work

In addition, NetWare 4 has specific rules about how menus are executed and what rights are necessary to get at them. These are the topics we're going to discuss in this section — starting with organizational commands.

ORGANIZATIONAL COMMANDS

It all starts with organizational commands. They provide the menu's look and feel. NetWare 4 supports two organizational commands:

- ▸ MENU — identifies the beginning of each menu screen and provides a title

- ▸ ITEM — defines the options that appear within the menu and includes a variety of built-in "squiggly" options

As you can see in Figure 6.5, the MENU command is left-justified and followed by a number. The menu number is then followed by a comma and the title of the menu. Next, options are listed under the MENU command using the organizational tool — ITEM. Items can be specific applications or other submenus — it doesn't matter. Using Figure 6.5 as a guide, let's explore these two organizational commands.

```
MENU 01, Guinevere's Main Menu
     ITEM  ^AApplications
           SHOW 10
     ITEM  ^EE-Mail {BATCH}
           EXEC WIN WMAIL
     ITEM  ^FFun Stuff
           SHOW 15
     ITEM  ^MAdmin Menu
           LOAD G:\GROUPS\ADMIN\ADMIN.DAT
     ITEM  ^LLogout
           EXEC LOGOUT

MENU 10, Guinevere's Applications
     ITEM  ^1Windows '95 {BATCH}
           EXEC WIN
     ITEM  ^2Network Utilities
           SHOW 20
     ITEM  ^3Word Perfect {CHDIR}
           EXEC WIN WPWIN

MENU 15, Guinevere's Fun Stuff
     ITEM  Pick your Doom
           GETO ENTER THE VERSION OF DOOM (1-3):{DOOM}1,1,{ }
           EXEC
     ITEM  Solitaire {BATCH}
           EXEC WIN SOL

MENU 20, Network Utilities
     ITEM  NetWare User Tools {BATCH}
           EXEC WIN NWUSER
     ITEM  Network Copy {PAUSE} {SHOW}
           GETP ENTER SOURCE FILE(S):{ }80,,{ }
           GETP ENTER DESTINATION FILE(S):{ }80,,{ }
           EXEC NCOPY %1 %2
```

MENU

MENU identifies the beginning of each menu screen. It is left-justified and followed by a number. A single NetWare 4 menu file can support 255 different menus — 1 through 255. The menu number is then followed by a comma and the title of the menu. As you can see in Figure 6.5, the first menu displays the title "Guinevere's Main Menu." Subsequent menus have systematically higher numbers (10, 15, and 20). Each menu number identifies the beginning of a new submenu for branching purposes (using the SHOW control command). Menu titles are limited to 40 characters.

> **REAL WORLD**
>
> The first menu defined in the source file is always the first menu displayed — no matter what number it uses. Subsequent submenus are referenced by their numbers. In Figure 6.5, the first menu has the number 01. This will be the first menu displayed for Guinevere — not because it's menu 01 but because it's the first menu shown in the source file. Branching to other submenus is accomplished with the SHOW command, not their numeric order. Bottom line: Menu numbers are for reference only; they don't have any systematical significance (there's a mouthful).

ITEM

Options are listed under each menu title using the ITEM command. Each item is preceded by a letter (from A through Z) and appears in the exact order in which it is written. If you'd like to force a different letter for any option, simply precede the text with a caret (^) and the desired letter. For example, refer to menu 01 in Figure 6.5. Notice how the five items are each preceded by a caret and a letter. This forces the letter E, for example, to appear in front of "E-mail." Otherwise, it would get the letter B. Numbers can also be used, as shown in Menu 10 of Figure 6.5. **Note**: If you force the letter assignment of one item, you should force the letter assignment of every item — but you don't have to. The menu program does not track forced assignments and might duplicate letters — this is a bad thing.

ITEM options can be customized using one of four built-in parameters. These are called "squiggly options" because they live inside cute "squiggly" brackets. Let's take a look:

- {BATCH} — shells the menu to disk and saves 32K of workstation RAM (see Figure 6.5)

- {CHDIR} — returns the user to the default directory upon completion of the item

- {PAUSE} — temporarily stops menu execution and displays the message

```
Press any key to continue.
```

ZEN

"Where's the Any key?"

Guinevere

> ▸ {SHOW} — displays DOS commands in the upper left-hand corner of
>   the screen when they're executed

Once you've created the "look and feel" of your menus, it's time to move on to
the real workhorses of NetWare 4 menuing — control commands.

CONTROL COMMANDS

The second NetWare 4 command type is control commands. These little wonders
are the workhorses of the menu system. They execute menu instructions and enable
branching to internal and external submenus. The NetWare 4 control commands
are

> ▸ EXEC — Executes any internal or external program.

> ▸ SHOW — Branches to another menu within this menu file. This is used
>   for submenuing.

> ▸ LOAD — Branches to a completely different external menu file (with the
>   .DAT extension).

> ▸ GETO — Supports optional user input.

> ▸ GETR — Supports required user input.

> ▸ GETP — Assigns user input to a programmable variable.

As you can see in Figure 6.5, the EXEC and SHOW control commands are the
most popular. In Guinevere's main menu, for example, she has the option of
branching to one of two submenus. This submenuing strategy continues throughout
her complex menu file. Let's take a closer look at how these little dynamos work.

EXEC

EXEC is the most popular NetWare 4 control command. It executes internal or external commands. These commands can be either an .EXE file, a .COM file, a DOS internal command, or one of four special EXEC options:

- EXEC CALL — Runs a batch file and returns to NMENU.

- EXEC DOS — Returns to the NetWare command line temporarily. Users must type **EXIT** to return to NMENU.

- EXEC EXIT — The only way to exit a NetWare 4 menu. Don't lock yourself in — use this command.

- EXEC LOGOUT — Exits NMENU and logs the user out. Guinevere is left at the DOS prompt without access to the network.

Be sure to include at least one of these EXEC commands toward the bottom of your main menu. As you can see in Figure 6.5, we're giving Guinevere the option of logging out. If you don't include one of these special EXEC options, the user will be trapped in the menu forever. This might not be a bad thing.

SHOW

SHOW is the second most popular NetWare 4 control command. Because you can create 255 submenus within a single script file, you need a way of getting to them. SHOW branches to another menu number from within any item. This is a way of submenuing from within the same script file. Notice in Figure 6.5 how the SHOW command is used with the Applications and Fun Stuff submenus. Also notice how Network Utilities is called as a submenu from within the Applications submenu.

TIP

Try not to confuse the SHOW control command with the SHOW squiggly option. It's unfortunate they share the same name. The SHOW control command is used for submenuing, whereas the SHOW squiggly option displays executed DOS commands in the upper left-hand corner of your screen.

LOAD

LOAD performs exactly the same function as SHOW, but in a slightly different way. Instead of executing submenus within the same script file, LOAD branches to submenus in completely different files. Refer to Figure 6.5 for an example of how the LOAD command is used. The Admin Menu item includes a branch to ADMIN.DAT. This external menu file must be in the default directory or specified with an exact path.

There is no limit to the number of menus that you can LOAD at any one time. But remember, you can only display 11 cascading menus simultaneously.

GETO

The final three control commands allow user input. This feature was previously not available in NetWare menus and is hard to find in MS Windows. GETO, GETR, and GETP are powerful tools, but their syntax is a little tricky:

```
GETx prompt{PREPEND}length,prefill,{APPEND}
```

- ▸ *x* is replaced with the type of GET command you wish to use — O for optional, R for required, and P for programmable user input.

- ▸ *prompt* is replaced by the message you want to send to the user. For example, in Figure 6.5, the last item asks Guinevere to "Enter source file(s):". This is the prompt.

- ▸ *{PREPEND}* data is attached *before* the user input. This works oppositely from *{APPEND}*. For example, in Figure 6.5, refer to the Pick your Doom item. The user is asked to enter the version of Doom he or she wishes to play. The number these choose is prepended by the DOOM command, and it executes a batch file to load the appropriate game. This is a *{PREPEND}*. If no *{PREPEND}* is necessary, use the braces without any characters between them. Refer to the last item in Figure 6.5.

- ▸ *length* is the maximum number of characters the user can enter. Again, a *length* is required and the maximum is 80 characters. In the DOOM example, users can only enter a one-character answer.

- *prefill* displays a default response if none is given. It is separated from *length* by a comma and no spaces. Again, in the DOOM example of Figure 6.5, you're forcing a 1 to appear if no input is given. This will run the original game.

- *{APPEND}* defines a value that will always be appended to the user input. Once again, these braces are required, and if no data are needed, type the brackets without any characters. Refer to the last item in Figure 6.5.

TIP

Wow, what a mind-boggling collection of NetWare 4 control commands. Don't GET too excited about using GETx. But if you have to, here are a few things to think about:

- **The GETO, GETR, and GETP commands must be entered between the ITEM line and the EXEC command associated with them.**

- **You can have a maximum of 100 GET commands per ITEM, although you want to limit each prompt to 1 line.**

- **Commands can be entered in either upper- or lowercase.**

- **You can enter up to 10 prompts in each dialog box. If you want a prompt to appear in its own dialog box, type a caret (^) at the beginning of the prompt text.**

- **During execution, the Enter key accepts input, but does not cause the command to execute. To activate the appropriate EXEC command, you must press F10.**

Now it's time to GET on with the show.

GETO allows for optional user input. As you can see in Figure 6.5, the Pick your Doom item uses an optional GET control command. If the user does not enter any input and simply presses Enter, NetWare executes the {*PREPEND*} and {*prefill*}, which is "DOOM1."

ZEN

"The computer is a great invention. There are just as many mistakes as ever. But now they are nobody's fault."

Anonymous

GETR

GETR requires user input. The menu will not continue until some valid information has been entered. However, the user can press Esc to return to the main menu.

GETP

GETP assigns user input to a programmable variable. If you need a variety of inputs from the user, assign each to a GETP prompt. The corresponding EXEC command can then use these prompts in combination with some valid external commands. As you can see in the final item of Figure 6.5, two GETP prompts are shown. The first input is assigned to %1 and the second to %2. The EXEC NCOPY command then uses these variables to satisfy the user's request. In addition, the {*PAUSE*} squiggly option enables the user to view the results as long as necessary.

Well, wasn't that fun? If you're feeling a little dizzy, now's a good time to put down the book and grab a soda . . . welcome back. Now that we've conquered the NetWare 4 menu syntax, let's take a look at how these babies execute.

MENU EXECUTION

So, how are NetWare 4 menu files executed? Good question. It all starts with the source file. Menu source files are created by using any text editor, and they must have the .SRC extension. As you can see in Figure 6.6, these source files are then compiled into .DAT files using MENUMAKE.EXE. The compiled files are smaller, more flexible, and easily swapped to and from the local disk. You cannot, however, edit .DAT files. You must edit the source file and recompile it for testing.

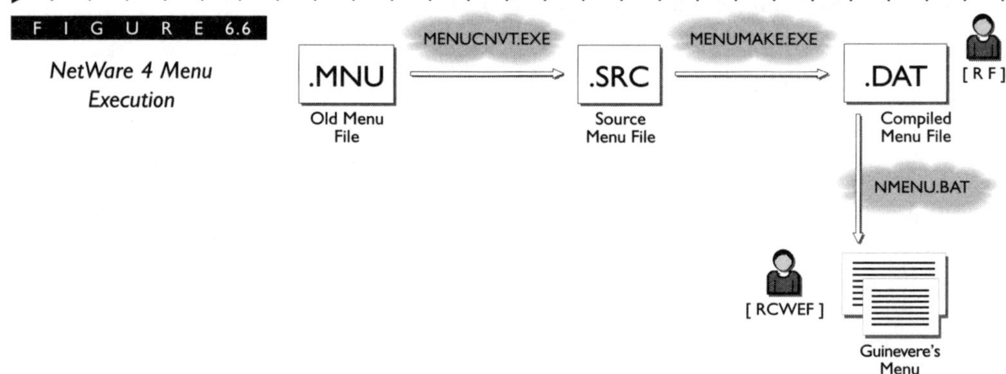

F I G U R E 6.6

NetWare 4 Menu Execution

The smaller, more flexible .DAT file is finally executed using NMENU.BAT. This step finally brings Guinevere's menu to life. (See Figure 6.7.)

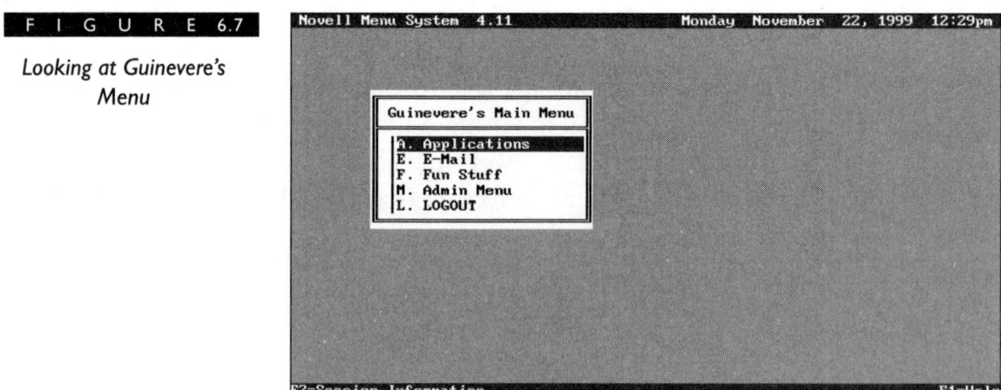

F I G U R E 6.7

Looking at Guinevere's Menu

That's not all — NetWare 4 also supports older menus. NetWare 3.11 menu files (with the extension .MNU) can be converted into NetWare 4 source files using MENUCNVT.EXE. These .SRC files are then compiled and displayed using MENUMAKE.EXE and NMENU.BAT. However, this is not the end of menu conversion. You must also edit some of the .SRC syntax changes, including invalid commands (such as SYSCON), preceding letters or numbers from the old menu system, and the conversion of "@1" variables into newer GETP statements.

So, what about security? The NMENU.BAT program is stored in SYS:PUBLIC so it can be accessed from anywhere by any NetWare user. In addition, there are access right issues concerning the location of .DAT files. Here's a summary:

▸ Users must have the Read and File Scan (RF) access rights to directories that hold the .DAT files. This is typically their home directory or a shared area such as SYS:PUBLIC.

▸ The NetWare 4 menu system creates many temporary files. For this reason, users need special rights in the current default directory when executing NMENU.BAT. These rights are Read, Create, Write, Erase, and File Scan (RWCEF). Typically, this is the user's home or temporary directory. Recall that in the previous discussion, you used EXIT to bail out of the Container login script and automatically accessed NMENU.BAT. You did this from Guinevere's home directory (with the DRIVE command) for security purposes. I knew there was a reason.

▸ If the menu file is going to be used by multiple users, it should be flagged as Sharable.

Once again, refer to Figure 6.6 for a summary of the access rights required at different points of menu execution.

So, what does Guinevere's menu look like? Check out Figure 6.7. As it shows, the NetWare 4 menu program creates an extremely NetWare-looking interface. As a matter of fact, it's difficult to tell the difference between Guinevere's main menu and NETADMIN. I just hope Guinevere can tell the difference. Let's review. NetWare 4 menu source files are created using any text editor. Their names contain the .SRC extension. These files are then compiled using MENUMAKE.EXE into a .DAT file.

The smaller, more flexible .DAT file is then executed using NMENU.BAT. Piece of cake.

ZEN

"Never eat more than you can lift."

Miss Piggy

Remember, "wherever you go, there you are." With that in mind, let's take a moment to reflect on our LAN's brief, but exciting, life so far. First, she was born (installation), and then she took her first step (workstation connectivity). Once she learned to talk (login scripts), we sent her off to preschool to learn how to get along with others (menu system).

Now, it's time for our talented toddler to scurry off to kindergarten. There she'll start her long and winding journey down the road known as "SCHOOL"! During this journey, Leia will expand her body and mind to new levels — gaining valuable skills in the process. She'll make friends, buy clothes, ignore you, go to the prom, and, finally, graduate. This all leads to one inevitable climax — adulthood. Where did all the time go?

Step 4: Installing Network Applications

Leia goes to school.

Aah, school:

"The chalice of wisdom, to drink once more from thee."

I don't know what's more memorable, school or all the extracurricular activities that surround it. Regardless, this is the fire in which we forge our personalities. So many memories — my fourth grade music teacher, recess, stomach-churning school lunches, mind-boggling math homework, field trips, sports, and the junior prom. As we help Leia through this phase of her childhood, we get an opportunity to live our own school days all over again. This is probably one of the most rewarding and excruciating experiences for any parent.

In addition to life lessons, school teaches you a few academic things. With knowledge comes productivity and wisdom. Suddenly, Leia's eyes open to the wonders and possibilities of calculus, art, and prepositional phrases. And sometimes the lessons aren't so obvious. I'm sure you'll never use algebra again in your life, but consider the problem-solving skills it taught you — skills that you'll put to good use as a NetWare 4 CNA.

As your LAN learns more and more from school, your users' productivity will increase as well. After all, a network is only as useful as the users who use it (that's a triple-word score). In Step 4 of NetWare 4 configuration, you will give Guinevere all the productivity tools she needs to get her job done. That includes network applications, utilities, and a consistent user environment. Don't underestimate the value of the latter. This means if Guinevere wants to use MS Windows, her application should be in Windows. However, if she breaks out in hives every time she touches the mouse, consider giving her DOS-based applications. Please try not to mix interfaces — it gets ugly fast.

Network applications are the productivity tools of your LAN — and NetWare 4 has great support for them. This is accomplished with the help of a simple seven-step model. For the most part, these seven steps help you foster synergy between user productivity and shared application software — I learned those big words in school.

1 • Make sure your applications are NetWare-compatible *before* you buy them.

2 • Ensure that the software is truly multiuser.

3 • Create an appropriate directory structure for the applications and all their support components.

4 • Install them.

5 • Establish file attributes for Sharable and Nonsharable network applications.

6 • In addition to file attributes, assign user access rights to network application subdirectories.

7 • Customize the workstation for specific application needs.

This is just a general discussion. Most network applications include specific instructions for making them work on a LAN. However, these guidelines are a great place to start.

STEP 1: ENSURING NETWARE COMPATIBILITY

It is important to determine whether your applications are NetWare-compatible before you buy them. Approximately 5,000 software packages are compatible and registered with Novell. This compatibility information is important, because NetWare makes demands on application software that can cause it to corrupt data or at least impede users' productivity. Information about NetWare compatibility and registration are available on NetWire or from your local Novell sales office. You should also consider contacting the software vendor directly. But be forewarned, the company might not have the full story.

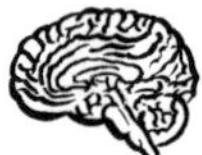

THE BRAIN

For more detailed information about Novell-certified hardware and software, consult the vendor forums on NetWire. In addition, the NSEPro CD-ROM has detailed results from Novell certification testing labs.

STEP 2: CHECKING MULTIUSERNESS

For the best results and highest level of user productivity, all applications should support multiple users simultaneously. If your application is designed to run on a stand-alone computer, don't assume it will work fine on the LAN. The good news is, most large software manufacturers routinely create multiuser versions of popular applications. Two signs of true multiuser capabilities are file sharing and multiuser access. Again, it is important to determine the level of multiuserness *before* you purchase the application. Also, be aware that almost all single-user software works in a NetWare environment — NetWare supports any DOS application. But don't expect these applications to offer data- or resource-sharing capabilities.

STEP 3: CREATING THE DIRECTORY STRUCTURE

Before you can install the application and configure its components, you must create an intelligent directory structure for it. As you learned in Chapter 4, the application directories must support software data as well as program files. Each application should have a specific subdirectory under the main SYS:APPS directory to avoid cluttering the root. This also organizes network applications for easy, efficient security implementation.

In addition, some applications create their own directory structure during the installation process. Unfortunately, these programs attack the root directory. That's fine in a local environment but doesn't work well in the NetWare-shared directory structure. Consider "MAP ROOTing" a network drive before installation. This way, the system will think that it's installing in [Root] when, in fact, it's installing under the SYS:APPS directory.

STEP 4: MANAGING THE INSTALLATION

The installation process is typically left up to the application. Many install programs perform file decompression as well as application customization. This is especially true in the MS Windows environment. Be sure you do not simply copy the files from the source diskette or CD-ROM. You haven't lived until you've had to manually customize the 342 .INI files configured by Windows 95. Let the application do it — that's what you paid for.

Once the network software has been installed, three more steps help define its special configurations.

STEP 5: ASSIGNING FILE ATTRIBUTES

Network applications must have the correct file attributes so that programs can share them without being locked out. Follow these simple guidelines:

- Shared application files — Sharable, Read-Only

- Shared data files — Sharable Read-Write

- Nonshared data files — Nonsharable Read/Write

Most of today's multiuser application programs provide detailed documentation about specific file attributes. I don't usually say this, but you might consider "reading the manual."

STEP 6: ASSIGNING ACCESS RIGHTS

In addition to file attributes, you'll need to assign user/group rights for access to network application directories. By default, users have *no* rights to the new directory structure you've created. If you install the application and walk away, users end up spinning their wheels trying to get work done. This also applies to NDS rights if they need access to other network resources, including printers and messaging objects.

As you recall from Chapter 5, most applications work fine with the Read and File Scan (RF) access rights. Also recall that these access rights can be inherited by all subdirectories under SYS:APPS. Next, you may consider assigning all rights except SAM (Supervisor, Access Control, and Modify) to data directories. Finally, consider these security guidelines:

- Application data should be stored under each application subdirectory (SYS:APPS\WP\DATA, for example).

- User-specific data should be stored in each user's home directory.

- Group-specific data should be stored in a corresponding SYS:GROUP subdirectory.

- Globally shared data should be stored in the SYS:DATA directory.

STEP 7: PERFORMING CUSTOMIZATION

The seventh and final step in network application support is workstation customization. Many programs require special DOS configurations in order to run properly. The most notable tool is CONFIG.SYS, which customizes the DOS environment. For example, device drivers might be loaded for programs that use a mouse. Here are a few other things to think about:

► You may need to increase environment space using the SHELL command:

```
SHELL=C:\COMMAND.COM /p /e:1024
```

► You may want to load HIMEM.SYS to activate the high memory area (HMA). Then you can use the following command in CONFIG.SYS to free 60K of conventional workstation RAM:

```
DOS=HIGH
```

► Many programs require special SET parameters for environment variables and temporary directories. Consult the application's documentation.

Once the application software has been installed, your LAN is well on its way to enlightenment: "sipping from the chalice of knowledge." In addition, the menu interface can provide a friendly, centrally managed arena for application launching. I know this is a lot of work, but "warm and fuzzy" is a good thing. Customization increases productivity by giving users the tools they need and decreasing their LAN-phobia — not to be confused with parent-phobia!

ZEN

"Actually I'm 18. I've just lived hard."

Clint Eastwood

Speaking of phobia, Guinevere is growing up way too fast. In the blink of an eye, the prom is over and she's ready for the fifth and final step of NetWare childhood — moving out.

Step 5: E-mail

The time has come. Your LAN becomes a woMAN (metropolitan area network).

It's inevitable. At some point, your child grows up and becomes an adult. The transition to adulthood is a scary time for everybody. She gets her first car, her first job, and her first apartment. Suddenly, the chalice of knowledge takes on a whole new importance. Her ability to survive depends on how many business classes she slept through. Suddenly all those nights you spent helping her with math homework equate to food on the table. Suddenly, Mom and Dad aren't so wrong anymore. It's weird how that happens — and it always does.

With adulthood comes new challenges and a new level of communication. To succeed, it's vital that you develop a high level of LAN synergy. All your users, configurations, workstations, and applications must work together as one cohesive unit. This is made possible through e-mail. The final step in NetWare 4 configuration focuses on tying all of these components together.

E-mail has become one of the most critical LAN services, next to filing and printing. That's because it

- ► Improves communication — E-mail enables employees to communicate even when business meetings, travel schedules, and distributed locations prevent them from seeing each other.

- ► Increases productivity — E-mail improves the success rate for communications because unlike other forms of communication, messaging does not require conversing participants to be available at the same time. No more "telephone tag."

- ► Maximizes the use of existing resources — E-mail leverages file, printing and connectivity services by providing a way of tying them all together. Much the same way as time ties together the fabric of our universe. (Is that *esoteric* enough for you?)

QUIZ

Speaking of esoteric, here's a doozy for you. There are five men — A, B, C, D, and E — each wearing a disc on his forehead selected from a total of five white, two red, and two black. Each man can see the colors of the discs worn by the other four, but he is unable to see his own.

They are all intelligent people, and they are asked to try to deduce the color of their own disc from the colors of the other four whom they can see. In fact, they are all wearing white discs. After a pause for reflection, C, who is even more intelligent than the others, says, "I reckon I must be wearing a white disc."

Huh? How did he do that?

(Q6-6)

E-mail in NetWare 4 relies on an integrated messaging platform called MHS Services for NetWare 4. MHS (Message Handling Service) stores, forwards, and routes user messages. These messages can be text, binary graphics, digitized video, or audio data. MHS Services is integrated with NDS and uses many NDS objects to accomplish these magic messaging tasks.

Let's take a closer look.

UNDERSTANDING MHS SERVICES

MHS Services for NetWare 4 is an "engine" that provides messaging capabilities. Various messaging programs can now take full advantage of this technology. In the simplest terms, this "engine" takes input from various e-mail applications and routes it to any user on the internetwork running any other type of e-mail interface. This is much like *the way* NetWare 4 file services stores a variety of different types of files from various network applications. However, unlike file services, MHS deals actively with the communication interactions between computer users. Instead of simply storing data files, MHS moves the data from point to point and notifies the user of waiting messages.

All of this magic is accomplished with three key components:

- ▸ Messaging server

- ▸ User mailboxes

- ▸ MHS applications

Messaging Server

The messaging server is NetWare 4's implementation of the MHS "engine." The server accepts data from a variety of user e-mail packages and delivers it to any type of mailbox (as Figure 6.8 shows). The server can deliver messages to local user mailboxes or route them through the internetwork to other messaging engines for eventual delivery. The main point is — MHS Services supports a variety of e-mail applications and can deliver to a variety of other engine types. Also, messages can be composed of text, graphics, video, or audio data.

*Understanding MHS
Services for NetWare 4*

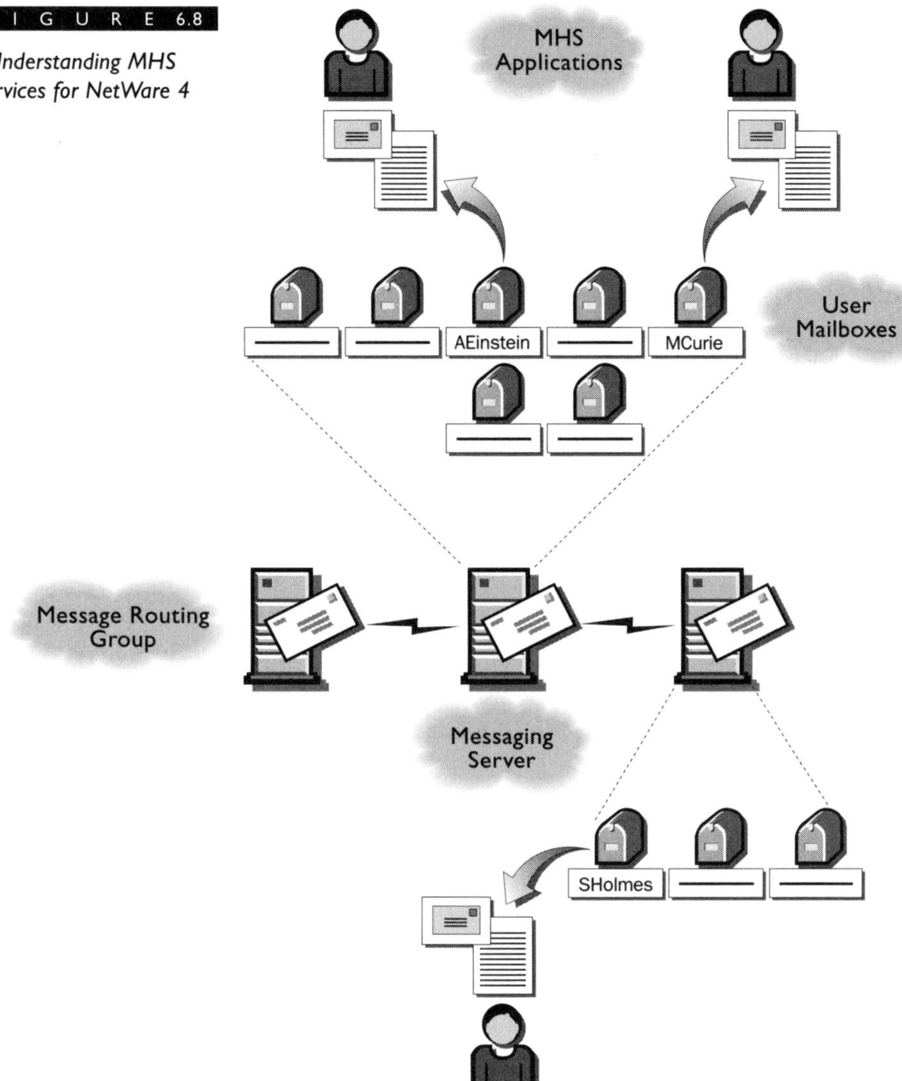

All of this fancy footwork occurs within the messaging server. Each network server that has MHS Services installed is called a *messaging server*. A *message routing group* is a group of messaging servers that communicate with each other directly — to transfer messages. In a large WAN such as that in Figure 6.8, for example, this would be all the NetWare 4 servers that share a common backbone. Each message routing group has one or more *Postmaster Generals*. This special user is automatically granted the privilege of modifying message routing groups and configuring all of the messaging servers. In addition, each of these servers has one or more *Postmasters* that configure and manage user mailboxes.

User Mailboxes

A *user mailbox* is a physical location on the messaging server where messages are delivered. You can use any MHS application to send messages to any NDS object that can be assigned a mailbox. This includes Users, Groups, Organizational Roles, and Organizational Units. Also, you can send mail to special *Distribution List objects*, which in turn copy the mail to multiple mailboxes. This reduces network traffic throughout the message routing group by creating and routing only one copy of the message and then replicating it for every mailbox on the list. Finally, user mailboxes can be configured and managed using either NWADMIN (MS Windows) or NETADMIN (DOS). Once again, refer to Figure 6.8 for an illustration of the relationship between messaging servers and user mailboxes.

MHS Applications

All this NetWare 4 messaging magic is made possible through a front-end e-mail application. Without these applications, there's no way to create or read MHS messages. Just your luck, NetWare 4 includes two rudimentary MHS applications — FirstMail for DOS and FirstMail for Windows. Both starter MHS applications are automatically installed in the SYS:PUBLIC subdirectory on each messaging server. The good news is, FirstMail automatically imports all user and group information from NDS. You don't need to lift a finger. This means that as soon as you install MHS Services, users can begin sending messages via FirstMail.

The bad news is, you get what you pay for. Although FirstMail for Windows has a nice interface (as shown later in Figure 6.12), it doesn't include any advanced messaging features. FirstMail is a simple starter application that can tide you over until you buy a real MHS front-end. Think of it as Guinevere's first broken-down VW or her one-room apartment under the train tracks. Even though it's not the Taj

Mahal, it does represent her first shot at freedom. For this reason, you'll probably never forget FirstMail or that adorable VW Bug.

There you have it. MHS Services in a nutshell. Even though I'm sure you absorbed it all the first time, let's take a quick review — just for the heck of it. Table 6.4 is your friend.

T A B L E 6.4	MHS COMPONENT	DESCRIPTION
Getting to Know MHS Services for NetWare 4	MHS Services for NetWare 4	"The Product"
	MHS engine	Implementation of "The Product"
	Messaging server	Each NetWare 4 server running "The Product." Also, the central communications point and storage location of user mailboxes
	Message routing group	A collection of interconnected messaging servers
	Postmaster General	Manages the message routing group
	Postmaster	Manages the messaging server
	User mailboxes	Physical storage location for MHS messages. They hang out on messaging servers
	MHS applications	E-mail front-ends that send and receive MHS messages
	Distribution list	A special NDS object that forwards messages to numerous user mailboxes

Now that you're a pro with MHS Services, let's explore the details of installing and managing it. Don't have any illusions; nobody said moving out would be easy.

INSTALLING MHS SERVICES

A complete set of MHS Services software is included on the NetWare 4.1 CD-ROM. It has no mailbox limit, which means you can identify as many user mailboxes as you wish. However, MHS Services for NetWare 4 does have a concurrent connection limit. This means the maximum number of users who can send simultaneous messages is limited by your NetWare 4.1 user license. If you need greater access, consider creating a centralized messaging server with a 500- or 1,000-user copy of NetWare 4.1 on it. This is a popular strategy for large organizations such as ACME.

Following is a brief list of prerequisites needed for installing MHS Services. Once you've digested these, we'll dive into the detailed installation steps themselves.

MHS Prerequisites

The NetWare 4.1 server where you install MHS Services is called the *host server*. The host server prerequisites differ for small-scale and large-scale implementations. A small-scale installation can handle about 10 users and 100 messages per day. Here's a list of the small-scale hardware prerequisites:

- 80386 processor or later.

- 12 MB of RAM for the server plus 500K for MHS Services.

- 65 MB of hard disk space for the default NetWare 4.1 installation plus 2.5 MB of disk space for MHS programs.

- Additional disk space requirements for user mailboxes. This number varies depending on how active users are.

- CD-ROM (required during installation only).

A large-scale MHS installation, on the other hand, can handle hundreds, even thousands, of messages per day. Following are the minimum hardware prerequisites for a large-scale MHS installation:

- 80386 processor or later.

- 16 MB of RAM plus any additional memory required to maintain more than 30 percent free cache buffers. Use MONITOR.NLM to determine availability of cache buffers.

- ► 65 MB of hard disk space for the default NetWare 4.1 installation plus 2.5 MB for MHS programs.

- ► An additional 5 MB of hard disk space for each user mailbox.

- ► CD-ROM (required during installation only).

REAL WORLD

Many large-scale MHS sites opt to create a centralized MHS server for delivery of all user messages. Following is a sample configuration that can easily handle 5,000 messages per hour:

- ► 80486-66 MHz processor

- ► 16 MB of RAM

- ► Two or three concurrent users

- ► No other server activities

Remember, the central MHS server doesn't provide file or printing services; it simply delivers mail.

Once you've established your minimum MHS prerequisites, it's time to get on with the installation. Here we go.

QUIZ

Which *Star Trek* character waited until the second season to beam aboard the Starship Enterprise?

(Q6-7)

MHS Installation Steps

You can install MHS Services during the custom NetWare 4.1 installation or afterward. In either case, it consists of four simple steps:

1 • Running INSTALL.NLM. Load INSTALL.NLM at the server console if you're not already there. Select Product Options and press Enter. Then select Choose an item or product listed above and press Enter. Finally, select the Install NetWare MHS option. You can accept the default path by pressing Enter, or specify your own directory. The product will most likely reside on the NetWare 4.1 installation CD-ROM.

TIP

If the MHS Services software is located on a different server, you'll need to log into that server at this point. After you've been authenticated, you can continue with MHS Services installation.

2 • Assigning the Postmaster General. Next, the Postmaster General Authentication window will appear. In the Name field, enter the complete name of the user who will be Postmaster General. This is typically Admin. For example, ACME's Postmaster General is

```
.CN=Admin.O=ACME
```

Next, enter the Postmaster General's password in the Password field and press Enter to continue.

3 • Selecting the host volume. MHS Services is typically installed on the SYS: volume of the host server. If you wish to specify a different volume, do so now. Also, you are given options for installing additional products at this point. When you're finished, exit INSTALL.NLM.

4 • Revising AUTOEXEC.NCF. To automatically activate MHS Services for NetWare 4, add the following line to the host server's AUTOEXEC.NCF file:

```
Load MHS
```

For a more detailed walk-through of MHS installation, refer to the messaging case study at the end of this chapter. When you're finished, a series of default MHS events will occur as if by magic. Table 6.5 lists the MHS objects that are created by default and actions that occur during installation. Note that Admin is assigned as the default owner of the Message Routing Group and Postmaster of the default messaging server. If you delete Admin, all heck breaks loose. In addition to 100 other NDS problems, you'll need to reassign these two MHS properties:

- ▸ Message Routing Group owner

- ▸ Messaging Server Postmaster

T A B L E 6.5	NDS OBJECT	ACTION
Life After MHS Installation	Default message routing group is created as MHS_ROUTING_GROUP	(1) This object is placed in the home container of the Host Server object.
		(2) Admin is assigned as the default owner.
	Messaging Server object is created	(1) This object is also placed in the home container of the Host Server object.
		(2) Postmaster is assigned to Admin.
		(3) Admin mailbox and ID are assigned to the default Messaging Server.
		(4) Default Messaging Server is assigned to default Message Routing Group and vice versa. Also, their respective MHS properties are updated.
		(5) Host server is assigned to Messaging Server and vice versa. Also, their respective MHS properties are updated.
	FirstMail	FirstMail for Windows and FirstMail for DOS are copied to the SYS:PUBLIC directory on the host server.

You will also notice that two FirstMail applications are copied to the SYS:PUBLIC directory on the host server — FirstMail for Windows and FirstMail for DOS. Later in this section, we'll take a closer look at using FirstMail and explore the steps for sending and receiving mail. For now, let's be content to bask in the glory of Table 6.5 and move on to MHS management.

MANAGING MHS SERVICES

So, you've learned about it and installed it. Now what do you do with it? Moving out can be such a traumatic experience. One morning you wake up and bam! It hits you that you're on your own. A thousand questions pop into your head: Who's going to make breakfast? What am I going to do with my life? Where's the laundry machine? In order to survive in this cruel and exciting world, you must have a plan and, above all, you must have friends.

Managing MHS Services is not so different. One day you'll come into work and bam! It hits you that you're using e-mail. Then a thousand questions pop into your head: Who's the Postmaster? Where's my mailbox? What's a Distribution List? Fortunately, NetWare 4 provides numerous NDS objects especially for MHS Services — your friends. They are:

- ▸ Message Routing Group

- ▸ Messaging Server

- ▸ Distribution List

- ▸ External Entity

In addition to these MHS-only objects, you'll need to create and manage various mailbox owners — Users, Groups, Organizational Roles, and Organizational Units.

Now let's take a closer look at how these MHS "friends" can help you get along in the cruel and exciting world of NetWare 4 messaging.

Message Routing Group

As you remember from our earlier discussions, the MHS Message Routing Group is a collection of interconnected messaging servers. As an NDS object, it represents a cluster of messaging servers that communicate directly with each other for transferring messages. A default Message Routing Group object is created during the installation of MHS Services and placed in the same container as the host NetWare 4 server. Subsequent messaging servers are defaulted to this group.

There are only a few important properties for the Message Routing Group object. They are

ACL	Full Name
Bindery Property	Login Script
CA Private Key	Mailbox ID
CA Public Key	Mailbox Location
CN	Member
Description	Owner
E-mail Address	See Also

Also recall that the Postmaster General manages the Message Routing Group (through NWADMIN — see Figure 6.9). This is usually the Admin user but can be assigned a unique name during initial MHS Services installation.

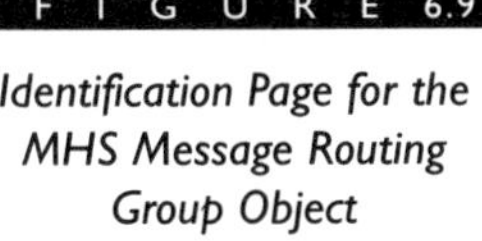

Identification Page for the MHS Message Routing Group Object

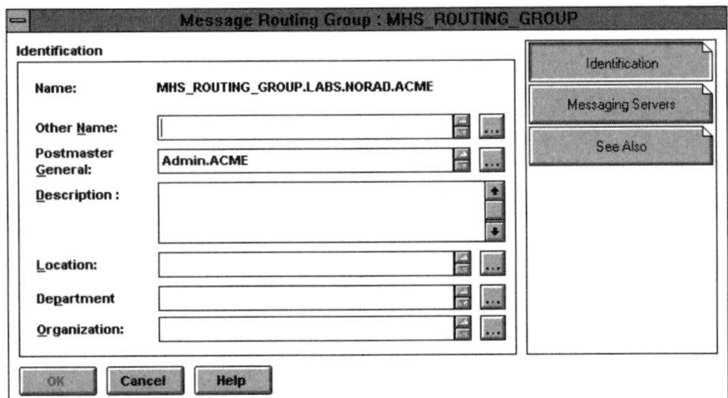

Messaging Server

In earlier discussions, you learned that the messaging server is the central communications point and storage location of MHS Services for NetWare 4. As an NDS object, it identifies the host NetWare 4 server and the location of the MHS directory structure (SYS:MHS). The SYS:MHS directory houses all user mailboxes assigned to this messaging server.

During a standard MHS Services installation, the Messaging Server object is created automatically and placed in the same container as the Host NetWare 4 Server object. As you can see in Figure 6.10, the Messaging Server object includes various interesting NDS properties, including

ACL	Messaging Server Type
Bindery Property	Network Address
Certificate Revocation	Postmaster
Certificate Validity Interval	Private Key
CN	Public Key
Cross Certificate Pair	Reference
Description	Security Equals To
Full Name	Security Equals To
Message Routing Group	See Also
Messaging Database Location	Status
	Supported Services

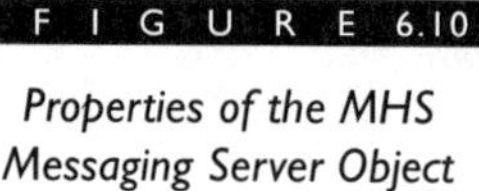

FIGURE 6.10

Properties of the MHS Messaging Server Object

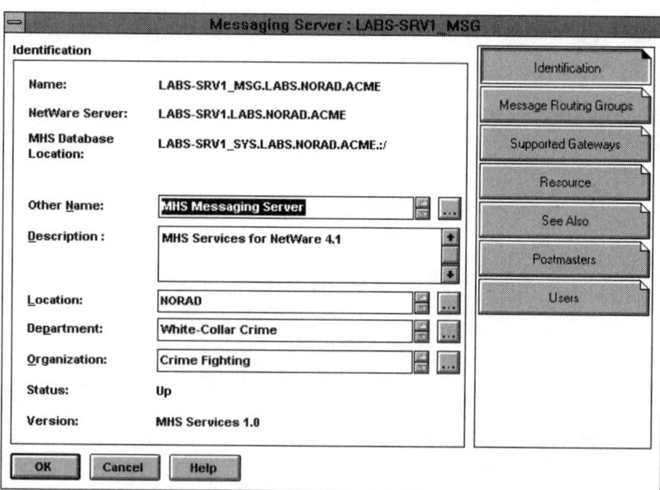

In order for numerous messaging servers to communicate with one another, they must be part of the same message routing group. Once these first two MHS objects have been created, you're well on your way to e-mail paradise. With the groundwork in place, it's time to turn our attention toward the people who will be sending and receiving MHS messages. Look out, Guinevere.

Distribution List

As you recall, the Distribution List is a special NDS object that forwards messages to numerous user mailboxes. It accomplishes this in an interesting way. Only one copy of the message is delivered to the Distribution List mailbox. The message is then replicated for every mailbox in the Distribution List. This decreases network traffic between messaging servers because multiple messages are routed with only a single packet.

Group objects can also be used for messaging, but they *do* increase network traffic. Unlike a Distribution List, Group objects generate a packet for every message routed between Messaging Servers. Distribution Lists also differ from Groups in that membership can be nested. In other words, a Distribution List can contain other Distribution Lists. This is not true for group NDS objects. As you can see in Figure 6.11, the Distribution List object only contains a few properties:

Name	Mailbox ID
Full Name	Foreign Mail Aliases
Owner	List Members
Description	See Also
Mailbox Location	

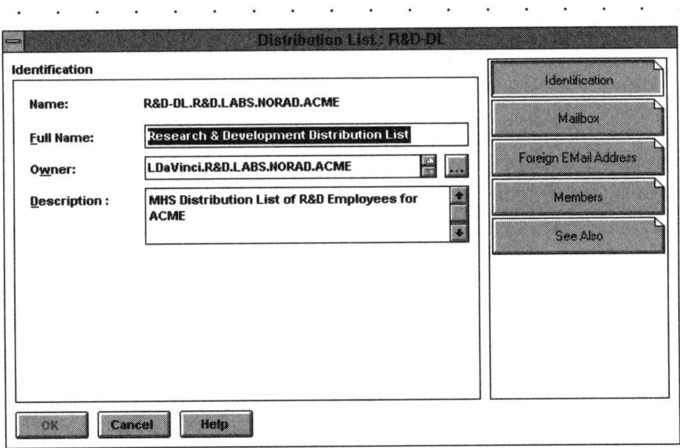

Properties of the MHS Distribution List Object

That completes our discussion of the three main MHS management objects — Message Routing Group, Messaging Server, and Distribution List. For a more practical hands-on approach toward MHS management, consult the case study at the end of this chapter. Now, let's take a quick look at the final two management objects: External Entity and Mailbox objects.

ZEN

"The only ZEN you can find on the tops of mountains is the ZEN you bring up there."

Robert M. Pirsig

External Entity

The *External Entity* object represents non-native NDS MHS objects. It's basically an NDS placeholder that enables you to send messages to users who are not part of the NDS tree. External Entity objects are not created during MHS Services installation; they are normally imported from special gateway software. This gateway software allows MHS to interface with other non-NDS systems.

Mailbox Objects

The discussion so far has focused on the key MHS management objects you need to deal with in order to make MHS Services work. But all of this lexicon doesn't mean a hill of beans if you don't have anyone to send the messages to. MHS Services for NetWare 4 supports four types of Mailbox objects:

- ► User

- ► Group

- ► Organizational Role

- ► Organizational Unit

Each of them can send and receive MHS mail with varying degrees of sophistication. In the exercise at the end of the chapter, we will explore how to assign mailboxes to each of these objects and use them in the grand MHS scheme of things. For now, suffice it to say that you probably fall into one of these four categories — maybe more.

USING FIRSTMAIL

As you learned earlier, MHS Services for NetWare 4 includes a rudimentary e-mail application called FirstMail, available by default in two versions (DOS and Windows), that are copied to the SYS:PUBLIC directory on each Messaging Server.

FirstMail for Windows is an intuitive messaging application with simple icons for sending, receiving, and reading e-mail. As seen in Figure 6.12, FirstMail lists all of your new messages and enables you to open, reply, forward, move, copy, or delete them. In addition, the Button Panel provides five management tasks:

- ▸ Send mail

- ▸ Read new mail

- ▸ Mail folders

- ▸ Address books

- ▸ Distribution Lists

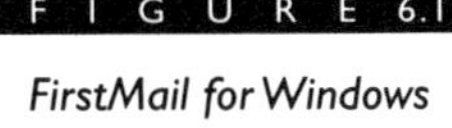

F I G U R E 6.12

FirstMail for Windows

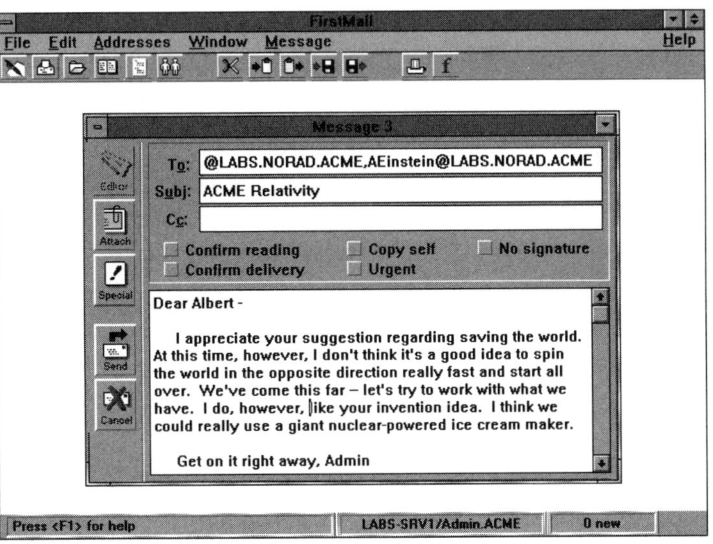

The greatest thing about FirstMail (other than it being free) is the fact that it's NDS-aware. This means you don't have to bother with user configurations; FirstMail gets everything it needs from the NDS database. Otherwise, if you're using an MHS-compatible application that's not NDS-aware, you have to register it with Directory Services and add the e-mail name to each user's list of applications. Too much work.

For a more extensive discussion of using FirstMail, refer to Exercise 6.4 at the end of the chapter. This will give you some valuable hands-on experience with NetWare 4 messaging.

ZEN

"Ring the bells that still can ring.
Forget your perfect offering.
There is a crack in everything.
That's how the light gets in."

Leonard Cohen

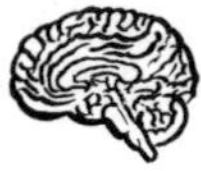

THE BRAIN

For more information on using MHS Services in NetWare 4, see the AppNote entitled "Integrating MHS Services with Other Novell Products" in the October 1995 issue of *Novell Application Notes*.

Well, there you have it. That completes the final step of NetWare 4 configuration. Childhood isn't so bad. Let's quickly review where we've been.

It all started with Leia's first step (workstation connectivity). Once she became connected to the network, Step 2 took over — Leia learned to talk. This involved Container, Profile, and User login scripts.

Leia went to preschool. The next stage in your network's development was dominated by a friendly NetWare 4 menu system. The menu system acted as a central repository for user interface, network applications, and e-mail. In Step 4, you installed and configured the network applications as Leia went to "real" school. This was the most important phase of the child's development. After all, without school (or network applications), there would be no productivity and purpose to life.

Finally, in Step 5, Leia moved out. She got her first car, her first apartment, and her first job. Although it seemed like a difficult time for everyone, moving out represented an important stage in Leia's life. She made a smooth transition from childhood to adulthood. In much the same way, your network needs a smooth transition from NetWare 4 configuration to management.

In a side story, we were tracking Guinevere as she started her day with a computer and cappuccino. As a CNA, it's your responsibility to establish the configuration so that Guinevere never knows what's happening while she's sipping her cappuccino. In an ideal world, Guinevere never suspects that when she turns on her computer, it initializes workstation connectivity files, runs login scripts, establishes a menu system, and provides transparent access to network applications and e-mail — just like a child never understands what her parents go through while she's growing up. Of course, life doesn't end there; this is only the beginning. Now that you've made it through childhood in one piece, it's time to move on to the third and final phase of life — adulthood.

Get out of the way, we're coming through!

EXERCISE 6-1: NETWARE 4 CHILDHOOD

Circle the 20 NetWare 4 configuration terms hidden in this word search puzzle using the hints provided.

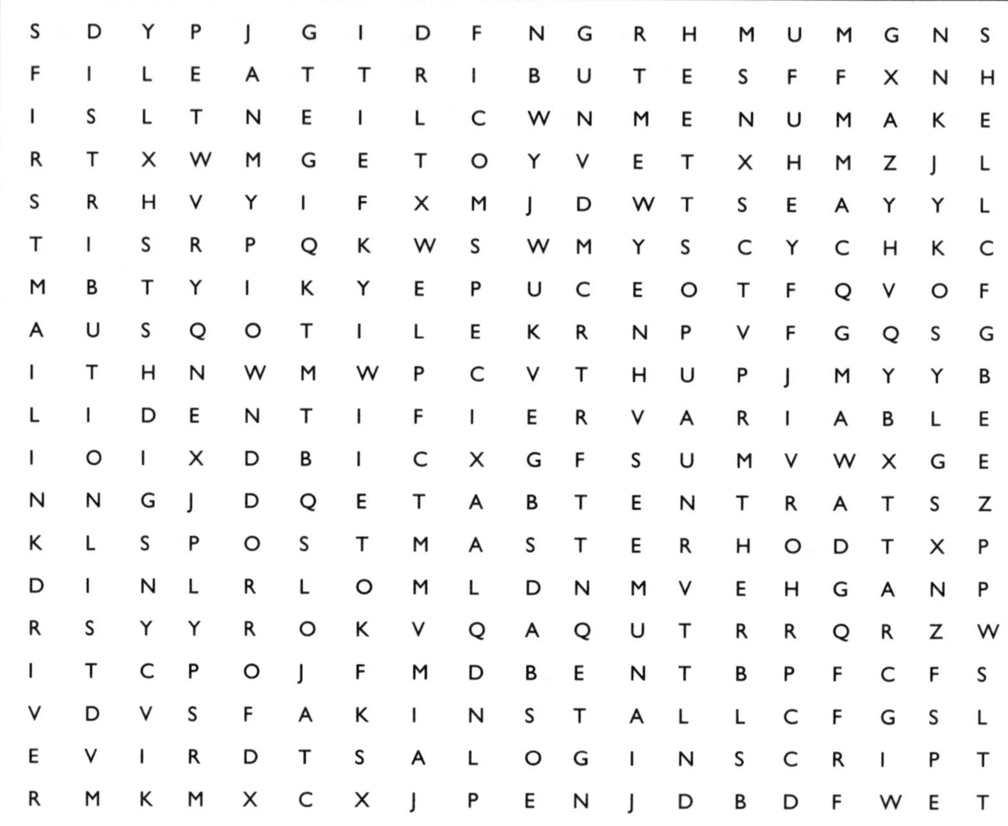

Hints:

1. Login script command used to indicate the location of the command specifier to be used (typically COMMAND.COM).
2. Leaf object that represents a list of E-mail recipients.
3. Menu system control command used to execute a DOS or NetWare command.

4. Set when installing network applications through use of the FLAG or FILER utility.
5. E-mail application that is included with NetWare 4.
6. Menu system command that requests (optional) information from the user before a menu item is executed.
7. Used in a login script instead of using literal values.
8. File that is used to create customized NET.CFG file during client installation.
9. Statement required in CONFIG.SYS for VLMs.
10. Section heading in NET.CFG.
11. File that is similar to a batch file and is executed when a user logs in.
12. Used to compile menu system source files.
13. Integrated messaging (e-mail) engine included in NetWare 4.
14. NET.CFG statement used to set workstation context prior to login.
15. Workstation boot file containing network-related information used by NetWare 4.
16. Workstation directory that contains NetWare client files.
17. Name of the supervisor for an MHS Server object.
18. Type of login script that can contain members that reside in different containers.
19. Workstation configuration file that was used in earlier versions of NetWare.
20. Batch file that is used to automate the loading of client connection files on the workstation.

See Appendix C for answers.

EXERCISE 6-2: WORKSTATION CONNECTIVITY FOR NETWARE 4

1. Ensure that the NetWare 4 connection files are not currently loaded in workstation memory. Display the TSRs currently in workstation memory by typing **MEM /C /P**. Ensure that LSL.COM, a LAN driver such as NE2000, IPXODI.COM, and/or VLM.EXE are not loaded. If they are, you must either unload them manually, boot off a "clean" bootable floppy, or comment out the @CALL STARTNET.BAT and related statements in your AUTOEXEC.BAT file and reboot. To manually unload these files, you must unload them in the reverse order from which they were loaded, namely by typing

```
C:
CD \NWCLIENT
VLM /U
IPXODI /U
NE2000 /U (or the appropriate LAN driver)
LSL /U
```

2. Load the NetWare 4 connection files:

   a. Switch to the C:\NWCLIENT directory by typing

   ```
   C:
   CD \NWCLIENT
   ```

   b. Load the Link Support Layer software by typing

   ```
   LSL
   ```

   What happens? Can you tell from the screen what the purpose is of LSL.COM? See Figure 6.13.

Understanding the Workstation Connection, Part I

```
C:\NWCLIENT>lsl
NetWare Link Support Layer v2.14 (941011)
(C) Copyright 1990-1994 Novell, Inc. All Rights Reserved.

The configuration file used was "C:\NWCLIENT\NET.CFG".
Max Boards 4, Max Stacks 4


C:\NWCLIENT>3c5x9
3Com EtherLink III MLID w/ DME   v1.51 (941003)
(C) Copyright 1994 3Com Corp.  All Rights Reserved

Int 10, Port 360, Node Address 20AFE84943 L
Max Frame 1514 bytes, Line Speed 10 Mbps
Board 1, Frame ETHERNET_802.2, LSB Mode

C:\NWCLIENT>ipxodi

NetWare IPX/SPX Protocol   v3.01 (941031)
(C) Copyright 1990-1994 Novell, Inc.  All Rights Reserved.

Bound to logical board 1 (3C5X9) : Protocol ID E0

C:\NWCLIENT>
```

c. Load the LAN driver by typing

   NE2000 *(or appropriate LAN driver)*

d. Load the IPX communications protocol by typing

   IPXODI

   What happens? Does IPXODI begin workstation communications, or do you have to wait for VLM.EXE?

e. Load the NetWare DOS Requester (and display the maximum amount of related information) by typing

   VLM /V4

   The "/V4" parameter defines the highest level of driver verbosity. This will display all loaded VLMs and some additional troubleshooting information. Refer to Figure 6.14 for more information. What does this tell you about the relationship between IPXODI and VLM?

*Understanding the
Workstation Connection,
Part II*

```
Patent pending.

The VLM.EXE file is pre-initializing the VLMs...............
The VLM.EXE file is using extended memory (XMS).
CONN.VLM       - NetWare connection table manager  v1.20 (941108)
IPXNCP.VLM     - NetWare IPX transport module   v1.20 (941108)
TRAN.VLM       - NetWare transport multiplexor module  v1.20 (941108)
SECURITY.VLM   - NetWare security enhancement module   v1.20 (941108)
NAME CONTEXT "WHITE.CRIME.TOKYO.ACME"
NDS.VLM        - NetWare directory services protocol module  v1.20 (941108)
BIND.VLM       - NetWare bindery protocol module  v1.20 (941108)
PREFERRED SERVER LABS-SRV1
PNW.VLM        - Personal NetWare protocol module  v1.20 (941108)
NWP.VLM        - NetWare protocol multiplexor module  v1.20 (941108)
FIO.VLM        - NetWare file input-output module  v1.20 (941108)
GENERAL.VLM    - NetWare general purpose function module v1.20 (941108)
FIRST NETWORK DRIVE F
REDIR.VLM      - NetWare DOS redirector module  v1.20 (941108)
FIRST NETWORK DRIVE F
PRINT.VLM      - NetWare printer redirection module  v1.20 (941108)
NETX.VLM       - NetWare workstation shell module  v4.20 (941108)
FIRST NETWORK DRIVE F
You are attached to server LABS-SRV1

C:\COLLDOS>
```

    f. Switch to your first network drive by typing

       `F:`

3. Log onto the network.

    a. Display the servers currently available on your network by typing

       `NLIST SERVER /B`

    b. Log into the network by typing

       `LOGIN .ADMIN.ACME`

    Notice that we're logging into the NDS tree and not the server. This is the fundamental advantage of NetWare 4. Why does it still reply with a "Servername"?

    c. Display your login name and connection number by typing

       `WHOAMI`

    d. Display users in your container that are currently logged into the network by typing

       `NLIST USER /A`

EXERCISE 6-3: UNDERSTANDING NET.CFG

The ACME R&D department has special WAN requirements. Also, it's made up of the most advanced — even sometimes dangerous — users. For these reasons, they've asked you to customize their workstation NET.CFG files. Fortunately, the hardware and software have already been sufficiently standardized. Now, you need to review their accessibility requirements and build an appropriate NET.CFG.

Be forewarned, it's not as easy as it looks. Following is a list of the R&D accessibility criteria. Good luck.

- ▶ A comment should be inserted at the top of the file indicating that it is the standard NET.CFG file for the R&D department It should also list the author of the file (who is you) and the date it is created.

- ▶ Each workstation will consist of a Dell 133 MHz Pentium using ODI drivers and a 3COM C35X9 network card set to use interrupt A, I/O port 320, and Ethernet frame type 802.2.

- ▶ The ACME_TREE will be the only NDS tree accessed by the R&D department at this time.

- ▶ R&D-SRV1 will be the primary server used by the R&D department.

- ▶ Users should have the following default context prior to login:

```
OU=R&D.OU=LABS.OU=NORAD.O=ACME
```

- ▶ The first network drive will be F:.

- ▶ Packet Buffers should be set to 10 to increase performance.

- ▶ The Signature Level for the NCP Packet Signature feature should be set to 3 for maximum security.

- ▶ The connection files should be loaded in low memory for better performance and stability.

> ▸ Users should be allowed to connect up to 10 servers simultaneously.

> ▸ Users should be allowed to capture up to a maximum of five printing ports.

> ▸ Microsoft Windows will be used on the workstations.

> ▸ The LONG MACHINE TYPE variable should be set to DELL.

For hints and a complete solution, refer to Appendix C. No cheating!

CASE STUDY: CONFIGURING ACME'S LOGIN SCRIPTS

Just as the day was winding down swimmingly at ACME (at 4:50 p.m.), FDR comes cruising into your office. "I'm sorry it's so late," he said, "but something's up with the Net. Can you take a quick look?" Grudgingly (because that's how you do things at 4:59 p.m.), you agree to check it out. "Oh right," he adds, "I want all the public relations managers to share some applications and report files — any ideas?"

Of course you have ideas; after all, you are a CNA! Quickly you discover that the PR Container script has been destroyed — fortunately, you have notes from the old one in your NetWare Log book.

1. Here's the PR Container login script notes:

    a. Insert a comment at the top of the login script indicating the purpose of the login script, the author (who is you), and the date the file was created.

    b. Set the DOS prompt to display the drive and directory name.

    c. Display a greeting that is displayed each time a user in this container logs in, including the username, day, and date.

d. Turn off the display of drive mappings and assign the following regular drive mappings:

   (1) Drive U: should point to the user's home directory.

   (2) Drive G: should point to the user's shared group directory.

e. Assign the following search drive mappings, making sure not to overwrite existing drive mappings in the DOS path:

   (1) S1: pointing to SYS:PUBLIC

   (2) S2: pointing to the DOS directory on the network

   (3) S3: pointing to the SYS:APPS\WINDOWS directory

f. Insert a COMSPEC command that points to the DOS directory on the network.

g. Prevent the Default login script from executing when a user logs in that has no User login script.

h. Set up a printer capture of the HP4SI-P1 printer, specifying no tabs, no banners, and a timeout of 20 seconds.

i. On Wednesdays, fire phasers and display a reminder to members of the PR-Group that the weekly Manager meeting is at 9:00 a.m. in Conference Room 3-D.

j. Every time a user logs onto the network, display a file called G:PR.NEW containing the important news of the day for the Public Relations department.

k. Set the default drive to U:.

l. Execute a custom menu called G:PRMAIN.DAT (which you will create in the next exercise).

m. General notes:

(1) Whenever you display a message, don't forget to insert a PAUSE statement so that the message doesn't scroll off the screen before the user has a chance to read it.

(2) Insert appropriate remarks through the login script so that someone else that looks at it can easily understand what you have done.

2. Next, you decide to create a PRMGRS-Profile login script for the public relations managers. Then you discover, astonishingly enough, that one already exists in the ACME container! Hmmmm. Must be those crazy ACME fairies again. Anyway, you might as well make FDR a member of the PRMGRS-Profile login script while you're there. (See Appendix C for hints on the basic steps involved.)

Log in FDR to check things out:

```
LOGIN .FDR.ADMIN.RIO.ACME
```

Watch the screen as the Container and Profile login scripts are automatically executed. Fix any errors that occur.

CASE STUDY: CONFIGURING THE ACME MENU SYSTEM

Well, the fun never stops. It seems as though FDR has opened Pandora's box. Now, for some unexplainable reason, the ACME gremlins have hit — the PR menu system has disappeared. If you don't get home soon, you're gonna miss "Friends." You'd better hurry.

Once again, the NetWare Log book has saved the day. Using the criteria outlined here, create a custom menu for the Public Relations department.

a. PR Main Menu

(1) Applications (which displays an Applications submenu)

(2) E-mail (which runs the Windows version of FirstMail)

(3) NetWare Commands (which displays a NetWare Commands submenu)

(4) Log off network (which exits the user from the menu and logs him/her off the network)

b. Applications Menu (submenu called by an option in the Main Menu)

(1) Database (where executable file is DB)

(2) Spreadsheet (where executable file is SS)

(3) Word Processing (where executable file is WP)

c. NetWare Utilities Menu (submenu called by an option in the Main Menu)

(1) File Management

(2) NCOPY

(3) NETUSER

(4) User Tools

(5) WHOAMI

Next, you'll need to quickly compile and debug the new menu. Once you're finished, you can place it in the default SYS:PUBLIC subdirectory and test it. Ensure that the new login script can automatically find and execute the menu system. After all, you don't want another visit from FDR tonight.

Sweet dreams.

Communication is the key to success in any business. It's even more important for ACME, considering the pressure the group is under — saving the world is a tough business.

One of the most important ACME divisions is R&D. This is where the ACME "brain trust" develops new technologies for making the Earth a better place. We can't do without antipollutants or NDS (Nuclear Disarmament Squads). To ensure that their critical WAN messaging works optimally, Leonardo Da Vinci has asked you to personally install MHS Services for NetWare 4 and assign mailboxes to all of his scientists. Also, he wants you to add another user to the R&D Container — "Nostradamus." The fate of the world (or at least its pollution) rests in your hands. Good luck.

Let's begin by installing MHS Services after the NetWare 4 server has been installed.

1. Activate the INSTALL.NLM utility. At the file server console, type **LOAD INSTALL** and press Enter. First, select Product Options from the Installation Options menu and press Enter. Then, select the "Choose an item or product listed above" option from the Other Installation Actions menu and press Enter. Finally, select the Install NetWare MHS Services option from the Other Installation Items/Products menu and press Enter.

2. Specify the source path. Next, you will be asked to specify the source path for the MHS Services software. Press F3 if you want to change the default path listed. Indicate the correct path and press Enter. If the path specified is on another server, you will be asked to log into that server. Next, a warning message may be displayed advising that there might be a conflict with the CD-ROM driver. If this message is displayed, select the Continue to Access the CD-ROM option and press Enter. (You'll probably find that you are able to continue despite the warning.) The installation program will then begin copying the appropriate files to the SYSTEM and PUBLIC directories on the SYS: volume.

3. Specify configuration information. The Postmaster General Authentication window will then be displayed. In the User Name field, indicate .ADMIN.ACME as the full name of the user that will act as Postmaster General and press Enter. Enter the password for the Postmaster General in the Password field and press Enter. After indicating the password, select the Press Enter to Continue field and press Enter. You may then be prompted to indicate whether this is the first MHS install in the NDS tree. If this is the first server, select Yes and press Enter. Otherwise, select No and press Enter. Next, if the server chosen has multiple volumes, you will be prompted to indicate the destination volume for the MHS subdirectory, which will contain the MHS Services database and mailboxes. Before doing so, make sure the volume selected meets the minimum space requirements for MHS Services. When you have indicated the correct volume and pressed Enter, the installation program will continue the installation of MHS Services.

   When the process is complete, a message will be displayed saying that the installation was completed successfully. When this message is displayed, press Enter to continue. An Installation Status Messages screen will be displayed. Press Enter to return to the Other Installation Items/Products menu. You can then continue installing optional products, or exit from the INSTALL.NLM utility.

4. Activate MHS Services. After you've installed the MHS software on the server, the next step is activate MHS Services by loading MHS.NLM and MHSLIB.NLM. To manually load MHS Services, type **LOAD MHS** and press Enter. You'll probably want to add this statement to the server's AUTOEXEC.NCF file so that MHS Services will be automatically activated each time the server is booted. Once MHS Services is activated, it will provide message-delivery services to all users with mailboxes.

5. Manage MHS mailboxes. After you load the MHS software and activate MHS services, you'll need to assign an MHS mailbox to each User, Group, Organizational Role, and Distribution List in the Labs division. You cannot assign MHS mailboxes to Organizations or Organizational Units. To assign a mailbox to a user, you'll need to define two properties for that user: the Mailbox Location (which indicates the messaging server on which the user's mailbox is located) and the Mailbox ID (which identifies the name of the subdirectory in which the user's incoming messages are stored). For performance reasons, you should always locate a user's mailbox on the server that contains his/her home directory or the server where the user stores most of his/her directories and files. In order to assign an MHS mailbox to an Organizational Role, Group, or Distribution List, you'll need to specify a mailbox location for the object's Mailbox Location property that identifies the MHS messaging server. The MHS messaging server has the ability to identify members or occupants of an object and make a copy of a message for each one.

a. Assign a mailbox to a user by using the Messaging Server object. From a workstation, log into the network as Admin by typing **LOGIN .ADMIN.ACME** and pressing Enter. Run MS Windows, then execute the NetWare Administrator utility by double-clicking on its icon. Expand the tree view by double-clicking on the NORAD Organizational unit, then double-clicking on the LABS container, then double-clicking on the LABS-SRV1_MSG Messaging Server object. Click on the Users property button on the right side of the screen, then click on the Add button at the bottom of the screen. An Object selection screen will be displayed. Double-click on the R&D Organization Unit icon on the right side of the screen to display the contents of the R&D container, then click on each of the members of the R&D department listed on the right side of the screen (such as Leonardo Da Vinci, Charles Darwin, Sir Isaac Newton, and Marie Curie). You'll find that if you hold down the Ctrl key while making your selections, you can make multiple selections at one time. When you've finished choosing the Users in the R&D container, click on the OK button at the bottom of the screen. Then, click on the OK button at the bottom of the next screen to return to the main NetWare Administrator screen.

b. Create a new User object in the R&D Organizational Unit container
called Nostradamus and assign him a mailbox. Click on the R&D
Organizational Unit container. Select the "Create" option from the
Objects menu. Select the User icon and click on the OK button at the
bottom of the screen. Click on the box in front of the Define Additional
Properties field. Type **Nostradamus** in the Login Name field and
Smarty-Pants in the Last Name field, then click on the CREATE button
at the bottom of the screen. Click on the Mailbox property screen
button. Click on the Browse button to the right of the Mailbox Location
field. You'll need to walk the tree to find the correct Messaging Server
object. First, double-click on the first entry in the Directory Context
section on the right side of the screen (as indicated by two side-by-side
periods), then double-click on the LABS-SRV1_MSG icon in the Objects
section on the left of the screen. Finally, click on the OK button at the
bottom of the User screen to return to the main NetWare Administrator
menu.

c. Create a Distribution List object named R&D-DL. Click on the R&D
Organizational Unit container. Select the "Create" option from the
Objects menu. Select the Distribution List icon and click on the OK
button at the bottom of the screen. Because this will be a Distribution
List for the members of the R&D department, type **R&D-DL** in the
Distribution List Name field, then click on the Browse button to the
right of the Mailbox Location field. You'll need to walk the tree to find
the correct Messaging Server object. First, double-click on the first entry
in the Directory Context section on the right side of the screen (as
indicated by two side-by-side periods), then double-click on the LABS-
SRV1_MSG icon in the Objects section on the left of the screen. Finally,
click on the CREATE button at the bottom of the Create Distribution
List screen to return to the main NetWare Administrator menu. Next,
highlight the Distribution List object you just created and click on it
with the right mouse button. Click on the Details option in the object
menu. Click on the Members screen button.

along the right edge of the screen, then click on the ADD button at the bottom of the screen. While holding down the Ctrl key, click on each user in the R&D department that is listed in the Objects section on the left side of the screen. When all of the users in the R&D department are highlighted, click on the OK button at the bottom of the screen, then click on the OK button at the bottom of the next screen in order to return to the NetWare Administrator main menu.

EXERCISE 6-4: USING FIRSTMAIL

Congratulations. You've successfully installed MHS Services for Leonardo Da Vinci and the R&D department. Now it's time to test FirstMail for Windows and make sure it's operating correctly. Follow these simple rules.

1. Execute FirstMail.

   a. MHS and FirstMail must be installed on your server in order to be able to complete this exercise. Although these products are bundled with NetWare 4, they are not automatically installed during the installation process.

   b. Log into the network as NOSTRADAMUS.R&D.LABS.NORAD.ACME.

   c. Run MS Windows, then double-click on the FirstMail icon. (If there is no FirstMail icon, you may want to create one in the Windows Program Group that contains your other NetWare tools, such as NetWare Administrator, DynaText, and User Tools. The executable file is called WMAIL and is located in the SYS:PUBLIC directory.)

2. Create a message and send it to a user.

   a. Select the New Message option from the File menu [or click on the first icon (pen and paper) on the button bar].

   b. Type **LDAVINCI** in the To: field and **Reporting for Duty** in the Subj: field.

   c. Click on the message area and type **I'm looking forward to working with the R&D team, Regards, Nostradamus**, then click the SEND button on the left side of the window when you're finished.

   d. Exit FirstMail and MS Windows.

3. Log in as LDAVINCI.R&D.LABS.NORAD.ACME, then read the message and save it.

a. Run MS Windows, then double-click on the FirstMail icon. Select the Read New Mail from the File menu [or click the second (envelope) icon on the button bar], then double-click on the message to read it.

b. Make sure that the message is highlighted. Click on the Move button in the New mail folder button bar. Select the Mail Folder. Your message will be stored in this folder.

NetWare 4 Management

"As a NetWare 4 CNA, I consider them part of the family."

Welcome to adulthood.

An interesting thing happens on the way to adulthood — we grow up. All through childhood we look forward to the days when we can drive our own car, eat junk food, and play loud music 24 hours a day — freedom!

Then it happens! What a shock. Once we grow up and become adults, we yearn for the days when life was simple. We dream of the simplicity and innocence of childhood. Wow, we need therapy. Well, you're an adult now, so deal with it. But being an adult doesn't mean you have to lose the child within. It just means the toys get bigger.

So, you have a new car, a new job, and a new apartment. Now your focus shifts from starting the "life span" (configuration) to keeping it going (management). As a CNA, you move into LAN adulthood with a new focus on NetWare management. Once the network is up and running, you can step back and shift your attention to the long term. Suddenly, your mind is filled with thoughts of a family (servers and workstations), a pension (SMS), and retirement (RMF). Aah, adulthood is a many-splendored thing.

NetWare 4 management is the most time-consuming aspect of being a CNA. Think about it: NetWare configuration occurs only once, but management dominates your life forever. In NetWare 4, network management occurs through four strategies:

▸ Server management

▸ Workstation management

▸ Storage Management Services (SMS)

▸ Remote Management Facility (RMF)

Server management is marriage. It involves daily tasks for protecting and maintaining your relationship with the NetWare 4 server. This includes NDS maintenance and console management. At this point, monitoring the server involves more than just walking by it once a day and making sure the green light is on.

Workstation management is like having children. It can be even more challenging than the other three strategies because you're dealing with the NetWare users (your children). And we all know that the user's primary purpose in life is to make CNAs miserable. In addition to battling users, our workstation management duties involve connectivity strategies, virus prevention, and diskless workstations. Finally, like it or not, you'll have to set up the LAN to support diverse client environments — DOS, Windows 95, OS/2, Macintosh, and UnixWare.

As the adage goes, "you never miss anything until it's gone." This holds especially true for NetWare data. Welcome to your pension plan. One of the most important things you can do as a NetWare 4 CNA is plan for the future by doing backups. *Storage Management Services (SMS)* is a NetWare 4 backup engine that provides data storage and retrieval from various front-end applications to numerous back-end storage devices. In this chapter, you'll learn about the fundamental architecture of SMS and explore the many features of SBACKUP.NLM.

Finally, *RMF (Remote Management Facility)* enables you to manage the server console from anywhere in the world — including Happy Acres. You've worked hard, and now it's time for retirement. RMF will become the cornerstone of your server maintenance schedule. Of course, it's hard to maintain the server when it's chained up and locked away in a hidden closet. Fortunately, by using RMF, you can access the server console from any distributed workstation.

ZEN

"Every wakeful step, every mindful act is the direct path to awakening. Wherever you go, there you are."

Anonymous

Like adulthood, NetWare 4 management doesn't always come naturally. You must work at it. Children have their parents to rely on, but now (as an adult) you're on your own. So, to help guide you through the minefield of CNA adulthood, I suggest these few management strategies.

First, build a NetWare Log book. Although few CNAs have one, it should become the foundation of your daily management life. The NetWare Log book is a detailed, step-by-step log of all activity from LAN conception to the present. It includes worksheets, floor plans, security restrictions, file management, pictures of LAN hardware, pictures of your mother, cabling layouts, application information, and weekly management tasks. It's vital that you take the Log book seriously because you never know when you might need it.

Next, use the worksheets provided with NetWare 4 documentation. The Installation manual includes various worksheets that can help you document LAN details, including file server hardware, workstation hardware, configuration files, NetWare directories, user and group information, default login restrictions, trustee assignments, and login scripts. Then put these worksheets in your NetWare Log book for future reference. I see a pattern forming here.

Reference material is the fodder of creative minds. I don't know what that means, but it sounds good. The bottom line is, you can't know everything. Create an extensive library of reference material so you don't have to know everything. Some of the best sources include Novell Press books, *Novell Application Notes*, NSEPro CD-ROM, Web Pages, documentation, and, of course, this book. Don't forget your library card.

Finally, your mindset has an important impact on NetWare 4 management. Psychologically, you need to be committed to the network and recognize management as an important aspect of your daily life. Take time to embrace these management tasks and make sure that everyone in the organization recognizes that you need time to do them. Many times, users and management don't understand why the network needs to be down for VREPAIR or SMS backup. Educate them gracefully.

With these strategies in mind, let's now dive into the wild and wacky world of NetWare 4 management. Remember, this is the foundation of your daily life as a CNA. NDS design happens once, installation happens once, and NetWare 4 configuration happens once. On the other hand, management happens every day until you win the lottery. So, without any further ado, let's start our jaunt through LAN adulthood, starting with marriage.

ZEN

"I know it is wet
And the sun is not sunny.
But we can have
Lots of good fun that is funny!"

Dr. Seuss

Server Management

Eventually you will find Mr./Ms. Right. Your eyes will meet across a crowded dance floor, you will feel that wonderful flutter in the pit of your stomach. Your knees will buckle and then bang — you're married! Marriage changes everything. Suddenly, your focus shifts from "me, me, me" to "the family." Your spouse becomes the center of your life. It's like sharing a lifeboat with that "special someone" while careening down the whitewater rapids of love. Yuck.

Similarly, the NetWare 4 server is at the center of your LAN. At some point, your focus shifts from "users, users, users" to "the server." After all, the entire WAN will crumble if your servers aren't running correctly.

NetWare 4 server management consists of three components:

- ▶ Server protection — keep users away from the server console

- ▶ Console commands — keep the server running at peak performance

- ▶ NetWare Loadable Modules — everything else

Because the server is at the heart of your WAN, you want to take any means possible to protect it. This includes locking up the server, preventing access to the keyboard with MONITOR.NLM, using the SECURE CONSOLE command, and adding a password for RMF. Also, don't forget to use The Club™. Server protection is a serious management task because of the vulnerability of the console — users can cause a lot of damage there. Many times, this security feature is overlooked and CNAs discover their inadequate security measures when it's too late — in the unemployment line.

The colon (:) prompt *is* the server console. This is where you'll spend most of your server management time. The colon prompt accepts two kinds of commands — console commands and NLMs. NetWare 4 includes numerous console commands for various server management and maintenance tasks, including NDS management, time synchronization, bindery services, sending messages, activating NLMs, server protection, and network optimization. This chapter explores most of the NetWare 4 console commands and gives you some hints on how to use them.

All remaining server activity is accomplished by using NLMs, which are modular Legos that provide supplemental functionality to the NetWare 4 server. There are four kinds of NLMs: disk drivers, LAN drivers, name space modules, and management utilities. In this chapter, we'll explore each of these and some key server management tools — INSTALL.NLM, MONITOR.NLM, SERVMAN.NLM, and DSREPAIR.NLM. You can think of NLMs as network management applications at the server.

As you can see, marriage takes a lot of work. Fortunately, the rewards greatly outweigh the pain. As a CNA, you must work hard at your network marriage to keep the server running and in peak condition (and, with luck, the rewards will also outweigh the pain). In both marriage and server management, communication (and protection) is the key. Let's take a closer look.

QUIZ

My first is in day, but not in night.
My second, in flame, but not in light.
My third is in milk, but not in tea.
My fourth in slip, but not in plea.
My last in yellow, not in whale.
My whole for love will tell a tale.
What am I?

(Q7-1)
(See Appendix C for all quiz answers.)

SERVER PROTECTION

If the server is at the heart of your NetWare 4 WAN, it makes sense to take all measures you can to protect it. As we saw in Chapter 5, NetWare 4 has an elaborate security system that protects NDS and data files from would-be hackers. This system does nothing, however, to protect the server console itself. Any user with mischievous intent and a little bit of knowledge can cause a lot of harm at the NetWare 4 server console. For this reason, you should take extra measure to install an impenetrable network armor at the file server console. Following are four scenarios that can go a long way in protecting your server:

▸ Physical — lock up the physical server

▸ MONITOR.NLM locking — use the password feature

▸ SECURE CONSOLE — restrict access to the DOS partition

▸ REMOTE.NLM — add a password to the built-in RMF facility

Now, let's take a closer look at how to create a "maximum security server."

Physical

No matter what security locks you put in place, someone's going to break them if he or she has physical access to the server. It's amazing how much information can be stolen from the physical server console including SERVER.EXE, NLMs, optimization data, and company secrets. The first step in creating a maximum security server is locking up the physical machine itself. This involves three steps:

1 • Lock the server in a wiring closet or other restricted room.

2 • Remove the keyboard to discourage physical access to the console.

3 • Remove the server monitor and leave the hacker "in the dark."

Although this is a great plan, you're probably wondering, "How am I supposed to manage server operations from within a locked closet and with no keyboard or monitor?" That is a good question. Fortunately, NetWare 4 includes a built-in Remote Management Facility (RMF) that provides virtual access to the file server console — from a direct workstation or asynchronously remote machine. Later in this chapter, we'll explore RMF and show you how it can be used to supplement the server protection plan. For now, let's move on to the next protection scenario — MONITOR.NLM.

MONITOR.NLM Locking

If locking up the server is not an option, or you want to increase your level of server protection, consider "locking" the console with MONITOR.NLM. This way, even if someone does get physical access to the machine, he/she can't access the console unless he/she has the MONITOR.NLM password. First, load the MONITOR.NLM utility by typing

```
LOAD MONITOR
```

at the file server console. Next, choose the Lock Server Console option from the main menu. NetWare will ask for a password. Enter a unique password and press Enter. All done. Now, anyone accessing the server console must first enter the MONITOR.NLM password.

By default, NetWare 4 accepts the bindery supervisor's password for unlocking the server console. As you learned earlier, this is the first password assigned to the Admin user when you install the first server in this NDS tree. Even if you delete Admin or change his/her password, the supervisor bindery password remains the same. You should specify a different password when you lock the monitor — just in case. You can also automate monitor locking by placing the following command in the server's AUTOEXEC.NCF configuration file:

```
LOAD MONITOR L
```

In this example, only the supervisor bindery password can be used to unlock the server console. Next, let's expand our server protection scheme to include the SECURE CONSOLE command.

TIP

If Intruder Detection/Lockout disables either the bindery supervisor or Admin account, the password won't unlock MONITOR. This is a bad thing. The only way to reactivate the accounts is to issue the ENABLE LOGIN console command at the server — but we can't get there! So, as a backup measure, consider issuing a different MONITOR locking password.

SECURE CONSOLE

To further enhance server protection, you can use the SECURE CONSOLE command at the colon prompt (:). This command accomplishes four things:

- ▶ Path specifiers are disabled. Only the SYS:SYSTEM search path remains in effect. This means NLMs can only be loaded from the SYS:SYSTEM directory. SECURE CONSOLE provides protection against Trojan horse modules that are loaded from DOS partitions or diskette drives. These modules enter the core OS and access or alter valuable server information. Remember, anyone can load an NLM at the server from diskette unless he/she is restricted from physically accessing it, or the SECURE CONSOLE command has been used.

- ▶ Keyboard entry into the NetWare 4 OS debugger is disabled. This stops super-nerdy hackers from altering the OS itself.

- ▶ This command prevents the server date and time from being changed by an intruder. This closes a loophole in the Intruder Detection/Lockout feature. Without SECURE CONSOLE, users whose accounts have been disabled can simply access the server colon prompt and manually expire their lockout period. Bad user.

- ▶ COMMAND.COM is removed from server memory. This protects files on the DOS partition by preventing access to it. Remember, one of your most important NetWare 4 files (SERVER.EXE) resides on the DOS partition.

I'm feeling more secure already. With the server locked up tight as a drum, there's only one more back door to close — RMF access.

REMOTE.NLM

The final server protection strategy involves restricting access to RMF — NetWare 4's built-in remote management facility. As you recall from our first protection strategy, we've already locked the server in a closet and removed the keyboard and monitor. Now the only way to perform daily monitoring tasks is RMF. We'll talk more about the details of RMF later in this chapter, but here's the "Cliff Notes" version.

RMF enables you to access the server console from a local or remote workstation. In either case, it relies on two key components — REMOTE.NLM at the server and RCONSOLE.EXE at the workstation. It's reasonable to assume that if *you* can access the server console from a remote workstation, so can any malevolent hacker. So, let's take measures to protect REMOTE.NLM.

When you activate REMOTE at the server console, you can specify a password using the following syntax:

```
LOAD REMOTE password
```

Replace *password* with any alphanumeric name you can remember. With the password in place, RCONSOLE prompts you for it before enabling access to the server console. Here's the catch — you'll probably want to automate this step by placing REMOTE in the AUTOEXEC.NCF file. Because AUTOEXEC.NCF is a text file in the SYS:SYSTEM subdirectory, it's reasonable to assume that any hacker worth his/her salt would be able to view the REMOTE password. Oops. But we have a solution. You can use null characters in the password or, better yet, encrypt it. Null characters appear as spaces, but are actual, valid, alphanumeric characters. You can issue a null character by pressing the Alt+255 keys simultaneously. When hackers view AUTOEXEC.NCF, they'll never know the difference between a null character and a space. Or, better yet, you can encrypt the REMOTE password using LDREMOTE. For more details, see the Real World that follows.

REAL WORLD

In previous versions of NetWare, REMOTE.NLM accepted the Supervisor's bindery password in addition to its own. This meant you could issue the LOAD REMOTE command in AUTOEXEC.NCF without having to disclose the password. This has changed in NetWare 4.1. Now the REMOTE password is required and the Supervisor bindery password no longer works. Fortunately, Novell has included an encryption scheme that enables you to encrypt what appears in AUTOEXEC.NCF. Here's how it works:

1 • Load REMOTE.NLM at the server console by typing LOAD REMOTE and pressing Enter. NetWare 4 will prompt you for an RMF password. Enter it now (for example, Cathy).

2 • RMF is now active, but your password is not protected. Next, you can encrypt the password by typing REMOTE ENCRYPT at the server console and pressing Enter. Once again, NetWare will ask you for a password. Enter the same one from above (Cathy).

3 • NetWare 4 then responds with an encrypted LOAD statement such as:

```
LOAD REMOTE -e 14572BFD3AFEAE4E4759
```

This is the encrypted representation of the password Cathy.

Next, REMOTE will ask you a simple question:

```
Would you like this command written to
SYS:SYSTEM\LDREMOTE.NCF?
```

You should probably answer Yes.

4 • Now you're ready to add the REMOTE statement to AUTOEXEC.NCF without any concerns about giving away the password. Simply enter these two commands toward the end of AUTOEXEC.NCF:

```
LDREMOTE

LOAD RSPX
```

There you have it! We've increased server protection by requiring an RMF password and closed a loophole by encrypting it. In summary, use LOAD REMOTE with the password, then issue the REMOTE ENCRYPT command to encrypt the password. Provide the same password again and have NetWare create the LDREMOTE configuration file. Finally, automate RMF by placing LDREMOTE in the AUTOEXEC.NCF file.

Don't you feel much better now, knowing that you have a maximum security server? Just like Alcatraz, it should be almost impossible for NetWare criminals to "break in." Now let's return to the final two stages of NetWare 4 marriage — console commands and NLMs. These are the tools that make a marriage work.

ZEN

"We could tell you what it's about. But then, of course, we'd have to kill you."

From the movie *Sneakers*

CONSOLE COMMANDS

To be successful in anything, you need the right tools. Marriage is no exception. In order to make any marriage work, you both have to bring the right tools — love, compassion, understanding, respect, flexibility, truth, and a spirit of compromise. But more important than anything is communication. You need to work together as a team and develop synergy. This strategy revolves around the single most important tool — "honey-do's." Honey-do's make the world go around. "Honey, do this," "honey, do that." As long as you pay attention to honey-do's, you'll never have to miss another Sunday football game or "mushy" movie like *On Golden Pond*. Don't forget those compromises.

NetWare 4 marriage is not any different. In order to develop server management synergy, you must bring along the right tools — console commands and NLMs. Console commands are internal management tools that enable you to perform various server management maintenance tasks, including NDS management, time synchronization, bindery services, sending messages, activating NLMs, server protection, and network optimization. NLMs, on the other hand, are the modular Legos that provide supplemental functionality to the core OS. NetWare 4 includes four kinds of NLMs — disk drivers, LAN drivers, name space modules, and management utilities. Let's start our discussion of NetWare 4 honey-do's with a look at some important console commands.

Console commands enable CNAs to interact directly with the NetWare 4 OS core. These commands are internal to SERVER.EXE and do not require any other support commands. One of the most powerful NetWare 4 console commands is SET. This utility enables you to customize the OS core with almost 100 advanced parameters. These parameters are organized into 11 categories ranging from communications to file system to time synchronization. Warning: don't mess around with SET unless you've been adequately trained and you're wearing protective gloves.

The syntax of console commands is relatively straightforward. The command itself is entered at the colon prompt and is followed by pressing the Enter key. Also, NetWare supports various command switches that customize their execution. Anyone can execute a console command as long as he/she has physical access to the file server console. This is a good reason to severely limit access to the machine and implement many of the protection schemes we discussed earlier. Also, console tools can be hazardous to the server if not handled correctly. You should ensure that they are kept out of the reach of small children and NetWare users. Fortunately, they have their own childproof cap (by being placed in the SYS:SYSTEM subdirectory by default).

Let's take a closer look at NetWare 4's top 15 console commands (provided here in alphabetical order). For a complete list of the console commands, refer to the *Novell NetWare 4 Utilities Reference Manual*.

TIP

Console commands are internal operating system tools similar to DOS's internal commands. They are built into SERVER.EXE just like CD or CLS is built into COMMAND.COM. You don't need to have any searching or NetWare directories available to access console commands.

BIND

BIND is an installation console command. As we saw earlier, it links LAN drivers to a communications protocol. Once the LAN driver is loaded, BIND must be issued to activate LAN communications. The default NetWare 4 communication protocol is IPX. Here's the syntax for activating communications on the 3C5X9 NIC:

```
BIND IPX to 3C5X9
```

When you issue the BIND statement at the server console, you'll be asked for the external network number.

BROADCAST

BROADCAST is an administrative console command that enables CNAs to send brief alert messages to all attached workstations. Another related command (SEND) enables you to broadcast messages to specific users or groups of users. In both cases, the message appears at the bottom of the workstation monitor and prompts the user to press Ctrl+Enter to clear it from the screen. Only users who are currently logged in will receive these messages. BROADCAST messages can be up to 40 characters, whereas SEND supports larger messages (55 characters maximum). Here's the syntax:

```
BROADCAST message
```

The downside of BROADCAST and SEND is that they lock up the destination computer until Ctrl+Enter is pressed. This lockup can create harmful effects if the computer is being used for unattended backups. To avoid having messages lock up unattended machines, consider issuing SEND with the following parameters:

/A=C — accept messages only from the server console

/A=N — accept no messages (dangerous)

/A=P — stores the last message sent until you poll to receive it

/P — polls the server for the last stored message

/A=A — accept all messages.

CLEAR STATION

CLEAR STATION is an administrative console command that enables you to abruptly clear a workstation's connection. Be forewarned — this command removes all file server resources from the workstation and can cause file corruption or data loss if it is executed while the workstation is processing transactions. This command is only useful if workstations have crashed, or if users have turned off their machines without logging out. Here's the syntax:

```
CLEAR STATION n
```

The *n* specifies the connection number of the workstation you want to clear. These connection numbers can be viewed from MONITOR.NLM or with the help of NLIST. Connection numbers are incrementally allocated as workstations attached to the server and are not the same from one session to another.

CONFIG

CONFIG is a maintenance console command. It displays hardware information for all internal communication components. Figure 7.1 shows the CONFIG information for ACME's first LABS-SRV1 server, and Table 7.1 describes CONFIG parameters.

FIGURE 7.1

```
LABS-SRV1:CONFIG
File server name: LABS-SRV1
IPX internal network number: 0BADCAFE
     Node address: 000000000001
     Frame type: VIRTUAL_LAN
     LAN protocol: IPX network 0BADCAFE
Server Up Time:  1 Minute 38 Seconds

3Com EtherLink III 3C5X9 Family
     Version 4.01b   October 19, 1994
     Hardware setting: I/O ports 320h to 32Fh, Interrupt Ah
     Node address: 0020AFE28F2D
     Frame type: ETHERNET_802.2
     Board name: 3C5X9_1_E82
     LAN protocol: IPX network 00001234

Tree Name: ACME_TREE
Bindery Context(s):
     LABS.NORAD.ACME

LABS-SRV1:
```

PARAMETER	VALUE	DESCRIPTION
File server name	LABS-SRV1	The name of the server.
IPX internal network number	BADCAFE	The eight-digit hexadecimal number used to uniquely identify this server.
Node address	000000000001 0020AFE28F2D	The internal server node and unique factory address for internal 3C5X9 NIC.
Frame type	VIRTUAL_LAN Ethernet_802.2	Modular communications within the server and external communications for this NIC.
LAN protocol	IPX 1234	Identifies the internal IPX address as BADCAFE and external cable segment as 1234.
Board name	3c5x9_1_E82	The unique board name given to this NIC's frame type and external address.
Tree name	ACME_TREE	The name of the NDS tree in which this server participates.
Server Up Time	1 minute 38 seconds	The amount of time the server has been active.

DOWN

DOWN is a dangerous administrative console command. It completely shuts down file server activity and closes all open files. This is probably one of the most dramatic and potentially harmful NetWare 4 console commands, so treat it with kid gloves. Before DOWN deactivates the server, it performs various tasks, including clearing all cache buffers and writing them to disk, closing all open files, updating appropriate directory and file allocation tables, dismounting all volumes, clearing all connections, and closing the operating system. Once DOWN has been entered at the file server console, you have various options:

- Type **EXIT** to return to the DOS partition.

- Type **RESTART SERVER** to bring things back up again.

- Type **UP** to reactivate the server console (really — take a look at the following Real World section).

> **REAL WORLD**
>
> In many of my trials and tribulations with the world of NetWare 4, I've seen frustrated users trying to reactivate the server by typing UP. I've come to the conclusion that Novell missed the boat in creating a cure for the DOWN command. Because turnabout is fair play, I offer this simple solution: Create a server batch file named UP.NCF. In it, place a single command: RESTART SERVER. Then add the following line to the end of your AUTOEXEC.NCF file:
>
> ```
> SEARCH ADD C:\NWSERVER
> ```
>
> Finally, copy UP.NCF to the C:\NWSERVER directory. Now whenever the server is brought DOWN, you can simply type UP to reactivate it. I just love it when a plan comes together.

ZEN

"Unformed people delight in the gaudy and in novelty. Cooked people delight in the ordinary."

Mao Pau Zen

DSTRACE

DSTRACE is a maintenance console command. It enables CNAs to monitor NDS replica-related activities, including advertising, synchronization, and replica-to-replica communications. As you can see in Figure 7.2, DSTRACE provides various statistics concerning ACME partitions and replicas. Here's a snapshot of some of the more interesting messages:

- Date and time — The date and exact second of replica synchronization is shown in parentheses.

- SYNC:Start sync of partition <RIO.ACME> — This indicates the start of a synchronization interval. A state of [0] indicates a normal synchronization check. A value greater than [0] (like [30]) shows replica activity such as a partition being created or a partition being merged back into its parent.

- SYNC:End sync of partition <RIO.ACME> — This line indicates the end of the synchronization interval. The message "All processed=YES" indicates that all updates were successfully incorporated into the master replica of this partition.

F I G U R E 7.2

Getting to Know
  DSTRACE

```
(99/12/24 03:24:06)
SYNC: Start sync of partition <RIO.ACME> state:[0] type:[1]
 SYNC: Start outbound sync with (1) [010000BC]<WHITE-SRV1.WHITE.CRIME.TOKYO.ACME
>
  SYNC: sending updates to server <CN=WHITE-SRV1>
 SYNC: update to server <CN=WHITE-SRV1> successfully completed
SYNC: End sync of partition <RIO.ACME> All processed = YES.

(99/12/24 03:24:06)
SYNC: Start sync of partition <SYDNEY.ACME> state:[0] type:[1]
 SYNC: Start outbound sync with (1) [010000BC]<WHITE-SRV1.WHITE.CRIME.TOKYO.ACME
>
  SYNC: sending updates to server <CN=WHITE-SRV1>
 SYNC: update to server <CN=WHITE-SRV1> successfully completed
SYNC: End sync of partition <SYDNEY.ACME> All processed = YES.

(99/12/24 03:24:06)
SYNC: Start sync of partition <TOKYO.ACME> state:[0] type:[1]
 SYNC: Start outbound sync with (1) [010000BC]<WHITE-SRV1.WHITE.CRIME.TOKYO.ACME
>
  SYNC: sending updates to server <CN=WHITE-SRV1>
 SYNC: update to server <CN=WHITE-SRV1> successfully completed
SYNC: End sync of partition <TOKYO.ACME> All processed = YES.
```

DSTRACE can be activated at the NetWare 4 server console by issuing the SET DSTRACE=ON statement.

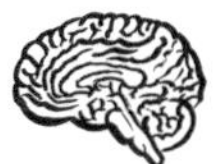

THE BRAIN

For more information on using DSTRACE and its parameters, consult the SET discussion in the *Novell NetWare 4 Utilities Reference Manual* or Chapter 5 of the *Novell NetWare 4 Supervising the Network I Manual.*

ENABLE/DISABLE LOGIN

ENABLE LOGIN and its counterpart, DISABLE LOGIN, are both maintenance console commands. DISABLE LOGIN enables you to prevent access to the server for troubleshooting or maintenance activities. DISABLE LOGIN is particularly useful when you are working on the NDS database, backing up files, loading software, or dismounting/repairing volumes. Keep in mind that DISABLE LOGIN does not affect users who are currently logged in. You may consider combining this command with the CLEAR STATION statement.

As I'm sure you've probably guessed, ENABLE LOGIN enables file server logins if they've been disabled. It also provides one other facility — supervisor unlocking. If the Supervisor bindery account has been locked because of intruder detection, ENABLE LOGIN will unlock it. This only works on the Supervisor bindery or Admin accounts.

EXIT

EXIT is an administrative console command. It enables you to return to the DOS partition once the file server has been brought DOWN. You may want to EXIT the file server console to prevent any other commands from being activated, or to reissue SERVER.EXE with new parameters. In addition, EXIT can be used in conjunction with REMOVE DOS to remotely reboot the file server. Of course, this facility has already been integrated into RESTART SERVER or our new UP.NCF utility. Who needs EXIT when you've got UP?

HELP

HELP is definitely an administrative console command. Many times when you feel the CNAship is weighing you down, simply type **HELP** at the server console and NetWare will come to your rescue. You can view help about a specific console command by identifying it with the HELP command or view a short description of all console commands by typing:

```
HELP ALL
```

Press Enter after each description to view the next command. Then press Esc to exit altogether.

LOAD/UNLOAD

LOAD is an installation console command. It is used to activate NLMs and attach them to the core OS. As you recall, the NetWare 4 architecture consists of two pieces — core OS and NLMs. The LOAD console command is used to activate these NLMs and bring them to life. You can also UNLOAD NLMs when you're finished with them and free up valuable server RAM.

MODULES

MODULES is a maintenance console command. It displays a list of currently loaded NLMs and some brief information about each, including the module short name, a descriptive string for each module, and the version number if it's a disk driver, LAN driver, or management utility. MODULES can be an important part of your NetWare 4 optimization strategy in that it enables you to identify which modules are occupying valuable server RAM. Also, it displays support NLMs you might not have known you're using.

MOUNT

MOUNT is an installation console command. It activates internal NetWare 4 volumes. The MOUNT command makes volumes available to users and can be used on specific volumes or all of them:

```
MOUNT ALL
```

MOUNTing and DISMOUNTing volumes can be used as a security feature for volumes that are rarely accessed. MOUNT them during access hours and DISMOUNT them when they are not in use. No matter how clever the hacker is, no one can access a dismounted volume. Murphy's Law Number 142 — never say "no one."

REMOVE DOS

REMOVE DOS is an administrative console command. As you learned earlier, REMOVE DOS eliminates COMMAND.COM from background file server RAM. This memory is then returned to NetWare 4 for file caching. REMOVE DOS can also be used to increase file server security. When DOS is removed, NLMs cannot be loaded from the DOS partition — it doesn't exist any more. Also, users cannot EXIT to the DOS partition. If they try, the file server is automatically rebooted back to the NetWare partition. Recall that the SECURE CONSOLE command automatically removes DOS from file server RAM.

RESTART SERVER

RESTART SERVER is an administrative console command. It can be used to reactivate the server after it has been DOWNed. This is most useful when your troubleshooting duties require that you frequently DOWN the server. RESTART SERVER is not one of your normal daily activities. This command also has a couple of interesting parameters that improve its troubleshooting value:

-NS — restart the server without invoking STARTUP.NCF.

-NA — restart the server without invoking AUTOEXEC.NCF.

Remember, this console command is the foundation of our earlier server UP.NCF scheme.

TRACK ON

TRACK ON is a maintenance console command. It activates the RIP tracking screen. This screen displays *router information protocol (RIP)* traffic on the NetWare 4 server. Keep in mind that NetWare 4 NDS activities do not rely on RIP and, therefore, broadcast their own information over separate channels. In addition, it's possible to filter RIP activity using additional products such as Novell's MultiProtocol Router. As you can see in Figure 7.3, TRACK ON fills up the server console very quickly. You can bounce between this and other screens by pressing the Alt+Esc keys simultaneously or using Ctrl+Esc to view a list of all active console screens.

Getting to Know TRACK
ON

```
Router Tracking Screen
OUT    [0BADCAFE:FFFFFFFFFFFF]    3:13:49 pm    00000DAD   2/3        00001234   1/2
OUT    [00001234:FFFFFFFFFFFF]    3:13:49 pm    0BADCAFE   1/2
IN     [0BADCAFE:000000000001]    3:13:56 pm    LABS-SRV1       1
IN     [00001234:0020AFE8B8B5]    3:13:56 pm    ACME_TREE___    1     ACME_TREE___    1
          WHITE-SRV1     1    WHITE-SRV1    1    WHITE-SRV1      1
IN     [00001234:0020AFC055F3]    3:14:07 pm    Get Nearest Server
OUT    [00001234:0020AFC055F3]    3:14:07 pm    Give Nearest Server LABS-SRV1
IN     [00001234:0020AFC055F3]    3:14:07 pm    Route Request
IN     [00001234:0020AFC055F3]    3:14:07 pm    Route Request
OUT    [00001234:0020AFC055F3]    3:14:07 pm    0BADCAFE   1/2
IN     [0BADCAFE:000000000001]    3:14:16 pm    ACME_TREE___    1
OUT    [0BADCAFE:FFFFFFFFFFFF]    3:14:19 pm    ACME_TREE___    2     ACME_TREE___    2
          WHITE-SRV1     2    WHITE-SRV1    2    WHITE-SRV1      2     ACME_TREE___    1
          LABS-SRV1      1
OUT    [00001234:FFFFFFFFFFFF]    3:14:19 pm    ACME_TREE___    1     LABS-SRV1       1
          LABS-SRV1      1
OUT    [0BADCAFE:FFFFFFFFFFFF]    3:14:19 pm    LABS-SRV1       1
IN     [0BADCAFE:000000000001]    3:14:23 pm    LABS-SRV1       1
IN     [0BADCAFE:000000000001]    3:14:25 pm    LABS-SRV1       1
IN     [00001234:0020AFE8B8B5]    3:14:26 pm    00000DAD   1/2
<Use ALT-ESC or CTRL-ESC to switch screens, or any other key to pause>
```

TRACK ON information is formatted according to whether the file server is receiving the information (IN) or broadcasting the information (OUT). Figure 7.3 shows the format of TRACK ON for the ACME LAB server and provides information about the many components it tracks, including sending file server's network address, node address, name, hops from that file server to this one, network addresses known by the sending file server, and the number of tics it takes to traverse the WAN. Refer to Table 7.2 for a more detailed discussion of these TRACK ON components. Finally, you can activate the RIP tracking screen by issuing the following command at the server colon prompt (:):

```
TRACK ON
```

If you haven't figured it out yet, almost every ON switch in the world has an OFF. TRACK ON is no exception. To deactivate the RIP tracking screen, simply issue the command:

```
TRACK OFF
```

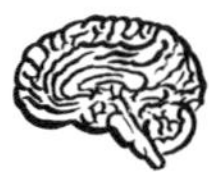

THE BRAIN

For more information on using TRACK ON and other server console commands, see the AppNote entitled "Using TRACK and Other Console Utilities in a Mixed NetWare Environment" in the October 1995 issue of _Novell Application Notes_.

That completes our discussion of NetWare 4 marriage tools. With this knowledge, comes responsibility. Remember, wield these tools wisely. Power corrupts and absolute power corrupts absolutely. Now, let's complete our journey through the world of NetWare 4 server management with a final discussion of "honey-do's."

ZEN

"The story of a girl who gets mad, gets big, and gets even."

From the movie _Attack of the 50-Foot Woman_

T A B L E   7.2

Understanding TRACK ON Parameters

PARAMETER	VALUE	DESCRIPTION
IN	IN [network address] 3:14:07 PM	Indicates inbound information originating outside this server and the time at which it was accepted.
OUT	OUT [network address] 3:14:07 PM	Indicates outbound information originating from this server and going across the WAN.
[network address]	[0BADCAFE:000000000001]	Identifies the IPX internal network address and node address of the internal virtual LAN. This is the server's unique internal network address.
	[00001234:FFFFFFFFFFFF]	The outbound network and node address for packets being sent from this server. The odd node address indicates this packet is meant to be broadcast to all workstations and servers on the 1234 external cabling segment.
	[00001234:0020AFC055F3]	Indicates a packet arriving from a specific machine — in this case, a workstation.

(continued)

T A B L E 7.2

Understanding TRACK ON Parameters
(continued)

PARAMETER	VALUE	DESCRIPTION
SAP Information	LABS-SRV1	Service advertising protocol information. This includes server names and a number. The number represents how many hops the server is from this server. Each router counts as a hop. Servers displaying SAP information include file servers, print servers, mail servers, and so on.
	WHITE-SRV1 2	SAP information showing the WHITE-SRV1 server as 2 hops from LABS-SRV1. Internal Parameter Value Description IPX routing does count as a hop.
RIP information	00001234 1/2	Routing information protocol data. The number 00001234 indicates the destination network address for this packet. The value 1/2 indicates the number of hops and ticks it will take to reach the network. A tick is 1/18th of a second and typically one more than the number of hops. If you're sending packets over a large WAN, the ticks could take much longer.
GET NEAREST SERVER	GET NEAREST SERVER	This is a broadcast from a client seeking a connection from any server. If you do not get this message, it indicates that the workstation is having trouble communicating with the server.
GIVE NEAREST SERVER	GIVE NEAREST SERVER LABS-SRV1	This server's response to the GET NEAREST SERVER request.

NETWARE LOADABLE MODULES

NLMs are NetWare 4 honey-do's. If you ever need any help, it's nice to know NLMs are there for you. These cute little server dynamos attach to the core OS and provide additional NetWare 4 functionality. As you can see in Figure 7.4, NetWare doesn't have much to offer without NLMs. The core operating system provides these basic network services:

- NetWare Directory Services (NDS)

- File server

- Security

- Authentication

- Routing

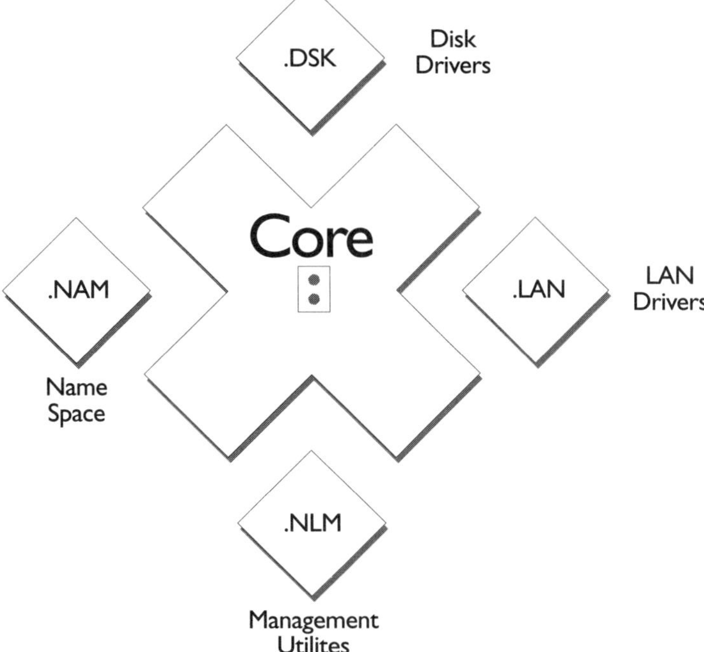

FIGURE 7.4

NetWare 4 Server Architecture

But none of these facilities are available until NLMs activate internal communications and mount the file system. In addition to saving the day, NetWare 4 NLMs have the following advantages:

▸ NLMs free up RAM by enabling CNAs to remove inactive modules.

▸ NLMs can be loaded and unloaded without bringing down the server — hence the Lego analogy.

▸ NLMs provide an easy method for outside developers to write their own modules for NetWare 4.

From Figure 7.4, you can see that NetWare 4 supports four NLM types: disk drivers, LAN drivers, name space, and management NLMs. Disk drivers are primarily responsible for the interface between NetWare and the internal hard disks. LAN drivers initiate communications with the internal NIC, whereas name space modules provide support for non-DOS naming schemes. Management NLMs are the real stars of the show. They're used for monitoring, maintenance, and configuration of the NetWare server environment. Let's take a closer look at each of these NLM types and explore how they can improve your quality of life — or at least your marriage.

Disk Drivers

As I just mentioned, disk drivers control communications between NetWare 4 and the internal shared disk. You can load and unload disk drivers as needed. Disk drivers activate the NetWare partition. They have the .DSK extension and are stored in the C:\NWSERVER directory. During the installation or startup process, your first task (after running SERVER.EXE) is to activate .DSK NLMs. This mounts the NetWare file system and makes all other utilities available from the SYS:SYSTEM directory. Some common .DSK drivers include ISADISK.DSK, IDE.DSK, and DCB.DSK for disk coprocessor boards. Newer disk modules written to the NetWare Peripheral Architecture (NPA) come in pairs and have .CDM and .HAM extensions.

LAN Drivers

LAN drivers, on the other hand, control communication between NetWare 4 and internal network interface cards (NICs). You can load and unload these drivers as needed to make communications available to all LAN users. Bear in mind that when you load the LAN driver, you must specify hardware configuration options such as interrupt, port address, memory address, and frame type.

Although disk drivers are automatically activated from STARTUP.NCF, LAN drivers reside in AUTOEXEC.NCF. This is because they are available from the SYS:SYSTEM directory once the NetWare partition has been activated. LAN drivers have the .LAN extension and include NE2000.LAN, TOKEN.LAN, 3C5X9.LAN, and TRXNET.LAN for ARCNet.

Name Space

Name space modules enable non-DOS naming conventions to be stored in the server file system. Name space is important so that Macintosh, Unix, and OS/2 names can be supported in cooperation with the default DOS environment. Name space modules have the .NAM extension and are stored in the SYS:SYSTEM directory with all other NLMs. Some common name space modules include MAC.NAM for Macintosh users and OS2.NAM for OS/2 users. Later in this chapter, we'll explore non-DOS workstations and review how name space works. For now, be aware that one other console command is required when you activate name space — ADD NAME SPACE.

INSTALL.NLM

This is where the fun begins. INSTALL.NLM is the first of a slew of management NLMs that help you install, manage, maintain, troubleshoot, and optimize the NetWare 4 server. As you can see in Figure 7.5, INSTALL consists of 10 options.

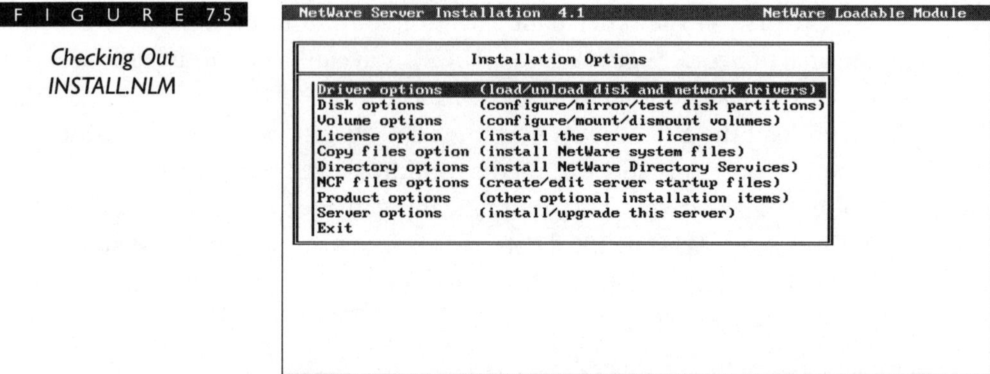

F I G U R E 7.5

*Checking Out
INSTALL.NLM*

These 10 INSTALL steps systematically walk you through the server install process, beginning with SERVER.EXE. Once the core OS has been activated, you load the disk driver and create the NetWare partition. Next, you create the default SYS: volume and activate the server license. Once you copy SYSTEM and PUBLIC files to the new volume, it's time to install NDS. This is the trickiest of the 10 installation options. Once time synchronization and server context have been established, you can automate the whole kit and caboodle with AUTOEXEC.NCF and STARTUP.NCF files. Finally, Product Options provides support for installing other products, and Server Options gives you the choice of starting all over again. Of course, like any management NLM, if things get too hairy, you can always EXIT.

This INSTALL.NLM utility is a dramatic improvement over earlier versions. In the past, the installation process wasn't nearly as systematic or organized. Also, you can jump to any point in the journey from the main menu. Some of the tasks you might want to perform after the NetWare 4 installation include:

- ▶ Disk duplexing

- ▶ Adding drives and volumes

- ▶ Redefining the hot-fix redirection area

- ▶ Editing server configuration files

▶ Loading an upgraded NetWare 4 license

▶ Installing and configuring additional products, including DynaText, MHS Services, Macintosh, or Unix support

MONITOR.NLM

MONITOR.NLM has always been the "mother of all server utilities." It provides a plethora of information about key memory and communication processes. The types of resources that can be tracked using MONITOR.NLM include file connections, memory, disk information, users, file lock activity, and processor usage. Of course, with the advent of SERVMAN, there's some competition at the top of the mountain.

ZEN

"My grandfather once told me that there are two kinds of people: those who do the work and those who take the credit. He then told me to try to be in the first group, there was much less competition there."

Indira Gandhi

As you can see in Figure 7.6, MONITOR.NLM consists of two main menu screens — General Information and Available Options. Like most MONITOR windows, General Information contains dynamic statistics that change every second or so. Some of the most interesting General Information statistics include:

▶ Utilization — Reflects CPU utilization. This number is roughly the amount of time the processor is busy. For a more accurate reading of CPU utilization, use the histogram displayed using the "Processor utilization" option in the main menu.

▶ Total cache buffers — The number of blocks available for file caching. This number decreases as modules and other server resources are loaded. Because file caching has the most dramatic impact on server file performance, you want this number to remain high. For a more accurate measure of available cache buffers, use the "Resource utilization" option in the main menu.

▸ Dirty cache buffers — The number of file blocks in memory waiting to be written to disk. If this number grows large, you may have a bottleneck problem with the internal file system. A server crash at this point would corrupt saved data.

▸ Current service processes — Indicates the number of task handlers NetWare allocates to service incoming requests. This can dramatically impact server performance, because requests must wait in line when service processes are busy. Consider what happens at the grocery store around 5:00 p.m. each evening. The default maximum number of service processes is 20, with a possible range of 5-100.

▸ Current licensed connections — The number of active licensed connections the server currently recognizes. This number will always be less than the maximum number of licensed connections your server supports. If this number approaches the maximum, consider upgrading your license using INSTALL.NLM.

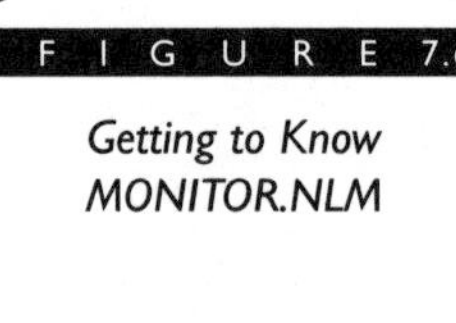

F I G U R E 7.6

Getting to Know
MONITOR.NLM

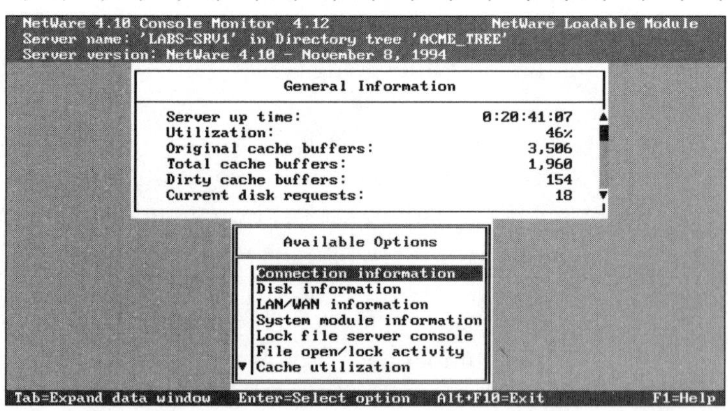

In addition to these general information statistics, MONITOR.NLM includes a plethora of Available Option submenus. Each submenu focuses on a specific subcomponent of the NetWare 4 server architecture. Here's a quick look:

▸ Connection information — Lists all active connections and tracks their current activity. CNAs can use this option to clear specific user workstation connections.

▸ Disk information — Lists all available internal disks and valuable hot-fix redirection statistics. CNAs can use this option to activate, deactivate, or modify internal disks.

▸ LAN/WAN information — Lists LAN driver configurations and statistics as well as node and network addressing.

▸ System module information — Lists all loaded modules by name, size, and version. In addition, you can track resource "tags" and memory usage for each module.

▸ Lock file server console — As you learned earlier, enables you to protect the console by specifying a password.

▸ File open/lock activity — Monitors files, lock activity, and status. It also enables you to view which stations have open files and general information about mounted volumes and directory structures.

▸ Cache utilization — View detailed caching statistics, including total cache block requests, the number of times a block request had to wait because there were no available cache blocks, long- and short-term cache hits, and dirty cache hits. This option enables you to assess the efficiency of server RAM and take corrective actions.

▸ Processor utilization — Provides a detailed histogram of all selected processes and their CPU usage.

▶ Resource utilization — View memory usage statistics for cache buffer pool, allocated memory, movable and nonmovable memory pools, and code/data memory. You can also view resource tags and determine which NLMs are "hogging" valuable server RAM.

▶ Memory utilization — View detailed memory statistics such as percent of allocated memory in use, memory blocks and bytes in use, and free blocks. This option also enables you to activate garbage collection routines. You never know when you might need it.

▶ Scheduling information — View and change the priority of a process by delaying CPU execution until a later time.

▶ EXIT — Sounds like a good time for this.

SERVMAN.NLM

Look out, there's a new superhero in Gotham. He is faster than a speedy microprocessor, has more storage than a CD-ROM, and is able to search huge databases in a single second. He's SERVMAN!

SERVMAN, the new SERVer MANager, is at the core of NetWare 4's new server utility strategy. It is the most exciting and versatile new server utility. SERVMAN provides a menu interface for SET parameters and displays valuable NetWare configurations. As you can see in Figure 7.7, SERVMAN includes two windows — Server General Information and Available Options. Each of the statistics in the Server General Information window is updated every second. Here's a quick look:

▶ Server uptime — Length of time the server has been running since it was last booted.

▶ Processor utilization — Percentage of time the server CPU is busy.

▶ Processor speed — Speed at which the processor is running based on CPU clock speed, CPU type, and the number of memory wait states. For example, the LABS-SRV1 server has a rating of 6576. This is an average setting for a Pentium 120 MHz machine.

▶ Server processes — The number of tasks handlers currently available to handle incoming user requests.

▶ Loaded NLMs — The number of modules currently loaded on the server.

▶ Mounted volumes — Number of volumes currently active on the server.

▶ Active queues — Number of active print queues currently servicing user print jobs.

▶ Logged in users — Number of users logged into the server.

▶ Loaded name spaces — Number of name spaces loaded on the server, and yes, DOS counts as one.

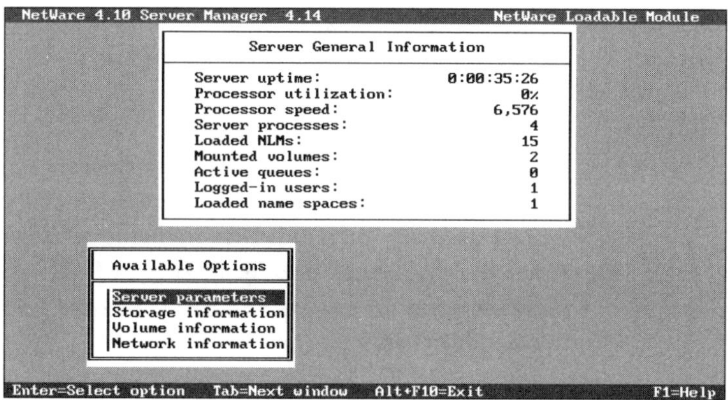

FIGURE 7.7

SERVMAN — The New NetWare 4 Superhero

> **REAL WORLD**
>
> The processor speed rating is a measurement of the server's processing capabilities as determined by the CPU clock speed (such as 120 MHz), the CPU type (such as Pentium), and the number of memory wait states (for example, 0). For instance, a 386/33 machine should get a rating of about 320, a 486/50 should get a rating of around 1370, and a Pentium/120 should get a rating of approximately 6576.

As you can see, there's a little overlap between MONITOR.NLM and SERVMAN.NLM. This is not where the similarities end. Throughout SERVMAN, you'll see references back to statistics displayed in INSTALL.NLM and MONITOR.NLM. And, of course, you'll see some new configurations not available anywhere else. The idea is this: With SERVMAN, you get a single management utility for all server maintenance and customization tasks. Although it doesn't provide a facility for *all* server management tasks, SERVMAN does help you accomplish *many* of them. Murphy's Law Number 342 — never say "all."

QUIZ

I was out house-hunting the other day, and this one really bothered me. There was this odd house, on which the two halves of the roof were unequally pitched. One half sloped downward at an angle of 60° (left) and the other half at an angle of 70° (right). I wondered, if a rooster layed an egg on the exact peak, where would the egg roll — left or right? Help.

(Q7-2)

The Available Options menu within SERVMAN offers some valuable management capabilities, including:

- Server parameters — You can view and configure "almost all" NetWare 4 operating system parameters. This includes SET parameters automated in AUTOEXEC.NCF and STARTUP.NCF. Changes you make in SERVMAN will automatically be reflected in the server configuration files. Cool! Plus, you can view a quick description of each SET parameter and its default settings from within a menu interface.

TIP

SET parameters are special console commands that customize internal core OS variables. You can get a list of the 11 NetWare 4.1 SET categories by typing "SET" at the file server console. Fortunately, SERVMAN provides the same customization features, but is an easy-to-use menu interface. SERVMAN is my hero!

- Storage information — View adapter, device, and partition information similar to INSTALL and MONITOR.

- Volume information — View information about volumes mounted on the file server (similar to INSTALL).

- Network information — View network information such as number of packets received and transmitted. This is a summary screen of the detailed LAN statistics provided by MONITOR.NLM.

All in all, SERVMAN is a great superhero. Remember, never tug on Superman's cape.

DSREPAIR

It's nice to know that if SERVMAN can't save the day, you can rely on DSREPAIR.NLM. This replaces the BINDFIX utility used in previous bindery-based versions of NetWare. DSREPAIR makes repairs and adjustments to the NDS database and solves inconsistencies with time and replica synchronization. Figure 7.8 shows the main menu of DSREPAIR and both synchronization options. In addition, the Advanced Options menu enables you to set advanced repair configurations, such as Log File Management, Pause on Errors, Validation, Scheme of Rebuilding, Remote Server ID List, and Scheduling. Finally, the Unattended Full Repair option attempts to repair corrupted databases with no interruption. If you're not sure you have a corrupted NDS database, consider the following symptoms:

- You cannot create, delete, or modify objects even though you have sufficient rights.

- You have unknown objects appearing in the tree that do not disappear after all servers are synchronized.

- You cannot create, merge, or modify partitions.

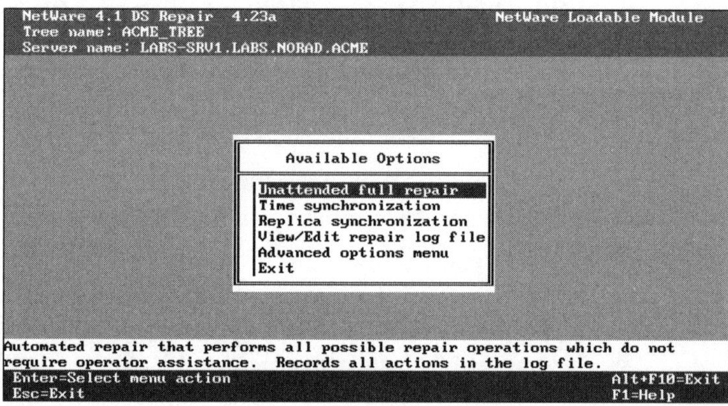

F I G U R E 7.8

If Only I Knew DSREPAIR.NLM

Once DSREPAIR is completed, you can read through the DSREPAIR log as the file DSREPAIR.LOG in the SYS:SYSTEM subdirectory. Remember, DSREPAIR is your friend, but should only be used in emergency situations.

ZEN

"Computers come in two varieties: the 'prototype' and the 'obsolete.'"

Anonymous

Well, there you have it — the tools of a good marriage. No matter what you do, remember: Communication is the key. And if you work hard at it and develop a synergistic team, I guarantee the rewards will greatly outweigh the pain. Speaking of pain, nothing grows a marriage more strongly than nine months of pregnancy.

Workstation Management

So, you're cruising along through life, minding your own business, and wham — it hits you. Suddenly, your family is twice as big as it was a few years ago. It's an abrupt wake-up call when you finally realize *you're* not the child anymore. A strange thing happens when children have children. Even though Leia is 27 years old — firmly planted in adulthood — she's still our little baby. We were there through the rough years — login scripts, menu system, and e-mail. Now Leia's having children of her own. Suddenly her focus shifts from marriage to her baby.

Now is a good time for your focus to shift as well — from the server to your NetWare children (workstations). As a CNA, you will spend just as much time managing the workstations as you will managing the server — probably more. In addition, managing workstations can be even more challenging because it encompasses a much more diverse collection of users, applications, and operating systems. And we all know users can act like babies sometimes.

In order to fully optimize the client connection and keep things running smoothly, you'll have to employ a stern, yet caring, workstation management strategy. Here are a few things to think about:

▸ ODI — As with most family matters, it all starts with communications. Using ODI, all your diverse clients can coexist on the same NetWare 4 LAN. As we saw in Chapter 6, ODI consists of three layers: MLID communications, the LSL switchboard, and various protocol stacks. Finally, ODI relies on NET.CFG for LAN driver configurations.

▸ NetWare DOS Requester — The NetWare DOS Requester is a connection point between the workstation operating system (WOS) and NetWare 4 services. It lies between the WOS and ODI to make transparent network communications obtainable. This is Leia making sure that Anakin doesn't get in any trouble. In addition, the NetWare DOS Requester is required to support NDS Services at the workstation. In this case, NETx just doesn't cut the mustard. The NetWare DOS Requester is implemented through a series of Virtual Loadable Modules (VLMs). These modular client Legos provide specific services for communications to file server and printing. All of these diverse VLMs are connected through VLM.EXE and NET.CFG.

▸ Non-DOS support — NetWare prides itself on its ability to transparently support a multitude of workstation environments. In addition to DOS, NetWare 4 supports Windows 95 (Windows 95 Requester), OS/2 (NetWare Client for OS/2), Macintosh (NetWare for Macintosh and MacNDS), and Unix (NetWare NFS). In addition, DOS workstations can share non-DOS files through an internal server naming scheme — name space. The bottom line is this: Any happy family is made up of many different kinds of children. These happy children can be found in the NetWare 4 Advanced Administration course, or *Novell's CNE Study Guide for NetWare 4.1*.

▸ Virus prevention — There will come a day when Anakin gets a cold. While it may seem like the end of the world, these things get better with time. The little one will just have to drink plenty of liquids and stay in bed (sounds like a cure for anything that ails you). Similarly, workstations can get hit by a virus and impart chaos on your WAN. It's paramount in network security to set standard procedures for protection against network viruses. In developing a workstation virus prevention strategy, consider limiting file server rights, monitoring the server disk, flagging executable files as Read-Only, and using virus-scanning software. If none of this works, go see the doctor. Unfortunately, our discussion of workstation management won't enable us to explore virus prevention in much depth. Please reference the Service and Support course, NetWare 4 documentation, or *Novell's CNE Study Guide for Core Technologies* for hints.

> ▸ Diskless workstations — Clients without a floppy or hard disk. This strategy can dramatically improve your quality of life by enhancing virus prevention, saving money, and, of course, centralizing NetWare administration. If you're one of the lucky people who convinces management to install diskless workstations, you'll need to set up the NetWare server for remote booting. Remote booting relies on two things — a remote boot PROM chip on the internal workstation NIC and a booting configuration file in the F:\LOGIN subdirectory. Once again, these details are in the Service and Support course or NetWare 4 documentation, or *Novell's CNE Study Guide for Core Technologies*.

ZEN

"If my heart can become pure and simple like that of a child, I think there probably can be no greater happiness than this."

Kitaro Nishida

Children aren't so bad. Once you get the hang of it, I think you might even enjoy adulthood. Having servers and workstations enables you to relive a little bit of your own childhood and adds years to your life (yeah, right). Of course, all the while you need to be thinking about the future and what happens when your children get children of their own. What a disaster. But let's not get ahead of ourselves. Now, we're going to explore the two main aspects of workstation management — ODI and the NetWare DOS Requester.

ODI

Of all the places you'll go in your life, few will be as interesting as the NetWare 4 client. There you'll find fun, adventure, and Virtual Loadable Modules (VLMs). The client is one of the most important aspects of a NetWare 4 system because it's where the users meet the network. Someday, I guarantee you'll get the question,

"Where's the ANY key?" In order to help you sleep at night, the interface should be as transparent as possible — avoid confusion and unnecessary support calls. In order to achieve client transparency, NetWare 4 breaks the workstation into two key components:

- ► NIC — The internal network interface card that provides communications between the local workstation operating system (WOS) and the NetWare server. This hardware device is managed by a series of workstation connectivity files called ODI (Open Datalink Interface).

- ► Workstation operating system — the WOS manages all local workstation services. It coordinates among local applications (word processing, spreadsheets, and databases) and local devices (file storage, screens, and printers). All of these local activities must somehow be orchestrated with network services. This is accomplished using the complex suite of workstation Legos called VLMs.

So, let's start with the NIC. As you can see in Figure 7.9, the internal workstation NIC attaches directly to network cabling. On the other end, it must somehow coordinate message transfer with the internal WOS. "So, how does it do this?," you say. Easy. With the help of our next superhero — ODI.

The Two Main Components of Workstation Connectivity

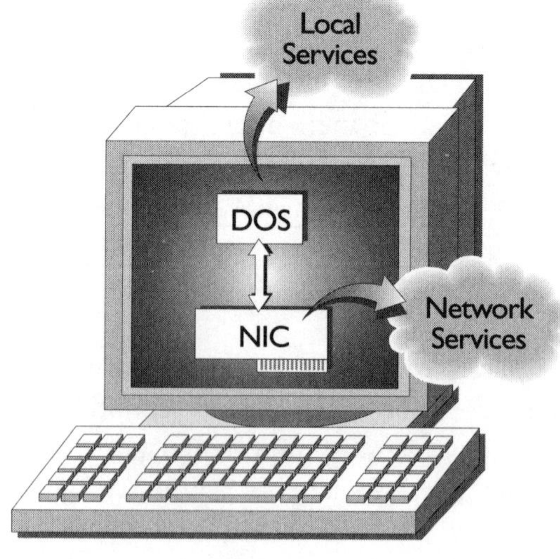

ODI stands for Open Datalink Interface. Interestingly, it's also the name of an old TV character and a cartoon dog. What does this mean? Using ODI, your network can run multiple protocols on the same cabling system. This enables devices that use different communication protocols to coexist on one WAN, thus increasing your network's functionality and flexibility. For example, both IPX and TCP/IP can run on the same workstation using the same NIC. This means that a user may concurrently access services from a NetWare server using IPX and a Unix host using TCP/IP. In general, ODI provides the following benefits:

- Concurrent communication with various workstations, servers, and mainframe computers that view different protocols

- Communication through any network board designed to meet ODI specifications

- Fewer hardware components to support

- Flexible configurations using NET.CFG file

As you can see in Figure 7.10, the workstation ODI architecture consists of three main components:

- MLID (the Multiple Link Interface Driver) — This component interfaces with the internal NIC.

- LSL (the Link Support Layer) — Acts as a switchboard to route packets between MLID and the protocol stack.

- Protocol stack — One of three protocol-specific files used to translate and negotiate network communications. This is the real star of the ODI show.

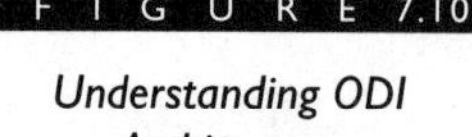

F I G U R E 7.10

*Understanding ODI
Architecture*

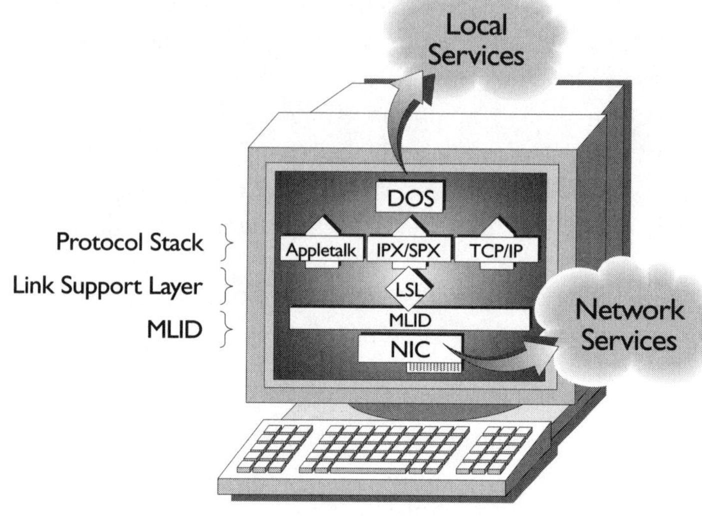

Let's take a closer look.

MLID

It all starts at the bottom of the ODI picture — MLID. Each physical NIC has its own specific MLID driver. MLIDs accept any type of packet and either send them up to LSL or down to the NIC. In either case, MLIDs handle workstation communications. In NetWare 4, MLIDs come in various shapes and sizes — each matching the specific NIC. The MLID driver NE2000.COM, for example, handles communications for the Novell NE2000 NIC. Similarly, the MLID driver 3C5X9.COM handles communications for the popular 3COM 3C5X9 NIC. The beauty of the modular ODI approach is that MLID drivers can be loaded and unloaded as needed. Also, their configuration settings are handled by a single text file — NET.CFG.

Link Support Layer

The Link Support Layer (LSL) is the next point in the ODI picture. It acts as a switchboard to route packets between the MLID driver and appropriate protocol stack. LSL identifies the packet and then passes it to either IPX/SPX, TCP/IP, or AppleTalk. At the DOS workstation, LSL is implemented as LSL.COM. A NetWare 4 client can use any of the three protocols shown in Figure 7.10

because LSL directs information to the appropriate one. Think of it as your client traffic cop.

Protocol Stack

The final ODI layer contains protocol stacks such as IPX/SPX, TCP/IP, and AppleTalk (see Figure 7.10). Once a packet arrives at the specific protocol stack, it either passes through and communicates with the NetWare DOS Requester, or is sent back down to another network. One of the main features of ODI is that it supports multiple protocols on the same cabling segment. This enables devices that allow different communication protocols to coexist on one network, thus increasing your WAN's functionality and flexibility. This is particularly important in NetWare 4 because it is the foundation of a multiprotocol, multinational, and multilingual operating system. Protocol implementation for the default IPX/SPX LAN is handled by IPXODI.COM, whereas TCP/IP implementation works through TCPIP.EXE.

ODI loading at the workstation works a little bit differently from the way the picture shows it. Although the MLID layer is at the bottom and is the first point of contact for incoming packets, it is not the first ODI driver loaded — go figure. Here's how it works:

- ▶ LSL.COM

- ▶ 3C5X9.COM (*or other MLID*)

- ▶ IPXODI.COM (or other *protocol stack*)

As you learned in Chapter 6, customization and configuration of the ODI files is implemented using NET.CFG. So, how do you unload them? It's easy. Simply type the name followed by a /U. Make sure, however, that you unload the drivers in reverse order, because they build on top of each other. And always unload the NetWare DOS Requester before unloading ODI drivers.

ZEN

"Dishes. Relationships. Wind. This guy breaks everything!"

From the movie _Drop Dead Fred_

Once the packet finds its way up through the correct protocol stack, it's time for the WOS to take over. WOS connectivity at the NetWare 4 client is handled by VLMs — the NetWare DOS Requester.

As a quick side note, let's talk frankly about the current state of ODI drivers and VLMs. They are relatively new additions to the NetWare 4 puzzle, but they have been around for a few years. Fortunately, these workstation connectivity strategies have been tested at great length in NetWare 3.12. The good news is the kinks have pretty much been ironed out. Chances are good that the latest release of ODI/VLM drivers will work just fine. This has not always been the case. If you're still a little bit skittish about introducing unproven technology in your workstations, consider a stepping stone — ODI drivers and NETX.EXE. Eventually, however, you will have to go to the VLMs, because they are required for NDS and the committed future of Novell client software. Go ahead, take the plunge — the water's fine. Really!

REAL WORLD

The ODI drivers have some interesting command line switches. Although these are not widely known, they can help you in special circumstances:

- IPXODI /C — indicates an alternate filename for configuration information. This way, you can specify a different NET.CFG for ODI settings. The /C parameter also works with LSL and VLM.

- IPXODI /A — eliminates the diagnostic responder and SPX communications. Although this reduces the memory size by 9K, it also eliminates support for RCONSOLE and dedicated print servers. Be careful when you use this option.

- IPXODI /D — eliminates the diagnostic responder, only reducing memory size by 3K.

- IPXODI /F — forcibly unloads IPXODI from memory even if other modules are loaded above it. Use this only in extreme circumstances, because it might cause the system to hang.

- IPXODI /? — all the ODI and VLM drivers have detailed help screens.

NETWARE DOS REQUESTER

The NetWare DOS Requester is a connection point between your WOS and network services. A DOS workstation, for example, is typically a stand-alone computer. It uses a local operating system to provide basic local services. These services include file storage to local disks, screen display access, printer access, and communications. DOS itself and most WOSs are not capable of communicating with the network. Therefore, they need a little help.

VLMs to the rescue! As you can see in Figure 7.11, the NetWare DOS Requester is a marshmallow-looking thing that surrounds DOS and provides transparent connectivity between user applications and the network. Interestingly, it looks as though it's two fingers squishing the life out of DOS. If I didn't know better, I would say this is a philosophical statement from Novell. Maybe I'm wrong.

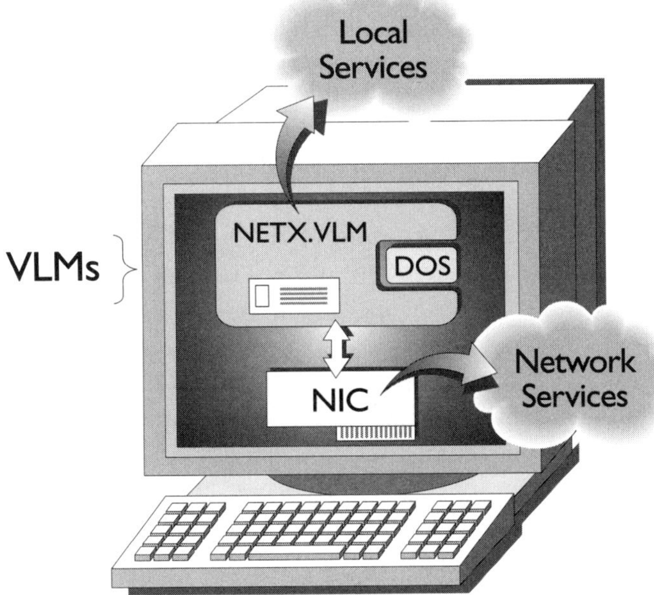

FIGURE 7.11

The NetWare DOS Requester Architecture

At the most basic level, think of the NetWare DOS Requester as your workstation's conscience. It takes requests from the user and decides whether they should be handled by the WOS or the NetWare server. If your request is destined for a server, the Requester will send it down through the ODI layers. If not, it will allow DOS to process the request and send it back to the user. In addition, valuable information about your network connection is stored in the Requester, such as environment variables and drive mappings. It's important to note that this information is virtual and session-specific, which means when you log in, log out, or disconnect from the network, all references to your information are deleted from the VLMs.

As you can see in Figure 7.11, the NetWare DOS Requester is oriented as a vise-like architecture that surrounds DOS. It shares drive table information with DOS, thereby reducing memory usage. The Requester performs such tasks as file and print redirection, connection maintenance, and packet handling. This is all made possible through various modular files, called VLMs. Each VLM performs a specific function including PRINT.VLM for printer redirection, CONN.VLM for connectivity, FIO.VLM for file services, and NETX.VLM for backward compatibility to NETx. Of course, none of this could be possible without the conductor of our orchestra — VLM.EXE.

All of the VLMs work together in synergy to provide a myriad of connectivity services, including:

- ▸ Modularity — Enables adopting third-party and future functionality, and takes advantage of expanded and extended memory in the form of protected-mode DOS extenders.

- ▸ Memory swapping — Enables efficient memory usage because the unnecessary items are not loaded. Also, VLMs can be placed in either conventional, expanded, or extended memory.

- ▸ DOS redirection — Eliminates the duplication of effort between VLMs and DOS. This also allows for direct communications between the local workstation operating system and NetWare 4 shells.

- ▸ System optimization — Includes packet bursting and large internetwork packet support.

- ▸ Compatibility with other versions of NetWare — Provides compatibility with previous versions of NetWare through NETX.VLM and current NetWare 4 features through NDS.VLM.

As you can see in Figure 7.11, the vise-like architecture consists of two main components — VLMs and NETX.VLM. The VLMs themselves have an interesting load-order architecture. As you can see in Figure 7.12, this model consists of three layers:

- ▸ Transport protocol

- ▸ Service protocol

- ▸ DOS redirection

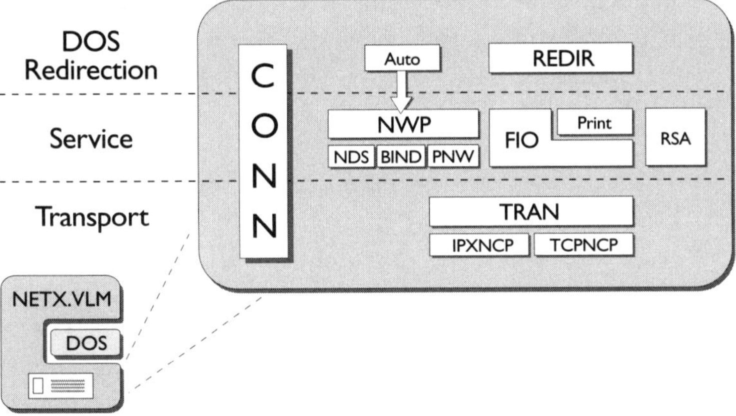

F I G U R E 7.12

Understanding NetWare 4 VLMs

CONN.VLM is used for connectivity among these three layers. Also, it's important to note that the NetWare DOS Requester supports two types of VLMs — parents and children. *Parent VLMs* route requests to applicable children. Parent VLMs (or *multiplexers*) also incorporate the services of multiple children. *Children*, on the other hand, handle a particular implementation of a logical group of functions. Let's take a closer look at the happy VLM family.

Transport Protocol VLMs

The Transport Protocol Layer maintains server connections and provides packet transmission and other transport-related services. As you can see in Figure 7.12, it consists of one parent and two children. The main parent, TRAN.VLM, is responsible for routing transport protocols to either of the two children — IPXNCP.VLM for IPX services or TCPNCP.VLM for TCP/IP services. In this example, the protocol-specific children are loaded before the TRAN.VLM parent.

Service Protocol VLMs

The Service Protocol Layer handles requests for specific services, such as broadcast messages, file reads and writes, and print redirection. Service protocol VLMs are the heart and soul of NetWare 4 client connectivity. Here's a list of some of the more important NetWare 4 service VLMs:

- NWP.VLM — The NetWare protocol multiplexer. It establishes and maintains connections, logins, and logouts. As a parent, it also handles network service implementations through the following children — NDS.VLM for NDS support, BIND.VLM for bindery services, and PNW.VLM for Personal NetWare.

- FIO.VLM — The file input/output module that implements basic transfer protocols for files. This VLM handles cached or non-cached reads and writes, and burst mode reads and writes for the client.

- PRINT.VLM — The print module provides printing services using the FIO module for its file writes. Print redirection is handled in various ways, including non-cached, cached, via packet burst protocol, or via file services.

- RSA.VLM — Provides system-level background authentication for NetWare 4 workstations.

- AUTO.VLM — Reconnects a client workstation to a server and rebuilds the workstation's environment to its original state prior to losing the connection. Although this is an optional VLM, it certainly has its merits.

TIP

In case you never knew, RSA is an acronym named for the three developers of the Public Key Encryption scheme — Rivest, Shamir, and Adleman. Now you can sleep at night.

DOS Redirection VLMs

REDIR.VLM is responsible for DOS redirection services. The Requester makes a NetWare server look like a DOS driver to the user by having REDIR.VLM make decisions about client requests. This is analogous to the major functionality of NETX.EXE.

QUIZ

The "Puzzler" strikes again:
What will you break even if you name it?
What fastens two people, yet touches only one?
What grows larger the more you take away?
What grows larger the more you contract it?

(Q7-3)

So, who's in charge here? The VLM manager — VLM.EXE. When you run it, it oversees the loading and sequencing of VLM files. Because VLMs are load-order dependent, you have to make sure VLM.EXE activates them in the correct order. In addition, the NetWare DOS Requester supports two types of VLMs — core and optional. *Core VLMs* are activated automatically in a specific order when you execute VLM.EXE. There are 13 of them shown in Table 7.3 — and they're listed in respective load order. *Optional VLMs*, on the other hand, can be activated by issuing the following command under the NetWare DOS Requester section heading of NET.CFG:

```
NETWARE DOS REQUESTER
        VLM=C:\NWCLIENT\AUTO.VLM
        VLM=C:\NWCLIENT\RSA.VLM
        VLM=C:\NWCLIENT\NMR.VLM
```

T A B L E 7.3

Load Order for Core VLMs

LOAD ORDER	VLM	DESCRIPTION
1	BIND.VLM	NetWare protocol implementation using bindery services. This is an optional core VLM for NetWare 4 NDS. (Child)
2	CONN.VLM	Connection table manager. Communicates between the three layers of VLM architecture. (Parent)
3	FIO.VLM	File input and output services. (Parent)
4	GENERAL.VLM	Miscellaneous functions for NETX.VLM and REDIR.VLM. (Child)
5	IPXNCP.VLM	Transport protocol using IPX/SPX. (Child)
6	NDS.VLM	NWP implementation using NDS support. This VLM is required for NetWare 4 NDS. (Child)
7	NETX.VLM	NetWare shell compatibility for previous versions of NetWare. (Parent)
8	NWP.VLM	NetWare protocol multiplexer. This VLM overlooks key NetWare 4 client services. (Parent)
9	PNW.VLM	NWP implementation for Personal NetWare. (Child)
10	PRINT.VLM	Printer redirector that provides CAPTURE capabilities for the DOS workstation. (Parent)
11	REDIR.VLM	DOS redirector. This VLM performs most of the tasks of earlier NETx. (Parent)
12	SECURITY.VLM	NetWare-enhanced security. (Parent)
13	TRAN.VLM	The transport protocol multiplexer that oversees IPX and TCP/IP communications. (Parent)

As you can see in Table 7.3, these are the three most popular optional VLMs. In addition, you can exclude core VLMs from loading, but only if you follow these two steps: First, add the following statement to the NetWare DOS Requester section of NET.CFG — USE DEFAULTS=OFF. Then, second, specify every VLM you do want to load in correct order. The bottom line is, you either load all 13 core VLMs, or specify the ones you want in correct order.

The Requester supports DOS 3.1 and above and works with extended, expanded, and conventional memory. VLM.EXE, by default, tries to load all VLMs in extended memory first. Expanded memory is the second choice, and if extended and expanded memory is unavailable, conventional memory is used. VLM.EXE itself can be loaded in high memory, but this is not the default state. In addition to memory support, VLM has various switches that customize its activities:

- /? — Displays the help screen.

- /Mx — Loads VLM.EXE and associated files in conventional (C), expanded (E), or extended (X) memory.

- /Vx — Displays the detailed level of messaging where x ranges from 0 to 4. Verbosity can display copyright messages and critical errors (0), warning messages (1), program load information (2), configuration information (3), or everything, including diagnostics (4).

- /PS — Specifies the preferred server during connection.

- /PT — Specifies the preferred tree during connection.

- /D — Displays file diagnostics, such as status information, memory type, current ID, and VLM manager functioning.

Well, that just about does it for the NetWare DOS Requester and ODI. Both of these workstation connectivity strategies rely on workstation-specific configuration files for implementation and customization. As you learned in Chapter 6, NET.CFG enables CNAs to increase user transparency and pinpoint communication problems. In summary, here's what it does for ODI and VLMs:

- ODI — NET.CFG provides vital information for NIC configuration. It includes a section heading called LINK DRIVER for ODI support. CNAs can use this section to name the MLID file and specify hardware and software settings, including interrupt, I/O port, memory address, and frame type. Fortunately, you only need to use NET.CFG if you plan on deviating from the established ODI defaults.

▶ VLMs — NET.CFG can also be used to customize default VLM settings. As we saw earlier, it includes a NetWare DOS Requester section heading for defining workstation connections, the first network drive, and activating specific core and optional VLMs.

I bet you never thought the marshmallow man could be so much fun. Well, that's connectivity in a nutshell. I wonder if Leia is enjoying parenthood yet.

ZEN

"In dwelling, live close to the ground.
In thinking, keep to the simple.
In conflict, be fair and generous.
In governing, don't try to control.
In work, do what you enjoy.
In family life, be completely present."

Tao Te Ching

Speaking of family, ours is growing quickly. We watched Leia go through a childhood of her own and now she's experiencing the growing pangs of parenthood. Of course, one of our most important parent responsibilities is the family. And we can learn an important lesson from the Girl Scouts of America — be prepared! Let's continue our journey through adulthood with a detailed look at the "second half" of life — pension and retirement.

Storage Management Services

Call it a pension, a "nest egg," or whatever you like, planning for the future is important business. With a family comes serious financial concerns — college education, emergency fund, and retirement. And these financial decisions aren't as simple as they used to be. You must choose among IRAs, annuities, mutual funds, pension plans, and (my old favorite) the "sock in the bedpost." Regardless of what you do, it's critical that you plan for the future.

One of the most exciting things about life is that you never know what's around the corner. To be prepared, you must have a backup plan. Also, as your network grows in complexity, the value of its services grows as well. And we all know nothing becomes more valuable until it is lost. That's Murphy's Law Number 193.

Welcome to NetWare 4 backup. Backup provides both a prevention and maintenance strategy:

▶ Prevention — Backup is a proactive strategy toward disaster recovery. You don't want to be wondering what to do *after* the data is lost.

▶ Maintenance — Backup doesn't always prevent a disaster from occurring; it simply expedites recovery.

As soon as your network data is lost, file backup should be the first thing that pops into your mind. In many cases, having current backups can spell the difference between a successful and prosperous CNA career and the unemployment line. *Never* neglect your NetWare backup duties. Fortunately, NetWare 4 includes a versatile new backup feature called Storage Management Services (SMS).

SMS is a combination of related services that enable data to be stored and retrieved. The SMS backup process involves a *host* server and a *target*. The host server is the NetWare 4 machine on which the backup program resides. The target is the NetWare server or client that contains the data needing to be backed up. In addition, SMS uses an application on the host server to communicate with modules on target devices — SBACKUP.NLM is included for free. This discussion first explores the fundamental architecture of SMS. Then we'll take a closer look at backing up and restoring data using the default SMS application — SBACKUP.NLM. What are we waiting for? Let's go.

SMS ARCHITECTURE

As you learned earlier, SMS is a combination of related services that enable you to store and retrieve data from various targets — Target Service Agents (TSAs). SMS operates as a backup engine that is independent from the front-end application and back-end device. As you can see in Figure 7.13, SMS supports various TSA front-ends, including NetWare file systems, NDS, DOS and OS/2 file systems, and BTRIEVE databases. Any or all of these resources can be backed up to various back-end devices, including DOS read/write disks, tape, and optical drives.

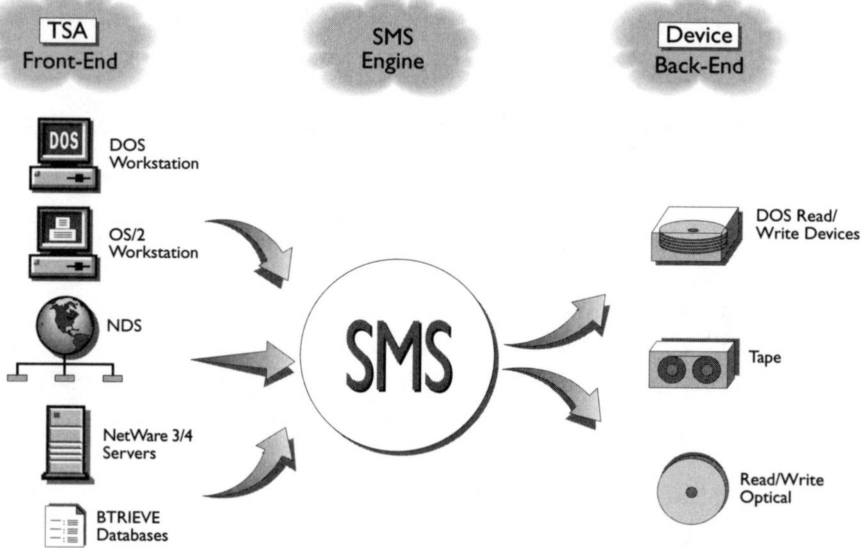

F I G U R E 7.13

SMS Architecture

There are three main components to the SMS architecture model:

- Device drivers

- SBACKUP.NLM

- Target Service Agents

You can see the interaction among these components in Figure 7.14. The device drivers interface between SBACKUP.NLM and the internal host device. Then, SBACKUP uses Target Service Agents to activate source file systems. Let's take a closer look.

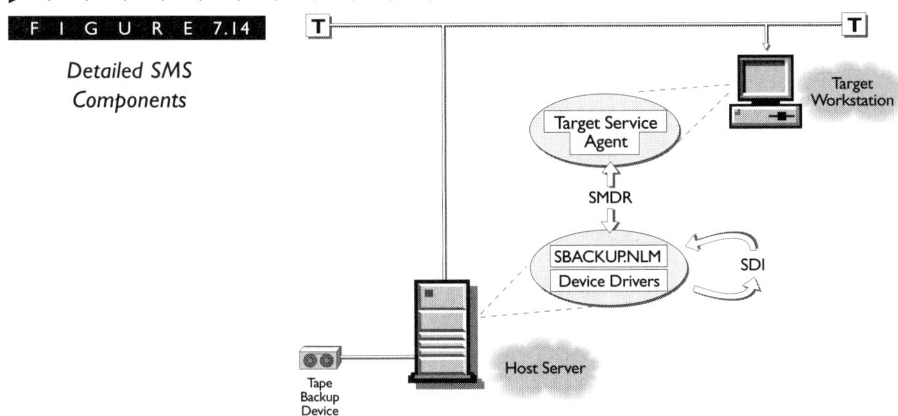

F I G U R E 7.14

*Detailed SMS
Components*

Device Drivers

Device drivers lie at the bottom of the SMS model. They control the mechanical operation of the host storage device. In addition, they must be specifically configured for each backup device and interface with the SBACKUP.NLM application. When device drivers are loaded, SBACKUP recognizes the storage device.

Device drivers are loaded at the host server and, therefore, must be NLMs. The following files are included with NetWare 4.1 — TAPEDAI.DSK (Novell's generic tape driver for most ASPI-compatible SCSI controllers), MNS*.DSK (Mountain Backup devices), PS2SCSI.DSK (for IBM PS2 SCSI controllers), and AHA*.DSK (Adaptec SCSI devices). Before SBACKUP.NLM recognizes the host device, you must register it with NetWare 4 using the following command:

```
SCAN FOR NEW DEVICES
```

SBACKUP.NLM

The backup application (SBACKUP, in our case) communicates with device drivers through SDI — the Storage Device Interface. It is loaded as an NLM on the host server. Once the backup device is activated, you can enter the SMS application — SBACKUP.NLM. This utility works within the SMS architecture to route data requests from the source and to the device through SDI. Interestingly, we are now backing up clients from the server — isn't this backward? Later in this section, we'll explore the ins and outs of using SBACKUP.NLM.

Target Service Agents

The final component in the SMS architecture model is TSAs — Target Service Agent. TSAs must be loaded on target servers or workstations. SBACKUP.NLM recognizes TSAs through the Storage Management Data Requester (SMDR). It is an NLM running on the host server. NetWare 4 supports various TSAs, including:

- NetWare 4 server — TSA410 or TSA400

- NetWare 3 server — TSA312 or TSA311

- DOS workstation — TSADOS and TSASMS

- OS/2 workstation — TSAPROXY and TSAOS2

- NDS database — TSANDS

Remember, if you're backing up data on the host server, you still have to load TSA410 and TSANDS. Finally, SBACKUP.NLM only recognizes targets that have loaded the appropriate TSA module.

ZEN

"Don't hurry, don't worry. You're only here for a short visit. So be sure to stop and smell the flowers."

Walter Hagen

Now that you understand the fundamental SMS architecture, let's explore SBACKUP.NLM in more depth. Keep in mind, any third-party backup application can be used with SMS, as long as it follows this fundamental design.

USING SBACKUP

At the heart of the SMS model is the backup application. NetWare 4 includes a starter program called SBACKUP.NLM. You can use any server application as long as it's SMS-compliant. SBACKUP, for example, is an NLM that operates at the

NetWare 4 server and communicates directly with the host backup device. Running SBACKUP at the server has its advantages. First, it supports multiple file server connections at one time. Also, it operates faster because it doesn't cause an additional communications load on the network. Because the tape unit is connected directly to the file server, SBACKUP doesn't route packets over the LAN. Finally, SBACKUP supports a wide variety of backup devices because of their independent *.DSK device drivers.

Just like any application, you'll have to learn the SBACKUP "lingo" to use it efficiently. Following are a few terms you should be aware of:

- ▸ Host — The NetWare 4 server running SBACKUP.NLM. Also, the backup device is attached to it.

- ▸ Target — Any NetWare 4 server, workstation, or NDS database that has a TSA loaded. This is where the backup source material resides.

- ▸ Parent — A data set that may have subordinate data sets. In NetWare 4, a parent would be a directory, a subdirectory, or a container.

- ▸ Child — A data set that has no subordinates. In NetWare 4, for example, a child would be a file or leaf object.

Let's explore SBACKUP.NLM by first learning about its four main backup strategies. Then we'll discuss some guidelines before diving into the detailed steps of SMS backup and restore.

Backup Strategies

So, how does it work? SBACKUP provides four strategies that can be used for backing up and restoring data. Each strategy provides a different balance of performance and efficiency. In Figure 7.15, you can see the three main strategies — full, incremental, and differential. Here's how they work.

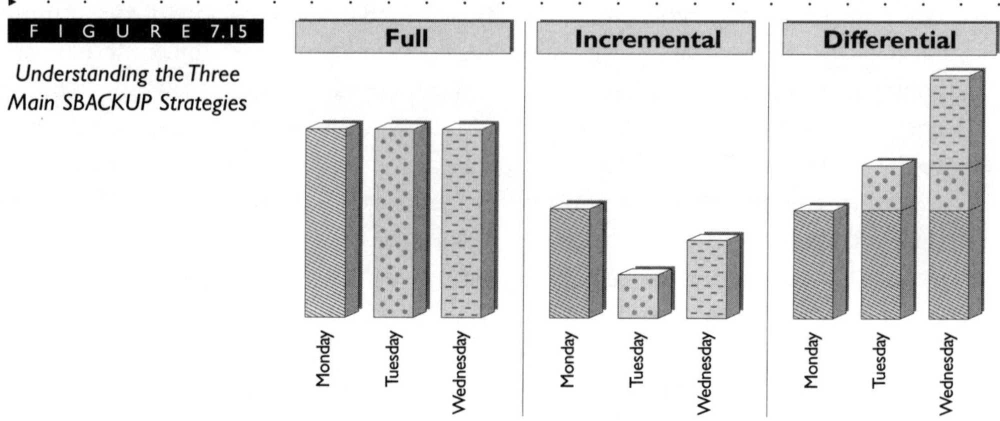

F I G U R E 7.15

Understanding the Three Main SBACKUP Strategies

As you can see in Figure 7.15, the full backup option is the most thorough. It is, however, not practical. During a full backup, all data is copied, regardless of when or if it has been previously backed up. While this option employs a slow backup performance, it does allow for very fast and easy restores — you only have to restore the latest full backup. During a full backup, the "modified bit" is cleared — we'll discuss why a little later.

The second option (incremental) backs up only the files that have changed since the last backup. Although this option offers a quick backup, restoring can be quite a nightmare. In order to get all the data, you must restore the last full and *every* incremental backup since then *in order*. If one is missing or doesn't work, you're up a creek. During an incremental backup, the "modified bit" is cleared, so SBACKUP skips it the next time. Only modified files activate the "modify" bit.

The differential backup is a new and interesting strategy. It backs up all the data that has been modified since the last full backup. Differential backup is the best balance of efficiency and performance because it minimizes the number of restore sessions. You only need to restore the last full and the latest differential. Also, the backup session is optimized because only the files that have changed are being copied.

The main difference when doing a differential backup is the state of the "modified bit" — it is *not* cleared. This way, all the files that have changed since the last full backup are copied each time. This is why the full backup strategy clears the modify bit. Notice in Figure 7.15 how the volume of data systematically increases. One word of warning, however — since the "modified bit" is also cleared during an incremental backup, this can mess up your differential strategy. Be sure never to perform an incremental backup between differential and full backups.

The fourth and final SBACKUP strategy is "custom." The custom method enables you to specify which files are backed up and whether the "modified bit" is cleared. This provides the ultimate level of flexibility.

Table 7.4 shows a comparison of the four SBACKUP strategies. The best combination is:

- ▸ Every day — differential

- ▸ Once a week on Friday — full

- ▸ Once a month — custom

T A B L E 7.4

*Understanding the Four Main SBACKUP
Strategies*

SBACKUP STRATEGY	BACKUP	RESTORE	MODIFIED BIT
Full	Slow	Easy	Cleared
Incremental	Quick	Hard	Cleared
Differential	Quick	Easy	Not cleared
Custom	Whatever	Your choice	Doesn't matter

Once you've chosen your backup strategy, you must follow some simple SBACKUP guidelines during backup and restore sessions. Let's take a look.

Guidelines

You've gotta have rules. Without rules, the world would be a very wacky place. Let me rephrase that — the world would be an even wackier place. SBACKUP is no exception. Here are a few guidelines you must follow when using this SMS application:

- ▶ Make sure you have enough disk space on the host server's SYS: volume for temporary files and log files (1 MB should be sufficient). Run the SBACKUP.NLM from a NetWare server and attach the backup device to the same host server. Also, be sure to run updated support NLMs, such as STREAMS, SPXS, TLI, CLIB, and NWSNUT.

- ▶ Limit access to SBACKUP to maintain the security of your NetWare server and to ensure data integrity. Also be aware that security can be compromised if a delayed backup session does not fit on inserted media. If you are prompted to insert another tape, the program pauses at that point and does not exit. To reduce this risk, set APPEND to NO.

- ▶ When you are entering a filename that has a non-DOS format, use the DOS equivalent naming scheme. SBACKUP does support OS/2 and Macintosh naming schemes, but the application interface doesn't. So even though you're backing up long filenames (September99, for example), they appear in their DOS equivalent (September, for example). You can track this by using the SBACKUP error and backup log files. They display both the DOS equivalent and the name space version of each directory or file.

- ▶ Monitor the size of SBACKUP temporary files. SBACKUP creates temporary files on the target server as well as the host machine. These temporary files may become quite large if you have extended attributes or linked Unix files.

- ▶ Do not mount or dismount volumes or unload drivers during a backup session. You may corrupt data or abend the host server — duh!

- ▶ Know the passwords assigned to target servers and workstations.

ZEN

"Don't wait for your ship to come in; swim out to it!"

Anonymous

Backup Steps

Once you understand these guidelines, you're ready to perform your first SMS backup using SBACKUP.NLM. I can hardly contain my excitement. Follow the bouncing ball as we outline the seven steps of an SMS backup. For a more detailed walkthrough, try it yourself. C'mon in, the water's fine.

1 • Load the backup device driver on the host server.

2 • Load appropriate TSA drivers on all target devices. This includes the host server, if you plan on backing it up. When you load the TSAs, all support modules are activated automatically.

3 • Load SBACKUP.NLM at the host server. Once you've activated SBACKUP, certain support modules are automatically loaded, including SMDR. The SBACKUP main menu is then displayed, as shown in Figure 7.16.

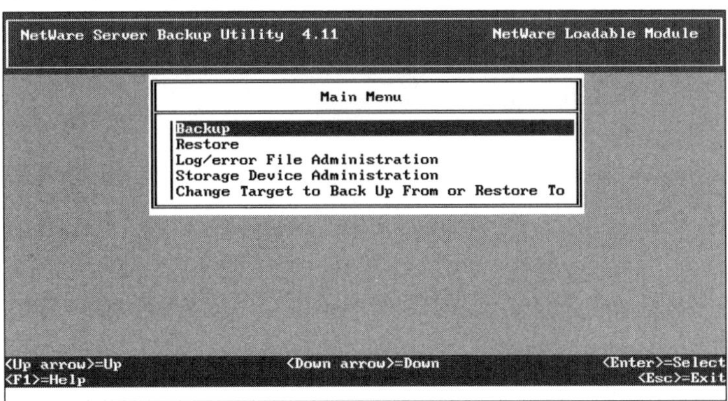

F I G U R E 7.16

NetWare 4 SBACKUP.NLM Main Menu

4 • Select a target to be backed up from the TSA list. **Note:** Targets will only appear if the appropriate TSAs have been loaded properly. You can get to the TSA list by choosing Change Target to back up from or restore to from the main menu of SBACKUP.NLM. If you choose a remote server, you'll be asked for a valid username and password for authentication. Recall that you can only back up files matching that user's access rights.

5 • Select the backup device from an Available Options list. The list should reflect all devices that are attached to the host server and have appropriate drivers loaded. If only one backup device driver is loaded, SBACKUP automatically selects this device. The list appears when you choose Storage Device Administration from the main menu of SBACKUP.NLM.

6 • Perform appropriate SBACKUP administration, including selecting a location for the log and error file, selecting the type of backup, and providing a session description. All of these tasks are accomplished using the Log/Error File Administration option within the main menu.

7 • Finally, you're ready to back up. You can either proceed "now" or "later." If you choose later, you'll be prompted for a date and time. If you choose now, you'll be asked to insert the backup media and enter a unique label for it.

You're finished. That wasn't so hard. Whatever you do, don't *trust* your backup. Always test SBACKUP tapes by selectively restoring them at regular intervals. This might involve restoring random files to a secondary volume or the entire SBACKUP session. Whatever you do, don't discover SBACKUP doesn't work after you've lost your disk.

Restore Steps

This is where "Murphy" comes in. If you need to restore, something bad happened. Let's hope you never have to implement the following seven steps. But before you begin, make sure the target server or workstation has enough free disk space. It must have approximately 20 percent *more* than the amount needed to restore. The overhead space stores temporary files and additional name space information. Here's a brief outline of the SBACKUP restore steps:

1 • Load the backup device driver on the host server (same as Backup Step 1).

2 • Load the appropriate TSA software on all targets you wish to restore to. This includes the host server if you plan on restoring to it.

3 • Load SBACKUP.NLM at the host server (same as Backup Step 3).

4 • Select a target to restore to. The Available Options within SBACKUP should reflect all devices which have loaded the appropriate TSA. Once again, this is accomplished using the Change Target to Backup From or Restore To option from the main menu of SBACKUP. Once you choose a TSA, a list of recognized restore sessions will appear. Select one.

5 • Perform SBACKUP administration including selecting a location for the log and error file and inserting the backup media.

6 • Select a restore device from the Available Options list. This list should match all attached devices and loaded drivers. If only one backup device driver is loaded, SBACKUP automatically selects this device.

7 • Now, we finally get to restore. First select the type of restore from the following list of three — One File or Directory, An Entire Session, or a Custom Restore. Second, choose the files and objects you wish to restore. Finally, select one of the following restore options — Proceed now or Later.

There you have it. Let's hope you never have to perform a "real" SBACKUP restore. You should practice, though — every week.

ZEN

"Learn not to sweat the small stuff."

Dr. Kenneth Greenspan

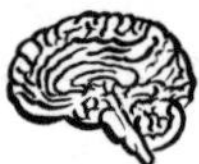

THE BRAIN

When backing up NDS with SBACKUP, there are a number of issues to be aware of. These are covered in detail in an AppNote entitled "Backing Up and Restoring Netware Directory Services in NetWare 4" in the August 1995 *Novell Application Notes*.

Well, that wasn't so hard, was it? That's SBACKUP.NLM in a nutshell. After you've completed the SBACKUP steps each day, you'll find a certain peace of mind knowing that you have these hot little tapes in your hands. It matches the peace of mind knowing that your children can go to college and someday you'll finally get to retire to the beaches of Tahiti. But that time is not now, so stop daydreaming and move on to the final section of NetWare 4 SMS — other SMS considerations.

OTHER SMS CONSIDERATIONS

We're not quite done yet. In order to take full advantage of NetWare 4's SMS feature, you'll need to explore a few other considerations. They are:

- ▸ Who does it?

- ▸ Workstation backup

- ▸ SMS management

So, who's the lucky person? Probably you. Count your blessings because you're the lucky person chosen to be the SBACKUP administrator. Remember, you wanted to be a CNA. In addition to understanding the rights needed for SMS duties, you'll need to understand the special drivers that load at the SMS workstation. Finally, there are a few SMS management issues that can help you troubleshoot and optimize SBACKUP duties. Any questions? Good, time to move on.

Who Does It?

Being assigned SBACKUP responsibility is a dubious distinction. Although it has its status in the NetWare 4 management realm, it does also have a price. You don't want to mess up here. The person you assign to back up your network must have certain qualifications and access privileges, including:

- The backup administrator needs Read and File Scan (RF) access rights to the files he/she plans to back up. The administrator will also need additional rights for restoring — (RWCEMF).

- The backup administrator will need the Browse Object Write and Read Property right for backing up NDS information.

- The backup administrator must know the password on all servers and workstations that act as hosts and targets. A standard naming scheme would be a great idea at this point.

If you're the lucky soul chosen as SBACKUP administrator, continue with the next two considerations. If not, go grab a soda.

Workstation Backup

As if by some inspiration, Novell finally allows workstation backup from the server. This long-awaited feature has been implemented in the new SMS. SMS uses SBACKUP.NLM to back up and restore information from local DOS disks or OS/2 workstations. You can back up certain directories or the entire workstation, including floppy and hard drives.

The DOS workstation TSA is a TSR (terminate-and-stay-resident) program that you can run on any target workstation. Some DOS TSA TSR options include /P for password, /T for no password, and /D for drive designation. Here's how the TSA works:

1. • Load TSADOS.NLM at the server for DOS workstations and TSAPROXY.NLM for OS/2.

2 • Load TSASMS.COM at the DOS workstation and TSAOS2.COM at the OS/2 workstation. This is where you specify the TSA parameters we just discussed. One additional parameter you may want to employ is /N to give the workstation a unique name. This name will appear in the TSA list of SBACKUP.NLM.

3 • Select the appropriate DOS TSA from the SBACKUP target list. The name that appears should match the name given in Step 2.

Workstation backup is a cool feature, but make sure that you use the correct parameters with the DOS TSA TSR, and that you remember to load the appropriate NLMs at the host server. And if those are not enough to worry about, check out the next discussion.

SMS Management

A few SMS management issues can help you journey through the SBACKUP jungle. Let's start with performance. The speed of SBACKUP varies depending on the configuration and location of the data being backed up. If a file server backs up its own data, for example, it runs about four times faster than if it backs up data from a remote server. This sluggishness is because communications are required between the host server and the target servers. The speed of communications also depends on the availability of packet receive buffers at the host server.

Next, let's talk about SBACKUP session files. Session files are "backup logs" that contain information to help you effectively manage SMS backups. The information also facilitates the restore process and helps you to troubleshoot anything that goes wrong. The two most important session files are the backup log and error log. The backup log consists of all data backed up during the session and the media ID, session date and time, session description, and location of data on the storage media.

The error file, on the other hand, is generated on the host server when a particular group of data is initially backed up. It contains the same header data as the backup log, but also provides error information, such as the names of files that were not backed up, files that were not restored, who accessed the NDS database, and error codes. As you recall from our earlier discussion, we identified the location of these session files during Step 6 of the backup process.

Now we're really done. Congratulations: You've been made SBACKUP administrator. I hope you understand the responsibility that accompanies this honor. But if you perform your duties admirably, everybody's going to treat you like a hero.

Pension planning works much the same way. Although it's a dubious honor to be responsible for the family's financial future, many times the rewards greatly outweigh the pain. I see a trend here. All I know is, retirement in Tahiti is sounding better and better all the time.

QUIZ

Here's a quick brain stretching exercise before you tackle NetWare 4 retirement:

A common English word can be made from the letters on the top row of a standard typewriter. For those of you who do not have a typewriter keyboard handy, the letters are Q, W, E, R, T, Y, U, I, O, P. Not all letters must be used and some letters may be used more than once.

(Q7-4)

Remote Management Facility

The final step in our life journey is retirement — RMF. Our life's been an exciting adventure and now it's time to kick back and put it on cruise control. Welcome to Happy Acres!

Now, no one is saying that retirement has to be boring. Quite the contrary: It provides us with an opportunity to enjoy all the adventures we never had time for in the past. You can learn to scuba dive, hang glide, golf, and even bungee jump. And the best part is, you get to do it on your own terms. It sure sounds appealing — where do I sign up?

RMF is the final step in NetWare 4 configuration and management. It enables you to manage all your NetWare file servers from one central location. This is particularly useful because file server security states that the machine should be locked away in a cabinet with no monitor or keyboard. Also, NetWare 4 prides itself on managing multiple servers spanning wide geographic boundaries. In both cases, you'll spend more time trying to access the servers than doing the important stuff — maintaining and managing them.

Now, let's take a moment to explore the details of RMF and learn how it can help you enjoy your new NetWare 4 retirement.

RMF ARCHITECTURE

So, how does it work? As you can see in Figure 7.17, RMF supports access from both the workstation and a modem. In either case, it consists of two main components: server NLMs and RCONSOLE.EXE.

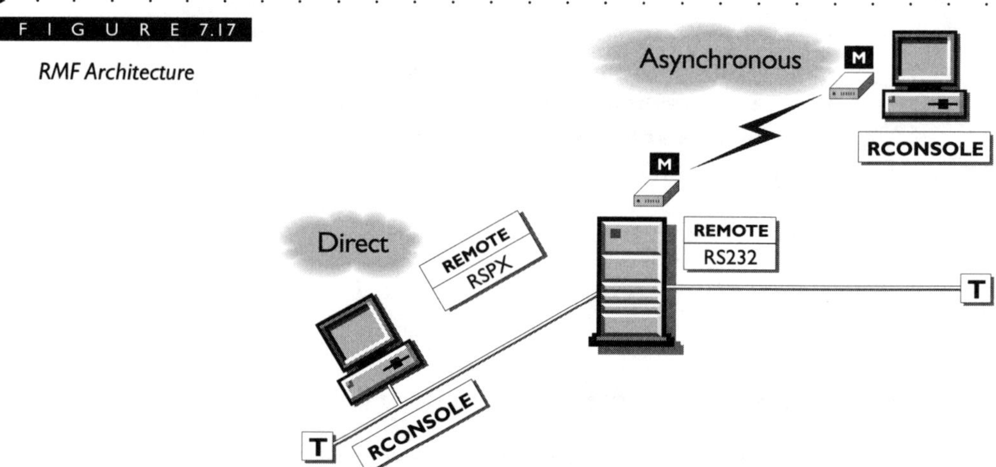

F I G U R E 7.17

RMF Architecture

The RMF server NLMs are broken into two functions — REMOTE and connection services. The REMOTE.NLM module manages information exchange to and from the workstation and the server. In addition, REMOTE.NLM enables you to specify an RMF password.

Connection services are a little bit trickier. As you remember from our earlier discussion, RMF supports access from both a direct workstation or from a modem. In either case, the connection NLM is different. When you access RMF from a direct workstation, connection services are provided by RSPX.NLM. This module provides communications support and advertises the server's availability for remote access. On the other hand, when you access RMF from an asynchronous modem, connection services are provided by RS232.NLM. This module initializes the server modem port and transfers screen and keystroke information to REMOTE.NLM.

Let's take a closer look.

ZEN

"Millions long for immortality who do not know what to do with themselves on a rainy Sunday afternoon."

Susan Ertz

SPX

The most popular RMF connection approach is direct — through SPX. Direct connection services are provided through the RSPX.NLM module. When you load RSPX, you have the option to require packet signatures — this ensures security. The default is ON, which means that packet signatures are required. However, packets with signatures are not compatible with NetWare 3.11. If your NetWare 4 server coexists with NetWare 3.11 machines, you'll need to deactivate packet signing by using the SIGNATURES OFF switch with RSPX.

In summary, the server modules required for a direct RMF connection are

```
LOAD REMOTE

LOAD RSPX
```

Finally, a quick note about REMOTE passwords. As you learned earlier in the chapter, REMOTE.NLM includes a password facility that enables you to restrict access to the server console. As a matter of fact, in NetWare 4.1, a REMOTE password is required. This creates a security loophole when the command is placed in AUTOEXEC.NCF. To work around this weakness, consider using LDREMOTE and encrypted passwords. See the earlier Server Protection discussion for more details.

TIP

If you use the IPXODI /A parameter to deactivate SPX and save workstation RAM, RCONSOLE won't work. I wouldn't want you to be surprised at a bad time.

Asynchronous

In addition to a direct connection, RMF supports asynchronous connectivity. As you can see in Figure 7.17, the remote workstation can be attached to the server via a modem. This means you really can manage the NetWare 4 server from Tahiti. In this case, connection services are provided by the RS232.NLM module. When you load RS232.NLM, NetWare will ask you for some simple modem configurations, including the communications port number, baud rate, and an option for callback.

A callback list enables you to create a list of authorized modem numbers that can be used to access the server. When a connection attempt is made, the server notes the number of the modem that is calling and then terminates the connection. The server then compares the number to the numbers in the call-back list. If the number is in the list, the server calls the modem at that number and reestablishes the connection. If it is not, the server ignores the call. This is another security feature that limits "hacker" access to your server console.

In summary, the following NLM command entries must be given at the NetWare 4 server to activate asynchronous RMF:

```
LOAD REMOTE

LOAD RS232 1 9600 C
```

In this example, 1 is the COM port, 9600 is the modem speed, and C activates the call-back option. The authorized list is defined as CALLBACK.LST in the SYS:SYSTEM directory.

Table 7.5 summarizes these two RMF options.

T A B L E 7.5	DIRECT SPX	ASYNCHRONOUS MODEM
Understanding RMF	REMOTE.NLM	REMOTE.NLM
	RSPX.NLM	RS232.NLM

Whether you're accessing RMF from a direct workstation or asynchronous modem, you're going to need RCONSOLE.EXE.

USING RCONSOLE

RCONSOLE is the front-end for NetWare 4 RMF. It provides direct access to the NetWare server console screen and enables you to perform any task as if you were standing right in front of it. In addition, RCONSOLE provides an Available Options menu with supplemental tasks, including changing screens, scanning server directories, and performing a remote install. All in all, RCONSOLE is your friend because it enables you to enjoy the good life without having to run around like a chicken with your head cut off.

Like most NetWare 4 utilities, RCONSOLE has both DOS and Windows versions. The DOS version is executed as RCONSOLE.EXE at any workstation DOS prompt. RCONSOLE.EXE resides in the SYS:SYSTEM subdirectory or any local hard disk.

Whether you access RCONSOLE from DOS or Windows, you'll get the same main screen asking the same simple question: What connection type do you want? The available choices are SPX for a direct connection or Asynchronous for a modem connection. The SPX option brings up a list of available servers, as shown in Figure 7.18. Once you choose a server, the password prompt appears. Upon entering the correct password, you'll find yourself staring at the all-too-familiar colon prompt (:).

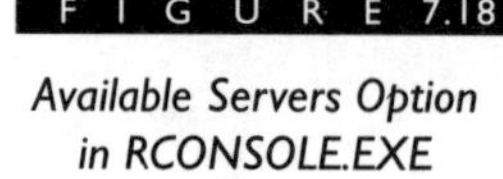

*Available Servers Option
in RCONSOLE.EXE*

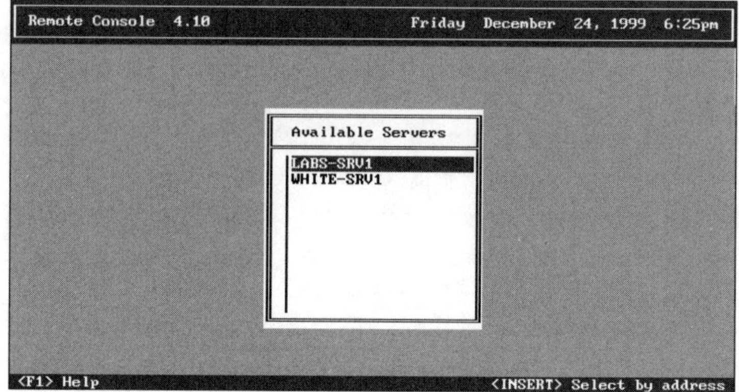

On the other hand, if you choose the asynchronous connection type, a different menu appears. The Asynchronous Options menu provides two choices: Connect to Remote Location and Configuration. From here, you can either dial a remote server or configure your local modem. Once your connection is established, a callback list will be activated and/or the password prompt will appear. Once again, after you enter the correct password, you'll find yourself staring down the barrel of the NetWare 4 console.

ZEN

"Go ahead: Make my day!"

Clint Eastwood

Once the RCONSOLE session is established, you can perform any available server task as if you were standing in the wiring closet yourself — closed quarters. In addition to standard console activities, you can perform various special RCONSOLE tasks, including:

- ▶ Change screens

- ▶ Scan server directories

- ▶ Transfer files

- ▸ Shell to DOS to view network directories

- ▸ View your local workstation address

- ▸ Configure keystroke buffering

- ▸ Copy NetWare files to the server

All of these fun-filled activities are accomplished using the RMF Available Options menu. This menu is activated by pressing the Alt+F1 keys simultaneously and can be seen in Figure 7.19. Also, a list of RCONSOLE function keys can be found in Table 7.6.

Available Options Menu
in NWADMIN

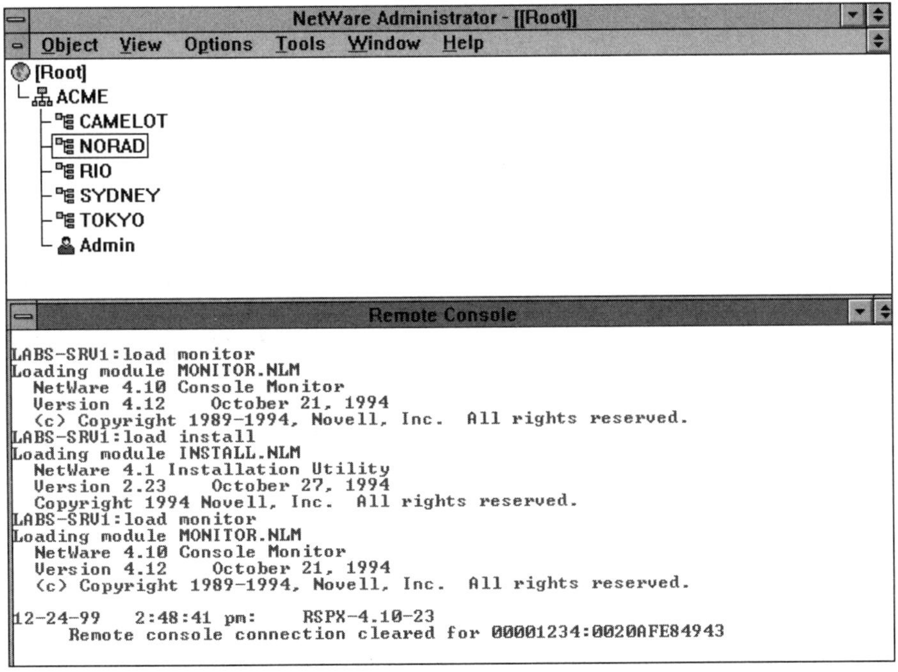

T A B L E 7.6	KEYS	TASK
NetWare 4 RCONSOLE Function Keys	Alt+F1	View the RMF Available Options menu.
	Alt+F2	Exit RCONSOLE.
	Alt+F3	Move forward through the server console screens. Similar to Alt+Esc at the physical server console itself.
	Alt+F4	Move backward through the server console screens.
	Alt+F5	Show your workstation address.
	F1	Display remote console help from within the Available Options menu.
	Esc	Resume remote session with the server.

Whenever a remote session is granted to RCONSOLE, the file server broadcasts a message to the error log and console prompt. This indicates that a remote session was attempted at a particular node address and that it was, in fact, granted or not. This is useful information if you like to track who's accessing the file server colon prompt using RMF — good idea!

REAL WORLD

RMF is cool. RMF is so cool, in fact, that it enables you to remotely install NetWare. Talk about extended vacations! This means you can actually install a NetWare 4 server in Camelot from Tahiti. Think of it. Sand between your toes and SERVER.EXE bouncing through your head. Just be sure to copy the public files locally, or you're in for an unhappy phone bill!

Well, that does it. Your life in a nutshell!

We've brought our LAN from birth through childhood and the rewards of adulthood. Through NetWare 4 configuration and management, we've transformed a relatively limp and lifeless LAN into a powerful and productive business tool. How did we do it?

In NetWare 4 configuration, we walked Leia through the five steps of childhood. She learned to walk (workstation connectivity), talk (login scripts), and get along with others in preschool (menu system). Then she enjoyed the many splendors of school (network applications) and finally moved out (e-mail).

In NetWare 4 management, Leia continued her "lifespan" through marriage (server management) and children of her own (workstation management). Now, in her later years, Leia planned her pension (SMS) and finally retired to Tahiti (RMF).

QUIZ

This pretty much sums up NetWare childhood and adulthood:

"Individuals who are completely devoid of sapience in all respects indicate a propensity to cast themselves without hesitation onto those areas where beings of a heavenly nature would reflect seriously and be timorous about proceeding."

(Q7-5)

It was a long and winding road but certainly an adventure for all of us. No matter how much you might want to, you can't just set up the server and walk away. You're a CNA and as one, your life is irrevocably bound to the childhood and adulthood of NetWare 4.

EXERCISE 7-1: NETWARE 4 ADULTHOOD

Circle the 20 NetWare 4 Management terms hidden in this word search puzzle using the hints provided.

```
S   B   A   C   K   U   P   N   Z   W   W   Q   X   Q   C
E   M   O   N   I   T   O   R   N   L   M   R   C   N   O
C   N   D   D   S   R   E   P   A   I   R   N   L   M   C
U   M   L   R   I   A   O   B   H   H   K   H   O   U   Z
R   N   A   M   E   S   P   A   C   E   H   J   C   I   Y
E   R   L   F   S   E   R   V   M   A   N   M   S   U   K
C   O   N   S   O   L   E   C   O   M   M   A   N   D   S
O   E   O   T   R   A   C   K   O   N   E   S   W   J   U
N   Y   H   O   S   T   H   K   L   N   X   T   B   O   T
S   V   L   M   P   A   A   C   V   B   X   S   W   S   Q
O   M   S   S   X   Q   E   R   X   D   L   O   X   K   N
L   C   T   T   L   C   U   M   H   Q   T   T   L   Y   G
E   L   S   P   F   I   W   M   K   L   U   G   S   E   N
```

Hints:

1. Executed at the colon prompt.
2. NLM used to detect and correct problems in the NDS database.
3. Term used to refer to the server to which a tape backup unit is attached.
4. ODI layer that acts as a switchboard to route packets between MLID and the protocol stack.
5. NLM used to view server RAM activity for troubleshooting and optimization purposes.
6. Module that is used to allow the storage of non-DOS files on a NetWare 4 server.
7. Modular server programs.

8. Architecture that allows multiple LAN drivers and protocols to coexist on network systems.
9. Workstation command line utility used to remotely access the server console.
10. NetWare 4 feature that allows remote access of the file server console.
11. NLM used to allow RCONSOLE to access a server over a direct connection.
12. Protocol used by servers to advertise their services on a NetWare internetwork.
13. NLM used to back up and restore data for a server, workstation, or service.
14. Console command used to increase security at the server console.
15. NLM used to view and configure system parameters. Can be used in place of the SET command.
16. Used to pass commands and information between SBACKUP and Target Service Agents.
17. NetWare 4 backup/restore engine used by the SBACKUP utility.
18. Console command used to display the RIP tracking screen.
19. Program used to process data moving between a target and an SMS-compliant backup engine such as SBACKUP.
20. Modular executable program that runs on a DOS workstation and enables communication with a NetWare server.

See Appendix C for answers.

EXERCISE 7-2: THE NETWARE WORKSTATION ARCHITECTURE

Not so fast. You passed the server test, but what about the workstations? You won't be able to enjoy ACME's exploratorium until you've studied the NetWare 4 workstation architecture model. Review Figure 7.20 and identify the correct components. I know it's painful, but this is for your own good: "tough love."

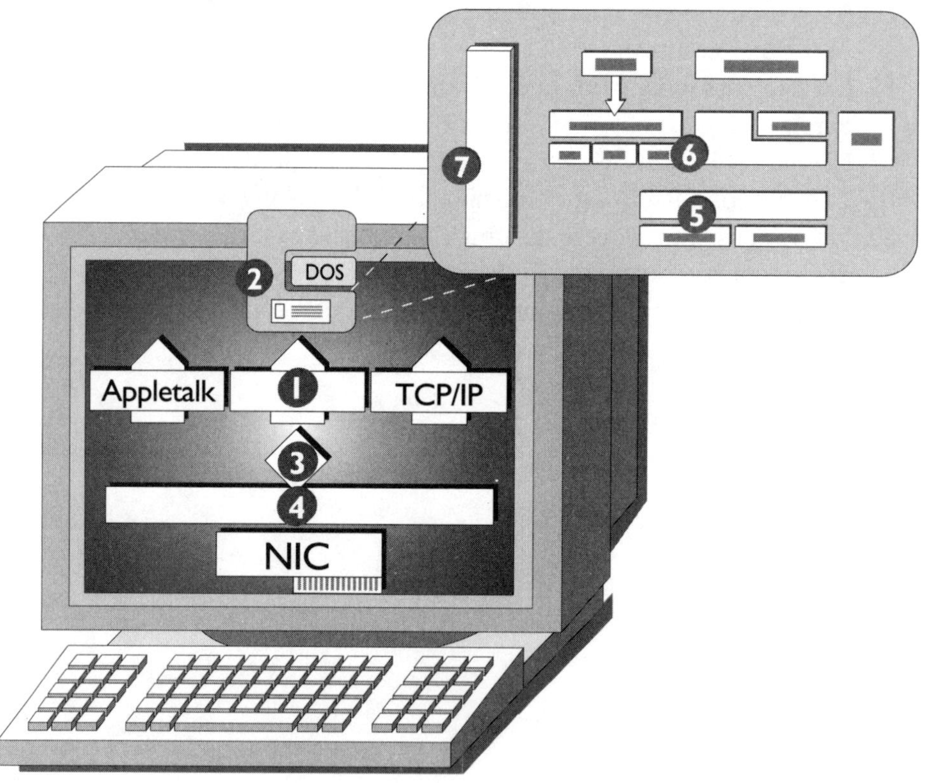

F I G U R E 7.20

The NetWare Workstation Architecture

CASE STUDY: CLIENT INSTALLATION FOR ACME

Your next mission, should you choose to accept it, is to install the NetWare Client on a DOS/Windows workstation. You will need a NetWare 3.1*x* or 4.*x* installation CD-ROM for this exercise. If you haven't purchased a copy of NetWare yet, just try to follow along anyway.

1. Install the CD-ROM drive. First, ensure that the CD-ROM drive is installed on the workstation as a DOS or network device, according to the manufacturer's instructions.

2. Execute the INSTALL.BAT utility. Insert the NetWare 4 Installation CD-ROM disk in the CD-ROM drive. Type **D**: (or the appropriate drive letter) and press Enter to switch to the CD-ROM drive. Next, type **CD ** and press Enter to switch to the root directory. Finally, type **INSTALL** and press Enter to begin the automated installation process.

3. Select the language. When you run INSTALL.BAT, you will be asked to choose the language to use during the installation process. Choose the Select this line to install in English option from the NetWare Install menu and press Enter if you want the installation instructions to be in English. Choose one of the other four languages (Deutsch, Español, Français, or Italiano) if you want the installation instructions to be displayed in another language. You will then be asked to indicate the type of installation desired. Choose the DOS/Windows Client Installation option from the Select the Type of Installation Desired menu and press Enter.

4. Provide configuration information. Next, a data entry screen will be displayed requesting workstation configuration information, as shown in Figure 7.21.

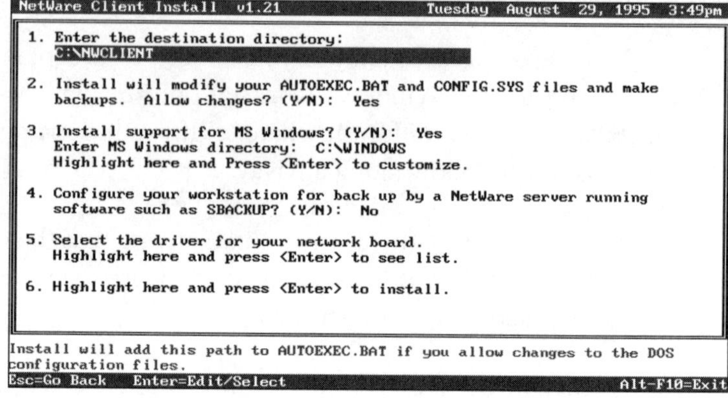

F I G U R E 7.21

The NetWare 4 Client Installation Configuration Screen

a. In Step 1, you are asked to supply the destination directory for the client software. Press Enter twice to accept the default directory of C:\NWCLIENT.

b. In Step 2, you are prompted to indicate whether to allow the INSTALL program to make changes to your AUTOEXEC.BAT and CONFIG.SYS files. Select Yes and press Enter twice.

c. In Step 3, you are asked whether to install support for MS Windows. Select Yes and press Enter. You will also be asked to indicate the path to the MS Windows software. Press Enter twice to accept the default path of C:\WINDOWS. Press the down-arrow key once to move down to Step 4.

d. In Step 4, you are asked to specify whether to configure the workstation to be backed up by the server running SBACKUP or other software. Select No and press Enter twice.

e. In Step 5, you are given the opportunity to select the appropriate LAN driver and associated settings. Press Enter to display a list of available LAN drivers. If the installation program detects an existing LAN driver in workstation RAM, it will display a screen similar to the one in Figure 7.22, advising you that it has detected an existing LAN driver and will install the newest version of the driver using the same options. If this is the case, press Enter to continue and skip to Step 6. If you do not already have a LAN driver loaded, indicate the appropriate LAN driver and related settings — making sure that the settings that you choose match those on the network board and that they do not conflict with other hardware. When you have finished entering your LAN driver settings, press Esc to continue.

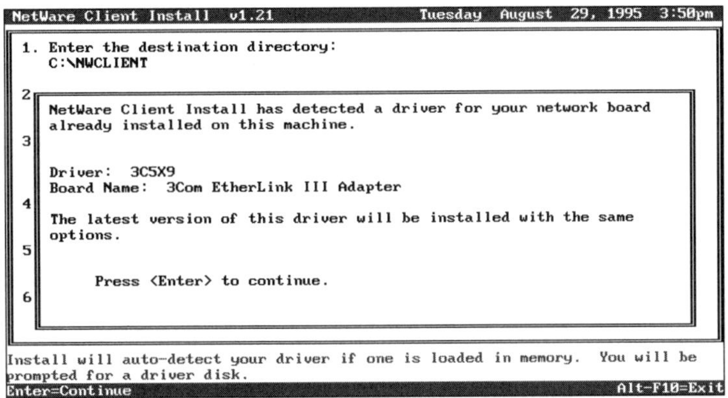

F I G U R E 7.22

Driver Detection
Notification

You'll notice that this screen provides you with information about files that have been created or changed, such as AUTOEXEC.BAT, CONFIG.SYS, NET.CFG, STARTNET.BAT, PROGMAN.INI, SYSTEM.INI, and WIN.INI. After you review the information listed, press Enter to exit to DOS. If you allowed the installation program to make changes to your AUTOEXEC.BAT and CONFIG.SYS files, press Ctrl+Alt+Del to reboot the computer and load the LAN driver into workstation RAM.

5. Complete the installation process. When all of the information on the data entry screen is correct, press Enter to continue. At this point, the installation program automatically copies the appropriate client software to the directory you specified (which in this case is C:\NWCLIENT). When the installation process is complete, a screen similar to the one in Figure 7.23 is displayed.

F I G U R E 7.23

*Installation Completion
Notification*

CASE STUDY: SERVER MANAGEMENT AT ACME

Let's go on an "incredible journey" through one of ACME's most exciting servers — CAM-CHR-SRV1. Don't blink; you might miss something. This NetWare 4 exploratorium is packed with console commands, NLMs, NDS, and pixie dust. Hold on tight!

Let's start at the beginning. As you know, before you can log into the network, you need to load the client connection files. When you originally install these files during the installation process, you tell the NetWare 4 client installation program to update your AUTOEXEC.BAT and CONFIG.SYS configuration files. Because of this, you'll find that these connection files are automatically loaded each time you boot your workstation. Let's investigate how this is accomplished.

First, take a look at your AUTOEXEC.BAT file. You'll notice that the Client Installation program added two lines: one to call the STARTNET.BAT batch file and the other to add C:\NWCLIENT to the path. Next, review the STARTNET.BAT file. You'll see that it designates the language to be used and loads the connection files and the NetWare DOS Requester. Finally, examine the CONFIG.SYS file. You'll find that the client installation program added a LASTDRIVE statement that is used by the DOS Requester to determine what drives are available to be used as NetWare drives.

Now that you understand how these files are loaded, try to accomplish the following tasks:

1. First, check to see if the files are currently loaded in workstation RAM by typing:

   ```
   MEM /C /P
   ```

2. Next, unload the connection files in the reverse order from which they were originally loaded, using the /U (that is, unload) switch with each command. (See the STARTNET.BAT file if you want to see how they were originally loaded.)

   Question 1: What commands did you use to unload the connection files from workstation RAM?

3. Finally, load all four of the connection files manually, specifying "maximum verbosity" for VLM.EXE. (If you don't remember which switch to use, use the command line help method for viewing options that can be used with VLM.EXE.)

   Question 2: What command did you use to list the options available for use with VLM.EXE?

   Question 3: What command did you use to load VLM.EXE with maximum verbosity?

   As soon as you execute VLM.EXE with the appropriate switch, various information will be displayed on the screen. Use the information displayed to answer the following questions:

   Question 4: What version of VLM.EXE are you running?

   Question 5: What type of RAM is being used to load the VLMs?

   Question 6: Which is the first VLM loaded by VLM.EXE? Which is the last?

4. Once you have successfully loaded the connection files, log into the network by typing:

```
F:

LOGIN .ADMIN.ACME
```

5. The next thing you want to do is to explore the Remote Management Facility (RMF). As you know, RMF is a wonderful feature you can use to access the file server console screen from your workstation. Because security is a concern, we will load this utility using an encrypted password.

   The first thing you need to do is to activate the RMF on the server by performing the following tasks at the server console:

   a. Load the REMOTE.NLM utility by typing:

      ```
      LOAD REMOTE
      ```

      NetWare 4 will prompt you for an RMF password. Enter it now:

      ```
      CATHY
      ```

   b. RMF is now active, but your password is not protected. You can encrypt the password by typing:

      ```
      REMOTE ENCRYPT
      ```

      Once again, NetWare will ask you for a password. Enter the same one:

      ```
      CATHY
      ```

   c. NetWare 4 then responds with an encrypted LOAD statement such as: LOAD REMOTE -e 14572BFD3AFEAE4E4759. (The number will be different every time you try this.) This is the encrypted representation of the password CATHY. Next, when you are asked whether you'd like for this command to be written to SYS:SYSTEM\LDREMOTE.NCF, type:

      ```
      Y
      ```

d. Load RSPX.NLM by typing:

```
LOAD RSPX
```

e. Now that you've activated the RMF on the server, you need to run the RCONSOLE utility on the workstation by typing:

```
RCONSOLE
```

Read the message that is displayed regarding the fact that MS Windows may cause RCONSOLE to behave erratically, then press Enter. Because our workstation is connected to the server via cable rather than via modem, select SPX when you are asked to choose the connection type. Next, choose the NetWare 4 file server from the Available Servers menu by selecting CAM-CHR-SRV1.

Finally, when you are asked to provide the password, type:

```
CATHY
```

At this point, the same information that is displayed on the file server console screen should be displayed on your workstation screen.

Question 7: How can you tell that you are viewing the file server console screen?

Question 8: What type of warning is displayed at the bottom of the screen? Why is this important?

Because you are running the RCONSOLE utility, you can now execute console commands at your workstation rather than having to type them at the file server console.

6. Next, let's take a look at the INSTALL.NLM utility. This utility is used for various functions such as installing the NetWare operating system and additional products, creating NetWare partitions and volumes, mirroring the hard disk, copying SYSTEM and PUBLIC files to the SYS: volume, and creating/editing AUTOEXEC.NCF and STARTUP.NCF configuration files. To load the INSTALL.NLM utility, type:

```
LOAD INSTALL
```

The first thing you want to do in this utility is to add the RMF commands to the AUTOEXEC.NCF file so that it will be activated with the encrypted password every time you boot the server. Select the "NCF Files options" choice from the Installation Options menu and press Enter, then Select the "Edit AUTOEXEC.NCF file" option from the Available NCF Files Options menu and press Enter. The AUTOEXEC.NCF file will then be displayed on the screen. Add the following two lines to the end of the file:

```
LDREMOTE
```

```
LOAD RSPX
```

Go ahead and save the file, and return to the Available NCF Files Options menu. Next, choose the appropriate options to view (edit) the AUTOEXEC.NCF and STARTUP.NCF configuration files so that you can answer the questions listed here:

Question 9: Which configuration file loads the LAN driver? Which one loads the disk driver?

Question 10: What time server type is designated for this server?

Question 11: If you have an Ethernet network board, what frame type is being used?

Next, press Esc once to return to the Installation options menu. Choose the appropriate options from this menu to answer the following questions:

Question 12: What percentage of the NetWare partition is reserved for the hot fix area?

Question 13: Is this disk mirrored?

Question 14: What volume block size is being used for SYS:, and why? On the SYS: volume, are file compression, block suballocation, and data migration turned on or off?

Question 15: For how many connections is this server currently licensed?

Question 16: Which menu choice would you select to install DOS/Windows Client files?

7. Let's leave INSTALL.NLM and move onto the MONITOR.NLM utility. To load the MONITOR.NLM utility, type:

    ```
    LOAD MONITOR
    ```

    Press the Tab key to expand the General Information window.

    Question 17: How long has your server been up and what do the four sets of numbers separated by colons represent? At what level is your CPU processor utilization? What is the total number of cache buffers currently being used? What is the number of current service processes in use? How many licensed connections are available at the moment? Press Esc to contract the General Information window.

    Question 18: What is the server's hot fix status? Have any blocks been redirected to the hot fix area?

    Question 19: What protocol(s) is/are currently supported on your server?

    Question 20: What is the load filename of the NetWare 4.1 Directory Services Module? What is the size of this file?

> **Question 21:** Finally, cruise over to Processor Utilization. Which NetWare 4 process occupies the most server CPU time?

8. Now let's exit MONITOR and warp ahead to SERVMAN. To load SERVMAN, type:

```
LOAD SERVMAN
```

> **Question 22:** Which general statistics overlap MONITOR functionality?

> **Question 23:** Explore some SET parameters. What console command could be used instead of SERVMAN to change SET parameters?

> **Question 24:** Next, switch to the server console without exiting SERVMAN. What method did you use? Next, check out the RMF Available Options menu. What method did you use to activate it?

> **Question 25:** Which option is similar to one found in INSTALL.NLM? How is this one different?

> **Question 26:** Press Esc to switch back to the server console. Use the appropriate console command to activate the RIP tracking screen. What command did you use? What's ACME's tree name? How about the IPX internal network number of CHARITY_INC? Where else can you get this information?

> **Question 27:** Switch to the server console and send yourself a message. What command did you use? Acknowledge receipt of the message. How did you do so? Aren't such messages annoying? How can you set your workstation so that it does not receive messages from other users?

> **Question 28:** What name spaces are loaded on the SYS: volume?

9. Turn off the RIP tracking screen and exit the SERVMAN utility.

Question 29: What method could you use to review a quick list of NetWare 4 console commands that are available?

Question 30: Use a console command to see what NLMs are currently loaded. Which console command did you use? What NLM would give you a count of the NLMs that are currently loaded?

10. Exit RCONSOLE, log off the network, and call it a day! Very good, you lived through the exploratorium without a scratch. Now, wasn't that fun?

See Appendix C for answers.

NetWare 4 Printing

Adding users to NetWare 4 printing is like putting Godzilla in a mosh pit.

Now that you've lived through the life span of a LAN, I think you're ready to discover one of the greatest mysteries of life — printing. The meaning of life? — Nah. The Great Pyramids? — Nah. The Sphinx? — No chance. Printing has them all beat. More brain cells have been lost pondering NetWare printing than any other philosophical question.

Why? It's not that printing itself is so puzzling. As a matter of fact, the concept of printing is fairly easy to comprehend — you click a button on the workstation, and a piece of paper comes out of the printer down the hall. No rocket science here. It's true, the fundamental architecture of NetWare 4 printing is solid — rock solid. So, why is it such a mystery? One word — users! It's the users' fault. They introduce so much complexity to printing, it's a wonder the paper finds its way anywhere, let alone to the correct printer. And to make matters worse, users expect too much:

▸ They want the page to be formatted correctly every time.

▸ They want their print jobs to arrive at the "correct" printer (when they don't even know what that means).

▸ They always want their jobs to come out first.

So, how can you possibly satisfy the lofty expectations of your users while maintaining a rock-solid NetWare 4 printing architecture? That's the greatest mystery of them all. Fortunately, Novell is on your side, and they've come up with some answers. The NetWare 4 printing system has been improved dramatically in several ways — easier setup, better management, more flexibility. They certainly haven't solved your mystery entirely, but they've given you some great tools to help you crack the case — and we're gonna learn all about them.

In this chapter, we're going to explore this great printing mystery and discover some startling answers. You're going to learn about the four steps of printing setup and everything you wanted to know about the great tools available for printing management. But first, we need to spend a few moments meditating on the true essence of printing. You must become one with the printer. It works, trust me.

The Essence of Printing

Now, repeat after me — I *am* a printer, I *am* a printer. The best way to handle NetWare 4 printing is to *be* NetWare 4 printing. This is the essence of printing.

Actually, the essence of printing is a little more technical than that. It is a wondrous journey from the user's workstation to the network printer down the hall. Here's how it works:

- Capturing — The job moves from the local workstation to the NetWare 4 server.

- Moving to the queue — It waits in line (first come; first served).

- The print server — The brains behind the process.

- At the printer — Finally, the print job arrives at the printer and prints correctly (fingers crossed).

This is the Printing Journey. But before we take a closer look at the Journey, let's take a history lesson in network printing. Get out your notebooks.

ZEN

"School, thank God for school. I need those seven hours of personal time. I mean, how can I continue to be the bright, vivacious Nanny everyone knows and loves if I have to spend all day with the kids?"

Nanny Fine

GETTING STARTED

We already know what a great job NetWare does with its file services, but printing is just as important to users. Initially, all users need access to file storage and shared print services to get the most out of NetWare.

Setting up and using printing services under NetWare can be a challenging part of setting up the network. But printing isn't as difficult as it seems — especially if you understand the system's essence. This chapter will give you some insight into the overall architecture of network printing, and, in the process, should make print services setup a whole lot easier.

Printing By Yourself

Most people are familiar with printing from a local workstation. In this scenario, a PC or other station has a stand-alone printer (a LaserJet, dot matrix, or other type of printer) that is dedicated to that station. With a dedicated printer, you have much less to worry about when it comes to printing documents. Issues such as *print drivers* or notification when the print job is complete do not apply. You can see the printer on your desk (or nearby, at least), and hopefully the correct print driver (with the proper version) has already been set up. When the document is printed, you need only reach over and grab it from the printer.

To better understand network printing, it helps to have a solid foundation of how local printing works. Starting from the beginning, the workstation has one or more local ports. Most PCs have at least one *parallel* port, labeled LPT1, LPT2, and so on. Many PCs also have a *serial* port as well. Serial ports typically are used as communication ports (that is, for modems), because they work faster than do parallel ports.

When you begin printing (if a printer is attached), the default output for printing is LPT1. LPT1 outputs to parallel port one, LPT2 outputs to parallel port two, and so on. Serial output is not enabled by default. If you print something, the software program you are using will usually default to LPT1. Otherwise, it may ask you which port you prefer (LPT1-LPT*n*).

Once you have hit the magic button to print something, the machine takes over. If you are running strictly DOS (no Windows in sight), then the machine may halt while printing. This is because DOS is set up to do only one thing at a time, but there are ways to trick DOS into not halting your machine, for example, by using the PRINT command. This command will take the print data and store it locally on the hard disk while it feeds the data to the printer in the background. This will allow you to do other things while the system is printing (for more information on the PRINT command, see your DOS reference manual). If you don't trick the computer, you'll have to wait for the document (or other print job) to finish printing before the machine will return control back to you (just like the old *Outer Limits* program, huh!).

If you are printing to a serial port under DOS, you'll need to do a bit of preparation. First, you must *redirect* the LPT output from the parallel port to a serial port. This is done using another DOS command called MODE. The MODE command works similarly to how network printing works in general. MODE simply takes LPT1 output and redirects it to the serial port. The program *thinks* it's sending to the LPT port. DOS takes the output, however, and streams it to the serial device (see Figure 8.1).

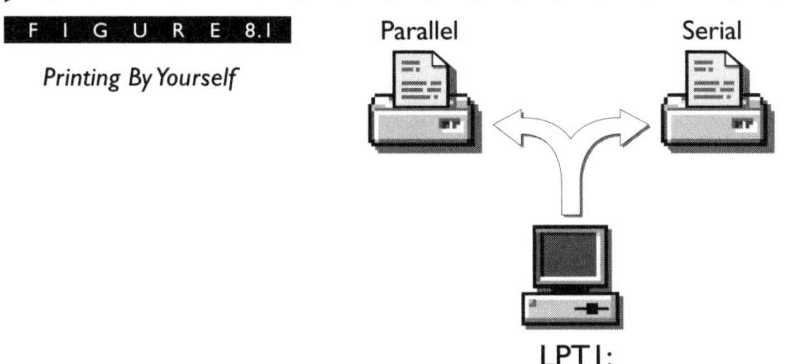

Printing By Yourself

If you are using Windows (3.x or Windows 95), there is a neat little program called Print Manager. Print Manager can be used to manage local printing from Windows. It also provides the same capabilities as the DOS PRINT program — such as the ability to spool the print data locally and feed it to the printer. Print Manager has a few more features than PRINT. For example, it will allow you to view the current printing job, delete it, or postpone it.

Typically, when you are printing to the network, those features are already provided by NetWare utilities, thereby making Print Manager functions unnecessary. Many users will disable Print Manager when using NetWare for this reason. Print Manager can actually slow network printing because the print job will be spooled once locally and then again to the network queue.

Instead of disabling Print Manager, you can select the Print Net Jobs Direct option (select Options and then Network Settings from the Print Manager). This will enable any network print jobs to spool directly to a NetWare queue and bypass local hard disk spooling. Check out the screen in Figure 8.2.

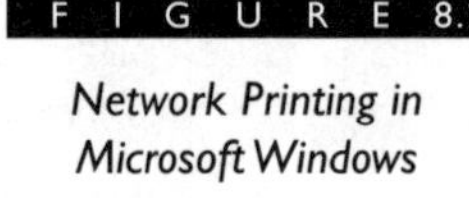

Network Printing in Microsoft Windows

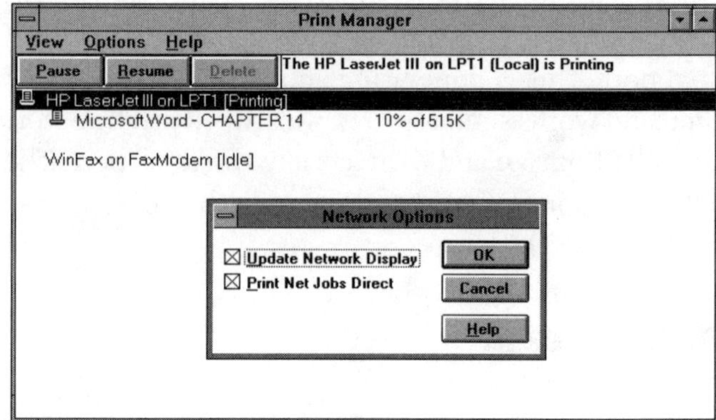

Once you attach a workstation to a network, the rules change a little. Some considerations are

1 • Does the workstation have the proper driver for the network printer?

2 • How will you know when the document has completed printing?

3 • How does the server know when you have stopped sending print data?

4 • What if the printer runs out of paper? How will you or the administrator be notified?

Printing on a Network

The flow for network printing works something like this. The user has enabled printing to a network device from the workstation, or the administrator has automatically enabled it via a batch file (AUTOEXEC.BAT) or a login script (Container, System, User, and so on). This is similar to using the MODE command under DOS except that when an application prints, the output gets redirected to a queue on a server somewhere. The workstation command line utility to enable printing is called CAPTURE.

When CAPTURE is executed, the local LPT port that is being redirected to the network is specified. By default, this is usually LPT1. With this approach, the application may send output via LPT2 and the NetWare shell knows to capture data coming from the LPT2 port and redirect it to the appropriate queue. As a default, the CAPTURE command automatically assumes that data will be sent via LPT1. Most applications also assume that this is the default port on which to send data. Remember, the LPT port is merely a channel, port, or stream as far as the application knows. It may *point* to a parallel port, a serial port, a file, or the network queue. This concept is shown in Figure 8.3.

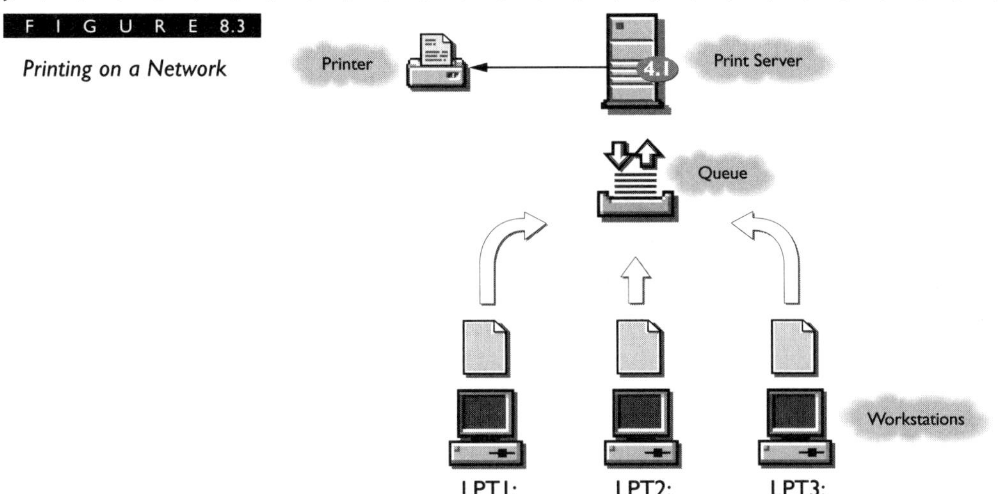

F I G U R E 8.3

Printing on a Network

Understanding Print Queues

Now that capturing is on, the user starts to print via the application, DOS, or Windows. The output can be an existing file (such as DATA.TXT) or raw data from a word processing program (such as WordPerfect). The data being printed will be sent to an area on a specified server called a *queue*. Queues are nothing more than a subdirectory with a *.QDR extension. The data will be spooled into an automatically created file. When the user signals that he/she is finished sending data, the file is closed and prepared for printing.

Understanding Print Servers

Now that the data file is closed and ready, it can be serviced from the QUEUE directory. A *print server* is a device that is assigned to watch a particular queue or queues. When it sees a job waiting to be serviced, it will open the job (file) and start to read from it. The print server will then print the data in the file to a printer attached to the print server. *Which* printer it sends the file to depends on the setup of the print server (see the "NetWare 4 Printing Setup" section). See Figure 8.4 for a quick preview.

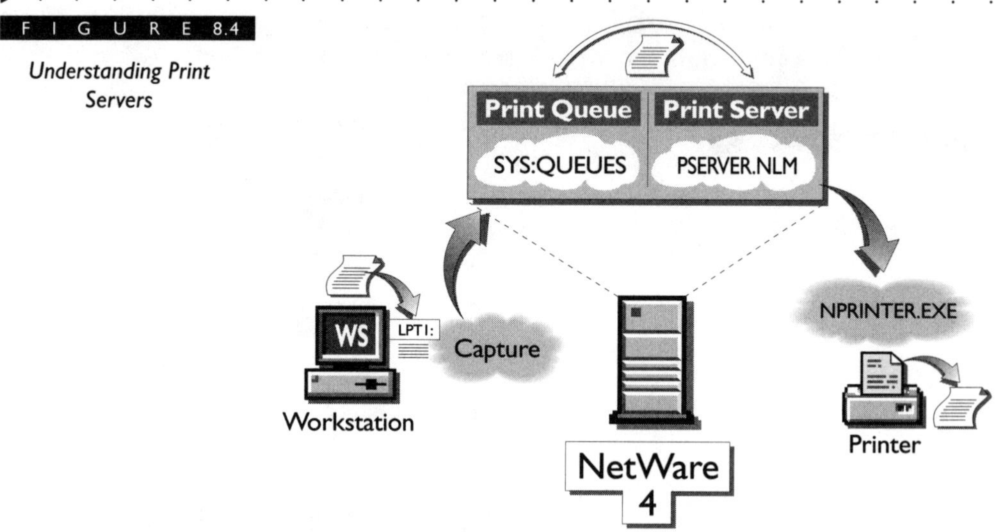

Understanding Print Servers

Understanding Printers

As the print server services the request, it attempts to print the data to a locally attached printer (physically attached to the print server) or a remotely attached printer (perhaps a printer attached to a workstation, but remotely attached via software to the print server). If the printer is a remote printer, the print server *thinks* it is attached locally, when, in fact, the data is being sent across the network to where the remote printer physically resides.

Once the contents of the data file have been printed, the data file residing in the queue will be deleted to recover the disk space. In addition, if it has been set up to do so, a notification will be sent to the user (and possibly others) that the job has been successfully printed and is ready to be picked up.

QUIZ

Let's begin our NetWare "sleuthing" with a simple one. Here goes. . . . At a college reunion, a group of men and women were discussing their lives after they had received their undergraduate degrees. It turned out that everyone in the group had gone on to receive an advanced degree, so each of them had two degrees. Each degree holder had both a B.A. and an M.S., an M.A., an M.B.A., or an M.F.A. Half of them had an M.S., one quarter had an M.A., one sixth had an M.B.A., and just one had an M.F.A. How many were there in total?

(Q8-1)
(See Appendix C for all quiz answers.)

THE PRINTING JOURNEY

This is the beginning of your printing journey. Hold on to your hat.

Now, we will cover the details of printing under a NetWare environment from a PC workstation perspective. Two areas will be covered: printing from DOS and printing from Windows. This discussion assumes that you have some knowledge of DOS and Windows in order to understand the elements of network printing.

This section also assumes that a printing system has already been set up (print server, print queue, and remote/local printer) and that the user has been granted access. If not, you can jump ahead to the section "NetWare 4 Printing Setup," then return to this section.

Capturing

To enable network printing, you must first tell the network client (for example, VLM or NETX) that you wish to print to the network. You can do this by using the (DOS) command, or by using NWUSER CAPTURE utility in windows (see Figure 8.5).

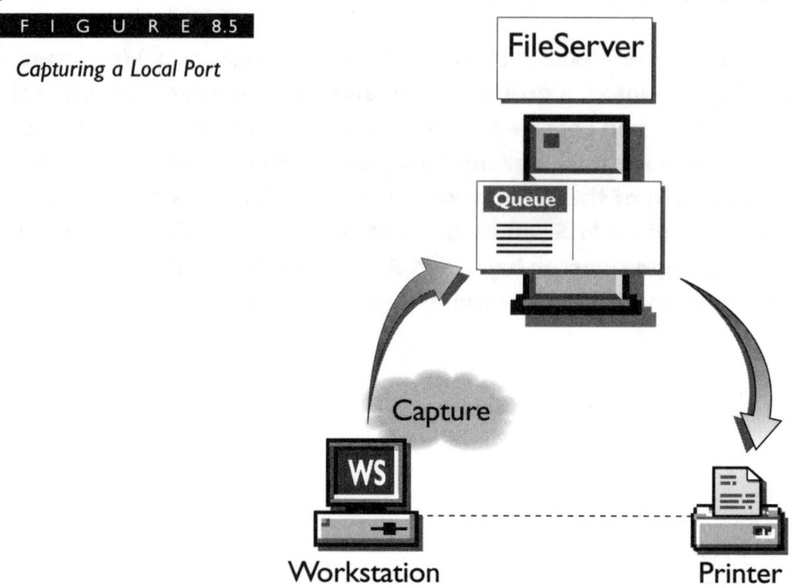

F I G U R E 8.5

Capturing a Local Port

Capturing with DOS

The CAPTURE command is included with NetWare, and allows you to start and end network printing. It can be used in a DOS-only environment, or it can be executed *before* starting Windows 3.x to allow capturing under Windows. In Windows 95 environments, you can use the Win95 Print Manager or NWUSER (a NetWare tool).

CAPTURE has several command line options that allow you to customize how the network capture will work. These options include:

- /? — This option will show help for the CAPTURE command if you need it. You can also use CAPTURE /? ALL to show every possible option and explanation for CAPTURE.

- /SH (Show) — This is a very useful command to see how you are currently captured to the network. CAPTURE /SH will show all LPT ports currently enabled for network printing, as well as other flags (such as banners, copies, and so on). The Show parameter will *not* initiate a print capture. It is for informational purposes only.

- ▶ /S (Server) — This option allows you to specify the server to which you want to print. In NetWare 4 environments, this is usually unnecessary because the user is oblivious to servers per se. When capturing, the user can just specify the printer name using a distinguished name (for example, HP5-P1.CRIME.TOKYO.ACME), and the server will automatically be found and attached. In a NetWare 3 environment, however, /S can be used to point to a server with a particular printer/ queue that you wish to use. If you are not logged in/attached to that particular server, then the CAPTURE command will attempt to log in as GUEST. If the GUEST account does not exist, printing on that server will be denied to the user. This is a good reason (in an open environment) to keep the GUEST account around on a public NetWare 3 server.

- ▶ /Q (Queue) — This command line option allows the user to specify the queue to which data should be sent. In a NetWare 3 environment, it can be combined with the /S option to specify a server name and queue name that the user desires. In a NetWare 4 network, the queue name can be a relative distinguished name (for example, HP5-PQ1) or a distinguished name (for example, HP5-PQ1.CRIME.TOKYO.ACME). If a distinguished name is used, there is much less of a chance of ambiguity between printer and queue names. For example, if the user is in context CYBER.WHITE.CRIME.TOKYO.ACME, and he/she wishes to print to a queue in BLUE.CRIME.TOKYO.ACME, there is a chance that the relative distinguished name HPIII-PQ1 may exist in both locations (and it does). In such a case, if a user types in the command CAPTURE /Q=HPIII-PQ1, the printer captured will be the one in CYBER.WHITE.CRIME.TOKYO.ACME.

- ▶ /AU (AutoEndCap) — This option allows the application to decide if the user is finished sending capture data. For example, when a user sends data, how does the network shell know when the application/user is finished sending data? There are three ways:

1. The user stops sending capture data (via the CAPTURE command — discussed later).

2. The application sends a NetWare-specific command to signal the end of capture data (this is the case with network-aware applications such as WordPerfect).

3. The shell assumes you are finished via AutoEndCap or timeouts. When AutoEndCap is enabled, the shell assumes you are finished sending data if you leave the application that began sending capture data. Consider a user who enables capture (via the CAPTURE command), sends a print job via the application (such as WordPerfect), and then exits the application. The shell can safely assume that, since the user exited, he/she was finished sending data. If AutoEndCap were *not* enabled, the user would still have to terminate CAPTURE to signal the end of capture data.

▶ /TI (TimeOut) — This option is similar to the AutoEndCap command, except that the user does not need to exit the application. Instead, a timeout is specified when capture was started (such as CAPTURE TI=8). This means the network shell will assume that once capture data has been sent, if no more data has been sent after 8 seconds, the job will automatically be completed and scheduled for printing. The only problem with this command is what happens when an application pauses between spurts of data. For example, if a database program were sending data and then paused 10 seconds before sending page totals, the first data would be sent as one print job and the page totals would be sent as a second, thereby violating the integrity of the job.

▶ /K (Keep/No Keep) — This option tells the shell what to do if something interrupts the flow of data from the workstation to the queue on the server. For example, if a print job were started and then interrupted when the workstation lost power, all data sent to the queue up to that point would be lost if Keep were not enabled. If Keep is enabled, any data sent up to that point will be printed.

- /T (Tabs) — The Tabs option was included from the earlier versions of NetWare when printing documents was not always done through the application. As a result, when a document was printed, the proper spaces were not inserted for a tab character. Therefore, the NetWare shell was enabled to observe a tab character during the print process, remove it, and send the proper number of spaces to the printer. This option was enabled in versions of NetWare 3.11 and below. The default amount of spaces per tab character was eight. Current versions no longer support this as a default. This is because most applications now format their own printing and convert tabs to the proper number of spaces. This option, if enabled, can cause printing problems since some graphics programs or other raw text may have characters that signify a tab. If T is enabled, the shell will strip the tab, send the spaces, and you'll end up with garbled print output. NT (No Tabs) is the default.

- /C (Copies) — This option specifies the number of copies you want of the printout. The default is 1.

- /B (Banner) — This option (enabled by default) will send a print banner at the beginning of the print job. You can specify the name of the person that submitted the document as well as the name of the job itself (B=<*user name*> and N=<*job name*>). If nothing is specified, then the document will either be the name of the file being printed (if an existing file is being printed) or PRN: if the print job is output from an application. The name will be the username of the person that submitted it.

- /NB (No Banner) — This option disables the Banner option. It is usually used when a small office is involved or with a local workgroup.

- /NFF (NoFormFeed) — This option prevents an additional page from being sent at the end of the print job. This may be necessary with some applications that do not send a form feed after a print job has been submitted.

- ▸ /FF (FormFeed) — This option sends a form feed after the job has been completed (default). This is necessary when the application doesn't do this automatically, since the last page of the document may not be ejected by the printer (especially when using a LaserJet printer). NFF (No Form Feed) turns off form feed.

- ▸ /L=n (Local Port Number) — DOS provides several channels for print output. The first and primary channel is LPT1. There can be more than one, however. Many applications today can output print data on LPT2-LPT*n*. Most default to LPT1. If your application is outputting on LPT2, you need to use this command to tell NetWare which LPT port is being used. For example, you might have a local printer attached to LPT1 and you want network printing to go out via LPT2. The CAPTURE command would look like this: CAPTURE /L=2. That way, through the application, you can print to LPT1 and the output will go to the local printer. If you print out to LPT2, however, the output will go to the network.

- ▸ /F (Form) — Forms allow network users to share the same printer for a variety of functions. When (and if) forms are defined, a user can submit a job of a particular form type and the print server will ensure that the printer being used is ready to accept a print job of that form type. For example, this option would allow one user to submit a purchase requisition (that requires a preprinted form), while another user could submit an invoice (also requiring a preprinted form). When the job is submitted, a form name or number is used to specify which form is to be used when printing the job. Form names and numbers are defined using the PRINTDEF utility.

- /CR (Create) — This option allows the user to send output to a file instead of to a print queue. When this option is specified, the user must also specify the filename to which output should be directed. If the file does not exist, it will be created automatically. After the first print job output has completed, subsequent print jobs will be sent to a normal queue. For example, if we typed **CAPTURE /CR=SYS:TEST.TXT /Q=.HP5-PQ1.CRIME.TOKYO.ACME**, the data will be captured to the printer HP5-P1, but the initial output will go to file TEST.TXT. We then submit data for print (through the application or an existing file). The data will go into the file TEST.TXT instead of being printed! If we print again, the data will be spooled to HP5-P1 and printed on the physical printer. This parameter is useful when you need to encapsulate an entire print job (printer escape codes and all) into a file. Another user could merely submit the entire file for printing (without the source application being available), and the data will print successfully.

- /NOTI (Notify) — With this option, provided the print server has been created to support it, a message will be sent to the user *after* the job has been printed successfully. In addition, the print server can be configured to notify the user or other responsible parties (such as Admin or the print server administrator) if any problems arise (for example, if the printer runs out of paper or if it is off-line). NNOTI disables notification.

- /EC (EndCapture) — This option is used to return LPT output to the local port (usually the local parallel port). Since the CAPTURE command could have been started for LPT2, LPT3, and so on, ENDCAP can be used with the L=n switch to turn off CAPTURE on a specific port.

A sample CAPTURE command might look like this:

```
CAPTURE /NB /L=2 /K /Q=HP5-PQ1.CRIME.TOKYO.ACME /TI=10
```

For this print job:

- No banner will be prefixed to the print job.

- Output will be via LPT2.

> ▸ Data will be kept and printed *if* the capture is not formally closed.

> ▸ The queue to be used is HP5-PQ1.CRIME.TOKYO.ACME.

> ▸ A timeout of 10 seconds will be used.

Capturing with Windows

There are two options for enabling CAPTURE under Windows:

> ▸ Use the CAPTURE command, and then start Windows.

> ▸ Use the NWUSER utility.

Since we have already covered CAPTURE, let's look at the NWUSER utility. To start NWUSER, you may find the icon under the NetWare Tools Program Group. This is installed as part of the NetWare client that was installed on your NetWare workstation. NWUSER is simply a launcher for the Novell Driver for Windows. Another option is to launch File Manager and choose Disk/Network Connections. This will also launch the NetWare Tools utility. Surprise!

TIP

If you have a sound card, choose the NetWare Settings option from the button bar (the one that has a key) and click once over the Novell icon in the upper left-hand corner! Surprise!

Once the tool is running, choose the printer icon (third icon from the left on the Button Bar). This will display all the printers available to you in the browser window to the right. You can also walk the tree to find other printers and queues in your network. You will also see any queues available for any 3.x/2.x servers that you are logged into.

To capture to a printer, you may do one of two things: Select the printer/queue you want and then select Capture or merely drag and drop the chosen printer from the right window to the desired LPT port on the left. Once completed, you can double-click on the newly captured printer and select printing options. These options correspond to the flags used under CAPTURE at the DOS prompt (see Figure 8.6).

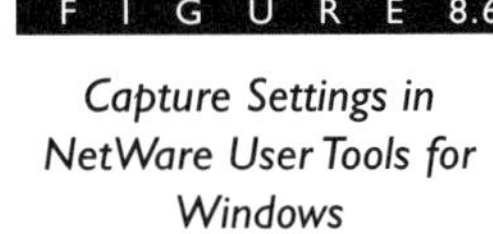

Capture Settings in NetWare User Tools for Windows

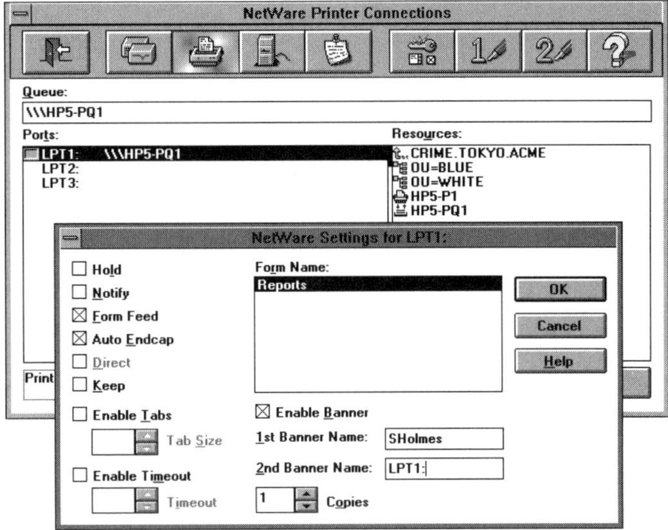

One other note: You can select the Permanent option after capturing a printer. This will automatically recapture the printer every time you start Windows. If it is a 3.x/2.x printer/queue, you may be required to log into the server again before capture is complete.

Note: Printers and queues are referred to in the same context here since they are so closely related. More will be explained later, but for clarification's sake, a print job always must be submitted to a queue before it can be serviced by a printer via a print server. To minimize complexity, Novell allows you to choose a printer by name and you will be captured automatically to the queue that services that printer. This way, you don't need to know which queue services which printer.

To end CAPTURE under Windows, you can drag the printer mapping from the left window to the right. You can also select the desired printer/queue and choose End Capture from the lower button bar.

ZEN

"Don't underestimate the power of these adenoids. I had next-door neighbors move closer to the airport."

Nanny Fine

Moving to the Queue

Once capturing has been started, data is sent either in the form of an existing file or by sending print output via an application.

Before the data is sent, however, a subtle thing may be happening. If you analyze the anatomy of a print stream (see Figure 8.7), you'll find there are three parts: the print header, the print body (data sent), and the print tail. The purpose of these other data become important when drivers are involved.

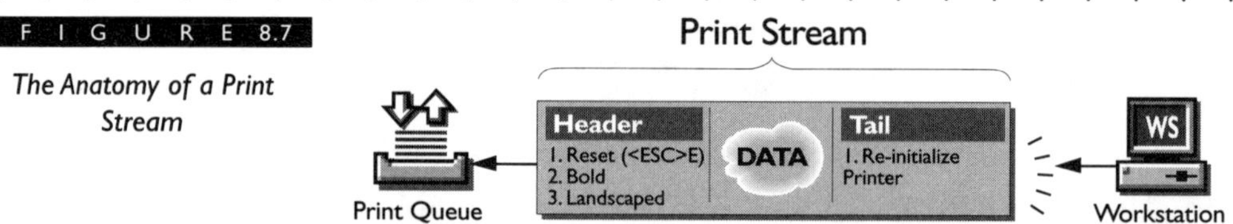

The Anatomy of a Print Stream

NetWare allows the user to specify escape codes that can be sent before the print data reaches the printer (a *print header*). And at the end of the print data, a *print tail* sends the proper escape codes to reset the printer to a default state. This leaves the printer ready for the next user. To use this feature of NetWare, two things must have been created: a PRINTDEF database, which includes escape code information for printers and modes of operation made up of these escape codes, as well as a Print Job Definition, which specifies details about how the capture should be handled. Remember the options for CAPTURE? Well these can be incorporated into a file stored in NDS that gets read and utilized when the user begins a CAPTURE. Any command line options used when executing the CAPTURE command will override the Print Job Definition options.

The print server's job is to control the flow of the print job from its beginning until it is finally printed on a printer *somewhere*. That somewhere is dictated by the queue typically.

Several server elements are involved in printing: the queue (which always resides on a server volume somewhere), the print server (which may reside on a file server, NetWare router, any other NLM platform, or even inside the printer itself), and finally the printer (which prints the data and notifies the print server of completion and any problems that may arise).

NetWare queue services are designed to provide more than just support for printing. Other applications can take advantage of the queue API under NetWare to service jobs based on a queuing mechanism. As a result, not all queue characteristics look related to printing.

A queue is basically comprised of a subdirectory stored on a server volume. Where the subdirectory exists is up to the person who creates it. In NetWare 3 and below, the directories always existed under the SYS:SYSTEM subdirectory. NetWare 4 allows them to be placed on any volume at any level.

Once a print job has begun from the client, the queue servicing the request (selected by the user via CAPTURE, Print Job Settings, or NWUSER) will create a temporary file inside the queue's subdirectory. This file is used to keep track of the job as it flows through the system. One type of data kept in the file is the *Job Entry Record*, which contains information such as:

- ▸ When the job was submitted

- ▸ Who submitted the job

- ▸ Size of the data

- ▸ Whether the job can be printed immediately

- ▸ How many copies to print

And more. This information can be obtained through NWADMIN or PCONSOLE. See Figure 8.8 for an example of the Print Job Detail screen in NWADMIN.

The queue also has security assigned to it. During setup, we can designate users, groups, or containers that may submit jobs to the queue. We can also restrict which print servers may service jobs from our queue. Finally, there is a security designation called Queue Manager. This entity, when designated, may delete jobs submitted by other users. In this manner, print queue administration may be delegated to other users.

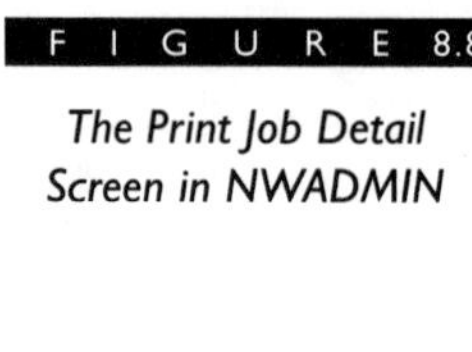

FIGURE 8.8

The Print Job Detail Screen in NWADMIN

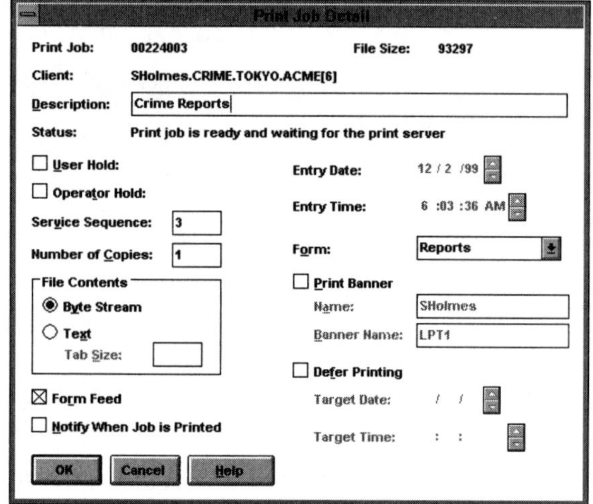

There are some utilities available that allow users and administrators to manage and view the flow of printing. These include PCONSOLE (under DOS) and NWADMIN (under Windows).

The Print Server

Once the print server is loaded and functioning, it must then log in to the servers it is servicing in order to poll the queues it has been assigned. It is a very good idea to password-protect all the print servers in the network to minimize security problems.

Once the server is fully initialized, it will begin polling the queues it has been assigned and service print jobs within those queues. Some factors may affect which queues get serviced first. They include:

- Queue priorities — When a queue is assigned to a print server, a priority can be assigned. This priority tells the print server that if any jobs are waiting in the highest priority queue, it must service them once the currently serviced job has completed. This can be set up as part of security, allowing certain users to have better access to a printer than others. This would be the case if two queues were servicing the same physical printer: Users having access to the higher priority queue will have their jobs completed before the users that submitted jobs to a lower priority queue.

- Forms servicing — This topic will be covered later in the chapter, but the Print Server Manager can designate how forms are serviced. As such, a print server may be required to service all forms of a particular type within a queue before it can move to the next queue. Or it may have to print all jobs that have a certain designated form type across all queues it is assigned to, before servicing jobs with a different form type.

TIP

Suppose print server Alpha were supporting Q1 and Q2. And further, assume it must service all jobs using a particular form before moving to the next form. If User1 submits a job of form type 0 into Q1 and User2 submits a job with form type 5 thereafter, User2 will have to wait if User3 submits a job of form type 0 into Q2 even if User3 submitted it *after* User2. Once User3's job is complete, the print server can begin to service jobs using form type 5.

Much like a print queue, print servers can have security designated.

- Print server users — These are users, groups, and containers that can view current jobs that are being serviced. Print server users can also abort their jobs if they wish.

- Print server operators — These are users, groups, and containers that can abort anyone's job currently being serviced. They can also view the status of any currently printing job.

Other things that can be controlled on print servers include how often the print server polls the assigned queues looking for jobs. As mentioned earlier, you can modify the queue priority and how forms get serviced using Admin utilities described later in this chapter.

When setting up print services, you should know the options available. The relationship of queues and print servers to printers can be:

- One to many

- One to one

- Many to many

- Many to one

At the Printer

Print servers usually reside at the file server, although they may reside as NLMs elsewhere, such as in a special third-party printer or NetWare router. Print servers, when created, are assigned the queues they are to service and which printers they will support. Unlike queues, print servers do not require disk storage; therefore, they can reside just about anywhere.

Once a print server has been initialized, it will first attempt to find any printers it is supposed to support. Print servers support two types of printers: local and remote. The print server software, in NLM form, is called PSERVER.NLM. PSERVER.NLM by itself does not know how to talk to a printer; therefore, a separate printer support module must be provided.

Local Printers

If the printer is local (as defined during print server creation), then PSERVER.NLM loads a local NLM called NPRINTER.NLM. NPRINTER.NLM has bidirectional communications with the print server, as well as a communication to the local port it is servicing. The local port is usually either a parallel or serial port.

This design has several advantages, including that:

- PSERVER can theoretically talk to devices other than serial and parallel ports.

- By design, NetWare SFTIII has two parts: one that talks to hardware (IOEngine) and one that is common to both servers. Using this method, the PSERVER resides in the shared engine and NPRINTER resides in the IOEngine.

Remote Printers

If the designated printer is a remote printer, PSERVER.NLM attempts to contact it using SPX as the communications method. This necessitates loading the NPRINTER.EXE module on a workstation that has the desired remote printer attached to it. Once NPRINTER.EXE has been loaded, communications will be established and remote printing can be supported.

ZEN

"Some people say Yoga is a great way to keep your energy up. For me, it's a Snickers and a Diet Coke."

Nanny Fine

Just when you think you're at the end of your journey, the tour guide throws in a few side stops. Don't you just hate that? In our case, it's time to explore third-party printing solutions.

Third-Party Printing Solutions

Several good add-ons are available for the NetWare printing system. These usually can augment the services already provided within the printing infrastructure.

For example, in a generic NetWare environment using remote printers, the job must go from the user to the queue, to the print server, and finally to the remote printer. Using a device that encapsulates these functions into one subsystem can greatly reduce the network traffic required to print. Two of these devices are the HP JetDirect Card and Intel's NetPort.

HP JetDirect

This device resides in a printer (such as an HP LaserJet4M or 4SI) and acts as a peer device on the network. It can be configured either as a print server or as a remote printer.

Ideally, the JetDirect card will be configured as a print server. This will reduce the flow of network printing, since the print job only has to go from the user to the queue, and then to the JetDirect card in the printer. The challenge is when you are running a system that the JetDirect card can't log into, for example, with an older JetDirect card and NetWare 4.

The other option is to set up the JetDirect as a remote printer. In this scenario, the JetDirect will have a name assigned to it when configured. This name must correspond to the name given to the remote printer when it was defined under NetWare. This way, the print server knows how to communicate with the JetDirect card. The down side is that you still have the same traffic, but you do not need a machine dedicated to support the remote printer.

Intel NetPort

Intel's solution is similar to HP's, except that an Intel NetPort can also be just a peer device on the network. It plugs into an Ethernet cable just like another node on the network. It can then have a standard parallel cable attached to it, enabling it to communicate with a standard printer (unlike the HP JetDirect card, which only plugs into HP printers).

The other options typically apply to the NetPort. Both modes can be supported, either as a remote printer or a print server.

These solutions also come with management software that allows the administrator to manage the print devices remotely. This software provides peer-to-peer communications with the print device.

Now, we're really at the end of our journey. They say, "A well-traveled person is an enlightened person." Do you feel well-traveled? Do you feel enlightened? You should feel *something* right about now.

So, that's the essence of printing. It's not so bad. I think NetWare printing gets a bad rap. It's not very mysterious — you click a button on the workstation and your document comes out of the printer down the hall. Assuming, of course, that you set it up correctly. Now would be a good time to explore that aspect of NetWare 4 printing.

NetWare 4 Printing Setup

Welcome to NetWare 4 printing setup. Now that you understand the essence of printing, it's time to do something about it. This is where the mystery begins to unfold. This is where the clues appear. This is "Sherlock Holmes 101."

Creating print services for a NetWare 4 network requires a little bit of planning. In a simple environment, NetWare allows you to create a basic printing system by using the DOS utility PCONSOLE.

Under Windows, you must create the items separately and associate them. This is a relatively simple process — once you understand how printing works under NetWare. If you have read the previous section, this should appear relatively obvious.

As you recall, there are three elements to the printing system that must be present in order to print. They are:

- The queue — Used to store print jobs on their way to the printer

- The print server — Polls the queue for jobs and prints them on assigned printers

- The printer — Defines whether the printer is local to the file server or remotely attached

You can use NWADMIN to create the NetWare 4 printing system. NWADMIN is a Windows-based graphical utility that integrates several aspects of managing NetWare (including rights assignments and user creation) into one easy-to-use application.

The order in which you create the print system items (queue, print server, and printer) really makes no difference. The most efficient way is to start with the queue, since it is central to the printing system under NetWare. Here's how I like to do it:

- Step 1: Create the print queue

- Step 2: Create the printer

▸ Step 3: Create the print server

▸ Step 4: Activate the printing system

There you have it. Four simple steps. No mystery here. Let's take a closer look, and don't forget your NetWare magnifying glass.

ZEN

"I've often wondered how the British know what everyone's feeling. They all must wear mood rings."

Nanny Fine

STEP 1: CREATE THE PRINT QUEUE

It is important to remember that when you create a queue, it should be central to the users who are going to use it. When using NDS, you usually want to keep the queues and print servers proximal to each other.

TIP

NetWare 4 Printing Setup is closely related to NDS and partitioning. It is more efficient to have the area where the jobs get stored (Queue Volume) as close to the users as possible. If you reside in Camelot, it makes no sense to print something to a queue in Tokyo (unless you *want* the print job to print in Tokyo).

The first step is to choose the context where you create the queue. This is usually in the container where the users reside who will be using the queue the most.

To create the queue under NWADMIN, select Object/Create or select the container and press Insert. You'll be presented with a dialog box asking for the type of object you wish to create. Choose Print Queue and press Enter (see Figure 8.9). The items you need to define next are shown in Table 8.1 and Figure 8.9.

Step 1: Create the Print Queue

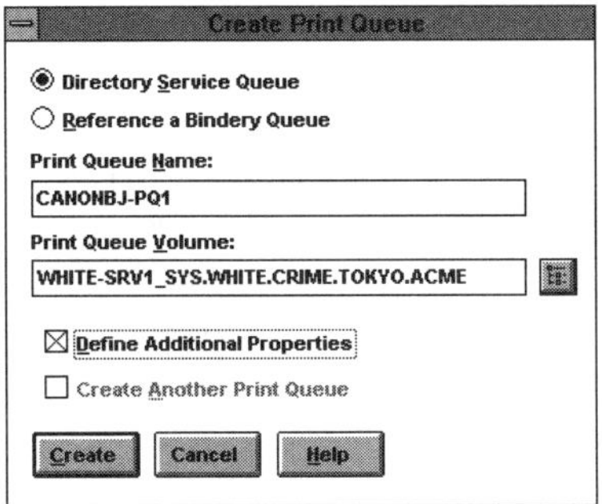

Important Print Queue Properties

PROPERTY	DESCRIPTION
Directory Queue vs. Bindery Queue	If you are creating a regular queue (and we are), choose Directory Services Queue. A Bindery Reference Queue can service jobs out of a queue that resides on a NetWare 2.x or 3.x server. This can be useful if you have a mixed environment and need to support queues from a single location. In addition, you can submit a job to Bindery Reference Queue and it will be sent automatically to the reference queue on the NetWare 3.x server.
Print Queue Name	Usually, you want to name a queue descriptively. It is easier to find a queue named CANONBJ-PQ1 than just Bubble Printer.
Print Queue Volume	This is the physical space where the job will be stored as it is spooled and when it is serviced. Therefore, this property must reference a volume somewhere in the NetWare 4 tree. In addition, the container in which the queue is created must have rights to that volume in order to create print jobs there.

REAL WORLD

In previous versions of NetWare, the queue was *always* stored under SYS:SYSTEM in the volume SYS:. In NetWare 4, the NWADMIN utility will create a subdirectory off of the root of the volume chosen (which can be other than SYS: now!) and call it QUEUES. This is where the data will be stored for the queue.

At this point, you can choose to define other queue properties (which will be brought up in a dialog box) or let NetWare create the queue and allow you to create another. For our example, let's click the Define Additional Properties check box, then click on Create.

Data added to the Print Queue Identification page (such as Other Name and Location) can be useful when searching for queues under NWADMIN. This allows the user to find a queue based on unique information entered here, but the additional data is purely optional (see Figure 8.10 and Table 8.2).

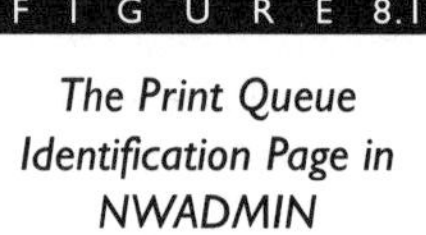

FIGURE 8.10

The Print Queue Identification Page in NWADMIN

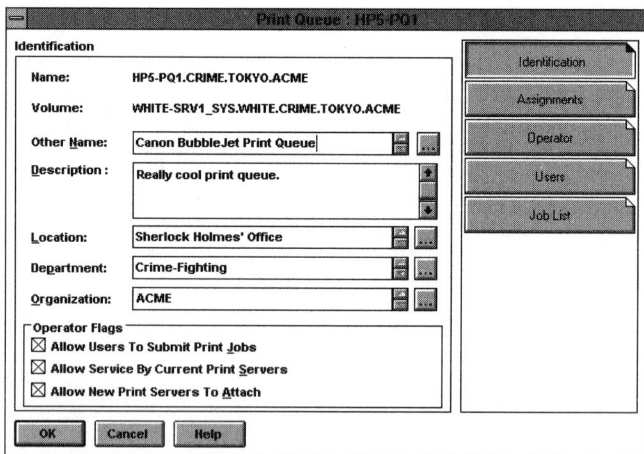

T A B L E   8.2

Additional Print Queue Pages

PRINT QUEUE PAGE	DESCRIPTION
Assignments	The Assignments page is a view-only screen used to show which printer(s) the queue is servicing and which print server is servicing this queue.
Operator	The Operator page contains some of the most important information for the queue. Print queue operators can do several valuable management items, such as: • Create new jobs in the queue • Delete jobs submitted by other users • Affect the availability of the queue • Place holds on their own submitted jobs • Place holds on jobs submitted by other users • Grant access to other users to use the queue By default, the user that created the queue is the queue operator. You can add other users if necessary.
Users	The Print Queue Users page is the most important item for the queue because it is where you designate who may use the queue (that is, who may submit jobs via CAPTURE or through Windows). By default, anyone in the container where the queue was created as well as any containers below this container may submit print jobs to this queue. To limit this, you can assign other objects such as Groups, Organizational Roles, or specific users the ability to submit print jobs to the queue.
Job List	Job List is a management function available to users and operators alike. It allows a user to view the current jobs in the queue as well as change details about the job. If you are a print queue operator, you can change aspects of jobs submitted by other users in addition to your own. To do this, highlight the job you wish to change and click on Job Details. If the job is not actively being serviced, you can change aspects of the job such as number of copies, form feed after print, and so on. A print queue operator can change the priority of a job by changing its *sequence number*. For example, changing a job from sequence 3 to sequence 1 bumps the first job to sequence 2, 3 to 4, and so on. More of this function will be covered in the section "NetWare 4 Printing Management."

STEP 2: CREATE THE PRINTER

The next step is to create a printer that will be serviced by the queue. Creating the printer is similar to creating the queue. Choose the container where the printer will be stored by selecting it with your mouse and pressing Insert (or choosing Create from the Object option on the toolbar). Choose Printer and give it a descriptive name. Click on Define Additional Properties and choose Create.

TIP

You don't have to create the printer, print server, and queue in the same container. You can locate them in three different areas and then associate them. For our example, it is easier to create them all in the same container.

You can use the Printer Identification page to provide information that NDS can use for searches as well as to provide more descriptive information for users and other administrators. Check out Figure 8.11 and Table 8.3.

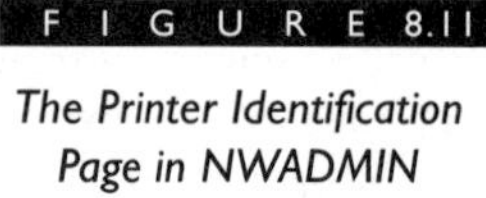

The Printer Identification Page in NWADMIN

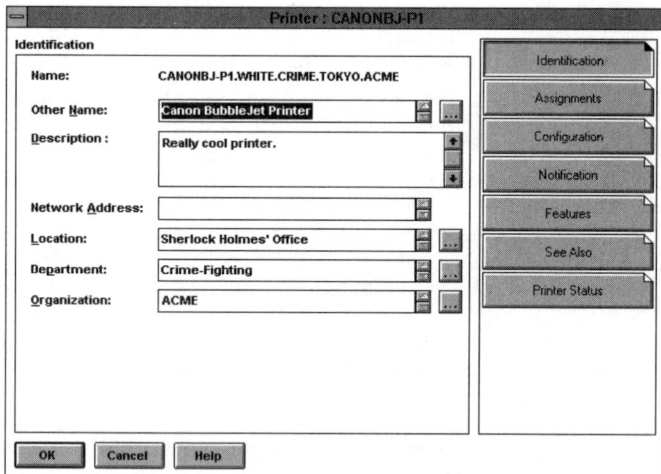

T A B L E 8.3

Additional Printer Pages

PRINTER PAGE	DESCRIPTION
Assignments	This page is where you tell the printer which queue(s) it will be servicing. You may have one printer that services multiple queues or multiple printers servicing one queue. If you have more than one queue per printer, you can assign a *priority,* the highest being 1. Any jobs submitted to a higher-priority queue will get serviced before any waiting jobs in a lower-priority queue (see Figure 8.12).
	The default queue is used when a user chooses to capture to the network by using a printer name instead of a queue name. When you choose a printer name, the job will be sent to the default queue.
	For this option, choose the queue that you just created.
Configuration	This option determines whether the printer is physically attached to the print server or remotely attached to a workstation.
	The first option, Printer Type, determines what kind of printer this is. Typically, it is either serial or parallel. The other options (such as AppleTalk and XNP) are configured and used with additional software.
	The Communication option specifies the local port that will be used. If the printer is polled, it will be sent printer output in a polled fashion instead of using interrupts to control print flow. Manual Load indicates that the remote printer software (NPRINTER.EXE) will be loaded instead of the local NPRINTER.NLM. If you choose Auto Load, the print server will know to load the NPRINTER.NLM at the server to service a locally attached printer.
	Another security feature of remote printers is the ability to limit the network address that the remote printer can use. This way, only the allowed address can load NPRINTER.EXE and support the print server as a remotely defined printer.
Notification	The Notification page is where you determine who will be notified in the event the printer has a problem. This is different than notifying the user when the print job submitted is complete.
	The default user is whoever submitted the print job. In a small office, this setting works just fine, but in a larger network, this setting is usually deleted and an IS group or person is added instead. This makes servicing the printer (for example, when it is out of paper) the job of such a person.
	You can also specify how often (in minutes) the person gets notified. First indicates how long before the first message is sent, and Next is the interval at which subsequent messages will be sent.

(continued)

T A B L E 8.3

Additional Printer Pages
(continued)

PRINTER PAGE	DESCRIPTION
Features	This page allows more descriptive data to be placed in NDS, which allows for better searching. For example, a user/administrator could search for printers supporting PCL with 4 MB memory and a fax card. This search could occur network-wide or could be limited to a subarea of the directory tree.

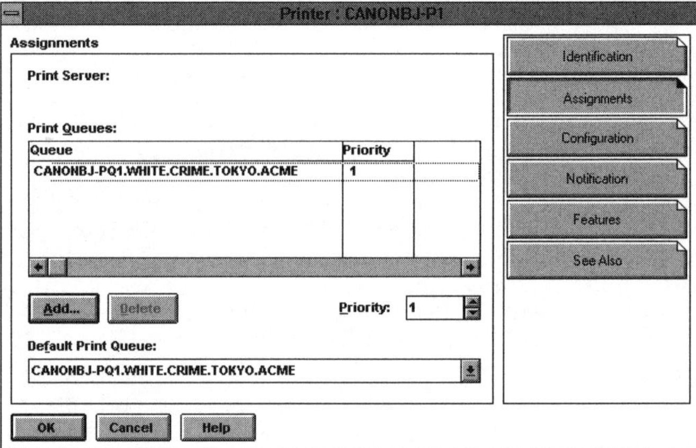

F I G U R E 8.12

The Printer Assignments Page in NWADMIN

REAL WORLD

The Printer Configuration page in NWADMIN is where you configure options for third-party printer support such as HP JetDirect cards or Intel's Netport. These devices can act either as a remote printer or as a print server to a NetWare server. Older versions of these products may only be used as remote printers and not as print servers in a NetWare 4 environment.

STEP 3: CREATE THE PRINT SERVER

To create a print server, use the NWADMIN utility. Select the container that will store the print server and press Insert while the container is highlighted. Choose Print Server off of the list and then choose OK.

First, you need to give the print server a name. Once again, descriptive names work best (such as WHITE-PS1). This will help you search for print servers later.

After entering the name, click on the Define Additional Properties check box and choose Create. The Print Server Identification page will appear (see Figure 8.13). Table 8.4 lists the basic information you will need to provide to complete print server creation.

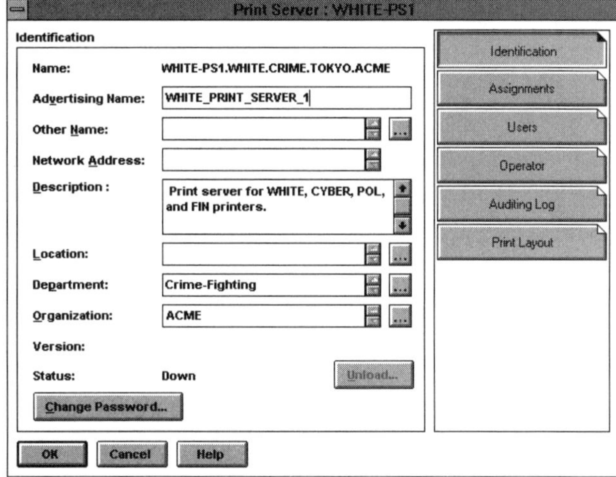

F I G U R E 8.13

The Print Server Identification Page in NWADMIN

T A B L E 8.4

Additional Print Server Pages

PRINTER	DESCRIPTION
Assignments	This page allows you to tell the print server which printers it will be servicing. Note that it may support several (up to 128) for one print server. Naturally, not all the printers can be attached physically to the print server. The rest would be attached remotely. Select the printer you just created by choosing Add (see Figure 8.14). The printer will be added with a *Printer Number*. Usually, this number is not be referenced on a day-to-day basis.
Users	Users information is not necessary for a user to print, even if this print server is servicing jobs in queues where the user has submitted a print job. This page is provided so that users can check the status of a print server using management utilities (such as NWADMIN). If the user never needs to do this (for example, if printer management is handled by IS), then the user doesn't need the print server user status. By default, all users in the container where the print server was created are given the print server user status.
Operator	Print server operators are similar to queue operators in that they can manage the print server. For example, print server operators may take printers off-line remotely, shut down the print server, and abort jobs in process.
Auditing Log	This page allows you to enable an auditing function for the print server. You can limit the size of the audit file as well as how many jobs it will keep in its auditing log. The file can be printed or it can be viewed under NWADMIN.
Print Layout	This is a very handy function in that you can graphically see the printing layout in one screen. This function works for all printers and queues associated with this print server. An additional function called Status allows the print server operator to view the status of all elements in the printing hierarchy. Simply select one of the printing components and click on Status. Figure 8.15 shows an example of the Print Server Status screen.

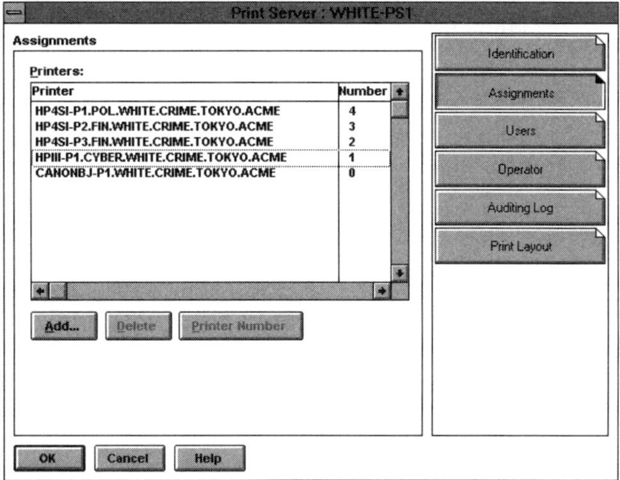

The Print Server Assignments Page in NWADMIN

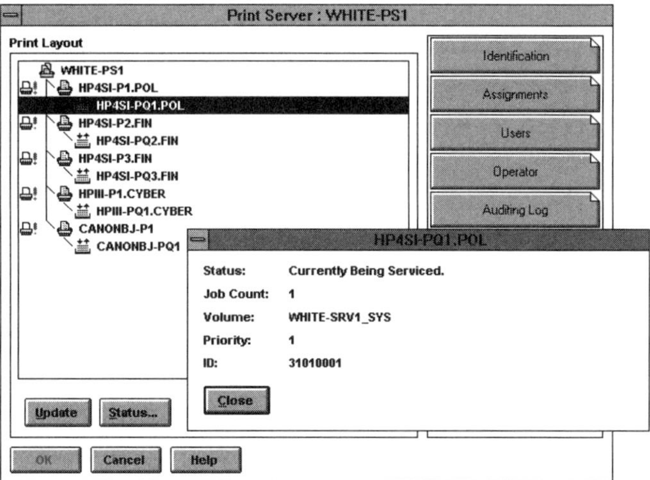

Monitoring Print Server Status in NWADMIN

When you create a print server, you should set a password for the print server for security reasons. You can set a password under the Print Server Creation screen by pressing the Change Password button. You will be asked for the password at server load time.

ZEN

"Danny bought me some lingerie for my birthday. It was so inappropriate. It's a good thing my mother's birthday was two days later or I'd still be stuck with the thing."

Nanny Fine

STEP 4: ACTIVATE THE PRINTING SYSTEM

Now that the configuration is set, the last step is to start the print server. This is done either at the server or remotely using RCONSOLE.

To start the print server, load PSERVER.NLM at the console by typing:

```
LOAD PSERVER
```

This will bring up the menu for PSERVER. It will show the context that the server is in within the directory tree. If you need to change where the print server is, you can either type in the new context or browse by pressing Enter. Selecting ".." moves up one level in the tree or you can select another container by choosing a container name and pressing Enter. Once you have found the print server, load it by highlighting it and pressing Enter.

Three things will happen:

1 • The print server will load. Any printers that are locally defined for this print server will be supported by NPRINTER.NLM. NPRINTER.NLM is loaded automatically if it is needed by local printers. The local printers will have a status of "Waiting for Jobs" once this is complete.

2 • Remote printers defined for this server will attempt to find a remote printer. If they cannot, they will wait for remote printer software to contact them (either NetWare's NPRINTER.EXE or a third-party solution such as HP's JetDirect card or Intel's Netport).

3 • The print server will ask for a password before loading. Passwords are desirable especially in larger networks. If you need to add or change a print server password, use NWADMIN and select the print server. PCONSOLE also allows you to change passwords as well.

The print server Main Menu provides you with two options: Printer Status and Print Server Information.

Printer Status

This option allows you to view the status of all printers defined for this print server (see Figure 8.16). You can also execute some printer management functions such as:

- ▸ Abort currently printing jobs

- ▸ Stop printer output

- ▸ Start printer output

- ▸ Eject a page (form feed)

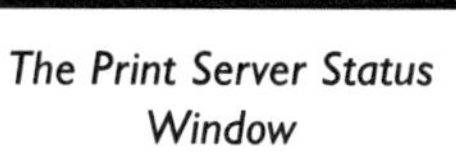

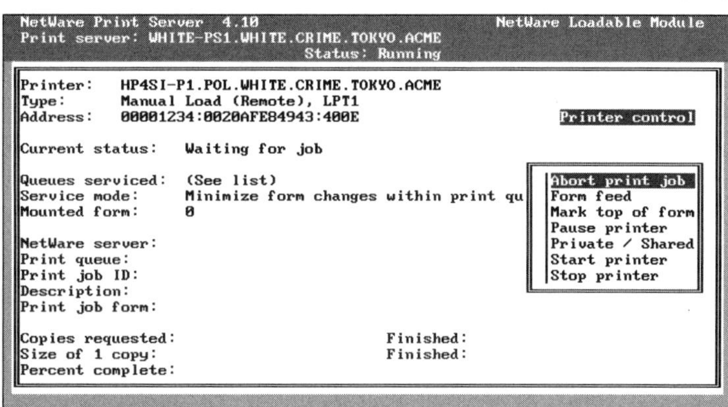

F I G U R E 8.16

The Print Server Status Window

In addition, you can change how forms (discussed later) get serviced on the selected printer. All of these functions can also be done via NWADMIN.

Print Server Information

The Print Server Information screen has two functions:

- ▸ Allows you to view print server information such as version and name

- ▸ Allows the print server to be shut down gracefully

Ideally, the print server should be shut down either remotely (via NWADMIN or PCONSOLE) or at the server using this option.

To shut down the print server, choose Current Status and press Enter. You can then shut down the print server in one of two ways:

1 • Immediately — With this option, any currently running jobs are suspended. They will continue when the print server is restarted.

2 • Unload after active print jobs — This allows any printing jobs to complete before the print server terminates.

In either case, the print server will advertise that it is no longer available and then terminate. Let's take a look at how changes to print servers take effect.

When you make the following changes, the print server must be unloaded and reloaded at the file server/router where the print server is running. This way, NetWare can read the new information and effect the changes:

Changes made directly to a print server:

- ▸ Assigned printers

- ▸ Passwords

Changes made to printers and queues assigned to a print server:

- ▸ Queue assignments

- ▸ Printer definition (parallel, serial, remote, or local)

- ▸ Forms servicing

- ▸ Notification of service alerts

Changes to the following take place immediately:

- ▸ Queue users

- ▸ Print server users

▸ Queue operators

▸ Print server operators

Understanding that some changes take place immediately and others take place after loading/reloading will help you avoid frustration when the print server appears to accept changes, but does not effect them immediately.

CUSTOMIZING NETWARE 4 PRINTING

Forms and devices add another dimension of printing for the NetWare printing system. You should be able to determine now if forms or device definitions are needed in your network.

The first step is to determine where in the tree the devices need to exist. If forms or devices do not exist in a particular context, the printing system will look into the next higher context until it finds a definition. This would allow an administrator to create forms and devices at the Organization level of the tree, and all users in the entire organization would benefit.

Users will always use the forms and devices in their own contexts if they exist. If they do exist within the context, then the users cannot see any others above their own context.

Creating forms and definitions can be done either under NWADMIN (graphically under Windows) or using the DOS menu command PRINTDEF. Once they have been created, you can assign forms or devices to users with either NWADMIN (under Windows) or PRINTCON (under DOS). This is accomplished by creating a print job configuration for the user or container.

Building Forms

1 • Choose the context where you wish the form or forms to exists. This could be at the [Root] or deep within the directory.

2 • Select the Organizational Unit (container) and click the right mouse button.

3 • Choose Details.

4 • Choose Printer Forms.

5 • Choose Create.

6 • Give the new form a descriptive name. Typically form 0 is the first form. Therefore, it should be the most commonly used form. This might be labeled BLANK or WORDPROC.

7 • The form number is used from the command line under CAPTURE, although CAPTURE can now use form names as well. Usually the form is referenced by name, not by number.

8 • Choose OK.

This will create the desired form within the selected context. The next step is to assign it to a user. This can be done two ways:

▸ Set up a *print job configuration*. This is a collection of printing attributes that the user can select by a given name. One of the attributes can be the form name used when submitting jobs.

▸ Select a form name when capturing a printer under NWUSER (Windows 3.1). This is usually chosen by the user before printing, as opposed to using a preset configuration such as print job configurations.

Creating print job configurations will be covered later (see the section "Tying It All Together").

Building Devices

Creating devices requires two steps:

▸ Step 1: Creating functions — These are printing specific. They include codes for things like Reset, Landscape, Portrait, Letter-size, Graphics mode and so on. To get these codes you must refer to the manual that came with your printer.

▸ Step 2: Creating modes — These are made up of one or more functions. They allow you to send a series of functions to the printer before your job prints. For example, you can

   ▸ Reset the printer

   ▸ Change to landscape

   ▸ Change to A4 format

Together, functions and modes constitute a *device* definition. The idea is that when you start to print to the network printer, NetWare will send these codes to the desired printer and properly initialize it for you.

TIP

As stated before, it is much more desirable to allow the application (such as WordPerfect) to send its own codes. If that is not possible, then NetWare can send them for you via this interface.

To create functions and modes, you must decide where you want them to be available. As with forms, you can create them once at the root of the tree and make them globally available, or deeper in the directory tree. Also as with forms, when looking for devices, NetWare looks in the current container, and, if none are found, it continues to look into superior containers until one is found. If none are found, no devices will be available.

REAL WORLD

NWUSER allows you to choose a form when capturing under Windows. However, NWUSER doesn't look into superior containers for other forms if none exist in the current context. Therefore, you may need to create a form in the users' context anyway, or change contexts.

To create a device, first choose the container where the device will be stored. As noted previously, this will have an impact on who will be able to see and use the device. Then create the device as follows:

1 • Click the right mouse button on the desired container.

2 • Choose Details.

3 • Choose Print Devices.

4 • Choose Create.

5 • Next, we need to create a device name (such as HP4SI). To do this, put in a name under Name and press Enter.

6 • Next, we'll need to create functions since modes are created from one or more functions. As a sample, we'll create a reset function. Choose Modify.

7 • Choose Create New Function (see Figure 8.17).

8 • First you need to give the function a name. This should be descriptive of the function. As described above, you can obtain the function codes from your printer manual. There are some codes that you cannot type in (such as ESCAPE). These codes are typed in within delimiters to tell NetWare that a special character is needed. For example, you can indicate ESCAPE in other ways:

    ▶ <ESC>

    ▶ <ESCAPE>

To represent a reset string of Escape E, you would represent it as <ESCAPE>E.

9 • Once you have created one or more functions, you can now create a mode. To create a mode, choose Create Mode. There is a default mode that is automatically created called *reinitialize*. This mode can be populated with the reset function (created earlier) for the print device you are defining. To add the reset function we just created, choose Add Above or Add Below.

TIP

Above and *Below* **will make a difference in how the mode works. Naturally, you would want to send a reset function before you send the function for Landscape. If the functions were reversed, it wouldn't do you any good (setting Landscape, then reset!). Add Above and Add Below allow you to place functions where they need to be in the mode list.**

10 • Be sure to give the mode a name. This should be descriptive of what the mode needs to do. In our case, the mode name Reset is perfect. You may also want to add the reset function to the predefined mode reinitialize.

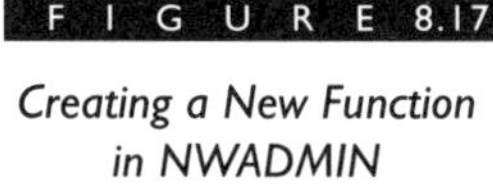

F I G U R E 8.17

Creating a New Function in NWADMIN

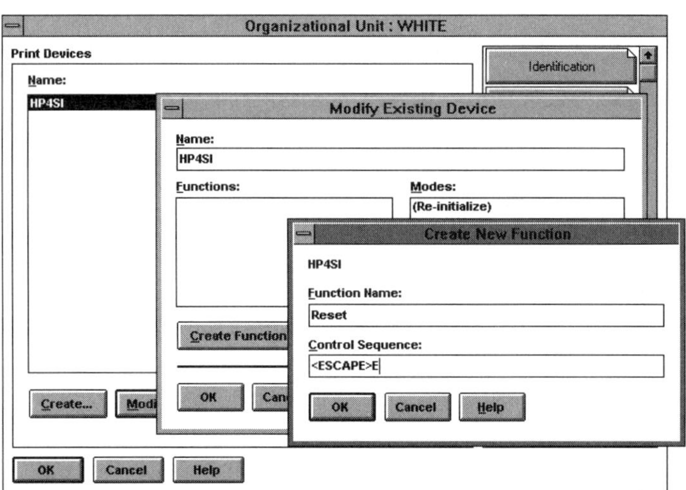

Importing Devices

A nice capability is importing predefined devices defined by someone else into the system. This does not include device drivers from application manufacturers. Only NetWare-defined devices can be imported (and exported).

An example might be where another administrator already went through the pain of creating a print driver for a new device. They can export that device (see the "Exporting Devices" section below) into a file that can then be imported into your system.

To do this follow these steps:

1 • Choose the container where you wish to import the device.

2 • Click the right mouse button and choose Details.

3 • Choose Print Devices.

4 • Choose Import.

5 • Under filename, type **Z:\PUBLIC** and press Enter (this step is shown in Figure 8.18).

TIP

Novell includes many predefined devices as examples for real applications. They are stored in SYS:PUBLIC during installation.

6 • Choose a device name, such as HPLJ4.PDF (PDF stands for Printer Definition File), then choose OK.

7 • The file will now be imported into NDS as a new device. To verify, check the modes and functions defined for this device.

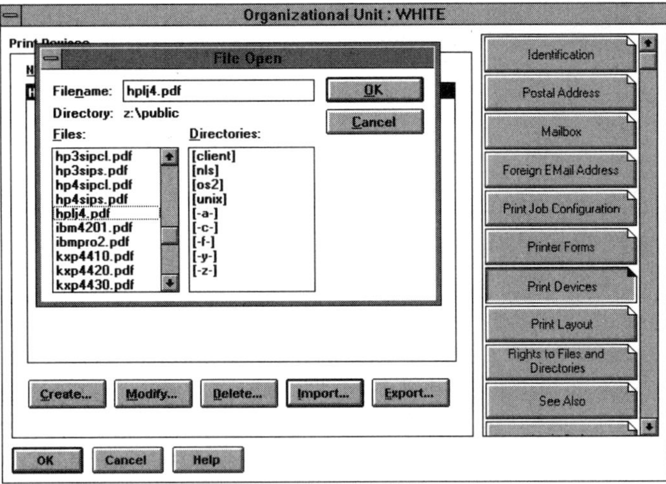

FIGURE 8.18

Importing Devices in NWADMIN

Remember that to utilize these forms and devices, you must create a print job configuration for a user and either make it a default for the user or allow the user to activate the configuration via a batch file or the command line.

Exporting Devices

This option is similar to import. The steps are as follows:

1 • Choose the container where the device exists.

2 • Open Details on the container.

3 • Choose Print Devices.

4 • Choose Export.

5 • Choose a filename and directory where you wish to store the exported device in the form of a file.

6 • Choose OK.

NWADMIN will then export all functions and modes for the device and store them in a file. At that point, you may copy it to a diskette, e-mail it, or otherwise make it available for other administrators.

QUIZ

Let's test your mystery-solving abilities. What English word can have four of its five letters removed and still retain the same pronunciation?

(Q8-2)

Tying It All Together

You now know how to create forms and devices, but how do you assign them to users? That is the next step. NetWare 4 has a method for integrating a series of printing options together into a named grouping of items. This is called a *print job configuration*. Print job configurations can be used in several ways:

- ▸ They can be created for a particular user.

- ▸ They can be created for a container. Then all users/objects in the container can use it.

- ▸ You can use a print job configuration defined for one user and assign it to another user in lieu of creating a duplicate configuration.

- ▸ You can make a print job configuration *default*. This means if the user issues a CAPTURE command (under a login script or command line), then the items defined in the job will take effect.

To create a print job (either for a user or a container):

1 • Choose the item in NWADMIN and select Details.

2 • Choose Print Job Configuration.

3 • Choose New.

4 • Give the job a name.

5 • You must choose a print queue for this job. Other options (for example, banners, copies, and form feed) are at the discretion of the creator. You can also assign a device, mode, and form (if they are created and within the scope of the configuration being created (see Figure 8.19).

6 • Choose OK

FIGURE 8.19

Creating Print Job Configurations in NWADMIN

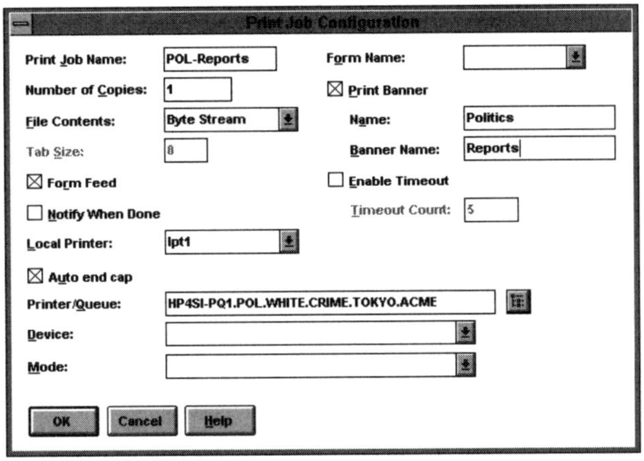

After creating the print job configuration, you can now optionally make it a default. For obvious reasons, there can be only one default. You can make other configurations the default if you wish.

To use a configuration other than the default, use the /J option with the CAPTURE command at the command line (or when using CAPTURE in a login script).

To select the default, highlight the configuration desired and click on Default. You should see a small printer icon next to the chosen configuration.

Congratulations! You've passed the first test. You successfully set up NetWare 4 printing. Now comes the fun part — keeping it running. This is the *real* mystery of life.

NetWare 4 Printing Management

NetWare 4 printing setup was a breeze. And now the system is working flawlessly. You've tested a few documents, and they printed fine. You're probably getting a little overconfident right about now. Be careful, it happens to the best of us.

Now for the real test — letting the users loose on your new, clean, "working" printing system. You know it can print in a vacuum, but what about in a war zone? Welcome to NetWare 4 printing management. In this section, we will explore five key management responsibilities, and learn about five key printing management tools. They are:

- ▸ Managing printing with PCONSOLE

- ▸ Managing printing with NWADMIN

- ▸ Configuring print jobs with PRINTCON

- ▸ Customizing printing with PRINTDEF

- ▸ Printing with NETUSER

With the release of NetWare 4, many of the DOS-based administration utilities that have been around since the beginning of NetWare were replaced by new utilities that support NDS. Even though the new NDS utilities have the same C-worthy look and feel, most of them have changed entirely — much to the dismay of some of us old NetWare junkies! Fortunately for those who prefer to work under DOS, the DOS-based printing utilities under NetWare 4 survived the cut with a few minor changes.

This section describes how NetWare print services can be managed in a distributed environment. We'll also cover some common printing issues and how to resolve them.

The main areas that can be managed are shown in Table 8.5. Let's take a look.

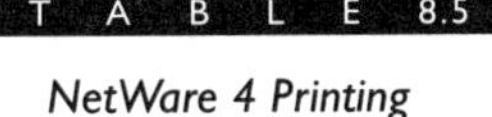

T A B L E 8.5

*NetWare 4 Printing
Management
Components*

COMPONENT	HOW YOU CAN MANAGE THIS COMPONENT
Print Servers	If you are a print server operator, you can: • Unload the print server • View auditing records
Queues	For queue operators and users, the queue allows for great flexibility in what can be seen and changed remotely (under NWADMIN and PCONSOLE). For example, you can: • Delete a job (NWADMIN and PCONSOLE) • Create a job (PCONSOLE) • Suspend a queue from receiving new jobs (NWADMIN and PCONSOLE) • Suspend servicing of jobs (NWADMIN and PCONSOLE) • Place an operator hold on a job (NWADMIN and PCONSOLE) • Place a user hold on a job (NWADMIN and PCONSOLE)
Printers	For printers, you can: • View how much of a job has been completed (NWADMIN and PCONSOLE) • Mount a new form (NWADMIN and PCONSOLE) • Pause and restart a printer (NWADMIN and PCONSOLE) • Abort a currently printing job

Most of the same general-purpose utilities that you used to create print services are the same ones that you will use for management. Table 8.6 summarizes these utilities.

T A B L E 8.6	TOOL	FUNCTION
NetWare 4 Printing Management Tools	NWADMIN	Used to do most print system component management. This includes: • Deleting jobs • Changing mounted forms • Stopping and starting printers • Checking the status of jobs in the queue • Placing holds on jobs • Aborting currently printing jobs
	PCONSOLE	This is a DOS/menu utility and encompasses most of the queue and print server creation and management functions. These include: • Deleting jobs from a queue • Submitting a new job (not possible under NWADMIN) • Placing holds on a job • Stopping and starting printers • Aborting currently printing jobs

For the most part, users are more interested in getting information about jobs than they are in completing particular tasks. Most of the time, users need to know when a job will complete or if the printer is available. They might need to delete a submitted job, but otherwise, they probably don't need to be able to do too many things to a printer or print job. The double-X's in Table 8.7 show the minimum rights needed to complete certain tasks.

T A B L E   8.7

NetWare 4 Printing Management Administrators

FUNCTION	QUEUE OPERATOR	QUEUE USER	PRINT SERVER OPERATOR	PRINT SERVER USER
Delete a submitted job (personal)		XX		
Delete another user's jobs	XX			
Create a new job		XX		
Prevent users from submitting jobs to a queue	XX			
Suspend servicing of print jobs	XX			
Abort a printing job on a printer			XX	
Stop a printer			XX	
Restart a printer			XX	
Mount a new form for a printer			XX	
Check printer status			XX	
Place a user hold on a job (personal)		XX		
Place an operator hold on a job	XX			
Check printer status				XX
Check percentage of the job printed				XX

Now that you've got your battle plan, let's arm you with some powerful printing management weapons. Starting with the strongest of them all — PCONSOLE.

ZEN

"Men can't be rushed. They're like children. You cook them too fast, they get tough. Whereas, you take your time, let them simmer for a while, they fall apart in your hands."

Nanny Fine

MANAGING PRINTING WITH PCONSOLE

PCONSOLE is the general of printing utilities. NetWare 4's print console allows for the configuration and administration of NDS printing objects. Let's take a look at the PCONSOLE main menu (see Figure 8.20).

F I G U R E 8.20

PCONSOLE Main Menu

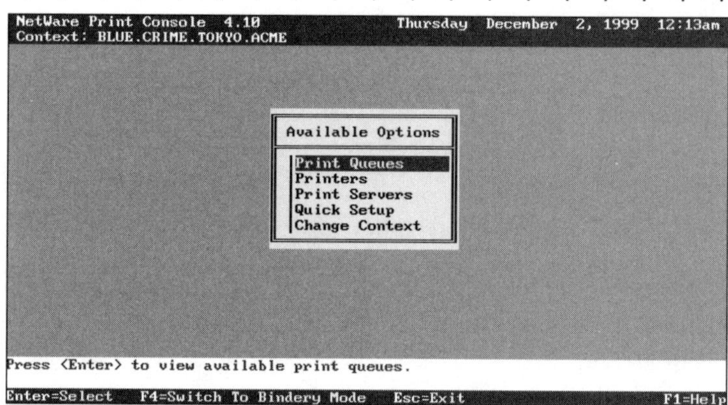

Before we begin exploring the PCONSOLE menu options, you need to be aware of a few important things about PCONSOLE. First, notice the top of the screen. In addition to the version of PCONSOLE that is running and the date and time, you will see your current context. This is very important because any menu option we choose at this point will affect this context only. For example, if we were to choose Print Queues, we would see the print queues configured in the current context only. A common mistake when using PCONSOLE is to be in the wrong context, then select one of the menu items and find yourself wondering, "What happened to all of my printing objects?" So, before beginning your printing administration, be sure you are in the proper context.

The default PCONSOLE context will be whatever context you were in when you ran PCONSOLE.EXE. Generally, this will be the context you were placed in at login. If your current context isn't correct, you can use the Change Context option to move to the proper context. Let's do that now. When you select Change Context you are prompted to either type the context you desire, or to use the Insert key to browse for the desired context. Using the Insert key is the easiest, most foolproof method since it eliminates any guessing. When you press Insert, you will be presented with the container object below your current context.

By selecting the Organizational Unit, you can move deeper in the tree. Just like in a DOS file system directory structure, the two dots indicate "parent," so, if you press Enter at the two dots, you'll move up the tree to the parent container. When you have finished browsing for the desired context, press F10 or Esc to save the new context.

The second important item to notice on the PCONSOLE main menu is the menu bar at the bottom of the screen. Most of the options are self-explanatory: press Enter to select, F10 or Esc to exit, F1 for help — but the one you should pay close attention to is F4=Switch To Bindery Mode. This option is a toggle switch. By pressing F4, PCONSOLE will change the display from NDS objects to Bindery objects. This option is normally used when you are logged into a bindery-based NetWare server (that is, NetWare 3 or NetWare 2). It can also be used if you are logged in as a user who is in the bindery context of the server to which you are authenticated. If you are not, when you press F4, you will receive a bindery context error message.

This option is useful in a mixed NetWare 3 and NetWare 4 environment because it allows you to toggle back and forth between NDS and bindery, and easily manage network printing in both environments.

Using Quick Setup

Before we get into the details of PCONSOLE, let's take a look at the best part of the utility — Quick Setup. One of the most frustrating parts of configuring network printing is trying to remember the next step in the process. Administrators frequently create all of the necessary printing objects correctly but miss one step in the process of linking print queues to printers and printers to print servers. The result: hours of trying to figure out why jobs go to the print queue but never print.

Quick Setup allows you to set up a print server, printer, and print queue very quickly (hence the name), making all of the necessary assignments for you. This option is great for the administrator who doesn't like to hop back and forth between menus, trying to remember the next step in the print setup process.

If you choose Quick Setup from a context that does not have print services configured, the system will present you with default print object names as shown in Figure 8.21.

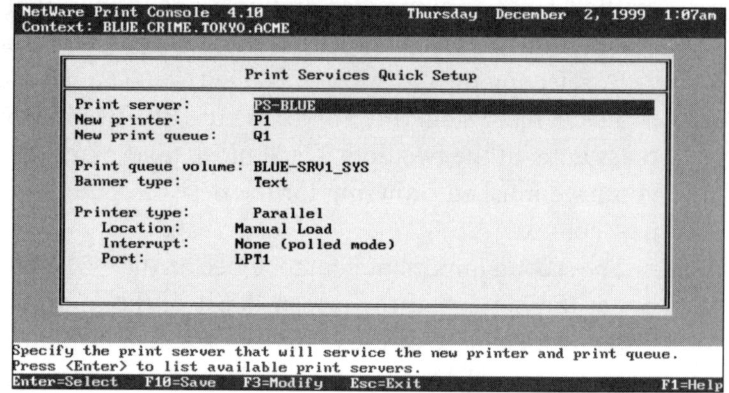

F I G U R E 8.21

The Print Services Quick Setup Screen in PCONSOLE

Print servers will be named PS-*<Container Name>*, the first printer will be named P1, and the first print queue will be named Q1. These defaults can be changed as necessary to match the naming standards of your organization.

Default assumptions will also be made about the print queue volume, banner type, and printer configuration. These defaults can also be changed as necessary.

To change the printer configuration, arrow down to Printer type and press Enter. Select the appropriate printer type — Parallel, Serial, or other printer type — and press Enter. You will also need to specify whether this printer is an Auto Load printer (directly attached to the print server) or a Manual Load (workstation or network attached).

Generally, the Interrupt field can be left at the default of None (polled mode). If you choose to use an interrupt method, this field can be configured to indicate the interrupt of the port hardware. This field must match the port hardware if an interrupt is used. The Port field must match the port that this printer is physically attached to — LPT1, LPT2, and so on.

Quick Setup is the foolproof method for configuring NetWare 4 printing. Unfortunately, this option is only available in PCONSOLE, not NWADMIN. So, for those of you who are die-hard GUI administrators, if you find yourself caught in a DOS utility, this is the easiest way to set up NetWare 4 printing.

Quick Setup is not the only way to create printing objects in PCONSOLE — it's just the easiest! The objects can also be created using the individual Print Queues, Printers, and Print Servers options from the PCONSOLE main menu as described in the following sections.

Managing Print Queues

By selecting the Print Queues option from the PCONSOLE main menu, you are shown a list of print queues currently configured in the current context. By pressing Insert, a new print queue can be created. When creating a new print queue, you will be asked for two pieces of information: print queue name and print queue volume.

The name assigned to a print queue can be any hexadecimal name from 1 to 64 characters, including spaces and underscores. Even though this gives you tremendous flexibility, it is recommended that you keep your print queue names short and descriptive. For example, a print queue that is serviced by an HPIII LaserJet printer might be named HPIII-PQ1.

The second piece of information that will be required when creating a new print queue is the print queue volume. This is the volume where the print jobs sent to this queue will be spooled. Since the volume name entered here must be the full NDS name of the volume, use the Insert key to browse the tree to find the appropriate volume. When you have found the volume on which you want to create this queue, press Enter or F10 to accept your selection.

Remember, before any new print queue created can be used, all of the proper printing assignments must be made, including assigning a print server to service this queue and attaching a printer. This process is described below.

By selecting Print Queues from the PCONSOLE Available Options menu, you can also manage existing NDS print queues. The left side of Figure 8.22 shows the print queues configured in the context .BLUE.CRIME.TOKYO.ACME.

F I G U R E 8.22

*The Print Queue
Information Screen in
PCONSOLE*

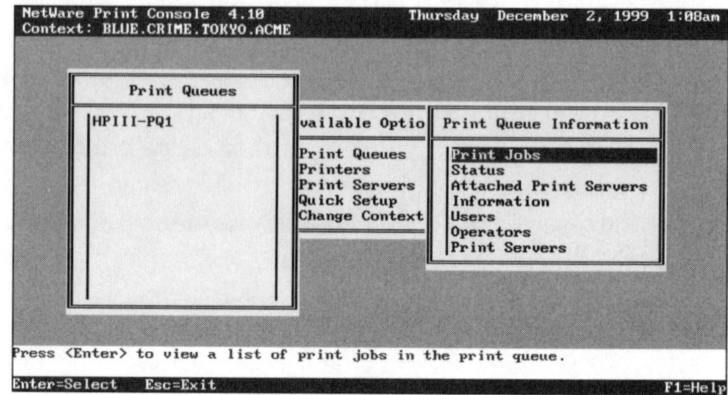

When you select an available print queue, you will see the available information about this print queue displayed on the right side of the screen (see Figure 8.22). Table 8.8 summarizes the information found in each menu option listed.

T A B L E 8.8

*Print Queue Information
Parameters*

MENU OPTION	PURPOSE
Print Jobs	Allows you to view the current print jobs in this queue. Also allows a print queue operator to delete jobs from the queue, reorder jobs in the queue and put an operator hold on the jobs in the queue. Regular users (non-operators) can only modify jobs that they have submitted.
Status	Allows you to view the status of this print queue, including number of jobs, number of print servers servicing this queue, and operator flags.
Attached Print Servers	Shows a list of active print servers servicing this print queue. The print server must be loaded in order to be active.

	MENU OPTION	PURPOSE
T A B L E 8.8 *Print Queue Information Parameters*	Information	Allows you to view the print queue identification number, and the server and volume in which this queue is created. The print queue ID number is the subdirectory name of this print queue plus a .QDR extension. This subdirectory will be in the QUEUES directory of the indicated volume.
	Users	Shows a list of users and groups who are authorized to submit jobs to this queue. Also allows you to add new users.
	Operators	Shows a list of users and groups who are authorized to manage this queue. Also allows you to add new operators.
	Print Servers	Allows you to view the print servers authorized to service this queue. Also allows you to authorize additional print servers to service this queue.

Viewing Jobs in a Print Queue

By selecting Print Jobs from the Print Queue Information menu, you can see all of the print jobs in this queue waiting to be serviced. Print queue operators will be shown all jobs in the queue. Regular users, or non-operators of the queue, will only be shown the jobs that they submitted. By selecting a specific print job, you will see information about that job, as shown in Figure 8.23.

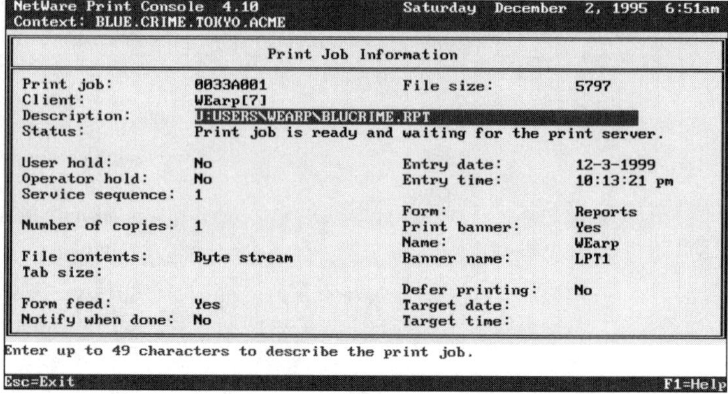

FIGURE 8.23

The Print Job Information Screen in PCONSOLE

This screen shows the print job ID number, who submitted the job, the filename, and the status of the job. This screen also allows a user or operator hold to be placed on the job. If the job is placed on hold, it will stay in the queue until the hold is removed.

The "Service sequence" field allows you to reorder jobs in the queue. In our example, there is only one job currently in the queue, so the service sequence is 1 — indicating that this job is next in line to be serviced by the print server. If there were jobs in the queue ahead of this one, we could change the service sequence number, thereby moving it up in the queue. Only print queue operators can place one user's job ahead of another's. Users can only reorder their own jobs.

If you look closely at the remaining options, you'll notice that these are all of the parameters used with CAPTURE. So, if you send a print job with CAPTURE parameters and would like to change the parameters after the job is sent, you can do that here.

The last option on this screen is "Defer printing." If this option is set to Yes, you will be able to specify the date and time at which you would like this job to print. This option is useful if you are printing large jobs that you would like to defer until a later, less busy time.

Putting Print Queues on Hold

Using the Status option of the Print Queue Information menu, a print queue operator can put the selected print queue on hold. There are three hold options in this menu:

▶ Allow users to submit print jobs — When set to No, this option prevents users from placing additional jobs in the queue. Any jobs already in the queue will continue to be serviced by the print server. This is useful when you are planning to do maintenance on a printer, or if you are planning to change print queue definitions.

▶ Allow service by current print servers — This option, when set to No, will allow users to continue to place jobs in the queue, but those jobs will not be printed until this flag is removed. Again, this option is useful when doing printer or print server maintenance.

▶ Allow new print servers to attach — This option prevents new print servers from attaching to this queue.

Assigning Print Queue Users and Operators

The Users option of the PCONSOLE Print Queue Information menu allows you to authorize users and groups to place jobs in this queue. When you select this option, you are presented with a list of current print queue users. Use the Insert key to browse the tree and then authorize new users, groups, or containers as users of this print queue by highlighting an object and pressing F10. Multiple objects can be selected by using the F5 key to mark them and F10 to select. To remove print queue users, highlight the object in the user list and press Delete.

Assigning print queue operators is done is a similar fashion. Select the Operators menu option and use the Insert key to browse and F10 to select.

Attaching Print Servers to a Queue

To assign a print server to service a queue, select the Print Servers option from the Print Queue Information menu. You will be shown a list of the print servers currently assigned to service this queue. Use the Insert key to browse the NDS tree to find the print server you would like to service this queue. To add a print server to the list, highlight the server name and press F10 or Esc. Before the print server will actively service this queue, it must be loaded at a file server.

ZEN

"Big hair makes your hips look smaller."

Nanny Fine

Managing Printers

When you select the Printer option from the PCONSOLE main menu, you will be shown a list of print queues configured in the current context. Use the Insert key to create a new printer. When you create a printer in PCONSOLE, the only information you are asked for at this point is the printer name. This can be a little deceiving because additional steps are required to complete the printer setup.

Once the printer is created, you will need to select the printer by pressing Enter and configure it from the resulting Printer Configuration screen (shown in the background of the screen in Figure 8.24).

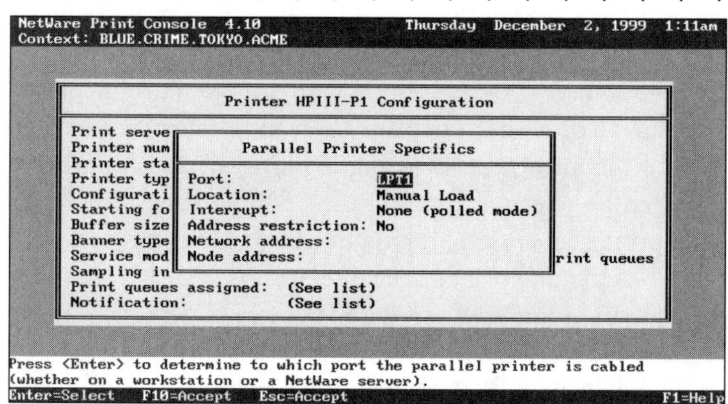

FIGURE 8.24

The Printer Configuration Screen in PCONSOLE

This default configuration assumes that you are configuring a parallel printer attached to LPT1 of a remote workstation. So, in order to complete the configuration, you will need to provide the following information if the default configuration is not correct.

- ▸ Printer type — Whether this printer is a parallel, serial, or other type of printer.

▸ Configuration — Which port this printer is attached to (LPT1, LPT2, and so on). The location of this printer [locally (directly) attached or remotely (workstation) attached].

▸ Interrupt — NetWare defaults to a polled mode when checking a print queue for new print jobs. If you choose to use an interrupt mode instead, this field can be configured to indicate the interrupt of the port hardware. This field must match the port hardware, if an interrupt is used.

▸ Address restriction — This optional field allows you to restrict this printer to being loaded on the specified workstation or network.

To complete the printer configuration, you must assign a print queue for this printer to service and link a print server.

To manage NDS printing objects with PCONSOLE, select the Printers option from the PCONSOLE main menu. This allows you to manage NDS printer objects in the current context. By selecting an available printer, you can see the current configuration of this printer (see Figure 8.25).

F I G U R E 8.25	NetWare Print Console 4.10 Thursday December 2, 1999 1:12am Context: BLUE.CRIME.TOKYO.ACME

Printer Configuration Screen for an HPIII LaserJet Printer

```
NetWare Print Console  4.10                    Thursday  December  2, 1999  1:12am
Context: BLUE.CRIME.TOKYO.ACME


                        Printer HPIII-P1 Configuration

       Print server:           BLUE-PS1
       Printer number:         0
       Printer status:         (See form)
       Printer type:           Parallel
       Configuration:          (See form)
       Starting form:          0
       Buffer size in KB:      3
       Banner type:            Text
       Service mode for forms: Minimize form changes within print queues
       Sampling interval:      5
       Print queues assigned:  (See list)
       Notification:           (See list)


 Specify the logical number (0-254, inclusive) assigned to this printer.

 Enter=Select    F10=Save    F8=Port Driver Name    Esc=Exit          F1=Help
```

Table 8.9 summarizes the information found in Figure 8.25.

T A B L E 8.9

Printer Configuration Parameters

PARAMETER	FUNCTION
Print server	Specifies the active print server currently servicing this printer.
Printer number	Displays the logical printer number assigned to this printer.
Printer status	Displays the status of this printer and the active print job. Also allows a print server operator to change the queue service mode, change the currently mounted form, and issue printer control commands.
Printer type	Displays the configured printer type. Available printer types include: parallel, serial, UNIX printer, AppleTalk printer, Other/Unknown, XNP, and AIO.
Configuration	Displays the configuration information about this printer, including port, location, and interrupt. For serial printers, this field also includes COM port configuration information such as baud rate, stop bits, data bits, and parity.
Starting form	Indicates the PRINTDEF form that the print server will assume is mounted on the printer when the print server starts.
Buffer size in KB	Indicates the size of the print server's internal buffer for this printer. Increasing this number may improve printer performance if the printer stops and restarts in the middle of a print job.
Banner type	Specifies the default banner type for this printer. Options are Text or Postscript.
Service mode for forms	Specifies how the print server will service jobs in the queue when forms are used.
Sampling interval	When the printer is idle, this number specifies how often, in seconds, that the print server will poll the queue assigned to this printer for new print jobs. When the printer is active the print server will automatically service the next job in the queue.
Print queues assigned	Allows you to view the print queues this printer is assigned to service. Also allows you to add new print queues to be serviced.
Notification	Displays the users and groups assigned to be notified if there is a problem with this printer. Also allows you to add users or groups to the notification list.

Assigning a Print Queue

Assigning a print queue to a printer can be done through the Printer Configuration screen as well. To do so, select the Print queues assigned option and press Enter. You can then use the Insert key to browse the directory tree for the print queue to which you would like to assign this printer. Once you have located the desired print queue, press Enter or F10 to select it.

When you assign a print queue to a printer, you can also set the priority level and default status of the queue. After you select the print queue, a Priority Configuration screen appears. The priority of this queue can be set to any number between 1 and 10, where Priority 1 is the highest and 10 is the lowest.

If this printer is servicing multiple queues, you can use the "Make this the default queue" option to define the default queue for this printer. When network users capture to this printer instead of a queue assigned to it, print jobs will be spooled to the default queue assigned here.

In the background you will see the priority this queue is set to and the state. As shown at the bottom of this screen, a printer's state can be one of the following:

- ▸ [A]: Active

- ▸ [C]: Configured

- ▸ [AC]: Active and configured

- ▸ [D]: Default

Using Forms

If you have defined print forms using NWADMIN or PRINTDEF, the Printers option under PCONSOLE will also allow you to configure how those forms are used. Referring back to the Printer Configuration screen (Figure 8.25), there are a number of areas that affect forms.

Under the "Printer status" option, there are two forms options. The first is "Service mode." This option determines how the printer will service the print queue when forms are being used. The next option is "Mounted form." This is the form that is currently mounted at this printer. You would use this option to change the currently mounted form through PCONSOLE. The currently mounted form can also be changed through NWADMIN.

The next option that affects forms from the Printer Configuration menu is "Starting form." This option defines the default starting form to be used when the printer starts up. This form number should represent the most commonly used form on this printer.

Finally, there is the "Service mode for forms" option. When you select this option, you are presented with the screen in Figure 8.26. Take a quick peek.

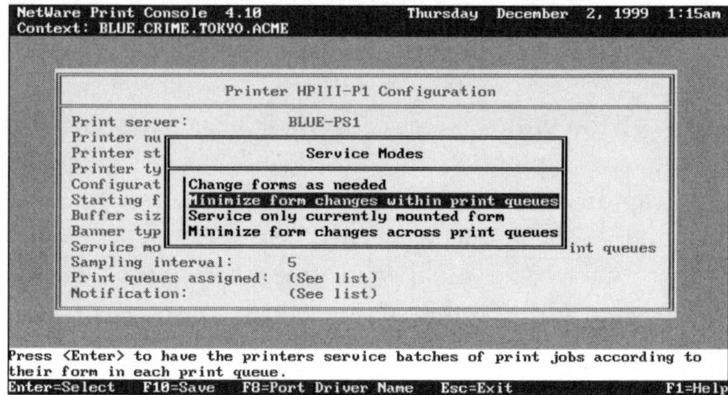

F I G U R E 8.26

Service Modes for Custom Forms in PCONSOLE

The first option, "Change forms as needed," requires you to mount a new form at this printer each time a print job with a different form number is submitted to the queue. The print jobs in the queue will be serviced based on priority (on a first-in, first-out basis). So, if many different form types are used, this option may require you to change forms often.

To minimize the number of times form changes occur, you may consider leaving the default ("Minimize form changes within print queues") enabled. With this option enabled, all of the print jobs with the same priority submitted to the queue with the currently mounted form requested will be serviced first. Lower priority jobs with a different form requested will require a form change before being serviced.

The next option, "Service only currently mounted form," will only service jobs submitted with the mounted form type. If this option is enabled, the print server will not prompt for a form change if a job with a different form type is submitted to the queue. These jobs will never be printed unless this option is changed to one of the other options above.

The final option on this menu, "Minimize form changes across print queues," is similar to the default option, except in this case, all jobs with the currently mounted form will be serviced first, regardless of priority.

ZEN

"If it ain't half off, it ain't on sale."

Nanny Fine

Managing Print Servers

When you select the Print Servers option from the PCONSOLE main menu, you are shown a list of print servers configured in the current context. When you press Insert, a prompt appears, at which you enter the print server name.

The print server can be any hexadecimal name from 1 to 64 characters, including spaces and underscores. Even though this gives you tremendous flexibility, you should keep your print server names short and descriptive. For example, the second print server created to service printers in the BLUE division might be named BLUE-PS2. When you press Enter to create the print server, a message appears on the screen indicating that it may take up to 60 seconds for the print server to be created. Though it rarely takes 60 seconds to create a new print server, this message is just to reassure you that the system is still working.

Once the print server is created, to complete the configuration you will need to assign this print server to service printers and print queues.

To manage NDS print servers with PCONSOLE, select the Print Servers option from the PCONSOLE main menu. By selecting Print Servers you can create new NDS print server objects or view existing print servers in the current context. The left side of Figure 8.27 shows the print servers configured in the current context.

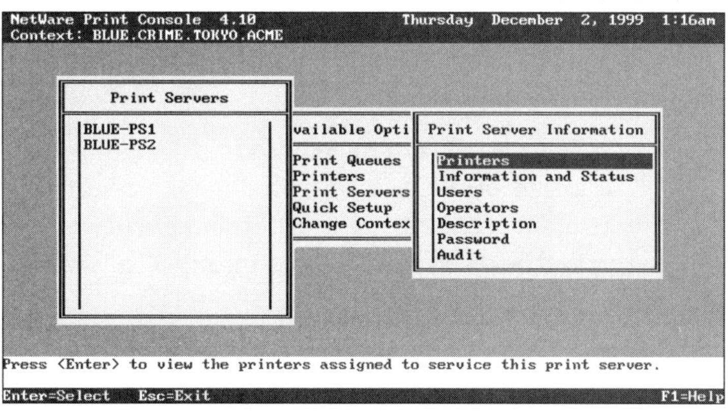

FIGURE 8.27

The Print Server Information Screen in PCONSOLE

After you select an available print server, all of the available information about that server will be displayed on the right side of the screen, as seen in Figure 8.27. Table 8.10 summarizes the information found in each menu option.

T A B L E 8.10	MENU OPTION	PURPOSE
Print Server Information Parameters	Printers	Displays the printers assigned to be serviced by this print server and their state. Also allows printers to be assigned or removed from this print server.
	Information and Status	Displays print server type, status, version, number of printers serviced, and advertising name. If the print server is running, this option also allows it to be taken down.
	Users	Displays users and groups who are authorized to view the print server's status and active configuration. Allows print server users to be added or removed.
	Operators	Displays users and groups who are authorized to manage the print server's status and active configuration. Allows print server operators to be added or removed.
	Description	Allows an optional text description to be entered for this print server.
	Password	Allows a print server password to be entered. This prevents unauthorized users from loading the print server.
	Audit	Allows you to view or modify this print server's auditing information.

Assigning Printers to Be Serviced

To assign printers to this print server, select Printers from the Print Server Information menu. A list of the printers currently being serviced by this print server will be displayed. Pressing Insert will allow you to browse the directory tree for the desired printer.

The Printers option will also show you the state of the attached printers. A printer's state can be one of the following:

- ▸ [A]: Active

- ▸ [C]: Configured

- ▸ [AC]: Active and configured

Selecting a configured printer from this screen will take you to the same Printer Configuration screen we saw when we were creating and configuring printers (see Figure 8.25). This is a nice shortcut when you are setting up printing services with this utility.

Assigning Print Server Users and Operators

Print server users are network users who have the ability to view the information and status of a print server. Print server operators have the ability to actually change that information. Selecting the Users option from the PCONSOLE Print Server Information menu allows you to authorize users and groups as print server users. You do not have to be a print server user to have print jobs routed by a particular print server, but you do to view its configuration and status. When you select the Users option, you will be presented with a list of current print server users. Use the Insert key to browse the tree for users, groups, or containers to be authorized as print server users. To select an object, highlight the object and press F10. Multiple objects can be selected by using the F5 key to mark them and then using F10 to select. To remove print server users, highlight the object in the user list and press Delete.

Assigning print server operators is done in a similar fashion. Select the Operators menu option and use the Insert key to browse and F10 to select. To remove a print server operator, use the Delete key.

Using the Auditing Feature

To keep track of printing transactions, print server auditing can be enabled. When auditing is enabled, information about each completed print job will be logged in an audit file called PSERVER.LOG. This log file can be viewed using PCONSOLE or NWADMIN. Also, because PSERVER.LOG is a text file, it can be viewed with any text editor.

To enable auditing or to view or delete the audit file for a particular print server, choose Audit from the Print Server Information menu. Figure 8.28 shows the resulting screen.

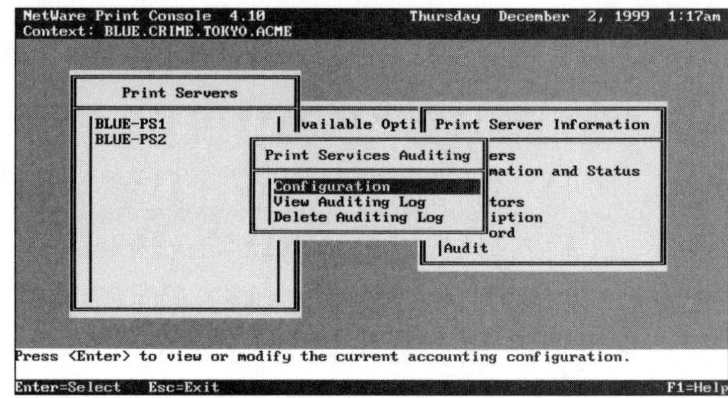

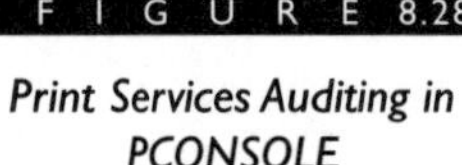

FIGURE 8.28

Print Services Auditing in PCONSOLE

To enable auditing, choose Configuration and set the Enable auditing field to Yes. When you enable auditing, you are given the option of limiting the size of the audit file. If you do not limit this file's size, it could grow to the maximum of the available disk space. To prevent the file from getting out of hand, you may want to limit its size. When the file size is limited, the print server will log entries until the maximum size is reached and then it will stop until the file is deleted or this field is changed.

Anytime a change is made in the Auditing Information screen, the print server will need to be taken down and restarted before the changes will take place.

QUIZ

To be a crack sleuth, you have to know your codes. Decode the following:

C V C C V C V!C V C   V C V C V C V C   V C
18 2 99 3 4 11 2   10 2 1515 1 2 2   15 5 22 2   15154 5   9920

C V C V C V C.
3 2 2 4 3 2 3

(Q8-3)

That completes our in-depth exploration of PCONSOLE. As you can see, it provides a lot of printing management punch. But for those of you who still prefer a GUI world, NWADMIN provides some printing management capabilities as well, albeit, not as many as PCONSOLE. Let's check it out.

MANAGING PRINTING WITH NWADMIN

Management under Windows is one of the easiest ways to track jobs and the status of print servers. NWADMIN and NWUSER are the main tools for doing this. Even though NWADMIN is primarily an administrator's tool, users can benefit from it as well.

Printing management under NWADMIN is broken into two sets of tasks:

- CNA tasks

- User tasks

Let's take a closer look.

CNA Tasks

As a manager of printers and queues, you will need to do several things:

- Mount new printer forms

- Stop/start printers

- Unload the print server

- Place a hold on a job

- Delete a job

Remember, you must be an operator (printer or queue) to carry out these management functions. Table 8.11 shows the steps required to accomplish these functions. This assumes you are already in NWADMIN and at the context where the objects resides.

T A B L E 8.11	TASK	STEPS INVOLVED
CNA Printing Tasks in NWADMIN	Mount new printer forms	1 • Choose the printer (highlight and double-click). 2 • Select Printer Status. 3 • Select Mount Form. 4 • Choose the form name (or number).
	Stop/start printers (see Figure 8.29)	1 • Choose the printer. 2 • Select Printer Status. 3 • Select Pause to stop or Start to resume printer output.
	Unload the print server	1 • Choose the print server. 2 • At the lower middle of the screen, choose Unload. 3 • Choose Immediately or After Jobs based on whether you wish current jobs to complete before the print server terminates.
	Place a hold on a job (see Figure 8.30)	1 • Select the queue that is servicing the job. 2 • Select Job List. 3 • Select Hold Job.
	Release a job hold	1 • Select the queue that is servicing the job. 2 • Select Job List. 3 • Select Resume.
	Delete a job	1 • Select the queue that is servicing the job. 2 • Select Job List. 3 • Highlight the specific job. 4 • Select Delete.

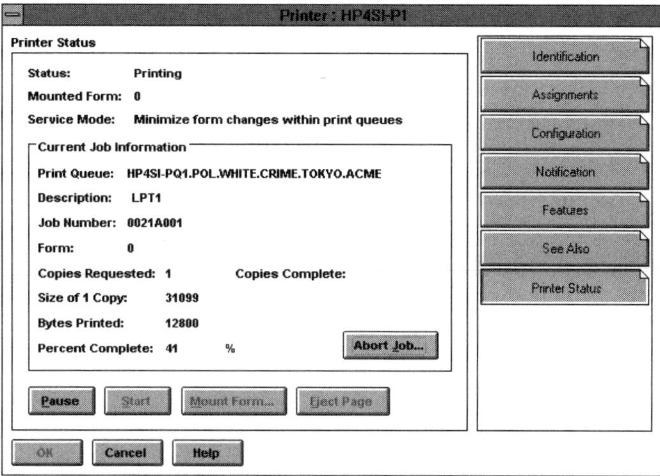

FIGURE 8.29

The Printer Status Screen in NWADMIN

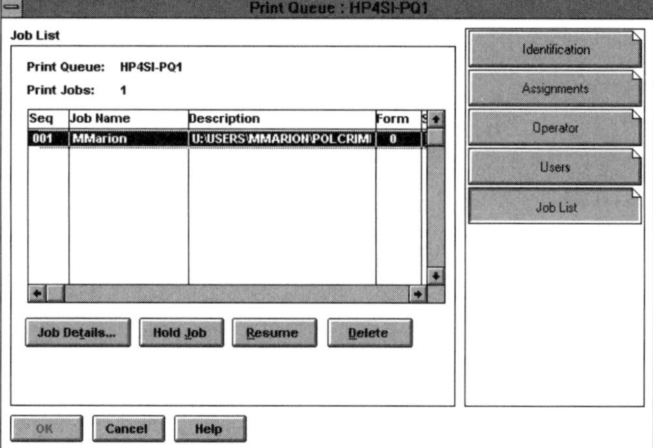

FIGURE 8.30

The Print Queue Job List Screen in NWADMIN

User Tasks

Some user management functions are similar to operator functions. Typically, they are basic view functions to check on the status of a job. These functions include:

- ▸ Viewing the status of a job in a queue

- ▸ Viewing the amount of job printed on a printer

▸ Deleting a job submitted

▸ Placing/releasing a user hold on the job

These functions require that you have at least user access on the print server or queue in question. Refer to Table 8.12 for a quick review.

TABLE 8.12	TASK	STEPS INVOLVED
User Printing Tasks in NWADMIN	View job status	1 • Select the queue that is servicing the job. 2 • Select Job List. 3 • Locate the job in question. 4 • Scroll right to view status (Active, Held, Ready).
	View percent completed	1 • Select the printer that is printing the job. 2 • Select Printer Status.
	Delete a job	1 • Select the queue that is servicing the job. 2 • Select Job List. 3 • Highlight the chosen job. 4 • Select Delete.
	Place/release a user hold (see Figure 8.31)	1 • Select the queue that is servicing the job. 2 • Select Job List. 3 • Select the job to hold/release. 4 • Select Hold Job to hold and Resume to release.

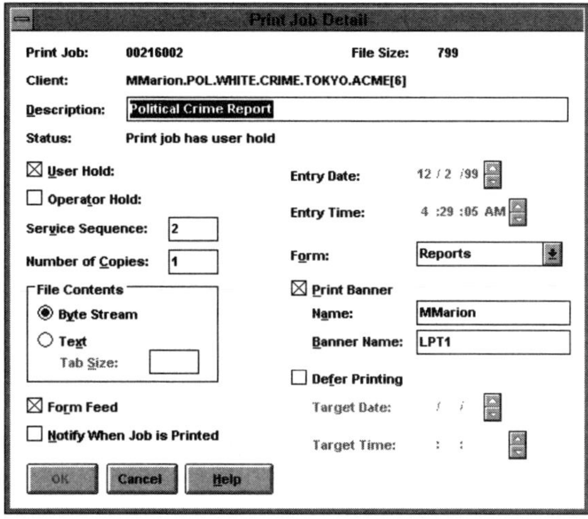

F I G U R E   8.31

*The Print Job Detail
Window in NWADMIN*

ZEN

*"Ma has plastic on the furniture. I think she's preserving it for the
afterlife!"*

Nanny Fine

That completes our discussion of general printing management with PCONSOLE
and NWADMIN. These two tools are the cornerstone of your arsenal. But you
never know when you might need a special utility. So, the next three topics deal
with less common printing management components — like print job configurations
and print forms customization. Ready, set, explore.

CONFIGURING PRINT JOBS WITH PRINTCON

Back in the days before NetWare supported Windows, the only way to capture
printers was with the CAPTURE command, either through a login script or a batch
file. To make this process easier, PRINTCON was used to create print job
configurations that consisted of common user CAPTURE statements. Then, rather
than having to enter long and cryptic CAPTURE statements, the CAPTURE
command was simply:

```
CAPTURE J=<job configuration>
```

Today, with the NWUSER Windows utility, we have an easier option: Just drag and drop to capture a printer once and select the Permanent option. But, even with this easier option, PRINTCON is still around for those who would like to use it. Figure 8.32 shows the PRINTCON main menu.

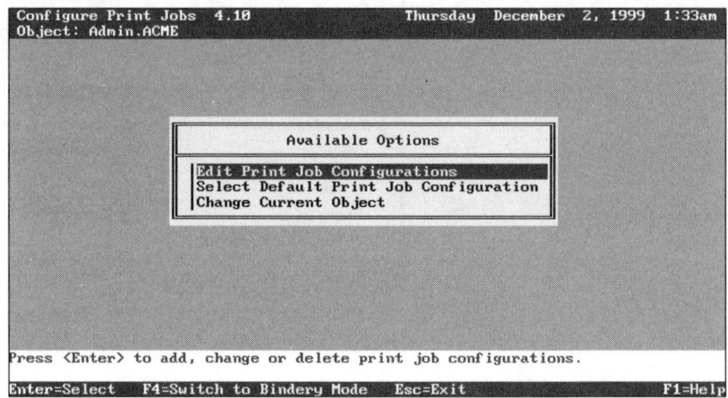

F I G U R E 8.32

PRINTCON Main Menu

CUSTOMIZING PRINT DEVICES AND FORMS WITH PRINTDEF

Now that everything is set up and running smoothly, we need to shift our printing focus to customization. These are the advanced tasks that separate NetWare 4 CNAs from pretenders. PRINTDEF is our friend. This DOS-based printing utility allows us to customize two important printing components:

- ▶ Print forms

- ▶ Print devices

Multiple print forms can be supported by attaching special instructions to specific print jobs. In addition, customized formatting is allowed with special print devices. All of this is accomplished using PRINTDEF.

The PRINTDEF utility is used to define and store printer definitions or command strings and printer form definitions. It's probably the least frequently used of all of the NetWare printing utilities, but it comes in handy when you have multiple paper types used on a single printer, or when you wish to exploit printer functionality that your application doesn't support. Let's take a look at the PRINTDEF main menu (see Figure 8.33).

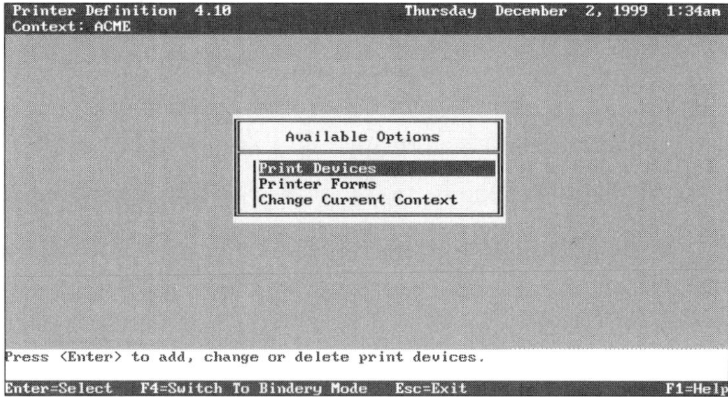

F I G U R E 8.33

PRINTDEF Main Menu

That pretty much finishes our journey through printing management LANd — otherwise know as the NetWare "war zone." The final utility deals with everyday, run-of-the-mill user printing. NETUSER is a pacifier for troublesome users. Use it or lose it (your mind, that is).

PRINTING WITH NETUSER

NWUSER makes network printing easier for Windows users, but what about DOS users? Are they limited to capturing from the DOS command line? Well, there is an option to simplify printing for the DOS user — NETUSER. Figure 8.34 shows the NETUSER main menu.

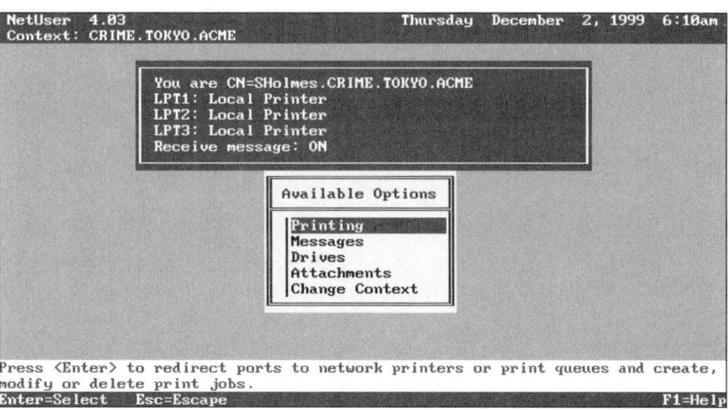

F I G U R E 8.34

NETUSER Main Menu

Just like with the other DOS utilities, it's important to note the context at the very top of the NETUSER screen. Anything done in NETUSER from this point on will be from the .WHITE.CRIME.TOKYO.ADMIN context.

You should also notice the box above the Available Options menu, indicating current user and capturing information. In Figure 8.34, we are currently logged in as Admin and LPT1 is captured to the queue servicing the Canon Bubble Jet.

Managing Print Jobs

When you select Printing from the Available Options menu, you are shown a list of the available LPT ports. If you select an LPT port, you are given two options: Print Jobs and Change Printers. Since we have already captured LPT1 to the CANONBJ-PQ1 queue, we can select the queue by pressing Enter and view a list of print jobs currently in the queue. If you select a print job, you are presented with the Printing Management menu.

Does this screen look familiar? It happens to be the same screen we saw when we selected a print job in PCONSOLE and also when we were setting up print job configurations in PRINTCON. The parameters shown here are the flags used with CAPTURE when the job was sent to the queue.

Capturing with NETUSER

To capture a printer port with NETUSER, under the Printers option, select the port you wish to capture and choose Change Printers. You are then presented with a list of printers and print queues in your current context.

To capture to a printer, use the arrow keys to highlight the printer you want (or the print queue assigned to it) and press Enter. Any capturing done through NETUSER will remain active during the current login session only. One disadvantage this utility has in comparison with its Windows counterpart is that there is no way to make the capturing permanent.

ZEN

"I just can't tame this darn charisma. Can I help it if I effervesce?"

Nanny Fine

That completes our discussion of NetWare 4's printing management tools. Wow, there's a lot to work with. We learned about PCONSOLE, NWADMIN, PRINTCON, PRINTDEF, and NETUSER. With all of these tools, it should be easy to keep NetWare printing running smoothly. It is. . . until someone tries to print something! That's when it gets a little out of hand.

I enjoy a good mystery, how about you? NetWare 4 printing is a great place to start. We discovered a lot of interesting things about it today, and I think you're definitely ready to attack it on your own. But if you're still feeling a little skittish, here's a quick review.

It all started with the essence of printing. In the old days, we used to print by ourselves. Now, we get to share this honor with hundreds of strangers. Network printing has probably had a major impact on the social fabric of humanity — we just don't notice it. We went on a little journey through the life of a print job — starting with CAPTURE, then to the queue, print server, and ultimately the printer. Wasn't that fun?

Then, we learned all the steps involved in printing setup. It's not so bad. There are only four steps and they're not very hard. First, you create the print queue, then the printer, and finally the print server. Then, to top it all off, you activate the print server. No sweat. We also discovered a few secrets about customizing NetWare 4 printing with print forms and devices.

Once it's up and running, the fun part starts — keeping it running. NetWare 4 printing management focused on five CNA and user tools, namely PCONSOLE, NWADMIN, PRINTCON, PRINTDEF, and NETUSER. We learned how to configure, manage, and customize the NetWare 4 printing system. I bet you didn't realize how much help there is out there! Don't worry — you're not alone.

ZEN

"I was thinking about the Pilgrims. How'd they know what to pack? I mean, you're going to a new world. Is it hot, . . . cold, . . . rainy? There are no brochures! So they all wear the same thing and what a mistake. Very few people look good in a big hat, a big collar, and a big buckle. What were they thinking?"

Nanny Fine

So, how do you feel now? A little better? Did all that wisdom from Nanny Fine soothe your brain? Well, if you're still a little worried about going out on your own, I have a surprise for you — exercises! You want practice, I've got practice. A bunch of hands-on exercises are just the cure for printing cold feet. Once you've cruised through the following six exercises, you'll be a printing pro. You'll be ready for anything. . . except a shopping spree with Nanny Fine — ouch!

ZEN

"All Good Things Must Come to An End!"

Q

Congratulations! You made it. Welcome to the next generation of NetWare 4. And more important, welcome to the end of this book. It's been a long and winding road, but we struggled through it together. We learned about NDS, the file system, security, the life span of a LAN, and printing. All in a day's work. Oh yeah... and we saved the world, too!

Oh, my goodness! Would you look at the time — where has it all gone? I've just been rambling away here. . . sorry, if you missed your train or something. I guess I'm done. There's not much more that can be said about life as a NetWare 4 CNA. But before you leave, let's take a quick moment to review our journey.

It's been quite a wild ride, and you should be very proud of yourself for surviving it in one piece — or so it seems. Do you still want to be a CNA? A NetWare 4 superhero? Good. Because the world needs a few good CNAs, and you're a great place to start. Speaking of starting. . . .

The journey began in Part I with a brief peek at "life as a CNA"! In this section, we learned about the reasons for becoming a CNA and acquired an appreciation for the tasks tackled each day by a CNA.

The journey really got rolling in Part II — "NetWare 4 Administration." It all started with a brief introduction of NetWare 4 and a detailed exploration of NetWare Directory Services (Chapter 3). In addition, we were introduced to ACME and learned about their plight — aka, saving the world! There's more to life as a NetWare 4 CNA than meets the eye.

In Chapter 4, we learned that the file system represents NetWare life *within* the server. All of our focus shifted to NetWare 4's big, electronic filing cabinet. Chapter 5 continued this journey with a look at security. Information is now the new commodity — more valuable than money. We need to take new measures to protect our information. We discovered NetWare 4's five-layered security model — login/ password authentication, login restrictions, NDS rights, file system access rights, and attributes. Think of it as your impenetrable network armor.

Once the LAN has been installed (born), it enters the second and third phases of its life span — configuration (childhood) and management (adulthood). In Chapter 6, the first of two related chapters, we walked through the five steps of configuration using Leia as an example. Then, in Chapter 7, we discovered the final phase of LAN life span — adulthood. Here your network got married, had children, planned for retirement, and finally retired. How about you?

In the final chapter, we ended the journey with NetWare 4 printing (Chapter 8). We learned that NetWare 4 printing is simple, and works great until... you add users. In Chapter 8, we explored some time-proven methods for successful NetWare 4 printing installation, management, and troubleshooting.

Well, that does it! The End... Finito... Kaput. Everything you wanted to know about the CNA but were afraid to ask. We hope you've had as much fun reading this book as we've had writing it. It's been a long and winding road — a life changer. Thanks for spending the last 800 pages with us, and we bid you a fond farewell in the only way we know how:

"See ya' later, alligator!"
"After a while, crocodile!"
"Hasta la vista, baby!"
"Live long and prosper!"
"So long and thanks for all the fish!"
"May the force be with you... "

EXERCISE 8-1: THE GREAT CHALLENGE WORD SEARCH

Circle the 20 printing terms hidden in this word search puzzle using the hints provided.

```
P  A  R  A  L  L  E  L  P  O  R  T  P  W  T  G  P  P  P
G  U  R  D  E  V  P  R  I  N  T  S  E  R  V  E  R  R  F
Y  T  L  F  Q  U  I  C  K  S  E  T  U  P  I  I  I  A  E
F  O  D  U  I  I  W  L  O  C  G  A  R  O  N  N  N  K  V
L  L  F  Y  I  W  F  F  K  N  M  X  R  T  T  N  T  C  T
O  O  L  I  H  L  T  J  L  M  S  O  J  Q  X  L  C  E  S
C  A  P  T  U  R  E  H  L  R  N  O  U  I  F  K  O  X  R
A  D  A  W  B  V  Q  Y  H  E  B  E  L  C  U  E  N  S  K
L  A  H  K  Z  K  T  G  U  A  U  Z  U  E  U  U  I  M  H
P  R  I  N  T  S  E  R  V  E  R  O  P  E  R  A  T  O  R
R  M  A  N  U  A  L  L  O  A  D  X  U  E  T  D  T  K  Y
I  B  U  D  M  P  P  P  D  L  R  Q  S  R  T  Z  X  M  D
N  A  V  C  Q  S  E  R  A  R  T  U  O  C  Y  X  U  S  F
T  J  L  B  O  R  L  C  I  N  W  X  Y  K  P  D  I  V  H
E  L  L  B  A  Y  P  R  I  N  T  D  R  I  V  E  R  X  U
R  X  Q  T  D  V  E  R  E  A  T  A  L  I  V  W  B  B  I
P  R  O  Z  D  L  P  O  L  L  E  D  M  O  D  E  P  G  P
R  R  X  H  S  W  D  P  S  E  R  V  E  R  N  L  M  L  D
E  A  G  X  T  P  E  Y  F  S  V  F  D  F  I  C  O  X  M
```

Hints:

1. Designation that indicates that a printer is directly connected to the print server.
2. Command line utility used to redirect DOS and OS/2 print jobs from applications designed to print to parallel ports.

3. Printer physically connected to the print server.

4. Designation that indicates that a printer is connected to a workstation, the network cable, or a server other than the print server.

5. Graphical utility running under MS Windows that can be used for printer redirection.

6. Type of port that typically provides better performance that a serial port.

7. Menu utility that can be used to set up the NetWare 4 printing environment.

8. Default NetWare 4 printer configuration option (where alternate choice is Interrupt mode).

9. Software that can be used to convert a print job into a format that can be used by a particular printer.

10. File stored in a print queue while waiting to be printed.

11. User or Group member who can edit the print jobs of other users, delete print jobs from the print queue, or modify the queue status.

12. Network directory used for storing print jobs.

13. User or Group member who has the rights needed to manage a print server.

14. Server used to direct print jobs from a print queue to a network printer.

15. Command line utility that can be used to create print job configurations for use with the CAPTURE, NETUSER, NPRINT, or PCONSOLE utilities.

16. Command line utility used to view, modify, import, or export print device definitions and create or modify printer forms.

17. A leaf object that represents a physical printing device on the network.

18. NLM used for loading print server software on a server.

19. Directory name extension used to indicate that a subdirectory is a NetWare print queue.

20. PCONSOLE option that provides a fast method for creating the initial printing environment.

See Appendix C for answers.

EXERCISE 8-2: NETWARE 4 CNA — THE GREAT CHALLENGE CROSSWORD

Across

2. Precedes print data to the printer
4. Print job has been placed on hold
6. Better than dot matrix
7. Used for printing multipart forms
11. Preferable application type
13. Connected directly to the print server
15. NetWare 3 print queue subdirectory
17. NetWare 4 RPRINTER equivalent
18. Cause of printing problems
20. Not attached to the network
21. Used for Autoload printers
22. NPRINTER loaded by print server

Down

1. Print job is ready to print
2. Language used for HP LaserJet printers
3. Print job is being printed
5. Only type of port that NetWare uses for printing
8. Transferring data from the computer to paper
9. Page Description Language for high quality printers
10. Computer containing print queues
11. Printing environment setup utility
12. NetWare 4 parent directory for print queues
14. Not directly connected to the print server
16. Follows print data to the printer
19. NetWare 4 context navigation tool
20. Typically used as communications port

See Appendix C for answers.

This exercise will walk you though the creation and loading of a basic print system using the NWADMIN (Windows) graphical interface. This assumes you have already created ACME's NDS tree. We'll be working in the Crime Fighting department today. Seems appropriate since we're trying to solve a mystery. Where's Sherlock Holmes when you need him?

For the exercise, we will assume the following names:

- *Print server*: WHITE-PS1

- *Print queue*: CANONBJ-PQ1

- *Printer*: CANONBJ-P1

First we will create the queue.

QUEUE CREATION

1. Select the container WHITE.CRIME.TOKYO.ACME with the mouse.
2. With the container WHITE selected, press Insert or choose Object/Create from the menu bar.
3. Choose Print Queue and click on OK.
4. Enter the queue name CANONBJ-PQ1.
5. Click on the browser button and select your server's volume SYS.
6. Click on the Define Additional Properties option.
7. For Other Name, type **MainQ**.
8. For Location, type **Downtown.**
9. Select Users.
10. Who is/are the existing queue users? Why?
11. Remove the allowed users and add yourself as the only queue user.
12. Select OK.
13. Go to a DOS box (under Windows). Type **DIR Q*.*** and notice what you see.

14. CD into the directory found. Count how many subdirectories exist with a
    QDR extension.

Next, we need to create the printer.

PRINTER CREATION

1. Return to NWADMIN.
2. Select the WHITE.CRIME.TOKYO.ACME container again.
3. Press Insert again (or Object/Create), and choose a printer this time.
4. Name the printer as noted above.
5. Click on Define Additional Properties and then on OK.
6. Under Other Name, type **Booking Printer**.
7. Click on Assignments.
8. Add the print queue just created.
9. Click on the Configuration button, then the Communication button, and
   choose the Auto Load button.
10. Choose OK.
11. Click on Notification.
12. Click on Notify Print Job Owner (deselect the option). Note what happens.
13. Click on Notify Print Job Owner again to reselect, and note what happens.
14. Click on Features.
15. Under Supported Cartridges, type **Fingerprint**.
16. Select OK.

Finally, it's time to build the print server.

PRINT SERVER CREATION

1. Select the WHITE.CRIME.TOKYO.ACME container again.
2. Press Insert again (or Object/Create), and choose a print server this time.
3. Name the print server as noted above.
4. Click on Define Additional Properties and click on OK.
5. Click on Change Password.

6. Enter the password Secret, and reconfirm. Then press OK.
7. Click on Assignments.
8. Add the CANONBJ-P1 printer.
9. Click on Users.
10. Who is the current print server user? Why?
11. Delete the current print server user and add yourself only.
12. Click on Operator. Who is the operator and why?
13. Click on Auditing Log.
14. Click on Enable Auditing.
15. Click on OK in the lowest left-hand corner (to save all changes).
16. Double-click on the print server WHITE-PS1.
17. Click on Print Layout.
18. Note the exclamation point next to the print server. Why do you think this is?
19. Click on the print server to select it and then click on Status. Note what you see.
20. Click on Close.
21. Click on Cancel to leave this screen.

Congratulations! You've built ACME's printing system. Now all you have to do is find the right printer and load the print server. Ready, set, print.

FINDING THE PRINTER

1. Click on the very [Root] of the tree.
2. Choose Object/Search from the menu bar.
3. Click on Search Entire Subtree.
4. Under Search For, choose Printer.
5. Under Property, choose Cartridge.
6. Under the blank entry box (to the right of Equal To), type **Fingerprint**.
7. Select OK.
8. Select Yes (Continue).

9. Note the results from the search.
10. Double-click on the printer to verify it's correct.

LOADING THE PRINT SERVER

1. At the server console, ensure you are at the colon prompt.
2. Type **LOAD PSERVER** and press Return.
3. Enter in the context where the print server resides (WHITE.CRIME.TOKYO.ACME) and press Return.
4. Choose the print server we've defined (WHITE-PS1).
5. What happens next?
6. Take steps to allow loading to continue.
7. Choose Printer Status.
8. Choose CANONBJ-P1.
9. Note status of the printer.
10. Escape back to the Available Options screen.
11. Choose Print Server Information.
12. Choose Current Status.
13. Choose Unload. What happens?
14. Reload the print server again.

See Appendix C for answers.

CASE STUDY: USING ACME'S PRINTING SYSTEM

This section assumes that you have two users set up in the WHITE.CRIME.TOKYO.ACME container. This will allow us to test capturing data and enabling print job configurations. You should have already completed the previous exercise.

You will log in as two different users in this exercise:

- ▶ Robin Hood (RHood)

- ▶ Maid Marion (MMarion)

You should also be created as yourself and currently logged in as such. You should not currently be captured.

1. Go to a DOS box under Windows.
2. Type **CAPTURE SH** and note the results.
3. Type **CAPTURE** and note what happens.
4. Change to the context where the CANONBJ-PQ1 exists. How do you do this?
5. CAPTURE to the CANONBJ-PQ1 using the Q option. What does the command look like?
6. End the capture using CAPTURE. How do you do this?
7. Return to Windows.
8. Run the NWUSER utility.
9. Click on the printer icon.
10. Use the browser on the right to locate the context WHITE.CRIME.TOKYO.ACME. Then click on the printer icon located on the top button bar.
11. Drag either the printer or the queue to the left onto LPT1:.
12. Double-click on the new printer mapping.
13. Note the default settings for the capture.
14. Leave the NWUSER utility.
15. Log out as the user and re-log in as RHood. Before you do this, ensure Sspeeders has at least Read and File Scan access to the volume SYS:.
16. From a DOS box, change to the WHITE.CRIME.TOKYO.ACME container using the CX command.
17. Attempt to CAPTURE to the CANONBJ-PQ1 queue. What happens and why?
18. Re-log in as yourself again. How would you grant access to the user RHood?
19. Change to the context WHITE.CRIME.TOKYO.ACME and reenable CAPTURE to the network queue CANONBJ-PQ1. How can you do this?
20. Start NWADMIN.
21. Choose Object/Print from the NWADMIN menu bar and print the current NWADMIN screen.

22. Ensure that CAPTURE is working. Where can you look in NWADMIN to verify this?
23. Return to a DOS box and ensure that CAPTURE is working. What is the command to do this?
24. Print a DOS text file to the network. How can you do this while CAPTURE is activated?
25. End the CAPTURE.
26. Return to Windows.
27. Create a print job configuration for the container WHITE.CRIME.TOKYO.ACME and call it Main. Where would this be done?
28. Grant the container WHITE.CRIME.TOKYO.ACME access to the print queue CANONBJ-PQ1. How would you do this?
29. Log in as RHood.
30. Under DOS, type **CAPTURE** and note what happens.
31. Log in as yourself to modify the queue.
32. Return to NWADMIN and again select the configuration under the container WHITE.CRIME.TOKYO.ACME. Highlight the configuration Main and click on Default. Note the printer icon that now appears next to the configuration. Note also the options for the configuration (copies, queue, notification). Press OK to save.
33. Log in as RHood again.
34. Return to a DOS box and execute CAPTURE. What happens now?
35. Type **CAPTURE SH**. What do you note about the settings?

See Appendix C for answers.

CASE STUDY: MANAGING ACME'S PRINTING SYSTEM

This assumes you have a printer attached to the print server ready to print (on-line, with paper). It also assumes the print server is running on the NetWare server.

1. Log in as yourself, start Windows, and run NWADMIN.
2. Select the printer CANONBJ-P1 by double-clicking.

3. Select Status for the printer.

4. Select Pause. What changes with the printer?

5. Send two jobs to the queue CANONBJ-PQ1.

6. Go to the queue CANONBJ-PQ1. Double-click on it and choose Job List. What do you see?

7. Select the first job and choose Details.

8. Click on the User Hold option. What does the status display?

9. Return to the printer CANONBJ-P1 and choose Status again.

10. Choose Resume to reenable the printer. What happens?

11. Place the printer off-line after the job has completed printing. Use the printer's on-line/off-line button for this.

12. View the printer CANONBJ-P1's status under NWADMIN.

13. Note the status of the printer.

14. With the printer status up (viewing percentage and such), place the printer back on-line and watch what happens.

15. Once the job has completed printing, select the print server WHITE-PS1 by double-clicking on it.

16. Select Print Layout.

17. Select each item and click on Status one at a time. What do you see?

18. Select the Identification button on the top right. Near the bottom is another button labeled Unload. Select it.

19. Choose Unload Print Server Immediately. Monitor the file server if you can. What happens?

20. Choose Cancel to leave the Print Server Detail screens.

21. Reselect the print server WHITE-PS1. Choose Print layout.

22. What do you notice that is different? What do you think this means?

23. Choose WHITE-PS1 and click on Status. Does this verify your assumption?

24. Submit another job to CANONBJ-PQ1.

25. Choose the CANONBJ-PQ1 and select Job List.

26. Select any job other than the first (Seq 001) and choose Job Details.

27. Locate Service Sequence on the middle left-hand side.

28. Change Service Sequence to 001.

29. Select OK.

30. What looks different?

See Appendix C for answers.

EXERCISE 8-3: USING QUICK SETUP IN PCONSOLE

The following exercise will walk you through the process of creating NetWare 4 printing objects using the Quick Setup option of PCONSOLE. Before beginning this exercise, be sure you are in the context that you wish to create new printing objects in, and that you are logged in as a user with sufficient rights to create objects.

1. From the DOS command line, run the PCONSOLE utility by typing **PCONSOLE** and pressing Enter.
2. Use the arrow keys to select Quick Setup and press Enter.
3. From the Print Services Configuration menu, modify the print server, printer, and print queue name to match the naming standards of your organization.
4. Verify the volume you wish this print queue to be created on. If necessary, use the Insert key to browse the tree and select the appropriate volume.
5. Specify the banner type. This should be based on the type of printer you are using. PCL printers use text banners.
6. Specify the printer type (parallel, serial, or other), location (manual load — workstation or network attached; or auto load — locally attached).
7. Specify the interrupt or polled mode (recommended). If interrupt is chosen it must match the configuration of the physical printer port.
8. Specify the port to which this printer is attached.
9. When configuration is complete, press Esc and Yes to save.

EXERCISE 8-4: MANUAL PRINTING SETUP IN PCONSOLE

The following exercise will walk you through the process of creating NetWare 4 printing objects using the individual print queues, printers, and print server options of PCONSOLE. Before beginning this exercise, be sure you are in the context that you wish to create new printing objects in, and that you are logged in as a user with sufficient rights to create objects.

1. From the DOS command line, run the PCONSOLE utility by typing **PCONSOLE** and then pressing Enter.
2. From the Available Options menu select Print Queues.
3. Use the Insert key to create a new print queue.
4. Enter a print queue name that matches the naming standards of your organization.
5. Enter the print queue's volume. Press the Insert key and browse the NDS tree to choose the appropriate volume and press Enter to select.
6. Press Esc to return to the Available Options menu.
7. Choose Printers.
8. Press the Insert key to create a new printer.
9. Enter a printer name that matches the naming standards of your organization.
10. Select the printer by pressing Enter.
11. Under Printer Configuration specify the port to which this printer is attached.
12. Specify the printer type (parallel, serial, or other) location (manual load — workstation or network attached; or auto load — locally attached).
13. Specify the interrupt or polled mode (recommended). If interrupt is chosen it must match the configuration of the physical printer port.
14. Specify an address restriction, if desired.
15. When configuration is complete, press Esc.
16. If forms are being used, specify the starting form number.
17. Specify the banner type. This should be based on the type of printer you are using. PCL printers use text banners.
18. If multiple form types are being used, specify the forms service mode you desire.

19. Press Enter at Print queues assigned and use the Insert key to add a print queue to service this queue.
20. Use the arrow keys to select the queue you created above and press Enter to select. When you have finished, press Esc.
21. Optional: Press Enter at Notification to add users or groups to be notified of printer problems. Use the Insert key to browse the NDS tree.
22. When you have completed the printer configuration, press Esc to save the changes.
23. Press Esc to return to the Available Options menu and select Print Servers.
24. Use the Insert key to add a new print server.
25. Enter a print server name that matches the naming conventions of your organization.
26. Under the Print Server Information menu, select Printers.
27. Use the Insert key to select the printer you created above.
28. Press Esc twice to return to the Available Options menu.

EXERCISE 8-5: CUSTOMIZING NETWARE 4 PRINTING WITH PRINTCON

This exercise will walk you through the process of creating a print job configuration for the user you are currently logged in as.

1. From the DOS command line, run the PRINTCON utility by typing **PRINTCON** and then pressing Enter.
2. Select Print Job Configurations.
3. Press the Insert key to create a new print job configuration.
4. Enter a name for this new print job configuration.
5. Press Enter to select the job configuration.
6. Use the arrow keys to select Local printer.
7. Enter the printer port you wish to capture (1=LPT1, 2=LPT2, and so on).
8. Use the arrow keys to select the print queue.
9. Press Insert and browse the NDS tree to find the desired print queue. Press Enter to select it.
10. Specify other desired options such as form feed, banner, and form number.
11. When you have finished, press Esc and Yes to save changes.
12. Press Esc to exit.

PART III

Appendixes

Overview of Novell Education and the CNA Program

In a world where people and businesses and organizations and governments and nations are being connected and sharing information at a dizzying rate, Novell's primary goal is to be the infrastructure that connects people and services together all over the world. By the year 2000, Novell is predicting that its networks and services will serve 1 billion connections.

ZEN

"Novell and its partners will create a world of pervasive computing that connects people with other people and the information they need, enabling them to act on it anytime, anyplace."

Bob Frankenberg, CEO of Novell, Inc.

To help fulfill this goal, Novell Education is providing quality education programs and products to help create a strong support base of trained networking professionals. By itself, the Novell Education department isn't nearly large enough to provide high-quality training to the vast number of people who will require it. Therefore, Novell Education has developed authorized training partnerships throughout the world to provide authorized training. In addition, Novell Education created certification programs to help ensure that the standard for networking skills is maintained at a high level.

Today, Novell has more than 1,500 authorized education partners worldwide, including colleges, universities, professional training centers, and the like.

This appendix describes Novell Education and the CNA program. It also provides some practical tips, such as alternatives to formal classes, finding out how to take the test, and so on.

Certification Partners

Two types of education partners work with Novell worldwide: Novell Authorized Education Centers (NAECs) and Novell Education Academic Partners (NEAPs). These education partners provide top-quality training on Novell products. In fact, Novell guarantees complete customer satisfaction for all Novell courses when they are taught at Novell-authorized training partners.

NAECs are private, independent training organizations that meet Novell's strict quality standards. Some NAECs are also Novell product resellers, but many operate independent of Novell's reseller channels.

The advantage of attending an NAEC is that these organizations typically have a great deal of experience in technology training, and since their livelihood depends on enticing students to take their courses, they are driven to provide quality education.

ZEN

"Don't waste time learning the 'tricks of the trade.' Instead, learn the trade."

H. Jackson Brown, Jr., *Life's Little Instruction Book*

To become an NAEC, the training organization must meet the following strict education guidelines:

- The facility must use Novell-developed course materials.

- The course must be taught within a recommended time frame.

- The facility itself must be Novell-authorized. Authorization is based on a strict set of standards for equipment, instructional soundness, and student comfort.

- The course must be taught by a Certified Novell Instructor (CNI), who is certified to teach the specific course.

In addition, the prospective NAEC must submit an extensive application to Novell Education. The training center also pays an initiation fee and annual licensing fees. NAECs are required to offer various courses in a consistent, timely manner.

NEAPs are colleges or universities that provide Novell-authorized courses in a semester- or quarter-length curriculum. There are more than 100 such colleges and universities in the United States, as well as some in Canada, and the list is growing.

NEAPs must follow the same strict guidelines as NAECs and provide Novell courses as part of their standard curriculum.

Both NAECs and NEAPs offer the same courses, based on the same education materials, objectives, and information. They also offer a wide variety of classes (more than 40) on various Novell products and technologies. If you want to pursue Novell-authorized training in a classroom setting, with hands-on labs and knowledgeable instructors, either type of education partner will be beneficial.

Novell-authorized courses (through either NAECs or NEAPs) often offer the best way to get direct, hands-on training, using approved techniques, technologies, and training materials.

Certification Levels

Because Novell has so many different products, and because networking professionals have different reasons for getting trained on those products, Novell offers four different certification levels.

Depending on the level of certification you want to achieve, you take different exams (and, if you desire, the associated courses to prepare for the exams). While one or more certain core exams are required for all levels, you may also take exams for additional "electives" to achieve the certification and specialization you want.

ZEN

"Argue for your limitations, and sure enough, they're yours."

Richard Bach, Illusions

The following certification levels are available for Novell products:

- ► CNA (Certified Novell Administrator)

- ► CNE

- Master CNE

- CNI (Certified Novell Instructor)

Within each of these levels, there are areas of specialization. Let's look at these four programs in more detail.

CNA (CERTIFIED NOVELL ADMINISTRATOR)

The CNA certification is the entry-level certification for network administrators. It prepares you to manage your own NetWare network on a day-to-day basis.

The CNA level does not delve into the more complex and technical aspects of NetWare network design, troubleshooting, and implementation. Instead, it is designed for people who perform day-to-day general network administration tasks (such as adding and deleting users, setting up desktop environments, backing up network data, and maintaining network security).

TIP

As a prerequisite to taking the NetWare 4.1 CNA exam, be sure you have a thorough knowledge of DOS, Windows, and general microcomputer concepts.

To prepare for the NetWare 4.1 CNA exam, you can take the Novell-authorized course entitled *NetWare 4 Administration* (course number 520). In addition to being the preparatory course for the CNA exam, this course is also a required course for the NetWare 4 track of the CNE certification level (described in the next section). So, if you have plans to continue past the CNA level to get your CNE certification, too, you're killing two birds with one stone.

For a list of the course objectives for the *NetWare 4 Administration* course, see Appendix B. That appendix cross-references all the course objectives with locations in this book that will help prepare you to meet those objectives.

 TIP

CNAs qualify for associate membership in the Network Professional Association (NPA), which is explained in Appendix D.

You can pursue five different CNA specialization tracks. This book deals exclusively with the NetWare 4.1 CNA track, of course, but you may be interested in knowing about the other tracks, too. Each CNA track involves a single exam that proves you have mastered the tasks associated with being a system administrator on that type of Novell product. You can achieve your CNA status in multiple tracks simply by passing the appropriate exam for each track.

Table A.1 shows the CNA tracks that are currently available.

T A B L E A.I		
Current CNA Tracks	**CNA TRACK**	**DESCRIPTION**
	NetWare 4	This track certifies that you understand and can administer features of your NetWare 4.1 network.
	NetWare 3	This track certifies that you understand and can administer features of your NetWare 3.12 network.
	GroupWise 4	This track certifies that you understand and can administer the GroupWise GroupWare product, including creating post offices and users, creating links between domains, installing GroupWise clients, and performing basic troubleshooting tasks.
	SoftSolutions 4	This track certifies that you understand and can administer the SoftSolutions product, including adding users, setting up basic applications, operating full-text indexers, and designing screens, reports, and workstation IDs.
	InForms 4	This track certifies that you understand and can administer the InForms product and its features, including creating forms, queries and reports; linking forms to the database; and creating simple macros.

CNE

The CNE certification ensures that you can adequately install and manage NetWare networks on a more advanced level than the CNA. The CNE starts with the basic CNA skills, then adds high-end skills that will allow you to support NetWare 4.1 networks more fully.

While pursuing your CNE certification, you "declare a major," meaning that you choose to specialize in any of the following three particular Novell product families:

- NetWare 4

- NetWare 3

- GroupWare

Some skills you are expected to master as a CNE include managing multiple networks, performing network upgrades, improving network printing performance, and managing network databases.

CNEs are expected to provide support at the network operating system and network applications level.

TIP

CNEs qualify for full membership in the Network Professional Association (NPA), which is explained in Appendix D.

MASTER CNE

The Master CNE certification level allows you to go beyond basic CNE certification. To get a Master CNE, you declare a "graduate major." These areas of specialization delve deeper into the integration- and solution-oriented aspects of running a network than the CNE level.

While CNEs provide support at the operating system and application level, Master CNEs are expected to manage advanced access, management, and workgroup integration for multiple environments. Master CNEs can support complex networks that span several different platforms, and can perform upgrades, migration, and integration for various systems.

There are three areas in which Master CNEs can specialize:

- Network management

- Infrastructure and advanced access

- GroupWare integration

TIP

Master CNEs qualify for membership in the Network Professional Association (NPA), which is explained in Appendix D.

The ECNE level is being phased out. The ECNE level's series of tests emphasized aspects of networking encountered in larger, enterprise-wide networks, such as routing, gateways, NetWare Directory Services, and so on.

The Master CNE program is replacing the ECNE level because it adds more flexibility to the type of specialization the candidate can pursue. If you've already achieved ECNE status, you will retain the title, and Novell will still recognize it. However, Novell stopped certifying new ECNEs on September 30, 1995.

CNI (CERTIFIED NOVELL INSTRUCTOR)

The CNI certification level qualifies instructors to teach authorized NetWare courses through NAECs. The tests and classes specific to this level ensure that the individual taking them will be able to adequately teach others how to install and manage NetWare.

This CNI program is designed for people who want to make a career of teaching others how to install, configure, and use Novell networking products.

CNI candidates must attend the Novell courses they wish to be certified to teach, and they must pass proficiency tests at a higher level than other certification candidates. (The course they attend must be taught by an official NAEC or NEAP, and must be taught in the standard Novell format.)

In addition, CNIs must successfully complete a rigorous Instructor Performance Evaluation, as well as meet continuing certification requirements (which include additional training and testing as Novell updates courses and releases new products).

Alternatives to Taking the Novell Authorized Course

If a typical course in a classroom or lab isn't your preferred method of learning, or if you are going through the course but like to have alternate study methods handy to reinforce your learning, you're in luck. You can use a variety of educational supplements to enhance your NetWare 4.1 education.

Such supplements allow networking professionals to train at their own pace in a more convenient manner.

ZEN

"You are never given a wish without also being given the power to make it true. You may have to work for it, however."

Richard Bach, *Illusions*

Some of the educational alternatives you can use include:

- Video training

- Computer-Based Training (CBT)

- Student Kits

- Practice Tests

- Courses from other training centers or consultants

VIDEO TRAINING

If you would rather learn the fundamentals of NetWare 4.1 administration in the comfort of your own testing lab (or in your home, for that matter), you're in luck. The NetWare 4.1 Administrator's course has been put on both videotape and CD-ROM formats.

Novell contracts its video training to an organization named J3 Learning. Some NAECs sell these video- and CD-ROM-based courses. Additionally, you can order them directly from J3 Learning at 1-800-532-7672 (toll-free in Canada and the USA) or 1-612-930-0330.

COMPUTER-BASED TRAINING (CBT)

Many of the authorized Novell courses are available in Computer-Based Training (CBT) form. If you'd rather work through the material at your own pace, on your own workstation, you may want to obtain the CBT for the NetWare 4.1 Administrator course.

Novell contracts their CBT coursework to a company named CBT Systems. Again, some NAECs sell these CBT courses, so you may want to contact your local NAEC to get a copy. You can also order the CBT course directly from CBT Systems by calling 1-800-929-9050 (toll free in Canada and the USA) or 1-415-737-9050.

STUDENT KITS

If you're interested in obtaining the materials that students of the authorized NetWare 4.1 Administrator course use during their training, you can order the corresponding Student Kit. The Student Kit for course 520 (the *NetWare 4.1 Administration* course) contains the following materials:

- The NetWare 4.1 Administrator student manual, which is designed to be used with the instructor-led course. (What this means is that this manual doesn't contain exhaustive information — it's more sketchy in nature, meant to be used in conjunction with class discussions, lectures, and labs.)

- A two-user version of NetWare 4.1 so that you can install it in your own testing lab and try things out on your own.

- A subset of the printed manuals (product documentation) that come with the NetWare 4.1 product:

  - Introduction to NetWare Directory Services

  - Utilities Reference

  - Concepts

  - Print Services

  - Supervising the Network (volumes 1 and 2)

  - Client for DOS/Windows User Guide

  - Quick Reference Card

- Marketing literature for Novell Press, Novell Application Notes, and so on

The Student Kit is only available from NAECs. Generally, NAECs sell them for approximately half of the cost of taking the course itself. (NAECs are at some liberty to set their own prices for the Student Kits, but the ballpark figure for the Student Kit is about $595.)

PRACTICE TESTS

Practice tests for the CNA and CNE exams are available, in case you want to see what you're in for before you tackle the exam itself. While they aren't exactly like the real exams, and don't substitute for study and experience, they can help you prepare for taking the exam.

Of course, we have also supplied you with the *Clarke Tests v2.0* on the CD-ROM that accompanies this book. The Clarke Tests v2.0 is a next-generation, interactive learning system. It contains practice tests and study sessions that combine a variety of question types with interactive graphics, sounds, and clues. Each interactive answer includes a full page or more of explanation and study material, plus great references to other resources. See Appendix D for more information about the *Clarke Tests v2.0*, or call 1-800-684-8858.

INDEPENDENT COURSES

Numerous "unauthorized" organizations provide classes and seminars on NetWare products. Some of these unauthorized classes are quite good. Others are probably of lower quality, since Novell does not have any control over their course content or instructor qualifications.

If you are interested in using an unauthorized provider for your NetWare classes, be sure you do some homework beforehand, to try to determine if the course will be beneficial. Here are some hints:

1 • Try to talk to others who've taken a class from the provider, and get a feel for how good they thought the class was.

2 • Get a copy of the course's syllabus or objectives, and compare them to the Novell-authorized course. Are there any glaring gaps?

3 • Find out if there is any lab-time associated with the class. It's important to get the hands-on experience that goes along with the "book-larnin'," or your education will be only superficial at best.

4 • Ask about the instructor's experience, both in the classroom and in the industry.

5 • Find out if the course covers the material in about the same time frame as the Novell course (four days), or if it is "accelerated." If you have plenty of hands-on experience in NetWare 4.1 already, and you're looking for a refresher course and some information to fill in a few of the missing pieces for you, an accelerated course may be just the ticket. If you are fairly new to the game, however, you'll want to find a course that will allow you the time to learn, practice, and digest the information. Don't shortchange yourself for the sake of a few hours of time.

If your homework reveals nothing worrisome about the course, then it may be a good investment. If you're hesitant about the course's quality, however, keep looking. There are plenty of courses and instructors out there that can do a good job of teaching you what you need to learn, so be picky. It's your life, after all.

Testing Your Mettle

Okay. You've finished the course, you've studied this book, you've spent hours in the lab or on your own network using the NetWare Administrator and other utilities to add users, change passwords, back up files, and the like. You're ready to show your stuff, and prove that you have the baseline of knowledge required to take on network administrator duties in the real world.

You're ready to take the test and become a CNA.

So how do you sign up for the exam?

The NetWare 4.1 Administrator exam is offered at NAECs and NEAPs all over the world. The first thing you must do is find one of these centers to administer the exam.

HOW DO YOU SIGN UP FOR AN EXAM?

All Novell exams are administered by a professional testing organization: Sylvan Prometric.

> **REAL WORLD**
>
> In the past, there were two testing organizations that Novell used to administer its tests: Sylvan Learning Systems and Drake Prometric. However, Drake Prometric was recently bought by Sylvan Learning Systems. The merged organization changed its name to Sylvan Prometric, so now it's all just one big, happy family.

If you take the Novell-authorized course, you may be able to sign up to the take the test at the same location, because some (but not all) NAECs are also affiliated with Sylvan Prometric. In fact, the instructor most likely can give you information about where to take the exam locally.

Otherwise, to find a location that administers this exam, simply call one of the following numbers:

- The Novell Education phone number at 1-800-233-EDUC (toll-free in Canada and the USA) or 1-801-222-7800

- Sylvan Prometric, at 1-800-RED-TEST (toll-free), 1-800-RED-EXAM (toll-free), or 1-410-880-8700

Outside of the USA and Canada, contact your local Novell office, or a local Sylvan Prometric office.

WHAT IS THE EXAM LIKE?

The NetWare 4.1 Administrator exam, like all Novell exams, is computer-based. You take the exam by answering questions on the computer. However, unlike more traditional tests, the NetWare 4.1 Administrator exam is *performance-based*. This means that instead of just asking you to regurgitate facts, the exam actually requires you to apply your knowledge to solve problems. For example, the exam may include simulations of network problems or tasks, such as adding a user. You must actually use NetWare 4.1 utilities to complete the task or solve the problem.

The exam is also *adaptive*. This means that the exam offers easier or more difficult questions to you based on your last answer, in an effort to determine just how much you know. In other words, the exam starts off asking you a fairly easy question. If you answer it correctly, the next question will be slightly harder. If you answer that one correctly, too, it will offer you a slightly harder one again, and so on. If you answer a question incorrectly, on the other hand, the next question will be slightly easier. If you miss that one, too, the next will be easier yet, until you get one right. Then the questions will get more difficult again.

The number of questions you'll be asked will vary, depending on your level of knowledge. If you answer all of the questions correctly, you will continue to be offered questions until you have been tested on the full range of knowledge. If you answer incorrectly, you'll only answer questions until your level of knowledge is determined. Obviously, the higher the level of knowledge the computer determines you have, the better score you receive.

It will probably take you from 20 to 40 minutes to take this exam.

ZEN

"Be brave. Even if you're not, pretend to be. No one can tell the difference."

H. Jackson Brown, Jr.

The exam is closed-book and is graded on a pass/fail basis. The standard fee for the exam is $85. When you go to take the exam, remember to take two forms of identification with you (one must be a picture ID). You will not be allowed to take any notes into or out of the exam room.

If you fail the test, take heart. You can take it again. In fact, you can take it again as many times as you want — there are no limits to repeating it. You can repeat it as soon as you like, and as many times as it takes to pass (or until your checkbook runs dry, whichever comes first). Because of the way the exam is designed, questions are randomly pulled from a giant database. Therefore, chances are slim that you will ever get the same test questions twice, no matter how often you take the exam.

After the Test — Now What?

Congratulations! You passed the exam with flying colors, just like we knew you would! Now comes the easiest part — getting your official certification.

To receive your official certification status, you must sign a Novell Education Certification Agreement.

The certification agreement contains the usual legal jargon you might expect with such certification. Among other things, it grants you permission to use the trademarked name "CNA" on your resume or other advertising, as long as you use the name in connection with providing network administration services on a NetWare 4.1 network. It also reminds you that if the network administration services you offer don't live up to Novell's high standards of quality, Novell can require you to meet those standards within "a commercially reasonable time."

After you've passed the exam, you can read the agreement, sign the "Signature Form," and mail it back to Novell. (Because Novell needs your legal signature on the form, they can't accept faxed copies of the form.) For your convenience, we've included a copy of the agreement, along with the signature form, at the end of this chapter (See Figure A.1). You can also receive additional copies of the form by calling your local NAEC, or by calling Novell's FaxBack phone line at 1-801-222-7800 or 1-800-233-EDUC and requesting a copy to be faxed to you. Novell Education, of course, reserves the right to change this form without notice.

For More Information...

You can get more information about Novell Education courses, exams, training supplements, programs, and so on, by using one of the following avenues:

- ► Call Novell Education at 1-801-222-7800 or 1-800-233-EDUC (toll free in the USA and Canada)

- ► Use Novell's FaxBack system to receive information by fax. The FaxBack system is available through the same numbers listed here. Select Option 3 for the FaxBack system, and follow the instructions to order the FaxBack master catalog of available documents. After you've received the FaxBack catalog of documents, you can call back and request the specific documents you want. You can order up to four documents per call.

- ► Call your local NAEC, NEAP, Drake Regional Service Center, or Sylvan Technology Center.

- ► Go on-line to Novell Education's Internet site. You can get to the Novell Education information either through Novell's Internet site (GO NETWIRE on CompuServe, or http://www.novell.com), or by going directly to http://education.novell.com. Figure A.1 shows the Novell Education forum on the Internet.

Novell Education Certification Agreement

1 **PURPOSE.** NOVELL is in the business of, among other things, manufacturing, distributing, selling, offering for sale, and promoting network computing products. Many of NOVELL's products are technically complex and require competent pre- and post-sales support. In order to provide adequate support, NOVELL has devised several programs under which individuals become certified to competently provide appropriate support. These are the Certified Novell Administrator (or "CNA"), the CNE, the Enterprise CNE (or "ECNE"), the Master CNE, and the Certified Novell Instructor (or "CNI") certification programs. Successful participants in these programs, through education, training, and/or testing become authorized to provide services and to use the NOVELL Marks pertaining to the particular certification program or programs that the participant has completed. Individuals may participate in one or more of these certification programs. Completion of one certification program does not entitle a participant to use the Marks or provide the services pertaining to any other certification program.

2 **DEFINITIONS.**

2.1 **Program** means one of the programs of certification that is offered by NOVELL, is available to participants, and may lead to certification under this Novell Education Certification Agreement ("Agreement"). The Programs include the CNA, CNE, Enterprise CNE, Master CNE, and CNI certification programs. As further provided in this Agreement, participants cannot administer Licensed Services under or otherwise use the Marks of a particular Program, claim any Program certification or status, or exercise any rights granted under this Agreement, except through the successful completion of NOVELL's requirements for that Program.

2.2 **MARKS** means, as the case may be, the Certified Novell Administrator and CNA marks and logos, the CNE marks and logos, Enterprise CNE and ECNE marks and logos, Master CNE marks and logos, and the Certified Novell Instructor and CNI marks and logos.

2.3 **LICENSED SERVICES** means the particular administration or pre- and post-sales service and support of NOVELL's network computing products that correspond with the Program or Programs successfully completed by the participant. The LICENSED SERVICES for each particular Program are described below. LICENSED SERVICES does not mean (i) any services provided with respect to non-NOVELL products or (ii) the teaching of courses relating to NOVELL products other than those courses permitted to be taught according to the CNI LICENSED SERVICES and described below.

2.3.1 **If YOU have successfully completed the CNA Program requirements, LICENSED SERVICES** means handling the day-to-day administration of the installed NOVELL networking product or products for which YOU have successfully completed a CNA Program. Successful completion of a particular CNA Program will allow YOU to administer the above services for one of several particular products, including (but not limited to) NetWare, GroupWare (GroupWise, InForms and SoftSolutions) and UnixWare.

2.3.2 **If YOU have successfully completed the CNE, Enterprise CNE and/or Master CNE Program requirements, LICENSED SERVICES** means the pre- and post-sales service and support of the NOVELL network computing product or products for which YOU have successfully completed a CNE, Enterprise CNE and/or Master CNE Program. Successful completion of a particular CNE Program will allow YOU to administer the above services in one of several particular products, including (but not limited to) NetWare, GroupWare (GroupWise, InForms and SoftSolutions) and UnixWare. Successful completion of a particular Master CNE Program will allow YOU to administer the above services in one of several particular service areas, including (but not limited to) Network Management, Infrastructure and Advanced Access, and GroupWare Integration.

2.3.3 **If YOU have successfully completed the CNI Program requirements, LICENSED SERVICES** means the teaching of NOVELL authorized courses under the auspices of a Novell Authorized Education Center. CNI Licensed Services does not mean the teaching of a course not authorized by NOVELL.

2.4 **NOVELL AUTHORIZED EDUCATION CENTER or NAEC** means any organization that has been approved by NOVELL as an authorized training facility and includes Novell Authorized Internal Training Organizations and Novell Education Academic Partners.

2.5 **NOVELL** means Novell Ireland Software Ltd. If YOU provide LICENSED SERVICES in Europe, the Middle East, or Africa (EMEA). If YOU do not provide LICENSED SERVICES in EMEA, Novell means Novell, Inc.

3 **CERTIFICATION.** YOUR Program certification is based on completing the required testing and complying with the requirements set forth in the brochure corresponding with the Program YOU have successfully completed. YOU acknowledge that NOVELL has the right to change the requirements for receiving Program certification, or

maintaining a Program certification, at any time. Once certification is granted, it will automatically renew if all continuing certification requirements are met. YOU are responsible for maintaining YOUR certification. To maintain certification, YOU must complete all Program continuing certification requirements, if any, corresponding with YOUR particular Program certification within the time frame specified by NOVELL. If YOU do not complete the continuing certification requirements within the time frame specified by NOVELL, YOUR certified Program status for that particular Program may expire, resulting in de-certification. NOTWITHSTANDING ANYTHING IN THIS AGREEMENT TO THE CONTRARY, NOVELL HAS THE RIGHT NOT TO GRANT OR RENEW YOUR CERTIFICATION IF NOVELL REASONABLY DETERMINES THAT YOUR CERTIFICATION OR USE OF THE MARKS WILL ADVERSELY AFFECT NOVELL. THIS AGREEMENT APPLIES TO ANY AND ALL PROGRAMS COMPLETED BY YOU.

4 WHAT HAPPENS WHEN YOU LEAVE AN ORGANIZATION? YOU retain YOUR Program certification if YOU move to a new organization.

5 GRANT AND CONSIDERATION. NOVELL grants to YOU a non-exclusive and non-transferable license to use the MARKS solely in connection with providing the LICENSED SERVICES corresponding to the Program certification YOU have achieved. YOU or YOUR agents may use the MARKS on such promotional display and advertising materials as may, in YOUR judgment, promote the LICENSED SERVICES corresponding to YOUR Program certification. YOU may not use the MARKS for any purposes that are not directly related to the provision of the LICENSED SERVICES corresponding to YOUR particular Program certification. YOU may not use the MARKS of any Program unless YOU have completed the Program certification requirements and have been notified by NOVELL in writing that YOU have achieved certification status for that particular Program. YOUR CNI certification, if applicable, is subject to the restrictions of Section 5.1 of this Agreement.

5.1 AFFILIATION WITH NAECS/CNI LICENSE GRANT

5.1.1 Affiliation with NAECs. YOU are authorized, if YOU achieve the status of CNI, to teach authorized Novell courses only at NAECs. YOU may be employed by one NAEC or YOU may work independently, contracting with one or more NAECs on a case-by-case basis. If YOU are employed by an NAEC and move to another NAEC or obtain independent status, YOU retain the CNI certification status. It is YOUR responsibility to notify NOVELL of any address or NAEC change.

6 TERM AND TERMINATION.

6.1 Term. This Novell Education Certification Agreement will commence on the date YOU receive written notice from NOVELL that YOU have met all the requirements necessary to attain YOUR particular Program certification and will terminate in accordance with the terms and provisions of this Agreement. YOU understand that, for convenience of processing, YOU will indicate assent to this Agreement via the use of a computer as indicated electronically prior to YOUR completion of the Program requirements, or, in certain circumstances and when authorized by NOVELL, YOU will indicate assent by signing this Agreement. YOU acknowledge that this Agreement will not take effect until NOVELL has notified YOU in writing that all Program requirements have been met. YOU further acknowledge that this Agreement will remain in effect in the event YOU upgrade YOUR status to include any other Program certifications, and that those subparagraphs specific to those certification(s) will also apply to YOU.

6.2 Termination by Either Party. Either party may terminate this Agreement without cause by giving thirty (30) days or more prior written notice to the other party.

6.3 Termination by NOVELL. Without prejudice to any rights it may have under this Agreement or in law equity or otherwise, NOVELL may terminate this Agreement upon the occurrence of any one or more of the following events (called "Default"):

6.3.1 If YOU fail to perform any of YOUR obligations under this Agreement;

6.3.2 If YOU render the LICENSED SERVICES without complying with the testing required under this Agreement, or if YOU discontinue offering the LICENSED SERVICES;

6.3.3 If any government agency or court finds that LICENSED SERVICES as provided by YOU are defective in any way, manner or form; or

6.3.4 If actual or potential adverse publicity or other information, emanating from a third party or parties, about YOU, the LICENSED SERVICES, or the use of the MARKS by YOU causes NOVELL, in its sole judgment, to believe that NOVELL's reputation will be adversely affected.

700

In the event any Default occurs, NOVELL will give YOU written notice of termination of this Agreement. In the event of a Default under Section 6.3.3 or 6.3.4, NOVELL may terminate this Agreement with no period for correction, and it will terminate automatically without further notice. In the event of a Default under Section 6.3.1 or 6.3.2, or at NOVELL's option under Section 6.3.3 or 6.3.4, YOU will be given thirty (30) days from receipt of notice in which to correct any Default. If YOU fail to correct the Default within the notice period, this Agreement will automatically terminate on the last day of the notice period.

6.4 **Return of Materials.** Upon termination of this Agreement, YOU agree to immediately cease to render the LICENSED SERVICES and to return all badges or other trademark collateral to NOVELL. Upon termination, all rights granted under this Novell Education Certification Agreement will immediately and automatically revert to NOVELL.

7 **CONDUCT OF BUSINESS.** YOU agree to (i) conduct business in a manner which reflects favorably at all times on the products, goodwill and reputation of NOVELL; (ii) avoid deceptive, misleading or unethical practices which are or might be detrimental to NOVELL or its products; and (iii) refrain from making any representations, warranties, or guarantees to customers that are inconsistent with the policies established by NOVELL. YOU further agree that YOU will not represent YOURSELF to possess the certification of any Program category until such time as YOU have completed all requirements for that Program and have been notified by NOVELL in writing that YOU have achieved the certification of that Program, including but not limited to the Program certifications of CNA, CNE, Enterprise CNE, Master CNE, and CNI.

8 **OWNERSHIP.** No title to or ownership of the MARKS or of any software or proprietary technology in hardware licensed to YOU pursuant to this Agreement is transferred to YOU. NOVELL, or the licensors through which NOVELL obtained the rights to distribute the products, owns and retains all title and ownership of all intellectual property rights in the products, including all software, firmware, software master diskettes, copies of software, documentation and related materials and, all modifications to and derivative works from software acquired as a Program certification holder which are made by YOU, NOVELL or any third party. NOVELL does not transfer any portion of such title and ownership, or any of the associated goodwill to YOU, and this Agreement should not be construed to grant YOU any right or license, whether by implication, estoppel or otherwise, except as expressly provided. YOU agree to be bound by and observe the proprietary nature of the products acquired as a CNA, CNE, Enterprise CNE, Master CNE, and/or CNI.

9 **QUALITY OF LICENSED SERVICES.** YOU agree that it is of fundamental importance to NOVELL that the LICENSED SERVICES be of the highest quality and integrity. Accordingly, YOU agree that NOVELL will have the right to determine in its absolute discretion whether the LICENSED SERVICES meet NOVELL's high standards of merchantability. In the event that NOVELL determines that YOU are no longer meeting accepted levels of quality and/or integrity, NOVELL agrees to so advise YOU and, except as otherwise provided in Section 6.3 of this Agreement, to provide YOU with a commercially reasonable time of no less than one (1) month to meet the above-referenced standards of quality and integrity.

10 **RESERVATION OF RIGHTS AND GOOD WILL IN NOVELL.** NOVELL retains all rights not expressly conveyed to YOU by this Agreement. YOU recognize the value of the publicity and goodwill associated with the MARKS and acknowledge that the goodwill will exclusively inure to the benefit of, and belong to, NOVELL. YOU have no rights of any kind whatsoever with respect to the MARKS licensed under this Agreement except to the extent of the license granted in this Agreement.

11 **NO REGISTRATION BY YOU.** YOU agree not to file any new trademark, collective mark, service mark, certification mark, and/or trade name application(s), in any class and in any country, for any trademark, collective mark, service mark, certification mark, and/or trade name that, in Novell's opinion, is the same as, similar to, or that contains, in whole or in part, any or all of Novell's trade names, trademarks, collective marks, service marks, and/or certification marks, including, without limitation, the MARKS licensed under this Agreement. This section will survive the expiration or other termination of this Agreement.

12 **PROTECTION OF RIGHTS.** YOU agree to assist NOVELL, to the extent reasonably necessary (and at NOVELL's expense), to protect or to obtain protection for any of NOVELL's rights to the MARKS. In addition, if at any time NOVELL requests that YOU discontinue using the MARKS and/or substitute using a new or different mark, YOU will immediately cease use of the MARKS and cooperate fully with NOVELL to ensure all legal obligations have been met with regards to use of the MARKS.

13 **INDEMNIFICATION BY YOU.** YOU agree to indemnify and hold NOVELL harmless against any loss, liability, damage, cost or expense (including reasonable legal fees) arising out of any claims or suits, whatever their nature and however arising, which may be brought or made against NOVELL (i) by reason of YOUR performance or non-performance of this Agreement; (ii) arising out of the use by YOU of the MARKS in any manner whatsoever except in the form expressly licensed under this Agreement; and/or (iii) for any personal injury, product liability, or other claim arising from the promotion

and/or provision of the LICENSED SERVICES. In the event NOVELL seeks indemnification under this Section, NOVELL will immediately notify YOU, in writing, of any claim or proceeding brought against it for which it seeks indemnification under this Agreement. In no event may YOU enter into any third party agreements which would in any manner whatsoever affect the rights of, or bind, NOVELL in any manner, without the prior written consent of NOVELL.

14 **REVISION OF TERMS.** NOVELL reserves the right to revise the terms of this Agreement from time to time. In the event of a revision, signing a new agreement may be a condition of continued certification.

15 **GENERAL PROVISIONS.**

15.1 **Governing Law and Venue.** This Agreement will in all respects be governed by the law of the country of Your residence, and venue of any actions will be proper either in the courts of the State of Utah of the United States of America or in those of the country of Your residence.

15.2 **Non-Waiver.** No waiver of any right or remedy on one occasion by either party will be deemed a waiver of such right or remedy on any other occasion.

15.3 **Course of Dealing.** This Agreement will not be supplemented or modified by any course of dealing or usage of trade.

15.4 **Assignment.** Neither this Agreement nor any of Your rights or obligations arising under this Agreement may be assigned without Novell's prior written consent. This Agreement is freely assignable by Novell, and will be for the benefit of Novell's successors and assigns.

15.5 **Independent Contractors.** YOU acknowledge that both parties are independent contractors and that YOU will not, except in accordance with this Agreement, represent YOURSELF as an agent or legal representative of NOVELL.

15.6 **Compliance with Laws.** YOU agree to comply, at YOUR own expense, with all statutes, regulations, rules, ordinances, and orders of any governmental body, department or agency which apply to or result from YOUR obligations under this Agreement. All holders of the CNE designation must not represent themselves as "engineers" or otherwise misrepresent the meaning of the CNE designation, which is an inventive and symbolic phrase only and not an acronym. Such holders must use only the "CNE" marks and logos, the "ECNE" or "Enterprise CNE" marks and logos, and/or the "Master CNE" marks and logos, as applicable and corresponding to your certification(s).

15.7 **Modifications.** Any modifications to the typewritten face of this Agreement will render it null and void. All modifications must be in writing and signed by both parties.

702

Signature Form

This Signature Form relates to and incorporates the terms and conditions of the Novell Education Certification Agreement ("Agreement") to which it is attached. YOU must either indicate assent electronically or sign this Agreement Signature Form and return it to the applicable address below:

Novell Education
c/o Agreements
5001 W 80th St, Suite 401
Bloomington, MN 55437
USA

Novell Education
c/o Agreements
Level 6, Suite 602
25 Bligh Street
Sydney, NSW 2000
Australia

Novell Education
c/o Agreements
Pelmolenlaan 12-14
3447 G W Woerden
The Netherlands

Please note: If YOU are a minor under the laws of the state or country (whichever applies) where you sign this Signature Form, it needs to be countersigned below by YOUR parent, court-appointed curator, or legal guardian. The Agreement will automatically terminate when YOU reach the age of majority *unless* you affirm the Agreement by completing and signing the Novell Education Certification Agreement being used generally by Novell at that time and returning it to Novell. If YOU allow the Agreement to lapse, YOU will be decertified.

Certification Candidate:

By signing this form, YOU confirm that YOU have read and agree to be bound by the terms and conditions of the Novell Education Certification Agreement, including, but not limited to, the terms relating to YOUR limited right to use Novell's Marks (as that term is defined in the Agreement).

Signature ______________________________

Print Name ____________________________

Date __________________________________

Test ID# _______________________________

Daytime Phone # ________________________

[ ] Parent / [ ] Curator / [ ] Legal Guardian:
(Check appropriate box)

By signing this form, the candidate's parent / curator / legal guardian confirms that he / she has read the Novell Education Certification Agreement and accepts full responsibility for the candidate's compliance with its terms and conditions and will be liable for any breach of the candidate's obligations thereunder.

Signature ______________________________

Print Name ____________________________

Date __________________________________

To receive a copy of the complete agreement from Certification Administration or by fax, call 1-800-233-EDUC or 1-801-222-7800.

Due to legal restrictions we cannot accept faxed copies of the signed form.

CNA Cross-Reference to Novell Course Objectives

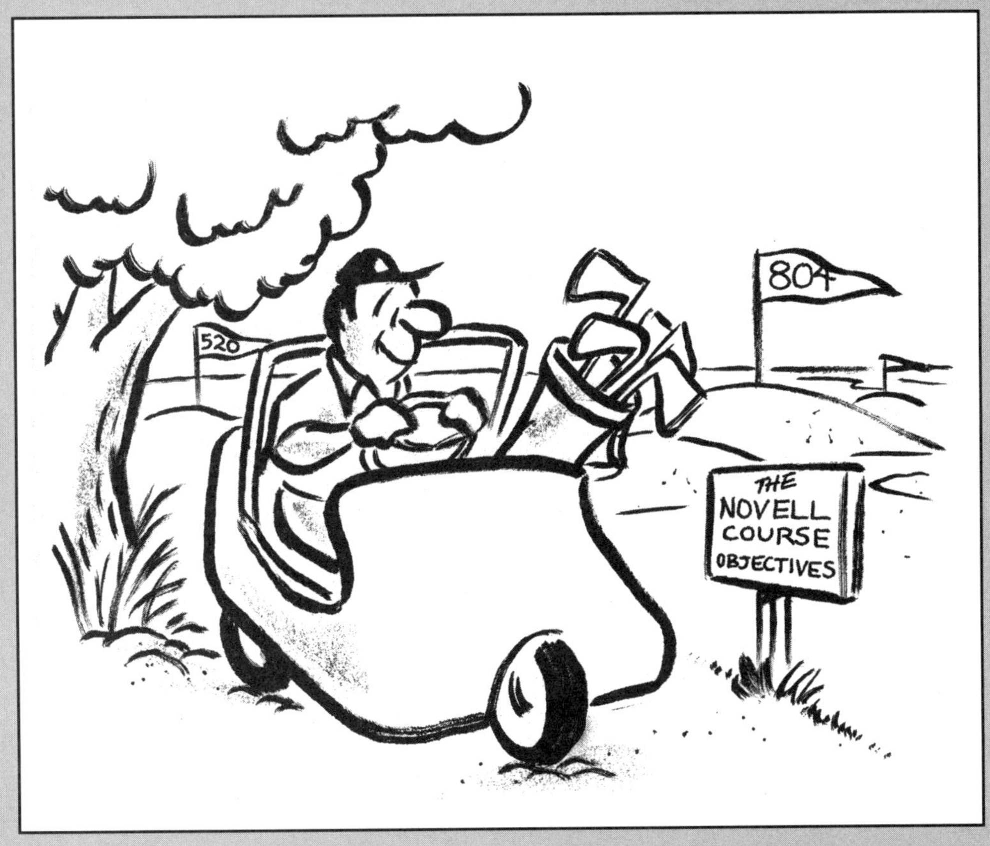

Following is a list of the Novell-authorized course objectives for the NetWare 4 CNA curriculum. Novell Education uses the objectives to write authorized courseware and to develop certification exams. In order to become a NetWare 4 CNA, you must be intimately familiar with every objective. Novell's CNA Study Guide for NetWare 4.1 enables you to learn these objectives (see page numbers cross-reference) in conjunction with Novell-authorized courseware. This appendix clarifies that relationship by pointing you in the right direction.

Have fun and good luck!

Course 520: NetWare 4 Administration

This is the foundation of the NetWare 4 curriculum. In the NetWare 4 Administration course, you are introduced to the fundamental technologies of NetWare 4, namely NetWare Directory Services, the File System, NDS and Server Security, Backup, Login Scripts, the "new" Menu System, Messaging, and, of course, Printing.

Good news — this represents the Entire CNA curriculum. Learn it, use it, become a CNA!

SECTION 1: INTRODUCTION TO NETWARE 4

1. Describe a network, including its basic function and physical components... **103**

2. List the NetWare 4 network services students will learn to administer in this course... **104–110**

3. Describe NetWare Directory Services (NDS) and explain its role on the network... **111–122**

4. Describe the Directory, including its function and basic components... **123**

5. Describe the Directory tree, including leaf and container objects... **120–144**

SECTION 2: CONNECTING TO THE NETWORK AND LOGGING IN

1. Describe how a workstation communicates with the network, and list the files required to connect a DOS workstation to the network... **406–418**

2. Describe the function of the software and hardware necessary to connect a workstation to the network, including local operating systems, NetWare DOS Requester, communications protocols, and network board... **531–546**

3. Connect a workstation to the network by loading the appropriate DOS workstation files... **480–482**

4. Explain and perform the login procedure... **480–482**

SECTION 3: ACCESSING DATA FILES AND APPLICATIONS ON THE NETWORK

1. Explain the basic concepts of network file storage, including volumes, directory structures, network drives, and search drives... **216–224**

2. Define NetWare command line utilities, describe how they are used, and activate Help information for them... **224–257**

3. Display volume, directory, and file information... **224–257**

4. Map a network drive to a volume using a Volume object and a Directory Map object, and navigate between the volumes... **257–279**

5. Map a network drive to a directory using a Volume object and a Directory Map object and navigate the directories of a volume... **257–279**

6. Map a search drive to a directory containing an application using a Volume object and a Directory Map object and run the application... **257–279**

SECTION 4: PRINTING TO A NETWORK PRINTER

SECTION 5: SETTING UP USER ACCOUNTS AND LOGIN SECURITY

SECTION 6: SETTING UP THE NETWORK FILE SYSTEM

1. Explain guidelines for planning and creating custom volumes and directories in the network file system... **206–214**

2. List the system-created volumes and directories; describe their contents and function... **214–218**

3. Identify the strengths and weaknesses of sample directory structures... **218–224**

4. Design and create a directory structure based on a given scenario... **277–278**

5. Explain guidelines for selecting and installing network applications... **454–458**

SECTION 7: MANAGING THE FILE SYSTEM

1. Manage the file system directory structure by creating, deleting, renaming, and moving directories... **235–246**

2. Manage files in the file system by copying, moving, deleting, salvaging, and purging files... **246–256**

3. Manage the use of volume space by viewing volume usage statistics; restricting space usage by user and directory; changing file ownership; locating files based on usage, owner, and size; setting compression attributes; and setting data migration attributes... **226–235**

SECTION 8: SETTING UP FILE SYSTEM SECURITY

1. Describe NetWare 4 file system security, including the concepts of directory and file rights, trustee assignments, inheritance, rights reassignment, Inherited Rights Filters (IRFs), security equivalence, and effective rights... **290–291**

2. Given a scenario, calculate a user's effective rights... **394–399**

3. Perform basic security implementation tasks, such as assigning a trustee and granting rights, setting a directory IRF, creating a group object and assigning members, and making a user security equivalent to another user... **378–388**

4. Describe guidelines for planning a directory structure based on security considerations... **219–224**

5. Given a directory structure and the function of its directories, recommend the rights that should be granted and the trustee object that will make security implementation and management easiest... **378–388**

6. Describe and set directory and file attributes that can be used to regulate access to files: Copy Inhibit, Delete Inhibit, Execute Only, Hidden, Purge, Read Only, Read Write, Rename Inhibit, Shareable, System, and Transactional... **291**

7. Activate, navigate NDS and file systems with, and get help for, NetWare Administrator... **378–388**

8. Based on a scenario, create and implement a file system security plan that appropriately grants directory and file rights to container, Group, and User objects, and set directory IRFs... **378–388**

SECTION 9: ACCESSING AND PROTECTING THE NETWARE SERVER CONSOLE

1. Describe the function of a NetWare 4 server and its interface... **499**

2. Define console command and NetWare Loadable Module (NLM) ... **500, 506–531**

3. Describe the function of the LOAD command... **514**

4. Describe remote console management; list the steps necessary to set up a server for both SPX and asynchronous remote connections... **561–565**

5. Use RCONSOLE.EXE to remotely access the server console, change between console screens, and activate the RCONSOLE Available Options menu... **565–569**

6. Describe security strategies for a NetWare 4 server, such as setting a password on the monitor, setting a password for Remote Console, and placing the server in a secure location... **500–506**

SECTION 10: SETTING UP NETWORK PRINTING

1. Set up a network printing environment by creating and configuring related Print Queue, Printer, and Print Server objects... **609–623**

2. Set up network printing hardware by bringing up a print server on a NetWare 4 server and connecting a printer to the network through a NetWare server or DOS workstation... **617–623**

3. Regulate who can do any of the following: print to a print queue, manage print jobs in the print queue, be notified by a printer when a problem occurs, view the status of the print server, or manage the print server... **632–657**

4. Manage the flow of print jobs into and out of a print queue by managing the status of the print queue... **632–657**

5. Manage print jobs in a print queue by pausing, rushing, delaying, and deleting print jobs in the print queue... **632–657**

6. Describe how to customize print jobs using print job configurations, printer definitions, and printer forms... **623–632**

SECTION 11: INSTALLING AND CONFIGURING NETWARE CLIENT ON A DOS WORKSTATION

1. Describe the appropriate options needed in the CONFIG.SYS, AUTOEXEC.BAT, and NET.CFG files to automate the network connection and login processes... **406–418**

2. Install NetWare Client for DOS and MS Windows using the NetWare Client installation software... **518–526**

3. Create a custom network connection by modifying the INSTALL.CFG and NET.CFG files... **410–418**

SECTION 12: CREATING LOGIN SCRIPTS

1. Describe the types of login scripts and how they coordinate at login... **419–427**

2. Recommend procedures that should be executed during login... **427–442**

3. Plan login scripts with correct login script command syntax, given an environment need... **427–442**

4. Create, execute, and debug a login script... **484–486**

SECTION 13: CREATING USER MENUS

1. Describe the process of creating menus... **442–454**

2. Plan a simple menu using correct command syntax... **442–454**

3. Build, compile, execute, and debug menus... **486–487**

4. Describe the process of converting menus from previous versions of NetWare to the new menu system... **451–453**

SECTION 14: MANAGING NDS SECURITY

1. Explain how access to the Directory is controlled by object trustees, object rights, and property rights... **321–352**

2. List and explain the automatic rights assignments that can occur in NDS... **321–325**

3. Explain guidelines and considerations for managing NDS security... **315–352**

4. Implement NDS security by making trustee assignments; modifying Object, All Property, and Selected Property rights; and setting Inherited Rights Filters... **378–388**

SECTION 15: MANAGING RESOURCES IN THE DIRECTORY TREE

1. Describe how the Directory tree structure affects network use and management skills... **111–129**

2. Describe sample Directory structures and discuss basic guidelines for organizing resources... **145–148**

3. Demonstrate correct object-naming techniques... **148–152**

4. Change the current context and navigate the Directory tree with CX... **154–156**

5. Log in, map network drives, and redirect print jobs to resources in other contexts... **195–201**

6. Grant rights to file system and network printing resources in other contexts... **195–201**

7. Create shortcuts to objects in other contexts using Directory Map and Alias objects... **138–143, 195–201**

8. Establish an initial context at login for a DOS workstation... **410–418**

9. Edit login scripts to access resources in other containers... **427–442**

SECTION 16: BACKING UP SERVERS AND WORKSTATIONS

1. Compare and contrast backup strategies... **550–553**

2. Describe the process of backing up a NetWare server's file system with SBACKUP... **546–558**

3. Describe the process of restoring lost file system information with SBACKUP... **546–558**

SECTION 17: PROVIDING MESSAGING SERVICES

1. Determine appropriate use of messaging services through MHS Services for NetWare 4... **460–465**

2. Describe the process of installing messaging services using MHS Services for NetWare 4... **4654–470**

3. Create a Distribution List object and assign members... **488–492**

4. Assign mailboxes to User, Group, Distribution List, and Organizational Role objects... **488–492**

5. Send and receive e-mail with FirstMail... **493–494**

Solutions to Quizzes, Puzzles, Exercises, and Case Studies

Chapter 3: Understanding NDS

ANSWERS TO QUIZZES

Q3-1

The only available matching color for the large present is red. Next, the only contrasting color available for the small wrapping is silver. Finally, that leaves green wrapping and a gold bow for the medium-sized gift. Happy birthday.

Q3-2

The only days the Lion can say "I lied yesterday" are Mondays and Thursdays. The only days the Unicorn can say "I lied yesterday" are Thursdays and Sundays. Therefore, the only day they can both say it is Thursday.

Q3-3

On no day of the week is this possible! Only on Mondays and Thursdays could he make the first statement; only on Wednesdays and Sundays could he make the second. So there is no day he could say both. Poor Alice is stuck in the Land of Forgetfulness forever.

Q3-4

This is a very different situation! It illustrates well the difference between making two statements separately and making one statement that is the conjunction of the two. Indeed, given any two statements X and Y, if the single statement "X and Y" is true, then it follows that X and Y are true separately. But if the conjunction "X and Y" is false, then at least one of them is false.

Now, the only day of the week it could be true that the Lion lied yesterday and will lie again tomorrow is Tuesday (this is the only day that occurs between two of the Lion's lying days). So, the day the Lion said that couldn't be Tuesday, for on Tuesdays that statement is true, but the Lion doesn't make true statements on Tuesdays. Therefore, it is not Tuesday. Hence, the Lion's statement is false, so the Lion is lying. Therefore, the day must be either Monday or Wednesday. Tricky little Lion.

Q3-5

A–4
B–5,8
C–1
D–2, 6
E–3

Q3-6

The Hint (Synergy) means the whole is greater than the sum of its parts. This means we must be dealing with a whole number. Therefore, half of "What I'd be" must be a whole number. "What I'd be" must be an even number. "What I am" cannot end in 1. There are four possible arrangements of the three digits:

	(a)	(b)	(c)	(d)
What I am	1?3	13?	31?	?13
What I'd be	3?4	34?	43?	?34

"What I am" is "Nine less than half what I'd be." So ("What I am" + 9) × 2 = "What I'd be." Examination shows that only "A" fits the bill and "What I am" must be 183.

No sweat.

EXERCISE 3-1: PLANT A TREE IN A CLOUD

```
G L E A D I N G P E R I O D N X G X T Q W
Y C O U N T R Y R F T I O V S I H R R I Q
M U X C P S K V O O U N K N O W N E L M F
G R S W A K S K F B U D A L I A S K A X J
E R N H T L W Y I N J P V M M U U A I I N
R E G A J R I B L U Z E C E P C W B E Q H
Y N L S N H P T E H D W C E X V X V Q X Q O
L T X P B F H R Y H H O R T A W V E S C T
I C B B F H I R X D N V G H R Q K E B Q E
B O R G A N I Z A T I O N A L R O L E T K
V N Y T L Y B X E S E R H F K F W G U Y K
J T D Y V R N X O T V G E E B T L Y E P X
K E T P S J T R W I L A N C S E J V B E U
R X F E H E S F G V H N A M T F B D Y L L
M T W F A S Q L H A Q I D K R O D Q I E R
T I N U L A N O I T A Z I N A G R O W S Z
M Y D L H S W N C X D A U Q I S N Y V S S
O D B N L R C G T J O T O O Y D A E M N M
R J P A A T J X N G F I T B V H J Y F A B
Q O H M H D I R E C T O R Y S C A N P M P
W U N E Z T R A I L I N G P E R I O D E V
```

1. ALIAS

2. COUNTRY

3. CURRENT CONTEXT

4. CX

5. DIRECTORY MAP

6. DIRECTORY SCAN

7. GROUP

8. LEADING PERIOD

9. LOCALITY

10. NAME CONTEXT

11. OBJECT

12. ORGANIZATION

13. ORGANIZATIONAL ROLE

14. ORGANIZATIONAL UNIT

15. PROFILE

16. SUPERVISOR

17. TRAILING PERIOD

18. TYPEFUL NAME

19. TYPELESS NAME

20. UNKNOWN

SOLUTIONS TO QUIZZES, PUZZLES, EXERCISES, AND CASE STUDIES

EXERCISE 3-2: NETWARE 4 CNE BASICS

A crossword puzzle with the following answers filled in:

1. CURRENT CONTEXT
4. COMMON NAME
6. BINDERY
7. AUTHENTICATION
8. TIMESERVERS
10. DYNATEXT
12. TIMESYNCHRONIZATION
13. CONTEXT
16. DATAMIGRATION
17. FILECOMPRESSION
18. SUBALLOCATION
19. DISTINGUISHEDNAME

Down answers include:
2. UTILIZATIONAL UNIT
3. CONTAINER
5. ORGANIZATION
9. TIMESTAMP
11. ALIAS
14. INDEXES
15. PARTITION

EXERCISE 3-3: "TREE WALKING" FOR TODDLERS

1a. Answers will vary in terms of what objects are displayed when you activate the NetWare Administrator utility. Your current context is the topmost icon displayed on the screen. (You may need to use the scrollbar on the right side of the screen to get to the top of the screen.) When you first activate the NetWare Administrator utility, your *current context* is the one that was in effect last time you used the utility on this workstation. Your current context in the NetWare Administrator utility is utility-specific. In other words, it is independent of your current context as displayed at the command line.

1b. Answers will vary for all questions in this section.

EXERCISE 3-4: UNDERSTANDING NDS NAMING

1. .BMasterson.BLUE.CRIME.TOKYO.ACME

2. .CN=RHood.OU=WHITE.OU=CRIME.OU=TOKYO.O=ACME

3. CRIME.TOKYO.ACME

4. CN=BLUE-SRV1.OU=BLUE.OU=CRIME.OU=TOKYO.O=ACME (since the default current context is the [Root])

5. SHolmes

6. LJohn.WHITE.CRIME

7. CN=SirKay.OU=CHARITY

8. Admin...

9. CN=Sirkay.OU=CHARITY..

10. CN=BLUE-SRV1_SYS.OU=BLUE.OU=CRIME.OU=TOKYO.O=ACME....

11. .BLUE.CRIME.TOKYO.ACME (since it's the context of the server)

SOLUTIONS TO QUIZZES, PUZZLES, EXERCISES, AND CASE STUDIES

LOGIN DHolliday.BLUE.CRIME.TOKYO.ACME

LOGIN DHolliday (since NetWare 4 searches the server's context by default)

12. CX CHARITY..

13. Add the following statement to his NET.CFG file:

NAME CONTEXT="OU=CHARITY.OU=TOKYO.O=ACME"

14. LOGIN .CN=SHolmes.OU=CRIME.OU=TOKYO.O=ACME

LOGIN .SHolmes.CRIME.TOKYO.ACME

LOGIN SHolmes.

LOGIN CN=SHolmes.

LOGIN SHolmes.CRIME..

LOGIN CN=SHolmes.OU=CRIME..

LOGIN SHolmes.CRIME.TOKYO...

LOGIN CN=SHolmes.OU=CRIME.OU=TOKYO...

LOGIN SHolmes.CRIME.TOKYO.ACME....

LOGIN CN=SHolmes.OU=CRIME.OU=TOKYO.O=ACME....

15. CX /R

Chapter 4: NetWare 4 File System

ANSWERS TO QUIZZES

Q4-1
28463

Q4-2
It doesn't matter what x is, because at some time during the calculation you will be multiplying by (x–x), which equals 0. Therefore, the product will be 0. Tricky!

Q4-3
69382

Q4-4
1, 4, 9, 6, 1, 5, 10, 4, 2
Now change to Roman numerals:
I, IV, IX, VI, I, V, X, IV, II
Very tricky, and I like it for that reason, and because the Roman numeral IV appears in my name. Touché.

EXERCISE 4-1: NETWARE 4 FILE CABINET

```
S Y S T E M C T E R R B
Y E U U J N E Q E K B U
S N E A K E R N E T S R
I W L L S J Q X Y F Q Z
X A U C P P T V Q L V G
T D E L E T E D S A V C
E M Z O V X V M W G P Q
E I F N C O P Y P L U N
N N N I G O L P R I B G
R I D N L S D U A A L Q
V Q U E U E S I M M I K
T A N B H K R W M E C D
```

1. DELETED.SAV
2. DOC
3. ETC
4. FILER
5. FLAG
6. LOGIN
7. MAIL
8. MAP
9. NCOPY
10. NDIR

11. NLS
12. NWADMIN
13. PUBLIC
14. QUEUES
15. RAID
16. SIXTEEN
17. SNEAKERNET
18. SYS:
19. SYSTEM
20. VOLUME

EXERCISE 4-2: UNDERSTANDING DRIVE MAPPING

1. MAP /?

2. MAP

3. MAP F:=SYS:USERS

4. MAP G:=SYS:\SHARED\POL

5. MAP J:=F:

6. MAP S:=.WHITE.SRV1_SYS.WHITE.CRIME.TOKYO.ACME:SHARED

7. MAP INS S1:=SYS:\PUBLIC

8. MAP INS S2:=SYS:\PUBLIC\IBM_PC\MSDOS\V6.22

9. MAP S3:=APPS\SS30

10. MAP ROOT S4:=SYS:\APPS\DB50

11. MAP

    In the map list, the false root has no space after the volume name but does have a space followed by a backslash after the name of the directory it points to.

12. MAP S5:=W:=SYS:\APPS\WP70

    Yes.

13. The MAP command didn't work. To fix the problem, type CD \PUBLIC

14. MAP DEL J:

15. MAP REM S3:

    The search drives with higher search drive numbers were renumbered accordingly.

    The network drive associated with the search drive was deleted.

16. MAP C S4:

    The search drive was deleted.

The network drive associated with the search drive was moved to the top portion of the map list.

Chapter 5: NetWare 4 Security

ANSWERS TO QUIZZES

Q5-1

"A road map tells you everything except how to refold it." (Start at *A* in center.)

Q5-2

36421

Q5-3

He is abstemious. We discovered that he only likes words with all five vowels in them — an odd bird.

Q5-4

That's easy, man. It's "wrong."

Q5-5

     ABORT: It is five letters long.
     ACT: Last letter cannot be placed first to form another word.
     AGT: Not an actual word.
     ALP: Does not end with a T.
     OPT: Does not start with A.
     APT: Not in alphabetical order with rest.

EXERCISE 5-1: HOW SECURE DO YOU FEEL?

```
S E C U R I T Y Z P R K C U G L S M Y
T J Z U N I Q U E P A S S W O R D S Y
A C M C K R S S Z P Z T V G O K B O W
T P R O O F S K P P W T T O M D R H P
I R U G R A C E L O G I N S N M X L Q
O I O B J E C T R I G H T S J U T H S
N V D Z L I L T U T I Y A B T Z W R
R A J S G I N H E R I T A N C E C T V
E T E F F E C T I V E R I G H T S J Q
S E C U R I T Y E Q U I V A L E N C E
T K R P R Y B V D N F D G M L F D W R
R E S B Q P G W P X G F W T W B H P J
I Y Y O B G V X L G O T B B M C A V M
C L H F W T Y N B B T G Y P T Q Y E K
T I M E R E S T R I C T I O N S U F P
I N T R U D E R D E T E C T I O N X U
O R U S T H G I R Y T R E P O R P Q F
N C P P A C K E T S I G N A T U R E F
S N W P B Z S T H G I R E E T S U R T
```

1. ACL	11. PROPERTY RIGHTS
2. EFFECTIVE RIGHTS	12. [PUBLIC]
3. GRACE LOGINS	13. RISK
4. INHERITANCE	14. SECURITY
5. INTRUDER DETECTION	15. SECURITY EQUIVALENCE
6. IRF	16. STATION RESTRICTIONS
7. NCP PACKET SIGNATURE	17. TIME RESTRICTIONS
8. OBJECT RIGHTS	18. TRUSTEE RIGHTS
9. PRIVATE KEY	19. TTS
10. PROOF	20. UNIQUE PASSWORDS

EXERCISE 5-2: NETWARE 4 MANAGEMENT

EXERCISE 5-3: CALCULATING NDS EFFECTIVE RIGHTS

CASE #I

See Figure C5.1 for answer to this case.

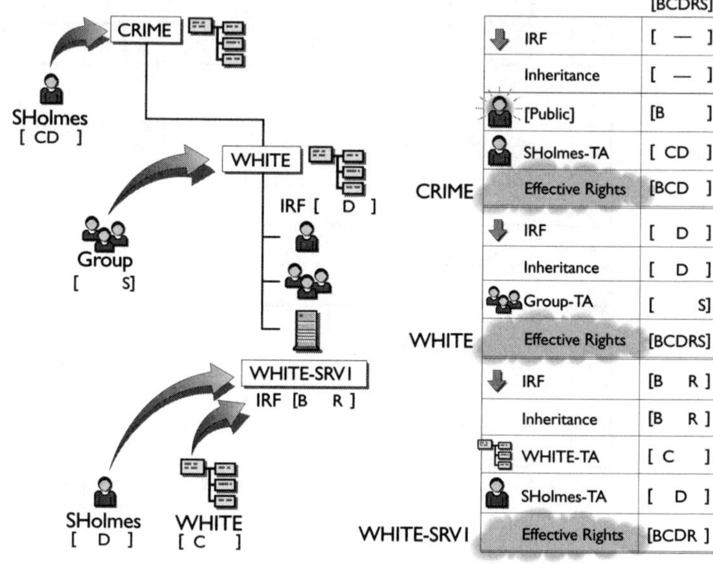

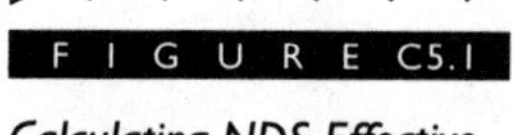

F I G U R E C5.I

Calculating NDS Effective Rights — CASE #I

CASE STUDY: ACME SECURITY

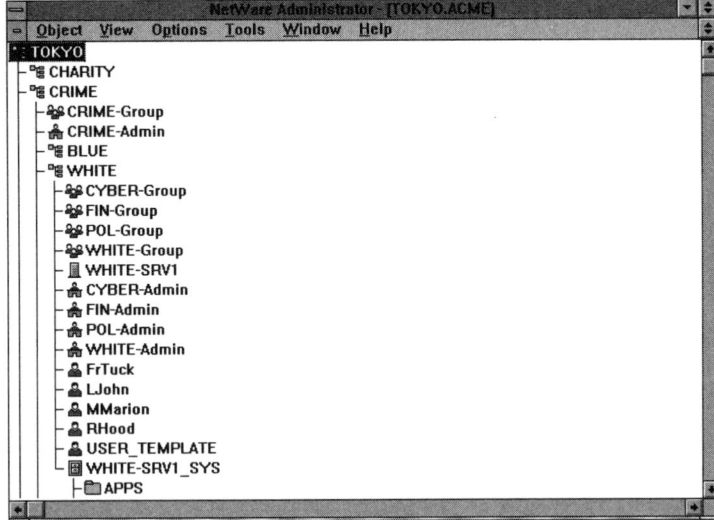

FIGURE C5.10

The .TOKYO.ACME NDS Directory Tree

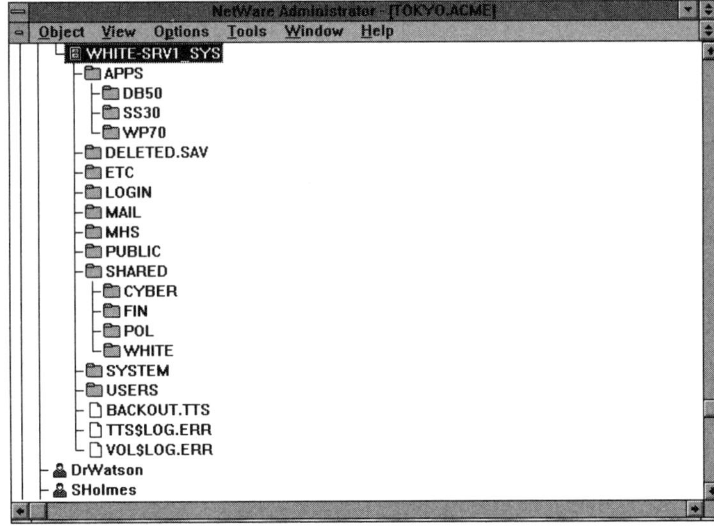

FIGURE C5.11

The WHITE-SRV1_SYS File System Directory Tree

FIGURE C5.12

Password Restrictions for the USER_TEMPLATE in .TOKYO.ACME

CASE #2

See Figure C5.2 for answer to this case.

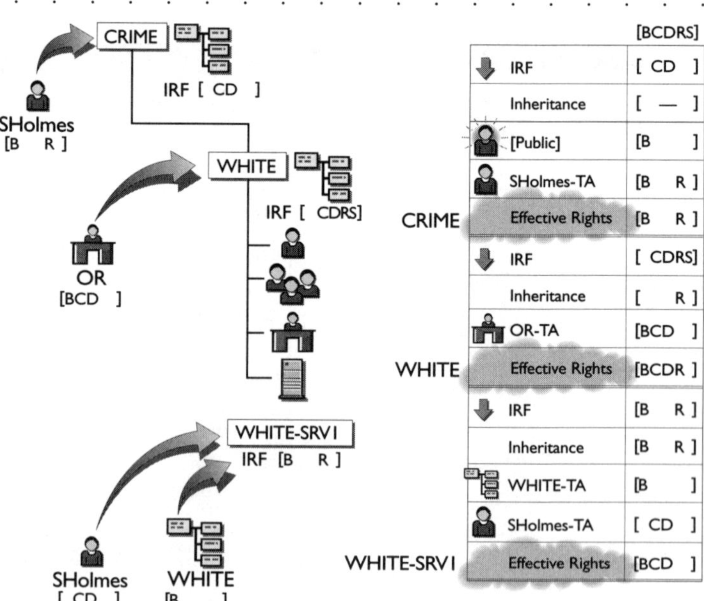

FIGURE C5.2

Calculating NDS Effective Rights — CASE #2

SOLUTIONS TO QUIZZES, PUZZLES, EXERCISES, AND CASE STUDIES

CASE #3

See Figure C5.3 for answer to this case.

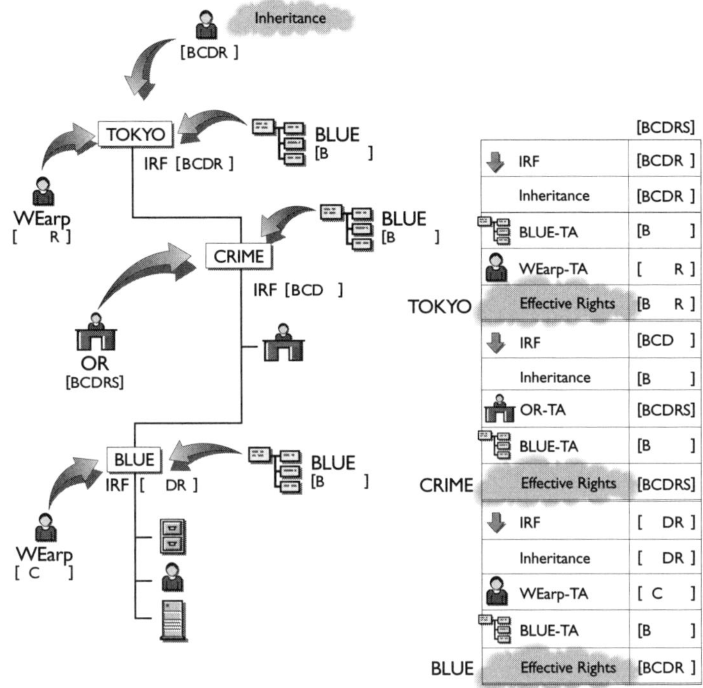

F I G U R E C5.3

Calculating NDS Effective Rights — CASE #3

		[BCDRS]
	IRF	[BCDR]
	Inheritance	[BCDR]
	BLUE-TA	[B]
	WEarp-TA	[R]
TOKYO	Effective Rights	[B R]
	IRF	[BCD]
	Inheritance	[B]
	OR-TA	[BCDRS]
	BLUE-TA	[B]
CRIME	Effective Rights	[BCDRS]
	IRF	[DR]
	Inheritance	[DR]
	WEarp-TA	[C]
	BLUE-TA	[B]
BLUE	Effective Rights	[BCDR]

EXERCISE 5-4: CALCULATING FILE SYSTEM EFFECTIVE RIGHTS

CASE #1

See Figure C5.4 for answer to this case.

Calculating File System Effective Rights — CASE #1

SYS:SHARED

	S	R	C	W	E	M	F	A
Inherited Rights Filter	S	R	C	W	E	M	F	A
Inherited Rights-User								
Inherited Rights-Group								
Trustee Assignment-User		R	C	W			F	
Trustee Assignment-Group								
Effective Rights		R	C	W			F	

SYS:SHARED\CYBER

	S	R	C	W	E	M	F	A
Inherited Rights Filter	S	R					F	
Inherited Rights-User		R					F	
Inherited Rights-Group								
Trustee Assignment-User								
Trustee Assignment-Group								
Effective Rights		R					F	

CYBER.DOC

	S	R	C	W	E	M	F	A
Inherited Rights Filter	S	R	C	W			F	
Inherited Rights-User		R					F	
Inherited Rights-Group								
Trustee Assignment-User								
Trustee Assignment-Group								
Effective Rights		R					F	

SOLUTIONS TO QUIZZES, PUZZLES, EXERCISES, AND CASE STUDIES

CASE #2

See Figure C5.5 for answer to this case.

FIGURE C5.5

Calculating File System Effective Rights — CASE #2

SYS:SHARED	S	R	C	W	E	M	F	A
Inherited Rights Filter	S	R	C	W	E	M	F	A
Inherited Rights-User								
Inherited Rights-Group								
Trustee Assignment-User								
Trustee Assignment-Group		R	C	W			F	
Effective Rights		R	C	W			F	

SYS:SHARED\FINAN	S	R	C	W	E	M	F	A
Inherited Rights Filter	S							
Inherited Rights-User								
Inherited Rights-Group								
Trustee Assignment-User		R	C	W	E	M	F	
Trustee Assignment-Group								
Effective Rights		R	C	W	E	M	F	

99QTR4.RPT	S	R	C	W	E	M	F	A
Inherited Rights Filter	S	R		W			F	
Inherited Rights-User		R		W			F	
Inherited Rights-Group								
Trustee Assignment-User								
Trustee Assignment-Group		R						
Effective Rights		R		W			F	

CASE #3

See Figure C5.6 for answer to this case.

Calculating File System Effective Rights — CASE #3

	S	R	C	W	E	M	F	A
SYS:SHARED								
Inherited Rights Filter	S	R	C	W	E	M	F	A
Inherited Rights-User								
Inherited Rights-Group								
Trustee Assignment-User		R	C	W			F	
Trustee Assignment-Group								
Effective Rights		R	C	W			F	

	S	R	C	W	E	M	F	A
SYS:SHARED\CRIME								
Inherited Rights Filter	S							
Inherited Rights-User								
Inherited Rights-Group								
Trustee Assignment-User								
Trustee Assignment-Group		R	C	W	E	M	F	
Effective Rights		R	C	W	E	M	F	

	S	R	C	W	E	M	F	A
CRIME.DB								
Inherited Rights Filter	S	R	C	W			F	
Inherited Rights-User								
Inherited Rights-Group		R	C	W			F	
Trustee Assignment-User								
Trustee Assignment-Group		R					F	
Effective Rights		R					F	

CASE #4

See Figure C5.7 for answer to this case.

*Calculating File System
Effective Rights —
CASE #4*

SYS:SHARED

	S	R	C	W	E	M	F	A
Inherited Rights Filter	S	R	C	W	E	M	F	A
Inherited Rights-User								
Inherited Rights-Group								
Trustee Assignment-User								
Trustee Assignment-Group		R	C	W	E		F	
Effective Rights		R	C	W	E		F	

SYS:SHARED\POLIT

	S	R	C	W	E	M	F	A
Inherited Rights Filter	S							
Inherited Rights-User								
Inherited Rights-Group								
Trustee Assignment-User						M		A
Trustee Assignment-Group		R	C	W	E		F	
Effective Rights		R	C	W	E	M	F	A

CRIME.RPT

	S	R	C	W	E	M	F	A
Inherited Rights Filter	S	R	C	W	E	M	F	A
Inherited Rights-User						M		A
Inherited Rights-Group		R	C	W	E		F	
Trustee Assignment-User								
Trustee Assignment-Group								
Effective Rights		R	C	W	E	M	F	A

CASE #5

See Figure C5.8 for answer to this case.

FIGURE C5.8

Calculating File System Effective Rights — CASE #5

	S	R	C	W	E	M	F	A
SYS:SHARED								
Inherited Rights Filter	S	R	C	W	E	M	F	A
Inherited Rights-User								
Inherited Rights-Group								
Trustee Assignment-User	S	R	C	W	E	M	F	A
Trustee Assignment-Group								
Effective Rights	S	R	C	W	E	M	F	A
SYS:SHARED\CRIME								
Inherited Rights Filter	S							
Inherited Rights-User	S	(R)	(C)	(W)	(E)	(M)	(F)	(A)
Inherited Rights-Group								
Trustee Assignment-User								
Trustee Assignment-Group		R	C	W			F	
Effective Rights	S	R	C	W	(E)	(M)	F	(A)
CRIME.DB								
Inherited Rights Filter	S	R					F	
Inherited Rights-User	S	R	(C)	(W)	(E)	(M)	F	(A)
Inherited Rights-Group		R					F	
Trustee Assignment-User								
Trustee Assignment-Group		R					F	
Effective Rights	S	R	(C)	(W)	(E)	(M)	F	(A)

CASE #6

See Figure C5.9 for answer to this case.

SYS:SHARED	S	R	C	W	E	M	F	A
Inherited Rights Filter	S	R					F	A
Inherited Rights-User								
Inherited Rights-Group or [Public]								
Trustee Assignment-User								
Trustee Assignment-Group or [Public]		R					F	
Effective Rights		R					F	

SYS:SHARED\WHITE	S	R	C	W	E	M	F	A
Inherited Rights Filter	S	R					F	
Inherited Rights-User								
Inherited Rights-Group or [Public]	S	R	C	W	E	M	F	A
Trustee Assignment-User	S	R	C	W	E	M	F	A
Trustee Assignment-Group or [Public]								
Effective Rights	S	R	C	W	E	M	F	A

SUMMARY.RPT	S	R	C	W	E	M	F	A
Inherited Rights Filter	S							
Inherited Rights-User	S	(R)	(C)	(W)	(E)	(M)	(F)	(A)
Inherited Rights-Group or [Public]								
Trustee Assignment-User		R	C	W	E	M		
Trustee Assignment-Group or [Public]								
Effective Rights	S	R	C	W	E	M	F	A

Chapter 6: NetWare 4 Configuration

ANSWERS TO QUIZZES

Q6-1

The most common wrong answer is 25. If the problem had been, "What is the smallest number I must pick in order to be sure of getting at least two socks of *different* colors," then the correct answer would have been 25. But the problem calls for at least two socks of the *same* color, so the correct answer is three. If I pick three socks, then either they are all of the same color (in which case I certainly have at least two of the same color), or else two are of one color and the third is of the other color — so I have two of the same color.

Q6-2

J.

Q6-3

The bear must be white — it must be a polar bear. The usual answer is that the bear must have been standing at the North Pole. Well, this is indeed one possibility, but it's not the only one. From the North Pole, all directions are south, so if the bear is standing at the North Pole and the man is 100 yards south of him and walks 100 yards east, then when he faces north, he will be facing the North Pole again. I'll buy that.

But, there are many more alternative solutions. It could be, for example, that the man is very close to the South Pole on a spot where the polar circle passing through that spot has a circumference of exactly 100 yards, and the bear is standing 100 yards north of him. Then if the man walks east 100 yards, he would walk right around that circle and be right back at the point he started from.

In addition, the man could be a little closer to the South Pole at a point where the polar circle has a circumference of exactly 50 yards, so if he walked east 100 yards, he would walk around that little circle twice and be back where he started. You get the idea.

Of course, in any of these solutions, the bear is sufficiently close to either the North Pole or the South Pole to qualify as a polar bear. There is, of course, the remote possibility that some mischievous human being deliberately transported a brown bear to the North Pole just to spite us — who's paranoid?

Q6-4

Cerebrum

Q6-5

1. The biologist is not Catherine and not from Canada. Therefore, she belongs to C house (she must have one C).

2. If Catherine were the doctor, then she would have to come from Brazil (we know she's not from Australia), and if she were the doctor, she couldn't be from Denmark. Therefore, the doctor is from Brazil — but we are told the doctor is not from Brazil. Therefore, Catherine is not the doctor. Therefore, she must be the author.

3. The biologist is not from Australia and not from Canada. Therefore, she must be from Denmark.

4. Since the biologist is from C house and from Denmark, she must be Alice.

5. Therefore, the doctor is not Alice, and the doctor is not Catherine. Therefore, the doctor is Brett, and Deirdre must be the cartoonist.

6. Since the doctor is Brett, she is not from B house. Therefore, the doctor is from A house (the only alternative left). Therefore, the doctor is from Canada.

7. Since the cartoonist is Deirdre, she cannot be from D house. Therefore, she is from B house. Therefore, the cartoonist is from Australia.

8. Therefore, Catherine, the author, is from Brazil and was in D house.

   Complete solution:

Alice	Biologist	C	Denmark
Brett	Doctor	A	Canada
Catherine	Author	D	Brazil
Deirdre	Cartoonist	B	Australia

Q6-6

OK, here's what was going on inside the cerebrum of "C." If anyone were to see two red and two black, he would know that he was white. If anyone were to see two red, one black, and one white, he would know that he could not be black. If he were, the man with the white disc would see two red and two black and would know that he was white. Similarly, if anyone were to see one red, two black, and two white.

If anyone were to see one red, one black, and two white, he would know that he could not be black. If he were, either of the men wearing white would see one red, two black, and one white, and would argue as above. If anyone were to see two red and two white, he would argue that he could not be black. If he were, someone would see two red, one black, and one white and would argue as above.

If anyone were to see one red and three white, he would argue that he could not be black. If he were, someone would see one red, one black, and two white and would argue as above; similarly, he would know that he could not be red. Therefore, if anyone sees me wearing red or black, he can deduce his color. Therefore, I must be white.

C really needs to get a life.

Q6-7

Ensign Chekov

EXERCISE 6-1: CHILDHOOD

```
S D Y P J G I D F N G R H M U M G N S
F I L E A T T R I B U T E S F F X N H
I S L T N E I L C W N M E N U M A K E
R T X W M G E T O Y V E T X H M Z J L
S R H V Y I F X M J D W T S E A Y Y L
T I S R P Q K W S W M Y S C Y C H K C
M B T Y I K Y E P U C E I T F Q V O F
A U S Q O T I L E K R N P V F G Q S G
I T H N W M W P C V T H U P J M Y Y B
L I D E N T I F I E R V A R I A B L E
I O I X D B I C X G F S U M V W X G E
N N G J D Q E T A B T E N T R A T S Z
K L S P O S T M A S T E R H O D T X P
D I N L R L O M L D N M V E H G A N P
R S Y Y R O K V Q A Q U T R R Q R Z W
I T C P O J F M D B E N T B P F C F S
V D V S F A K I N S T A L L C F G S L
E V I R D T S A L O G I N S C R I P T
R M K M X C X J P E N J D B D F W E T
```

1. COMSPEC

2. DISTRIBUTION LIST

3. EXEC

4. FILE ATTRIBUTES

5. FIRST MAIL

6. GETO

7. IDENTIFIER VARIABLE

8. INSTALL.CFG

9. LASTDRIVE

10. LINK DRIVER

11. LOGIN SCRIPT

12. MENUMAKE

13. MHS SERVICES

14. NAME CONTEXT

15. NET.CFG

16. NWCLIENT

17. POSTMASTER

18. PROFILE

19. SHELL.CFG

20. STARTNET.BAT

EXERCISE 6-2: WORKSTATION CONNECTIVITY FOR NETWARE 4

2B.   Look at Figure 6.13. You'll see that LSL.COM loads the Link Support Layer, provides version information, and activates the default NET.CFG file. From this, we can surmise that the Link Support Layer is in control of the client connection somehow. It's the traffic cop.

2D.   No. When IPXODI loads, it activates the internal NIC, but you still can't talk to the server without VLM.EXE.

2E.   IPXODI activates communications at the NIC level, whereas VLMs activate communications at the higher DOS level. Neither one is any good without the other.

3B.   Regardless of what you might think about the "logical" nature of NetWare 4 NDS, you still have to attach to a server. In this case, LABS-SRV1 is our host server for all NDS resource access. Any other necessary server attachments will be made for you automatically in the background. You only need to attach to the initial host server.

EXERCISE 6-3: UNDERSTANDING NET.CFG

```
; Standard R&D Dept. NET.CFG file
; Created for LDaVinci on 10/28/99

SHOW DOTS = ON
LONG MACHINE TYPE = DELL

LINK DRIVER C35X9
     INT A
     PORT 320
     FRAME Ethernet_802.2
```

```
NETWARE DOS REQUESTER
      PREFERRED TREE=ACME_TREE
      PREFERRED SERVER=R&D-SRV1
      NAME CONTEXT="OU=R&D.OU=LABS.OU=NORAD.O=ACME"
      FIRST NETWORK DRIVE=F:
      PACKET BUFFERS = 10
      SIGNATURE LEVEL = 3
      LOAD CONN TABLE LOW = ON
      CONNECTIONS = 10
      NETWORK PRINTERS = 5
```

Note: Be sure you don't put a preceding period (.) in the NAME CONTEXT statement.

CASE STUDY: CONFIGURING ACME'S LOGIN SCRIPTS

1. Create the Container login script for the PR Organizational Unit. (If you already did this step, proceed to Step 2.)

    a. Log in as the Admin user and run MS Windows. Switch to the first network drive on the server by typing **F:** and pressing Enter. Login to the network as the Admin user by typing **LOGIN .ADMIN.ACME** and pressing Enter. Run MS Windows by typing **WIN** and pressing Enter.

    b. Execute the NetWare Administrator utility.

        1) Locate the Program Group icon containing the NetWare Tools, and double-click on it. Then, double click on the NetWare Administrator Program Item icon to run the NetWare Administrator utility.

        2) Double-click on the NORAD Organizational Unit using the right mouse button. A menu should be displayed. Select the Details option from the menu and press Enter.

3) Use the scroll bar along the right edge of the screen to display the Login Script button and click on it. Next, single-click in the upper-right corner of the window located in the center of the screen.

c. Create the System (Container) login script for the Public Relations department.

1) Key in the appropriate statements for the Public Relations department Container login script using the clues in the Chapter 6 case study. (If you need help with what each script should look like, see Figures C6.1 and C6.2.)

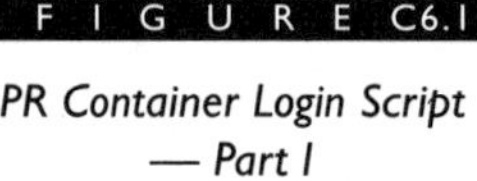

F I G U R E C6.1

PR Container Login Script — Part I

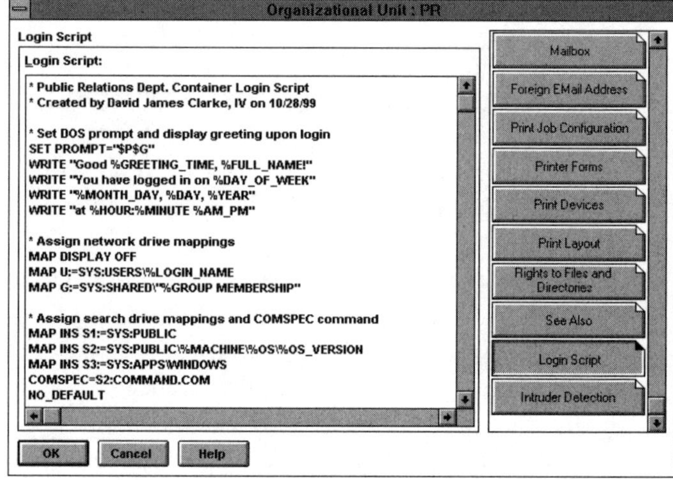

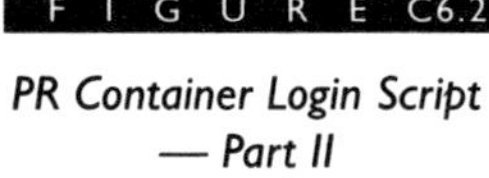

FIGURE C6.2

*PR Container Login Script
— Part II*

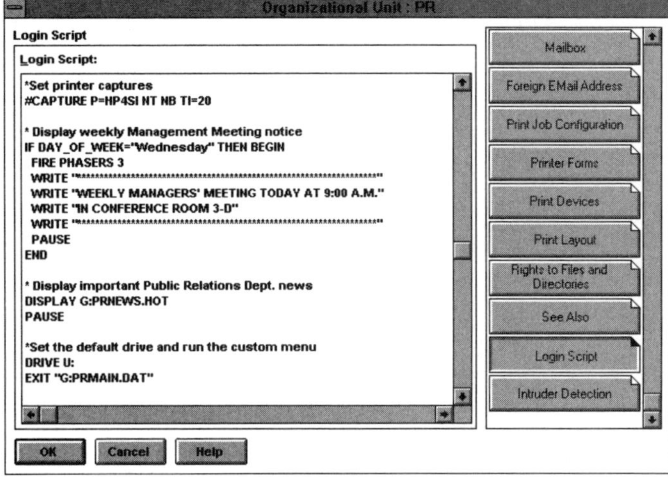

2. Make the FDR user a member of the PRMGRS-Profile login script. (The PRMGRS-Profile login script is located in the ACME container.)

    a. Identify PRMGRS-Profile as the name of the Profile Login Script object in the Profile login script field of the FDR's User's login script screen (see Figure C6.3).

FIGURE C6.3

*Adding FDR to the
PRMGRS Profile Login
Script Object*

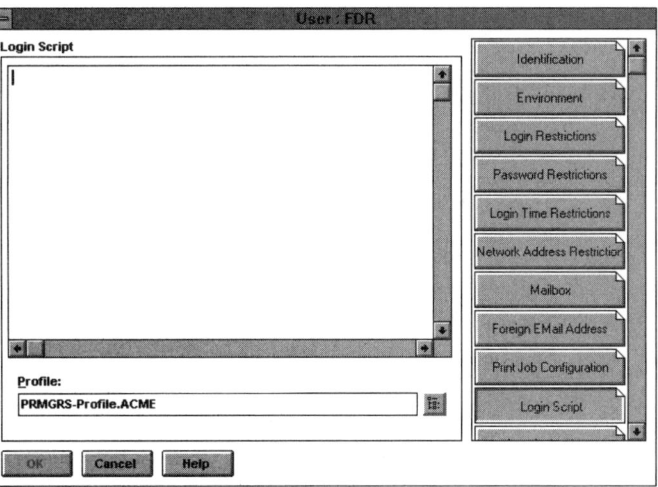

    b. Grant the User the R property right to the Login Script property of the Profile. Also, make sure that the B right to the Profile Login Script object that was granted by default to [Public] at the [Root] has not been blocked by an IRF.

3. Login as the FDR user by typing **LOGIN .FDR.PR.RIO.ACME** and pressing Enter. Watch as the Container and Profile login scripts are automatically executed. Fix any errors that occur.

CASE STUDY: CONFIGURING THE ACME MENU SYSTEM

1. Create a custom menu:

```
; PR Main Menu
; Created by David James Clarke, IV on 10/28/99

MENU 01,Public Relations Main Menu
  ITEM  ^AApplications
        SHOW 10
  ITEM  ^EE-Mail
        EXEC WIN WMAIL
  ITEM  ^NNetWare Commands
        SHOW 20
  ITEM  ^LLog off the network
        EXEC LOGOUT

MENU 10,Applications
  ITEM  Database
        EXEC DB
  ITEM  Spreadsheet
        EXEC SS
  ITEM  Word Processing
        EXEC WP
```

```
MENU 20,NetWare Utilities
    ITEM  File Management
          EXEC FILER
    ITEM  NCOPY
          GETP Enter Source File(s): { }80,,{}
          GETP Enter Destination File(s): { }80,,{}
          EXEC NCOPY %1 %2
    ITEM  NLIST
          GETO Enter Class Name and Option:
          { }25,USER/A,{}
          EXEC NLIST
    ITEM  User Tools
          EXEC WIN NWUSER
    ITEM  WHOAMI
          EXEC WHOAMI
```

2. Compile and execute the custom menu (and debug any problems):

```
MENUMAKE PRMAIN.SRC <Enter>
NMENU PRMAIN.DAT <Enter>
```

(See Figure C6.4 for a sample of what the PR Main Menu should look like.)

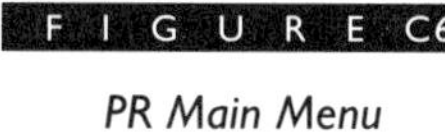

F I G U R E C6.4

PR Main Menu

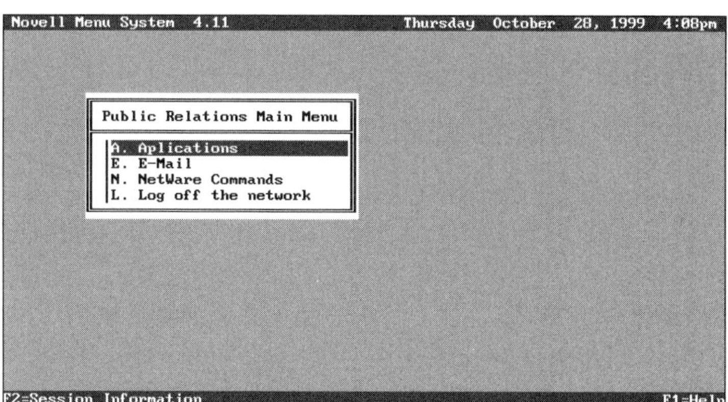

Chapter 7: NetWare 4 Management

ANSWERS TO QUIZZES

Q7-1
DAISY

Q7-2
Nice try. Roosters don't lay eggs.

Q7-3
Silence, Wedding Ring, Hole, Debt.

Q7-4
TYPEWRITER

Q7-5
Fools rush in where angels fear to tread. Which one are you?

SOLUTIONS TO QUIZZES, PUZZLES, EXERCISES, AND CASE STUDIES

EXERCISE 7-1: ADULTHOOD

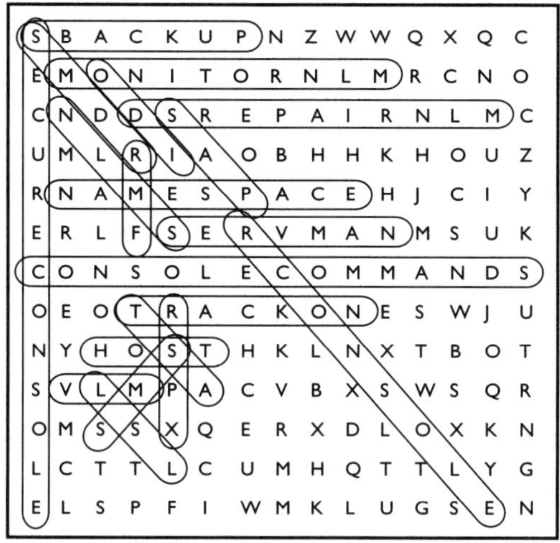

1. CONSOLE COMMANDS

2. DSREPAIR.NLM

3. HOST

4. LSL

5. MONITOR.NLM

6. NAME SPACE

7. NLMS

8. ODI

9. RCONSOLE

10. RMF

11. RSPX

12. SAP

13. SBACKUP

14. SECURE CONSOLE

15. SERVMAN

16. SMDR

17. SMS

18. TRACK ON

19. TSA

20. VLM

EXERCISE 7-2: THE NETWARE WORKSTATION ARCHITECTURE

1. Protocol Stack — IPXODI.COM

2. The NetWare DOS Requester — VLM.EXE

3. Link Support Layer — LSL.COM

4. MLID — 3C5X9.COM

5. Transport Multiplexer — TRAN.VLM

6. File System Multiplexer — FIO.VLM

7. Connectivity Module — CONN.VLM

CASE STUDY: SERVER MANAGEMENT AT ACME

1. VLM /U

   IPXODI /U

   NE2000 /U (or appropriate LAN driver)

   LSL /U

2. VLM /?

3. VLM /4

4. v1.20 (answers will vary)

5. Extended Memory (XMS)

6. CONN.VLM; NETX.VLM

7. The file server console prompt is displayed (that is, CHARITY_INC:)

8. A message is displayed indicating that a remote (RCONSOLE) connection has been granted. This is important to know in case unauthorized personnel (or worse yet, a hacker) have gained access to your file server console through the RMF utility.

9. AUTOEXEC.NCF; STARTUP.NCF

10. Single

11. 802.2

12. 2 percent

13. No, this disk is not mirrored.

14. 4K. This server was migrated from a NetWare 3.12 server where the default block size was 4K. (Your block size may vary.) On the SYS: volume, file compression, block suballocation, and data migration are turned off.

15. 10 (Answers will vary.)

16. Product options

17. 10 days, 2 hours, 6 minutes, and 34 seconds (answers will vary). The elapsed time since the server was last restarted is represented in the format DD:HH:MM:SS, where DD = number of days, HH = number of hours, MM = number of minutes, and SS = number of seconds. Current server utilization is at 8 percent (answers will vary). What is the total number of cache buffers currently being used? What is the number of current service processes in use? Eight licensed connections are available at the moment (10 minus 2 in use).

18. Normal; no. (Answers may vary.)

19. IPX

20. DS.NLM; 598,515 bytes. (Size may vary.)

21. Idle loop (that is, polling)

22. Processor Uptime (called Server Up Time in MONITOR.NLM), Processor Utilization (called Utilization in MONITOR.NLM), Server Processes (called Server Processes in MONITOR.NLM), and Users logged in (called Connection Information in MONITOR.NLM).

23. SET command

24. Alt+F3; Alt+F1

25. The Transfer files to server option in SERVMAN performs a similar function to the Copy SYSTEM and PUBLIC files option in INSTALL.NLM. The difference between the two is that the SERVMAN option copies the SYSTEM and PUBLIC files from the workstation's drive rather than the server's.

26. TRACK ON; ACME_TREE; DAD; Server Information in SERVMAN, AUTOEXEC.NCF in INSTALL.NLM, and CONFIG console command.

27. BROADCAST or SEND. You can acknowledge an incoming BROADCAST or SEND message displayed on the screen by pressing Ctrl+Enter. You can turn off receipt of incoming messages from other users by typing **SEND / A=N** at the workstation prompt after you exit RCONSOLE.

28. HELP ALL

29. MODULES; SERVMAN.NLM

Chapter 8: NetWare 4 Printing

ANSWERS TO QUIZZES

Q8-1
There were 12 friends in the group

Q8-2
QUEUE — pretty sneaky, huh?

Q8-3
V (vowel) 1 = A, and so on
C (consonant) 1 = B, and so on
"Well done! Message successfully decoded."

EXERCISE 8-1: THE GREAT CHALLENGE WORD SEARCH

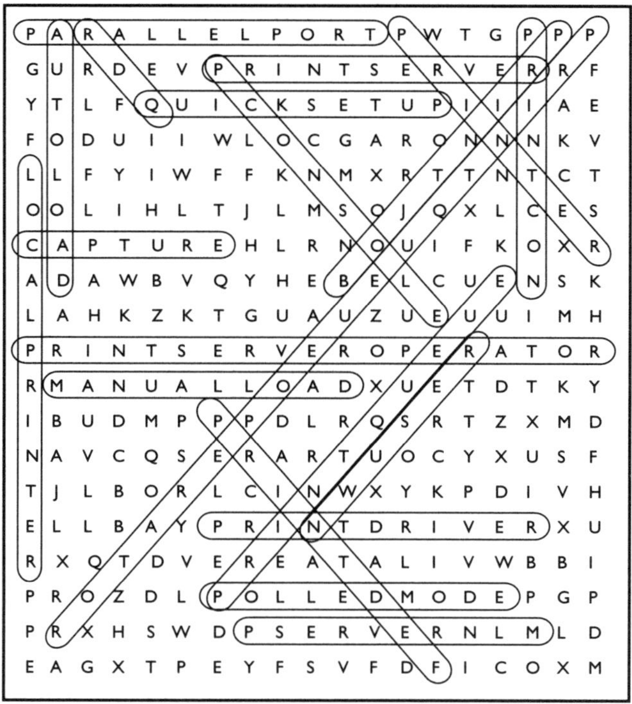

1. AUTOLOAD
2. CAPTURE
3. LOCAL PRINTER
4. MANUAL LOAD
5. NWUSER
6. PARALLEL PORT
7. PCONSOLE
8. POLLED MODE
9. PRINT DRIVER
10. PRINT JOB
11. PRINT QUEUE
12. PRINT QUEUE OPERATOR
13. PRINT SERVER
14. PRINT SERVER OPERATOR
15. PRINTCON
16. PRINTDEF
17. PRINTER
18. PSERVER.NLM
19. QDR
20. QUICK SETUP

NOVELL'S CNA STUDY GUIDE FOR NETWARE 4.1

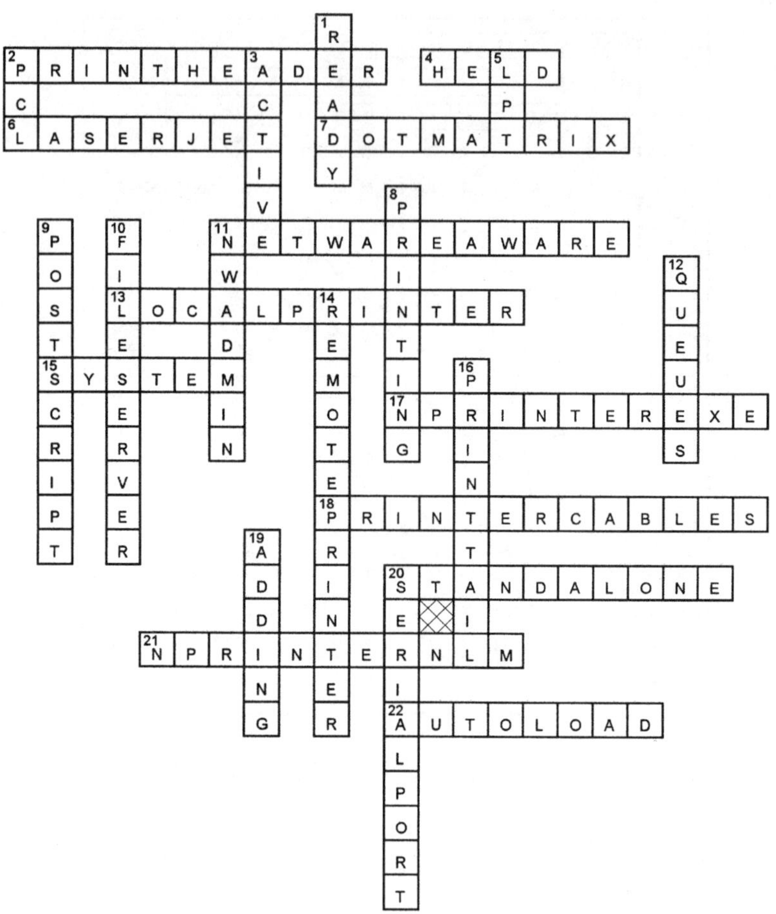

CASE STUDY: BUILDING ACME'S PRINTING SYSTEM

Queue Creation

10. The container where the queue was created. Because all users in the container usually need access.

13. There is a QUEUES directory off the root.

14. One or more.

Printer Creation

12. The job owner as the person notified disappears.

13. It reappears.

Creating the Print Server

10. The context where the print server was created. Because everyone in the container usually has access.

12. You are, because you created it!

18. Because the print server hasn't been loaded yet. It isn't yet running.

19. The print server is down.

Loading the Print Server

5. It asks for a password.

6. Enter the password **Secret**.

9. It should be off-line or waiting for job if no printer is attached.

13. The print server unloads back to a colon prompt.

CASE STUDY: USING ACME'S PRINTING SYSTEM

2. All LPTs should be set to local ports.

3. Error. Default Configuration cannot be found.

4. CX .WHITE.CRIME.TOKYO.ACME

5. CAPTURE Q=CANONBJ-PQ1

6. CAPTURE Endcap

17. Access not authorized. The only user authorized during print queue creation was the person doing the exercise.

18. Use NWADMIN or PCONSOLE to give the entire container access to the queue as a queue user or give it specifically to Speeders.

19. Either under NWUSER or CAPTURE in a DOS box.

22. Click on the print queue and choose Job List.

23. CAPTURE SH

24. Use the DOS PRINT command. PRINT DOSFIL.TXT.

25. CAPTURE Endcap

27. Right-mouse click on the container WHITE.CRIME.TOKYO.ACME and choose Details. Choose Print Job Configuration. Choose Create. Choose the CANONBJ-PQ1 for the queue. Save the new configuration.

28. Choose the print queue by double-clicking. Choose Users. Add the context WHITE.CRIME.TOKYO.ACME to the list of allowed users.

30. CAPTURE still doesn't automatically set you up.

34. The station is captured with the settings of the job configuration.

35. They match the print job configuration.

CASE STUDY: MANAGING ACME'S PRINTING SYSTEM

4. The printer shows Stopped in the status screen.

5. Use NWUSER to drag and drop, then send a print out from NWADMIN under Object/Print twice.

6. Two jobs submitted.

8. Job shows Held.

10. The second job now prints on the printer — the first is still held.

12. Double-click on the printer CANONBJ-P1 and view status.

13. Off-line/paper out.

14. The status screen shows the percentage of the job being printed as it prints.

17. Each has a status that can be seen now that it's running.

19. The print server unloads automatically.

22. The print server has an exclamation point next to it. This means the server is not available.

23. The print server should show that it's down.

24. Use either CAPTURE or NWUSER to start network capture. Then print from NWADMIN using Object/Create.

30. The jobs have reordered themselves to place the job just modified at the top of the queue.

For More Information and Help

Whenever a product becomes as popular and as widely used as NetWare, an entire support industry crops up around it. If you are looking for more information about NetWare 4.1, you're in luck. There is a wide variety of places you can go for help, advice, information, or even just camaraderie.

NetWare information is as local as your bookstore or local user group, and as international as the Internet forums that focus on NetWare. It can be as informal as articles in a magazine, or as structured as a college course. Best of all, it's easy to tap into most of these resources, wherever you may happen to be on the planet.

There is no point in trudging along through problems by yourself, when there is such a vast array of helpful people and tools at your fingertips.

ZEN

"Worrying is like standing in a mud hole; it gives you something to do, but it doesn't get you anywhere."

Texas Bix Bender, *Laughing Stock, A Cow's Guide to Life*

This chapter describes the following ways you can get more information or technical support for NetWare. With a little digging, you can probably turn up even more resources than these, but these will get you started.

- General Novell product information

- *The Novell Buyer's Guide*

- The NetWare 4.1 manuals

- Novell and NetWare information on the Internet

- Novell technical support

- The *Novell Support Encyclopedia*

- DeveloperNet (Novell's developer support)

- Novell *Application Notes*

- NetWare Users International (NUI)

- NetWork Professional Association (NPA)

- Novell Press books and other publications

- World Wire

- Cyber State University

General Novell Product Information

The main Novell information number, 1-800-NETWARE, can be your inroad to all types of information about Novell and its products. By calling this number, you can obtain information about Novell products, the locations of your nearest resellers, pricing information, technical support (see the section, "Novell Technical Support," later in this chapter), and so on.

The *Novell Buyer's Guide*

If you are responsible for helping find networking solutions for your organization, you may want to get a copy of the *Novell Buyer's Guide*. This guide is a complete book on everything you could possibly want to buy from Novell.

The *Novell Buyer's Guide* explains all the products Novell is currently offering, complete with rundowns on the technical specifications, features, and benefits of those products.

The *Guide* is available in a variety of formats, too. It is available on-line through Novell's on-line service on the Internet and through CompuServe. (From Novell's home page on the Internet, http://www.novell.com, select the NetWire Technical Support Services icon, then open up the Sales and Marketing information.)

The *Novell Buyer's Guide* also comes on CD-ROM with the NSEPro (explained later in this chapter). A sample from the *Buyer's Guide* is shown in Figure D.1. If you prefer the written version, you can order the *Novell Buyer's Guide* by calling one of the following phone numbers (which are all toll-free in Canada and the USA):

- ► 1-800-NETWARE

- ► 1-800-544-4446

- ► 1-800-346-6855

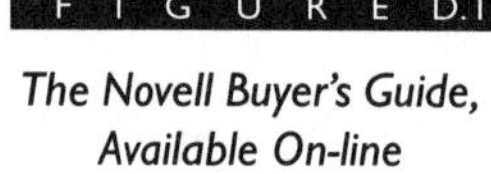

F I G U R E D.1

The Novell Buyer's Guide, Available On-line

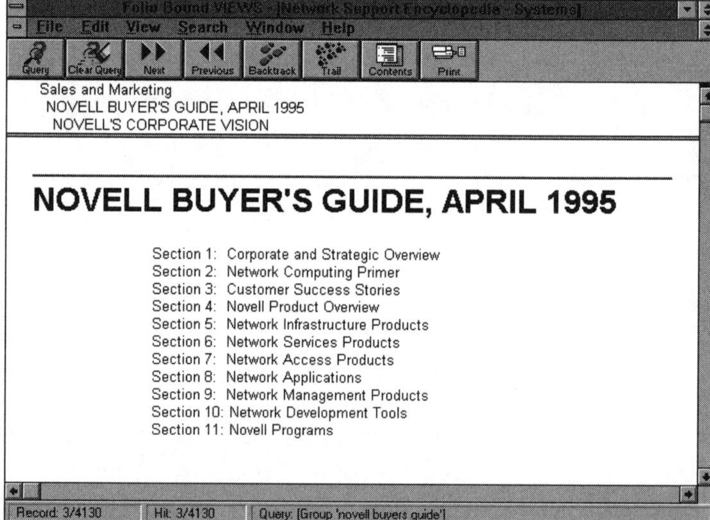

There may be a small charge to purchase the printed version of the *Buyer's Guide*.

The NetWare 4.1 Manuals

The NetWare 4.1 manuals are the complete reference guides to the features and workings of NetWare 4.1. In your NetWare 4.1 package, you should have received a handful of printed manuals (just enough to get you started), plus a CD-ROM containing the full set of manuals on-line (see Figure D.2).

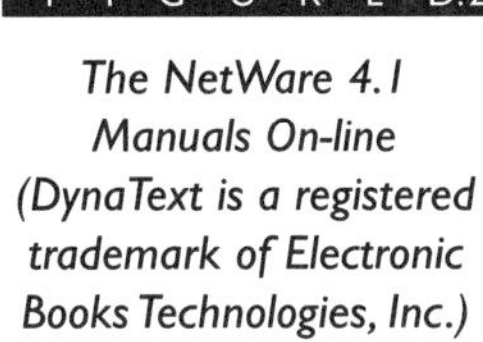

The NetWare 4.1 Manuals On-line (DynaText is a registered trademark of Electronic Books Technologies, Inc.)

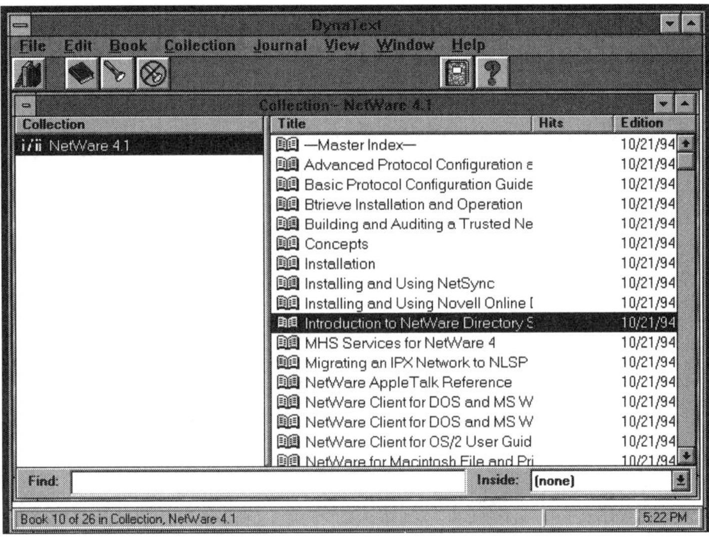

If you install the on-line documentation on your server, you'll be able to access the manuals from any workstation on the network that has the DynaText viewer installed. If you have a laptop computer, you may want to install the on-line documentation on it, so that you can carry the entire set around with you.

If you really like having printed documentation, you can order the full printed set of manuals from Novell.

TIP

The only manual that is not included in the printed set is the *System Messages* manual. Believe me, you don't want to see how big that book would be if it were printed.

To order the printed manuals for NetWare 4.1, you can use the order form that came in your NetWare 4.1 box, or call one of the following phone numbers:

- ▶ 1-800-336-3892 (toll-free in Canada and the USA)

- ▶ 1-512-834-6905

Novell on the Internet

A tremendous amount of information about Novell and NetWare products (both official and unofficial) is on the Internet. Officially, you can obtain the latest information about Novell from Novell's home page on the Internet (also called NetWire), as well as from the NetWire forums on CompuServe and Spaceworks. Unofficially, there are several active user forums that deal specifically with NetWare, or generally with computers. (NetWire will also be on the AT&T NetWare Connect Services when it becomes available.)

Novell's on-line forums offer you access to a wide variety of information and files dealing with NetWare and other Novell products (such as GroupWise, LAN Workplace, Nested NetWare, and Novell's Multiprotocol Router). You can receive information such as technical advice from sysops (system operators) and other users, updated files and drivers, and the latest patches and workarounds for known problems in Novell products.

ZEN

"Though a program be but three lines long, some day it will have to be maintained."

Geoffrey James, *The Zen of Programming*

Novell's on-line sites also provide a database of technical information from the Novell Technical Support division, as well as information about programs such as Novell Education classes and NetWare Users International (NUI). In addition, you can find marketing and sales information about the various products that Novell produces.

Novell's Internet and CompuServe sites are very dynamic, well-done, and packed with information. They are frequently updated with new information about products, education programs, promotions, and the like. In fact, the technical support features of NetWire on the Internet even garnered a place on the "What's Cool" list of Internet sites from Netscape.

NetWire is managed by Novell employees and by sysops who have extensive knowledge about NetWare. Public forums can be quite active, with many knowledgeable users offering advice to those who experience problems.

TIP

To get technical help with a problem, post a message and address the message to the NetWire sysops. (But don't send the sysops a personal e-mail message asking for help—the public forums are the approved avenue for help.)

To access NetWire on CompuServe, you need a CompuServe account. There is no additional monthly fee for using NetWire, although you are charged the connection fee (on an hourly rate) for accessing the service. To get to NetWire, use GO NETWIRE. There, you will find information for new users, telling you how the forums are set up, how to get technical help, and so on.

If you have a connection to the Internet, you can access NetWire in one of the following ways:

- **World Wide Web:** http://www.novell.com

- **Gopher:** gopher.novell.com

- **File Transfer Protocol (FTP):** anonymous FTP to ftp.novell.com

(Users in Europe should replace .com with .de.)

To get to NetWire on the Microsoft Network, use GO NETWIRE.

For information about Spaceworks, call 1-800-577-2235.

Novell Technical Support

If you encounter a problem with your network that you can't solve on your own, there are several places you can go for immediate technical help.

ZEN

"When you find yourself in over your head, don't open your mouth. Swim!"

Texas Bix Bender, *Laughing Stock, A Cow's Guide to Life*

Try some of the following resources:

- ▶ Try calling your reseller or consultant.

- ▶ Go on-line, and check out the Technical Support areas of NetWire. There, you will find postings and databases of problems and solutions. Someone else may have already found and solved your problem for you.

- ▶ While you're on-line, see if anyone in the on-line forums or Usenet forums knows about the problem or can offer a solution. The knowledge of people in those forums is broad and deep. Don't hesitate to take advantage of it, and don't forget to return the favor if you know some tidbit that might help others.

- ▶ Call Novell Technical Support. You may want to reserve this for a last resort, simply because Novell Technical Support charges a fee for each incident (an "incident" may involve more than one phone call, if necessary). The fee depends on the product for which you're requesting support.

When you call Technical Support, make sure you have all the necessary information ready (such as the versions of NetWare and any utility or application you're using, the type of hardware you're using, network or node addresses and hardware settings for any workstations or other machines being affected, and so on). You'll also need a major credit card.

To get to Novell's Technical Support, call 1-800-NETWARE.

The *Novell Support Encyclopedia*

A subscription to the *Novell Support Encyclopedia Professional Volume* (*NSEPro*) can update you every month with the latest technical information about Novell products. The *NSEPro* is a CD-ROM containing technical information such as:

- ▶ Novell technical information documents

- ▶ Novell Labs hardware and software test bulletins

- ▶ On-line product manuals

- ▶ *Novell Application Notes*

- ▶ All available NetWare patches, fixes, and drivers

- ▶ The *Novell Buyer's Guide*

- ▶ Novell corporate information (such as event calendars and press releases)

The *NSEPro* includes Folio information-retrieval software that allows you to access and search easily through the *NSEPro* information from your workstation using DOS, Macintosh, or Microsoft Windows.

ZEN

"If computers get too powerful, we can organize them into a committee—that will do them in."

from "Bradley's Bromide"

To subscribe to the *NSEPro*, contact your Novell Authorized Reseller or Novell directly at 1-800-377-4136 (in the United States and Canada) or 1-303-297-2725. To whet your appetite, Figure D.3 shows an example screen from the *NSEPro*.

The NSEPro

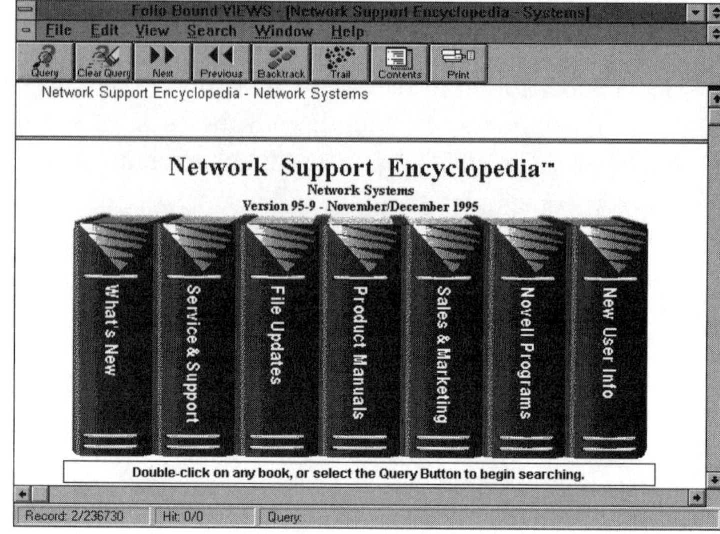

DeveloperNet: Novell's Developer Support

If you or others in your organization develop applications that need to run on a NetWare 4.1 network, you can tap into a special information resource created just for developers.

DeveloperNet is a support program specifically for professional developers who create applications designed to run on NetWare. Subscription fees for joining DeveloperNet vary, depending on the subscription level and options you choose. If you are a developer, some of the benefits you can receive by joining DeveloperNet include:

- The Novell SDK (Software Development Kit) CD-ROM, which contains development tools you can use to create and test your application

- The *DeveloperNet Handbook*

- Special technical support geared specifically toward developers

- *Novell Developer Notes,* a bimonthly publication from the Novell Research department that covers software-development topics for NetWare products

- Discounts on various events, products, and Novell Press books

For more information, to apply for membership, or to order an SDK, call 1-800-REDWORD or 1-801-429-5281, or contact the program administrator via e-mail at devprog@novell.com.

TIP

More information about DeveloperNet is available on-line on CompuServe (GO NETWIRE) or on the World Wide Web . On the Web, you can connect to the DeveloperNet information through Novell's home site, at http://www.novell.com, or you can go directly to the DeveloperNet information at http://developer.novell.com. Both addresses get you to the same place.

Novell Application Notes

Novell's Research department produces a monthly publication called the *Novell Application Notes.* Each issue of *Novell Application Notes* contains research reports and articles on a wide range of topics. The articles delve into topics such as network design, implementation, administration, and integration.

A year's subscription costs $95 ($135 outside the United States), which includes access to the *Novell Application Notes* in their electronic form on CompuServe. An electronic-only subscription costs $35 (plus access charges).

To order a subscription, call 1-800-377-4136 or 1-303-297-2725. You can also fax an order to 1-303-294-0930.

NetWare Users International (NUI)

NetWare Users International (NUI) is a nonprofit association for networking professionals. With more than 250 affiliated groups worldwide, NUI provides a forum for networking professionals to meet face-to-face, to learn from each other, to trade recommendations, or just to share "war stories."

ZEN

"I believe in computer dating, but only if the computers are truly in love."

Groucho Marx

By joining the NetWare user group in your area, you can take advantage of the following benefits:

- Local user groups that hold regularly scheduled meetings.

- *NetWare Connection,* a bimonthly magazine that provides feature articles on new technologies, network management tips, product reviews, NUI news, and other helpful information.

- A discount on Novell Press books through the *NetWare Connection* magazine and also at NUI shows.

- NUInet, NUI's home page on the World Wide Web (available through Novell's home site, under "Programs," or directly at http:// www.nuinet.com), which provides NetWare 3 and NetWare 4 technical information, a calendar of NUI events, and links to local user group home pages.

- Regional NUI conferences, held in different major cities throughout the year (with a 15 percent discount for members).

The best news is, there's usually no fee or only a very low fee for joining an NUI user group.

For more information or to join an NUI user group, call 1-800-228-4NUI or send a fax to 1-801-228-4577.

For a free subscription to *NetWare Connection*, fax your name, address, and request for a subscription to 1-801-228-4576. You can also mail NUI a request at:

NetWare Connection
P.O. Box 1928
Orem, UT 84059-1928
USA

REAL WORLD

You don't even have to officially join NUI to get a subscription to *NetWare Connection*, but don't let that stop you from joining. "Networking" with other NetWare administrators can help you in ways you probably can't even think of yet.

Network Professional Association (NPA)

If you've achieved (or are working toward) your CNA or CNE certification, you may want to join the Network Professional Association (NPA), formerly called CNEPA. The NPA is an organization for network computing professionals. Its goal is to keep its members current with the latest technology and information in the industry.

If you're a certified CNE, you can join the NPA as a full member. If you're a CNA, or if you've started the certification process, but aren't finished yet, you can join as an associate member. Associate members have all the benefits of full membership, except that they cannot vote or hold offices in the NPA.

ZEN

"The more I want to get something done, the less I call it work."

Richard Bach, Illusions

When you join the NPA you can enjoy the following benefits:

- ► Local NPA chapters (more than 100 worldwide) that hold regularly scheduled meetings that include presentations and hands-on demonstrations of the latest technology

- ► *Network News*, a monthly publication that offers technical tips for working with NetWare networks, NPA news, classified ads for positions, and articles aimed at helping CNEs make the most of their careers

- ► Discounts on NPA Satellite Labs (satellite broadcasts of presentations)

- ► Product discounts from vendors

- ► Hands-On Technology Labs (educational forums at major trade shows and other locations as sponsored by local NPA chapters)

- ► Discount or free admission to major trade shows and conferences

Membership in NPA costs $150 per year. For more information or to join NPA, call 1-801-379-0330.

Novell Press Books and Other Publications

Every year, more and more books are being published about NetWare and about networking in general. Whatever topic you can think up, someone's probably written a book about it.

Novell Press itself has an extensive selection of books written about NetWare and other Novell products. For an up-to-date Novell Press catalog, you can send an e-mail to Novell Press at novellpress@novell.com.

You can also peruse the selection of books on-line. From Novell's main Internet site (http://www.novell.com), you can get to the Novell Press area (located under "Programs"). You can also get to the same location by going directly to http://corp.novell.com/programs/press.

In addition to books, there are a wide variety of magazines that are geared specifically toward networking and general computing professionals, such as *Network News*, *NetWare Connection* (From NUI), *LAN Times*, *PCWeek*, and so on.

World Wire

World Wire is an on-line service that gives you incredible new educational avenues for learning about NetWare. It provides you with technical support, technical information, Internet access, testing, and other benefits.

In addition, World Wire gives you access to actual, on-line NetWare 3.1*x* and NetWare 4.1 LANs so that you can get some hands-on experience in the safety of a practice environment, rather than in your real, production environment.

For more information, call 1-510-254-7283.

Cyber State University

Cyber State University is a service that uses the World Wire to connect students and provide comprehensive, multimedia training on-line. The Cyber State University uses several different tools to help train students in NetWare 4.1 skills: video, lectures, virtual classes, lab exercises, testing, and so on.

For more information, call 1-510-253-TREK.

WHAT'S ON THE CD-ROM?

The CD-ROM included with this book contains two resources that can help you in your quest for NetWare knowledge.

First, you'll find *The Clarke Tests v2.0*, a next-generation interactive learning system. These tests a wide variety of topics and study sessions. Each study session combines a variety of question types with interactive graphics, sounds, and clues. Even better, each interactive answer includes a full page or more of explanation and study material, plus page references to Novell-authorized courseware, NetWare documentation, or other resources.

To install The Clarke Tests v2.0, go to the directory CLARKE on the CD-ROM. In that directory, you'll find the readme file (README.CLK), which contains installation instructions.

The other exciting component of the CD-ROM is the Novell Messenger. The Novell Messenger brings you a variety of information, such as white papers, data sheets, phone numbers for key Novell departments, and success stories (which tell how customers have successfully implemented Novell products in their organizations). You can also find lists of third-party hardware and software products that have been certified to work with Novell products.

To install the Novell Messenger, choose Run from the File menu (in Windows' Program Manager). Click the Browse button, and choose the SETUP.EXE file, located in the NOVELL directory. Press the Enter key, then follow the instructions that appear. In Windows 95, click on the Setup icon in the Novell directory.

*I*ndex

(continued)

Archive Needed (A) feature attribute, 369
assigning
  access rights to network applications, 458
  file attributes for network applications, 458
  print queue priorities, 605-606, 647
  print queue users and operators, 613
assigning file system trustee rights, 359-363
  from directory point-of-view, 361
  inheritance, 362
  overview of, 359-360
  security equivalence, 362-363
  from user point-of-view, 360-361
  See also file system security
assigning NDS trustee rights, 289, 316,
    326-340
  inheritance
    blocking with Inherited Rights Filter (IRF),
      332, 337-340
    blocking with trustee assignments, 332-333,
      339-340
    overview of, 289, 321, 326, 331-332
  overview of, 326-327
  security equivalences, 334-336
    ancestral inheritance (AI), 334, 362
    Directory Map objects, 336
    groups, 335-336
    Organizational Roles, 335
    overview of, 334
  trustee assignments, 327-331
    blocking inheritance with, 332-333, 339-340
    container trustees, 327
    group trustees, 327
    from object point-of-view, 328-331
    Organizational Role trustees, 327
    [Public] trustees, 327
    from user point-of-view, 328-330
    user trustees, 327
  See also NetWare Directory Services security
asynchronous modems, 564-566
attributes, 286, 291, 366-373
  assigning for network applications, 458
  customizing, 371-372
  disk management attributes, 370-371
  feature attributes, 369
  overview of, 366-367
  security attributes, 367-369
  See also security
auditing feature
  in managing printing with PCONSOLE, 651-652
  tracking network transactions with, 108
authentication. See login/password
    authentication
AUTO.VLM, 542
AUTOEXEC.BAT file, 408
AUTOEXEC.NCF file
  automating passwords with, 504-505
  changing SET parameters in, 89-90
  LAN drivers and, 521
  and monitoring processor utilization, 44
automatic call distribution, 63

B

background login/password authentication,
  287, 297-298
backups
  documenting, 90-91
  in network maintenance, 48-49
  See also Storage Management Services
bad block tracking documentation, 85-87
batch file documentation, 89
[BATCH] option, in ITEM organizational
  command, 446
BIND console command, 507-508
BIND.VLM, 541-542, 544
bindery emulation, 103
bindery leaf object, 143
bindery mode, switching to in PCONSOLE
  utility, 637
bindery queue leaf object, 144
Bindery Services [Supervisor] file system
  security right, 357
BINDFIX. See DSREPAIR.NLM

(continued)

(continued)

(continued)

E

(continued)

G

(continued)

H

I

J

K

L

(continued)

(continued)

(continued)

(continued)

O

(continued)

(continued)

(continued)

R

(continued)

U

(continued)

(continued)

X

IDG BOOKS WORLDWIDE LICENSE AGREEMENT

Important — read carefully before opening the software packet. This is a legal agreement between you (either an individual or an entity) and IDG Books Worldwide, Inc. (IDG). By opening the accompanying sealed packet containing the software disc, you acknowledge that you have read and accept the following IDG License Agreement. If you do not agree and do not want to be bound by the terms of this Agreement, promptly return the book and the unopened software packet(s) to the place you obtained them for a full refund.

1. __License__. This License Agreement (Agreement) permits you to use one copy of the enclosed Software program(s) on a single computer. The Software is in "use" on a computer when it is loaded into temporary memory (i.e., RAM) or installed into permanent memory (e.g., hard disk, CD-ROM, or other storage device) of that computer.

2. __Copyright__. The entire contents of this disc and the compilation of the Software are copyrighted and protected by both United States copyright laws and international treaty provisions. You may only (a) make one copy of the Software for backup or archival purposes, or (b) transfer the Software to a single hard disk, provided that you keep the original for backup or archival purposes. The individual programs on the disc are copyrighted by the authors of each program respectively. Each program has its own use permissions and limitations. To use each program, you must follow the individual requirements and restrictions detailed in Appendix D of this Book. Do not use a program if you do not want to follow its Licensing Agreement. None of the material on this disc or listed in this Book may ever be distributed, in original or modified form, for commercial purposes.

3. __Other Restrictions__. You may not rent or lease the Software. You may transfer the Software and user documentation on a permanent basis provided you retain no copies and the recipient agrees to the terms of this Agreement. You may not reverse engineer, decompile, or disassemble the Software except to the extent that the foregoing restriction is expressly prohibited by applicable law. If the Software is an update or has been updated, any transfer must include the most recent update and all prior versions. Each shareware program has its own use permissions and limitations. These limitations are contained in the individual license agreements that are on the software discs. The restrictions include a requirement that after using the program for a period of time specified in its text, the user must pay a

registration fee or discontinue use. By opening the package which contains the software disc, you will be agreeing to abide by the licenses and restrictions these programs. Do not open the software package unless you agree to be bou by the license agreements.

4. <u>Limited Warranty</u>. IDG warrants that the Software and disc are free fr defects in materials and workmanship for a period of sixty (60) days from the d of purchase of this Book. If IDG receives notification within the warranty period defects in material or workmanship, IDG will replace the defective disc. IDG's ent liability and your exclusive remedy shall be limited to replacement of the Softwa which is returned to IDG with a copy of your receipt. This Limited Warranty void if failure of the Software has resulted from accident, abuse, or misapplicatio Any replacement Software will be warranted for the remainder of the origin warranty period or thirty (30) days, whichever is longer.

5. <u>No Other Warranties</u>. To the maximum extent permitted by applicable la IDG and the author disclaim all other warranties, express or implied, includi but not limited to implied warranties of merchantability and fitness for a particul purpose, with respect to the Software, the programs, the source code contain therein and/or the techniques described in this Book. This limited warranty giv you specific legal rights. You may have others which vary from state/jurisdiction state/jurisdiction.

6. <u>No Liability For Consequential Damages</u>. To the extent permitted applicable law, in no event shall IDG or the author be liable for any damag whatsoever (including without limitation, damages for loss of business profi business interruption, loss of business information, or any other pecuniary los arising out of the use of or inability to use the Book or the Software, even if IDG h been advised of the possibility of such damages. Because some states/jurisdictio do not allow the exclusion or limitation of liability for consequential or incident damages, the above limitation may not apply to you.

7. <u>U.S.Government Restricted Rights</u>. Use, duplication, or disclosure of th Software by the U.S. Government is subject to restrictions stated in paragraph (c) ((ii) of the Rights in Technical Data and Computer Software clause of DFARS 252.22 7013, and in subparagraphs (a) through (d) of the Commercial Computer - Restricted Rights clause at FAR 52.227-19, and in similar clauses in the NASA FA supplement, when applicable.

IDG BOOKS WORLDWIDE REGISTRATION CARD

Title of this book: **Novell's® CNA Study Guide for NetWare® 4.1**

My overall rating of this book: ❑ Very good [1] ❑ Good [2] ❑ Satisfactory [3] ❑ Fair [4] ❑ Poor [5]

How I first heard about this book:

❑ Found in bookstore; name: [6]   ❑ Book review: [7]

❑ Advertisement: [8]   ❑ Catalog: [9]

❑ Word of mouth; heard about book from friend, co-worker, etc.: [10]   ☒ Other: [11] _For a class._

What I liked most about this book:

What I would change, add, delete, etc., in future editions of this book:

Other comments:

Number of computer books I purchase in a year: ❑ 1 [12] ☒ 2-5 [13] ❑ 6-10 [14] ❑ More than 10 [15]

I would characterize my computer skills as: ❑ Beginner [16] ❑ Intermediate [17] ☒ Advanced [18] ❑ Professional [19]

I use ☒ DOS [20] ☒ Windows [21] ❑ OS/2 [22] ❑ Unix [23] ❑ Macintosh [24] ❑ Other: [25] _______________
(please specify)

I would be interested in new books on the following subjects:
(please check all that apply, and use the spaces provided to identify specific software)

❑ Word processing: [26]   ❑ Spreadsheets: [27]

❑ Data bases: [28]   ❑ Desktop publishing: [29]

❑ File Utilities: [30]   ❑ Money management: [31]

☒ Networking: [32]   ☒ Programming languages: [33]

❑ Other: [34]

I use a PC at (please check all that apply): ☒ home [35] ❑ work [36] ☒ school [37] ❑ other: [38] _______________

The disks I prefer to use are ❑ 5.25 [39] ☒ 3.5 [40] ❑ other: [41] _______________

I have a CD ROM: ☒ yes [42] ❑ no [43]

I plan to buy or upgrade computer hardware this year: ☒ yes [44] ❑ no [45]

I plan to buy or upgrade computer software this year: ☒ yes [46] ❑ no [47]

Name: _______________ Business title: [48] _______________ Type of Business: [49] _______________

Address (❑ home [50] ❑ work [51] /Company name: _______________)

Street/Suite# _______________

City [52] /State [53] /Zipcode [54]: _______________ Country [55] _______________

❑ **I liked this book!** You may quote me by name in future
IDG Books Worldwide promotional materials.

My daytime phone number is _______________

IDG BOOKS

THE WORLD OF
COMPUTER
KNOWLEDGE

❏ YES!

Please keep me informed about IDG's World of Computer Knowledge
Send me the latest IDG Books catalog.